The 4th Table Representation Learning Workshop (TRL 2025)

Vienna, Austria
31 July 2025

ISBN: 979-8-3313-2419-3

Printed from e-media with permission by:

Curran Associates, Inc.
57 Morehouse Lane
Red Hook, NY 12571

Some format issues inherent in the e-media version may also appear in this print version.

Association for Computational Linguistics
209 N. Eighth Street
Stroudsburg, Pennsylvania 18360

Phone: 1-570-476-8006
Fax: 1-570-476-0860

acl@aclweb.org

Additional copies of this publication are available from:

Curran Associates, Inc.
57 Morehouse Lane
Red Hook, NY 12571 USA
Phone: 845-758-0400
Fax: 845-758-2633
Email: curran@proceedings.com
Web: www.proceedings.com

TRL 2025

The 4th Table Representation Learning Workshop at ACL 2025

Proceedings of the Workshop

July 31, 2025

The TRL organizers gratefully acknowledge the support from the following sponsors.

Introduction

We are excited to welcome you to TRL 2025, the Workshop on Table Representation Learning, held in conjunction with ACL 2025. This year, the workshop takes place on July 31st, 2025, in Vienna, Austria, and brings together researchers working on all aspects of modeling, understanding, and reasoning over tabular data.

TRL serves as a forum for recent advances in table representation learning, spanning a wide range of topics including pretraining and foundation models for tables, table-based retrieval and question answering, table-to-text generation, semantic parsing, and applications in both textual and multimodal settings.

This year, we received 30 submissions, reflecting the growing interest in this area. Following a thorough review process, 24 papers were accepted for presentation, including 6 selected for oral presentations. The overall acceptance rate was 80%. The accepted papers represent both the breadth and depth of current research, and we are excited to showcase them during the workshop.

We are honored to feature invited talks by Edward Choi, Ruoxi Sun, Tao Yu, and Jiani Zhang, whose insights help frame the ongoing challenges and opportunities in table representation learning. We thank them for accepting our invitation and for their generous contributions to the program.

The workshop program includes oral presentations, a poster session, and invited talks. The oral sessions are organized thematically to highlight emerging directions and shared challenges across subfields. We hope these discussions foster new connections and inspire future research.

We thank all authors for their contributions and all attendees for their participation. We are especially grateful to our Program Committee for their thoughtful and timely reviews—their efforts were essential in shaping a strong and balanced program.

Finally, we thank our sponsors, SAP and Snowflake, for their generous support in making TRL 2025 possible.

We hope you enjoy the workshop!

Madelon Hulsebos, Qian Liu, Shuaichen Chang, Wenhu Chen, Huan Sun Organizers of TRL 2025

Organizing Committee

Organizers

Madelon Hulsebos, Centrum voor Wiskunde en Informatica
Qian Liu, Tiktok
Shuaichen Chang, AWS AI Lab
Wenhu Chen, University of Waterloo
Huan Sun, The Ohio State University

Program Committee

Reviewers

Rajat Agarwal, Amazon
Simran Arora, Stanford University, University of Pennsylvania, University of Pennsylvania and The Wharton School, University of Pennsylvania
Sebastian Bordt, Eberhard-Karls-Universität Tübingen
Shuaichen Chang, AWS AI Lab
Jiajing Chen, New York University
Sharad Chitlangia, Amazon
Naihao Deng, University of Michigan
Yuntao Du, Purdue University
Till Döhmen, University of Amsterdam and Rheinisch Westfälische Technische Hochschule Aachen
Katharina Eggensperger, Eberhard-Karls-Universität Tübingen
Moonjung Eo, LG AI Research
Matthias Feurer, Ludwig Maximilian University of Munich
Yury Gorishniy, Moscow Institute of Physics and Technology and Yandex
Yiqun Hu, AWS AI Labs
Zezhou Huang, Columbia University
Mouxiao Huang, Huawei Technologies Ltd.
Xiangjian Jiang, University of Cambridge
Myung Jun Kim, Inria
Andreas Kipf, University of Technology Nuremberg
Aneta Koleva, Siemens
Gaurav Kumar, Moveworks
Kyungeun Lee, LG AI Research
Gyubok Lee, Korea Advanced Institute of Science and Technology
Alexander Hanbo Li, Amazon
Tianyang Liu, University of California, San Diego
Xinyuan Lu, national university of singaore, National University of Singapore
Sazan Mahbub, Carnegie Mellon University
Sascha Marton, Technical University of Clausthal
Amine Mhedhbi, École Polytechnique de Montréal, Université de Montréal
Akshata Kishore Moharir, Microsoft
Mira Moukheiber, Massachusetts Institute of Technology
Andreas C Mueller, Microsoft
Simone Papicchio, Politecnico di Torino
Paolo Papotti, Eurecom
Panupong Pasupat, Google
Yuxin Qiao, Northern Arizona University
Ivan Rubachev, Yandex Research
Maximilian Schambach, SAP
Sebastian Schelter, BIFOLD & TU Berlin
Ananya Singha, Research, Microsoft
Gerardo Vitagliano, Computer Science and Artificial Intelligence Laboratory, Electrical Engineering & Computer Science
Liane Vogel, Technische Universität Darmstadt
Tianshu Wang, Chinese Academy of Sciences

Katarzyna Woźnica, Warsaw University of Technology
Jiani Zhang, Google
Tianshu Zhang, The Ohio State University
Ye Zhang, University of Pittsburgh
Zecheng Zhang, Kumo.AI
Fuheng Zhao, University of California, Santa Barbara
Mingyu Zheng, University of Chinese Academy of Sciences
Shuhan Zheng, Hitachi, Ltd.
Mengyu Zhou, Microsoft Research
Fengbin Zhu, National University of Singapore

Invited Speakers

Edward Choi, KAIST
Ruoxi Sun, Google
Tao Yu, HKU
Jiani Zhang, Google

Table of Contents

Theme-Explanation Structure for Table Summarization using Large Language Models: A Case Study on Korean Tabular Data

TaeYoon Kwack[1*] **Jisoo Kim**[1*] **Ki Yong Jung**[1] **DongGeon Lee**[2] **Heesun Park**[1†]
[1]Sungkyunkwan University [2]Pohang University of Science and Technology
{njj05043, clrdln, wjdrldyd0213}@g.skku.edu
donggeonlee@postech.ac.kr hspark20@skku.edu

Abstract

Tables are a primary medium for conveying critical information in administrative domains, yet their complexity hinders utilization by Large Language Models (LLMs). This paper introduces the **T**heme-E**x**planation Structure-based Table Summarization (**Tabular-TX**) pipeline, a novel approach designed to generate highly interpretable summaries from tabular data, with a specific focus on Korean administrative documents. Current table summarization methods often neglect the crucial aspect of human-friendly output. Tabular-TX addresses this by first employing a multi-step reasoning process to ensure deep table comprehension by LLMs, followed by a journalist persona prompting strategy for clear sentence generation. Crucially, it then structures the output into a Theme Part (an adverbial phrase) and an Explanation Part (a predicative clause), significantly enhancing readability. Our approach leverages in-context learning, obviating the need for extensive fine-tuning and associated labeled data or computational resources. Experimental results show that Tabular-TX effectively processes complex table structures and metadata, offering a robust and efficient solution for generating human-centric table summaries, especially in low-resource scenarios.

1 Introduction

Tables are essential for presenting core information, especially within the administrative domain, where critical data is frequently structured in tabular formats (Musumeci et al., 2024). The ability of Large Language Models (LLMs) to accurately summarize and elucidate the contents of these tables is becoming increasingly significant for data utilization. An important aspect of effective table summarization is the generation of human-understandable output. This necessitates not only the LLM's profound comprehension of the input table, but also the crafting of summaries that are both intuitive and concise, delivering key information without ambiguity.

Despite the critical need for human-centric summaries, recent research in table-to-text generation has often overlooked this aspect. Many existing approaches prioritize other metrics or model architectures, without sufficiently addressing how the generated text will be perceived and understood (Liu et al., 2024; Zhang et al., 2024b). Consequently, while the output can be factually correct, they lack the clarity, conciseness, or intuitive structure that facilitates effortless human comprehension, particularly when dealing with specialized data such as Korean administrative tables (NIKL, 2024).

To address this gap and emphasize the generation of human-friendly summaries, we propose the **T**heme-E**x**planation Structure-based Table Summarization (**Tabular-TX**) pipeline. Our approach is meticulously designed to guide LLMs towards producing summaries that are not only accurate but also exceptionally interpretable. First, to ensure a deep understanding of the input table, we decompose the LLM's reasoning process into a multi-step procedure, where each step focuses on a specific inferential task, thereby simplifying the complex table interpretation process. Second, we employ a "Journalist Persona" prompting strategy to encourage the generation of clear, objective, and well-phrased sentences. Finally, and most critically, we transform these generated insights into a highly structured Theme-Explanation (TX) format, where each summary segment consists of a thematic adverbial phrase followed by a predicative explanatory clause, enhancing readability and directness.

The Tabular-TX pipeline offers significant advantages, particularly in resource-constrained environments where extensive fine-tuning is unfeasible. Our primary contributions are threefold:

- We introduce a novel pipeline that leverages

*Both authors contributed equally to this work.
†Corresponding author.

Proceedings of the 4th Table Representation Learning Workshop, pages 1–12
July 31, 2025 ©2025 Association for Computational Linguistics

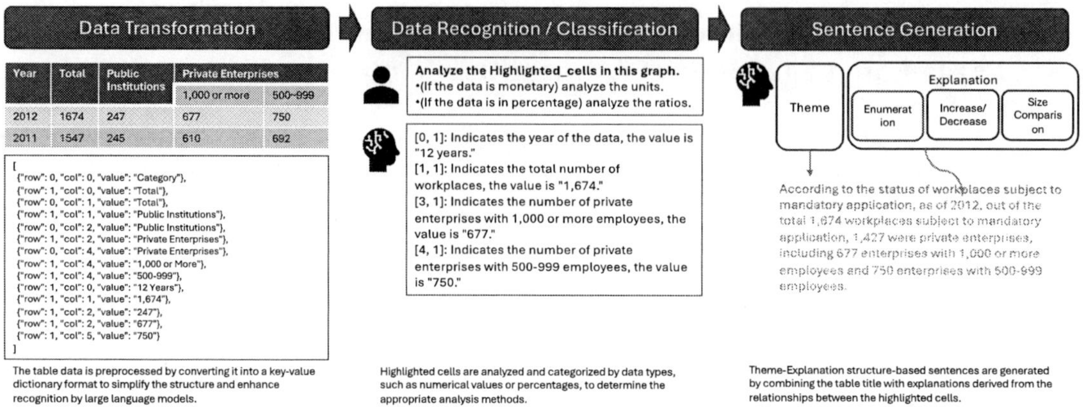

Figure 1: An overall pipeline of Theme-Explanation Structure-based Table Summarization (Tabular-TX).

multi-step reasoning and a journalist persona to generate high-quality textual explanations from complex tabular data.

- We propose the Theme-Explanation (TX) sentence structure, a new format for table summaries designed to maximize human interpretability.

- Through empirical evaluation, we demonstrate that our In-Context Learning (ICL)-based approach enables LLMs to achieve strong performance in table data processing and summarization without the need for task-specific fine-tuning.

2 Related Work

Table-to-Text Generation To enable complex reasoning over tabular data, Wang et al. (2024) proposed the Chain-of-Table framework as an extension of the text-based Chain-of-Thought method (Wei et al., 2022). This approach simplifies inference by reordering, extracting, and filtering table data, ultimately integrating relevant information into a structured table format. While this method excels in structured table processing and mathematical reasoning, it has limitations in generating interpretations for sections that require metadata or background knowledge.

TableLlama (Zhang et al., 2024b) aims to generalize table-based models beyond task-specific constraints by fine-tuning 14 datasets across 11 tasks, including Highlighted Cells question-answering. The model achieved performance comparable to or surpassing task-specific models and even outperformed GPT-4 (OpenAI, 2023) on unseen tasks. However, despite its effectiveness, the model suffers from high computational costs.

Among table-based interpretation benchmarks, FeTaQA (Nan et al., 2022) serves as a key reference dataset. While Chain-of-Table and TableLlama utilize in-context learning (Brown et al., 2020) and fine-tuning, respectively, they struggle to incorporate metadata into their interpretations effectively.

3 Theme-Explanation Structure

Unlike conventional approaches that treat table summaries as isolated text generation tasks, our method ensures structural consistency by explicitly organizing content into a **Theme Part** and an **Explanation Part**.

3.1 Theme Part

The Theme Part serves as a crucial contextual anchor, ensuring that numerical or categorical values in the table are interpreted correctly. It is structured as an adverbial phrase, combining the noun phrase of the table title (`table_title`) with a citation or basis expression[1]. This structure is essential because the table title provides the sole comprehensive context in table summaries. Unlike general text summaries, table cells alone are insufficient to provide meaningful context, making the resulting sentence ambiguous without additional background information.

3.2 Explanation Part

Following the Theme Part, the Explanation Part delivers a structured analysis of the highlighted cells,

[1]Comparison of summarization sentence with and without theme part is illustrated at Figure 4.

forming the core content of the summary. Depending on the data type, this section uses a specific analytical technique, such as enumeration, magnitude comparison, or trend analysis. The choice of method is determined based on the comparability of the highlighted cells, ensuring that the summary provides meaningful insights rather than just raw cell values.

4 Tabular-TX Pipeline

Generating summaries with the theme-explanation structure in Tabular-TX involves multiple processing steps to transform tabular data into structured natural language summaries.[2]

4.1 Chain-of-Thought (CoT)

After data transformation, the actual sentence generation process begins using Chain-of-Thought (CoT) reasoning. Large Language Models (LLMs) generally face performance degradation when handling tabular data summarization, as this task simultaneously requires multiple capabilities such as table recognition, mathematical reasoning, and commonsense inference. This issue, known as the Compositional Deficiency problem (Zhao et al., 2024), occurs because individual data points tend to be analyzed separately without adequately integrating their relationships into a holistic interpretation. CoT mitigates this by systematically guiding the model to tackle one reasoning step at a time, thereby improving interpretative accuracy and contextual completeness.

Specifically, CoT first classifies the types of highlighted cells, distinguishing among monetary values, percentages, categorical data, and textual explanations. This classification step prevents potential errors, such as misinterpreting percentages as plain numbers. Then, depending on the classified data type, the most appropriate analytical method—such as enumeration for listing individual items, magnitude comparison for numerical rankings, or trend analysis for temporal changes—is selected and applied. For instance, monetary values are converted into consistent units, and percentages are appropriately formatted for clarity.

In the context of Korean administrative table data, these challenges are further complicated by the language's implicit nature, the potential gap between administrative and everyday terminology, and morphological complexities (e.g., absent subjects or ambiguous particle usage). CoT systematically decomposes these linguistic hurdles by (1) classifying specialized terms, (2) normalizing numeric expressions in line with Korean usage conventions, and (3) incrementally integrating contextual cues, such as clarifying administrative vocabulary or disambiguating omitted referents. Through this stepwise process, the model avoids misinterpretations caused by either unfamiliar terms or implicit structures, ultimately generating summaries that better align with Korean textual norms.

By addressing each reasoning subtask explicitly and sequentially, CoT ensures the final table summary captures data relationships clearly and coherently, resulting in an accurate and contextually meaningful summary.

4.2 Journalist Persona for Structured Generation

In last step of pipeline we assign a journalist persona to the LLM to generate Theme-Explanation structured summaries. This persona is particularly effective because table summaries share key characteristics with straight news articles, which prioritize conciseness, objectivity, and fact-based clarity. Rather than generating overly detailed or speculative content, the model produces well-structured and neutral summaries that adhere to journalistic reporting conventions when guided by this persona.

Figure 2 demonstrates the impact of the journalist persona on table summarization. With a generic prompt, the model generates an ambiguous summary that captures core information but lacks contextual clarity and coherence. In contrast, applying the journalist persona produces a structured and contextually enriched summary. This improvement occurs because the journalist persona explicitly guides the model to state information sources, clearly define numerical constraints, and incorporate contextual details, closely resembling news article formats.

5 Experiment

5.1 Experimental Setup

Dataset For training and evaluation, we utilized the Korean table interpretation benchmark (NIKL, 2024), which focuses on summarizing highlighted table segments into coherent sentences. An example of the dataset is shown in Figure 3. The dataset consists of 7,170 training tables, 876 validation ta-

[2]Within Tabular-TX, data is preprocessed before using LLMs. Further details on data preprocessing are discussed in Appendix C.1.

Model	ROUGE-1	ROUGE-L	BLEU	Average
KoBART - Fine-tuned	0.37	0.28	0.35	0.33
EXAONE 3.0 7.8B - ICL	0.21	0.14	0.01	0.12
EXAONE 3.0 7.8B - LoRA	0.27	0.21	0.05	0.17
EXAONE 3.0 7.8B - Tabular-TX	**0.51**	**0.39**	**0.44**	**0.45**
llama-3-Korean-Bllossom-8B - ICL	0.33	0.25	0.27	0.28
llama-3-Korean-Bllossom-8B - Tabular-TX	**0.48**	**0.37**	**0.42**	**0.43**

Table 1: Evaluation results on the Korean Korean table interpretation benchmark for each model.

bles, and 876 test tables. Each data point contains metadata such as the document title, table title, publication date, publishing organization, table source URL, highlighted cell information, table data, and a reference summary sentence describing the highlighted portions' key contents.

Evaluation Metrics We employ ROUGE-1, ROUGE-L, and BLEU to evaluate the performance of table segment interpretation. These metrics assess how effectively the summaries convey the key content of the table while achieving high semantic quality.

Models To evaluate the effectiveness of the Tabular-TX pipeline, we utilize EXAONE 3.0 7.8B (An et al., 2024) and llama-3-Korean-Bllossom-8B[3] models as base models. EXAONE 3.0 7.8B, a successor to EXAONE-LM-v1.0, has demonstrated state-of-the-art performance in Korean TableQA, ranking first on the KorWikiTableQuestions (Jun et al., 2022). Similarly, llama-3-Korean-Bllossom-8B is the top-performing sub-10B model in a Korean multi-domain reasoning benchmark. We compare the performance of these models with and without Tabular-TX, assessing whether structured generation enhances performance in table summarization. Additionally, we analyze whether Tabular-TX reduces reliance on extensive fine-tuning while maintaining high-quality summaries.

5.1.1 Additional Adaptation Approaches

In-Context Learning (ICL) We begin by applying ICL to each model, providing a few table-summarization examples without explicit fine-tuning. This approach tests how effectively the model can generate coherent sentences for highlighted table cells based solely on a small set of demonstrations.

Low-Rank Adaptation (LoRA) Next, we assess the computational efficiency and performance of the Tabular-TX pipeline by introducing LoRA (Hu et al., 2022). We trained the EXAONE 3.0 7.8B by applying LoRA to see if we could maintain high-quality table summaries with fewer resources.

Full Model Fine-Tuning Finally, we evaluate the KoBART (Korean BART)[4] model under a full model fine-tuning setup to determine whether a smaller-scale language model can achieve comparable performance when all its parameters are trained on the Korean table interpretation benchmark.

5.2 Experimental Results

Table 1 presents the performance of various models evaluated using ROUGE-1, ROUGE-L, BLEU, and their average scores. The KoBART recorded an average score of 0.33 after fine-tuning. In contrast, EXAONE 3.0 7.8B achieved 0.12 with the ICL method, 0.17 after fine-tuning, and 0.45 when combined with the Tabular-TX method. Similarly, llama-3-Korean-Bllossom-8B, which was also tested with Tabular-TX, showed a notable improvement, reaching an average score of 0.43. These results demonstrate that Tabular-TX consistently outperforms alternative methods, achieving the highest overall performance across different model configurations.

The performance gap between EXAONE 3.0 7.8B and KoBART, despite both being fine-tuned on the same dataset, can be explained through the multiplicative joint scaling law (Zhang et al., 2024a). This principle suggests that when the dataset size is insufficient relative to the model size, the performance gains from fine-tuning remain limited. Since KoBART has 124M parameters, while EXAONE 3.0 is approximately 63 times larger, the

[3]https://huggingface.co/MLP-KTLim/llama-3-Korean-Bllossom-8B

[4]https://huggingface.co/gogamza/kobart-base-v2

dataset required to achieve a comparable performance boost must be proportionally scaled up by a factor of 63. The inability to meet this scaling requirement explains why the performance of the fine-tuned KoBART plateaued, while EXAONE 3.0 7.8B demonstrated more significant gains with the same dataset.

This study confirms that the proposed Tabular-TX method enhances table data analysis performance without fine-tuning. Notably, Tabular-TX outperforms traditional fine-tuned models despite relying on significantly smaller datasets, demonstrating its efficacy in resource-constrained learning environments. Moreover, Tabular-TX achieved approximately four times higher average performance compared to standard ICL methods, further reinforcing its role as a scalable and efficient alternative for structured table summarization tasks.

6 Conclusion

This study introduced the Theme-Explanation Table Summarization (Tabular-TX) pipeline, a novel approach to improve table summarization tasks with low-resource requirements. Moreover, the proposed pipeline effectively overcame unique challenges in Korean administrative table processing.

Experimental results signify that Tabular-TX enhances table summarization performance. This study contributed to the summarization of complex table data by introducing a novel sentence generation method based on the theme-explanation structure. Furthermore, Tabular-TX achieved excellent performance without fine-tuning, by incorporating ICL. This indicates its potential as a significant contribution to table data analysis, even in resource-constrained environments, without requiring direct model training.

Limitations

We acknowledge a few limitations in this study. First, Tabular-TX was only evaluated on EXAONE 3.0 7.8B and llama-3-Korean-Bllossom-8B, leaving the question of its effectiveness across a broader range of LLMs open. Second, this study primarily focused on Korean administrative table data, and further research should investigate whether the Theme-Explanation structure is equally effective for diverse tabular data formats in other languages or specialized domains. Finally, Tabular-TX currently relies on predefined structural components (Theme and Explanation parts) to enforce interpretability. Future work should explore more dynamic approaches that allow for adaptive sentence structuring based on different types of tables, potentially improving performance across varied tabular structures.

References

Soyoung An, Kyunghoon Bae, Eunbi Choi, Stanley Jungkyu Choi, Yemuk Choi, Seokhee Hong, Yeonjung Hong, Junwon Hwang, Hyojin Jeon, Gerrard Jeongwon Jo, Hyunjik Jo, Jiyeon Jung, Yountae Jung, Euisoon Kim, Hyosang Kim, Joonkee Kim, Seonghwan Kim, Soyeon Kim, Sunkyoung Kim, and 18 others. 2024. EXAONE 3.0 7.8b instruction tuned language model. *CoRR*, abs/2408.03541.

Tom B. Brown, Benjamin Mann, Nick Ryder, Melanie Subbiah, Jared Kaplan, Prafulla Dhariwal, Arvind Neelakantan, Pranav Shyam, Girish Sastry, Amanda Askell, Sandhini Agarwal, Ariel Herbert-Voss, Gretchen Krueger, Tom Henighan, Rewon Child, Aditya Ramesh, Daniel M. Ziegler, Jeffrey Wu, Clemens Winter, and 12 others. 2020. Language models are few-shot learners. In *Advances in Neural Information Processing Systems 33: Annual Conference on Neural Information Processing Systems 2020, NeurIPS 2020, December 6-12, 2020, virtual.*

Edward J. Hu, Yelong Shen, Phillip Wallis, Zeyuan Allen-Zhu, Yuanzhi Li, Shean Wang, Lu Wang, and Weizhu Chen. 2022. Lora: Low-rank adaptation of large language models. In *The Tenth International Conference on Learning Representations, ICLR 2022, Virtual Event, April 25-29, 2022*. OpenReview.net.

Changwook Jun, Jooyoung Choi, Myoseop Sim, Hyun Kim, Hansol Jang, and Kyungkoo Min. 2022. Korean-specific dataset for table question answering. In *Proceedings of the Thirteenth Language Resources and Evaluation Conference, LREC 2022, Marseille, France, 20-25 June 2022*, pages 6114–6120. European Language Resources Association.

Tianyang Liu, Fei Wang, and Muhao Chen. 2024. Rethinking tabular data understanding with large language models. In *Proceedings of the 2024 Conference of the North American Chapter of the Association for Computational Linguistics: Human Language Technologies (Volume 1: Long Papers), NAACL 2024, Mexico City, Mexico, June 16-21, 2024*, pages 450–482. Association for Computational Linguistics.

Emanuele Musumeci, Michele Brienza, Vincenzo Suriani, Daniele Nardi, and Domenico Daniele Bloisi. 2024. LLM based multi-agent generation of semi-structured documents from semantic templates in the public administration domain. In *Artificial Intelligence in HCI*, pages 98–117, Cham. Springer Nature Switzerland.

Linyong Nan, Chiachun Hsieh, Ziming Mao, Xi Victoria Lin, Neha Verma, Rui Zhang, Wojciech Kryscinski, Hailey Schoelkopf, Riley Kong, Xiangru Tang, Mutethia Mutuma, Ben Rosand, Isabel Trindade, Renusree Bandaru, Jacob Cunningham, Caiming Xiong, and Dragomir R. Radev. 2022. Fetaqa: Free-form table question answering. *Trans. Assoc. Comput. Linguistics*, 10:35–49.

National Institute of Korean Language, NIKL. 2024. A corpus for evaluating the generation of interpretations for part of a table. `https://kli.korean.go.kr/corpus/taskOrdtm/taskDownload.do?taskOrdtmId=109&clCd=ING_TASK&subMenuId`.

OpenAI. 2023. GPT-4 technical report. *CoRR*, abs/2303.08774.

Elias Stengel-Eskin, Kenton W. Murray, Sheng Zhang, Aaron Steven White, and Benjamin Van Durme. 2021. Joint universal syntactic and semantic parsing. *Trans. Assoc. Comput. Linguistics*, 9:756–773.

Zilong Wang, Hao Zhang, Chun-Liang Li, Julian Martin Eisenschlos, Vincent Perot, Zifeng Wang, Lesly Miculicich, Yasuhisa Fujii, Jingbo Shang, Chen-Yu Lee, and Tomas Pfister. 2024. Chain-of-table: Evolving tables in the reasoning chain for table understanding. In *The Twelfth International Conference on Learning Representations, ICLR 2024, Vienna, Austria, May 7-11, 2024*. OpenReview.net.

Jason Wei, Xuezhi Wang, Dale Schuurmans, Maarten Bosma, Brian Ichter, Fei Xia, Ed H. Chi, Quoc V. Le, and Denny Zhou. 2022. Chain-of-thought prompting elicits reasoning in large language models. In *Advances in Neural Information Processing Systems 35: Annual Conference on Neural Information Processing Systems 2022, NeurIPS 2022, New Orleans, LA, USA, November 28 - December 9, 2022*.

Biao Zhang, Zhongtao Liu, Colin Cherry, and Orhan Firat. 2024a. When scaling meets LLM finetuning: The effect of data, model and finetuning method. In *The Twelfth International Conference on Learning Representations, ICLR 2024, Vienna, Austria, May 7-11, 2024*. OpenReview.net.

Tianshu Zhang, Xiang Yue, Yifei Li, and Huan Sun. 2024b. Tablellama: Towards open large generalist models for tables. In *Proceedings of the 2024 Conference of the North American Chapter of the Association for Computational Linguistics: Human Language Technologies (Volume 1: Long Papers), NAACL 2024, Mexico City, Mexico, June 16-21, 2024*, pages 6024–6044. Association for Computational Linguistics.

Jun Zhao, Jingqi Tong, Yurong Mou, Ming Zhang, Qi Zhang, and Xuanjing Huang. 2024. Exploring the compositional deficiency of large language models in mathematical reasoning through trap problems. In *Proceedings of the 2024 Conference on Empirical Methods in Natural Language Processing, EMNLP 2024, Miami, FL, USA, November 12-16, 2024*, pages 16361–16376. Association for Computational Linguistics.

Table title : 보건복지부 관서 운영비 한도 Ministry of Health and Welfare's office operating expense limits

예산과목 Budget Category	용 도 Usage
운영비(210) Operating Expenses (210)	건당 500만원이하의 경비(단, 공관금 및 위원회 참석비, 선거 관련 용품제작·인쇄 비용·우편요금, 청사임차료, 기업특별회계 당해 사업에 직접 소요되는 경비는 금액 제한 없음). Expenses of up to 5 million KRW per case (However, there is no spending limit for embassy fees, committee attendance fees, election-related item production/printing costs, postage fees, building rental fees, and
여비(220) Travel Expenses (220)	전체 Entirely covered
업무추진비(240) Business Promotion Expenses (240)	건당 500만원 이하의 경비(단, 기업특별회계의 당해 사업에 직접 소요되는 경비는 금액제한 없음) Expenses of up to 5 million KRW per case (However, there is no spending limit for expenses directly related to projects under the corporate special accounting).

highlighted_cells : [(0,1), (1,1)]

Generic prompt

위의 표에서 highlighted_cells를 모두 언급하여 내용을 요약해줘
Summarize the contents of the table above by mentioning all highlighted_cells in the table above.

운영비(210)는 500만 원 이하의 경비가 기업 특별회계 사업에 직접 소요되는 경비로 사용되며, 후자의 경우 금액 제한이 없습니다.

Operating expenses (210) are expenses of 5 million won or less and are used directly for corporate special accounting projects, and in the case of the latter, there is no limit to the amount.

Generic Prompt with Specific Instructions

위 표에서 highlighted_cells를 모두 언급하여 정확하고 객관적 사실만 담아서 내용을 요약해줘.
Summarize the content with only accurate and objective facts, while mentioning all highlighted_cells in the table

보건복지부 관서 운영비 한도에 따르면, 운영비(210)는 건당 5백만 원 이하로 제한되나 기획특별회계 사업 직접 경비는 제한이 없고, 여비(220)는 전액 적용됩니다.

According to the Ministry of Health and Welfare's office operating expense limits, operating expenses (210) are limited to 5 million won or less per case, but there is no limit to direct expenses for planning and special accounting projects, and travel expenses (220) are fully applied.

Journalist persona-applied prompt

너는 한 문장짜리 기사를 쓰는 신문 기자야. 이 표에서 highlighted_cells를 모두 언급하여 한 문장으로 기사를 써줘.
You are a newspaper journalist writing a one-sentence news article. Write a single sentence mentioning all the highlighted_cells in the table.

보건복지부 관서 운영비 한도에 따르면 운영비(210)는 공관금 및 위원회 참석비, 선거 관련 용품 제작·인쇄 비용·우편요금, 청사 임차료 등을 포함하여 건당 500만원 이하로 제한되며, 여비(220)는 전체적으로 적용된다.

According to the Ministry of Health and Welfare's office operating expense limits, operating expenses (210) are restricted to 5 million KRW per case, including embassy fees, committee attendance fees, election-related item production and printing costs, postage fees, and building rental fees, while travel expenses (220) are fully covered.

Figure 2: An example of how a persona-applied prompt generates more accurate summaries. (Gray text indicates the English translation.)

A Korean table interpretation benchmark


```
{
 "id": "nikluge-gtps-2023-train",
 "input": {
  "metadata": {
   "title": "Tax Environment Changes and Policy Issues due to the 4th Industrial Revolution",
   "table_title": "Major Legislative Proposals in Taxation Related to the 4th Industrial Revolution",
   "date": "2020-06-09",
   "publisher": "National Assembly Budget Office",
   "url": "https://www.nabo.go.kr/Sub/01/Report/01_01_Board.jsp",
   "highlighted_cells": [[10, 13], [1, 14], [3, 14]]
  },
  "table": [
   { "value": "Special Tax Limitation Act", "is_header": true, "col": 0, "colspan": 4, "row": 0, "rowspan": 1 },
   { "value": "2009580", "is_header": false, "col": 0, "colspan": 1, "row": 1, "rowspan": 1 },
   { "value": "Special Deduction/Registration Fee", "is_header": false, "col": 1, "colspan": 1, "row": 1, "rowspan": 1 },
   { "value": "Income Tax Act Disclosure", "is_header": false, "col": 1, "colspan": 1, "row": 1, "rowspan": 1 }
  ]
 },
 "output": [
  "The content of the VAT law issued on November 6, 2018, covers the electronic application scope for VAT...",
  "For VAT law, the scope of electronic application includes internet ads, cloud computing services, ...",
  "On November 6, 2018, the VAT law was revised to include internet ads, cloud computing services,..."
 ]
}
```


Figure 3: An example from the corpus for evaluating interpretation generation of table segments (originally in Korean, translated into English) (NIKL, 2024).

We leverage the Korean table interpretation benchmark provided by the National Institute of Korean Language (NIKL, 2024).

As shown in Figure 3, an objective of the dataset is to summarize the highlighted cells, which are labeled in the metadata as `highlighted_cells`, into a single coherent sentence.

B Examples of the Theme Part & Explanation Part

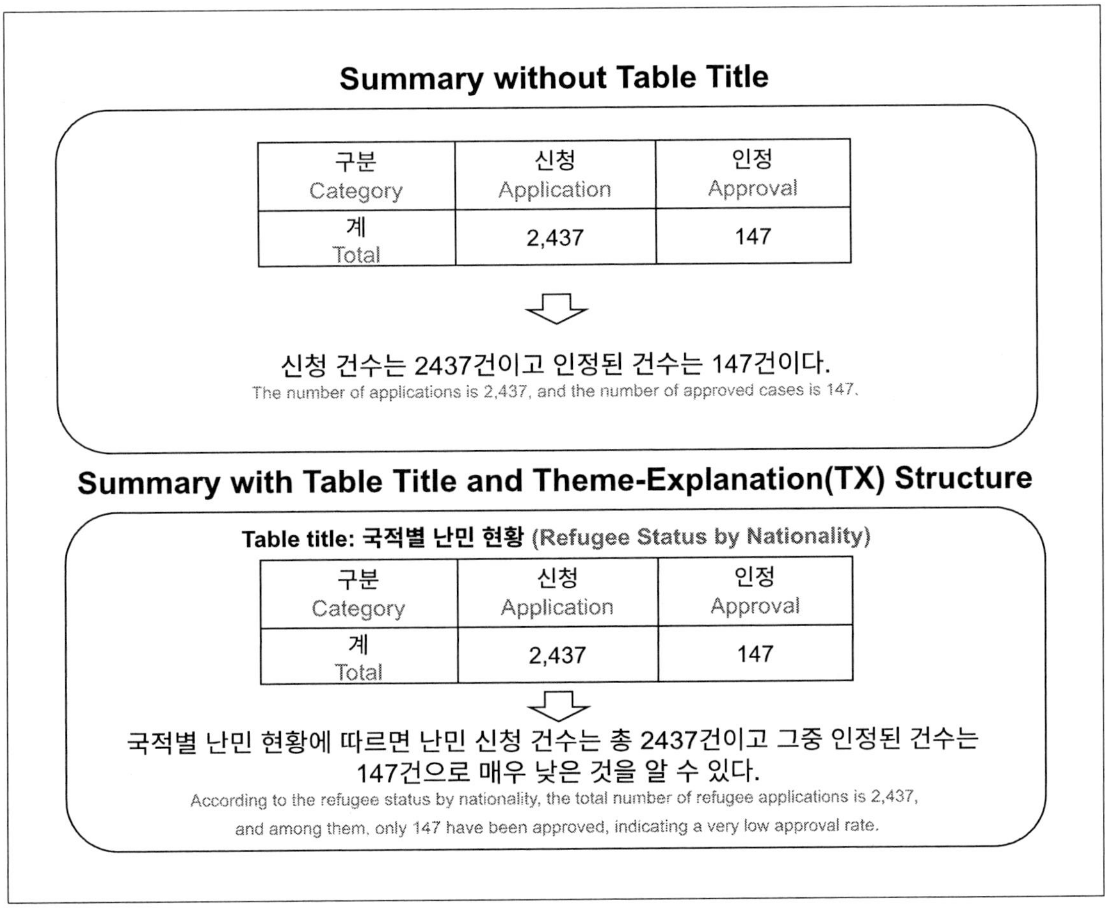

Figure 4: A sentence including the table title conveys the context more accurately. (Gray text indicates the English translation.)

B.1 Theme Part

For example, in the sentence: *"According to the refugee status by nationality, the total number of refugee applications is 2,437, and among them, only 147 have been approved, indicating a very low approval rate."* Here, the Theme Part is: *"According to the refugee status by nationality,"* This phrase, introduced with the citation expression *"According to"*, provides essential context for the numerical values that follow. Without this structured introduction, the reader may struggle to understand the significance of the numbers. Figure 4 illustrates how omitting the Theme Part results in an unclear or misleading summary.

B.2 Explanation Part

For instance, in the previous example, the Explanation Part is: *"the net fiscal cost increased by 9.435 trillion KRW from the previous year, reaching a total of 61.301 trillion KRW."* Here, the Explanation Part is derived by comparing the numerical changes between the two cells. Here, a trend analysis is applied to highlight the increase in fiscal cost.

C Implementation Details

C.1 Data Preprocessing

The first step is preprocessing the table to simplify its structure for better LLM comprehension. Since LLMs primarily operate on sequential text representations, directly processing raw tabular formats can lead to misinterpretation of hierarchical relationships within the data. To address this, we convert table data into a key-value pair dictionary format, which is commonly used in natural language processing tasks. This transformation significantly enhances LLMs' ability to recognize table semantics, improving summarization accuracy (Stengel-Eskin et al., 2021).

Then, we process merged cells to clarify the table structure. Merged cells span multiple rows or columns and are defined by 'rowspan' and 'colspan.' As shown in Figure 5, LLMs infer relationships between data through row or column alignment. However, incorrect handling of merged cell ranges can lead to misinterpretation. For example, in Figure 6, the cell labeled "2020" should cover columns 3 and 4, but it appears only in column 3. To resolve this, merged cells are replicated across their ranges, allowing LLMs to recognize cell dependencies and hierarchical structures correctly.

Finally, the transformed dictionary list retains only the highlighted and related cells, where "related cells" refer to all header cells sharing the same row/column as the highlighted cells. This process reduces data complexity and enhances LLMs' recognition of table structures.

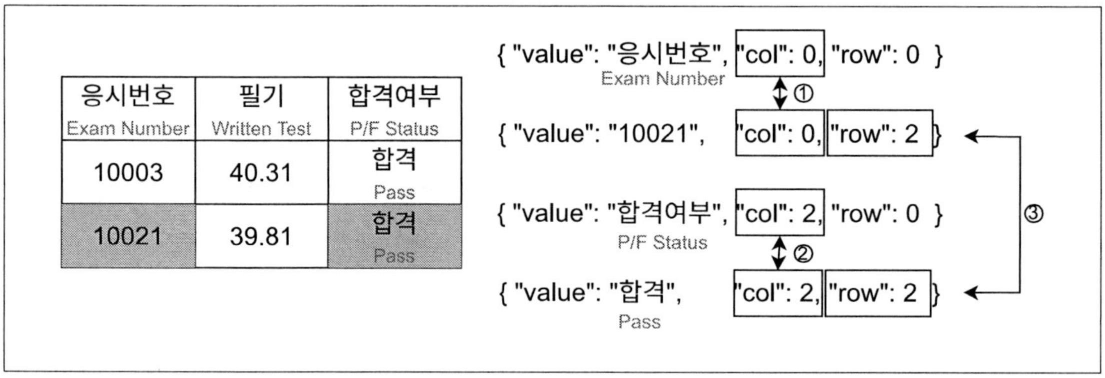

Figure 5: An example of inferring relationships between data sharing the same row or column. Through inference in ①, it is deduced that '10021' represents the 'Exam number.' In ②, the meaning of 'pass' is inferred. In ③, it is deduced that the exam with the 'Exam number' '10021' has 'passed.' (Gray text indicates the English translation.)

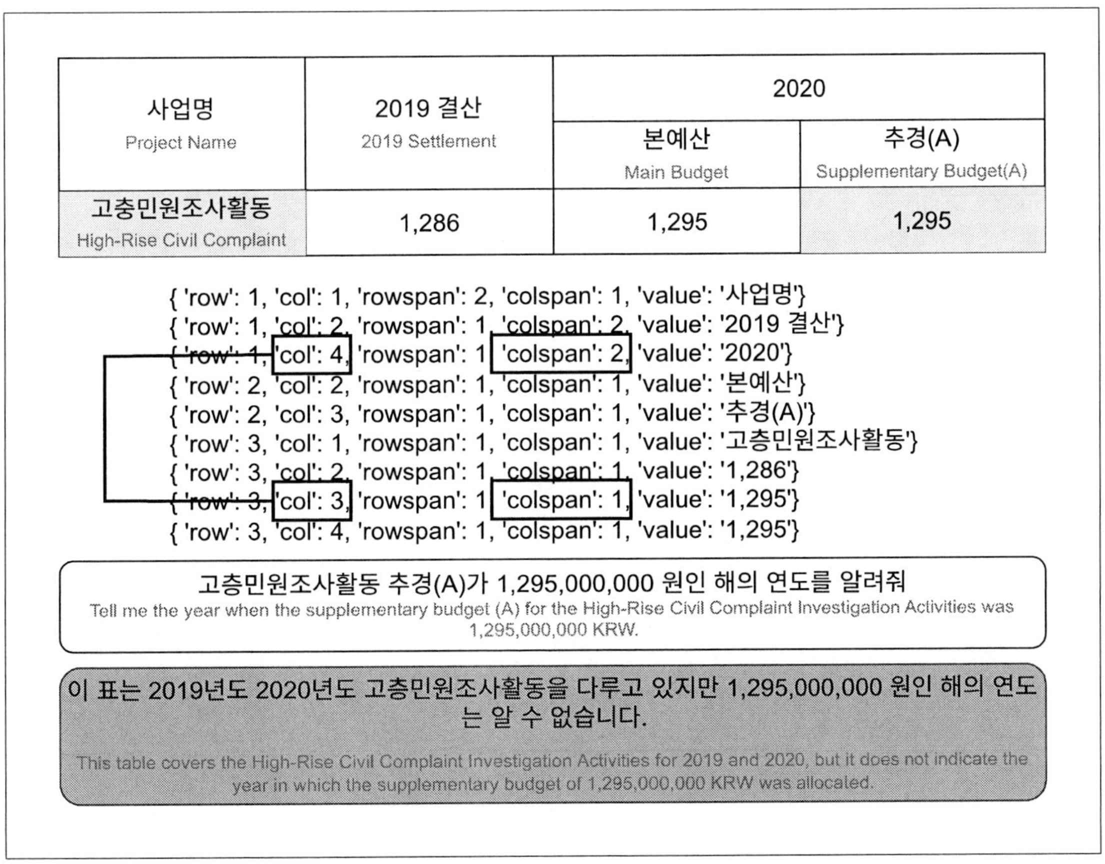

Figure 6: An example of how merged cells hinder table recognition. (Gray text indicates the English translation.)

C.2 Prompt Details

Tabular-TX generates table summaries in two steps. First, the **Data Recognition / Classification** step identifies key data from highlighted cells (Figure 7). Second, the **Sentence Generation** step forms a summary in the Theme-Explanation format (Figure 8).

Title: {'title'}

Table Title: {'table_title'}

Table: {'table data}

highlighted_cells: {'highlighted_cell coordinates'}

highlighted_cells are in (col, row) format and indicate the location of important data within the table.

if 'Δ' in Table [{', '.join(increased_cells)}] values contain the Δ symbol, which indicates an increase.

if 'monetary unit' in Table [{', '.join(money_cells)}] values represent monetary amounts.

if 'percentage data' in Table [{', '.join(percent_cells)}] values represent percentages and should be displayed with a % symbol.

Figure 7: Summarizing key data points from the table in a single sentence for a news article. (originally in Korean, translated into English)

You are a newspaper reporter writing an article based on the table. You must convey the information in a single sentence. Mention all the highlighted_cells in the table and write the sentence in a declarative form. Do not say anything other than the one sentence.

Figure 8: Writing a one-sentence summary of a table by embodying news reporter persona. (originally in Korean, translated into English)

Generating Synthetic Relational Tabular Data via Structural Causal Models

Frederik Hoppe and **Astrid Franz** and **Lars Kleinemeier** and **Udo Göbel**
CONTACT Software GmbH, Wiener Str. 1-3, 28359 Bremen, Germany
frederik.hoppe@contact-software.com

Abstract

Synthetic tabular data generation has received increasing attention in recent years, particularly with the emergence of foundation models for tabular data. The breakthrough success of TabPFN (Hollmann et al., 2025), which leverages vast quantities of synthetic tabular datasets derived from structural causal models (SCMs), demonstrates the critical role synthetic data plays in developing powerful tabular foundation models. However, most real-world tabular data exists in relational formats spanning multiple interconnected tables — a structure not adequately addressed by current generation methods. In this work, we extend the SCM-based approach by developing a novel framework that generates realistic synthetic relational tabular data including causal relationships across tables. Our experiments confirm that this framework is able to construct relational datasets with complex inter-table dependencies mimicking real-world scenarios.

1 Introduction

The development of synthetic data generation techniques has seen remarkable progress with the advent of foundation models, particularly in domains such as images and text. However, generating realistic tabular data - especially relational tabular data with properly linked entries - remains an underexplored challenge in machine learning research. While large language models and diffusion models have revolutionized synthetic data generation across various domains, structured tabular data has received comparatively less attention despite its prevalence in real-world applications.

In this paper, we develop a novel synthetic relational data generation framework for creating arbitrarily large amounts of relational datasets with complex, realistic dependencies, suitable, e.g., for foundation model training and benchmark creation. In order to systematically model both intra-table correlations and inter-table relationships, our method constructs data independently from real-world datasets, overcoming accessibility limitations. Our method is inspired by the SCM-based approach for single tables of TabPFN (Hollmann et al., 2025). However, we introduce critical changes to the original SCM framework, and extend it to generate multiple tables connected through shared key columns. Based on these extensions, we provide an automated framework for creating synthetic relational datasets that comprise both statistical properties within individual tables and structural relationships between them. This contribution enables the creation of realistic relational tabular data that can be used for developing models capturing inter-table relationships.

2 Related Work

Synthetic tabular data generation has evolved significantly to address challenges like data scarcity and privacy concerns. Earlier work (Patki et al., 2016) presented the Synthetic Data Vault, which builds generative models of relational databases through recursive conditional parameter aggregation. It is the first learning-based approach for generating relational data. Recently, (Hudovernik, 2024) proposed an approach that combines graph neural network embeddings with diffusion models, exploiting a graph representation of relational data induced by foreign key constraints. The method captures topological structure and statistical properties across multiple linked tables. These approaches require a (real-world) dataset as a basis to extract statistical and relational patterns, which are then used to generate new data with the same statistical properties. However, due to the lack of accessible real-world datasets, these methods seem to be unsuited for producing huge amounts of relational datasets with manifold intra- and inter-table relationships. A generation method independent of

Proceedings of the 4th Table Representation Learning Workshop, pages 13–18

real-world data was proposed in (Hollmann et al., 2025), generating synthetic datasets through SCMs (Pearl, 2010), which naturally allow for simulating wide-ranging causal dependencies. However, the method is restricted to single, unrelated tables.

3 Data Generation Method

Our structured data generation approach is based on an SCM, represented by a directed acyclic graph (DAG) $\mathcal{G}$ with directed edges, connecting parent nodes (causes) to child nodes (effects). For every node $i = 1, \ldots, N$, a structural assignment

$$x_i = f_i(x_{\text{pa}(i)}, \varepsilon_i) \in \mathbb{R}^n \tag{1}$$

is used to propagate the data in $\mathcal{G}$, where n denotes the hidden dimension of the data at each node, f_i a deterministic mapping, $x_{\text{pa}(i)}$ the realization of the parent data of node i, and ε_i an independent n-dimensional noise vector. First, we sample the structure of the model, i.e. the nodes and the directed edges. Second, for every independent sample, i.e. table row, we initialize the data as multi-dimensional vectors at the root nodes and propagate it, including random noise, through the graph. In the final step, we readout the data by projecting the n-dimensional vectors to scalars. Thus, we obtain a two-dimensional data scheme where the number of rows corresponds to the number of samples and the number of columns to the number of nodes. Subsections 3.1, 3.2 and 3.3 describe these construction steps in more detail. Algorithm 1 provides a high-level overview.

After these steps, the data of the final tabular format could be additionally processed via bias induction, disturbance by additional noise, wrong data incorporation or the methods mentioned in (Hollmann et al., 2025) in order to mimic real-world data challenges.

3.1 Structure Sampling

To sample a directed graph, we utilize the Barabási Albert model (Barabási and Albert, 1999). After removing isolated nodes and edges (i, j) with $j > i$, we obtain a DAG. The sinks of the resulting graph represent the targets, and the remaining nodes are considered as features for the future dataset.

The data associated with the root nodes are initialized as n-dimensional vectors, drawn from a range of distributions, including normal distributions with random means and standard deviations as well as gamma distributions with random shapes and scales. This initialization data will be propagated through the graph. For every node $i = 1, \ldots, N$, we define a function

$$g_i : \mathbb{R}^{|\text{pa}(i)| \cdot n} \to \mathbb{R}^n \tag{2}$$

that propagates the concatenated parent data. In contrast to (Hollmann et al., 2025), we do not incorporate categorical feature generation into the set of propagation functions (2), since this restricts the variety of states at successive nodes. In our approach, the data is propagated through the graph as multi-dimensional (continuous) vectors. Only when we observe the data, it may become categorical, i.e. discretized. Thus, we construct categorical data without restricting the number of different data vectors at the subsequent nodes to the number of categories. In principle, propagation functions (2) could be arbitrarily defined. In this work, propagation functions (2) are considered to be one-layer fully-connected neural networks followed by randomly chosen (non-)linear activation functions, e.g., ReLU, logabs.

Once each node has processed the data, the information from the resulting vectors $x_1, \ldots, x_N$ is stored in a tabular format. To this end, we define a set of pooling functions $p_i : \mathbb{R}^n \to \mathbb{R}$, to reduce dimensionality, i.e., for every node $i = 1, \ldots, N$, we independently select a continuous pooling function p_i such as norm, mean, median or variance of the vector, or a categorical pooling function, defined in Subsection 3.2.

Algorithm 1 Generating Synthetic Datasets

Structure Sampling: ▷ cf. Subsec. 3.1
  Sample DAG $\mathcal{G}$
  Initialize root node distributions
    Define propagation fct g_i (e.g. neural net)
    Define pooling fct p_i (e.g. norm, categorical)
Pre-Sampling: ▷ cf. Subsec. 3.2
  Sample root data and propagate it by g_i
  for every node i **do**
    Compute component-wise 10%- and 90%-quantiles $q_{0.1}(i), q_{0.9}(i)$
    if i categorical node
      Choose number of categories K
      Cluster data into K categories
      Refine p_i as in (4)
Main Data Sampling: ▷ cf. Subsec. 3.3
  Sample root data and propagate it by f_i (cf. (3))
  Read out data at every node by p_i

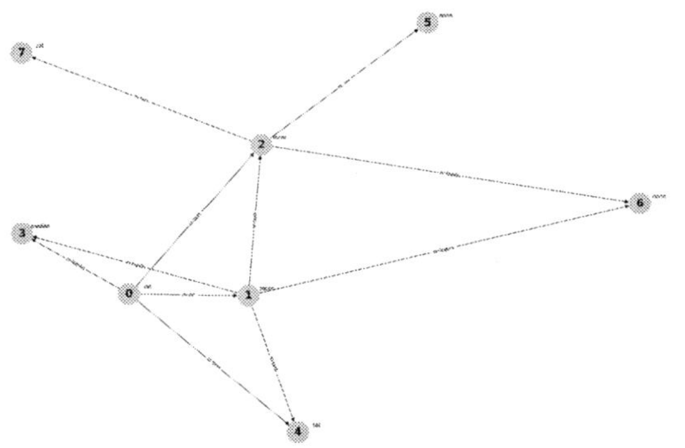

Figure 1: Example of a DAG illustrating the SCM. Nodes represent the structural assignments, see Equation (1), annotated with the corresponding pooling function (Euclidean **norm**, **mean**, **median** or **cat**egorical projection). Edges indicate the flow of the data vectors, with edge labels specifying the applied (non)-linear activation function. The green nodes symbolize the targets, while the blue nodes correspond to the features.

The selection of initialization and pooling functions is stored in the graph structure to assure reproducability and allow for a detailed analysis of parameter influence. An example of such a DAG is presented in Fig. 1.

3.2 Pre-Sampling

Propagating the data in the DAG $\mathcal{G}$ according to Equation (1) involves noise vectors ε_i. In order to align the magnitude of the noise influence with the data distribution, we conduct the data generation process via a low-sample pre-run without noise. We independently sample the root data according to the pre-defined distribution and propagate the data through the entire graph. Then, we estimate the corresponding data distribution of each node with the sampling data of the pre-run. More concretely, for every node i we compute the 10%- and 90%-quantiles component-wise, denoted by vectors $q_{0.1}$ and $q_{0.9}$. In the main data generation run, this information enables us to tailor the noise level to the distribution of the corresponding node, i.e., x_i is given by

$$\begin{aligned} x_i &= f_i(x_{\mathrm{pa}(i)}, \varepsilon_i) \\ &= g_i(x_{\mathrm{pa}(i)}) + (q_{0.9}(i) - q_{0.1}(i))\varepsilon_i. \end{aligned} \quad (3)$$

By introducing this noise scaling we ensure a balanced noise integration into the data vector, such that $g_i(x_{\mathrm{pa}(i)})$ remains the primary source of information. The degree of perturbation could be adjusted by computing different quantiles.

Moreover, the estimation of the node distributions allows for a semantically meaningful discretization of the data into categories. For every categorical node i, we randomly select the number of categories $K(i)$, and cluster the pre-sampled data into these $K(i)$ categories, for instance by the k-means algorithm. Then, we define a categorical pooling function, assigning the continuous n-dimensional data vectors to the categories:

$$p_i(x_i) = \mathrm{argmin}_{l=1,\ldots,K(i)} \|x_i - v_l\|_2, \quad (4)$$

where $v_1, \ldots, v_{K(i)}$ denote the cluster centroids. It is important to note that the categorization of the data occurs only for the readout and does not affect the subsequent propagation through the child nodes.

With the information collected by the pre-run, we are able to perform the main sampling run.

3.3 Main Data Sampling

During the main run, we initialize independently data at the root nodes and propagate it through the entire graph according to Equations (1) and (3). Utilizing the pooling functions mentioned above, we project the n-dimensional vector at each node to a scalar, which yields one data sample. The procedure is repeated for the desired sample size, resulting in a table, where the rows correspond to the samples and the columns to the graph nodes.

We consider the columns, represented by the sinks of the graph (colored green in Fig. 1), as potential targets whereas the remaining columns (indicated blue in Fig. 1) are considered as features. On the one hand, this allows for a complete usage of the dataset, e.g., to train a tabular foundation model. On the other hand, the single targets could be used independently, e.g., for handling end-to-end scenarios.

4 Extensions to Relational Data

This section extends the previously described methodology to generate relational tables, summarized in Algorithm 2. The objective is to create

Algorithm 2 Generating Relational Datasets

Sample DAGs $\mathcal{G}_{\text{main}}$ and $\mathcal{G}_{\text{add}}$
Connect via coupling node C: $\mathcal{G}_{\text{add}} \to \text{C} \to \mathcal{G}_{\text{main}}$
Link feature nodes of $\mathcal{G}_{\text{add}}$ to target nodes of $\mathcal{G}_{\text{main}}$
Sample dataset w.r.t. Algorithm 1 for merged graph
Sample dataset w.r.t. Algorithm 1 for $\mathcal{G}_{\text{add}}$ (incl. C)

two tables with different sample sizes that share a common feature, represented as a coupling node. First, we independently sample two DAGs, denoted by $\mathcal{G}_{\text{main}}$ and $\mathcal{G}_{\text{add}}$, according to the procedure described in Subsection 3.1. Then, we introduce a coupling node C that is caused by a sink of $\mathcal{G}_{\text{add}}$ and directs to a feature of $\mathcal{G}_{\text{main}}$. In this way, we establish a relationship between these graphs and assure, that information propagates from $\mathcal{G}_{\text{add}}$ to $\mathcal{G}_{\text{main}}$.

To incorporate *latent* causal influence from $\mathcal{G}_{\text{add}}$ to $\mathcal{G}_{\text{main}}$, we connect feature nodes of $\mathcal{G}_{\text{add}}$ to target nodes of $\mathcal{G}_{\text{main}}$. An example of two coupled graphs is illustrated in Fig. 2. Nodes belonging to the main graph $\mathcal{G}_{\text{main}}$ are labeled M1, M2, ..., forming the same graph as shown in Fig. 1. The nodes in the additional graph $\mathcal{G}_{\text{add}}$ are denoted by A1, A2, ... In the same way, more than two relational tables can be generated. The data samples are generated once for the merged graph (including node C) and once for graph $\mathcal{G}_{\text{add}}$ (including node C), both with separate sample sizes. Although we utilize the merged graph to generate the data together with the (latent) causal relationships, the main table contains only the data corresponding to the nodes of $\mathcal{G}_{\text{main}}$ (including node C). The headers of the resulting main and additional tables for the example graphs of Fig. 2 are presented in Tables 1 and 2. The edges representing the latent causality effectively link the two tables. Consequently, a comprehensive understanding of the affected targets requires integrating information from both tables, as demonstrated in Section 5. Without the latent causality links, the information propagated through node C would be sufficient to represent the relationships in $\mathcal{G}_{\text{main}}$.

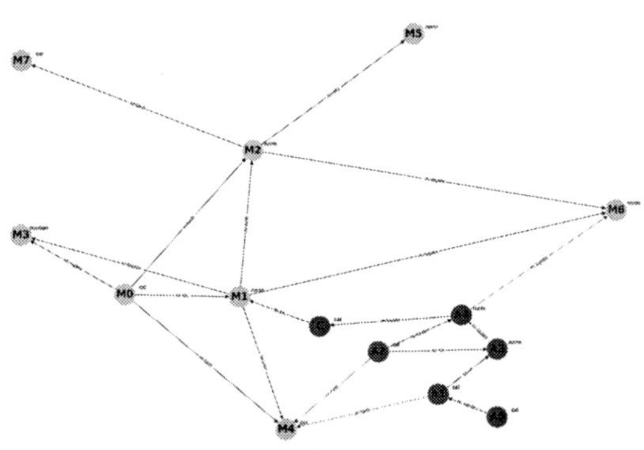

Figure 2: Example graph for generating relational tables. The DAG from Fig. 1 with renamed nodes M1, M2, ... is extended by an additional DAG with feature nodes A1, A2, ... Both graphs are linked via the connection node C and latent relationships indicated by yellow edges.

5 Evaluation

We exemplary analyze one relational dataset consisting of two coupled tables constructed as stated in Section 4. This example dataset is based on the DAG shown in Fig. 2. We sample the main dataset with 100,000 rows, described and illustrated in Appendix A and Table 1. The first 90,000 rows serve as training set, while the remaining 10,000 rows are excluded from embedding training and serve as a test set. The additional dataset, including the C-column, is sampled with 500 rows, see Table 2. In order to measure how the data in the main table is influenced by the data in the additional table, we perform the classical ML tasks classification and regression, first using the main table only and second using the data of the additional table, too.

In order to perform regression or classification tasks for several target columns, we compute task-independent table entry embeddings with respect to the EmbDI procedure (Cappuzzo et al., 2020), for a variety of embedding dimensions. First, we consider the main table only. For each training row, we compute a row embedding vector by averaging the embeddings of all entries in this row, excluding the target columns to be task-independent. This row embedding procedure can be applied not only to training rows but also to test rows, as the entries in the test rows are drawn from the same underlying distribution as the entries in the training rows. For all target columns, we then perform a regression or classification task, depending on the type of pooling function (numerical as mean, median, norm, ... or categorical). For any test row, we search for 10 nearest neighbors in the row embedding space of the training rows. The prediction is computed as an average of the target values of the selected 10 training rows, weighted by the inverse distance of the test row embedding vector to the 10 nearest training

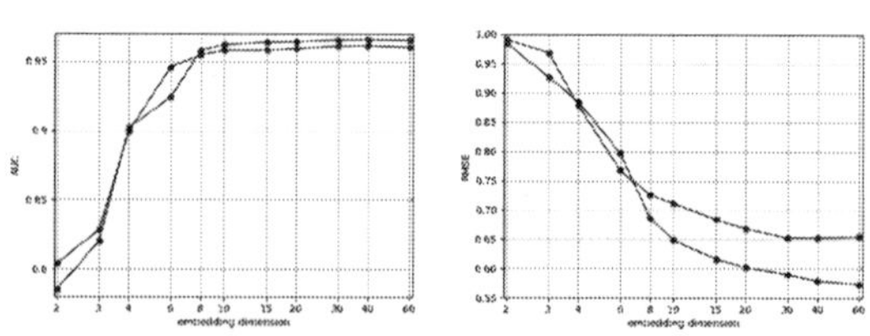

(a) Results for node M4 (b) Results for node M6

Figure 3: Quality measures as a function of the embedding dimension (logarithmically scaled) when using just the main table (red) and using the combined information of both tables (green).

row embedding vectors. The quality of the prediction is measured by the root-mean-squared error (RMSE) for numerical targets and by the area under the receiver operating characteristic curve (AUC) for categorical targets. These quality measures for two nodes of the example dataset are shown in red in Fig. 3 with respect to the embedding dimension.

Second, we apply the EmbDI embedding procedure to the main and additional table simultaneously. We use all the rows of the additional table for training, while for the main table we reserve 10% for testing as before. Again, regression and classification tasks are conducted for the target columns of the main table. The results for the two selected nodes are highlighted in green in Fig. 3. As the merged information requires a higher embedding dimension to be fully represented, the comparison of the two curves in Fig. 3 is meaningful for sufficiently high embedding dimensions. There, involving the additional table improves the results for targets influenced by latent information from the additional dataset.

Hence, we showed that our method for synthetic relational dataset generation is able to construct realistic related tables in the sense that the additional table contains information that is not present in the main table, but influences the target columns of the main table. This is an essential, frequently occurring property of real-world relational datasets. We emphasize that further research should include a more comprehensive evaluation with more datasets and further methods for downstream tasks, see Section 7.

6 Discussion and Conclusion

In this work, we presented an approach for generating relational datasets based on SCMs. The corresponding graph controls the causality between features and targets, involving latent causal relationships to model inter-table dependencies. Our approach serves as a scalable methodology to provide huge amount of data with various statistical properties for robust training of a tabular foundation model for relational tabular data.

The main advantage to use SCMs is the ability to model causal relationships. Thus, we are able to control the dependence between certain targets and features. Additionally, by incorporating isolated sub-graphs, we can generate data that is irrelevant to the targets mimicking real-world redundancy.

The quality of generated data is determined by several parameters. Choosing a large hidden dimension n and projecting the data to a one-dimensional output may significantly increase the difficulty of predicting a target based on the feature nodes. Furthermore, the choice of the activation function of the neural networks influences data complexity.

A key strength of our approach lies in its ability to generate relational tables that capture complex causal relationships, including those mediated by latent variables. This simulation of inter-table dependencies, often lacking in simpler methods, is crucial for developing robust table representation learning models that can effectively handle the complexities of real-world data, commonly encountered in database management systems.

7 Limitations

Our approach successfully generates relational datasets with numerical and categorical features. However, a more detailed experimental analysis with varying parameters, that would go beyond the scope of this short paper, is desirable. Real-world databases often contain multimodal elements like images and text. Extending our framework to incorporate these diverse data types represents an important research direction. Furthermore, a comprehensive evaluation for three or more relational tables, including cross-connections, needs to be conducted.

References

Albert-László Barabási and Réka Albert. 1999. Emergence of scaling in random networks. *Science*, 286(5439):509–512.

Riccardo Cappuzzo, Paolo Papotti, and Saravanan Thirumuruganathan. 2020. Creating embeddings of heterogeneous relational datasets for data integration tasks. In *ACM SIGMOD/PODS Conference*, pages 1335–1349.

Noah Hollmann, Samuel Müller, Lennart Purucker, Arjun Krishnakumar, Max Körfer, Shi Bin Hoo, Robin Tibor Schirrmeister, and Frank Hutter. 2025. Accurate predictions on small data with a tabular foundation model. *Nature*, 637:319–326.

Valter Hudovernik. 2024. Relational data generation with graph neural networks and latent diffusion models. In *NeurIPS 2024 Third Table Representation Learning Workshop*, Vancouver, Canada.

Neha Patki, Roy Wedge, and Kalyan Veeramachaneni. 2016. The synthetic data vault. In *2016 IEEE International Conference on Data Science and Advanced Analytics (DSAA)*, pages 399–410, Montreal, QC, Canada. IEEE.

Judea Pearl. 2010. An introduction to causal inference. *The International Journal of Biostatistics*, 6(2).

A Example of Generated Relational Tables

Based on the graph in Fig. 2, we sample two relational tables. The hidden dimension is set to $n = 2$. For the root node M0, the data follows a gamma distribution with shape $\alpha = 2.245$ and scale $\theta = 1.780$. The data at root node A0 is drawn from a normal distribution with mean $\mu = -0.029$ and standard deviation $\sigma = 0.816$, and for each component of the data vector at root node A2, we choose randomly with $p = 0.5$ if the component is drawn from a standard normal or an exponential distribution with scale $\lambda = 0.584$. A randomly chosen fraction of 10% of the data is affected by noise, where the noise standard deviation is set to 0.1. The pre-sampling run described in Subsection 3.2 is conducted with 1,000 samples. For the categorical nodes, the following numbers of categories are chosen: M0: 6, M4: 2, M7: 6, A0: 3, A1: 4, A2: 2. All these numbers are drawn randomly from a normal distribution with mean $\mu = 4$ and standard deviation $\sigma = 2$. For the categorical coupling node C, the number of categories is 175, chosen randomly from a normal distribution with mean $\mu = 100$ and standard deviation $\sigma = 50$, mimicking a foreign key column.

M0	M1	M2	M3	M4	M5	M6	M7	C
4	-0.831	1.281	0.669	0	1.722	2.418	0	53
0	-0.556	1.190	0.239	0	1.630	2.204	3	46
5	-0.243	1.325	0.932	0	1.765	2.100	0	48
2	-0.627	1.276	0.927	0	1.718	2.563	0	46
3	-0.398	1.154	0.295	0	1.591	2.020	3	15

Table 1: Main Table for the DAG shown in Fig. 2, the first 5 out of 100,000 rows are displayed.

A0	A1	A2	A3	A4	C
0	0	1	0.499	0.355	46
0	0	0	1.005	2.903	76
0	3	0	0.661	0.711	59
1	2	0	0.567	0.577	103
2	3	1	0.271	0.691	146

Table 2: Additional Table for the DAG shown in Fig. 2, the first 5 out of 500 rows are displayed.

Table as Thought: Exploring Structured Thoughts in LLM Reasoning

Zhenjie Sun, **Naihao Deng**, **Haofei Yu**, **Jiaxuan You**
University of Illinois Urbana-Champaign, University of Michigan

Abstract

Large language models' reasoning abilities benefit from methods that organize their thought processes, such as chain-of-thought prompting, which employs a sequential structure to guide the reasoning process step-by-step. However, existing approaches focus primarily on organizing the sequence of thoughts, leaving structure in individual thought steps underexplored. To address this gap, we propose Table as Thought, a framework inspired by cognitive neuroscience theories on human thought. Table as Thought organizes reasoning within a tabular schema, where rows represent sequential thought steps and columns capture critical constraints and contextual information to enhance reasoning. The reasoning process iteratively populates the table until self-verification ensures completeness and correctness. Our experiments show that Table as Thought excels in planning tasks and demonstrates a strong potential for enhancing LLM performance in mathematical reasoning compared to unstructured thought baselines. This work provides a novel exploration of refining thought representation within LLMs, paving the way for advancements in reasoning and AI cognition.

1 Introduction

Recent advancements in reasoning have demonstrated that the reasoning capabilities of large language models (LLMs) can be enhanced by introducing structure into the reasoning process (Wei et al., 2023; Yao et al., 2023; Besta et al., 2024). For instance, the chain-of-thought approach organizes textual reasoning in a step-by-step manner using a linear chain structure (Wei et al., 2023). Building on this, following works have shown that incorporating more complex organizational structures further improves reasoning performance (Besta et al., 2024; Yao et al., 2023). However, these approaches structure reasoning only at the level of connections between distinct reasoning steps (inter-thought level) and leave the content of individual steps (thought level) unstructured. This raises the critical question: ***Can LLMs' reasoning abilities be further enhanced by introducing structure within individual thoughts?***

To address this question, we draw inspiration from cognitive neuroscience theories of human thought. Neuroscientists have found that humans think in a structured way, with the brain's organization facilitating sequential and goal-oriented reasoning. Christoff and Gabrieli (2000) provided early evidence that the prefrontal cortex supports structured reasoning through a rostrocaudal hierarchy, enabling the processing of increasingly abstract concepts and complex goal-directed behavior. Later, Friston (2005)'s predictive coding framework demonstrated how structured cognition emerges from the brain's ability to build hierarchical models, combining experiences with current input to predict results. More recently, Jeff Hawkins (Hawkins, 2021) argued that humans think in a structured manner, with the neocortex organizing knowledge in certain structures, and thinking arises from neurons activating sequential locations in these frames. Building on these insights, we propose investigating whether similarly structured representations can be incorporated into LLMs to enhance their reasoning and planning capabilities.

In this work, we adopt a simple yet effective structural format—a tabular schema—to approximate the structured nature of human thinking processes. In our approach, the schema of a table serves as a framework for organizing and navigating knowledge. Inspired by the sequential processes described in neuroscience—where neurons activate specific patterns step by step (Hawkins, 2021)—we model these processes as the sequential population of rows in a table, moving across columns according to a predefined schema. A single table can encapsulate one or more such structured thought processes, providing a coherent con-

Proceedings of the 4th Table Representation Learning Workshop, pages 19–33
July 31, 2025 ©2025 Association for Computational Linguistics

tainer for organizing and connecting thinking steps and associated information. Tables not only represent step-by-step processes for achieving specific goals but also serve as robust frameworks for planning tasks. Moreover, utilizing tables as structured representations enables schema design that ensures organization and data integrity, thereby facilitating efficient verification and analysis.

The contributions of our paper are as follows:

- Motivated by insights from cognitive neuroscience regarding the structured nature of human thinking, we propose a novel framework, Table as Thought, that injects structure at the thought level. To the best of our knowledge, this is the first exploration and demonstration of integrating structured representations directly into the reasoning process of large language models.
- We demonstrate the advantages of Table as Thought in tasks requiring planning, highlighting its potential to enhance performance on tasks that demand sequential and goal-oriented thought processes.
- We provide a detailed and comprehensive analysis of Table as Thought, offering insights into its functionality and strengths, and comparing the benefits of structured versus unstructured thought representations. We hope these findings inspire future research into the nature and representation of thought processes in artificial intelligence and computational linguistics.

2 Related Work

Structures in LLM Reasoning. Recent advancements in large language models (LLMs) have increasingly focused on integrating structured processes to enhance reasoning capabilities. Chain-of-Thought prompting (Wei et al., 2023) introduces a step-by-step framework that organizes thoughts in a sequential manner, enabling more coherent reasoning. Building on this, Tree of Thoughts (Yao et al., 2023) and Graph of Thoughts (Besta et al., 2024) employ hierarchical and networked structures to further enhance problem-solving, leveraging branching and interconnected paths. Moreover, self-consistency (Wang et al., 2023) improves reliability by sampling multiple reasoning paths and selecting the most consistent outcome, thereby addressing variability in generated responses.

While these methods excel at organizing reasoning at a macro level—such as through chaining, branching, or aggregating thought paths—they do not address the internal structure of individual thoughts. Our work is distinct in that it introduces structure directly at the thought level, refining the granularity of reasoning processes in LLMs. By focusing on the internal organization of individual reasoning steps, we provide a novel perspective on enhancing the depth and precision of structured reasoning in LLMs.

Representations of Tables in LLM Inference. Tables have traditionally played a significant role in LLMs for tasks involving the understanding and processing of tabular data, such as knowledge retrieval (Cong et al., 2024), question answering over structured data (Yin et al., 2020; Zhang et al., 2024b), and tabular reasoning (Herzig et al., 2020; Deng et al., 2024). In these tasks, tables are leveraged only as input for interpretation and manipulation.

The Chain-of-Table framework (Wang et al., 2024) extends the application of tables by employing them as proxies for intermediate thoughts in reasoning tasks involving tabular data. In this framework, LLMs iteratively update a table, forming a dynamic reasoning chain where the table evolves based on intermediate results. While this approach has proven effective on tabular-specific datasets, it remains inherently tied to tasks where tabular data is part of the input or reasoning context.

In contrast, our work redefines the role of tables by utilizing them as a universal framework for structuring and representing the internal thought processes of LLMs in non-table-specific tasks, such as planning and mathematical reasoning. Unlike prior approaches that depend on pre-existing tabular inputs, we employ tables as dynamic containers to organize and manipulate thoughts step by step. This approach enables structured reasoning even in tasks where no tabular data is initially present, bridging the gap between unstructured text-based reasoning and structured problem-solving paradigms. By generalizing the utility of tables beyond table-specific reasoning tasks, our work marks a significant departure from previous methods and demonstrates the versatility of this novel framework.

3 Table as Thought

We present the design of the Table as Thought framework, which introduces a novel approach to reasoning in large language models by leveraging tables as structured representations of

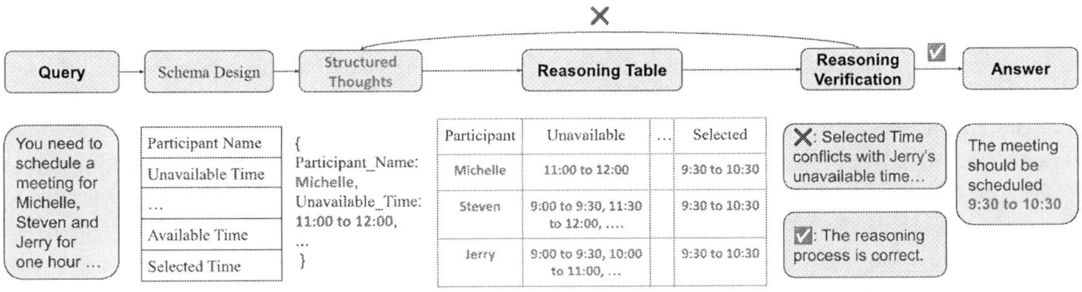

Figure 1: The Overall Pipeline for Table as Thought Reasoning. The figure illustrates how Table as Thought structures reasoning by iteratively populating a reasoning table based on the schema, verifying consistency, and updating the table until the final answer is achieved.

thoughts.

Table as Thought. Table as Thought employs a table as a container to represent one or more structured thoughts. These tables, referred to as **"reasoning tables"**, encapsulate thoughts and provide a transparent representation of the reasoning process. A reasoning table T is initialized with an original table schema S, which is defined by the LLM for a given query Q. Structured thoughts Θ are then generated based on S, with each thought corresponding to a row in the reasoning table T. The table T is subsequently populated and updated according to these structured thoughts Θ.

The overall reasoning workflow using the reasoning table is illustrated in Figure 1 and formalized in Algorithm 1.

Algorithm 1 Table as Thought

Require: Query Q
Ensure: A table T that satisfies Q

```
1: S ← DESIGNSCHEMA(Q)              // Define table schema
2: Initialize an empty table T with schema S.
3: while not SUFFICIENT(T, Q) do
4:     Θ ← REFLECT(T, Q)   // Generate possible updates
5:     T ← UPDATETABLE(T, Θ)        // Apply updates if needed
6: end while
7: return T
```

Schema Development Module. The Schema Development Module dynamically adapts table schemas to accommodate various queries across different reasoning tasks. For constraint-planning tasks, where the primary objective is to satisfy constraints, we prompt LLMs to identify the constraints explicitly before designing the schema. This ensures that both explicit and implicit constraints are addressed in the reasoning process. For mathematical reasoning tasks, the schema is tailored to reflect the logical progression of the reasoning steps, enabling systematic organization of critical information.

The headers in the table schemas are designed to represent essential reasoning steps and key information pertinent to the task. These headers act as anchors for organizing and verifying intermediate and final reasoning outputs.

For example, consider the travel planning query:

```
I plan to travel alone, and my
planned budget for the trip is
around $1,100.
```

In this case, a key constraint is that the total cost should not exceed \$1,400. To address this constraint, the schema must include a header such as `Cost`, with the type `Number`, ensuring that the relevant information is captured and evaluated against the budgetary constraint.

For a mathematical reasoning task, such as a question from the GSM8K dataset:

```
A robe takes 2 bolts of blue fiber
and half that much white fiber.
How many bolts in total does it
take?
```

Here, the reasoning process requires consideration of the quantities of blue and white fibers. The schema should therefore include keys such as `Blue Fiber` and `White Fiber`, ensuring that all relevant elements are systematically tracked and calculated.

Reasoning Verification Module. Our preliminary experiments reveal that existing LLMs may fail to generate a consistent reasoning path. Therefore, we introduce a verification module to verify the completeness and correctness of the reasoning process.

For constrained reasoning tasks, such a module verifies whether the constraints identified in the schema development phase are satisfied. Constraint checking is typically performed by the LLM through reflective reasoning. The structured nature of thoughts in Table as Thought brings a natural benefit: **Auto-Check Constraints**, which are constraints set that can be externally verified. In Table as Thought, Auto-Check Constraints facilitate the systematic validation of intermediate steps and final outputs.

For math reasoning tasks, such a module ensures that the table reflects an accurate and logically correct reasoning path toward solving the problem. This involves checking whether the intermediate and final outputs align with the expected reasoning steps outlined in the schema.

Table Construction Module. The Table Construction Module iteratively generates structured thoughts and constructs the reasoning table by incorporating the schema and feedback from the reasoning verification module. This process involves dynamically adding new thoughts to the table, modifying existing entries, or removing entries that do not align with the schema or query requirements.

The iterative process terminates under one of the following conditions:

1. The reasoning table is verified as complete and correct by the reasoning verification module.

2. The maximum number of iterations, which we set empirically as 10 in all our experiments, is reached.

4 Experiments

4.1 Tasks and Language Models

For all tasks, we adopt the original evaluation methods to ensure consistency and comparability.

Constraint Planning Tasks. The goal of constraint planning tasks is to generate plans that satisfy both explicit and implicit constraints. We evaluate our approach on two datasets, each presenting different levels of complexity in the expected plans. The TravelPlanner dataset (Xie et al., 2024) requires LLMs to generate detailed travel plans that adhere to explicit constraints provided in the query, such as budget limitations, as well as implicit constraints derived from common sense. The expected travel plans are highly complex, encompassing multi-day agendas that include transportation, accommodations, and daily attractions. Due to the exceptionally long context required for this task, which results in substantial token costs, we conduct experiments exclusively with GPT-4-o-mini. The calendar scheduling task from the NaturalPlan benchmark (Zheng et al., 2024) focuses on generating single-object plans. In this task, LLMs must determine an appropriate meeting time based on explicit constraints, such as the company's working hours and the unavailable time slots of each participant.

Math Reasoning Tasks. We evaluate LLMs using GSM-8K and MATH500 to assess structured mathematical reasoning. GSM-8K (Cobbe et al., 2021) contains 8,000 grade-school-level word problems, testing multi-step reasoning and numerical precision. MATH500 (Lightman et al., 2023) features 500 advanced problems from the MATH dataset (Hendrycks et al., 2021), covering algebra, calculus, and geometry. It challenges models with tasks requiring symbolic manipulation and deep mathematical understanding. These datasets help evaluate our approach across diverse scenarios, from simple arithmetic to complex problems.

Language Models. The schema design and table construction modules in Table as Thought require LLMs capable of generating complex, structured outputs that conform to intricate schemas. This capability is natively supported by OpenAI's Structured Outputs Mode, which allows for precise alignment with defined schema requirements. Consequently, our experiments are conducted exclusively on OpenAI's GPT-4-o-mini and GPT-4-o-2024-08-06 models (OpenAI et al., 2024). Expanding the evaluation to include open-source models with similar capabilities remains an area for future work.

4.2 Text Thought Baselines

Direct Prompting. Direct Prompting involves solving queries by directly generating an answer from the input, without prompting for any intermediate reasoning steps.

CoT Prompting. Chain-of-Thought (CoT) Prompting organizes reasoning as a sequential chain of thoughts.

Text as Thought. This approach differs from Table as Thought only in its use of unstructured representations for thoughts. **Text as Thought** employs text as the medium for reasoning. This method extends CoT prompting by iteratively updating the reasoning process based on reflection. Each iteration involves generating intermediate reasoning steps, reflecting on their correctness, and refining the reasoning path as needed. The streamlined process is formalized in Algorithm 2.

Algorithm 2 Text as Thought

Require: Query Q
Ensure: A text T that satisfies Q
1: Initialize an empty text T.
2: **while** not $\text{SUFFICIENT}(T, Q)$ **do**
3: $\Theta \leftarrow \text{REFLECT}(T, Q)$ // Generate possible updates
4: $T \leftarrow \text{UPDATETEXT}(T, \Theta)$ // Apply updates if needed
5: **end while**
6: **return** T

4.3 Variations of Table as Thought

To fully explore and understand the boundaries of Table as Thought, we introduce two variations to the TravelPlanner task. These variations include Table as Thought with auto check constraint, which adds complexity to schema design, and Table as Thought with given schema, which simplifies the task by providing a predefined schema.

Table as Thought with Auto-Check Constraint. This variation builds on the vanilla Table as Thought by requiring the LLM to add additional constraints during schema design to ensure data integrity and reflect the constraints present in the query. For instance, if a TravelPlanner query includes budget constraints, the LLM is expected to design a schema with headers like `Cost` and enforce a rule ensuring that the sum of the column does not exceed the specified budget. By introducing this variation, we aim to explore the boundaries of LLMs in designing complex reasoning structures and handling intricate schema requirements.

Table as Thought with Given Schema. In this variation, the LLM is provided with a predefined schema, as shown in Table 7, rather than designing the schema independently. The given schema is derived from the evaluation pipeline of the TravelPlanner task (Xie et al., 2024), where answers are processed into tables following this schema before evaluation. This variation serves as a comparative baseline to assess the effectiveness and adaptability of schemas designed by LLMs compared to fixed, predefined schemas.

5 Results

5.1 Calendar Scheduling Task

Table as Thought achieves the highest performance among all prompting methods on the Calendar Scheduling Task, as shown in Table 2. On GPT-4o, Table as Thought improves performance by 10.8% over Direct Prompting and achieves a 5.4% improvement compared to the Text as Thought baseline. This highlights the advantage of using tables as structured representations for planning over unstructured text-based representations. A similar trend is observed with GPT-4o-mini, where Table as Thought outperforms other methods, suggesting the robustness of table-based reasoning for simpler constraint reasoning tasks like calendar scheduling.

For GPT-4o, the improvement from Direct Prompting to CoT Prompting is minimal (0.5%). In contrast, incorporating self-verification through Text as Thought yields a 4.9% improvement. When transitioning from unstructured thoughts to structured tables, there is a substantial performance boost (5.4%), underscoring the benefits of structured representations in reasoning tasks.

For GPT-4o-mini, CoT Prompting achieves a moderate 2.2% improvement over Direct Prompting, but Text as Thought fails to provide any additional gains. In contrast, Table as Thought demonstrates a significant 4.4% improvement over CoT Prompting, demonstrating the effectiveness of introducing structure at the thought level over chain-like structures at the reasoning level.

5.2 TravelPlanner Task

Table 1 shows that Table as Thought with a given schema achieves the best performance on metrics for commonsense and hard constraint in the TravelPlanner task. The results reveal an important trend: on a challenging task like TravelPlanner, which demands complex reasoning, introducing increasingly sophisticated structures into the reasoning process can lead to performance degrada-

Metric	Direct	CoT	Text as Thought	Table as Thought		
				Vanilla	w/ Auto-Check constraint	w/ Given Schema
Delivery Rate (%)	100.0	100.0	100.0	100.0	99.4	**100.0**
Commonsense Constraint Micro Pass Rate (%)	68.3	69.0	68.3	64.4	63.8	**70.1**
Commonsense Constraint Macro Pass Rate (%)	2.22	2.22	0.556	0.0	0.0	**3.33**
Hard Constraint Micro Pass Rate (%)	**7.62**	6.19	3.81	3.33	1.90	5.95
Hard Constraint Macro Pass Rate (%)	4.44	4.44	2.78	1.67	0.556	**5.00**
Final Pass Rate (%)	0.556	0.556	0.0	0.0	0.0	**1.11**

Table 1: Evaluation results for different models and prompt methods on TraverPlanner Tasks on GPT4o-mini

	Direct	CoT	Text as Thought	Table as Thought
GPT-4o	64.0	64.5	69.4	**74.8**
GPT-4o-mini	36.2	38.4	38.4	**42.3**

Table 2: Performance of GPT-4o and GPT-4o-mini models under different prompting methods for calendar scheduling.

	Direct	CoT	Text as Thought	Table as Thought
MATH500				
GPT-4o	75.0	72.2	72.6	64.2
GPT-4o-mini	65.4	65.2	63.4	47.8
GSM8K				
GPT-4o	95.4	95.9	95.7	94.1
GPT-4o-mini	93.9	93.6	92.9	92.4

Table 3: Performance of GPT-4o and GPT-4o-mini models under different prompting methods for MATH500 and GSM8K.

	Direct	CoT	Text as Thought
MATH500			
GPT-4o	4.4/25.0	5.4/27.8	4.4/27.4
GPT-4o-mini	2.0/36.6	2.4/34.6	2.8/34.8
GSM8K			
GPT-4o	1.59/4.62	1.29/4.09	1.60/4.33
GPT-4o-mini	1.59/6.14	2.12/6.37	2.50/7.13

Table 4: The Percentage of Questions that Table as Thought successfully work out while other prompting methods failed vs failed rate of other prompting methods.

tion. Specifically, methods that incorporate additional complexity—such as chain-of-thought (CoT) prompting, self-reflection in Text as Thought, and rule-constrained structured thoughts in Table as Thought with Auto-Check constraint—tend to perform worse compared to simpler approaches. The exception is Table as Thought with a given schema, which avoids this degradation by relieving the LLM of the need to design its own schema, allowing it to focus solely on reasoning within a predefined structure.

5.3 Math Reasoning Tasks

Table 3 highlights a general trend in the MATH500 and GSM8K tasks: introducing additional complexity into the reasoning process often leads to a performance drop, particularly for GPT-4o-mini. For instance, on MATH500, the performance of both GPT-4o and GPT-4o-mini decreases as the reasoning structures become more complicated, from Direct Prompting to Text as Thought to Table as Thought. This effect is especially pronounced for GPT-4o-mini, where the performance of Table as Thought falls to 47.8%, compared to 65.4% with Direct Prompting. A similar trend is observed on GSM8K, where the addition of more structured reasoning methods results in marginal performance degradation. These results suggest that LLMs may already be overfitted to math reasoning tasks, as noted in recent studies (Mirzadeh et al., 2024; Zhang et al., 2024a).

Despite this general trend, Table as Thought demonstrates its potential to improve performance by successfully solving questions that text-thought-based methods fail to address, particularly with more capable models like GPT-4o. Table 4 provides a detailed breakdown of the percentage of questions that Table as Thought solves, which were missed by other methods. On MATH500, Table as Thought resolves approximately 20% of such questions, while on GSM8K, this figure exceeds 30%. These findings underscore the utility of structured reasoning in identifying alternative pathways to solutions that text-based reasoning methods may overlook.

6 Analysis

6.1 Effect of Schema Design

Schema design plays a pivotal role in structuring the reasoning paths of Calendar Scheduling tasks. Different schemas determine the granularity of the reasoning process, which in turn affects model performance.

	Schema Example
One Row	Time Slot, Jesse Availability Kathryn Availability, Megan Availability All Participants Available, Earliest Availability
Multi Row	Participant Name, Availability Start Time Availability End Time, Meeting Duration Work Hours Constraint, Schedule Constraint Preference Constraint, Proposed Meeting Time

Table 5: Schema examples for Multi Row Thought and One Row Thought.

	GPT-4o-mini	GPT-4o
One Row	45.05	72.93
Multi Row	43.46	80.28

Table 6: Performance Comparison of Multi Row and One Row Schemas for GPT-4o-mini and GPT-4o on Calendar Scheduling.

Table 5 shows that in the **one-row schema**, the reasoning process is concise: the LLM identifies all available time slots for participants in a single step and selects a suitable meeting time. This schema produces a single-row table, encapsulating the reasoning process in a compact form. In contrast, the **multi-row schema** divides the process into finer-grained steps. The LLM first extracts unavailable and preferred time slots for each participant. It then computes available time slots before aggregating this information to finalize the meeting time. This approach results in a table with multiple rows, each representing an intermediate reasoning step, and provides a more detailed reasoning path.

In Table 6, for GPT-4o, the multi-row schema outperforms the one-row schema, achieving 80.28% accuracy compared to 72.93%. In contrast, GPT-4o-mini performs better with the simpler one-row schema (45.05% vs. 43.46% for the multi-row schema). This highlights that schema complexity impacts performance differently for the two models.

6.2 LLM Struggles to Design Effective Schema for Complex Planning

Unlike Calendar Scheduling, which focuses on selecting a single time slot, TravelPlanner involves generating a comprehensive travel itinerary, which is much more complex. Our findings indicate that tasking the LLM with designing a table schema results in a notable performance drop compared to using direct prompting with a pre-defined schema.

	Schema Example
Given Schema	days, current_city, attraction, transportation, breakfast, lunch, dinner, accommodation
LLM Developed Schema	Day, Date, Location, Transportation Details, Accommodation Details, Activities/Attractions, Dining Options, Estimated Cost, Notes/Preferences

Table 7: Given Schema and Example of GPT-4o developed Schema.

Schema Designing	Resoning Verification	ACC(%)
✓	✓	**42.3**
✓	×	38.5 (↓ 3.8)
×	✓	36.2 (↓ 6.1)
×	×	32.7 (↓ 9.6)

Table 8: Ablation study results for GPT-4o-mini with schema designing and reasoning verification effects on performance of calendar scheduling.

This suggests that the insufficient capability of LLM in designing table schemas may hinder its performance on complex planning tasks.

Although the provided schema is not perfect—omitting some critical columns, such as "cost" for budget constraints—it is generally more effective than most LLM-designed schemas. For instance, as shown in Table 7, the LLM-developed schema and the given schema are structurally similar. However, a key difference is the use of "Dining Options" in the LLM-designed schema, as opposed to separating dining into specific categories like "breakfast," "lunch," and "dinner." In practice, this simplification often leads the LLM to allocate only a single meal per day, which contradicts commonsense expectations for travel planning.

6.3 Ablation Study

We conducted an ablation study using GPT-4o-mini on the Calendar Scheduling task to evaluate the individual contributions of schema design and reasoning verification . Table 8 shows that when reasoning verification is removed, accuracy drops from 42.3% to 38.5% (↓ 3.8%). This indicates that without explicitly verifying constraints, the LLM may overlook key restrictions in the query, leading to false positives during self-checking. The absence of schema design leads to a larger performance drop, from 42.3% to 36.2% (↓ 6.1%), and further to 32.7% (↓ 9.6%) when both schema design and reasoning verification are removed. This highlights

	Column Headers
wo/ Schema Design	Participant, Available Time Slots, Selected Meeting Time
w/ Schema Design	Participant Name, Participant Availability, Meeting Duration, Meeting Day, Proposed Meeting Time, Work Hours Start, Work Hours End, Conflict Check, Final Meeting Time , Notes/Comments

Table 9: Example of Column Headers of Table Thoughts w/wo Schema Design.

the critical role of schema design in structuring the reasoning process. Table 9 shows that without a schema, the LLM tends to create tables with fewer columns, omitting key information necessary for constraint checking. While the table without schema design contains basic headers such as `Participant` and `Selected Meeting Time`, the schema-designed table includes additional headers like `Conflict Check`, `Work Hours Start/End`, and `Notes/Comments`. These additional columns capture critical reasoning steps and constraints, enabling more effective verification and selection of a valid meeting time.

7 Conclusion

We proposed Table as Thought, a novel framework that introduces structured reasoning at the thought level. The framework centers on the design and utilization of table schemas, where the LLM is tasked with constructing a schema and generating structured thoughts based on it. Our results demonstrate that Table as Thought excels in constraint planning tasks, showcasing its ability to manage complex constraints effectively. Moreover, the framework exhibits significant potential for further improving performance in math reasoning tasks, particularly in addressing unsolved problems through structured reasoning.

Additionally, we conducted detailed analyses of the results, exploring the interplay between schema design, reasoning complexity, and model capabilities. These insights pave the way for future research into the nature and representation of thought processes, offering a promising direction for the development of more robust reasoning frameworks in LLMs.

Limitations

Our proposed methods are currently supported only by models capable of generating structured data with complex schemas. This limitation restricts our experiments to a small set of closed-source models, such as those provided by OpenAI. Consequently, the generalizability of our findings to open-source LLMs remains unexplored. Future work should investigate approaches for adapting Table as Thought to a broader range of models, including those with limited native support for structured data generation.

Ethical Statement

This research was conducted using publicly available datasets (e.g., GSM-8K, MATH500, TravelPlanner) in compliance with their terms of use, ensuring no personally identifiable information (PII) was processed. While our proposed framework, Table as Thought, aims to enhance structured reasoning in LLMs, we acknowledge the potential risks of misuse in harmful applications, such as deceptive planning or adversarial reasoning. To mitigate this, we advocate for responsible deployment with appropriate safeguards.

Acknowledgement

The GPT experiments are supported by credit from OpenAI through OpenAI Researcher Access assigned to Naihao Deng. We thank Hanchen Xia and Ruiqi He for their assistance with reviewing and offering helpful feedback during the development process.

References

Maciej Besta, Nils Blach, Ales Kubicek, Robert Gerstenberger, Lukas Gianinazzi, Joanna Gajda, Tomasz Lehmann, Michał Podstawski, Hubert Niewiadomski, Piotr Nyczyk, and Torsten Hoefler. 2024. Graph of Thoughts: Solving Elaborate Problems with Large Language Models. *Proceedings of the AAAI Conference on Artificial Intelligence*, 38(16):17682–17690.

Kalina Christoff and John D. E. Gabrieli. 2000. The frontopolar cortex and human cognition: Evidence for a rostrocaudal hierarchical organization within the human prefrontal cortex. *Psychobiology*, 28:168–186.

Karl Cobbe, Vineet Kosaraju, Mohammad Bavarian, Mark Chen, Heewoo Jun, Lukasz Kaiser, Matthias Plappert, Jerry Tworek, Jacob Hilton, Reiichiro Nakano, Christopher Hesse, and John Schulman. 2021. Training verifiers to solve math word problems. *arXiv preprint arXiv:2110.14168*.

Tianji Cong, Madelon Hulsebos, Zhenjie Sun, Paul Groth, and H. V. Jagadish. 2024. Observatory: Characterizing embeddings of relational tables. *Preprint*, arXiv:2310.07736.

Naihao Deng, Zhenjie Sun, Ruiqi He, Aman Sikka, Yulong Chen, Lin Ma, Yue Zhang, and Rada Mihalcea. 2024. Tables as texts or images: Evaluating the table reasoning ability of LLMs and MLLMs. In *Findings of the Association for Computational Linguistics: ACL 2024*, pages 407–426, Bangkok, Thailand. Association for Computational Linguistics.

Karl Friston. 2005. A theory of cortical responses. *Philosophical Transactions of the Royal Society of London. Series B, Biological Sciences*, 360(1456):815–836.

Jeff Hawkins. 2021. *A Thousand Brains: A New Theory of Intelligence*, first edition edition. Basic Books, Hachette Book Group, Inc., New York, NY.

Dan Hendrycks, Collin Burns, Saurav Kadavath, Akul Arora, Steven Basart, Eric Tang, Dawn Song, and Jacob Steinhardt. 2021. Measuring mathematical problem solving with the math dataset. *Preprint*, arXiv:2103.03874.

Jonathan Herzig, Pawel Krzysztof Nowak, Thomas Müller, Francesco Piccinno, and Julian Eisenschlos. 2020. TaPas: Weakly supervised table parsing via pre-training. In *Proceedings of the 58th Annual Meeting of the Association for Computational Linguistics*, pages 4320–4333, Online. Association for Computational Linguistics.

Hunter Lightman, Vineet Kosaraju, Yura Burda, Harri Edwards, Bowen Baker, Teddy Lee, Jan Leike, John Schulman, Ilya Sutskever, and Karl Cobbe. 2023. Let's verify step by step. *Preprint*, arXiv:2305.20050.

Iman Mirzadeh, Keivan Alizadeh, Hooman Shahrokhi, Oncel Tuzel, Samy Bengio, and Mehrdad Farajtabar. 2024. Gsm-symbolic: Understanding the limitations of mathematical reasoning in large language models. *Preprint*, arXiv:2410.05229.

OpenAI, Josh Achiam, Steven Adler, Sandhini Agarwal, Lama Ahmad, Ilge Akkaya, Florencia Leoni Aleman, Diogo Almeida, Janko Altenschmidt, Sam Altman, Shyamal Anadkat, Red Avila, Igor Babuschkin, Suchir Balaji, Valerie Balcom, Paul Baltescu, Haiming Bao, Mohammad Bavarian, Jeff Belgum, Irwan Bello, Jake Berdine, Gabriel Bernadett-Shapiro, Christopher Berner, Lenny Bogdonoff, Oleg Boiko, Madelaine Boyd, Anna-Luisa Brakman, Greg Brockman, Tim Brooks, Miles Brundage, Kevin Button, Trevor Cai, Rosie Campbell, Andrew Cann, Brittany Carey, Chelsea Carlson, Rory Carmichael, Brooke Chan, Che Chang, Fotis Chantzis, Derek Chen, Sully Chen, Ruby Chen, Jason Chen, Mark Chen, Ben Chess, Chester Cho, Casey Chu, Hyung Won Chung, Dave Cummings, Jeremiah Currier, Yunxing Dai, Cory Decareaux, Thomas Degry, Noah Deutsch, Damien Deville, Arka Dhar, David Dohan, Steve Dowling, Sheila Dunning, Adrien Ecoffet, Atty Eleti, Tyna Eloundou, David Farhi, Liam Fedus, Niko Felix, Simón Posada Fishman, Juston Forte, Isabella Fulford, Leo Gao, Elie Georges, Christian Gibson, Vik Goel, Tarun Gogineni, Gabriel Goh, Rapha Gontijo-Lopes, Jonathan Gordon, Morgan Grafstein, Scott Gray, Ryan Greene, Joshua Gross, Shixiang Shane Gu, Yufei Guo, Chris Hallacy, Jesse Han, Jeff Harris, Yuchen He, Mike Heaton, Johannes Heidecke, Chris Hesse, Alan Hickey, Wade Hickey, Peter Hoeschele, Brandon Houghton, Kenny Hsu, Shengli Hu, Xin Hu, Joost Huizinga, Shantanu Jain, Shawn Jain, Joanne Jang, Angela Jiang, Roger Jiang, Haozhun Jin, Denny Jin, Shino Jomoto, Billie Jonn, Heewoo Jun, Tomer Kaftan, Łukasz Kaiser, Ali Kamali, Ingmar Kanitscheider, Nitish Shirish Keskar, Tabarak Khan, Logan Kilpatrick, Jong Wook Kim, Christina Kim, Yongjik Kim, Jan Hendrik Kirchner, Jamie Kiros, Matt Knight, Daniel Kokotajlo, Łukasz Kondraciuk, Andrew Kondrich, Aris Konstantinidis, Kyle Kosic, Gretchen Krueger, Vishal Kuo, Michael Lampe, Ikai Lan, Teddy Lee, Jan Leike, Jade Leung, Daniel Levy, Chak Ming Li, Rachel Lim, Molly Lin, Stephanie Lin, Mateusz Litwin, Theresa Lopez, Ryan Lowe, Patricia Lue, Anna Makanju, Kim Malfacini, Sam Manning, Todor Markov, Yaniv Markovski, Bianca Martin, Katie Mayer, Andrew Mayne, Bob McGrew, Scott Mayer McKinney, Christine McLeavey, Paul McMillan, Jake McNeil, David Medina, Aalok Mehta, Jacob Menick, Luke Metz, Andrey Mishchenko, Pamela Mishkin, Vinnie Monaco, Evan Morikawa, Daniel Mossing, Tong Mu, Mira Murati, Oleg Murk, David Mély, Ashvin Nair, Reiichiro Nakano, Rajeev Nayak, Arvind Neelakantan, Richard Ngo, Hyeonwoo Noh, Long Ouyang, Cullen O'Keefe, Jakub Pachocki, Alex Paino, Joe Palermo, Ashley Pantuliano, Giambattista Parascandolo, Joel Parish, Emy Parparita, Alex Passos, Mikhail Pavlov, Andrew Peng, Adam Perelman, Filipe de Avila Belbute Peres, Michael Petrov, Henrique Ponde de Oliveira Pinto, Michael, Pokorny, Michelle Pokrass, Vitchyr H. Pong, Tolly Powell, Alethea Power, Boris Power, Elizabeth Proehl, Raul Puri, Alec Radford, Jack Rae, Aditya Ramesh, Cameron Raymond, Francis Real, Kendra Rimbach, Carl Ross, Bob Rotsted, Henri Roussez, Nick Ryder, Mario Saltarelli, Ted Sanders, Shibani Santurkar, Girish Sastry, Heather Schmidt, David Schnurr, John Schulman, Daniel Selsam, Kyla Sheppard, Toki Sherbakov, Jessica Shieh, Sarah Shoker, Pranav Shyam, Szymon Sidor, Eric Sigler, Maddie Simens, Jordan Sitkin, Katarina Slama, Ian Sohl, Benjamin Sokolowsky, Yang Song, Natalie Staudacher, Felipe Petroski Such, Natalie Summers, Ilya Sutskever, Jie Tang, Nikolas Tezak, Madeleine B. Thompson, Phil Tillet, Amin Tootoonchian, Elizabeth Tseng, Preston Tuggle, Nick Turley, Jerry Tworek, Juan Felipe Cerón Uribe, Andrea Vallone, Arun Vijayvergiya, Chelsea Voss, Carroll Wainwright, Justin Jay Wang, Alvin Wang, Ben Wang, Jonathan Ward, Jason Wei, CJ Weinmann, Akila Welihinda, Peter Welinder, Jiayi Weng, Lilian Weng, Matt Wiethoff, Dave Willner, Clemens Winter, Samuel Wolrich, Hannah Wong, Lauren Workman, Sherwin Wu, Jeff Wu, Michael Wu, Kai Xiao, Tao Xu, Sarah Yoo, Kevin Yu, Qiming Yuan, Wojciech Zaremba, Rowan Zellers, Chong Zhang, Marvin Zhang, Shengjia Zhao, Tianhao Zheng, Juntang Zhuang, William Zhuk, and Barret Zoph. 2024. Gpt-4 technical report. *Preprint*, arXiv:2303.08774.

Xuezhi Wang, Jason Wei, Dale Schuurmans, Quoc Le, Ed Chi, Sharan Narang, Aakanksha Chowdhery, and Denny Zhou. 2023. Self-consistency improves chain of thought reasoning in language models. *Preprint*, arXiv:2203.11171.

Zilong Wang, Hao Zhang, Chun-Liang Li, Julian Martin Eisenschlos, Vincent Perot, Zifeng Wang, Lesly Miculicich, Yasuhisa Fujii, Jingbo Shang, Chen-Yu Lee, and Tomas Pfister. 2024. Chain-of-table: Evolving tables in the reasoning chain for table understanding. *Preprint*, arXiv:2401.04398.

Jason Wei, Xuezhi Wang, Dale Schuurmans, Maarten Bosma, Brian Ichter, Fei Xia, Ed Chi, Quoc Le, and Denny Zhou. 2023. Chain-of-thought prompting elicits reasoning in large language models. *Preprint*, arXiv:2201.11903.

Jian Xie, Kai Zhang, Jiangjie Chen, Tinghui Zhu, Renze Lou, Yuandong Tian, Yanghua Xiao, and Yu Su. 2024. Travelplanner: A benchmark for real-world planning with language agents. *Preprint*, arXiv:2402.01622.

Shunyu Yao, Dian Yu, Jeffrey Zhao, Izhak Shafran, Thomas L. Griffiths, Yuan Cao, and Karthik Narasimhan. 2023. Tree of thoughts: Deliberate problem solving with large language models. *Preprint*, arXiv:2305.10601.

Pengcheng Yin, Graham Neubig, Wen-tau Yih, and Sebastian Riedel. 2020. TaBERT: Pretraining for joint understanding of textual and tabular data. In *Proceedings of the 58th Annual Meeting of the Association for Computational Linguistics*, pages 8413–8426, Online. Association for Computational Linguistics.

Hugh Zhang, Jeff Da, Dean Lee, Vaughn Robinson, Catherine Wu, Will Song, Tiffany Zhao, Pranav Raja, Charlotte Zhuang, Dylan Slack, Qin Lyu, Sean Hendryx, Russell Kaplan, Michele Lunati, and Summer Yue. 2024a. A careful examination of large language model performance on grade school arithmetic. *Preprint*, arXiv:2405.00332.

Tianshu Zhang, Xiang Yue, Yifei Li, and Huan Sun. 2024b. Tablellama: Towards open large generalist models for tables. *Preprint*, arXiv:2311.09206.

Huaixiu Steven Zheng, Swaroop Mishra, Hugh Zhang, Xinyun Chen, Minmin Chen, Azade Nova, Le Hou, Heng-Tze Cheng, Quoc V. Le, Ed H. Chi, and Denny Zhou. 2024. Natural plan: Benchmarking llms on natural language planning. *Preprint*, arXiv:2406.04520.

A Completion Rate Analysis of Table as Thought on Closed and Open Source LLMs

We investigate the completion rate of Table as Thought when using both closed-source and open-source LLMs in calendar scheduling tasks. Despite advancements in open-source models such as LLaMA 3.1-8B and LLaMA 3.1-70B, these models encounter significant challenges in adhering to the tool schema required for the schema design and table construction modules. Specifically, they fail to generate the expected outputs due to the complexity of the tool schema, leading to errors in the intermediate pipeline.

In a set of 100 test examples, we observe that Table as Thought fails 100% and 63% of the time when using LLaMA 3.1-8B and LLaMA 3.1-70B, respectively. These high failure rates make experiments with open-source models infeasible because:

1. **High Computational Cost:** The need for repeated retries significantly increases computational overhead.

2. **Result Bias:** Retrying may introduce bias, as incorrect reasoning processes may be verified as correct, prematurely terminating the pipeline and artificially increasing the success rate.

In contrast, closed-source models such as GPT-4 variants demonstrate much higher success rates. The results are summarized in Table 10.

Table 10: Success Rates of Table as Thought with Different LLMs on Calendar Scheduling Tasks.

Model	Completion Rate (%)
LLaMA 3.1-8B	0
LLaMA 3.1-70B	37
GPT-4o	100
GPT-4o-mini	99

B Example of Table as Thought on TraverPlanner Task

B.1 Table as Thought w/ Given Schema

Query: Please draw up a 3-day travel itinerary for one person, beginning in Oakland and heading to Tucson from March 15th to March 17th, 2022, with a budget of $1,400.
Raesoning table:

```
"day1": {
    "days": 1,
    "current_city": "Oakland",
    "transportation": "Flight Number: F4002752, from Oakland to Tucson,
        Departure Time: 15:07, Arrival Time: 17:00",
    "breakfast": "-",
    "attraction": "-",
    "lunch": "-",
    "dinner": "Pizza Street, Tucson",
    "accommodation": "Private room with private bathroom, Tucson",
    "total_cost": 270,
    "id": "day1"
},
"day2": {
    "days": 2,
    "current_city": "Tucson",
    "transportation": "-",
    "breakfast": "Mocha, Tucson",
    "attraction": "Pima Air & Space Museum, Tucson",
    "lunch": "Pizza Street, Tucson",
    "dinner": "Canteen Till I Die, Tucson",
    "accommodation": "Room for rent shared bathroom, Tucson",
    "total_cost": 61,
    "id": "day2"
},
"day3": {
    "days": 3,
    "current_city": "Tucson",
    "transportation": "Self-driving from Tucson to Oakland, Duration: 12 hours
        42 mins, Cost: $68",
    "breakfast": "-",
    "attraction": "-",
    "lunch": "-",
    "dinner": "-",
    "accommodation": "-",
    "total_cost": 68,
    "id": "day3"
}
```

B.2 Table as Thought w/ Self-designed Schema

Query: Please draw up a 3-day travel itinerary for one person, beginning in Oakland and heading to Tucson from March 15th to March 17th, 2022, with a budget of $1,400.
Raesoning table:

```
"1": {
    "Day": "Day 1",
    "Date": "2022-03-15",
    "Travel Mode": "Flight",
    "Departure Location": "Oakland",
    "Destination": "Tucson",
    "Travel Duration": "1 hour 53 minutes",
    "Travel Cost": 190,
    "Accommodation Name": "Private room with private bathroom",
    "Accommodation Cost": 58,
    "Room Type": "Private room",
    "House Rules": "No smoking",
```

```
        "Attractions": "Pima Air & Space Museum (Cost: $15), Reid Park Zoo (Cost:
            $10)",
        "Dining Options": "Villa Tevere (Cost: $37), Magic Spice Wok (Cost: $31)",
        "Total Trip Cost": 341,
        "Budget Remaining": 1059,
        "id": "1",
        "Maximum Occupancy": "2 people"
    },
    "2": {
        "Day": "Day 2",
        "Date": "2022-03-16",
        "Travel Mode": "Self-driving",
        "Departure Location": "Tucson",
        "Destination": "Oakland",
        "Travel Duration": "12 hours 40 minutes",
        "Travel Cost": 68,
        "Accommodation Name": "Private room with private bathroom",
        "Accommodation Cost": 58,
        "Room Type": "Private room",
        "House Rules": "No smoking",
        "Attractions": "Tucson Botanical Gardens (Cost: $15), Old Tucson (Cost:
            $20)",
        "Dining Options": "La Plage (Cost: $93), Ooh Lala! (Cost: $70)",
        "Total Trip Cost": 324,
        "Budget Remaining": 735,
        "id": "2",
        "Maximum Occupancy": "2 people"
    },
    "3": {
        "Day": "Day 3",
        "Date": "2022-03-17",
        "Travel Mode": "Self-driving",
        "Departure Location": "Tucson",
        "Destination": "Oakland",
        "Travel Duration": "12 hours 42 minutes",
        "Travel Cost": 68,
        "Accommodation Name": "None",
        "Accommodation Cost": 0,
        "Room Type": "Private room",
        "House Rules": "No smoking",
        "Attractions": "Arizona-Sonora Desert Museum (Cost: $15), Children's
            Museum Tucson (Cost: $10)",
        "Dining Options": "Pirates of Grill (Cost: $52), Mood 4 Food (Cost: $20)",
        "Total Trip Cost": 165,
        "Budget Remaining": 570,
        "id": "3",
        "Maximum Occupancy": "N/A"
    }
```

C Example of Table as Thought on Calendar Scheduling Task

C.1 Table as Thought w/ One Row Schema

Query: You need to schedule a meeting for Roy, Kathryn and Amy for half an hour between the work hours of 9:00 to 17:00 on Monday.
Here are the existing schedules for everyone during the day: Roy has blocked their calendar on Monday during 9:00 to 9:30, 10:00 to 10:30, 11:00 to 11:30, 12:30 to 13:00; Kathryn has meetings on Monday during 9:30 to 10:00, 16:30 to 17:00; Amy has blocked their calendar on Monday during 9:00 to 14:30, 15:00 to 16:00, 16:30 to 17:00;
Amy would rather not meet on Monday after 15:30. Find a time that works for everyone's schedule and constraints.
Raesoning table:

```
"1": {
    "Meeting Duration": "30 minutes",
    "Work Hours Start": "9:00",
    "Work Hours End": "17:00",
    "Roy's Unavailable Times": "9:00-9:30, 10:00-10:30, 11:00-11:30,
        12:30-13:00",
    "Kathryn's Unavailable Times": "9:30-10:00, 16:30-17:00",
    "Amy's Unavailable Times": "9:00-14:30, 15:00-16:00, 16:30-17:00",
    "Amy's Preference": "Prefers not to meet after 15:30",
    "Proposed Meeting Time": "14:30-15:00"
}
```

C.2 Table as Thought w/ Multi Row Schema

Query: You need to schedule a meeting for Kathryn, Charlotte and Lauren for half an hour between the work hours of 9:00 to 17:00 on Monday.
Here are the existing schedules for everyone during the day: Kathryn has blocked their calendar on Monday during 9:00 to 9:30, 10:30 to 11:00, 11:30 to 12:00, 13:30 to 14:30, 16:30 to 17:00; Charlotte has blocked their calendar on Monday during 12:00 to 12:30, 16:00 to 16:30; Lauren has blocked their calendar on Monday during 9:00 to 10:00, 12:00 to 12:30, 13:30 to 14:30, 15:00 to 16:00, 16:30 to 17:00;
Charlotte do not want to meet on Monday after 13:30. Find a time that works for everyone's schedule and constraints.
Raesoning table:

```
"1": {
    "Participant Name": "Kathryn",
    "Unavailable Time Slots": "9:00-9:30, 10:30-11:00, 11:30-12:00,
        13:30-14:30, 16:30-17:00",
    "Preferred Meeting Time": "None",
    "Meeting Duration": "30 minutes",
    "Work Hours": "9:00-17:00",
    "Available Time Slots": "9:30-10:30, 11:00-11:30, 12:00-13:30,
        14:30-16:30",
    "Constraints Satisfied": true,
    "Proposed Meeting Time": "10:00-10:30"
},
"2": {
    "Participant Name": "Charlotte",
    "Unavailable Time Slots": "12:00-12:30, 16:00-16:30",
    "Preferred Meeting Time": "Before 13:30",
    "Meeting Duration": "30 minutes",
    "Work Hours": "9:00-17:00",
    "Available Time Slots": "9:00-12:00, 12:30-16:00, 16:30-17:00",
    "Constraints Satisfied": true,
    "Proposed Meeting Time": "10:00-10:30"
},
"3": {
    "Participant Name": "Lauren",
    "Unavailable Time Slots": "9:00-10:00, 12:00-12:30, 13:30-14:30,
        15:00-16:00, 16:30-17:00",
    "Preferred Meeting Time": "None",
    "Meeting Duration": "30 minutes",
    "Work Hours": "9:00-17:00",
    "Available Time Slots": "10:00-12:00, 12:30-13:30, 14:30-15:00",
    "Constraints Satisfied": true,
    "Proposed Meeting Time": "10:00-10:30"
}
```

D Comparison of Table as Thought and Direct Prompting on GSM-8k

D.1 Example where Direct Prompting succeceds while Table as Thought Fails

Query: Stephen placed an online order for groceries. His final bill came to $40.00. Because this was through a delivery vendor, they tacked on a 25% fee to his final total and charged him $3.00 in delivery fees. Stephen also added a $4.00 tip. After the extra fees, what was the final price of Stephen's groceries?
Raesoning table:

```
"1": {
    "Base_Price": 40.0,
    "Delivery_Fee_Percentage": 0,
    "Delivery_Fee_Amount": 0,
    "Tip_Amount": 0,
    "Total_Fee_Percentage": 0,
    "Total_Fee_Amount": 0,
    "Final_Price": 40.0
}
```

Direct Prompting response:
To find the final price of Stephen's groceries after all the extra fees, we need to calculate each component and add them together.
1. **Original Bill**: Stephen's original grocery bill was $40.00.
2. **Vendor Fee**: The vendor adds a 25% fee to the original bill. To calculate this fee:

$$\text{Vendor Fee} = 0.25 \times 40.00 = 10.00$$

3. **Delivery Fee**: The delivery fee is a flat $3.00.
4. **Tip**: Stephen added a $4.00 tip.
Now, we add all these amounts together to find the final price:

$$\text{Final Price} = \text{Original Bill} + \text{Vendor Fee} + \text{Delivery Fee} + \text{Tip}$$

$$\text{Final Price} = 40.00 + 10.00 + 3.00 + 4.00 = 57.00$$

Therefore, the final price of Stephen's groceries, after all the extra fees, is $57.00.

D.2 Example where Table as Thought succeceds while Direct Prompting Fails

Query: Jamal's phone can hold 6 times more photographs than can Brittany's phone. The maximum number of photographs that Brittany's phone can hold is 50 times more than the number of birds in Jamal's photograph of the ducks at the zoo. If Jamal's phone can hold 1800 photographs, how many ducks can be seen in Jamal's photograph of ducks at the zoo?
Raesoning table:

```
"1": {
    "Jamal_Phone_Capacity": 1800,
    "Brittany_Phone_Capacity": 300,
    "Ducks_in_Photograph": 6,
    "Brittany_Phone_Additional_Capacity": 50,
    "Equation": "300 = 50D",
    "Solution_Steps": "1. Jamal's phone can hold 6 times more photographs than
        Brittany's phone. 2. Jamal's phone can hold 1800 photographs. 3. Let
        B be the number of photographs Brittany's phone can hold. Then, 6B =
        1800. 4. Solve for B: B = 1800 / 6 = 300. 5. Brittany's phone can hold
        50 times more photographs than the number of ducks in Jamal's
        photograph. 6. Let D be the number of ducks in Jamal's photograph. B =
        50D. 7. Substitute B = 300 into the equation: 300 = 50D. 8. Solve for
        D: D = 300 / 50 = 6.",
```

```
    "Final_Answer": 6
}
```

Direct Prompting response:
To solve the problem, we need to determine the number of ducks in Jamal's photograph.
First, let's define the variables:

- Let B be the maximum number of photographs Brittany's phone can hold.
- Let D be the number of ducks in Jamal's photograph.

According to the problem, Jamal's phone can hold 6 times more photographs than Brittany's phone. Therefore, we have the equation:

$$J = 6B$$

where J is the number of photographs Jamal's phone can hold. We know from the problem that $J = 1800$. Substituting this into the equation gives:

$$1800 = 6B$$

To find B, divide both sides by 6:

$$B = \frac{1800}{6} = 300$$

Next, the problem states that Brittany's phone can hold 50 more photographs than the number of ducks in Jamal's photograph. This gives us the equation:

$$B = D + 50$$

We already found that $B = 300$. Substituting this into the equation gives:

$$300 = D + 50$$

To find D, subtract 50 from both sides:

$$D = 300 - 50 = 250$$

Thus, the number of ducks in Jamal's photograph is $\boxed{250}$.

R^3 : "This is My SQL, Are You With Me?" A Consensus-Based Multi-Agent System for Text-to-SQL Tasks

Hanchen Xia*, **Feng Jiang***, **Naihao Deng**, **Cunxiang Wang**, **Guojiang Zhao**
Rada Mihalcea, **Yue Zhang**
School of Mathematical Science, Shanghai Jiao Tong University
School of Engineering, Westlake University
University of Michigan   Carnegie Mellon University

Abstract

Large Language Models (LLMs) have demonstrated exceptional performance across diverse tasks. To harness their capabilities for Text-to-SQL, we introduce $\boldsymbol{R}^3$ (Review-Rebuttal-Revision), a consensus-based multi-agent system for Text-to-SQL tasks. $\boldsymbol{R}^3$ achieves the new state-of-the-art performance of 89.9 on the Spider test set. In the meantime, $\boldsymbol{R}^3$ achieves 61.80 on the Bird development set. $\boldsymbol{R}^3$ outperforms existing single-LLM and multi-agent Text-to-SQL systems by 1.3% to 8.1% on Spider and Bird, respectively. Surprisingly, we find that for Llama-3-8B, $\boldsymbol{R}^3$ outperforms chain-of-thought prompting by over 20%, even outperforming GPT-3.5 on the Spider development set. We open-source our codebase at https://github.com/1ring2rta/R3.

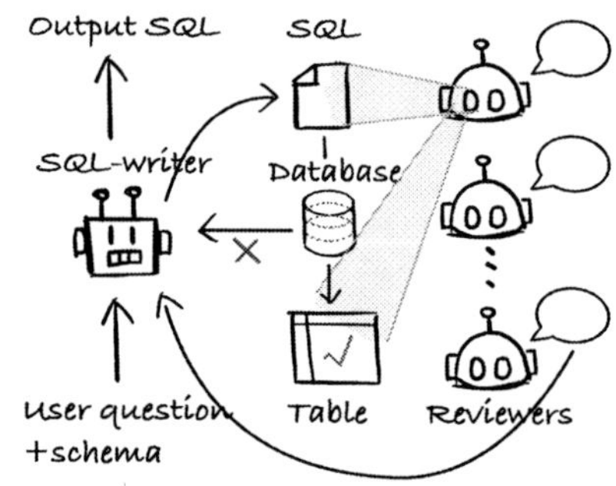

Figure 1: $\boldsymbol{R}^3$ Architecture. n Reviewer agents, each with distinct characteristics, are created to review the generated SQL and its execution result. The process continues until the master node (SQL-Writer agent) and the other nodes reach a consensus, at which point the system outputs the final SQL.

1 Introduction

Text-to-SQL, the task of converting natural language to SQL queries, enables non-technical users to access databases with natural language (Deng et al., 2022; Katsogiannis-Meimarakis and Koutrika, 2023). Recently, Large Language Models (LLMs) have made significant progress on various tasks (Touvron et al., 2023; OpenAI, 2023).

Although various methods were proposed to enhance the reasoning abilities of LLMs (Wei et al., 2022; Yao et al., 2023; Besta et al., 2024), they are still facing challenges with Text-to-SQL tasks (Li et al., 2023b; Hong et al., 2024). The LLM-based multi-agent system leverages collective intelligence from a group of LLMs and has achieved exceptional performance across various tasks (Park et al., 2023; Hong et al., 2023; Xu et al., 2023), but little work explores using them on Text-to-SQL. The existing multi-agent Text-to-SQL system first decomposes the task into multiple subtasks, which are then accomplished step-by-step in a pipeline by agents (Wang et al., 2023). While achieving remarkable performance, such decomposition-based systems necessitate extensive prompt engineering and logic design.

We propose $\boldsymbol{R}^3$, a consensus-based multi-agent system for Text-to-SQL tasks that draws inspiration from the peer-review mechanism. In our designed framework, the LLM does not need to be divided into sub-tasks such as column selection, schema linking, and so on. Instead, it is split into an SQL Writer and multiple Reviewers who provide feedback based on the execution results. Once the generated SQL query is confirmed to be executable, the system enters a review process, where the execution results guide the SQL Writer and reviewers to refine the SQL. Through rounds of "review," "negotiation or rebuttal," and "revision," the SQL Writer and reviewers ultimately reach a consensus and deliver a solution with collective agreement (see Figure 1).

We test $\boldsymbol{R}^3$ on the popular Spider and Bird benchmarks. $\boldsymbol{R}^3$ outperforms the existing single LLM as well as the multi-agent Tex-to-SQL systems by 1.3% to 8.1% on Spider and Bird, and set new state-of-the-art (SOTA) performance of 89.9 on Spider

Proceedings of the 4th Table Representation Learning Workshop, pages 34–46
July 31, 2025 ©2025 Association for Computational Linguistics

dataset. Surprisingly, we find that for Llama-3-8B, $\boldsymbol{R}^3$ outperforms chain-of-thought prompting by over 20%, even outperforming GPT-3.5 on the Spider-Dev set.

In summary, our contributions are several-fold:

1. To the best of our knowledge, $\boldsymbol{R}^3$ is the first Text-to-SQL system to use the execution result for SQL refinements, and the first Text-to-SQL system to equip agents with memory sequences to enhance SQL generation.

2. $\boldsymbol{R}^3$ offers a consensus-based multi-agent system for Text-to-SQL tasks. Using very succinct prompts, $\boldsymbol{R}^3$ sets the new SOTA performance of 89.9 on the Spider dataset. In the meantime, $\boldsymbol{R}^3$ achieves 61.80 on the Bird-Dev dataset. In addition, $\boldsymbol{R}^3$ effectively helps open-source LLMs such as Llama-3-8B on SQL generation. When using Llama-3-8B as the backbone model, $\boldsymbol{R}^3$outperforms direct CoT prompting Llama-3-8B by 20%, and outperforms GPT-3.5 on the Spider-Dev set.

3. We provide a detailed error analysis of $\boldsymbol{R}^3$ on the existing Text-to-SQL benchmarks, shedding light on future research on the Text-to-SQL task.

2 Related Works

Traditional Methods for Text-to-SQL. The Text-to-SQL conversion task has enjoyed a long history dating back to 1970s (Androutsopoulos et al., 1995), and researchers have kept working on this problem for the past few decades (Dahl et al., 1994; Zelle and Mooney, 1996; Popescu et al., 2003; Zhong et al., 2017; Yu et al., 2018). Before the advent of LLMs, systems like RATSQL (Wang et al., 2019) and LGESQL (Cao et al., 2021) adapt BERT (Devlin et al., 2018) architecture to acquire better representations, and carefully design their techniques to link schema in the database system. Later, approaches like PICARD (Scholak et al., 2021), RASAT (Qi et al., 2022), and RESD-SQL (Li et al., 2023a) adapt the T5 model (Raffel et al., 2020) to translate user questions into SQL query in an end-to-end fashion. Additionally, researchers propose a variety of task-specific strategies like relation-aware self-attention (Qi et al., 2022), schema selection (Li et al., 2023a), and constrained decoding (Scholak et al., 2021) to improve the performance of the Text-to-SQL systems.

LLMs for Text-to-SQL. Recent years have witnessed LLMs' breakthroughs in many fields (Ouyang et al., 2022; Touvron et al., 2023; Dubey et al., 2024). Moreover, Brown et al. (2020); Chen et al. (2022); Liu and Liu (2021) have observed that these LLMs can learn in context with a few examples during their inference time. The strong reasoning and in-context learning capabilities of these LLMs have brought a paradigm shift to the Text-to-SQL community, which now focuses on leveraging LLMs' ability to handle Text-to-SQL tasks. For instance, Pourreza and Rafiei (2023) propose DIN-SQL to few-shot prompt GPT-4; Dong et al. (2023) introduce C3, which zero-shots GPT-3.5 with hints and checks output consistency; DAIL-SQL (Gao et al., 2023) comprehensively evaluates the efficiency and effectiveness of various prompting techniques.

Output Consistency. Recent works have applied the consistency principle (Wang et al., 2022) to enhance the reasoning ability of LLMs through in-context learning, such as chain-of-thought (CoT) (Wei et al., 2022) or tree-of-thoughts (ToT) (Yao et al., 2023). In addition, Chen et al. (2023) adopt program-of-thoughts (PoT), which uses Python code to assist LLMs in the reasoning process and surpasses CoT on math reasoning.

3 $\boldsymbol{R}^3$ Architecture

SQL-Writer We task SQL-Writer (SW) agents to: (1) compose the original SQL query based on the user question and database schema; (2) ensure that the SQL query is executable, and correct it when errors occur; (3) respond to reviewer agents' feedback and revise the SQL query accordingly. Specifically, we prompt SW agent through Prompt 1 in Appendix A.6. For task (1), we feed the Prompt 1 to SW agent directly. Given a user question x and the database schema $\mathcal{S}$, task (1) can be formalized as:

$$y = \texttt{SW}(x, \mathcal{S}),$$

where y is the generated SQL query. For steps (2) and (3), we maintain a truncated dialogue history, denoted as $\mathcal{H}$, which is initially set to $\mathcal{H} = [(x, \mathcal{S}), y]$. Specifically, if an error e occurs during SQL execution, $\texttt{DB}(y)$, we append e to the history, updating $\mathcal{H} \leftarrow \mathcal{H} + e$. Subsequently, we obtain the updated output, y', via the following process:

$$y' = \texttt{SW}(\mathcal{H}).$$

Given $x, \mathcal{S}$
$y = \texttt{SW}(x, \mathcal{S})$
$i = 0$
while $i \leq 5$ **do**
    $o = \texttt{DB}(y)$; $\{r_k\}_{k=1}^{n} = \texttt{RE}(x, y, o, \mathcal{S})$
    $\hat{y} = \texttt{SW}(x, \{r_k\}_{k=1}^{n}, \mathcal{S})$
    if $y = \hat{y}$ **then**
        break
    else
        $y \leftarrow \hat{y}$
    end
    $i \leftarrow i + 1$
end

Algorithm 1: $\boldsymbol{R}^3$-Loop

We then concatenate y' to the history, resulting in the update $\mathcal{H} \leftarrow \mathcal{H} + y'$. Furthermore, in consideration of the context window limitations of LLMs, we truncate the dialogue history $\mathcal{H}$ when the length of the prompt exceeds the model's context limit.

Reviewers. We generate the reviewer agent's (REs) professions using an LLM (see Prompt 3 in Appendix A.6) based on the database schema and the content of the SQL query, for instance, "Senior Database Engineer specialized in writing various clauses" and "Data Analyst in the automotive industry", etc. We incorporate these professions in the system prompt for the REs to make them focus on different aspects of the SQL query. These REs are prompted to provide their professional comments based on the database schema, the user's question, the predicted SQL, and its execution result in the table format.

Overall Architecture. After several rounds of "negotiation" between the SQL-writer and REs, we decide whether there is a consensus by checking if the SQL-writer agent generates the same SQL query as in the previous round. When there is a consensus, we terminate the negotiation loop and output the final SQL query. Algorithm 1 depicts the overall process of our system.

Appendix A.6 provides the detailed prompts we use in $\boldsymbol{R}^3$. In addition, we incorporate:

1. Program of Thoughts (PoT) (Chen et al., 2023) to prompt the SQL-writer agent to generate Python code before SQL query (see Prompt 2 in Appendix A.6). Therefore, the agents may leverage Python in their reasoning process for better SQL query generation.

2. k-shots example selection based on similarity of the user question embeddings. Specifically, when our system infers the SQL query in the test set, we select the k most similar use questions and their corresponding SQL queries from the training set (k-shots) and use them for in-context learning.

4 Experimental Setup

	Spider-Dev	Spider-Test	Bird-Dev
	(Yu et al., 2018)		(Li et al., 2023b)
#QA	1,034	2147	1,534
#Domain	138	-	37
#DB	200	206	95
DB Size	879.5 MB	906.5 MB	1.76 GB

Table 1: Statistics of two Text-to-SQL benchmarks we use in our experiments. "#QA", "#Domain" and "#DB" refer to the number of samples, domains and databases, respectively.

Datasets. We conduct experiments on two cross-domain Text-to-SQL benchmarks, Spider and Bird, detailed in Table 1.

Baselines. We conduct our experiments based on LLMs including GPT-3.5-Turbo, GPT-4 (OpenAI, 2023) and Llama-3 (AI@Meta, 2024). As for the compared methods, the raw performance for GPT-3.5 ("-") was evaluated by Li et al. (2023b); C3 employs schema linking filtering (Dong et al., 2023); DAIL selects few-shot demonstrations based on their skeleton similarities (Gao et al., 2023), and "SC" represents Self-Consistency (Wang et al., 2022); PET uses cross-consistency (Li et al., 2024); DIN decomposes the Text-to-SQL task into smaller subtasks (Pourreza and Rafiei, 2023); MAC, as previously mentioned, is the first to apply a Multi-Agent system to Text-to-SQL tasks (Wang et al., 2023).

Metrics. We employ test-suite execution evaluation[1] (Zhong et al., 2020), the standard evaluation protocol for Spider, and the official SQL execution accuracy evaluation for Bird[2].

5 Results and Analysis

5.1 General Results

Table 2 compares $\boldsymbol{R}^3$'s performance with existing baseline methods when we use GPT-3.5-Turbo or GPT-4 as our backbone models. Our best performed system with GPT-4 as the backbone

[1] github.com/taoyds/test-suite-sql-eval
[2] bird-bench.github.io/

Backbone	Method	Spider		Bird
		Dev	*Test*	*Dev*
GPT-3.5 Turbo	-	72.1	-	37.22
	C3 (2023)	81.8	82.3	-
	MAC (2023)	80.6	75.5	50.56
	R^3 (ours)	81.4	81.1	52.15
GPT-4	DAIL (2023)	83.6	86.6	-
	PET (2024)	82.2	87.6	-
	DIN (2023)	82.8	85.3	50.72
	MAC (2023)	86.8	82.8	59.39
	R^3 (ours)	**88.1**	**89.9**	**61.80**

Table 2: Execution accuracy across existing Text-to-SQL systems. We use the GPT-3.5-Turbo in our experiment. The results for plain GPT-3.5-Turbo (first row) are taken from Li et al. (2023b).

Backbone	Method	Spider	
		Dev	*Test*
GPT-3.5 Turbo	Li et al. (2023b)	72.1	–
	R^3	**81.4**	**81.1**
Llama-3-8B Instruct	CoT	52.1	53.5
	R^3	**72.8**	**72.6**

Table 3: Execution accuracy comparison when we employ open-source LLMs as the backbone models with R^3on Spider-Dev and Spider-Test. We highlight that R^3 significantly boosts the open-source LLM's capability on SQL generation.

achieves 88.1%, 89.9%, and 61.8% on the Spider-Dev, Spider-Test, and Bird-Dev respectively, surpassing the existing multi-agent Text-to-SQL systems.

5.2 Discussions

Generalizability of R^3 framework. We test our system with open-source Llama-3 models on Spider and report the results in Table 3. To our surprise, with the help of R^3, zero-shot Llama-3-8B outperforms GPT-3.5 performance reported by Li et al. (2023b) on Spider-Dev set. This demonstrates the effectiveness of our proposed R^3 system.

CoT versus PoT. We conduct an ablation study on the impact of CoT, PoT with one or three reviewer agents in the discussion and report the results in Table 4. The results in Table 4 show that the n-Reviewer(s) Loop (nR-Lp) plays a major role in performance improvement, with the 3R-Lp configuration significantly outperforming the 1R-Lp setup. The proposed R^3 system achieves a 10.54% improvement over the baseline GPT-4 + CoT. We

	GPT-3.5-Turbo		GPT-4	
	Spider	Bird	Spider	Bird
CoT	78.2	37.22	79.7	53.30
PoT	78.5	36.96	80.0	54.61
1R-Lp + CoT	78.3	44.13	82.3	57.89
1R-Lp + PoT	79.3	46.35	85.4	58.34
R^3: 3R-Lp + PoT	**81.4**	**52.15**	**88.1**	**61.80**

Table 4: Ablation Studies on Spider-Dev and Bird-Dev (Execution Accuracy). The 1-Reviewer Loop (1R-Lp) represents that only one reviewer agent participates in the discussion, while the 3-Reviewers Loop (3R-Lp) represents three in the discussion, which is also the default configuration of R^3. We conduct all the experiments here under the 5-shot setting.

provide the statistical significant test for these results in Appendix A.1. Appendix A.2 provides a sensitivity analysis of the impacts of the k value in k-shots.

5.3 Error Analysis

In total, GPT-4+R^3 fails to generate the gold SQL queries for 123 instances in Spider-Dev. Table 5 shows the error case distribution for our system on Spider-Dev (more in Appendices A.3 and A.4). Note that though we have spotted issues with the gold SQL queries, we still adopt the original set to calculate the performance of our system to ensure a fair comparison.

Gold Error. We notice that though the annotation quality of Spider is good, there are still cases where the gold SQL queries are not correct. Specifically, among the 151 examples, 30.5% are due to incorrect gold SQL queries (4.5% of all the examples in Spider-Dev). To facilitate future research, we catalog the instances with incorrect gold SQL, correct the errors, and share the details.

Ambiguity. We observe that there are a few questions involving ambiguities, a phenomenon spotted on a wide range of NLP tasks (Plank, 2022; Deng et al., 2023). In Table 5.3, both `FullName` and `Maker` columns hold the information for the "name of makers", except that `FullName` holds the full names while `Maker` holds the name abbreviations. Therefore, both the gold and predicted SQL queries should be considered correct if there is no further clarifications. Such ambiguous requests may be common in real-world applications as the

Error Types	Question, Gold & Prediction	Explanation
Gold Error (30.5%)	**Q:** What are the Asian countries which have a population **larger than that of any country in Africa**? **Gold:** ✗ ... `AND population > (SELECT min(population) FROM country WHERE Continent = "Africa")` **Pred:** ☑ ... `AND population > (SELECT max(population) FROM country WHERE Continent = "Africa")`	Judged as incorrect because of the incorrect gold SQL query.
Logic (29.8%)	**Q:** How many owners **temporarily do not** have any dogs? **Gold:** ☑ `SELECT count(*) FROM Owners WHERE owner_id NOT IN (SELECT owner_id FROM Dogs)` **Pred:** ✗ `SELECT (SELECT COUNT(DISTINCT owner_id) FROM Owners) - (SELECT COUNT(DISTINCT owner_id) FROM Dogs WHERE date_departed IS NULL)`	The predicted SQL query wrongly assumes that all owners have had dogs.
Ambiguity (13.2%)	**Q:** What are the **names** of all makers with more than 3 models? **Gold:** ☑ `SELECT T1.FullName ... HAVING count(*) > 3;` **Pred:** ☑ `SELECT T1.Maker ... HAVING count(*) > 3;`	Both `FullName` and `Maker` columns hold the information for "names".
Inaccuracy (11.3%)	**Q:** What are the **arriving date** of the dogs who have gone through a treatment? **Gold:** ☑ `SELECT T1.date_arrived, FROM ...` **Pred:** ✗ `SELECT T1.date_arrived, T1.Name FROM ...`	The selected `Name` is not asked by the question.
DB Value (10.6%)	**Q:** Which city and country is the **Alton** airport at? **Gold:** ☑ `SELECT ... WHERE AirportName = "Alton" ;` **Pred:** ✗ `SELECT ... WHERE AirportName LIKE "%Alton%" ;`	Our framework notices there is a space for `Alton` in the DB, therefore employing a fuzzy match.
Others (4.6%)		

Table 5: Error Analysis of $\boldsymbol{R}^3$ on Spider-Dev. We make the part in the question red when it is either annotated incorrectly in the gold SQL query (Gold) or predicted incorrectly in the predicted SQL query (Pred).

lay users may not be familiar with the database schema. This requires future research on interactive Text-to-SQL systems that can understand and deal with such ambiguities in user questions.

Dirty Database Value. We observe that due to the Database (DB) setup for Spider, certain DB values may deviate from what is asked in the question. For instance, in Table 5.5, $\boldsymbol{R}^3$ notices a space for `Alton` in DB, therefore employing a fuzzy match. But this deviates the SQL query's execution results from the gold SQL query's results.

Logic. In Table 5.2, we present an example of the logic error made by $\boldsymbol{R}^3$. We notice that LLMs may solve the problems using a more complicated logic, which is prone to mistakes. For instance, in Table 5.2, instead of directly counting the owners who do not own dogs, the LLMs try to subtract the number of dog owners from the total number of owners. This ignores the possibility that some owners may have never had any dogs before. This addresses an issue with the multi-agent system that if the system comes up with a complicated initial SQL query, the following discussion process may try to polish the complicated SQL query instead of switching to an easier solution. In cases like Table 5.2, there is no way to reach a perfect SQL query with the subtraction logic.

Inaccuracy. We observe that the LLMs may incorporate more information than what is asked by the end user. For instance, in Table 5.4, the user does not ask for the name of the dogs, but the LLMs present such information along with the requested arrival date. We hypothesize that since such extra information can potentially be helpful to the end user, LLMs may be biased towards including it.

Our findings indicate that the existing evaluation protocols for Text-to-SQL generation may not authentically capture the capabilities of these sophisticated systems. Therefore, we advocate for a reassessment and enhancement of Text-to-SQL evaluation methods. We provide further error analysis of $\boldsymbol{R}^3$ on Bird in Appendix A.4.

6 Conclusion

In this paper, we propose $\boldsymbol{R}^3$, a consensus-based multi-agent system for Text-to-SQL generation. $\boldsymbol{R}^3$ sets the new SOTA performance on Spider (89.9) and achieves 61.80 on the Bird Dev set. In addition, we find that $\boldsymbol{R}^3$ significantly enhances open-source LLMs such as Llama-3-8B (over 20% improvement on Spider Dev set). Last but not least, we conduct a comprehensive error analysis and identify issues with the current Text-to-SQL evaluation, underscoring the necessity for a more refined evaluation protocol, as the LLMs and LLM-based methods become more powerful than ever.

Limitations

Due to the scope of the study, we only test a limited number of LLMs. In this paper, we study the performance gap between 1R-Lp and 3R-Lp. We leave further studies on the effects of the number of reviewers to future research.

Ethical Statements

In this paper, we propose strategies to improve the SQL generation capabilities of LLMs. To the best of our knowledge, we do not expect our system would have negative impacts on society.

References

AI@Meta. 2024. Llama 3 model card.

Ion Androutsopoulos, Graeme D Ritchie, and Peter Thanisch. 1995. Natural language interfaces to databases–an introduction. *Natural language engineering*, 1(1):29–81.

Maciej Besta, Nils Blach, Ales Kubicek, Robert Gerstenberger, Michal Podstawski, Lukas Gianinazzi, Joanna Gajda, Tomasz Lehmann, Hubert Niewiadomski, Piotr Nyczyk, et al. 2024. Graph of thoughts: Solving elaborate problems with large language models. In *Proceedings of the AAAI Conference on Artificial Intelligence*, volume 38, pages 17682–17690.

Tom Brown, Benjamin Mann, Nick Ryder, Melanie Subbiah, Jared D Kaplan, Prafulla Dhariwal, Arvind Neelakantan, Pranav Shyam, Girish Sastry, Amanda Askell, et al. 2020. Language models are few-shot learners. *Advances in neural information processing systems*, 33:1877–1901.

Ruisheng Cao, Lu Chen, Zhi Chen, Yanbin Zhao, Su Zhu, and Kai Yu. 2021. Lgesql: line graph enhanced text-to-sql model with mixed local and non-local relations. *arXiv preprint arXiv:2106.01093*.

Mingda Chen, Jingfei Du, Ramakanth Pasunuru, Todor Mihaylov, Srini Iyer, Veselin Stoyanov, and Zornitsa Kozareva. 2022. Improving in-context few-shot learning via self-supervised training. *arXiv preprint arXiv:2205.01703*.

Wenhu Chen, Xueguang Ma, Xinyi Wang, and William W. Cohen. 2023. Program of thoughts prompting: Disentangling computation from reasoning for numerical reasoning tasks. *Transactions on Machine Learning Research*.

Deborah A. Dahl, Madeleine Bates, Michael Brown, William Fisher, Kate Hunicke-Smith, David Pallett, Christine Pao, Alexander Rudnicky, and Elizabeth Shriberg. 1994. Expanding the scope of the ATIS task: The ATIS-3 corpus. In *Human Language Technology: Proceedings of a Workshop held at Plainsboro, New Jersey, March 8-11, 1994*.

Naihao Deng, Yulong Chen, and Yue Zhang. 2022. Recent advances in text-to-SQL: A survey of what we have and what we expect. In *Proceedings of the 29th International Conference on Computational Linguistics*, pages 2166–2187, Gyeongju, Republic of Korea. International Committee on Computational Linguistics.

Naihao Deng, Xinliang Zhang, Siyang Liu, Winston Wu, Lu Wang, and Rada Mihalcea. 2023. You are what you annotate: Towards better models through annotator representations. In *Findings of the Association for Computational Linguistics: EMNLP 2023*, pages 12475–12498, Singapore. Association for Computational Linguistics.

Jacob Devlin, Ming-Wei Chang, Kenton Lee, and Kristina Toutanova. 2018. Bert: Pre-training of deep bidirectional transformers for language understanding. *arXiv preprint arXiv:1810.04805*.

Xuemei Dong, Chao Zhang, Yuhang Ge, Yuren Mao, Yunjun Gao, Jinshu Lin, Dongfang Lou, et al. 2023. C3: Zero-shot text-to-sql with chatgpt. *arXiv preprint arXiv:2307.07306*.

Abhimanyu Dubey, Abhinav Jauhri, Abhinav Pandey, Abhishek Kadian, Ahmad Al-Dahle, Aiesha Letman, Akhil Mathur, Alan Schelten, Amy Yang, Angela Fan, et al. 2024. The llama 3 herd of models. *arXiv preprint arXiv:2407.21783*.

Dawei Gao, Haibin Wang, Yaliang Li, Xiuyu Sun, Yichen Qian, Bolin Ding, and Jingren Zhou. 2023. Text-to-sql empowered by large language models: A benchmark evaluation. *arXiv preprint arXiv:2308.15363*.

Sirui Hong, Xiawu Zheng, Jonathan Chen, Yuheng Cheng, Jinlin Wang, Ceyao Zhang, Zili Wang, Steven Ka Shing Yau, Zijuan Lin, Liyang Zhou, et al. 2023. Metagpt: Meta programming for multi-agent collaborative framework. *arXiv preprint arXiv:2308.00352*.

Zijin Hong, Zheng Yuan, Qinggang Zhang, Hao Chen, Junnan Dong, Feiran Huang, and Xiao Huang. 2024. Next-generation database interfaces: A survey of llm-based text-to-sql. *arXiv preprint arXiv:2406.08426*.

George Katsogiannis-Meimarakis and Georgia Koutrika. 2023. A survey on deep learning approaches for text-to-sql. *The VLDB Journal*, 32(4):905–936.

Haoyang Li, Jing Zhang, Cuiping Li, and Hong Chen. 2023a. Resdsql: Decoupling schema linking and skeleton parsing for text-to-sql. In *Proceedings of the AAAI Conference on Artificial Intelligence*, volume 37, pages 13067–13075.

Jinyang Li, Binyuan Hui, Ge Qu, Binhua Li, Jiaxi Yang, Bowen Li, Bailin Wang, Bowen Qin, Rongyu Cao, Ruiying Geng, et al. 2023b. Can llm already serve as a database interface. *A big bench for large-scale database grounded text-to-sqls. CoRR abs/2305.03111*.

Zhishuai Li, Xiang Wang, Jingjing Zhao, Sun Yang, Guoqing Du, Xiaoru Hu, Bin Zhang, Yuxiao Ye, Ziyue Li, Rui Zhao, et al. 2024. Pet-sql: A prompt-enhanced two-stage text-to-sql framework with cross-consistency. *arXiv preprint arXiv:2403.09732*.

Yixin Liu and Pengfei Liu. 2021. Simcls: A simple framework for contrastive learning of abstractive summarization. *arXiv preprint arXiv:2106.01890*.

Henry B Mann and Donald R Whitney. 1947. On a test of whether one of two random variables is stochastically larger than the other. *The annals of mathematical statistics*, pages 50–60.

R OpenAI. 2023. Gpt-4 technical report. *arXiv*, pages 2303–08774.

Long Ouyang, Jeffrey Wu, Xu Jiang, Diogo Almeida, Carroll Wainwright, Pamela Mishkin, Chong Zhang, Sandhini Agarwal, Katarina Slama, Alex Ray, et al. 2022. Training language models to follow instructions with human feedback. *Advances in neural information processing systems*, 35:27730–27744.

Joon Sung Park, Joseph O'Brien, Carrie Jun Cai, Meredith Ringel Morris, Percy Liang, and Michael S Bernstein. 2023. Generative agents: Interactive simulacra of human behavior. In *Proceedings of the 36th Annual ACM Symposium on User Interface Software and Technology*, pages 1–22.

Barbara Plank. 2022. The "problem" of human label variation: On ground truth in data, modeling and evaluation. In *Proceedings of the 2022 Conference on Empirical Methods in Natural Language Processing*, pages 10671–10682, Abu Dhabi, United Arab Emirates. Association for Computational Linguistics.

Ana-Maria Popescu, Oren Etzioni, and Henry Kautz. 2003. Towards a theory of natural language interfaces to databases. In *Proceedings of the 8th international conference on Intelligent user interfaces*, pages 149–157.

Mohammadreza Pourreza and Davood Rafiei. 2023. Din-sql: Decomposed in-context learning of text-to-sql with self-correction. *arXiv preprint arXiv:2304.11015*.

Jiexing Qi, Jingyao Tang, Ziwei He, Xiangpeng Wan, Yu Cheng, Chenghu Zhou, Xinbing Wang, Quanshi Zhang, and Zhouhan Lin. 2022. Rasat: Integrating relational structures into pretrained seq2seq model for text-to-sql. *arXiv preprint arXiv:2205.06983*.

Colin Raffel, Noam Shazeer, Adam Roberts, Katherine Lee, Sharan Narang, Michael Matena, Yanqi Zhou, Wei Li, and Peter J Liu. 2020. Exploring the limits of transfer learning with a unified text-to-text transformer. *The Journal of Machine Learning Research*, 21(1):5485–5551.

Torsten Scholak, Nathan Schucher, and Dzmitry Bahdanau. 2021. Picard: Parsing incrementally for constrained auto-regressive decoding from language models. *arXiv preprint arXiv:2109.05093*.

Hugo Touvron, Louis Martin, Kevin Stone, Peter Albert, Amjad Almahairi, Yasmine Babaei, Nikolay Bashlykov, Soumya Batra, Prajjwal Bhargava, Shruti Bhosale, et al. 2023. Llama 2: Open foundation and fine-tuned chat models. *arXiv preprint arXiv:2307.09288*.

Bailin Wang, Richard Shin, Xiaodong Liu, Oleksandr Polozov, and Matthew Richardson. 2019. Rat-sql: Relation-aware schema encoding and linking for text-to-sql parsers. *arXiv preprint arXiv:1911.04942*.

Bing Wang, Changyu Ren, Jian Yang, Xinnian Liang, Jiaqi Bai, Qian-Wen Zhang, Zhao Yan, and Zhoujun Li. 2023. Mac-sql: Multi-agent collaboration for text-to-sql. *arXiv preprint arXiv:2312.11242*.

Xuezhi Wang, Jason Wei, Dale Schuurmans, Quoc Le, Ed Chi, Sharan Narang, Aakanksha Chowdhery, and Denny Zhou. 2022. Self-consistency improves chain of thought reasoning in language models. *arXiv preprint arXiv:2203.11171*.

Jason Wei, Xuezhi Wang, Dale Schuurmans, Maarten Bosma, Fei Xia, Ed Chi, Quoc V Le, Denny Zhou, et al. 2022. Chain-of-thought prompting elicits reasoning in large language models. *Advances in Neural Information Processing Systems*, 35:24824–24837.

Zelai Xu, Chao Yu, Fei Fang, Yu Wang, and Yi Wu. 2023. Language agents with reinforcement learning for strategic play in the werewolf game. *arXiv preprint arXiv:2310.18940*.

Shunyu Yao, Dian Yu, Jeffrey Zhao, Izhak Shafran, Thomas L Griffiths, Yuan Cao, and Karthik Narasimhan. 2023. Tree of thoughts: Deliberate problem solving with large language models. *arXiv preprint arXiv:2305.10601*.

Tao Yu, Rui Zhang, Kai Yang, Michihiro Yasunaga, Dongxu Wang, Zifan Li, James Ma, Irene Li, Qingning Yao, Shanelle Roman, et al. 2018. Spider: A large-scale human-labeled dataset for complex and cross-domain semantic parsing and text-to-sql task. *arXiv preprint arXiv:1809.08887*.

John M. Zelle and Raymond J. Mooney. 1996. Learning to parse database queries using inductive logic programming. In *Proceedings of the Thirteenth National Conference on Artificial Intelligence - Volume 2*, pages 1050–1055.

Ruiqi Zhong, Tao Yu, and Dan Klein. 2020. Semantic evaluation for text-to-sql with distilled test suites. *arXiv preprint arXiv:2010.02840*.

Victor Zhong, Caiming Xiong, and Richard Socher. 2017. Seq2sql: Generating structured queries from natural language using reinforcement learning. *arXiv preprint arXiv:1709.00103*.

A Appendix

A.1 Significance Test

We divided the generated SQL by several strategies in Table 4 into 10 equal parts and calculated the execution accuracy for each. To test whether our strategy can indeed improve execution accuracy, we conduct a significance test between the "CoT" and "3R-Lp+PoT" strategies. The null hypothesis of the test is that the median execution accuracy obtained by the two strategies is the same. The Mann-Whitney U Test (Mann and Whitney, 1947) is a non-parametric statistical method used to compare whether there is a significant difference in the medians of two independent samples. Compared to the Analysis of Variance (ANOVA), it does not require the data to be normally distributed, making it suitable for small samples or data with unknown distribution.

The p-value of the test is 0.0024, which is below the commonly accepted significance level of 0.05. Therefore, we have reason to reject the null hypothesis, indicating that the "3R-Lp+PoT" strategy leads to a significant performance improvement.

Effects of the number of "reviewer" agents.

A.2 Effects of k in k-shot.

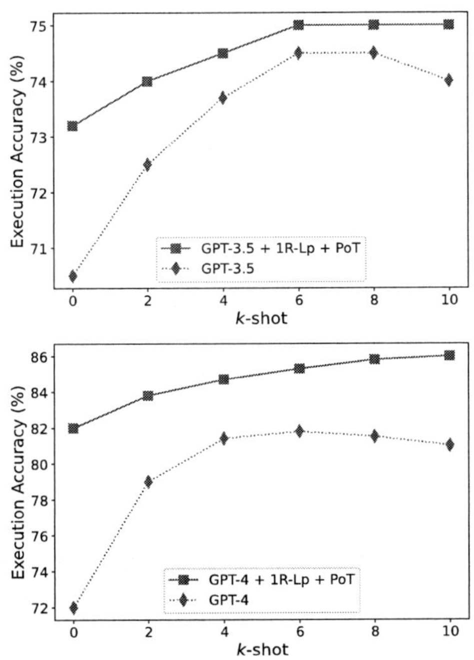

Figure 2: k-shot Sensitivity Analysis.

We test various k values on 200 random samples from Spider-Dev. As shown in Figure 2, compared to CoT, the performance of the $\boldsymbol{R}^3$ system remains relatively stable regardless of the number of examples, which corroborates our previous findings from the 0-shot experiments with Llama-3.

A.3 Spider Error Cases

Error Type	Question, Gold & Prediction	Reason
DB Value	**Q:** Find the last name of the students who currently live in the state of North Carolina but have not registered in any degree program. **Gold:** `SELECT ... WHERE T2.state_province_county = 'NorthCarolina' EXCEPT ...` **Pred:** `SELECT ... WHERE T2.state_province_county = 'North Carolina' EXCEPT ...`	The filtering condition in the question does not match the database value, string "NorthCalifornia" in database do not have a space in between.
Gold Error	**Q:** What are the first names of all players, and their average rankings? **Gold:** `SELECT avg(ranking), T1.first_name FROM players AS T1 JOIN rankings AS T2 ON T1.player_id = T2.player_id GROUP BY T1.first_name` **Pred:** `SELECT avg(ranking), T1.first_name FROM players AS T1 JOIN rankings AS T2 ON T1.player_id = T2.player_id GROUP BY T1.player_id`	The individuals in the table can be uniquely determined by column player_id not first_name, when `GROUP BY`.
Gold Error	**Q:** Find the id and cell phone of the professionals who operate two or more types of treatments. **Gold:** `SELECT T1.professional_id, T1.cell_number FROM Professionals AS T1 JOIN Treatments AS T2 ON T1.professional_id = T2.professional_id GROUP BY T1.professional_id HAVING count(*) >= 2` **Pred:** `SELECT T1.professional_id, T1.cell_number FROM Professionals AS T1 JOIN Treatments AS T2 ON T1.professional_id = T2.professional_id GROUP BY T1.professional_id HAVING COUNT( DISTINCT T2.treatment_type_code) >= 2`	The gold only finds professionals who have two or more records in the treatment table does not ensure that the records are for different types of treatments
Ambiguity	**Q:** What are the names and ids of all makers with more than 3 models? **Gold:** `SELECT T1.FullName, T1.Id FROM CAR_MAKERS AS T1 JOIN MODEL_LIST AS T2 ON T1.Id = T2.Maker GROUP BY T1.Id HAVING count(*) > 3;` **Pred:** `SELECT T1.Maker, T1.Id FROM CAR_MAKERS AS T1 JOIN MODEL_LIST AS T2 ON T1.Id = T2.Maker GROUP BY T1.Id HAVING count(*) > 3;`	Both column "Maker" and column "FullName" can answer the question about the "names of makers" in the query.
Imprecise	**Q:** What are the arriving date and the departing date of the dogs who have gone through a treatment? **Gold:** `SELECT DISTINCT T1.date_arrived, T1.date_departed FROM Dogs AS T1 JOIN Treatments AS T2 ON T1.dog_id = T2.dog_id` **Pred:** `SELECT DISTINCT T1.date_arrived, T1.date_departed, T1.Name FROM Dogs AS T1 JOIN Treatments AS T2 ON T1.dog_id = T2.dog_id`	The question do not require listing the specific names of the students, but only ask to list the students' arrival and departure dates. This falls under information redundancy.

Table 6: Spider error cases.

A.4 BIRD Error Cases

Error Type	Question, Gold & Prediction	Reason
DB Value	**Q:** How many cards with unknown power that can't be found in foil is in duel deck A? **Gold:** `SELECT SUM(CASE WHEN power LIKE '%*%' OR power IS NULL THEN 1 ELSE 0 END) FROM cards WHERE hasFoil = 0 AND duelDeck = 'a'` **Pred:** `SELECT COUNT(*) FROM cards WHERE (power IS NULL OR power = '*') AND hasFoil = 0 AND duelDeck = 'a'`	Values in database cannot exact match with the question and evidence.
Gold Error	**Q:** How many artists have designed a card with a black border color and is available in both "arena" and "mtgo" printing type? **Gold:** `SELECT COUNT(CASE WHEN availability LIKE '%arena,mtgo%' THEN 1 ELSE NULL END) FROM cards` **Pred:** `SELECT COUNT(DISTINCT artist) FROM cards WHERE borderColor = 'black' AND availability LIKE '%arena,mtgo%'`	The gold missed one filtering condition.
Ambiguity	**Q:** Among black card borders, which card has full artwork? **Gold:** `SELECT id FROM cards WHERE borderColor = 'black' AND isFullArt = 1` **Pred:** `SELECT name FROM cards WHERE borderColor = 'black' AND isFullArt = 1;`	Both column "name" and column "id" can answer the question about the "the card has full artwork" in the query.
Logic	**Q:** Which cities have the top 5 lowest enrollment number for students in grades 1 through 12? **Gold:** `SELECT T2.City FROM frpm AS T1 INNER JOIN schools AS T2 ON T1.CDSCode = T2.CDSCode GROUP BY T2.City ORDER BY SUM(T1.'Enrollment (K-12)') ASC LIMIT 5` **Pred:** `SELECT T2.City, T1."Enrollment (K-12)" FROM frpm AS T1 JOIN schools AS T2 ON T1.CDSCode = T2.CDSCode ORDER BY T1."Enrollment (K-12)" ASC LIMIT 5;`	The Pred query is incorrect because it lacks grouping and aggregation. It directly selects cities and their corresponding "Enrollment (K-12)" without summing up the enrollment numbers across all schools within each city. As a result, it returns the cities of the five schools with the lowest enrollment numbers, which does not accurately answer the question seeking the top 5 cities with the lowest total enrollment for students in grades 1 through 12.

Table 7: Bird error cases.

A.5 Interactive Correction Cases

Before	After	Reason
Q: What is the phone number of the school that has the highest number of test takers with an SAT score of over 1500?		
Before: SELECT schools.Phone FROM satscores JOIN schools ON satscores.cds = schools.CDSCode WHERE satscores.NumGE1500 > 1500 GROUP BY schools.School ORDER BY COUNT(*) DESC LIMIT 1;	**After:** SELECT schools.Phone FROM satscores JOIN schools ON satscores.cds = schools.CDSCode ORDER BY satscores.NumGE1500 DESC LIMIT 1;	The WHERE clause is checking if the number of test takers with an SAT score over 1500 is greater than 1500, which is not what the question is asking. The question is asking for the school with the highest number of test takers who scored over 1500. Additionally, the GROUP BY clause is grouping by the school name, which may not be unique. It would be better to group by the school code (CDSCode) which is unique for each school.
Q: List the top five schools, by descending order, from the highest to the lowest, the most number of Enrollment (Ages 5-17). Please give their NCES school identification number.		
Before: SELECT T1."School Name", T2.NCESSchool FROM frpm AS T1 JOIN schools AS T2 ON T1.CDSCode = T2.CDSCode ORDER BY T1."Enrollment (Ages 5-17)" DESC LIMIT 5;	**After:** SELECT T2.NCESSchool FROM frpm AS T1 JOIN schools AS T2 ON T1.CDSCode = T2.CDSCode ORDER BY T1."Enrollment (Ages 5-17)" DESC LIMIT 5;	The question asks for the top five schools with the most number of Enrollment (Ages 5-17), and their NCES school identification number. However, the SQL query provided returns the school name, which is not required by the question.
Q: find the package option of the tv channel that do not have any cartoon directed by Ben Jones.		
Before: SELECT TV_Channel.Package_Option FROM TV_Channel LEFT JOIN Cartoon ON TV_Channel.id = Cartoon.Channel WHERE Cartoon.Directed_by IS NOT 'Ben Jones';	**After:** SELECT TV_Channel.Package_Option FROM TV_Channel WHERE TV_Channel.id NOT IN (SELECT Cartoon.Channel FROM Cartoon WHERE Cartoon.Directed_by = 'Ben Jones');	The current query is selecting all channels where the director is not Ben Jones, but it should exclude channels that have any cartoons directed by Ben Jones. This can be achieved by using a subquery to find all channels that have cartoons directed by Ben Jones, and then excluding these channels in the main query. Here is the corrected SQL:
Q: List the earnings of poker players in descending order.		
Before: SELECT * FROM poker_player ORDER BY Earnings DESC;	**After:** SELECT Earnings FROM poker_player ORDER BY Earnings DESC;	The question only asks for the earnings of poker players. Therefore, we should only select the 'Earnings' column to make the result more concise and relevant to the question.
Q: How many countries speak both English and Dutch?		
Before: SELECT COUNT(DISTINCT CountryCode) FROM countrylanguage WHERE Language = 'English' AND CountryCode IN (SELECT CountryCode FROM countrylanguage WHERE Language = 'Dutch')	**After:** SELECT COUNT(*) FROM (SELECT CountryCode FROM countrylanguage WHERE Language = 'English' INTERSECT SELECT CountryCode FROM countrylanguage WHERE Language = 'Dutch')	The SQL query provided uses the 'IN' clause, which selects countries that speak either English or Dutch. However, the question asks for countries speaking both languages. Using IN results in a union of sets (either English or Dutch), not an intersection (both English and Dutch). This could be done with two separate queries joined by an 'INTERSECT' clause.

Table 8: Interactive correction cases.

A.6 Prompt Examples

```
Describe how you understand the question based on the evidence, and
 help me write an SQL to answer the question.
### EVIDENCE: {evidence}
### USER_QUESTION: {question}

### RELATED SQL:
{related_sql}

### DATABASE STRUCTURE:
{schema}
```

Prompt 1: CoT-SQL-Writer

```
Write an to answer the question.

Program of Thoughts (PoT) is a variant of Chain of Thought (CoT),
pre-generating Python code to assist in the creation of SQL. Please
 apply PoT (and PoT only) before generating an SQL.
In your python code, `Table %s` is stored in `db_dict['%s']`, `
db_dict` is of type dict[pandas.DataFrame].

### RELATED SQL:
{related_sqls}

### DATABASE STRUCTURE:
{schema}

### EXAMPLES:
QUESTION: What is %s in the earliest year and what year was it?
SQL:
earliest_year = db_dict[%s]['Year'].min()
year_filtered_data = step1_result[step1_result['Year'] ==
earliest_year]
result = year_filtered_data[[%s, 'Year']]
```sql
SELECT T1.%s, T2.Year FROM %s AS T1 JOIN %s AS T2 ON T1.Id = T2.Id
WHERE T2.Year = (SELECT min(YEAR) FROM %s);
```

QUESTION: Show names for all %s except for %s having a %s in year
2023.
SQL:
%s_2023 = db_dict['%s'][db_dict['%s']['year'] == '2023']
result = db_dict[%s][~db_dict[%s][%s].isin(%ss_2023[%s])]
```sql
SELECT name FROM %s EXCEPT SELECT T2.name FROM %s AS T1 WHERE T1.
year = 2023
```

QUESTION: Find the %s that %s is A and B?
SQL:
```

```
condition_a_data = db_dict[%s][db_dict['Cartoon'][%s] == 'A']
condition_b_data = db_dict[%s][db_dict['Cartoon'][%s] == 'B']
result = pd.merge(condition_a_data, condition_b_data, how='inner')
```sql
SELECT T1.%s FROM %s AS T1 WHERE %s = 'A'
INTERSECT
SELECT T1.%s FROM %s AS T1 WHERE %s = 'B'
```

EVIDENCE: {evidence}
USER_QUESTION: {question}
SQL:
```

Prompt 2: PoT-SQL-Writer

```
You are the manager of a Database project. You are going to invite
{n} experts to review an SQL query.
Who would you invite?

considering:
(1) the domain of this database;
(2) the structure of this SQL.
Please write your invitation as a JSON format dictionary, Enclose
the JSON within ```json...```.

### DATABASE STRUCTURE:
{schema}

### QUESTION: {question}
### SQL:
{pred_sql}

### EXAMPLES:
```json
{
  "Reviewer PVsg": "Data Analyst in automotive industry",
  "Reviewer 2KtR": "Senior Database Engineer specialized in writing
    various clauses",
  "Reviewer LmN3": "Senior Database Engineer specialized in writing
    filtering conditions"
}
```
INVITATION:
```

Prompt 3: Invitation

SQLong: Enhanced NL2SQL for Longer Contexts with LLMs

Dai Quoc Nguyen, Cong Duy Vu Hoang, Duy Vu, Gioacchino Tangari
Thanh Tien Vu, Don Dharmasiri, Yuan-Fang Li, Long Duong
Oracle Corporation
{dai.nguyen,vu.hoang,duy.vu,gioacchino.tangari}@oracle.com
{thanh.v.vu,don.dharmasiri,yuanfang.li,long.duong}@oracle.com

Abstract

Open-weight large language models (LLMs) have significantly advanced performance in the Natural Language to SQL (NL2SQL) task. However, their effectiveness diminishes when dealing with large database schemas, as the context length increases. To address this limitation, we present SQLong, a novel and efficient data augmentation framework designed to enhance LLM performance in long-context scenarios for the NL2SQL task. SQLong generates augmented datasets by extending existing database schemas with additional synthetic CREATE TABLE commands and corresponding data rows, sampled from diverse schemas in the training data. This approach effectively simulates long-context scenarios during finetuning and evaluation. Through experiments on the Spider and BIRD datasets, we demonstrate that LLMs finetuned with SQLong-augmented data significantly outperform those trained on standard datasets. These imply SQLong's practical implementation and its impact on improving NL2SQL capabilities in real-world settings with complex database schemas.[1]

1 Introduction

The NL2SQL task focuses on translating natural language questions into SQL queries, enabling non-experts to interact with databases seamlessly (Deng et al., 2022). Recent advances leverage LLMs, finetuned on structured input prompts (*e.g., task instructions, database schema, and natural language question*), to achieve state-of-the-art performance (Yang et al., 2024b; Liu et al., 2024) on benchmarks such as Spider (Yu et al., 2018) and BIRD (Li et al., 2023). Despite significant progress, a critical challenge persists: LLMs finetuned on existing benchmarks still struggle with large database schemas due to limited context handling. Current datasets primarily feature small schemas, failing to represent real-world complexities. Additionally, the absence of publicly available large-schema datasets further hinders progress. Addressing this, we propose SQLong, a data augmentation framework designed to enhance LLM performance in long-context NL2SQL tasks by extending schemas to meet predefined context thresholds.

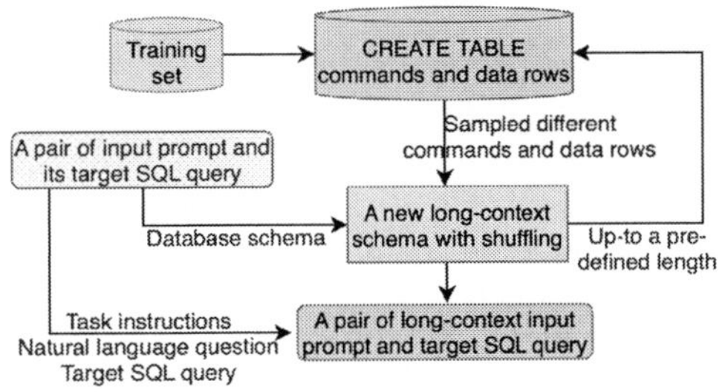

Figure 1: Our proposed SQLong Pipeline.

SQLong constructs augmented data by sampling CREATE TABLE commands and data rows from diverse schemas. These datasets enable LLMs to effectively manage large schemas and maintain robustness in long-context scenarios. Our experiments with *CodeQwen1.5-7B-Chat* (Bai et al., 2023) and *Llama-3.1-8B-Instruct* (Dubey et al., 2024) show SQLong consistently outperforms baseline finetuning, achieving an average accuracy improvement of over 2.2% on benchmarks like `Spider-dev`, `Spider-test`, and `BIRD-dev`.

Moreover, SQLong enables the creation of 45 long-context test sets, with context lengths up to 128k tokens. Models finetuned with SQLong exhibit significant performance gains, achieving an 11% improvement over base models and a 6% improvement over larger-scale models within the same family. These results highlight SQLong's effectiveness in real-world, large-schema scenarios.

In this paper, we focus on demonstrating that SQLong-augmented models outperform their unaugmented counterparts across varying context

[1]Table Representation Learning Workshop at ACL 2025

Proceedings of the 4th Table Representation Learning Workshop, pages 47–55
July 31, 2025 ©2025 Association for Computational Linguistics

```
Given an input Question, create a syntactically correct
SQLite SQL query to run.
Pay attention to using only the column names that you can
see in the schema description.
Be careful to not query for columns that do not exist. Also,
pay attention to which column is in which table.
Please double check the SQLite SQL query you generate.
DO NOT use alias in the SELECT clauses.
Only use the tables listed below.

CREATE TABLE grades (
   "student_id" INTEGER,
   "student_name" TEXT,
   "subject" TEXT,
   "grade" TEXT,
   PRIMARY KEY ("student_id")
)
/* 3 rows from grades table:
student_id    student_name subject    grade
1    Alice      math        A
2    Bob        math        B
3    David      science     B
*/

Question: Show me all the students getting an A in math

SELECT student_name FROM grades WHERE subject =
'math' AND grade = 'A'
```

Figure 2: Prompt template for the NL2SQL task.

lengths. While direct comparisons to retrieval-augmented generation (RAG) schema linking are beyond this paper's scope, our findings suggest combining SQLong with RAG could unlock further gains. Our main contributions include:

- **Introducing long-context NL2SQL:** A challenging new task for evaluating LLM performance on large database schemas.
- **SQLong pipeline:** A novel, scalable data augmentation approach for generating long-context training and test datasets.
- **Empirical insights:** Comprehensive experiments validating SQLong's effectiveness in enhancing LLM robustness and accuracy in long-context scenarios.
- **Resource sharing:** Plans to release SQLong datasets and code to support further research.

2 The Proposed SQLong Pipeline

The NL2SQL task aims to translate a natural-language question about a database schema into a corresponding SQL query. Following the standardized prompt template (Rajkumar et al., 2022), we represent the input prompt to LLMs in the format of *(task instructions, database schema, natural language question)*.[2] As illustrated in Figure 2, the database schema is represented by CREATE TABLE commands and three sample data rows for each corresponding table.

Using supervised finetuning (SFT) (Wei et al., 2022), LLMs can be trained on pairs of input prompts and target SQL queries to optimize their performance on the NL2SQL task. Specifically, given a training set $\mathbf{T}$ comprising pairs of input prompts x and corresponding target SQL queries s, the supervised finetuning process can be formulated as minimizing the log-likelihood loss (Wei et al., 2022), as shown below:

$$\mathbb{E}_{(\mathrm{x},\mathrm{s})\sim\mathbf{T}}\left[\sum_{i=1}^{|\mathrm{s}|}\log p_\theta\left(s_i|\mathrm{s}_{<i},\mathrm{x}\right)\right]$$

wherein $|\mathrm{s}|$ is the length of s, s_i is the i-th token, $\mathrm{s}_{<i}$ is the prefix of s up to the i-th position, and θ denotes the given LLM's parameters.

In this work, we introduce **SQLong**, a novel approach for constructing long-context finetuning and benchmark datasets, as illustrated in Figure 1. SQLong augments database schemas to enable large language models (LLMs) to effectively handle long-context scenarios in natural language to SQL (NL2SQL) tasks.

The SQLong pipeline has three main steps:

1. Schema Collection. We collect all CREATE TABLE commands and three sample data rows for each table from the training database schemas, compiling them into a comprehensive schema set.

2. Schema Augmentation. For each training pair, consisting of an input prompt (task instructions, database schema, natural language question) and its target SQL query, SQLong randomly samples items from the schema set. These sampled items contain table names distinct from those in the given database schema. The sampled items are combined with the original schema, and the resulting schema is randomly shuffled to produce a new, long-context database schema. This shuffling introduces variability in the positions of the original tables and columns.

3. Long-Context Prompt Generation. SQLong generates an augmented input prompt in the format of task instructions, the long-context database schema, and the natural language question, while keeping the target SQL query unchanged. It ensures that the combined length of the long-context input prompt and the target SQL query does not exceed a predefined context length (e.g., 32k tokens), maintaining compatibility with the model's tokenizer constraints.

[2] In datasets with additional complexity, such as BIRD, the question may be supplemented with extra information, such as evidence. For simplicity, this additional information is omitted in Figure 2.

By systematically extending and diversifying the context, SQLong enhances the robustness and effectiveness of LLMs in handling long-context NL2SQL tasks. We summarise the steps involved in SQLong in Algorithm 1 in Appendix A.1.

3 Evaluation

We assess the effectiveness of our proposed SQLong model in enhancing NL2SQL performance in both short-context and long-context scenarios.

3.1 Experimental Setup

Datasets For the short-context evaluation, we utilize widely adopted benchmark datasets, including Spider (Yu et al., 2018), Spider-realistic (Deng et al., 2020), Spider-syn (Gan et al., 2021), and BIRD (Li et al., 2023). [3] It is noted that Spider-Syn is manually created based on Spider training and development sets using synonym substitution in the original questions, while Spider-realistic is created based on Spider development set by manually removing the explicit mention of column names in the original questions. The BIRD-test set is not publicly available.

For the long-context evaluation, we extend each of the Spider-dev, Spider-test, Spider-realistic, Spider-syn, and BIRD-dev datasets by applying SQLong with a pre-defined context length. Specifically, we generate augmented long-context test sets for nine context lengths: 8k, 16k, 24k, 32k, 40k, 48k, 56k, 64k, and 128k. This process results in a total of 45 long-context test sets, constructed in accordance with the tokenizer of the base model.

Importantly, the long-context test sets are constructed with distinct database schema alignments. To build Spider-based long-context test sets, we use the database schemas from the BIRD training set, whereas for the BIRD-dev long-context test sets, we use the database schemas from the Spider training set. This ensures a robust evaluation across diverse schema configurations and context lengths. The data statistics of the experimental datasets are presented in Figure 3 and Tables 1 and 2.

Baseline Models and Evaluation Metrics We evaluate SQLong using two powerful base models: CodeQwen1.5-7B-Chat (Bai et al., 2023), which supports a context length of up to 64k, and Llama-3.1-8B-Instruct (Dubey et al., 2024), which supports a context length of up to 128k. Following Yu

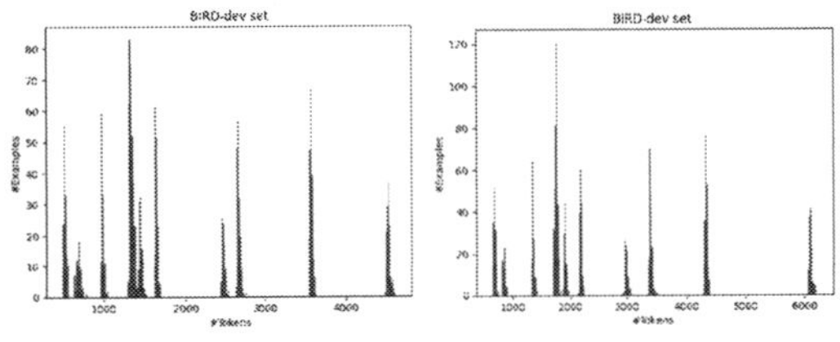

Figure 3: Statistics of input prompt lengths with respect to Llama-3.1-8B-Instruct's tokenizer (left) and CodeQwen1.5-7B-Chat's tokenizer (right) on the original BIRD-dev set. Similarly, the maximum input prompt lengths for the original Spider-related sets are approximately 2,000 tokens for Llama-3.1-8B-Instruct's tokenizer and 2,500 tokens for CodeQwen1.5-7B-Chat's tokenizer.

Dataset	#DB	#tables	#training	#dev	#test
Spider	200	5 ± 3	6,712	1,034	2,019
Spider-syn	200	5 ± 3	6,712	1,034	–
Spider-realistic	200	5 ± 3	6,712	508	–
BIRD	98	7 ± 3	9,428	1,534	–

Table 1: Statistics of the experimental datasets. **#DB** denotes the number of databases. **#tables** denotes the mean and standard deviation of numbers of tables in the databases.

Length	CodeQwen1.5-7B-Chat		Llama-3.1-8B-Instruct	
	Spider-related	BIRD-dev	Spider-related	BIRD-dev
8k	37 ± 4	35 ± 8	48 ± 5	48 ± 8
16k	72 ± 6	76 ± 8	94 ± 7	102 ± 9
24k	107 ± 7	118 ± 8	141 ± 8	157 ± 9
32k	142 ± 8	159 ± 9	186 ± 8	211 ± 9
40k	177 ± 8	200 ± 9	233 ± 9	269 ± 9
48k	212 ± 9	242 ± 9	279 ± 9	320 ± 10
56k	247 ± 9	283 ± 9	326 ± 9	374 ± 9
64k	283 ± 9	324 ± 9	372 ± 8	429 ± 9
128k	551 ± 4	639 ± 7	725 ± 9	843 ± 8

Table 2: Mean and standard deviation statistics of the numbers of tables in input prompts for our augmented long-context test sets with respect to each model's tokenizer.

et al. (2018), we report execution-match accuracy on both the original short-context test sets and the augmented long-context test sets.

Training Protocol For each original training set, we use SQLong to create an augmented *long-context finetuning* dataset with context lengths of up to 32k.[4] The augmented dataset is combined with the original training set to form the final

[3]We use the latest BIRD-dev dataset, updated on June 27, 2024. The BIRD-test set is not publicly available.

[4]Due to computational constraints, we limit finetuning to context lengths of up to 32k. Specifically, for each training example, the context length is randomly sampled from a range starting at 4,096 and increasing by 512 increments up to 32,768.

Model	Spider-dev	Spider-realistic	Spider-syn	Spider-test	BIRD-dev	Average
Qwen2-72B-Instruct	82.7	80.7	73.0	82.9	53.7	74.6
CodeQwen1.5-7B-Chat	76.4	70.1	62.7	75.1	44.3	65.7
Finetuned without SQLong	81.9	76.2	68.7	79.6	51.4	71.6
Finetuned with SQLong	**83.4**	**79.7**	**71.2**	**81.3**	**53.3**	**73.8**
Llama-3.1-70B-Instruct	80.7	78.0	73.0	83.7	61.5	75.4
Llama-3.1-8B-Instruct	71.1	63.8	61.0	65.7	40.9	60.5
Finetuned without SQLong	79.2	76.4	69.6	80.4	51.9	71.5
Finetuned with SQLong	**83.2**	**78.0**	**73.1**	**81.8**	**53.3**	**73.9**

Table 3: Execution-match accuracy results (in %) across different datasets and model configurations. Finetuning with SQLong consistently improves performance, with the best results highlighted in **bold**.

dataset used for finetuning the base models.[5]

We experiment with two base models: CodeQwen1.5-7B-Chat (Bai et al., 2023), which supports a 64k context length, and Llama-3.1-8B-Instruct (Dubey et al., 2024), which supports a 128k context length. Finetuning is performed with a batch size of 1, gradient accumulation steps of 8, a learning rate chosen from $1 \times 10^{-6}, 5 \times 10^{-6}, 1 \times 10^{-5}$, and up to 5 epochs on 8×H100 80GB GPUs.

We use Huggingface's TRL (von Werra et al., 2020) for supervised finetuning, employing 8-bit AdamW (Dettmers et al., 2021), Flash Attention v2 (Dao, 2023), and DeepSpeed ZeRO-3 Offload (Ren et al., 2021). For a fair comparison, we also finetune the base models on the original training set (i.e., without SQLong) under the same settings.

Inference Protocol We utilize vLLM (Kwon et al., 2023) for the inference process. For long-context test sets, we employ dynamic NTK RoPE scaling (Peng et al., 2023) to extend support up to a 128k context length for CodeQwen1.5-7B-Chat and its finetuned variants.

3.2 Main Results

Performance on Original Datasets Table 3 summarizes the results on the original development and test sets, comparing base models with larger LLMs such as Llama-3.1-70B-Instruct (Dubey et al., 2024) and Qwen2-72B-Instruct (Yang et al., 2024a). Models finetuned using long-context augmentation via SQLong consistently outperform their counterparts finetuned on original contexts. On average, SQLong delivers an absolute improvement of over 2.2% across five benchmark datasets. Additionally, SQLong-finetuned models achieve performance comparable to much larger LLMs on specific datasets, showcasing the scalability and efficiency of the approach.

Performance on Long-Context Datasets Figure 4 illustrates the experimental results on long-context test sets. The full details are presented in Tables 4 and 5 in Appendix A.2. Across all datasets, models finetuned with SQLong demonstrate superior performance compared to those trained without SQLong. For instance, on the Spider-test datasets with 8k and 24k context lengths, the Llama-3.1-8B-Instruct model achieves outstanding results of 77.1% and 72.3%, reflecting absolute gains of 7.2% and 13.3%, respectively. Notably, the SQLong-finetuned Llama-8B model outperforms the larger Llama-70B model on 41 out of 45 long-context test sets, with minor exceptions on Spider-realistic 8k and BIRD-dev 8k, 16k, and 24k sets. Similar performance trends are observed with the Qwen models.

On average, SQLong finetuning delivers an 11% absolute improvement over models without SQLong and a 6% advantage over 70B models within the same model family. These results underscore the efficacy of SQLong in handling long-context scenarios and advancing the performance of NL2SQL systems.

Positional robustness We conduct an experiment wherein each original database schema is placed at different positions within the input prompt, assessing the models' ability to detect it regardless of its location.

We select a set of 124 samples from Spider-dev, Spider-realistic, and Spider-syn, ensuring each sample has a maximum input prompt and target SQL query length of 384 tokens according to CodeQwen1.5-7B-Chat's tokenizer. Using SQLong, we augment this set to a 64k context

[5]For Spider, we finetune the base models on the Spider training set and evaluate performance on Spider-dev, Spider-test, Spider-realistic, and Spider-syn.

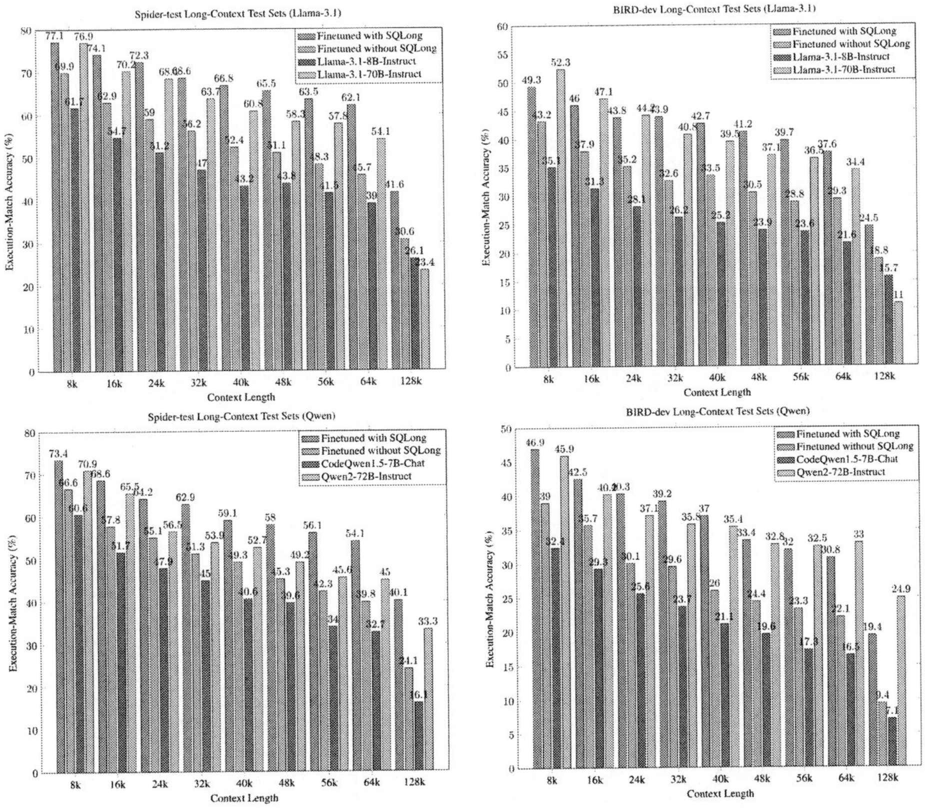

Figure 4: Execution-match accuracy (in %) for Llama-3.1 (top) and Qwen (bottom) families on Spider-test (left) and BIRD-dev (right) long-context test sets.

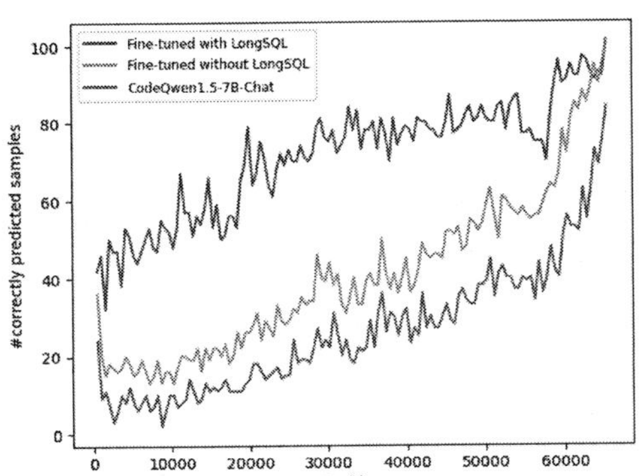

Figure 5: Robust impact of fine-tuned models.

length. In each augmented set, the original database schemas are positioned at specific offsets, starting from 512 and incrementing by 512 up to 64k. This results in 125 new test sets, each containing 124 samples with a 64k context length, corresponding to a distinct schema position.

We compute the number of correctly executed samples for each test set, as shown in Figure 5. The results demonstrate that the long-context fine-tuned model with SQLong is significantly more robust compared to the model without fine-tuning.

4 Conclusion and Future Work

Handling large database schemas poses a significant challenge for NL2SQL models. In this paper, we introduce long-context NL2SQL generation, a novel task that reflects real-world scenarios, and propose SQLong, a simple yet effective augmentation approach for creating long-context finetuning and benchmark datasets. Experiments show that LLMs finetuned with SQLong significantly outperform their counterparts on benchmarks like Spider, BIRD, and our long-context test sets (up to 128k context length).

Future work includes leveraging a RAG-based schema linking approach to retrieve relevant schema elements, enabling more concise and efficient inputs for SQLong-tuned models.

References

Jinze Bai, Shuai Bai, and 1 others. 2023. Qwen technical report. *arXiv preprint arXiv:2309.16609*.

Tri Dao. 2023. Flashattention-2: Faster attention with better parallelism and work partitioning. *arXiv preprint arXiv:2307.08691*.

Naihao Deng, Yulong Chen, and Yue Zhang. 2022. Recent advances in text-to-SQL: A survey of what we have and what we expect. In *Coling*, pages 2166–2187.

Xiang Deng, Ahmed Hassan Awadallah, Christopher Meek, Oleksandr Polozov, Huan Sun, and Matthew Richardson. 2020. Structure-grounded pretraining for text-to-sql. *arXiv preprint arXiv:2010.12773*.

Tim Dettmers, Mike Lewis, Sam Shleifer, and Luke Zettlemoyer. 2021. 8-bit optimizers via block-wise quantization. *arXiv preprint arXiv:2110.02861*.

Abhimanyu Dubey, Abhinav Jauhri, Abhinav Pandey, Abhishek Kadian, Ahmad Al-Dahle, Aiesha Letman, Akhil Mathur, Alan Schelten, Amy Yang, Angela Fan, and 1 others. 2024. The llama 3 herd of models. *arXiv preprint arXiv:2407.21783*.

Yujian Gan, Xinyun Chen, Qiuping Huang, Matthew Purver, John R Woodward, Jinxia Xie, and Pengsheng Huang. 2021. Towards robustness of text-to-sql models against synonym substitution. In *ACL-IJCNLP*, pages 2505–2515.

Woosuk Kwon, Zhuohan Li, Siyuan Zhuang, Ying Sheng, Lianmin Zheng, Cody Hao Yu, Joseph E. Gonzalez, Hao Zhang, and Ion Stoica. 2023. Efficient memory management for large language model serving with pagedattention. In *SOSP*.

Jinyang Li, Binyuan Hui, Ge Qu, Jiaxi Yang, Binhua Li, Bowen Li, Bailin Wang, Bowen Qin, Ruiying Geng, Nan Huo, and 1 others. 2023. Can llm already serve as a database interface? a big bench for large-scale database grounded text-to-sqls. *NeurIPS 2023 Track on Datasets and Benchmarks*, 36.

Xinyu Liu, Shuyu Shen, Boyan Li, Peixian Ma, Runzhi Jiang, Yuyu Luo, Yuxin Zhang, Ju Fan, Guoliang Li, and Nan Tang. 2024. A survey of nl2sql with large language models: Where are we, and where are we going? *arXiv preprint arXiv:2408.05109*.

Bowen Peng, Jeffrey Quesnelle, Honglu Fan, and Enrico Shippole. 2023. Yarn: Efficient context window extension of large language models. *arXiv preprint arXiv:2309.00071*.

Nitarshan Rajkumar, Raymond Li, and Dzmitry Bahdanau. 2022. Evaluating the text-to-sql capabilities of large language models. *arXiv preprint arXiv:2204.00498*.

Jie Ren, Samyam Rajbhandari, Reza Yazdani Aminabadi, Olatunji Ruwase, Shuangyan Yang, Minjia Zhang, Dong Li, and Yuxiong He. 2021. {Zero-offload}: Democratizing {billion-scale} model training. In *USENIX ATC*, pages 551–564.

Leandro von Werra, Younes Belkada, Lewis Tunstall, Edward Beeching, Tristan Thrush, Nathan Lambert, and Shengyi Huang. 2020. Trl: Transformer reinforcement learning. `https://github.com/huggingface/trl`.

Jason Wei, Maarten Bosma, Vincent Zhao, Kelvin Guu, Adams Wei Yu, Brian Lester, Nan Du, Andrew M Dai, and Quoc V Le. 2022. Finetuned language models are zero-shot learners. In *ICLR*.

An Yang, Baosong Yang, and 1 others. 2024a. Qwen2 technical report. *arXiv preprint arXiv:2407.10671*.

Jiaxi Yang, Binyuan Hui, Min Yang, Jian Yang, Junyang Lin, and Chang Zhou. 2024b. Synthesizing text-to-sql data from weak and strong llms. *arXiv preprint arXiv:2408.03256*.

Tao Yu, Rui Zhang, Kai Yang, Michihiro Yasunaga, Dongxu Wang, Zifan Li, James Ma, Irene Li, Qingning Yao, Shanelle Roman, and 1 others. 2018. Spider: A large-scale human-labeled dataset for complex and cross-domain semantic parsing and text-to-sql task. In *EMNLP*, pages 3911–3921.

A Appendix

A.1 The algorithm steps in SQLong

Algorithm 1: The algorithm steps involved in the proposed SQLong.

Input: A training set $\mathbf{T}$ of pairs of input prompts and target SQL queries: $\mathbf{T} = \{((instructions_i, database\_schema_i, question_i), target\_sql_i)\}_{i=1}^{N}$, wherein each $database\_schema_i$ is a set of CREATE TABLE commands and three data rows for each corresponding table; a set $\mathcal{T} = \{((instructions_j, database\_schema_j, question_j), target\_sql_j)\}_{j=1}^{M}$; the base model's tokenizer tk, a starting number s_n (default 4096), an ending number e_n (default 32768), an increasing number i_n (default 512), and a pre-defined number p_n (default 8192).

Output: The augmented long-context set $\mathcal{T}'$.

$schema\_set \leftarrow$ collect_unique_commands_and_data_rows($\{database\_schema_i\}_{i=1}^{N}$)

$table\_names \leftarrow$ get_table_names($schema\_set$)

$item\_lengths \leftarrow \{\}$

for $item \in schema\_set$ **do**

  $item_lengths \leftarrow item_lengths \cup \{$get_length($item$, tk)$\}$

$\mathcal{T}' \leftarrow \{\}$

$diverse\_lengths \leftarrow$ range(s_n, $e\_n + 1$, i_n)

for $((instructions, database\_schema, question), target\_sql) \in \mathcal{T}$ **do**

  $original\_length \leftarrow$ get_length($instructions + database\_schema + question + target\_sql$, tk)

  $certain\_length \leftarrow$ randomly_select_value($diverse\_lengths$) // This aims to construct long-context fine-tuning data with $\mathbf{T} = \mathcal{T}$. Otherwise, $certain\_length$ is set to p_n to construct long-context benchmark data.

  $local\_table\_names \leftarrow$ get_table_names($database\_schema$)

  $augmented\_schema \leftarrow \{\}$

  for $idx \in$ shuffle_list(range(0, get_size($schema\_set$))) **do**

    if $schema\_set[idx] \notin database\_schema$ and $table\_names[idx] \notin local\_table\_names$ and $original\_length + item\_lengths[idx] < certain\_length$ **then**

      $original\_length \leftarrow original\_length + item\_lengths[idx]$

      $augmented\_schema \leftarrow augmented\_schema \cup \{schema\_set[idx]\}$

  $augmented\_long\_context\_schema \leftarrow$ shuffle_list($augmented\_schema \cup database\_schema$)

  $\mathcal{T}' \leftarrow \mathcal{T}' \cup \{((instructions, augmented\_long\_context\_schema, question), target\_sql)\}$

A.2 Full execution-match accuracy results for all long-context test sets

Model	Context length	Spider-dev	Spider-realistic	Spider-syn	Spider-test	BIRD-dev	Average across 45 sets
Llama-3.1-8B-Instruct	8k	61.9	53.5	45.1	61.7	35.1	37.2
	16k	58.5	47.0	38.9	54.7	31.3	
	24k	53.2	43.1	32.7	51.2	28.1	
	32k	49.6	42.9	29.9	47.0	26.2	
	40k	48.7	38.4	28.4	43.2	25.2	
	48k	46.9	35.8	24.9	43.8	23.9	
	56k	45.5	32.1	23.8	41.5	23.6	
	64k	42.6	33.1	22.5	39.0	21.6	
	128k	28.0	17.9	10.3	26.1	15.7	
Our model fine-tuned Without SQLong	8k	71.7	63.4	49.3	69.9	43.2	43.8
	16k	66.6	54.7	39.9	62.9	37.9	
	24k	63.6	52.4	35.5	59.0	35.2	
	32k	59.4	48.0	33.1	56.2	32.6	
	40k	57.0	45.1	30.2	52.4	33.5	
	48k	55.9	43.7	28.0	51.1	30.5	
	56k	52.5	40.4	25.7	48.3	28.8	
	64k	51.4	40.9	25.3	45.7	29.3	
	128k	34.7	23.6	13.5	30.6	18.8	
Our model fine-tuned With SQLong	8k	**77.4**	67.1	**61.7**	**77.1**	49.3	**54.8**
	16k	**75.2**	**66.1**	**53.4**	**74.1**	46.0	
	24k	**71.8**	**64.2**	**50.0**	**72.3**	43.8	
	32k	**68.3**	**61.6**	**46.5**	**68.6**	**43.9**	
	40k	**67.5**	**62.8**	**44.9**	**66.8**	**42.7**	
	48k	**66.9**	**56.7**	**40.2**	**65.5**	**41.2**	
	56k	**63.3**	**52.6**	**38.4**	**63.5**	**39.7**	
	64k	**61.3**	**52.2**	**39.3**	**62.1**	**37.6**	
	128k	**43.0**	**33.7**	**21.7**	**41.6**	**24.5**	
Llama-3.1-70B-Instruct	8k	73.9	**67.3**	55.0	76.9	**52.3**	48.5
	16k	67.7	59.4	48.9	70.2	**47.1**	
	24k	62.4	54.9	43.8	68.4	**44.2**	
	32k	60.9	49.6	41.7	63.7	40.8	
	40k	59.0	52.6	37.4	60.8	39.5	
	48k	57.6	46.9	35.0	58.3	37.1	
	56k	55.3	46.3	32.3	57.8	36.5	
	64k	55.0	43.9	31.7	54.1	34.4	
	128k	28.0	25.6	12.3	23.4	11.0	

Table 4: Execution-match accuracy results (in %) on the augmented long-context test sets with respect to the Llama-3.1 model family.

Model	Context length	Spider-dev	Spider-realistic	Spider-syn	Spider-test	BIRD-dev	Average across 45 sets
		Dataset					
CodeQwen1.5-7B-Chat	8k	61.7	49.6	38.1	60.6	32.4	
	16k	55.9	42.1	30.7	51.7	29.3	
	24k	51.5	37.8	27.9	47.9	25.6	
	32k	48.0	30.9	22.8	45.0	23.7	
	40k	46.7	28.9	21.0	40.6	21.1	31.7
	48k	42.4	27.8	18.7	39.6	19.6	
	56k	36.4	24.0	17.5	34.0	17.3	
	64k	36.4	21.3	15.8	32.7	16.5	
	128k	19.2	7.9	6.4	16.1	7.1	
Our model fine-tuned Without SQLong	8k	68.9	57.1	39.5	66.6	39.0	
	16k	62.6	51.4	31.8	57.8	35.7	
	24k	57.6	49.0	29.3	55.1	30.1	
	32k	53.0	41.5	25.6	51.3	29.6	
	40k	53.7	38.4	23.5	49.3	26.0	37.8
	48k	48.7	34.6	22.3	45.3	24.4	
	56k	44.5	33.1	20.9	42.3	23.3	
	64k	43.8	30.3	18.4	39.8	22.1	
	128k	26.1	15.6	9.2	24.1	9.4	
Our model fine-tuned With SQLong	8k	**75.9**	**65.7**	**53.2**	**73.4**	**46.9**	
	16k	**72.9**	**62.6**	**46.6**	**68.6**	**42.5**	
	24k	**68.9**	**58.5**	**43.0**	**64.2**	**40.3**	
	32k	**67.5**	**54.3**	**40.0**	**62.9**	**39.2**	
	40k	**63.4**	**53.7**	**37.4**	**59.1**	**37.0**	**50.2**
	48k	**63.9**	**52.8**	**35.3**	**58.0**	**33.4**	
	56k	**60.3**	**51.0**	**33.6**	**56.1**	32.0	
	64k	**60.6**	**52.4**	**31.0**	**54.1**	30.8	
	128k	**43.4**	**33.7**	**19.4**	**40.1**	19.4	
Qwen2-72B-Instruct	8k	70.6	63.4	47.2	70.9	45.9	
	16k	69.1	58.7	40.6	65.5	40.2	
	24k	60.9	53.3	34.1	56.5	37.1	
	32k	59.6	45.5	31.1	53.9	35.8	
	40k	55.8	45.7	29.5	52.7	35.4	44.2
	48k	52.3	43.7	27.8	49.2	32.8	
	56k	50.8	39.4	27.6	45.6	**32.5**	
	64k	47.3	34.6	25.1	45.0	**33.0**	
	128k	36.8	28.3	18.6	33.3	**24.9**	

Table 5: Execution-match accuracy results (in %) on the augmented long-context test sets with respect to the Qwen mdoel family.

iTBLS: A Dataset of Interactive Conversations Over Tabular Information

Anirudh Sundar[1] **and Christopher Richardson**[2] * **and Adar Avsian**[1] **and Larry Heck**[1]
[1] Georgia Institute of Technology, USA
[2] Google Inc., USA
asundar34, larryheck@gatech.edu

Abstract

This paper introduces Interactive Tables (iTBLS), a dataset of interactive conversations that focuses on natural-language manipulation of tabular information sourced from academic preprints on ArXiv. The iTBLS dataset consists of three types of tabular tasks – interpretation, modification, and generation. Interpretation focuses on tabular understanding, modification focuses on manipulating tabular information, and generation focuses on the addition of new natural-language evidence. In addition, the paper presents a novel framework that reformulates tabular operations as question-answering, where an appropriate question is formulated based on the nature of interaction and the question is answered using the user request as evidence. The developed approach results in an improvement on all tasks on a sequence-to-sequence modeling baseline on iTBLS. In addition, the question-answering-based reformulation is applied to datasets from prior work for the text-to-table task where textual paragraphs are summarized into tables. The novel approach results in up to 13% improvement in Exact-Match accuracy and up to 16% improvement in BERTScores compared to the prior state-of-the-art.

1 Introduction

Recent research on Conversational AI has focused on adding enhanced multi-task capabilities to large language models (LLMs). This research includes building systems capable of situated interactions over structured knowledge sources such as tabular information (Sundar and Heck, 2022). Automated methods for tabular interpretation, manipulation, and generation empower users by saving time and reducing errors in managing tabular content (Kardas et al., 2020). Previous studies have focused on individual aspects of tabular data management: representation learning for interpretation tasks like grounded question answering, manipulation for data wrangling, and generation for summarizing textual information independently (Nakamura et al., 2022a; Sundar and Heck, 2023; Fang et al., 2024).

The development of situated conversational interactions over tables necessitates a suite of approaches to unify tabular interpretation, modification, and generation in a conversational context. Additionally, an important yet largely unaddressed challenge in interacting with tabular sources is the ability to modify existing tabular content using conversational natural language commands.

To address these challenges, this paper introduces Interactive Tables (iTBLS) [1], a dataset of interactive conversations in English situated in tabular information. iTBLS decomposes the challenge into three distinct tasks: *interpretation*, which involves understanding tabular content within a conversational framework; *modification*, which entails manipulating tabular content through natural language commands; and *generation*, which focuses on integrating new natural language information into existing tables. The tabular information in iTBLS is sourced from scientific articles hosted on arXiv [2], an open-access repository of academic preprints.

Beyond factoid question-answering, iTBLS encompasses tasks such as comparison, determining absolute and relative positions, and mathematical reasoning. Previous research primarily examined procedural command generation for spreadsheets or the alignment of tabular data through LLMs. iTBLS integrates these functionalities into a unified task, enabling the manipulation of existing tables through natural-language commands. On tabular generation, while prior work addressed the summarization of natural language paragraphs in a tabular format, iTBLS focuses on generating row

*Work done while at Georgia Tech

[1] https://huggingface.co/datasets/avalab/iTBLS
[2] https://arxiv.org

Proceedings of the 4th Table Representation Learning Workshop, pages 56–70
July 31, 2025

or column data conversationally.

In addition to building iTBLS, this paper develops a novel approach to address tabular operations by reformulating the task as conditional question answering. Furthermore, the question-answering-based reformulation is applied to other datasets introduced in prior work (Wu et al., 2022) and results in better performance in terms of both table-cell accuracy and BERTScore.

The contributions of this work are as follows:

- Creating iTBLS, a dataset of tabular interactions unifying interpretation, modification, and generation.
- Extending prior tabular datasets by collecting information from arXiv
- Broadening the scope of interactions to include mathematical reasoning, natural language manipulation, and natural language expansion.
- Introducing a novel approach for table generation tasks through a two-stage reformulation that first identifies the cells to be manipulated and generates a question based on the requested operation, then answers those questions using the user request and the input table as evidence.
- Demonstrating up to 13% improvement in table-cell accuracy and up to 16% improvement in BERTScore using the novel approach on the text-to-table task introduced by prior work.

2 Related Work

A detailed survey of LLMs for tabular data is available in (Fang et al., 2024). Related work on paired natural-language and tabular data can be broadly classified by the nature of the interaction: tabular interpretation, tabular modification, and tabular generation.

2.1 Tabular Interpretation

Tabular interpretation involves a dialogue turn focused on extracting information from a specific cell in a table, such as identifying a cell satisfying certain criteria. Prior research on tabular interpretation focused on grounded question-answering. An important challenge in the collection of such datasets is the availability of large-scale tabular data. Consequently, many tabular datasets are constructed from online resources such as Wikipedia including WIKITABLEQUESTIONS (Pasupat and Liang, 2015), ManyModalQA (Hannan et al., 2020), TABERT (Yin et al., 2020), NQ-Tables (Herzig et al., 2021), FEVEROUS (Aly et al., 2021), FeTaQA (Nan et al., 2022), HYBRIDIALOGUE (Nakamura et al., 2022b), and HiTab (Cheng et al., 2022). Other tabular datasets are constructed from financial reports including TAT-QA (Zhu et al., 2021), FINQA (Chen et al., 2021), MULTIHIERTT (Zhao et al., 2022), or scientific reviews (Sundar et al., 2024).

Proposed approaches to address the tabular interpretation task include architectures based off of the Transformer encoder (Yin et al., 2020; Herzig et al., 2020; Chen et al., 2019b; Eisenschlos et al., 2020; Liu et al., 2021; Gu et al., 2022; Yang et al., 2022), decoder (Gong et al., 2020; Akhtar et al., 2023; Zha et al., 2023; Jiang et al., 2023; Zhang et al., 2023; Sui et al., 2024; Cremaschi et al., 2025), or both (encoder-decoder) (Nakamura et al., 2022b; Deng et al., 2022; Sundar and Heck, 2023).

2.2 Tabular Modification

Tabular modification concerns the manipulation of the content within an existing table without altering the overall structure of rows and columns. Early work on tabular modification explored the generation of procedural commands for spreadsheets using synthesis algorithms (Singh and Gulwani, 2012; Shigarov et al., 2019). Tools utilizing programming-by-example to parse user intents into executable commands have also been explored (Scaffidi et al., 2009; Kandel et al., 2011; Jin et al., 2017; Petricek et al., 2023; Chen et al., 2023; Xing et al., 2024). More recent work has shifted focus towards leveraging LLMs to synthesize commands for tools (Huang et al., 2024), reformat tabular information (Dargahi Nobari and Rafiei, 2024), and execute programming commands (Liu et al., 2024).

2.3 Tabular Generation

Tabular generation focuses on expanding an existing table by adding a new row or column. Research on tabular generation initially employed discriminative techniques, such as tree-based methods for generating tables of contents (Branavan et al., 2007) and SVMs to classify text across various labels Aramaki et al. (2009). Recent approaches have shifted towards neural techniques including Generative Adversarial Networks (GANs) (Xu and Veeramachaneni, 2018; Park et al., 2018; Chen et al., 2019a;

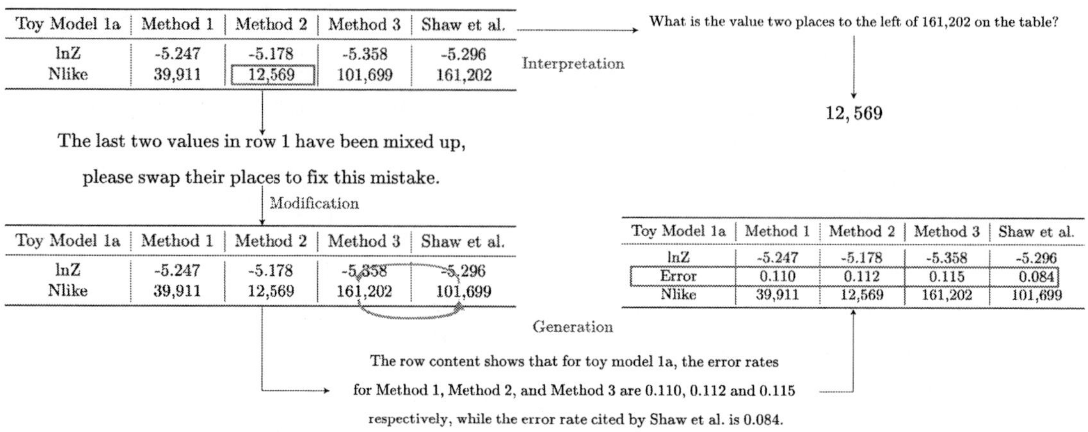

Figure 1: Examples of interactions from the Interactive Tables (iTBLS) dataset.

Zhao et al., 2021), Autoencoders (Li et al., 2019; Darabi and Elor, 2021), Diffusion models (Kotelnikov et al., 2023), and LLMs (Borisov et al., 2023; Solatorio and Dupriez, 2023; Gulati and Roysdon, 2023; Zhao et al., 2023; Seedat et al., 2024; Deng et al., 2024).

A similar line of research also explores the generation of tabular data from associated textual information. Wu et al. (2022) introduced four datasets and proposed a modification to the Transformer's attention mechanism to summarize textual information in a tabular format by inverting datasets created for the dual task of converting tables to text, (as opposed to new conversational evidence). Other approaches to summarize textual information in a tabular format include the addition of learnable bias parameters (Pietruszka et al., 2022) and structure-aware instruction-tuning (Tang et al., 2023).

In contrast to prior work addressing a single mode of interaction, iTBLS is a dataset unifying tabular interpretation, modification, and generation in a conversational format. Additionally, iTBLS broadens the range of interactions to include mathematical reasoning, natural language manipulation, and the expansion of tables using natural language. Furthermore, by leveraging scientific articles from arXiv as a primary source, iTBLS introduces a novel and rich source of information that is not present in existing datasets.

3 The iTBLS Dataset

The Interactive Tables (iTBLS) dataset features conversational interactions situated in tabular data, covering the three distinct types of interactions described in Section 2: *interpretation*, *modification*, and *generation*. Each example type is exemplified in Figure 1 and described below. In addition, since the mode of interaction is not known a priori, any proposed approach using iTBLS must effectively identify the interaction type, either explicitly or implicitly. In the following sections, we provide a detailed description of each type of interaction and outline the dataset collection process.

3.1 Tasks

Tabular Interpretation: In iTBLS, interpretive interactions are structured as question-answer pairs, where the goal is to identify the cell referred to by the question. The references could be absolute (referring to a specific row or column), or relative (referring to one cell in the context of another). Appendix A.5 details absolute and relative references in iTBLS.

Tabular modification: We conceptualize modification in iTBLS as a series of cell swaps, positing that any content rearrangement can ultimately be reduced to such exchanges. This approach allows for both explicit references, where specific row and column numbers are cited, and implicit references, which rely on the content or relative positions of cells. Table 9 in Appendix A.5 showcases examples from iTBLS. As observed, there is a mix of explicit and implicit references to the specific contents to be manipulated.

Tabular generation: In iTBLS, table generation is guided by new natural language evidence. This evidence clarifies appending a row or column, defines the suitable header, and supplies the data entries for the new row (or column) relative to existing columns (or rows). This process ensures that the added elements are contextually relevant and accurately integrated into the table. Table 10 in Appendix A.5 provides examples of such interactions, demonstrating how users can request the incorporation of new row and column data into an established table framework.

In iTBLS, the mode of interaction is not explicitly stated by the user, introducing an additional task: **interaction identification**. This task involves predicting whether the interaction is intended for interpretation, modification, or generation based solely on the user's request.

3.2 Dataset Collection

To collect the dataset, first we use AXCELL (Kardas et al., 2020) an automatic machine learning pipeline for extracting results from papers. AXCELL is used to parse tabular information from papers on arXiv to populate online leaderboards comparing scientific methods. Using AXCELL, we collect 20,000 tables from academic papers in Mathematics, Physics, and Computer Science over a period spanning from 2007 to 2014. The tables are processed to remove stray characters resulting from the conversion from LaTeX. Additionally, only tables with at least three rows and three columns to at most ten rows or ten columns are retained. The final dataset consists of 4000 tables split between train, development, and test sets.

For each table, we generate three sequential edits corresponding to different types of interaction. Interpretation involves generating a dialogue turn (question-answer pair) grounded on a single cell of the table. Modification involves manipulating two cells of an existing table by swapping them. Finally, generation encompasses the task of appending either a new row or a column to an existing table based on a natural language utterance.

To enhance the quality of the dataset and minimize errors, we implement a strategic selection process for the table components involved in each interaction. In *interpretation*, a cell is randomly selected to ground the dialogue. For *modification*, two cells are chosen and their positions are swapped to simulate a realistic table manipulation scenario. In *generation*, all cells in a randomly masked row or column are used as the basis for appending new table data. All of the interactions are based on cells that do not belong to row or column headers, that is, they reside in the body of the table.

For our dataset creation, we employ two distinct sources for generating dialogue turns based on the type of interaction and the specific table component involved. For tasks related to tabular interpretation and modification, we engage crowd-workers from Amazon Mechanical Turk (AMT). These workers are tasked with formulating questions or commands that pertain to the pre-identified cell(s) designated for each interaction. We recruit workers from Australia, Canada, Ireland, New Zealand, the United Kingdom, and the USA. Each crowdworker is compensated at a rate of $0.15 per Human Intelligence Task (HIT), with the average completion time for each HIT being approximately 40 seconds. Detailed information on the AMT interface used for these tasks is included in Appendix A.7.

For generation, GPT-4 is prompted to write a dialogue turn summarizing a row or column of the table. The prompt is as follows:

The string contains information from a table [table]. Describe the content in this [row/column] for a visually impaired user in one line. Make sure to include all information from the rows and columns and appropriate headers so the user can understand the content.

Each sample in the dataset contains the source arXiv ID, the table that the conversation is situated in, the index of that table within the paper (e.g. Table X), the utterance describing the interaction, the ground truth cell(s) involved in the interaction, and finally the expected output. Statistics of the datasets are provided in Table 1.

Statistic	Interpret	Modify	Generate
# Samples	4168	4168	4168
# Per utterance			
Words	10.6	13.4	31.6
Tokens	14.3	18.3	59.1
# Per table			
Cells	28.1	28.1	25.31
(Cols/Rows)	5.0/5.5	5.0/5.5	4.8/5.3

Table 1: Statistics of the iTBLS dataset

4 Methods

4.1 Table operations through conditional question answering

We also present a novel approach that reformulates operations on tables as question answering. A primary challenge in tabular operations using LLMs lies in ensuring the syntactic validity of the produced tables. Every row and column in a table must contain the same number of cells, with row and column headers delineating relationships between cells. Failing to adhere to this constraint invalidates the structure of the table and the information presented. Prior work addresses this constraint by including additional parameters like row and column relation embeddings (Wu et al., 2022) or positional bias (Pietruszka et al., 2022) to get the model to attend to header cells while generating content. However, this results in highly specialized architectures for a singular task. Breaking the task down into question-answering results in a more interpretable framework while ensuring validity of the generated tables.

The first step identifies the mode of interaction and the cell(s) the user is referring to, which is used to formulate a question. The second step converts the table into a pandas dataframe, parses the table and the question generated from the previous step to obtain a pandas command corresponding to the task, and executes the command on the dataframe to generate the final table. Generating a valid command ensures that the final table is syntactically valid as well (that is, the number of columns across all rows is consistent).

For the *interpret* task, the question-answer reformulation is trivial, since all interpretive queries and associated responses are naturally question-answer pairs. For the *modify* task, the question is of the form *To which cells is the user referring?*. A language model is then fine-tuned to generate a response containing the cells (indexed by row and column). Then, the LLM response is reformatted into an appropriate pandas command. Finally, for the *generate* task, the question-answering is more nuanced. First, the user request is parsed to identify whether a row or a column is to be appended. The header of the corresponding row is then extracted from the user request. Using the extracted header and the other header cells of the table, questions are generated for each of the empty cells to be filled in the form *What is the row value for column?*. The user request is parsed to obtain the answers to these generated questions, forming the corresponding row or column to be appended.

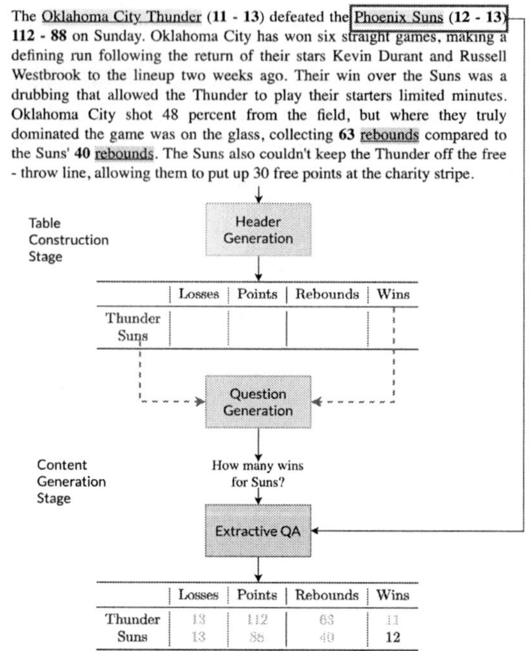

Figure 2: Overview of the novel question-answering reformulation to perform table operations

5 Results

5.1 Experimental Setup

For our experiments, we utilize Gemma models (Team et al., 2024). We fine-tune the instruction-tuned base model `gemma-2-9b-it` using LoRA (Hu et al., 2022). Hyperparameters for our training setup as well as LoRA parameters are shown in Appendix A.

5.2 Datasets

In addition to the iTBLS dataset, we also evaluate our method on five datasets to summarize textual paragraphs to tables (Wu et al., 2022). While iTBLS is a table-to-table or table-to-text task, the datasets proposed by Wu et al. (2022) address the dual problem of text-to-table. The datasets consist of textual paragraphs containing some information that is to be converted into a tabular format by determining both the appropriate header cells and the content that the table is filled with.

Wu et al. (2022) present datasets for the text-to-table task by inverting datasets created for the dual problem of generating textual descriptions from tables. Each dataset consists of textual paragraphs paired with tabular information summarizing content in the text. Dataset statistics are available in Appendix A.3. Each dataset is described below.

E2E (Novikova et al., 2017) concerns restaurant descriptions, requiring summarization of information into tables with descriptors like restaurant name, customer rating, and location. WikiTableText (WTT) (Bao et al., 2018), sourced from Wikipedia, consists of natural language descriptions generated from tabular data across various topics. WikiBio (Lebret et al., 2016) comprises introductions of individuals from Wikipedia alongside tabular summaries extracted from the same page's information box. In contrast to E2E, the table headers in the WikiTableText and WikiBio datasets vary widely across data samples.

Example textual paragraphs and associated tables from each dataset are presented in A.4.

5.3 Metrics

Exact-Match (EM): On the iTBLS dataset, we report exact-match, that is, whether or not the generated table matches the ground-truth table exactly.

BERTScore: On the E2E, WTT, WikiBio and RotoWire datasets, we report BERTScore (Zhang et al., 2020) in addition to EM to be consistent with prior work. BERTScore is a measure of semantic similarity which computes the similarity of embeddings in a latent space obtained using an encoder language model.

Consistent with prior work, all our evaluations are order-invariant. That is, credit is given as long as the generated cells are indexed by the correct row and column headers, even if the headers themselves are in different positions between the model-generated response and the ground-truth.

5.4 iTBLS

Results on the iTBLS dataset using a vanilla sequence-to-sequence approach and the question-answering-based method are presented in Table 2. As observed in the results, the generate task is the hardest, with performance slightly lower on the generate task when compared to interpret and modify. This is a result of the fact that the exact-match metric only provides credit when all cells are correct (necessitating that all cells in the output are identical to the ground truth) and does not provide partial credit for getting some of the cells right, and the fact that the generate task requires getting more cells right in comparison to the other tasks.

5.5 Text-to-table

The results on the text-to-table datasets proposed by Wu et al. (2022) are available in Table 3. Our method performs on par with or better than the prior state-of-the-art method in terms of BERTScore and is competitive with prior work in terms of Exact-Match. The exact-match score does not reflect true performance on the WikiBio dataset since synonyms are penalized under this framework. A deep-dive into the results is presented in Section 5.6.

Split	Approach	Exact-Match
Interpret	Seq2seq	88.29
	iTBLS as QA	90.98
Modify	Seq2seq	74.65
	iTBLS as QA	89.58
Generate	Seq2seq	48.94
	iTBLS as QA	73.32

Table 2: Comparison between the question-answering reformulation and a vanilla sequence-to-sequence modeling approach on the iTBLS dataset

Dataset	Approach	EM	BS
WTT	Wu et al. (2022)	62.71	80.74
	Ours	75.96	95.52
Wikibio	Wu et al. (2022)	69.71	76.56
	Ours	66.65	92.60
E2E	Wu et al. (2022)	97.94	98.57
	Ours	97.64	99.35

Table 3: Comparison between our method and prior work on the text to table task in terms of Exact-Match and BERTScore

5.6 Analysis of Errors

An analysis of the difference in performance between the prior state of the art and our approach is presented in Table 6. As observed, the dataset is inconsistent in the description of individuals, with no consistent pattern when middle and last names are present. Furthermore, the use of quantifying information in the header as opposed to the table cell results in no credit using the exact-match metric, though the information contained is exactly the same between the prediction and the ground-truth. Finally, the datasets often contain textual examples with multiple possible tabular summarizations, all of which are equally valid, further complicating evaluation. In the third example in Table 6, the model correctly generates the 'Occupation' as a table header while the ground truth contains an erroneous sample, using the phrase 'Known for' instead of 'Known as'.

Examples of errors in the iTBLS dataset are provided in Tables 4, 5, and 13. On the interpret task, the model incorrectly understand the user request, and produces the cell immediately to the right instead of three columns over. On the modify task (Table 5), the model incorrectly understands the references and swaps index (2,3) with (3,2) instead of swapping indices (2,2) and (3,3). On the generate task (Table 13), the model incorrectly places a tuple and hallucinates a value instead of performing the requested action.

Text: What is the value of the cell in row 1 that is three cells to the right of the cell with a value of 12%?

Input Table:

row ID	$\sigma\mu[IO]$	$\mu[\tau s]$	$\sigma[\tau s]$	$\sigma\mu[\tau s]$
0	13%	912.5 μs	91.9 μs	10.1%
1	12%	18335.7 μs	90.7 μs	10.0%
2	12%	903.1 μs	1832.7 μs	10.0%

Ground Truth: 10.0%

Prediction: 18335.7 μs

Table 4: Example error for iTBLS interpret task. Table source: `https://arxiv.org/pdf/1411.5458`

Text: Swap row 1 in the second column with row 2 in the third column

Input Table:

row ID	col 1	col 2	col 3
0	X	O	X
1	NaN	O	O
2	O	X	X

Ground Truth:

row ID	col 1	col 2	col 3
0	X	O	X
1	NaN	X	O
2	O	X	O

Prediction:

row ID	col 1	col 2	col 3
0	X	O	X
1	NaN	O	X
2	O	O	X

Table 5: Example error for iTBLS modify task. Table source: `https://arxiv.org/pdf/1411.4023`

6 Conclusion

This paper introduces Interactive Tables (iTBLS), a dataset of interactive conversations addressing three types of tasks – interpretation, modification, and generation. In contrast to prior tabular datasets that are sourced from Wikipedia or financial reports, iTBLS is situated in tabular data obtained from scientific pre-prints on ArXiv. Success on the iTBLS dataset requires understanding both ordinal and cardinal references to cell positions, and understanding implicit references. Additionally, the paper introduces a novel framework that reformulates tabular operations as question-answering. Appropriate questions are created based on the input table and the nature of interaction, and the user request is used as evidence to obtain the answers. The developed approach demonstrates an improvement over a sequence-to-sequence modeling approach on the iTBLS dataset. In addition, the question-answering-based reformulation is evaluated on datasets for the text-to-table task, obtaining up to 13% improvement in terms of exact-match accuracy and 16% improvement in terms of BERTScore compared to the prior state-of-the-art.

Limitations

While iTBLS introduces a dataset for interactive conversations over tabular information, there are some avenues for improvement. In this dataset, modification is modeled as a series of swaps. A more comprehensive sequence of manipulations includes in-place modification of values and modifying a cell's value based on other cells using both absolute and relative references. While sourcing tabular information from arXiv provides a cost-efficient approach, LLMs are often pre-trained on LaTeXsources from arXiv. This paper alleviates the issue by sourcing natural language commands from crowdworkers. Future work could look at collecting tabular information from crowdworkers as well. While we present a suite of baseline approaches for iTBLS, there is still headroom between the presented approaches and perfect performance. We identify the closure of this gap as an avenue for future work.

Acknowledgments

This work was supported by CoCoSys, one of seven centers in JUMP 2.0, a Semiconductor Research Corporation (SRC) program sponsored by DARPA.

1. Text: Walter Clarence Henderson (28 February 1891 – 20 September 1968) was a progressive conservative party member of the Canadian house of commons. He was born in Carberry, Manitoba and became a farmer by career. He was elected at the Cariboo riding in the 1958 general election, defeating social credit incumbent Bert Leboe.
Generated Table:

Predicted Header	Prediction - iTBLS	Ground Truth Header	Ground Truth
Name	Walter Henderson	Name	Walter Clarence Henderson
Profession	Farmer	Profession	Farmer
Party	Progressive Conservative	Party	Progressive Conservative

2. Text: The production of Tautona mine is 235,000 ounces in 2013.
Generated Table:

Predicted Header	Prediction - iTBLS	Ground Truth Header	Ground Truth
Title	Tautona mine	Title	Tautona mine
Subtitle	Production	Subtitle	Production
Year	2013	Year	2013
Production (ounces)	235,000	Production	235,00 ounces

3. Text: Elango Nagarajah, also known as "Thaimann Elango", is a Tamil film actor, director, producer and lyricist in the Tamil film industry. He began his career in his early ages as a producer for the Tamil film Anbudan, starred Arun Vijay, Meena, Rambha (actress) in the main was released in the year 2000.
Generated Table:

Predicted Header	Prediction - iTBLS	Ground Truth Header	Ground Truth
Name	Elango Nagarajah	Name	Elango
Occupation	actor, director, producer, lyricist	Known for	Thaimann

Table 6: Difference between the tables generated by the Zero Shot (ZS) and Fine-Tuned (FT) approaches with respect to the Ground Truth on the WikiBio and WikiTableText datasets with additions and deletions represented using red and green.

References

Mubashara Akhtar, Abhilash Shankarampeta, Vivek Gupta, Arpit Patil, Oana Cocarascu, and Elena Simperl. 2023. Exploring the numerical reasoning capabilities of language models: A comprehensive analysis on tabular data. In *Findings of the Association for Computational Linguistics: EMNLP 2023*, pages 15391–15405, Singapore. Association for Computational Linguistics.

Rami Aly, Zhijiang Guo, Michael Sejr Schlichtkrull, James Thorne, Andreas Vlachos, Christos Christodoulopoulos, Oana Cocarascu, and Arpit Mittal. 2021. The fact extraction and VERification over unstructured and structured information (FEVEROUS) shared task. In *Proceedings of the Fourth Workshop on Fact Extraction and VERification (FEVER)*, pages 1–13, Dominican Republic. Association for Computational Linguistics.

Eiji Aramaki, Yasuhide Miura, Masatsugu Tonoike, Tomoko Ohkuma, Hiroshi Mashuichi, and Kazuhiko Ohe. 2009. TEXT2TABLE: medical text summarization system based on named entity recognition and modality identification. In *Proceedings of the Workshop on BioNLP - BioNLP '09*, page 185, Boulder, Colorado. Association for Computational Linguistics.

Junwei Bao, Duyu Tang, Nan Duan, Zhao Yan, Yuanhua Lv, Ming Zhou, and Tiejun Zhao. 2018. Table-to-Text: Describing Table Region with Natural Language. *arXiv preprint*. ArXiv:1805.11234 [cs].

Vadim Borisov, Kathrin Sessler, Tobias Leemann, Martin Pawelczyk, and Gjergji Kasneci. 2023. Language Models are Realistic Tabular Data Generators. In *The Eleventh International Conference on Learning Representations*.

S. R. K. Branavan, Pawan Deshpande, and Regina Barzilay. 2007. Generating a table-of-contents. In *Proceedings of the 45th Annual Meeting of the Association of Computational Linguistics*, pages 544–551, Prague, Czech Republic. Association for Computational Linguistics.

Haipeng Chen, Sushil Jajodia, Jing Liu, Noseong Park, Vadim Sokolov, and V. S. Subrahmanian. 2019a. FakeTables: Using GANs to Generate Functional Dependency Preserving Tables with Bounded Real Data. In *Proceedings of the Twenty-Eighth International Joint Conference on Artificial Intelligence*, pages 2074–2080, Macao, China. International Joint Conferences on Artificial Intelligence Organization.

Ran Chen, Di Weng, Yanwei Huang, Xinhuan Shu, Jiayi Zhou, Guodao Sun, and Yingcai Wu. 2023. Rigel: Transforming tabular data by declarative mapping. *IEEE Transactions on Visualization and Computer Graphics*, 29(1):128–138.

Wenhu Chen, Hongmin Wang, Jianshu Chen, Yunkai Zhang, Hong Wang, Shiyang Li, Xiyou Zhou, and William Yang Wang. 2019b. Tabfact: A large-scale dataset for table-based fact verification. *arXiv preprint arXiv:1909.02164*.

Zhiyu Chen, Wenhu Chen, Charese Smiley, Sameena Shah, Iana Borova, Dylan Langdon, Reema Moussa, Matt Beane, Ting-Hao Huang, Bryan Routledge, and William Yang Wang. 2021. FinQA: A dataset of numerical reasoning over financial data. In *Proceedings of the 2021 Conference on Empirical Methods in Natural Language Processing*, pages 3697–3711, Online and Punta Cana, Dominican Republic. Association for Computational Linguistics.

Zhoujun Cheng, Haoyu Dong, Zhiruo Wang, Ran Jia, Jiaqi Guo, Yan Gao, Shi Han, Jian-Guang Lou, and Dongmei Zhang. 2022. HiTab: A hierarchical table dataset for question answering and natural language generation. In *Proceedings of the 60th Annual Meeting of the Association for Computational Linguistics (Volume 1: Long Papers)*, pages 1094–1110, Dublin, Ireland. Association for Computational Linguistics.

Marco Cremaschi, Fabio D'Adda, and Andrea Maurino. 2025. steellm: An llm for generating semantic annotations of tabular data. *ACM Trans. Intell. Syst. Technol.* Just Accepted.

Sajad Darabi and Yotam Elor. 2021. Synthesising multimodal minority samples for tabular data. *arXiv preprint arXiv:2105.08204*.

Arash Dargahi Nobari and Davood Rafiei. 2024. Dtt: An example-driven tabular transformer for joinability by leveraging large language models. *Proceedings of the ACM on Management of Data*, 2(1):1–24.

Yang Deng, Wenqiang Lei, Wenxuan Zhang, Wai Lam, and Tat-Seng Chua. 2022. PACIFIC: Towards proactive conversational question answering over tabular and textual data in finance. In *Proceedings of the 2022 Conference on Empirical Methods in Natural Language Processing*, pages 6970–6984, Abu Dhabi, United Arab Emirates. Association for Computational Linguistics.

Zheye Deng, Chunkit Chan, Weiqi Wang, Yuxi Sun, Wei Fan, Tianshi Zheng, Yauwai Yim, and Yangqiu Song. 2024. Text-tuple-table: Towards information integration in text-to-table generation via global tuple extraction. *Preprint*, arXiv:2404.14215.

Julian Eisenschlos, Syrine Krichene, and Thomas Müller. 2020. Understanding tables with intermediate pre-training. In *Findings of the Association for Computational Linguistics: EMNLP 2020*, pages 281–296, Online. Association for Computational Linguistics.

Xi Fang, Weijie Xu, Fiona Anting Tan, Jiani Zhang, Ziqing Hu, Yanjun Qi, Scott Nickleach, Diego Socolinsky, Srinivasan Sengamedu, and Christos Faloutsos. 2024. Large language models on tabular data–a survey. *arXiv e-prints*, pages arXiv–2402.

Heng Gong, Yawei Sun, Xiaocheng Feng, Bing Qin, Wei Bi, Xiaojiang Liu, and Ting Liu. 2020. TableGPT: Few-shot table-to-text generation with table structure reconstruction and content matching. In *Proceedings of the 28th International Conference on Computational Linguistics*, pages 1978–1988, Barcelona, Spain (Online). International Committee on Computational Linguistics.

Zihui Gu, Ju Fan, Nan Tang, Preslav Nakov, Xiaoman Zhao, and Xiaoyong Du. 2022. PASTA: Table-operations aware fact verification via sentence-table cloze pre-training. In *Proceedings of the 2022 Conference on Empirical Methods in Natural Language Processing*, pages 4971–4983, Abu Dhabi, United Arab Emirates. Association for Computational Linguistics.

Manbir S. Gulati and Paul F. Roysdon. 2023. TabMT: Generating tabular data with masked transformers. In *Thirty-seventh Conference on Neural Information Processing Systems*.

Darryl Hannan, Akshay Jain, and Mohit Bansal. 2020. Manymodalqa: Modality disambiguation and qa over diverse inputs. In *Proceedings of the AAAI conference on artificial intelligence*, volume 34, pages 7879–7886.

Jonathan Herzig, Thomas Müller, Syrine Krichene, and Julian Eisenschlos. 2021. Open domain question answering over tables via dense retrieval. In *Proceedings of the 2021 Conference of the North American Chapter of the Association for Computational Linguistics: Human Language Technologies*, pages 512–519, Online. Association for Computational Linguistics.

Jonathan Herzig, Pawel Krzysztof Nowak, Thomas Müller, Francesco Piccinno, and Julian Eisenschlos. 2020. TaPas: Weakly supervised table parsing via pre-training. In *Proceedings of the 58th Annual Meeting of the Association for Computational Linguistics*, pages 4320–4333, Online. Association for Computational Linguistics.

Edward J Hu, Yelong Shen, Phillip Wallis, Zeyuan Allen-Zhu, Yuanzhi Li, Shean Wang, Lu Wang, Weizhu Chen, et al. 2022. Lora: Low-rank adaptation of large language models. *ICLR*, 1(2):3.

Yanwei Huang, Yunfan Zhou, Ran Chen, Changhao Pan, Xinhuan Shu, Di Weng, and Yingcai Wu. 2024. Interactive table synthesis with natural language. *IEEE Transactions on Visualization and Computer Graphics*, 30(9):6130–6145.

Jinhao Jiang, Kun Zhou, Zican Dong, Keming Ye, Xin Zhao, and Ji-Rong Wen. 2023. StructGPT: A general framework for large language model to reason over structured data. In *Proceedings of the 2023 Conference on Empirical Methods in Natural Language Processing*, pages 9237–9251, Singapore. Association for Computational Linguistics.

Zhongjun Jin, Michael R. Anderson, Michael Cafarella, and H. V. Jagadish. 2017. Foofah: Transforming data by example. In *Proceedings of the 2017 ACM International Conference on Management of Data*, SIGMOD '17, page 683–698, New York, NY, USA. Association for Computing Machinery.

Sean Kandel, Andreas Paepcke, Joseph Hellerstein, and Jeffrey Heer. 2011. Wrangler: interactive visual specification of data transformation scripts. In *Proceedings of the SIGCHI Conference on Human Factors in Computing Systems*, CHI '11, page 3363–3372, New York, NY, USA. Association for Computing Machinery.

Marcin Kardas, Piotr Czapla, Pontus Stenetorp, Sebastian Ruder, Sebastian Riedel, Ross Taylor, and Robert Stojnic. 2020. AxCell: Automatic extraction of results from machine learning papers. In *Proceedings of the 2020 Conference on Empirical Methods in Natural Language Processing (EMNLP)*, pages 8580–8594, Online. Association for Computational Linguistics.

Akim Kotelnikov, Dmitry Baranchuk, Ivan Rubachev, and Artem Babenko. 2023. TabDDPM: modelling tabular data with diffusion models. In *Proceedings of the 40th International Conference on Machine Learning*, pages 17564–17579.

Rémi Lebret, David Grangier, and Michael Auli. 2016. Neural text generation from structured data with application to the biography domain. In *Proceedings of the 2016 Conference on Empirical Methods in Natural Language Processing*, pages 1203–1213, Austin, Texas. Association for Computational Linguistics.

Szu-Chuang Li, Bo-Chen Tai, and Yennun Huang. 2019. Evaluating Variational Autoencoder as a Private Data Release Mechanism for Tabular Data. In *2019 IEEE 24th Pacific Rim International Symposium on Dependable Computing (PRDC)*, pages 198–1988.

Qian Liu, Bei Chen, Jiaqi Guo, Morteza Ziyadi, Zeqi Lin, Weizhu Chen, and Jian-Guang Lou. 2021. Tapex: Table pre-training via learning a neural sql executor. *arXiv preprint arXiv:2107.07653*.

Tianyang Liu, Fei Wang, and Muhao Chen. 2024. Rethinking tabular data understanding with large language models. In *Proceedings of the 2024 Conference of the North American Chapter of the Association for Computational Linguistics: Human Language Technologies (Volume 1: Long Papers)*, pages 450–482, Mexico City, Mexico. Association for Computational Linguistics.

Kai Nakamura, Sharon Levy, Yi-Lin Tuan, Wenhu Chen, and William Yang Wang. 2022a. HybriDialogue: An information-seeking dialogue dataset grounded on tabular and textual data. In *Findings of the Association for Computational Linguistics: ACL 2022*, pages 481–492, Dublin, Ireland. Association for Computational Linguistics.

Kai Nakamura, Sharon Levy, Yi-Lin Tuan, Wenhu Chen, and William Yang Wang. 2022b. HybriDialogue: An information-seeking dialogue dataset grounded on tabular and textual data. In *Findings of the Association for Computational Linguistics: ACL 2022*, pages 481–492, Dublin, Ireland. Association for Computational Linguistics.

Linyong Nan, Chiachun Hsieh, Ziming Mao, Xi Victoria Lin, Neha Verma, Rui Zhang, Wojciech Kryściński, Hailey Schoelkopf, Riley Kong, Xiangru Tang, Mutethia Mutuma, Ben Rosand, Isabel Trindade, Renusree Bandaru, Jacob Cunningham, Caiming Xiong, Dragomir Radev, and Dragomir Radev. 2022. FeTaQA: Free-form table question answering. *Transactions of the Association for Computational Linguistics*, 10:35–49.

Jekaterina Novikova, Ondřej Dušek, and Verena Rieser. 2017. The E2E Dataset: New Challenges For End-to-End Generation. *arXiv preprint*. ArXiv:1706.09254 [cs].

Noseong Park, Mahmoud Mohammadi, Kshitij Gorde, Sushil Jajodia, Hongkyu Park, and Youngmin Kim. 2018. Data synthesis based on generative adversarial networks. *Proceedings of the VLDB Endowment*, 11(10):1071–1083.

Panupong Pasupat and Percy Liang. 2015. Compositional semantic parsing on semi-structured tables. In *Proceedings of the 53rd Annual Meeting of the Association for Computational Linguistics and the 7th International Joint Conference on Natural Language Processing (Volume 1: Long Papers)*, pages 1470–1480, Beijing, China. Association for Computational Linguistics.

Tomas Petricek, Gerrit J. J. van den Burg, Alfredo Nazábal, Taha Ceritli, Ernesto Jiménez-Ruiz, and Christopher K. I. Williams. 2023. Ai assistants: A framework for semi-automated data wrangling. *IEEE Transactions on Knowledge and Data Engineering*, 35(9):9295–9306.

Michał Pietruszka, Michał Turski, Łukasz Borchmann, Tomasz Dwojak, Gabriela Pałka, Karolina Szyndler, Dawid Jurkiewicz, and Łukasz Garncarek. 2022. STable: Table Generation Framework for Encoder-Decoder Models. *arXiv preprint*. ArXiv:2206.04045 [cs].

Christopher Scaffidi, Brad Myers, and Mary Shaw. 2009. Intelligently creating and recommending reusable reformatting rules. In *Proceedings of the 14th International Conference on Intelligent User Interfaces*, IUI '09, page 297–306, New York, NY, USA. Association for Computing Machinery.

Nabeel Seedat, Nicolas Huynh, Boris van Breugel, and Mihaela van der Schaar. 2024. Curated LLM: Synergy of LLMs and Data Curation for tabular augmentation in ultra low-data regimes. _eprint: 2312.12112.

Alexey O. Shigarov, Vasiliy V. Khristyuk, Andrey A. Mikhailov, and Viacheslav V. Paramonov. 2019. Tabbyxl: Rule-based spreadsheet data extraction and transformation. In *International Conference on Information and Software Technologies*.

Rishabh Singh and Sumit Gulwani. 2012. Learning semantic string transformations from examples. *arXiv preprint arXiv:1204.6079*.

Aivin V. Solatorio and Olivier Dupriez. 2023. REaLTabFormer: Generating Realistic Relational and Tabular Data using Transformers. *arXiv preprint*. ArXiv:2302.02041 [cs].

Yuan Sui, Mengyu Zhou, Mingjie Zhou, Shi Han, and Dongmei Zhang. 2024. Table meets llm: Can large language models understand structured table data? a benchmark and empirical study. In *Proceedings of the 17th ACM International Conference on Web Search and Data Mining*, WSDM '24, page 645–654, New York, NY, USA. Association for Computing Machinery.

Anirudh Sundar and Larry Heck. 2022. Multimodal conversational AI: A survey of datasets and approaches. In *Proceedings of the 4th Workshop on NLP for Conversational AI*, pages 131–147, Dublin, Ireland. Association for Computational Linguistics.

Anirudh Sundar, Jin Xu, William Gay, Christopher Richardson, and Larry Heck. 2024. cpapers: A dataset of situated and multimodal interactive conversations in scientific papers. *Advances in Neural Information Processing Systems*, 37:66283–66304.

Anirudh S. Sundar and Larry Heck. 2023. cTBLS: Augmenting large language models with conversational tables. In *Proceedings of the 5th Workshop on NLP for Conversational AI (NLP4ConvAI 2023)*, pages 59–70, Toronto, Canada. Association for Computational Linguistics.

Xiangru Tang, Yiming Zong, Jason Phang, Yilun Zhao, Wangchunshu Zhou, Arman Cohan, and Mark Gerstein. 2023. Struc-Bench: Are Large Language Models Really Good at Generating Complex Structured Data? *arXiv preprint*. ArXiv:2309.08963 [cs].

Gemma Team, Thomas Mesnard, Cassidy Hardin, Robert Dadashi, Surya Bhupatiraju, Shreya Pathak, Laurent Sifre, Morgane Rivière, Mihir Sanjay Kale, Juliette Love, et al. 2024. Gemma: Open models based on gemini research and technology. *arXiv preprint arXiv:2403.08295*.

Xueqing Wu, Jiacheng Zhang, and Hang Li. 2022. Text-to-Table: A New Way of Information Extraction. *arXiv preprint*. ArXiv:2109.02707 [cs].

Junjie Xing, Yeye He, Mengyu Zhou, Haoyu Dong, Shi Han, Dongmei Zhang, and Surajit Chaudhuri. 2024. Table-llm-specialist: Language model specialists for tables using iterative generator-validator fine-tuning. *arXiv preprint arXiv:2410.12164*.

Lei Xu and Kalyan Veeramachaneni. 2018. Synthesizing Tabular Data using Generative Adversarial Networks. *arXiv preprint*. ArXiv:1811.11264 [cs, stat].

Jingfeng Yang, Aditya Gupta, Shyam Upadhyay, Luheng He, Rahul Goel, and Shachi Paul. 2022. TableFormer: Robust transformer modeling for table-text encoding. In *Proceedings of the 60th Annual Meeting of the Association for Computational Linguistics (Volume 1: Long Papers)*, pages 528–537, Dublin, Ireland. Association for Computational Linguistics.

Pengcheng Yin, Graham Neubig, Wen-tau Yih, and Sebastian Riedel. 2020. Tabert: Pretraining for joint understanding of textual and tabular data. *arXiv preprint arXiv:2005.08314*.

Liangyu Zha, Junlin Zhou, Liyao Li, Rui Wang, Qingyi Huang, Saisai Yang, Jing Yuan, Changbao Su, Xiang Li, Aofeng Su, et al. 2023. Tablegpt: Towards unifying tables, nature language and commands into one gpt. *arXiv preprint arXiv:2307.08674*.

Tianshu Zhang, Xiang Yue, Yifei Li, and Huan Sun. 2023. Tablellama: Towards open large generalist models for tables. *arXiv preprint arXiv:2311.09206*.

Tianyi Zhang, Varsha Kishore*, Felix Wu*, Kilian Q. Weinberger, and Yoav Artzi. 2020. BERTScore: Evaluating Text Generation with BERT. In *International Conference on Learning Representations*.

Yilun Zhao, Yunxiang Li, Chenying Li, and Rui Zhang. 2022. MultiHiertt: Numerical reasoning over multi hierarchical tabular and textual data. In *Proceedings of the 60th Annual Meeting of the Association for Computational Linguistics (Volume 1: Long Papers)*, pages 6588–6600, Dublin, Ireland. Association for Computational Linguistics.

Yilun Zhao, Yitao Long, Hongjun Liu, Linyong Nan, Lyuhao Chen, Ryo Kamoi, Yixin Liu, Xiangru Tang, Rui Zhang, and Arman Cohan. 2023. DocMath-Eval: Evaluating Numerical Reasoning Capabilities of LLMs in Understanding Long Documents with Tabular Data. _eprint: 2311.09805.

Zilong Zhao, Aditya Kunar, Robert Birke, and Lydia Y Chen. 2021. Ctab-gan: Effective table data synthesizing. In *Asian Conference on Machine Learning*, pages 97–112. PMLR.

Fengbin Zhu, Wenqiang Lei, Youcheng Huang, Chao Wang, Shuo Zhang, Jiancheng Lv, Fuli Feng, and Tat-Seng Chua. 2021. TAT-QA: A question answering benchmark on a hybrid of tabular and textual content in finance. In *Proceedings of the 59th Annual Meeting of the Association for Computational Linguistics and the 11th International Joint Conference on Natural Language Processing (Volume 1: Long Papers)*, pages 3277–3287, Online. Association for Computational Linguistics.

A Appendix

A.1 AI Assistance Acknowledgment

We acknowledge the use of GitHub Copilot to assist in code completion.

A.2 Compute

All fine-tuning and inference was run on Nvidia A40 GPUs with 48GB GDDR6 memory. Fine-tuning took 1-2 hours on 8 GPUs in parallel with pytorch distributed data parallel (DDP).

A.3 Dataset Statistics

Statistics of the text-to-table datasets:

Dataset	Train	Valid	Test
E2E	42.1k	4.7k	4.7k
WikiTableText	10k	1.3k	2.0k
WikiBio	582.7k	72.8k	72.7k

Table 7: Statistics of the E2E, WikiTableText, WikiBio, and RotoWire datasets, number of samples across splits

A.4 Dataset Examples – Text to Table

This section details example textual paragraphs and associated tables from the different datasets.

E2E:
The Eagle is a low rated coffee shop near Burger King and the riverside that is family friendly and is less than £20 for Japanese food.

Name	The Eagle
Food	Japanese
Price range	Less than £20
Customer Rating	Low
Area	Riverside
Family friendly	Yes
Near	Burger King

WikiTableText:
Michelle Schimel was New York State assemblywoman in Portuguese Heritage Society.

Title	Potuguese Heritage Society
Subtitle	Other activities
Name	Michelle Schimel

WikiBio:
Leonard Shenoff Randle (born February 12, 1949) is a former Major League Baseball player. He was the first-round pick of the Washington Senators in the secondary phase of the June 1970 Major League Baseball draft, tenth overall.

Debut team	Washington Senators
Name	Lenny Randle
Birth Date	12 February 1949

A.5 Dataset Examples – iTBLS

	Example
1	What is the 2nd cell value for row 4?
2	Tell me the final value in the column labeled k
3	What is the value of the cell to the left of the cell in the bottom right of the table.

Table 8: Example interactions in iTBLS *Interpret*

	Example
1	The rows 1 and 4 in the Column "Citation" were accidentally switched. Please rectify the positions of these values so they are where they need to be.
2	Swap the contents of the second and last cell under repetitions.
3	Two values in the MCBLp column were put in the reverse spots. I need the values for the FM and PCC rows flipped.

Table 9: Example interactions in iTBLS *Modify*

	Example
1	The row 3 of the table shows the values for Peak as 4, X coordinate as 0.100, Y coordinate as -0.150, A as 0.5, standard deviation (σ) as 0.02, and Local lnZ as -7.824.
2	The column "Method 2 (with sub-clustering)" contains the 'Nlike' values in different rows: 27,658 in the second row, 69,094 in the third row, 579,208 in the fourth row, and 43,093,230 in the fifth row, while the remaining rows from six to nine contain no data (NaN).
3	The column R contains eight numerical values in increasing order: 3.34, 3.40, 3.66, 5.06, 6.02, 6.61, 4.05, and 4.11.

Table 10: Example interactions in iTBLS *Generate*

A.6 Hyperparameters

Hyperparameters used during training are listed here.

Parameter	Value
Rank	2
α	2
Dropout	0.01
Target modules	`all-linear`

Table 11: LoRA Hyperparameters

Parameter	Value
Learning Rate	2e-4
Batch size	4
Warmup Schedule	Constant
Warmup Ratio	0.03
Epochs	5
Optimizer	`paged_adamw_32bit`[3]

Table 12: Training Hyperparameters

A.7 Mechanical Turk Interface

[3]https://huggingface.co/docs/bitsandbytes/main/en/reference/optim/adamw

B Example error on the generate task of iTBLS

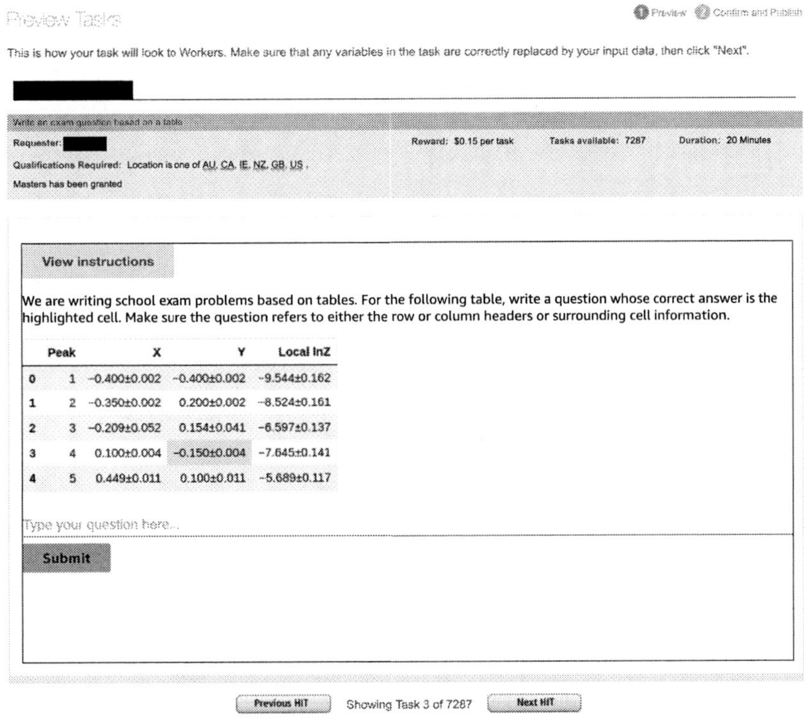

Figure 3: Amazon Mechanical Turk Interface to collect iTBLS interpretation

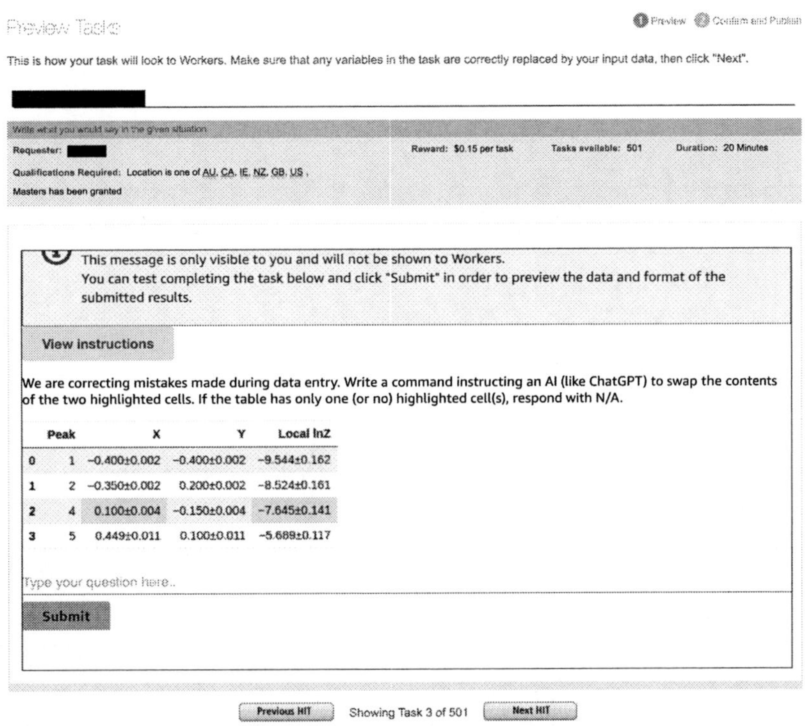

Figure 4: Amazon Mechanical Turk Interface to collect iTBLS modification

Text: The column 'Standard deviation' contains entries which are both numbers and number sequences: first has 0.45, 0.75, 0, 0.57, second has 0.36, 0.5, 0, 0.34, third is exactly 0, the fourth one is 0.77, fifth is 0.49, and the last one is 0.22.

Input Table:

row ID	Questions	Average score
0	Q. 1 (a-d)	(3.6 3.93 5 4)
1	Q. 2 (a-d)	4.26
2	Q. 3	5
3	Q. 4	3.64
4	Q. 5	(4.04 4.44 5 4.86)
5	GQ	4.35

Ground Truth:

row ID	Questions	Average score	Standard deviation
0	Q. 1 (a-d)	(3.6 3.93 5 4)	(0.45 0.75 0 0.57)
1	Q. 2 (a-d)	4.26	(0.36 0.5 0 0.34)
2	Q. 3	5	0
3	Q. 4	3.64	0.77
4	Q. 5	(4.04 4.44 5 4.86)	0.49
5	GQ	4.35	0.22

Prediction:

row ID	Questions	Average score	Standard deviation
0	Q. 1 (a-d)	(3.6 3.93 5 4)	(0.45 0.75 0 0.57)
1	Q. 2 (a-d)	4.26	(0.36 0.5 0 0.34)
2	Q. 3	5	0
3	Q. 4	3.64	0.77
4	Q. 5	(4.04 4.44 5 4.86)	(0.49 0.22)
5	GQ	4.35	0

Table 13: Example error for iTBLS generate task. Table source: `https://arxiv.org/pdf/1411.4925`

Something's Fishy In The Data Lake: A Critical Re-evaluation of Table Union Search Benchmarks

Allaa Boutaleb, Bernd Amann, Hubert Naacke and Rafael Angarita

Sorbonne Université, CNRS, LIP6, F-75005 Paris, France
{firstname.lastname}@lip6.fr

Abstract

Recent table representation learning and data discovery methods tackle table union search (TUS) within data lakes, which involves identifying tables that can be unioned with a given query table to enrich its content. These methods are commonly evaluated using benchmarks that aim to assess semantic understanding in real-world TUS tasks. However, our analysis of prominent TUS benchmarks reveals several limitations that allow simple baselines to perform surprisingly well, often outperforming more sophisticated approaches. This suggests that current benchmark scores are heavily influenced by dataset-specific characteristics and fail to effectively isolate the gains from semantic understanding. To address this, we propose essential criteria for future benchmarks to enable a more realistic and reliable evaluation of progress in semantic table union search.

1 Introduction

Measurement enables scientific progress. In computer science and machine learning, this requires the creation of efficient benchmarks that provide a stable foundation for evaluation, ensuring that observed performance scores reflect genuine capabilities for real-world tasks.

Table Union Search (TUS) aims to retrieve tables C from a corpus that are semantically unionable with a query table Q, meaning they represent the same information type and permit vertical concatenation (row appending) (Nargesian et al., 2018; Fan et al., 2023a). As a top-k retrieval task, TUS ranks candidate tables C by a table-level relevance score $R(Q, C)$. This score is typically obtained by aggregating column-level semantic relevance scores $R(C_Q, C_C)$ computed for each column C_Q of the query table Q and each column C_C of the candidate table C. The aggregation often involves finding an optimal mapping between the columns of Q and C, for instance via maximum bipartite matching (Fan et al., 2023b). Successful TUS facilitates data integration and dataset enrichment (Khatiwada et al., 2023; Castelo et al., 2021).

Recent research has introduced sophisticated TUS methods with complex representation learning (Fan et al., 2023b; Khatiwada et al., 2025; Chen et al., 2023) designed to capture deeper semantics. However, current benchmarks often exhibit excessive schema overlap, limited semantic complexity, and potential ground truth inconsistencies, which raises questions about whether they provide a reliable environment to evaluate advanced TUS capabilities. While state-of-the-art methodologies leverage semantic reasoning to reflect the task specific challenges, observed high performance may be significantly attributed to model adaptation to specific statistical and structural properties inherent within the benchmark datasets. This phenomenon can confound the accurate assessment and potentially underestimate the isolated contribution of improvements specifically targeting semantics-aware TUS.

In this paper, we examine prominent TUS benchmarks [1], using simple baselines to assess the benchmarks themselves. Our research questions are:

1. Do current TUS benchmarks necessitate deep semantic analysis, or can simpler features achieve competitive performance?
2. How do benchmark properties and ground truth quality impact TUS evaluation?
3. What constitutes a more realistic and discriminative TUS benchmark?

Our analysis[2] reveals that simple baseline methods often achieve surprisingly strong performance by leveraging benchmark characteristics rather than demonstrating sophisticated semantic reasoning.

[1] Preprocessed benchmarks used in our evaluation are available at https://zenodo.org/records/15499092

[2] Our code is available at: https://github.com/Allaa-boutaleb/fishy-tus

Proceedings of the 4th Table Representation Learning Workshop, pages 71–85
July 31, 2025 ©2025 Association for Computational Linguistics

Our contributions include:

- A systematic analysis identifying limitations in current TUS benchmarks.
- Empirical evidence showing simple embedding methods achieve competitive performance.
- An investigation of ground truth reliability issues across multiple TUS benchmarks.
- Criteria for developing more realistic and discriminative benchmarks.

2 Related Work

We review existing research on TUS methods and the benchmarks used for their evaluation, with a focus on how underlying assumptions about table unionability have evolved to become increasingly nuanced and complex.

2.1 Methods and Their Assumptions

2.1.a) Foundational Approaches: Following early work on schema matching and structural similarity (Sarma et al., 2012), Nargesian et al. (2018) formalized TUS by assessing attribute unionability via value overlap, ontology mappings, and natural language embeddings. Bogatu et al. (2020) incorporated additional features (e.g., value formats, numerical distributions) and proposed a distinct aggregation method based on weighted feature distances. Efficient implementations of these methods rely on Locality Sensitive Hashing (LSH) indices and techniques like LSH Ensemble (Zhu et al., 2016) for efficient table search.

2.1.b) Incorporating Column Relationships: Beyond considering columns individually, Khatiwada et al. (2023) proposed SANTOS, which evaluates the consistency of inter-column semantic relationships (derived using an existing knowledge base like YAGO (Pellissier Tanon et al., 2020) or by synthesizing one from the data itself) across tables to improve TUS accuracy.

2.1.c) Deep Table Representation Learning: Recent approaches use deep learning for tabular understanding. Pylon (Cong et al., 2023) and Starmie (Fan et al., 2023b) use contrastive learning for contextualized column embeddings. Hu et al. (2023) propose AutoTUS, employing multi-stage self-supervised learning. TabSketchFM (Khatiwada et al., 2025) uses data sketches to preserve semantics while enabling scalability. Graph-based approaches like HEARTS (Boutaleb et al., 2025) leverage HyTrel (Chen et al., 2023), representing tables as hypergraphs to preserve structural properties.

2.2 Benchmarks and their Characteristics

Benchmark creators make design choices at every stage of the construction process that reflect their understanding and assumptions about how and when tables can and should be meaningfully combined. We identify three primary construction paradigms applied for building TUS benchmarks:

2.2.a) Partitioning-based: $\text{TUS}_{\text{Small}}$ and $\text{TUS}_{\text{Large}}$ (Nargesian et al., 2018), as well as the SANTOS benchmark (referring to $\text{SANTOS}_{\text{Small}}$, as $\text{SANTOS}_{\text{Large}}$ is not fully labeled) (Khatiwada et al., 2023) partition seed tables horizontally or vertically, labeling tables from the same original seed as unionable with the seed table. This approach likely introduces significant schema and value overlap, potentially favoring methods that detect surface-level similarity rather than deeper semantic alignment.

2.2.b) Corpus-derived: The PYLON benchmark (Cong et al., 2023) curates tables from GitTables (Hulsebos et al., 2023) on specific topics. While this avoids systematic partitioning overlap, the focus on common topics may result in datasets with a general vocabulary that is well-represented in pre-trained models. This can reduce the comparative advantage of specialized table representation learning and data discovery methods.

2.2.c) LLM-generated: UGEN (Pal et al., 2024) leverages Large Language Models (LLMs) to generate table pairs, aiming to overcome limitations of previous methods by crafting purposefully challenging scenarios, including hard negatives. However, this strategy introduces the risk of ground truth inconsistency, as LLMs may interpret the criteria for unionability differently across generations, affecting label reliability.

2.2.d) Hybrid approaches: LAKEBENCH (Deng et al., 2024) uses tables from OpenData[3] and WebTable corpora[4] alongside both partitioning-based synthetic queries and real queries sampled from the corpus. However, such hybrid approaches can inherit the limitations of their constituent methods: partitioning still risks high overlap, candidate-based labeling may yield incomplete ground truth,

[3] `https://data.gov/`

[4] `https://webdatacommons.org/webtables/`

Benchmark		Overall Statistics					Column Type (%)				Size (MB)
		Files	Rows	Cols	Avg Shape	Missing%	Str	Int	Float	Other	
SANTOS	NQ	500	2,736,673	5,707	5473 × 11	9.96	65.39	17.00	11.46	6.15	*~422*
	Q	50	1,070,085	615	21402 × 12	5.79	73.17	15.93	8.46	2.44	
$\text{TUS}_{\text{Small}}$	NQ	1,401	5,293,327	13,196	3778 × 9	6.77	85.43	5.93	4.77	3.86	*~1162*
	Q	125	577,900	1,610	4623 × 13	6.86	82.05	7.08	5.84	5.03	
$\text{TUS}_{\text{Large}}$	NQ	4,944	8,416,415	53,133	1702 × 11	12.53	90.12	5.10	3.57	1.21	*~1459*
	Q	100	213,229	1,792	2132 × 18	14.87	90.46	3.68	4.13	1.73	
PYLON	NQ	1,622	85,282	16,802	53 × 10	0.00	58.74	25.36	15.90	0.00	*~22*
	Q	124	11,207	880	90 × 7	0.00	75.68	22.95	1.36	0.00	
UGEN_{V1}	NQ	1,000	7,609	10,315	8 × 10	5.79	91.68	3.27	4.29	0.76	*~4*
	Q	50	405	546	8 × 11	5.87	90.48	4.58	4.21	0.73	
UGEN_{V2}	NQ	1,000	18,738	13,360	19 × 13	8.16	82.40	11.71	5.50	0.39	*~8*
	Q	50	5,363	665	107 × 13	4.14	84.96	10.23	2.41	2.41	
LB-OpenData	NQ	4,832	351,067,113	89,757	72655 × 19	3.44	52.50	22.56	22.37	2.57	*~80834*
	Q	3,138	238,576,481	61,815	76028 × 20	2.90	40.60	26.28	27.60	5.53	
LB-Webtable	NQ	29,686	1,039,347	387,432	35 × 13	0.01	61.07	26.28	12.64	0.01	*~170*
	Q	5,488	335,187	56,174	61 × 10	0.00	40.43	43.06	16.51	0.01	

Table 1: Table Union Search Benchmarks Summary. NQ = Non-query table, Q = Query table.

and the large scale of these benchmarks can introduce practical evaluation challenges.

3 Methodology

As TUS methods become increasingly sophisticated, the benchmarks used for their evaluation may contain inherent characteristics that hinder the accurate assessment of progress in semantic understanding. This section outlines our approach to examining prominent TUS benchmarks through analysis of their construction methods and strategic use of simple baselines as diagnostic tools. The goal of advanced TUS methods is to capture deep semantic compatibility between tables, beyond simple lexical or structural similarity. Our investigation first analyzes the various benchmark construction processes to identify potential structural weaknesses, then employs computationally inexpensive baseline methods to reveal how these characteristics enable alternative pathways to high performance, thereby influencing evaluation outcomes.

3.1 Analyzing Benchmark Construction

We examine five prominent families of TUS benchmarks and formulate hypotheses about their potential limitations based on their construction methodologies (Table 1). We identify three issues stemming from these methodologies: **(1) excessive overlap**, **(2) semantic simplicity**, and **(3) ground truth inconsistencies**, which we detail below:

3.1.a) Excessive Overlap: Benchmarks like $\text{TUS}_{\text{Small}}$, $\text{TUS}_{\text{Large}}$, SANTOS, and the *synthetic* query portion of the LAKEBENCH derivatives are created by partitioning seed tables horizontally and vertically, with tables derived from the same original seed designated as unionable pairs. We hypothesize that this methodology inherently leads to significant overlap in both schema (column names) and content (data values) between query tables and their ground truth unionable candidates.

To quantify this, we measure overlap using the Szymkiewicz–Simpson coefficient for exact column names ($Overlap_c$, Eq. 1) and for values of a given data type d ($Overlap_v$, Eq. 2) between ground truth pairs.

$$Overlap_c(Q, C) = \frac{|Cols_Q \cap Cols_C|}{\min(|Cols_Q|, |Cols_C|)} \quad (1)$$

$$Overlap_v(Q, C) = \frac{|V_Q^d \cap V_C^d|}{\min(|V_Q^d|, |V_C^d|)} \quad (2)$$

where $Cols_Q$ and $Cols_C$ denote the sets of column names in the query table Q and candidate table C respectively, and V_Q^d, V_C^d represent the sets of unique values of data type d in each table. The coefficient equals 1.0 when one set is fully contained within the other. Figure 1 shows the distribution of overlap coefficients, with values $\geq$ 50% indicating substantial overlap. As expected, partitioning-based benchmarks exhibit high overlap: over 90% of ground truth pairs share $\geq$ 50% of exact column names. For value overlap, we focus on string data types, which dominate the benchmarks (Table 1). Here too, 45–60% of query-candidate pairs share $\geq$ 50% of string tokens. LAKEBENCH derivatives (LB-OPENDATA, LB-WEBTABLE) show similar trends. Appendix A provides a detailed breakdown by data type. This high surface similarity favors simple lexical methods

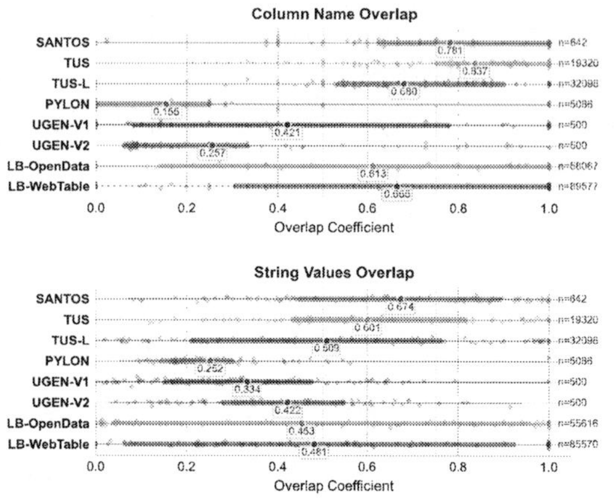

Figure 1: Distribution of Exact Column Name Overlap (Top) and String Value Overlap (Bottom) Coefficients for Ground Truth Unionable Pairs Across Benchmarks. Colored circles represent mean values; numbers on the right indicate total pairwise relationships considered.

and also influences advanced models by introducing repeated patterns in serialized inputs (Starmie), data sketches (TabSketchFM), and graph structures (HEARTS). Though designed for deeper semantics, these models are affected by strong benchmark-induced surface signals, making it hard to attribute performance gains purely to nuanced reasoning.

3.1.b) Semantic Simplicity: Benchmarks derived directly from large corpora, such as PYLON (Cong et al., 2023) using GitTables (Hulsebos et al., 2023) or the *real* query portions of LAKEBENCH derivatives using diverse public datasets, avoid the systematic overlap introduced by partitioning. However, we hypothesize that this construction method introduces other limitations since (1) it often focuses on relatively common topics with simpler semantics, reducing the need for specialized domain knowledge, and (2) it generally draws from public data sources likely included in the pre-training corpora of large foundation models. Evidence from specific benchmarks supports this concern. PYLON's construction indeed avoids high overlap (Figure 1 shows lower overlap than partitioning-based benchmarks). For LAKEBENCH, while the distinction between *real* and *synthetic* queries was unavailable during our analysis[5], the significant overall observed overlap suggests that synthetic, partitioning-based queries constitute a large portion of the benchmark. The semantic simplicity evident in PYLON's topics and the public origins of data in both PYLON and LAKEBENCH could favor general-purpose models like BERT (Devlin et al., 2019) or SBERT (Reimers and Gurevych, 2019), which have with a high, however unverifiable, probability encountered similar content during pre-training. Consequently, the semantic challenge presented by these benchmarks might be relatively low for models with strong general language understanding – a contrast to documented LLM struggles with non-public, enterprise-specific data characteristics (Bodensohn et al., 2025), potentially allowing off-the-shelf embedding models to achieve high performance without fine-tuning.

3.1.c) Noisy Ground Truths: Ensuring accurate and complete ground truth labels is challenging, especially with automated generation or large-scale human labeling efforts as used in LLM-generated benchmarks (UGEN) and large human-labeled ones (LAKEBENCH derivatives). We hypothesize that ground truth in these benchmarks may suffer from reliability issues, including incorrect labels (false positives/negatives) or incompleteness (missed true positives). For UGEN, generating consistent, accurate positive and negative pairs (especially hard negatives) is difficult. LLMs might interpret unionability rules inconsistently across generations, leading to noisy labels. For large-scale human labeling with LB-OPENDATA and LB-WEBTABLE, the process introduces two risks: *incompleteness*, if the initial retrieval misses true unionable tables; and *incorrectness*, if human judgments vary or contain errors despite validation efforts. Evaluating performance on UGEN and LAKEBENCH derivatives thus requires caution. Scores are affected by label noise or incompleteness; low scores reflect ground truth issues and are therefore not solely attributable to benchmark difficulty, while the maximum achievable recall is capped by unlabeled true positives.

3.2 Baseline Methods for Benchmark Analysis

Based on the hypothesized benchmark issues identified above, we select some simple baseline methods to test benchmark sensitivity to different information types. While the (1) overlap and (2) general semantics limitations can be directly examined through baseline performance, (3) the ground truth integrity issue requires separate validation of labels, which we address in Section 5.2. Detailed implementation choices for all baseline methods are in Appendix B.1.

[5] https://github.com/RLGen/LakeBench/issues/9

3.2.a) Bag-of-Words Vectorizers: To test whether the *Excessive Overlap* enables methods sensitive to token frequency to perform well on partitioning-based benchmarks, we employ standard lexical vectorizers (`HashingVectorizer`, `TfidfVectorizer`, and `CountVectorizer`) from scikit-learn[6]. These generate column embeddings based on sampled string values, with a single table vector obtained via *max pooling* across column vectors. These baselines test whether high performance can be achieved primarily by exploiting surface signals without semantic reasoning.

3.2.b) Pre-trained Sentence Transformers: To examine whether the *Semantic Simplicity* allows benchmarks from broad corpora to be effectively processed by pre-trained language models, we use a Sentence-BERT model (`all-mpnet-base-v2`[7]) with three column-to-text serializations: (1) SBERT (V+C): input includes column name and sampled values; (2) SBERT (C): input is only the column name; and (3) SBERT (V): input is only concatenated sampled values. Column embeddings are aggregated using mean pooling to produce a single table vector. These baselines assess whether general semantic embeddings, without task-specific fine-tuning, suffice for high performance on benchmarks with general vocabulary.

4 Experimental Setup

To evaluate our hypotheses about benchmark limitations, we employ both simple baseline methods (Section 3.2) and advanced SOTA methods in a controlled experimental framework. This section details the benchmark datasets used, any necessary preprocessing, the comparative methods, and our standardized evaluation approach.

4.1 Benchmarks

Our analysis uses the benchmarks described in Section 2.2, with post-preprocessing statistics summarized in Table 1. Most benchmarks were used as-is, but the large-scale LAKEBENCH derivatives (LB-OPENDATA and LB-WEBTABLE) required additional preprocessing for feasibility and reproducibility. The original datasets were too large to process directly and included practical issues, such as missing files, as well as characteristics that complicated evaluation, such as many unreferenced tables. We removed ground truth entries pointing to missing files (58 in LB-WEBTABLE), and excluded unreferenced tables from the retrieval corpus (removing ~5,300 and >2.7M files from LB-OPENDATA and LB-WEBTABLE, respectively). This latter step was done purely for computational feasibility; as a side effect, it simplifies the benchmark by eliminating tables that would otherwise be false positives if retrieved. We also ensured that each query table was listed as a candidate for itself. These steps substantially reduced corpus size while preserving evaluation integrity. The LAKEBENCH variants considered in our study are those available as of May 20, 2025[8]. Future updates to the original repository may modify dataset contents, which yield different evaluation results.

Additionally, for LB-OPENDATA, we created a smaller variant with tables truncated to 1,000 rows, which we use in experiments alongside the original version (Table 2). For $\text{TUS}_{\text{Small}}$ and $\text{TUS}_{\text{Large}}$, we followed prior work (Fan et al., 2023b; Hu et al., 2023), sampling 125 and 100 queries, respectively. For the other benchmarks, all queries were used.

4.2 Comparative Methods

To evaluate our baseline methods (Section 3.2), we compare them against key TUS models previously discussed in Section 2.1, focusing on SOTA methods. For each method, we optimize implementation using publicly available code for fairness:

- **Starmie** (Fan et al., 2023b): We retrained the RoBERTa-based model for 10 epochs on each benchmark using recommended hyperparameters and their "Pruning" bipartite matching search strategy for generating rankings, which achieves optimal results according to the original paper.
- **HEARTS** (Boutaleb et al., 2025): We utilized pre-trained HyTrel embeddings (Chen et al., 2023) with a contrastively-trained checkpoint. For each benchmark, we adopted the best-performing search strategy from the HEARTS repository: Cluster Search for SANTOS, PYLON, and UGEN benchmarks, and ANN index search with max pooling for the TUS and LAKEBENCH benchmarks.
- **TabSketchFM** (Khatiwada et al., 2025): Results for the $\text{TUS}_{\text{Small}}$ and SANTOS were reported directly from the original paper, as the pretrained checkpoint was unavailable at the time of our experiments.

[6]Scikit-Learn Vectorizers Documentation
[7]all-mpnet-base-v2 on Hugging Face
[8]LakeBench commit df7559d used in our study

These methods represent significant advancements in table representation learning. AutoTUS (Hu et al., 2023) wasn't included due to code unavailability at the time of writing. We provide further implementation details in Appendix B.2.

4.3 Evaluation Procedure

We use a consistent evaluation procedure for all baseline and SOTA methods to ensure fair comparison. Table vectors are generated per method (Section 3.2 for baselines; SOTA-specific procedures otherwise) and L2-normalized for similarity via inner product. For similarity search, baseline methods use the FAISS library (Douze et al., 2024) with an exact inner product index (`IndexFlatIP`); each query ranks all candidate tables by similarity. SOTA methods use FAISS or alternative search strategies (Appendix B.2). Following prior work (Fan et al., 2023b; Hu et al., 2023), we report Precision@k (P@k) and Recall@k (R@k), averaged across queries. Values of k follow prior works and are shown in results tables (e.g., Table 2). We also evaluate computational efficiency via offline (training, vector extraction, indexing) and online (query search) runtimes, with hardware details in Appendix B.3.

5 Results and Discussion

Our empirical evaluation revealed significant patterns across benchmarks that expose fundamental limitations in their ability to measure progress in semantic understanding. Tables 2 and 3 present effectiveness and efficiency metrics respectively.

5.1 Evidence of Benchmark Limitations

The most compelling evidence for our benchmark limitation hypotheses emerges from the unexpectedly strong performance of simple baselines. On partitioning-based benchmarks ($\text{TUS}_{\text{Small}}$, $\text{TUS}_{\text{Large}}$, SANTOS), lexical methods achieve near-perfect precision, matching or exceeding sophisticated models at a fraction of the cost. This directly validates our overlap issue hypothesis: the high schema and value overlap (Figure 1) creates trivial signals that simple lexical matching can exploit. While advanced methods like Starmie or HEARTS also achieve high scores here, the fact that much simpler, non-semantic methods perform nearly identically leads us to conclude that the benchmark itself does not effectively differentiate methods based on deep semantic understanding. This phenomenon, where simpler approaches can achieve comparable or even better results than more complex counterparts, especially when computational costs are considered, has also been observed in related data lake tasks such as table augmentation via join search (Cappuzzo et al., 2024).

For PYLON, a different pattern emerges: lexical methods perform considerably worse due to the much lower exact overlap, but general-purpose semantic embeddings excel. SBERT variants, particularly SBERT(V+C) combining column and value information, outperform specialized SOTA models like Starmie. This confirms our general semantics hypothesis that these benchmarks employ vocabulary well-represented in standard pre-trained embeddings, diminishing the advantage of specialized tabular architectures for the TUS task.

LB-OPENDATA and LB-WEBTABLE exhibit both limitations despite their scale. Simple lexical methods remain surprisingly competitive, while SBERT variants consistently outperform specialized models. The computational demands of sophisticated models create additional practical barriers: Starmie requires substantial offline costs (training and inference) plus over 16 hours to process the queries on the truncated LB-OPENDATA, and over 21 hours to evaluate the queries of LB-WEBTABLE. HEARTS performs better computationally by leveraging a pre-trained checkpoint without additional training, resulting in a shorter offline processing time, but still under-performs SBERT variants.

5.2 Ground Truth Reliability Issues

A notable observation across UGEN and LAKEBENCH derivatives is the significant gap between the R@k achieved by all methods and the IDEAL recall (Table 2). This discrepancy led us to question the reliability of the benchmarks' ground truth labels. We hypothesized that such gaps might indicate not only the limitations of the search methods or the inherent difficulty of the benchmarks but also potential incompleteness or inaccuracies within the ground truth itself. Examining discrepancies at small values of k is particularly revealing, as this scrutinizes the highest-confidence predictions of a system. If a high-performing method frequently disagrees with the ground truth at these top ranks, it may signal issues with the ground truth labels.

To investigate this, we defined two heuristic metrics designed to help identify potential ground truth flaws. Let $\mathcal{Q} = \{Q_1, \ldots, Q_N\}$ be N query tables. For $Q_i \in \mathcal{Q}$, $C_{Q_i,k}$ is the set of top-k candidates

Method	SANTOS		TUS		TUS_{Large}		PYLON		$UGEN_{V1}$		$UGEN_{V2}$		LB-OPENDATA$_{1k}$		LB-OPENDATA		LB-WebTable	
	P@10	R@10	P@60	R@60	P@60	R@60	P@10	R@10	P@10	R@10	P@10	R@10	P@50	R@50	P@50	R@50	P@20	R@20
IDEAL	1.00	0.75	1.00	0.34	1.00	0.23	1.00	0.24	1.00	1.00	1.00	1.00	0.39	1.00	0.39	1.00	0.81	0.95
Non-specialized Embedding Methods																		
HASH	0.98	0.74	0.99	0.33	**0.99**	**0.23**	0.64	0.15	0.59	0.59	0.43	0.43	0.21	0.60	0.21	0.60	0.21	0.25
TFIDF	**0.99**	**0.74**	**1.00**	**0.34**	**0.99**	**0.23**	0.70	0.17	0.58	0.58	0.50	0.50	0.21	0.61	0.21	0.61	0.23	0.27
COUNT	**0.99**	**0.74**	**1.00**	**0.34**	**0.99**	**0.23**	0.68	0.17	0.58	0.58	0.50	0.50	0.21	0.60	0.21	0.60	0.23	0.27
SBERT (V+C)	0.98	0.74	**1.00**	**0.34**	**0.99**	**0.23**	**0.91**	**0.22**	**0.61**	**0.61**	**0.68**	**0.68**	**0.23**	**0.66**	**0.23**	**0.66**	**0.26**	**0.31**
SBERT (V)	0.94	0.71	**1.00**	**0.34**	**0.99**	**0.23**	0.84	0.20	0.58	0.58	0.58	0.58	0.22	0.62	0.22	0.62	0.25	0.29
SBERT (C)	0.98	0.74	**1.00**	**0.34**	0.98	0.23	0.85	0.21	0.60	0.60	0.65	0.65	0.22	0.64	0.22	0.64	0.16	0.20
Specialized Table Union Search Methods																		
Starmie	0.98	0.73	0.96	0.31	0.93	0.21	0.81	0.20	0.57	0.57	0.58	0.58	0.18	0.51	‡	‡	0.25	0.30
HEARTS	0.98	0.74	**1.00**	**0.34**	**0.99**	**0.23**	0.65	0.16	0.56	0.56	0.37	0.37	0.19	0.61	0.19	0.60	0.23	0.28
TabSketchFM	0.92	0.69	0.97	0.32	*	*	*	*	*	*	*	*	*	*	*	*	*	*

Table 2: Precision and Recall across benchmarks. Highest values in **bold**, second highest underlined. IDEAL represents the maximum possible P@k and R@k achievable for each benchmark at the specified k. $*$: Results unavailable as checkpoint was not publicly accessible. ‡ : Not reported due to excessive computational requirements.

Method	SANTOS		TUS		TUS_{Large}		PYLON		$UGEN_{V1}$		$UGEN_{V2}$		LB-OPENDATA$_{1K}$		LB-OPENDATA		LB-WebTable	
	Offline	Online	Offline	Online	Offline	Online	Offline	Online	Offline	Online	Offline	Online	Offline	Online	Offline	Online	Offline	Online
Non-specialized Embedding Methods																		
HASH	0m 15s	0m 0s	0m 43s	0m 1s	1m 45s	0m 2s	0m 19s	0m 1s	0m 12s	0m 0s	0m 14s	0m 0s	7m 56s	0m 31s	12m 4s	0m 22s	6m 3s	0m 21s
TFIDF/COUNT	0m 53s	0m 0s	1m 45s	0m 1s	3m 10s	0m 2s	0m 22s	0m 1s	0m 9s	0m 0s	0m 12s	0m 0s	22m 22s	0m 31s	37m 14s	0m 21s	6m 21s	0m 22s
SBERT	1m 45s	0m 0s	3m 30s	0m 0s	9m 21s	0m 15s	3m 18s	0m 0s	1m 41s	0m 0s	2m 20s	0m 0s	27m 47s	0m 4s	82m 13s	0m 4s	30m 45s	0m 3s
Specialized Table Union Search Methods																		
STARMIE	19m 3s	1m 2s	4m 24s	8m 59s	14m 43s	20m 29s	7m 56s	3m 27s	2m 8s	1m 0s	2m 45s	1m 45s	131m 48s	1220m 53s	–	–	48m 11s	1311m 43s
HEARTS	0m 21s	0m 34s	1m 1s	0m 0s	3m 10s	0m 0s	0m 57s	0m 36s	0m 23s	0m 40s	0m 30s	0m 35s	21m 33s	0m 3s	76m 12s	0m 5s	29m 28s	0m 3s

Table 3: Computational efficiency across benchmarks. Times are averaged over 5 runs due to runtime variability. Offline includes vector generation, indexing, and training times where applicable; Online is total query search time.

retrieved by a search method for Q_i, and G_{Q_i} is the set of ground truth candidates labeled unionable with Q_i.

1. **GTFP@k (Ground Truth False Positive Rate)**: This measures the fraction of top-k candidates retrieved by a search method that are not labeled as unionable in the original ground truth. A high GTFP@k, especially at small k, suggests the method might be identifying valid unionable tables missing from the ground truth, thereby helping us pinpoint its possible *incompleteness*. It is calculated as:

$$\frac{\sum_{i=1}^{N} |C_{Q_i,k} \setminus G_{Q_i}|}{N \cdot k}$$

Here, $|C_{Q_i,k} \setminus G_{Q_i}|$ counts retrieved candidates for Q_i that are absent from its ground truth set G_{Q_i}. The denominator is the total top-k slots considered across all queries.

2. **GTFN@k (Ground Truth False Negative Rate)**: This quantifies the fraction of items labeled as positives in the ground truth that a well-performing search method fails to retrieve within its top-k results (considering a capped expectation up to k items per query). It is calculated as:

$$\frac{\sum_{i=1}^{N}(\min(k, |G_{Q_i}|) - |G_{Q_i} \cap C_{Q_i,k}|)}{\sum_{i=1}^{N} \min(k, |G_{Q_i}|)}$$

The term $\min(k, |G_{Q_i}|)$ represents the capped ideal number of ground truth items we would expect to find in the top k for Q_i. The numerator sums the "misses" for each query: the difference between this capped ideal and the number of ground truth items actually retrieved. The denominator sums this capped ideal across all queries. A high GTFN@k at small k is particularly insightful when investigating ground truth integrity. If we trust the method's ability to discern relevance, a high GTFN@k implies that the method correctly deprioritizes items that, despite being in the ground truth, might be less relevant or even incorrectly labeled as positive. Thus, it can signal potential *incorrectness* within the ground truth. GTFN@k is equivalent to "1 − CappedRecall@k" (Thakur et al., 2021).

These metrics assume discrepancies between a strong search method and the ground truth may indicate flaws in the latter. While not highly accurate, they helped us identify a smaller, focused subset of query-candidate pairs with disagreements for deeper manual or LLM-based inspection. Results are shown in Table 4.

Beyond heuristic metrics, we also conduct a more direct–though still imperfect–assessment of UGEN's ground truth using an LLM-as-a-judge approach. While this method may not capture the same conflicts identified by the cheaper GTFP/GTFN heuristics, it provides a complementary perspective that can offer more precise insights in certain cases. We use `gemini-2.0-flash-thinking-exp-01-21`[9], chosen for its 1M-token context window, baked-in reasoning abilities, and low hallucination rate[10]. This LLM-as-a-judge approach has become increasingly common in recent works (Gu et al., 2024; Wolff and Hulsebos, 2025). We gave the LLM both tables in each query-candidate pair, along with a detailed prompt including curated unionable and non-unionable examples from UGEN (see Appendix D) to condition the LLM's understanding of unionability based on the benchmark. Each pair was evaluated in 5 independent runs with `temperature=0.1`. A sample of 20 LLM outputs was manually validated and showed strong alignment with human judgment. Comparison with original UGEN labels (Table 5) revealed substantial inconsistencies. Our manual inspection (Appendix C.1) suggested the LLM often provided more accurate assessments, indicating notable noise in the original ground truth.

Given the scale of LB-OPENDATA and LB-WEBTABLE, full LLM adjudication was impractical. Instead, we used SBERT(V+C) as our reference search method to compute GTFP@k, focusing on top-ranked pairs not labeled as unionable in the ground truth. As shown in Table 4, such cases were frequent even at top ranks ($2 < k < 5$). To assess ground truth completeness, we manually inspected 20 randomly sampled top-2 and top-3 disagreements. Of these, 19 were genuinely unionable but missing from the ground truth; the remaining pair was correctly non-unionable, with SBERT likely misled by its numeric-only columns. These results suggest non-negligible *incompleteness* in the LAKEBENCH ground truth. Example cases are shown in Appendix C.2.

In summary, our investigations, combining heuristic metrics, LLM-based adjudication, and manual inspection, reveal the presence of non-negligible noise and incompleteness within the original benchmark labels for both UGEN and LAKEBENCH. Consequently, performance metrics reported on these benchmarks may be influenced by these underlying ground truth issues, potentially misrepresenting true task difficulty or method capabilities.

5.3 Implications for Measuring Progress

Our experiments reveal several critical issues. Benchmark scores often fail to measure true semantic capabilities, as simple lexical or general embedding methods can match or outperform specialized models by exploiting excessive domain overlap, semantic simplicity, or ground truth inconsistency. This suggests that current benchmarks may inadvertently reward adaptation to these characteristics, making it difficult to quantify the practical benefits of progress on sophisticated TUS methods capabilities within these settings. These persistent issues also point to a fundamental challenge, the lack of a precise, operational definition for unionability, mirroring broader difficulties in dataset search (Hulsebos et al., 2024) and highlighting the need to address the subjective, context-dependent nature of table compatibility in practice.

Benchmark (Metric)	@1	@2	@3	@4	@5
UGEN_{V1} (GTFP)	0.160	0.210	0.247	0.275	0.308
UGEN_{V1} (GTFN)	0.160	0.210	0.247	0.275	0.308
UGEN_{V2} (GTFP)	0.060	0.080	0.093	0.140	0.156
UGEN_{V2} (GTFN)	0.060	0.080	0.093	0.140	0.156
LB-OPENDATA (GTFP)	0.000	0.059	0.092	0.123	0.154
LB-OPENDATA (GTFN)	0.000	0.054	0.080	0.105	0.132
LB-WEBTABLE (GTFP)	0.000	0.110	0.198	0.296	0.377
LB-WEBTABLE (GTFN)	0.000	0.110	0.197	0.295	0.376

Table 4: Disagreement rates of top-k retrieved results between SBERT and the ground truth across different benchmarks. For UGEN, the query table is not considered a candidate to itself, so values at @1 reflect actual disagreement. For LAKEBENCH variants, the ground truth is normalized to include the query table as a valid candidate for itself. Therefore, the top-1 match is always correct by construction, yielding no disagreement @1.

GT Label	LLM Judge	UGEN V1	UGEN V2
Unionable	Non-unionable	24.8%	0.0%
Non-unionable	Unionable	33.8%	23.6%
Non-unionable	Non-unionable	16.2%	76.4%
Unionable	Non-unionable	25.2%	0.0%

Table 5: Breakdown of agreement and disagreement between ground truth labels and LLM-based judgments.

6 Towards Better TUS Benchmarks

In industry practice, unionability judgments are inherently subjective, depending on analytical goals, domain contexts, data accessibility constraints (Martorana et al., 2025), and user preferences (Mirzaei and Rafiei, 2023). Yet current benchmarks impose fixed definitions, creating a disconnect with practical utility: methods excelling on benchmarks often falter in real-world scenarios demanding different compatibility thresholds. Addressing this requires benchmark designs that embrace contextual variability and provide a stable foundation for

[9] Gemini 2.0 Flash Thinking Model Card

[10] Vectara Hallucination Leaderboard

evaluation, lest even advanced methods fall short in practice.

Rethinking Benchmark Design Principles: Overcoming current benchmark limitations requires a shift in design focusing on three key principles: (1) actively reducing artifactual overlap while introducing controlled semantic heterogeneity to better reflect real-world schema and value divergence; (2) incorporating realistic domain complexity beyond general vocabularies, addressing challenges like non-descriptive schemas and proprietary terms where LLMs struggle (Bodensohn et al., 2025), thus emphasizing domain-specific training that may require industry collaboration; and (3) rethinking ground truth representation by replacing brittle binary labels with richer, nuanced formats validated through multi-stage adjudication to improve completeness and consistency.

Exploring Implementation Pathways: Translating these principles into practice requires concrete strategies for benchmark design and evaluation. One approach is to develop (1) scenario-driven micro-benchmarks targeting specific challenges such as schema drift simulation or value representation noise, enabling more granular analysis than coarse end-to-end metrics. Another is (2) advancing controllable synthetic data generation, following LLM-based methods like UGEN (Pal et al., 2024), to verifiably embed semantic constraints or domain knowledge, supporting diverse testbeds when real data is unavailable or sensitive. Equally important is (3) exploring adaptive, interactive evaluation frameworks such as human-in-the-loop systems, which would dynamically adjust relevance criteria based on user feedback to better capture the subjective nature of unionability. Tools like LakeVisage (Hu et al., 2025) further enhance usability and trust by recommending visualizations that help users interpret relationships among returned tables, improving transparency and interpretability in union search systems.Incorporating natural language preferences is also key. The recent NLCTABLES benchmark (Cui et al., 2025) advances this by introducing NL conditions for union and join searches on column values and table size constraints. However, its predicate-style conditions may be better addressed via post-retrieval filtering (e.g., translating NL to SQL predicates with an LLM), avoiding early discard of unionable candidates and unnecessary retrieval model complexity. To drive further advancement, benchmarks should incorporate (4) natural language conditions that capture key aspects of unionability and joinability, including specifications about the characteristics of the final integrated table or conditional integration logic. For example, a challenging predicate might require identifying tables that can be "joined with a query table on column A, unioned on columns B and C, and also contain an additional column D providing specific contextual information about a particular attribute." Such conditions would demand deeper reasoning capabilities from data integration systems and encourage the development of more sophisticated methods for Table Union and Join Search. Finally, moving beyond binary success metrics, future benchmarks could adopt (5) multi-faceted evaluation frameworks using richer ground truth representations to assess unionability across dimensions like schema compatibility, semantic type alignment, value distribution similarity, and task-specific relevance, offering a more holistic evaluation than current standards.

7 Conclusion

Our analysis of TUS benchmarks highlights three major limitations: excessive overlap in partitioning-based datasets, semantics easily captured by pre-trained embeddings, and non-negligible ground-truth inconsistencies. The first two allow simple baselines to rival sophisticated models with far lower computational cost, showing that high performance isn't necessarily tied to advanced semantic reasoning. The third undermines evaluation validity, as scores may reflect misalignment with flawed ground truth rather than actual benchmark difficulty. This gap between benchmark performance and true semantic capability suggests current evaluations often reward adaptation to benchmark-specific artifacts. To address this, we propose design principles that better reflect the complex, subjective nature of real-world table union search.

Limitations: Our study examined selected benchmarks and methods, with broader evaluation potentially revealing more insight. Our investigation of ground truth issues in UGEN and LAKEBENCH, while systematic, identifies certain patterns without exhaustive quantification.

Future Work: Developing benchmarks aligned with our proposed criteria represents the next step towards ensuring that measured progress translates to meaningful real-world utility.

References

Jan-Micha Bodensohn, Ulf Brackmann, Liane Vogel, Anupam Sanghi, and Carsten Binnig. 2025. Unveiling challenges for llms in enterprise data engineering. *Preprint*, arXiv:2504.10950.

Alex Bogatu, Alvaro A. A. Fernandes, Norman W. Paton, and Nikolaos Konstantinou. 2020. D3L: Dataset Discovery in Data Lakes. In *2020 IEEE 36th International Conference on Data Engineering (ICDE)*, pages 709–720. ArXiv:2011.10427 [cs].

Allaa Boutaleb, Alaa Almutawa, Bernd Amann, Rafael Angarita, and Hubert Naacke. 2025. HEARTS: Hypergraph-based related table search. In *ELLIS workshop on Representation Learning and Generative Models for Structured Data.*

Riccardo Cappuzzo, Gaël Varoquaux, Aimee Coelho, and Paolo Papotti. 2024. Retrieve, merge, predict: Augmenting tables with data lakes. *CoRR*, abs/2402.06282.

Sonia Castelo, Rémi Rampin, Aécio Santos, Aline Bessa, Fernando Chirigati, and Juliana Freire. 2021. Auctus: a dataset search engine for data discovery and augmentation. *Proceedings of the VLDB Endowment*, 14(12):2791–2794.

Pei Chen, Soumajyoti Sarkar, Leonard Lausen, Balasubramaniam Srinivasan, Sheng Zha, Ruihong Huang, and George Karypis. 2023. Hytrel: Hypergraph-enhanced tabular data representation learning. *Advances in Neural Information Processing Systems*, 36:32173–32193.

Tianji Cong, Fatemeh Nargesian, and H. V. Jagadish. 2023. Pylon: Semantic table union search in data lakes. *CoRR*, abs/2301.04901.

Lingxi Cui, Huan Li, Ke Chen, Lidan Shou, and Gang Chen. 2025. Nlctables: A dataset for marrying natural language conditions with table discovery. *CoRR*, abs/2504.15849.

Yuhao Deng, Chengliang Chai, Lei Cao, Qin Yuan, Siyuan Chen, Yanrui Yu, Zhaoze Sun, Junyi Wang, Jiajun Li, Ziqi Cao, Kaisen Jin, Chi Zhang, Yuqing Jiang, Yuanfang Zhang, Yuping Wang, Ye Yuan, Guoren Wang, and Nan Tang. 2024. LakeBench: A Benchmark for Discovering Joinable and Unionable Tables in Data Lakes. *Proceedings of the VLDB Endowment*, 17(8):1925–1938.

Jacob Devlin, Ming-Wei Chang, Kenton Lee, and Kristina Toutanova. 2019. BERT: Pre-training of deep bidirectional transformers for language understanding. In *Proceedings of the 2019 Conference of the North American Chapter of the Association for Computational Linguistics: Human Language Technologies, Volume 1 (Long and Short Papers)*, pages 4171–4186, Minneapolis, Minnesota. Association for Computational Linguistics.

Matthijs Douze, Alexandr Guzhva, Chengqi Deng, Jeff Johnson, Gergely Szilvasy, Pierre-Emmanuel Mazaré, Maria Lomeli, Lucas Hosseini, and Hervé Jégou. 2024. The faiss library.

Grace Fan, Jin Wang, Yuliang Li, and Renée J. Miller. 2023a. Table Discovery in Data Lakes: State-of-the-art and Future Directions. In *Companion of the 2023 International Conference on Management of Data*, pages 69–75, Seattle WA USA. ACM.

Grace Fan, Jin Wang, Yuliang Li, Dan Zhang, and Renée J. Miller. 2023b. Semantics-aware dataset discovery from data lakes with contextualized column-based representation learning. *Proc. VLDB Endow.*, 16(7):1726–1739.

Daniel Gomm and Madelon Hulsebos. 2025. Metadata matters in dense table retrieval. In *ELLIS workshop on Representation Learning and Generative Models for Structured Data.*

Jiawei Gu, Xuhui Jiang, Zhichao Shi, Hexiang Tan, Xuehao Zhai, Chengjin Xu, Wei Li, Yinghan Shen, Shengjie Ma, Honghao Liu, Yuanzhuo Wang, and Jian Guo. 2024. A survey on llm-as-a-judge. *CoRR*, abs/2411.15594.

Xuming Hu, Shen Wang, Xiao Qin, Chuan Lei, Zhengyuan Shen, Christos Faloutsos, Asterios Katsifodimos, George Karypis, Lijie Wen, and Philip S. Yu. 2023. AUTOTUS: Automatic Table Union Search with Tabular Representation Learning. In *Findings of the Association for Computational Linguistics: ACL 2023*, pages 3786–3800, Toronto, Canada. Association for Computational Linguistics.

Yihao Hu, Jin Wang, and Sajjadur Rahman. 2025. Lakevisage: Towards scalable, flexible and interactive visualization recommendation for data discovery over data lakes. *CoRR*, abs/2504.02150.

Madelon Hulsebos, Çagatay Demiralp, and Paul Groth. 2023. Gittables: A large-scale corpus of relational tables. *Proc. ACM Manag. Data*, 1(1):30:1–30:17.

Madelon Hulsebos, Wenjing Lin, Shreya Shankar, and Aditya Parameswaran. 2024. It Took Longer than I was Expecting: Why is Dataset Search Still so Hard? In *Proceedings of the 2024 Workshop on Human-In-the-Loop Data Analytics*, pages 1–4, Santiago AA Chile. ACM.

Aamod Khatiwada, Grace Fan, Roee Shraga, Zixuan Chen, Wolfgang Gatterbauer, Renée J. Miller, and Mirek Riedewald. 2023. SANTOS: Relationship-based Semantic Table Union Search. *Proceedings of the ACM on Management of Data*, 1(1):1–25.

Aamod Khatiwada, Harsha Kokel, Ibrahim Abdelaziz, Subhajit Chaudhury, Julian Dolby, Oktie Hassanzadeh, Zhenhan Huang, Tejaswini Pedapati, Horst Samulowitz, and Kavitha Srinivas. 2025. Tabsketchfm: Sketch-based tabular representation learning for data discovery over data lakes. *IEEE ICDE.*

Margherita Martorana, Tobias Kuhn, and Jacco van Ossenbruggen. 2025. Metadata-driven table union search: Leveraging semantics for restricted access data integration. *CoRR*, abs/2502.20945.

Leland McInnes, John Healy, Steve Astels, and 1 others. 2017. hdbscan: Hierarchical density based clustering. *J. Open Source Softw.*, 2(11):205.

Leland McInnes, John Healy, Nathaniel Saul, and Lukas Großberger. 2018. UMAP: uniform manifold approximation and projection. *J. Open Source Softw.*, 3(29):861.

Hamed Mirzaei and Davood Rafiei. 2023. Table union search with preferences. In *Joint Proceedings of Workshops at the 49th International Conference on Very Large Data Bases (VLDB 2023), Vancouver, Canada, August 28 - September 1, 2023*, volume 3462 of *CEUR Workshop Proceedings*. CEUR-WS.org.

Fatemeh Nargesian, Erkang Zhu, Ken Q. Pu, and Renée J. Miller. 2018. TUS: Table union search on open data. *Proceedings of the VLDB Endowment*, 11(7):813–825.

Koyena Pal, Aamod Khatiwada, Roee Shraga, and Renée J Miller. 2024. Alt-gen: Benchmarking table union search using large language models. *Proceedings of the VLDB Endowment. ISSN*, 2150:8097.

Thomas Pellissier Tanon, Gerhard Weikum, and Fabian Suchanek. 2020. Yago 4: A reason-able knowledge base. In *The Semantic Web*, pages 583–596, Cham. Springer International Publishing.

Nils Reimers and Iryna Gurevych. 2019. Sentence-BERT: Sentence embeddings using Siamese BERT-networks. In *Proceedings of the 2019 Conference on Empirical Methods in Natural Language Processing and the 9th International Joint Conference on Natural Language Processing (EMNLP-IJCNLP)*, pages 3982–3992, Hong Kong, China. Association for Computational Linguistics.

Anish Das Sarma, Lujun Fang, Nitin Gupta, Alon Y Halevy, Hongrae Lee, Fei Wu, Reynold Xin, and Cong Yu. 2012. Finding related tables. In *SIGMOD Conference*, volume 10, pages 2213836–2213962.

Nandan Thakur, Nils Reimers, Andreas Rücklé, Abhishek Srivastava, and Iryna Gurevych. 2021. BEIR: A heterogeneous benchmark for zero-shot evaluation of information retrieval models. In *Thirty-fifth Conference on Neural Information Processing Systems Datasets and Benchmarks Track (Round 2)*.

Cornelius Wolff and Madelon Hulsebos. 2025. How well do llms reason over tabular data, really? *arXiv preprint arXiv:2505.07453*.

Erkang Zhu, Fatemeh Nargesian, Ken Q. Pu, and Renée J. Miller. 2016. LSH ensemble: Internet-scale domain search. *Proc. VLDB Endow.*, 9(12):1185–1196.

A Benchmark Overlap

As discussed in section 3.1.a), the degree of lexical overlap (both in column names and values) between query and candidate tables in benchmark ground truths can significantly influence model performance. Methods sensitive to surface-level similarity might perform well on benchmarks with high overlap without necessarily capturing deeper semantic relationships. This section provides a more detailed breakdown of overlap coefficients by data type across the different benchmarks evaluated. Figure 2 presents these distributions.

B Implementation and Evaluation Details

This appendix provides supplementary details regarding the implementation of baseline methods, SOTA models, and the evaluation procedure used in our experiments, complementing the core methodology described in Sections 3.2 and 4.3.

B.1 Lexical Baselines (Hashing, TF-IDF, Count) Implementation Details

Vectorizers: We used implementations from scikit-learn[11]. All vectorizers were configured with `lowercase=True`.

- `TfidfVectorizer` and `CountVectorizer`: Used an `ngram_range=(1, 2)`. Their vocabulary was constructed by first collecting unique tokens from all columns across the entire corpus (query tables included), ensuring a consistent feature space.
- `HashingVectorizer`: Used an `ngram_range=(1, 1)` and `alternate_sign=False`.

Input Data: For each table, we randomly sampled up to 1000 unique non-null cell values per column.

Vectorization: Each column's sampled values were treated as a document and vectorized into a 4096-dimensional vector using the appropriately fitted or configured vectorizer.

B.2 SOTA Method Implementation Details

B.2.a) Starmie: [12] We utilized the implementation and recommendations from the original Starmie paper (Fan et al., 2023b).

[11] `https://scikit-learn.org/stable/api/sklearn.feature_extraction.html`

[12] Starmie GitHub Repository

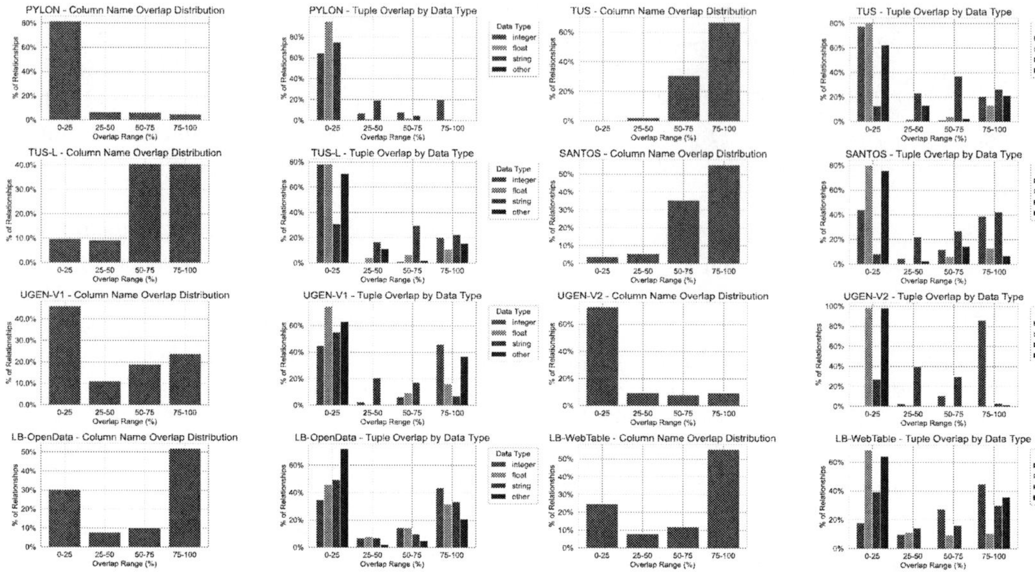

Figure 2: Distribution of exact column name and tuple overlap across different benchmarks, broken down by data type (String, Numeric, Datetime, Other). Each subplot represents a benchmark, showing the percentage of ground truth pairs falling into different overlap ranges.

Training Setup: The provided RoBERTa-based model was retrained for 10 epochs on each benchmark. Key hyperparameters included: batch size 32, projection dimension 768, learning rate 5e-5, max sequence length 256, and fp16 precision.

Sampling and Augmentation Strategies: Starmie employs specific strategies during contrastive pre-training to generate positive pairs (views of the same column). The strategies, based on the definitions in the original paper, are:

- *TF-IDF Entity Sampling ('tfidf_entity'):* Samples cells in columns that have the highest average TF-IDF scores calculated over their tokens.
- *Alpha Head Sampling ('alphaHead'):* Samples the first N tokens sorted alphabetically.
- *Column Dropping Augmentation ('drop_col'):* Creates augmented views by dropping a random subset of columns from the table.
- *Drop Cell Augmentation ('drop_cell'):* Creates augmented views by dropping random cells within the table.

We followed the paper's recommendations for each benchmark, detailed in Table 6. For benchmarks not explicitly mentioned in the original paper (PYLON, UGEN, LAKEBENCH derivatives), we applied the same strategies recommended for the SANTOS benchmark.

Evaluation: We used the "Pruning" search strategy described in the Starmie paper, also referred to as "bounds" in the original implementation. This involves a maximum bipartite matching approach on a pruned set of candidate column pairs to calculate table similarity, offering higher efficiency compared to naive matching, while remaining more precise than approximate search approaches.

Benchmark	**Sampling**	**Augmentation**
SANTOS	tfidf_entity	drop_col
TUS (Small)	alphaHead	drop_cell
TUS$_{Large}$	tfidf_entity	drop_cell
PYLON	tfidf_entity	drop_col
UGEN$_{V1}$	tfidf_entity	drop_col
UGEN$_{V2}$	tfidf_entity	drop_col
LB-OPENDATA	tfidf_entity	drop_col
LB-WEBTABLE	tfidf_entity	drop_col

Table 6: Starmie sampling and augmentation strategies applied per benchmark.

B.2.b) HEARTS: [13]

Model: Employs pre-trained HyTrel embeddings (Chen et al., 2023), utilizing a publicly available checkpoint trained with a contrastive learning objective[14]. No further finetuning was performed.

[13] HEARTS GitHub Repository

[14] https://github.com/awslabs/hypergraph-tabular-lm/tree/main/checkpoints

Evaluation Strategy: We adopted the best-performing search strategy reported in the HEARTS repository for each benchmark:

- **Cluster Search (for SANTOS, PYLON, UGEN$_{V1}$, UGEN$_{V2}$):** This strategy first reduces the dimensionality of the pre-trained HyTrel column embeddings using UMAP (McInnes et al., 2018) and then performs clustering using HDBSCAN (McInnes et al., 2017). Default parameters provided in the HEARTS repository were used for both UMAP and HDBSCAN within this search method. Table similarity is derived based on cluster assignments.
- **FAISS + Max Pooling (for TUS$_{Small}$, TUS$_{Large}$, LB-OPENDATA, LB-WEBTABLE):** This strategy uses FAISS (Douze et al., 2024) for efficient similarity search. Table vectors are computed by max-pooling the embeddings of their constituent columns before indexing and searching.

B.3 Hardware

Our experiments were conducted using the following setup:

- CPU: Intel Xeon Gold 6330: 4 cores / 8 threads @ 2.00 GHz.
- GPU: 40GB MIG partition of NVIDIA A100 (used for SBERT embedding generation and SOTA models training/inference).
- 64 Go DDR4 RAM.

C Inconsistent Ground Truth Examples

This section provides illustrative examples of the ground truth inconsistencies identified in the UGEN and LAKEBENCH benchmarks during our analysis (Section 5.2). We categorize these into False Positives (pairs incorrectly labeled as unionable) and False Negatives (pairs incorrectly labeled as non-unionable or missed).

C.1 UGEN Benchmark Inconsistencies

Figures 3 and 4 showcase examples from UGEN variants.

C.2 Lakebench Benchmark Inconsistencies

This subsection presents examples of GTFPs from the LAKEBENCH benchmarks, where semantically and structurally compatible tables were not labeled as unionable in the ground truth but were correctly retrieved by search methods. Figures 5 and 6 show such cases from the WebTable and OpenData subsets, respectively.

Query: Anthropology_FGTNBDWF.csv
Candidate: Anthropology_N30U114M.csv

Age	Culture	Arena	Domain	Meaning	Origin	Activity
1	Neo.	Arch.	Past	Prim.	Africa	Hunt.
2	Islam.	Artif.	Hist.	Cplx.	Asia	Farm.

Artifact	Language	Technology	Education	Society
1	English	GPS	Political	Communal
2	Latin	Smartphone	Scientific	Global

(a) UGEN$_{V1}$ Example: Tables discussing structurally and semantically distinct aspects of Anthropology (historical cultures vs. social technology), originally labeled unionable despite conceptual incompatibility.

Query: Anthropology_N7BS08I4.csv
Candidate: Anthropology_VS4SJ2VH.csv

Site Name	Location	Period	Culture
Olduvai Gorge	Tanzania, Africa	Pliocene	Hominin
Teotihuacan	Central Mexico	Early Classic	Teotihuacanos

Age Group	Clothing	Food	Housing
Children (0-12)	Tunics, hides	Porridge, roots	Huts (branch)
Teenagers (13-19)	Garments, beads	Grains, stews	Huts (woven)

(b) UGEN$_{V2}$ Example: Tables about archaeological sites versus demographic lifestyles, representing fundamentally different entity types despite the shared Anthropology topic.

Figure 3: Examples of UGEN where pairs labeled unionable in the original ground truth exhibit significant semantic/structural divergence suggesting non-unionability.

D LLM Adjudicator

D.1 Prompt Details

To systematically re-evaluate potential ground truth inconsistencies in the UGEN benchmarks, we employed an LLM-based adjudicator. This process targeted disagreements identified during our analysis, specifically Ground Truth False Positives (GTFPs, pairs retrieved as potentially unionable within a rank threshold k' but not labeled as unionable in the ground truth, $k' < k$) and Ground Truth False Negatives (GTFNs, pairs labeled as unionable in the ground truth but retrieved within a rank threshold k', $k' > k$, or not retrieved at all).

For each query-candidate pair under review, we provided the LLM with the full content of both tables. The table data was serialized into a Markdown format using the `MarkdownRawTableSerializer` recipe from the Table Serialization Kitchen library[15](Gomm and Hulsebos, 2025). This serialized data was inserted into specific placeholders (`'<Query Table Data>'`, `'<Candidate Table Data>'`) within

[15]Table Serialization Kitchen Github Repository

Query: Archeology_2LWSQ5A2.csv
Candidate: Archeology_3ML53C0M.csv

Discovery	Item	Artifact	Date	Culture	Region
Giza Pyramid	Scroll	Diamond	~2500 BC	Anc. Egypt	N. Africa
Tut. Tomb	Knife	Stone Tab.	1323 BC	Anc. Egypt	N. Africa

Item	Discovery	Artifact	Date	Culture	Region
Scroll	Giza Pyramid	Diamond	~2500 BC	Anc. Egypt	N. Africa
Knife	Tut. Tomb	Stone Tab.	1323 BC	Anc. Egypt	N. Africa

(a) UGEN$_{V1}$ Example: Two archaeology tables with identical information and permuted but perfectly alignable columns, incorrectly labeled non-unionable despite clear semantic compatibility.

Query: Veterinary-Science_YP1NJGLN.csv
Candidate: Veterinary-Medicine_GVNM098Q.csv

Animal Type	Breed	Age	Health Status	Symptoms	Diagnosis
Dog	Labrador Retr.	3 years	Healthy	No symptoms	Routine check-up
Cat	Domestic SH	5 years	Overweight	Lethargy...	Obesity

Animal Type	Breed	Age	Gender	Symptoms	Diagnosis
Dog	Labrador	3 years	Male	Aggression...	Rabies
Cat	Siamese	8 years	Female	Limping...	Arthritis

(b) UGEN$_{V2}$ Example: Two veterinary case tables with highly alignable core columns (Animal Type, Breed, Age, Symptoms, Diagnosis) representing the same fundamental entity type (animal patients).

Figure 4: Examples of UGEN Pairs explicitly labeled as non-unionable in the original ground truth exhibiting strong compatibility suggesting unionability.

Query: csvData10212811.csv
Candidate: csvData1066748.csv

Player	Team	POS	G	AB	H	HR	...	OPS
B Dean	GL	1B	96	350	83	7	...	0.657
Y Arbelo	SB	1B	134	461	114	31	...	0.877

Player	Team	POS	G	AB	H	HR	...	OPS
J Colina	WS	2B	59	216	66	3	...	0.832
B Friday	LYN	SS	85	341	98	2	...	0.752

(a) WebTable Example 1: Baseball player statistics tables with identical, rich schemas (including Player, Team, POS, G, AB, H, HR, OPS, etc.). These tables represent the same entity type (player season stats) and are highly unionable, but were not labeled as such in the ground truth.

Query: csvData10025189.csv
Candidate: csvData20099586.csv

Player	Team	POS	AVG	G	AB	R	...	OPS
A Ramirez	MIL	3B	0.285	133	494	47	...	0.757
E Chavez	ARI	3B	0.246	44	69	6	...	0.795

Player	Team	POS	AVG	G	AB	R	...	OPS
L Castillo	NYM	2B	0.245	87	298	46	...	0.660
R Durham	MIL	2B	0.289	128	370	64	...	0.813

(b) WebTable Example 2: More baseball player statistics tables with identical schemas, clearly unionable but not labeled as such.

Figure 5: Examples of LB-WEBTABLE Ground Truth Incompleteness.

Source: OpenData (Canada)
Query: CAN_CSV0000000000000659.csv
Candidate: CAN_CSV0000000000000562.csv

REF_DATE	GEO	Age group	Sex	...	VALUE
2003	Canada	Total, 12 years and over	Both sexes	...	20723896.0
2003	Canada	Total, 12 years and over	Both sexes	...	20632799.0

REF_DATE	GEO	Age group	Sex	...	VALUE
2003	Canada	Total, 12 years and over	Both sexes	...	26567928.0
2003	Canada	Total, 12 years and over	Both sexes	...	26567928.0

(a) OpenData Example 1: Canadian health survey tables sharing key demographic columns (REF_DATE, GEO, Age group, Sex) for the same population. This pair represents unionable statistics about that population but was not labeled as unionable in the ground truth.

Source: OpenData (Canada)
Query: CAN_CSV0000000000000686.csv
Candidate: CAN_CSV0000000000005304.csv

Sex	Type of work	Hourly wages	UOM	UOM_ID	...	VALUE
Both	Both full- and part...	Total employees, all wages	Persons	249	...	10921.0
Males	Both full- and part...	Total employees, all wages	Persons	249	...	5645.4

Sex	Type of work	Weekly wages	UOM	UOM_ID	...	VALUE
Both	Both full- and part...	Total employees, all wages	Persons	249	...	11364.5
Males	Both full- and part...	Total employees, all wages	Persons	249	...	5954.5

(b) OpenData Example 2: Canadian employment statistics. The query table (data related to 'Hourly wages') and candidate table (data related to 'Weekly wages') share key dimensions like Sex, Type of work, and UOM. The cell values within their respective 'Hourly wages'/'Weekly wages' columns (e.g., 'Total employees, all wages') describe similar employee groups. This pair, differing mainly in wage aggregation period (hourly vs. weekly) and slightly in REF_DATE format (YYYY vs YYYY-MM), is potentially unionable for comprehensive wage analysis but was not labeled as such in the ground truth.

Figure 6: Examples of LB-OPENDATA Ground Truth Incompleteness.

the prompt detailed below. Crucially, the original table names were *not* included in the prompt. This decision was made to avoid potentially biasing the LLM by providing explicit hints about the table's topic beforehand, thereby ensuring the adjudication relies solely on the semantic and structural information present in the table content itself.

The prompt utilizes few-shot learning, incorporating hand-selected positive and negative examples of unionability from the UGEN benchmarks themselves to guide the LLM's judgment (these examples are represented by a placeholder in the verbatim prompt below for brevity). The prompt defines the LLM's role, outlines core principles for assessing conceptual coherence and semantic column alignment, and specifies the required output format.

The complete prompt structure provided to the LLM adjudicator is shown below:

```
You are an experienced data curator evaluating
    if two database tables can be meaningfully
    combined vertically (unioned). The goal of
    unioning is to create a single, larger
    dataset containing the same kind of
    information or describing the same type of
    entity/event.

Your task is to determine if TABLE 1 and TABLE
    2 are conceptually compatible enough for a
    union operation.

CORE PRINCIPLES FOR UNIONABILITY:

1. Conceptual Coherence: Do both tables
    fundamentally describe the same type of
    entity (e.g., customers, products, logs) or
    record the same type of event (e.g., sales,
    website visits)? Appending rows from one
    table to the other should result in a
    dataset that makes logical sense.

2. Meaningful Column Alignment: There must be a
    reasonable set of columns across the two
    tables that represent the same underlying
    attributes or concepts.
   * These columns can have DIFFERENT NAMES
      (e.g., "Cust_ID" vs.
      "ClientIdentifier").
   * They can have DIFFERENT FORMATS (e.g.,
      "2023-01-15" vs. "1/15/2023").
   * They may have LITTLE TO NO OVERLAP in
      actual data values.
   * Focus on the semantic meaning of the
      columns in the context of their
      respective tables.

3. Sufficient Column Matching: The alignment
    shouldn't rely on just one incidental or
    minor column. There should be enough
    matching among key columns to confidently
    conclude that the tables represent the same
    underlying information. More aligned
    columns representing core attributes
    increase confidence.

4. Distinction from Joins: We are NOT looking
    for keys to join tables horizontally. We
    are assessing if they can be stacked
    vertically.

[EXAMPLES OF UNIONABILITY/NON-UNIONABILTY:]
(Hand-selected positive/negative examples from
    \textsc{Ugen} benchmark were inserted here
    in the actual prompt)

YOUR TASK:

Examine the following two tables based on the
    principles and examples above:

TABLE 1:
<Query Table Data (Serialized)>

TABLE 2:
<Candidate Table Data (Serialized)>

PROVIDE YOUR ANSWER IN THE FOLLOWING FORMAT:

1. First line: `UNIONABLE: Yes` or `UNIONABLE:
    No`
2. Second line: `EXPLANATION:` followed by a
    brief justification focusing on the
    conceptual coherence and the sufficiency of
    semantic column alignment. Explain why they
    are or are not the same kind of data.
```

D.2 Example LLM Outputs

Below are illustrative examples of the outputs generated by the LLM adjudicator based on the prompt above for some table pairs showcased in Appendix C.1.

Example 1: Archeology_2LWSQ5A2.csv vs. Archeology_3ML53C0M.csv (UGEN-V1)

```
UNIONABLE: Yes
EXPLANATION: Both tables describe archeological
    artifacts and their attributes (discovery
    location, item type, date, culture,
    material, etc.). They represent the same
    kind of data - records of archeological
    findings. Unioning them would create a
    consolidated dataset of such findings.
    There is strong semantic alignment across
    almost all columns, even though the column
    order differs.
```

Example 2: Anthropology_FGTNBDWF.csv vs. Anthropology_N30U114M.csv (UGEN-V1)

```
UNIONABLE: No
EXPLANATION: TABLE 1 categorizes
    anthropological concepts based on
    dimensions like 'Age', 'Culture', 'Arena',
    'Domain', 'Meaning', 'Origin', and
    'Activity'. TABLE 2, on the other hand,
    lists categories such as 'Artifact',
    'Language', 'Technology', 'Education', and
    'Society' as columns. While both tables are
    related to Anthropology, they represent
    different perspectives and categorizations
    within the field. There is insufficient
    semantic overlap in the columns to suggest
    they describe the same type of entity or
    event. Unioning them would likely result in
    a table that is not conceptually coherent,
    as the rows from each table represent
    different kinds of anthropological
    classifications.
```

RITT: A Retrieval-Assisted Framework with Image and Text Table Representations for Table Question Answering

Wei Zhou[1,3] **Mohsen Mesgar**[1] **Heike Adel**[2] **Annemarie Friedrich**[3]
[1]Bosch Center for Artificial Intelligence, Renningen, Germany
[2]Hochschule der Medien, Stuttgart, Germany [3]University of Augsburg, Germany
{wei.zhou|mohsen.mesgar}@de.bosch.com
annemarie.friedrich@uni-a.de adel-vu@hdm-stuttgart.de

Abstract

Tables can be represented either as text or as images. Previous works on table question answering (TQA) typically rely on only one representation, neglecting the potential benefits of combining both. In this work, we explore integrating textual and visual table representations using multi-modal large language models (MLLMs) for TQA. Specifically, we propose RITT, a retrieval-assisted framework that first identifies the most relevant part of a table for a given question, then dynamically selects the optimal table representations based on the question type. Experiments demonstrate that our framework significantly outperforms the baseline MLLMs by an average of 13 Exact Match and surpasses two text-only state-of-the-art TQA methods on four TQA benchmarks, highlighting the benefits of leveraging both textual and visual table representations.

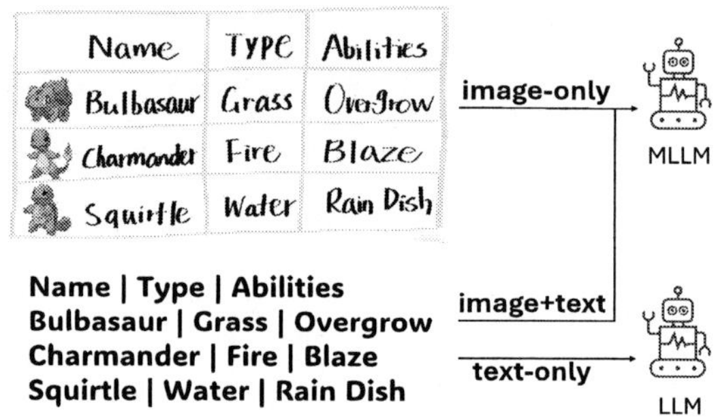

Figure 1: Three current approaches for representing and processing tables. Our framework RITT uses both table images and texts.

1 Introduction

Previous approaches in table question answering (TQA) represent tables as either textual sequences (Herzig et al., 2020; Jiang et al., 2022; Zhang et al., 2023a) or as images (Zheng et al., 2024; Deng et al., 2024a), and process them by large language models (LLMs) or multi-modal large language models (MLLMs) accordingly. However, in real-life scenarios, tables often exist in both forms (e.g., HTML tables), or one form can be easily converted to the other via optical character recognition (OCR) or HTML rendering. This leads to increased interest in approaches that leverage both visual and textual table representations (Deng et al., 2024b; Liu et al., 2025; Zhou et al., 2025).

Current approaches using both representations either fine-tune an existing MLLM using preference data collected by prompting MLLMs with different table representations of a TQA problem (Liu et al., 2025), or leverage instance-level features (e.g., table size) to determine the best representation for an MLLM to process (Zhou et al., 2025). The former requires careful data collection and training (Feng et al., 2024), while the latter struggles to effectively handle large tables due to the inherent limitations of current MLLMs (Li et al., 2023; Zhou et al., 2025).

This work builds upon the latter approach, focusing on designing a training-free framework that can be easily applied across different datasets. We adopt the core idea proposed in FRES (Zhou et al., 2025) to select the most suitable table representation of a TQA problem based on its question type. Questions are classified as either retrieval questions, which only require locating information to be solved, or reasoning questions, which require both retrieval and reasoning.

However, unlike FRES, we introduce a novel **a sub-table retriever** that selects the most relevant part of a table to reduce input size. The module produces relevant table texts and images, which can be combined with the original full table and passed to an MLLM for reasoning. To determine the optimal representation combinations for an MLLM, we **extend the analysis** from Zhou et al. (2025) to explore combinatorial scenarios, such as pairing retrieved table images with original textual representations and vice versa. Our results indicate

Proceedings of the 4th Table Representation Learning Workshop, pages 86–97
July 31, 2025 ©2025 Association for Computational Linguistics

that combining textual and visual representations yields the best performance for reasoning questions, while textual representation alone is sufficient for retrieval questions.

Based on these findings, we propose RITT, a training-free Retrieval-assisted framework leveraging Image and Text representations of Tables. It comprises four modules: a sub-table retriever, a question classifier, a table reformatter, and an MLLM reasoner. Experimental results show that RITT outperforms baseline MLLMs by an average of 13 exact match (EM) points, and surpasses two state-of-the-art text-only TQA systems, demonstrating the clear benefits of leveraging both table representations. Lastly, we provide an ablation study highlighting the contribution of each component.

2 Related Work

Sub-table Retrieval. Both LLMs and MLLMs have been shown to struggle with large tables (Lin et al., 2023; Wang et al., 2024a). To address this issue, prior work either fine-tunes smaller retriever models using annotated gold sub-tables (Lin et al., 2023; Lee et al., 2024), or utilizes LLMs as retrievers via in-context learning (Chen et al., 2024; Li et al., 2024b; Ye et al., 2023). In this work, we propose an LLM-based sub-table retriever. Unlike existing approaches that rely solely on semantic matching between headers and cells (Chen et al., 2024; Li et al., 2024b), our method further narrows down relevant cells by explicitly formulating and executing filtering logic. In contrast to methods that directly output relevant row indices using an LLM (Ye et al., 2023), our retriever ensures faithful generation using code execution for relevant content filtering.

Table Representations for TQA. Most prior work processes tables as texts (Zhang et al., 2023a; Wang et al., 2024c) or as images (Zheng et al., 2024). Liu et al. (2025) fine-tune an existing MLLM using preference data collected by prompting an MLLM with different table representations. Zhou et al. (2025) propose a rule-based framework FRES to select the best table representation for an MLLM. They obtain the rules by comparing different representations under varying scenarios controlled by table size and question type. Their findings indicate that different representations perform differently under varying conditions. For instance, passing large tables in textual format to LLMs can lead to better performance than passing large tables in images to MLLMs. Though the textual format is more robust than the visual format when handling larger tables, it still faces challenges with large tables. In this work, we propose a sub-table retriever to mitigate the impact of table size on representation selection. Moreover, we extend existing analyses to cover combinatorial cases where retrieved sub-tables are combined with original tables.

3 Framework

Figure 2 shows an overview of our proposed system RITT. It contains four parts: a *sub-table retriever* that filters for the most relevant cells, a *question classifier* to determine a question type, a *table reformatter* to reformat a retrieved sub-table based on question type, and a *table reasoner* MLLM to output an answer to a given TQA problem.

3.1 Sub-table Retrieval

We define a table T as a set of headers H, values V, and a schema function S that maps values to their corresponding headers. H can be further represented as $\{\emptyset, \{ht_1, \dots, ht_m\}\} \cup \{\emptyset, \{hl_1, \dots, hl_n\}\}$, where ht and hl stands for top and left headers, respectively, and m and n represent the number of columns and rows, respectively. We use $\emptyset$ to denote the absence of a header. For instance, the table in Figure 2 features only top headers. As a result, H can be represented as $\{$"Country", "Result", "Year", "Score"$\}$. The task of sub-table retrieval involves locating relevant top headers, ht_r, relevant left headers hl_r, and a set of cell values V_r indexed by those headers. As shown in the yellow box in Figure 2, an LLM takes in a TQA problem and can perform two tasks: header prediction and question parsing. Header prediction requires an LLM to predict the most relevant headers given a problem. Prompts for header prediction are shown in Figure 4. For a table that features both ht and hl, we directly aggregate cells indexed by predicted headers as a sub-table.

However, when either ht or hl is missing,[1] simply filtering based on available headers may still yield overly large sub-tables. To address this issue, we additionally ask the LLM to parse a question into filtering conditions in natural language (A prompt is shown in Figure 5). The same LLM then translates these conditions into executable Python code (A prompt is shown in Figure 6), which is run

[1]It is more common to have missing hl, e.g., relational tables, than missing ht.

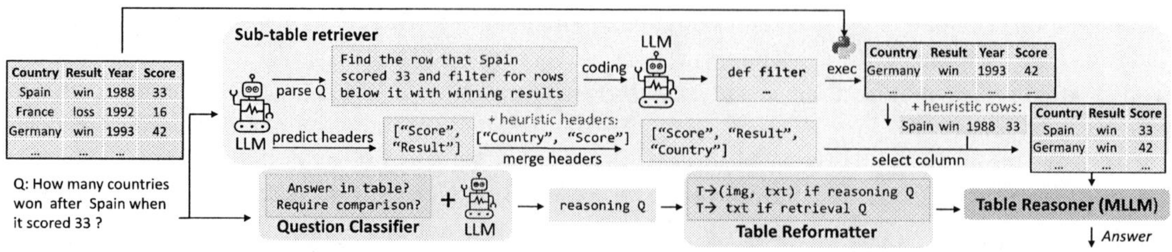

Figure 2: Given a table and question pair, a sub-table retriever outputs relevant cells. A question classifier is applied to distinguish retrieval and reasoning questions. Based on the question type, a table reformatter prepares an input table for a table reasoner, which outputs a final answer based on relevant cells and a question.

via a Python interpreter to further filter a table. If the code execution fails, we revert to the original table. Finally, we filter a retrieved sub-table based on relevant headers predicted by the LLM previously to produce a final sub-table.

To ensure the retrieved sub-table preserves essential information to solve a question, we also apply a heuristic: we include rows and columns that contain tokens in the question (referred to as heuristic rows/columns). For example, as shown in Figure 2, the heuristic headers "Country" and "Score" and heuristic rows mentioning "Spain" and "33" are added back to the final sub-table.

3.2 Question Classifier & Table Reformatter

Given a retrieved sub-table in textual format, the next step is to determine which table representations to pass to the table reasoner. Motivated by previous findings that MLLMs with table images manifest stronger reasoning abilities (Zhou et al., 2025), we consider determining table representations based on question type. Following Zhou et al. (2025), we classify questions into two categories: retrieval and reasoning. Retrieval questions are those whose answers can be directly located verbatim in the table cells, whereas reasoning questions require additional inference, involving numerical, temporal, or commonsense reasoning.

To investigate the effectiveness of table representations with different question types, we use the dataset provided by Zhou et al. (2025), which contains 1,600 instances from six common TQA datasets: WTQ (Pasupat and Liang, 2015), TabFact (Chen et al., 2020), HiTab (Cheng et al., 2022), CRT (Zhang et al., 2023b), TabMWP (Lu et al., 2022), and TempTabTQA (Gupta et al., 2023), with 800 instances for each question type. We examine multiple methods of passing retrieved sub-tables to the table reasoner: *rc*: passing only relevant headers in a prompt. *rt*: passing only relevant cells in

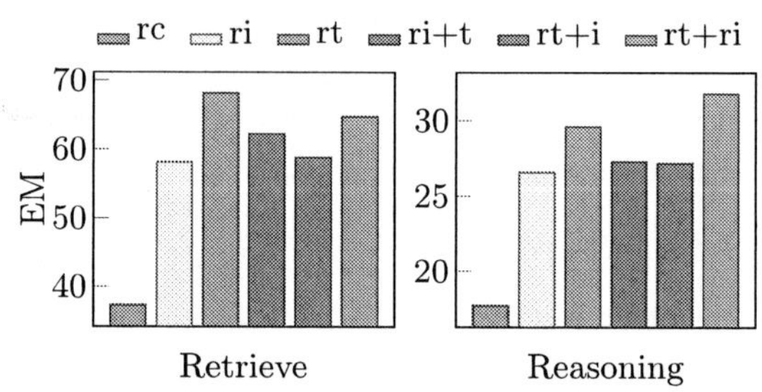

Figure 3: Comparing the effectiveness of different methods under varying question types. rc stands for passing relevant headers in a prompt. ri and rt represent passing only relevant table images and texts, respectively. ri+t stands for passing relevant cells as images and a full table as text. rt+i refers to passing relevant cells as texts and passing the original table as images. Lastly, rt+ti refers to passing both relevant cells as texts and images. We employ the Exact Match (EM) metric.

a prompt. *ri*: passing relevant cells converted into image format. *rt+ri*: passing relevant cells in both text and image formats. Since providing only relevant cells may result in information loss, we also explore combining relevant cells with the original table: *ri+t*: passing relevant cells as images and the original table as text. *rt+i*: passing relevant cells as text and the original table as an image.

We evaluate these methods using six open-weight MLLMs as in Zhou et al. (2025): Qwen-2-VL-7b (Wang et al., 2024b), Pixtral-12b (Agrawal et al., 2024), Phi-3.5-vision-instruct-4b (Abdin et al., 2024), LLaVA-Next-7b (Li et al., 2024a), GLM-4v-9b (Zeng et al., 2024), and InternVL2-8b.[2] Exact Match is used for evaluation, which checks if a predicted answer and a ground truth are the same. To obtain relevant cells, we apply the method proposed in Section 3.1 on the evaluation dataset, with Qwen-2-72b as the backbone LLM.

[2] https://internvl.github.io/blog/2024-07-02-InternVL-2.0/

As Figure 3 shows, different question types benefit from different representations. For reasoning questions, passing relevant cells simultaneously as texts and images (rt+ri) to MLLMs achieves the best performance. In contrast, table text representation suffices when a question is of type retrieval. The observations align with findings in (Zhou et al., 2025). We do not observe a clear advantage from combining relevant table information with the original table information. We suspect this might be because adding the original table information back increases the input size. Detailed results for each MLLM are reported in Appendix A.3. Based on these observations, our table reformatter encodes sub-tables as both images and texts when a question is of type reasoning. Otherwise, only table texts are passed to the final reasoner. We adopt the question type classifier proposed by Zhou et al. (2024), which combines rule-based heuristics and an LLM. Details are represented in Appendix A.2.

4 Experiments

Datasets. We evaluate RITT with the **test sets** of three aforementioned TQA benchmarks used during our analysis in Section 3.2: WTQ, TabFact (small test), and HiTab. We also include one additional dataset, WikiSQL (Zhong et al., 2017), that has not been used in our analysis to test the generalizability of our method.

Models and Baselines. Our framework contains an MLLM table reasoner and an LLM retriever/classifier.[3] For MLLMs, we choose the best performing MLLM from our previous analysis: **Pixtral-12b** (see A.3 for individual model's performance) as well as a fine-tuned MLLM for TQA: **TableLlaVA-7b** (Zheng et al., 2024). We use Qwen-2-72b as the LLM backbone in our framework. As baselines, we choose the backbone MLLM without applying RITT. In addition, we compare RITT with two SoTA frameworks that use only table text representations: TableRAG (Chen et al., 2024) and GraphOTTER (Li et al., 2024b). Both frameworks involve relevant cell retrieval and are inference-based methods utilizing LLMs. For fair comparisons, we replace the LLM backbones used in previous work and this work with an MLLM (Qwen-2-VL-72b).[4] As a result, all compared frameworks use the same backbone model.

Systems	WTQ	TabFact	HiTab	WiKiSQL
Pixtral-12b	52.5	75.9	62.2	60.1
+RITT	54.4 (+1.9)	76.8 (+0.9)	68.0 (+5.8)	62.7 (+2.6)
TableLlaVA-7b	17.2	60.9	16.3	29.5
+RITT	39.7(+22.5)	64.5 (+3.6)	61.8 (+45.5)	52.0 (+22.5)
Qwen2-VL-72b	62.6	**86.7**	73.4	77.6
+RITT	**63.4**	86.0	**76.4**	**78.0**
TableRAG	60.8	79.3	65.3	77.9
GraphOTTER	59.4	81.8	71.6	75.6

Table 1: Model performances on four TQA benchmarks. The first four rows show the results of direct inference with MLLMs and applying our framework. The last four rows compare the performance of our framework with two SoTA systems using the same model.

5 Results and Discussions

Results. Table 1 shows the results averaged across three runs. The top section of the table compares direct inference using the backbone MLLMs against the same models enhanced by RITT. The bottom section compares our method to two state-of-the-art frameworks (TableRAG and GraphOTTER) using the same underlying backbone model. Applying RITT consistently improves performance, with notable gains on the HiTab dataset, achieving increases of 5.8 and 45.5 EM points for Pixtral-12b and TableLLaVA-7b, respectively. Differences in improvement can be attributed to the capabilities of the base models: Pixtral-12b generally exhibits stronger multi-modal reasoning capabilities than TableLlaVA and can handle longer inputs, resulting in smaller performance improvements. Moreover, our framework consistently outperforms both TableRAG and GraphOTTER across all four datasets. When using a larger MLLM model (Qwen-2-72b), we still observe improvements in three out of four datasets, though these improvements are relatively smaller compared to those observed with smaller models. We hypothesize this is because larger models inherently have stronger capabilities in handling longer and more complex table-question instances, leaving less room for improvement from additional retrieval steps.

Ablation. We conduct an ablation study to analyze the contribution of each component. We present results categorized by table size to understand how each component performs on tables of

[3]The retriever/classifier can be replaced by the MLLM reasoner. We do not find big performance differences between an LLM and an MLLM of the same size and series.

[4]We do not find a significant performance difference when switching from a text-only model to a multi-modal model.

System	0-50	50-100	100-200	>200
#Instances	187	413	466	518
MLLM	74.3	63.7	61.6	57.3
+ st	+4.1	+1.6	+2.9	+7.5
+ st+tr	+3.8	+2.9	+4.3	+10.3
+ st+tr (oracle)	+4.3	+3.1	+5.1	+11.7

Table 2: Ablation study of our framework on HiTab using Pixtral-12b. st stands for sub-table retriever, and tr stands for table reformatter. tr (oracle) refers to passing the oracle question type obtained from the dataset.

Methods	Precision	Recall	F_1	# Cells
GraphOTTER	**47.4**	51.1	46.8	4.56
TableRAG	17.6	40.3	22.7	13.8
RITT	41.0	**92.6**	**51.2**	8.65

Table 3: Comparing our sub-table retriever with two state-of-the-art sub-table retrievers.#Cells shows the average number of identified relevant cells. For gold relevant cells, the number is 5.34.

varying sizes. When ablating the table reformatter, retrieved sub-tables are passed to an MLLM as both images and texts. We pass the oracle question types obtained from the dataset annotation to investigate the effectiveness of the question classifier. Table 2 shows results on the HiTab dataset, chosen as it exhibits the largest performance gains using RITT. We observe that both the sub-table retriever and table reformatter contribute to the overall performance. The sub-table retriever demonstrates greater performance enhancement compared to the table reformatter. Additionally, we note that overall system performance tends to decline as the table size increases, aligning with previous findings (Lin et al., 2023). Interestingly, the benefit provided by the sub-table retriever becomes more pronounced on larger tables, highlighting its effectiveness in handling large tables.

Effectiveness of Sub-table Retriever. We compare our proposed sub-table retriever with two current state-of-the-art LLM-based retrievers (introduced in Section 4) on 800 instances from the HiTab evaluation subset described in Section 3.2. We chose this dataset as it provides manual annotations of relevant table cells required to answer each question. The results are shown in Table 3. Our proposed sub-table retriever achieves the highest F_1 score among the three methods, demonstrating its effectiveness in accurately identifying relevant table cells. Nevertheless, the high recall and relatively large average number of cells (8.65 compared to the gold standard of 5.34) indicate that our sub-table retriever identified irrelevant cells with regard to answering a question.

Error Analysis. We randomly sample 100 instances on which applying RITT with Pixtral-12b fails, with each investigated dataset 25 instances, and perform an error analysis. For each instance, we manually check (1) whether a retrieved sub-table contains the relevant information needed to answer a question, and (2) whether the question type is predicted correctly. We find that for approximately 23% of instances, the retrieved sub-tables do not contain the information needed to answer questions, leading to information loss. In contrast, only 7% of instances are predicted with wrong question types, suggesting the task is relatively easy. We observe that in the majority of cases, the relevant information is present in the retrieved sub-tables, and the question type is correctly identified. However, Pixtral-12b still fails to provide the correct answer. This might be because the retrieved sub-tables are still large, due to code execution errors during row filtering. The failure affects instances with reasoning questions more than retrieval questions, given that both table images and table texts are passed when a question is of type reasoning. An example is provided in Figure 7. Our analysis suggests that future work should focus on developing methods that reduce table sizes effectively without losing necessary information.

6 Conclusions

In this paper, we explored leveraging both textual and visual table representations using MLLMs for TQA. To handle the challenges of large table inputs and representation selection, we proposed RITT, a retrieval-assisted framework that retrieves the most relevant sub-table, classifies the question type, and dynamically determines the optimal representations to an MLLM reasoner based on the question type. Extensive experiments on four TQA benchmarks demonstrated the advantages of our framework over baseline MLLMs as well as frameworks utilizing only textual representations. Ablation studies further confirmed the effectiveness of each proposed component. Our findings highlight the benefits and promising potential of integrating both table representations for TQA.

Limitation

We explore utilizing both textual and visual table representations. Nevertheless, the underlying assumption that table images and table texts both exist and can be easily converted might not hold for every case. For instance, converting large table images to texts using OCR tools can suffer from information loss. We leave these for further exploration. Secondly, due to a limited number of existing large MLLMs, we specifically focus on evaluating and designing methods for small MLLMs. Last but not least, RITT is a pipeline method, consisting of several components. As a result, it requires longer inference time than end-to-end systems.

References

Marah Abdin, Sam Ade Jacobs, Ammar Ahmad Awan, Jyoti Aneja, Ahmed Awadallah, Hany Hassan Awadalla, Nguyen Bach, Amit Bahree, Arash Bakhtiari, Harkirat Singh Behl, Alon Benhaim, Misha Bilenko, Johan Bjorck, Sébastien Bubeck, Martin Cai, Caio C'esar Teodoro Mendes, Weizhu Chen, Vishrav Chaudhary, Parul Chopra, Allison Del Giorno, Gustavo de Rosa, Matthew Dixon, Ronen Eldan, Dan Iter, Abhishek Goswami, Suriya Gunasekar, Emman Haider, Junheng Hao, Russell J. Hewett, Jamie Huynh, Mojan Javaheripi, Xin Jin, Piero Kauffmann, Nikos Karampatziakis, Dongwoo Kim, Young Jin Kim, Mahoud Khademi, Lev Kurilenko, James R. Lee, Yin Tat Lee, Yuanzhi Li, Chen Liang, Weishung Liu, Eric Lin, Zeqi Lin, Piyush Madan, Arindam Mitra, Hardik Modi, Anh Nguyen, Brandon Norick, Barun Patra, Daniel Perez-Becker, Thomas Portet, Reid Pryzant, Heyang Qin, Marko Radmilac, Corby Rosset, Sambudha Roy, Olli Saarikivi, Amin Saied, Adil Salim, Michael Santacroce, Shital Shah, Ning Shang, Hiteshi Sharma, Xianmin Song, Olatunji Ruwase, Praneetha Vaddamanu, Xin Wang, Rachel Ward, Guanhua Wang, Philipp Witte, Michael Wyatt, Can Xu, Jiahang Xu, Sonali Yadav, Fan Yang, Ziyi Yang, Donghan Yu, Cheng-Yuan Zhang, Cyril Zhang, Jianwen Zhang, Li Lyna Zhang, Yi Zhang, Yunan Zhang, and Xiren Zhou. 2024. Phi-3 technical report: A highly capable language model locally on your phone. *ArXiv*, abs/2404.14219.

Pravesh Agrawal, Szymon Antoniak, Emma Bou Hanna, Devendra Singh Chaplot, Jessica Chudnovsky, Saurabh Garg, Théophile Gervet, Soham Ghosh, Am'elie H'eliou, Paul Jacob, Albert Q. Jiang, Timothée Lacroix, Guillaume Lample, Diego de Las Casas, Thibaut Lavril, Teven Le Scao, Andy Lo, William Marshall, Louis Martin, Arthur Mensch, Pavankumar Reddy Muddireddy, Valera Nemychnikova, Marie Pellat, Patrick von Platen, Nikhil Raghuraman, Baptiste Rozière, Alexandre Sablayrolles, Lucile Saulnier, Romain Sauvestre, Wendy Shang, Roman Soletskyi, Lawrence Stewart, Pierre Stock, Joachim Studnia, Sandeep Subramanian, Sagar Vaze, and Thomas Wang. 2024. Pixtral 12b. *ArXiv*, abs/2410.07073.

Si-An Chen, Lesly Miculicich, Julian Martin Eisenschlos, Zifeng Wang, Zilong Wang, Yanfei Chen, Yasuhisa Fujii, Hsuan-Tien Lin, Chen-Yu Lee, and Tomas Pfister. 2024. Tablerag: Million-token table understanding with language models. *ArXiv*, abs/2410.04739.

Wenhu Chen, Hongmin Wang, Jianshu Chen, Yunkai Zhang, Hong Wang, Shiyang Li, Xiyou Zhou, and William Yang Wang. 2020. Tabfact : A large-scale dataset for table-based fact verification. In *International Conference on Learning Representations (ICLR)*, Addis Ababa, Ethiopia.

Zhoujun Cheng, Haoyu Dong, Zhiruo Wang, Ran Jia, Jiaqi Guo, Yan Gao, Shi Han, Jian-Guang Lou, and Dongmei Zhang. 2022. HiTab: A hierarchical table dataset for question answering and natural language generation. In *Proceedings of the 60th Annual Meeting of the Association for Computational Linguistics (Volume 1: Long Papers)*, pages 1094–1110, Dublin, Ireland. Association for Computational Linguistics.

Chunyuan Deng, Yilun Zhao, Xiangru Tang, Mark Gerstein, and Arman Cohan. 2024a. Investigating data contamination in modern benchmarks for large language models. In *Proceedings of the 2024 Conference of the North American Chapter of the Association for Computational Linguistics: Human Language Technologies (Volume 1: Long Papers)*, pages 8706–8719, Mexico City, Mexico. Association for Computational Linguistics.

Naihao Deng, Zhenjie Sun, Ruiqi He, Aman Sikka, Yulong Chen, Lin Ma, Yue Zhang, and Rada Mihalcea. 2024b. Tables as texts or images: Evaluating the table reasoning ability of LLMs and MLLMs. In *Findings of the Association for Computational Linguistics: ACL 2024*, pages 407–426, Bangkok, Thailand. Association for Computational Linguistics.

Duanyu Feng, Bowen Qin, Chen Huang, Zheng Zhang, and Wenqiang Lei. 2024. Towards analyzing and understanding the limitations of dpo: A theoretical perspective.

Vivek Gupta, Pranshu Kandoi, Mahek Vora, Shuo Zhang, Yujie He, Ridho Reinanda, and Vivek Srikumar. 2023. TempTabQA: Temporal question answering for semi-structured tables. In *Proceedings of the 2023 Conference on Empirical Methods in Natural Language Processing*, pages 2431–2453, Singapore. Association for Computational Linguistics.

Jonathan Herzig, Pawel Krzysztof Nowak, Thomas Müller, Francesco Piccinno, and Julian Eisenschlos. 2020. TaPas: Weakly supervised table parsing via pre-training. In *Proceedings of the 58th Annual Meeting of the Association for Computational Linguistics*, pages 4320–4333, Online. Association for Computational Linguistics.

Zhengbao Jiang, Yi Mao, Pengcheng He, Graham Neubig, and Weizhu Chen. 2022. OmniTab: Pretraining with natural and synthetic data for few-shot table-based question answering. In *Proceedings of the 2022 Conference of the North American Chapter of the Association for Computational Linguistics: Human Language Technologies*, pages 932–942, Seattle, United States. Association for Computational Linguistics.

Wonjin Lee, Kyumin Kim, Sungjae Lee, Jihun Lee, and Kwang In KIm. 2024. Piece of table: A divide-and-conquer approach for selecting sub-tables in table question answering.

Feng Li, Renrui Zhang, Hao Zhang, Yuanhan Zhang, Bo Li, Wei Li, Zejun Ma, and Chunyuan Li. 2024a. Llava-next-interleave: Tackling multi-image, video, and 3d in large multimodal models. *ArXiv*, abs/2407.07895.

Qianlong Li, Chen Huang, Shuai Li, Yuanxin Xiang, Deng Xiong, and Wenqiang Lei. 2024b. Graphotter: Evolving llm-based graph reasoning for complex table question answering.

Zhang Li, Biao Yang, Qiang Liu, Zhiyin Ma, Shuo Zhang, Jingxu Yang, Yabo Sun, Yuliang Liu, and Xiang Bai. 2023. Monkey: Image resolution and text label are important things for large multi-modal models. *2024 IEEE/CVF Conference on Computer Vision and Pattern Recognition (CVPR)*, pages 26753–26763.

Weizhe Lin, Rexhina Blloshmi, Bill Byrne, Adria de Gispert, and Gonzalo Iglesias. 2023. An inner table retriever for robust table question answering. In *Proceedings of the 61st Annual Meeting of the Association for Computational Linguistics (Volume 1: Long Papers)*, pages 9909–9926, Toronto, Canada. Association for Computational Linguistics.

Zhenghao Liu, Haolan Wang, Xinze Li, Qiushi Xiong, Xiaocui Yang, Yu Gu, Yukun Yan, Qi Shi, Fangfang Li, Ge Yu, and Maosong Sun. 2025. Hippo: Enhancing the table understanding capability of large language models through hybrid-modal preference optimization.

Pan Lu, Liang Qiu, Kai-Wei Chang, Ying Nian Wu, Song-Chun Zhu, Tanmay Rajpurohit, Peter Clark, and A. Kalyan. 2022. Dynamic prompt learning via policy gradient for semi-structured mathematical reasoning. *ArXiv*, abs/2209.14610.

Panupong Pasupat and Percy Liang. 2015. Compositional semantic parsing on semi-structured tables. In *Proceedings of the 53rd Annual Meeting of the Association for Computational Linguistics and the 7th International Joint Conference on Natural Language Processing (Volume 1: Long Papers)*, pages 1470–1480, Beijing, China. Association for Computational Linguistics.

Hengyi Wang, Haizhou Shi, Shiwei Tan, Weiyi Qin, Wenyuan Wang, Tunyu Zhang, Akshay Uttama Nambi, Tanuja Ganu, and Hao Wang. 2024a. Multimodal needle in a haystack: Benchmarking long-context capability of multimodal large language models. *ArXiv*, abs/2406.11230.

Peng Wang, Shuai Bai, Sinan Tan, Shijie Wang, Zhihao Fan, Jinze Bai, Ke-Yang Chen, Xuejing Liu, Jialin Wang, Wenbin Ge, Yang Fan, Kai Dang, Mengfei Du, Xuancheng Ren, Rui Men, Dayiheng Liu, Chang Zhou, Jingren Zhou, and Junyang Lin. 2024b. Qwen2-vl: Enhancing vision-language model's perception of the world at any resolution. *ArXiv*, abs/2409.12191.

Zilong Wang, Hao Zhang, Chun-Liang Li, Julian Martin Eisenschlos, Vincent Perot, Zifeng Wang, Lesly Miculicich, Yasuhisa Fujii, Jingbo Shang, Chen-Yu Lee, and Tomas Pfister. 2024c. Chain-of-table: Evolving tables in the reasoning chain for table understanding. *ArXiv*, abs/2401.04398.

Yunhu Ye, Binyuan Hui, Min Yang, Binhua Li, Fei Huang, and Yongbin Li. 2023. Large language models are versatile decomposers: Decomposing evidence and questions for table-based reasoning. In *Proceedings of the 46th International ACM SIGIR Conference on Research and Development in Information Retrieval*, SIGIR '23, page 174–184, New York, NY, USA. Association for Computing Machinery.

Team Glm Aohan Zeng, Bin Xu, Bowen Wang, Chenhui Zhang, Da Yin, Diego Rojas, Guanyu Feng, Hanlin Zhao, Hanyu Lai, Hao Yu, Hongning Wang, Jiadai Sun, Jiajie Zhang, Jiale Cheng, Jiayi Gui, Jie Tang, Jing Zhang, Juanzi Li, Lei Zhao, Lindong Wu, Lucen Zhong, Ming yue Liu, Minlie Huang, Peng Zhang, Qinkai Zheng, Rui Lu, Shuaiqi Duan, Shudan Zhang, Shulin Cao, Shuxun Yang, Weng Lam Tam, Wenyi Zhao, Xiao Liu, Xiaoyu Xia, Xiaohan Zhang, Xiaotao Gu, Xin Lv, Xinghan Liu, Xinyi Liu, Xinyue Yang, Xixuan Song, Xunkai Zhang, Yi An, Yifan Xu, Yilin Niu, Yuantao Yang, Yueyan Li, Yushi Bai, Yuxiao Dong, Zehan Qi, Zhaoyu Wang, Zhenyi Yang, Zhengxiao Du, Zhen-Ping Hou, and Zihan Wang. 2024. Chatglm: A family of large language models from glm-130b to glm-4 all tools. *ArXiv*, abs/2406.12793.

Tianshu Zhang, Xiang Yue, Yifei Li, and Huan Sun. 2023a. Tablellama: Towards open large generalist models for tables. In *North American Chapter of the Association for Computational Linguistics*.

Zhehao Zhang, Xitao Li, Yan Gao, and Jian-Guang Lou. 2023b. CRT-QA: A dataset of complex reasoning question answering over tabular data. In *Proceedings of the 2023 Conference on Empirical Methods in Natural Language Processing*, pages 2131–2153, Singapore. Association for Computational Linguistics.

Mingyu Zheng, Xinwei Feng, Qingyi Si, Qiaoqiao She, Zheng Lin, Wenbin Jiang, and Weiping Wang. 2024. Multimodal table understanding. In *Proceedings of the 62nd Annual Meeting of the Association for Computational Linguistics (Volume 1: Long Papers)*, pages 9102–9124, Bangkok, Thailand. Association for Computational Linguistics.

Victor Zhong, Caiming Xiong, and Richard Socher. 2017. Seq2sql: Generating structured queries from natural language using reinforcement learning. *CoRR*, abs/1709.00103.

Wei Zhou, Mohsen Mesgar, Heike Adel, and Annemarie Friedrich. 2024. FREB-TQA: A fine-grained robustness evaluation benchmark for table question answering. In *Proceedings of the 2024 Conference of the North American Chapter of the Association for Computational Linguistics: Human Language Technologies (Volume 1: Long Papers)*, pages 2479–2497, Mexico City, Mexico. Association for Computational Linguistics.

Wei Zhou, Mohsen Mesgar, Heike Adel, and Annemarie Friedrich. 2025. Texts or images? a fine-grained analysis on the effectiveness of input representations and models for table question answering.

A Appendix

A.1 Prompts

We present prompts used in sub-table retriever in Figure 4, 5 and 6.

A.2 Datasets

Question Type Classification. We use the question type classifier proposed in Zhou et al. (2024): a rule-based method is applied first. If an answer is not in a table, a question is classified as a reasoning question. If a question contains comparative terms (detected using NLTK), the question is classified into a reasoning question. Next, an LLM takes in a question and table and returns a predicted question type. We replace the LlaMA-2-13b used in the original paper with Qwen-2-72b for its better general capabilities but keep the prompt the same.

Dataset Licenses WTQ (Pasupat and Liang, 2015), TabFact (Chen et al., 2020), HiTab (Cheng et al., 2022) and WikiSQL (Zhong et al., 2017), they are under the license of CC-BY-SA-4.0[5], MIT, BSD-3 CLAUSE[6] and C-UDA[7] respectively.

[5] https://creativecommons.org/licenses/by-sa/4.0/

[6] https://opensource.org/license/bsd-3-clause

[7] https://github.com/microsoft/HiTab?tab=License-1-ov-file

A.3 MLLMs

Table 4 shows performances of individual MLLMs on the evaluation set. We find that Pixtral 12b performs the best among all evaluated small models.

Header prediction prompt for hierarchical tables:
Your task is to find out the relevant headers based on the question.
Return the answer in json format: {'top_header':[(relevant top header tuple),...], 'left_header':[(relevant left header tuple),...]}
Below is an example:
top header: [('club',),('season',),('league','division'),('league','apps'),('league', 'goals'), ('total','apps'), ('total','goals')]
left header: [('Gillingham',),('Stevenage',),('Bristol City',)]
question: How many goals did this player score in total for Bristol City and Stevenage in League One?
answer: {'top_header':[('club,'), ('league', 'division'), ('league','goals'), ('total', 'goals')], 'left_header':[('Stevenage',),('Bristol City',)]}
now find out the relevant headers for the following instance:
top header: {top_header}
left header: {left_header}
question: {question}
answer:

Header prediction prompt for flat tables:
Your task is to find out the relevant headers to answer the question.
Return the answer in list format: ["relevant_header_a", "relevant_header_b",...] and nothing else.
Below is an example:
table: | country | result | year | score |
Example Row 1: | Spain | win | 2000 | 33 |
Example Row 2: | Germany | win | 2001 | 17 |
question: What is the next country to win after Germany?
Answer: ["country", "result", "year"]
now find the relevant headers for the following instance:
table: {table}
question: {question}

Figure 4: Prompts for header selection.

Model	QT	rc	rt+i	rt	ri+t	ri	rt+ri
Qwen2 7b	Retrieve	50.7	57.2	**81.2**	79.8	75.9	79.7
	Reasoning	24.4	29.1	37.0	35.8	38.2	**42.0**
Pixtral 12b	Retrieve	57.1	**77.9**	76.5	71.4	68.4	72.7
	Reasoning	32.2	40.1	39.7	41.1	39.9	**41.6**
Phi-3.5 4b	Retrieve	52.8	71.9	**77.4**	74.9	69.8	76.1
	Reasoning	17.4	28.3	28.2	27.3	24.7	**30.9**
LlaVA 7b	Retrieve	10.8	48.3	**68.5**	51.9	49.3	67.7
	Reasoning	3.85	12.0	20.4	12.9	9.9	**23.2**
GLM-4 9b	Retrieve	22.8	26.8	**33.0**	22.1	22.3	23.5
	Reasoning	10.5	12.2	12.6	11.1	13.3	**13.9**
Intern-8b	Retrieve	29.8	71.1	72.4	**73.2**	63.1	68.9
	Reasoning	18.3	37.7	**40.2**	34.7	34.1	39.5
Average	Retrieve	37.3	58.8	**68.1**	62.2	58.1	64.7
	Reasoning	17.7	26.5	29.6	27.2	26.6	**31.8**

Table 4: Exact Match of different MLLMs. QT stands for question type. rc refer to passing relevant column names in a prompt. ri and rt represent passing only relevant table images and texts, respectively. ri+t stands for passing relevant cells as images and full table as texts. rt+i refers to passing relevant cells as texts and passing original table as images. rt+ti refers to passing both relevant cells as texts and images. We employ the Exact Match (EM) metric.

Prompt for generating filtering conditions:

You are skilled at translating questions into filtering conditions and adhering to instructions. Your task is to convert a question into a dictionary containing filtering conditions and relevant columns. The dictionary should be structured as: {"general filtering statement: specific instructions for filtering":[list of relevant headers]}. Adhere strictly to this format. Use only words from the table's header when listing relevant columns. Only a portion of the table is shown for data type reference. Do not provide an answer to the question. Examples are provided below for clarity:

Example 1:
Table Header: | country | result | year |
Example Row 1: | Spain | win | 2000 |
Example Row 2: | Germany | win | 2001 |
Question: How many times did Spain win after 2001?
Answer: The question requires filtering for occurrences where Spain won after 2001. This involves checking rows where "country" is "Spain", "result" is "win", and "year" is after 2001. Relevant columns are ["country", "result", "year"]. Hence, the dictionary is: {"filter for rows where Spain won after 2001: find rows where country is Spain, result is win, and year is after 2001":["country", "result", "year"]}

Example 2:
Table Header: | country | result | year |
Example Row 1: | Spain | win | 2000 |
Example Row 2: | Germany | win | 2001 |
Question: What is the next country to win after Germany?
Answer: This question seeks the next winning country after Germany. It requires identifying when Germany won, then filtering for rows where "year" is greater than that year and "result" is "win". Relevant columns are ["country", "result", "year"]. The dictionary is: {"filter for rows where a win occurred after Germany: first identify the year Germany won, then find rows where year is later and result is win":["country", "result", "year"]}

Example 3:
Table Header: | team | scores |
Example Row 1: | Navi | 3 |
Example Row 2: | Spirit | 5 |
Question: What is the total score for Navis and G2?
Answer: This question asks for the total score of Navi and G2, requiring filters for rows where the team is either 'Navi' or 'G2'. Relevant column is ["team"]. The dictionary is: {"filter for rows where team is either Navis or G2: find rows where team is either Navi or G2":["team"]}

Now, based on the given table and question, compose the filtering conditions:
Table: {table}
Question: {question}
Answer:

Figure 5: Prompts for generating filtering conditions.

Prompt for code parsing:

Your task is to write a function 'filtering' to filter out irrelevant rows from a dataframe object, based on a given condition.
The given condition might not match the values or datatype in the dataframe. Therefore, you will have to translate the given condition into the dataframe operatable Python code or converting the data (type) in the dataframe. Return the filtered df in the variable 'df_filtered'
Below is an example:

df = pd.DataFrame.from_dict({{'country':['Spain', 'Germany', 'France', 'Norway'], 'year':['2000', '2001', '2002','1998']}})
condition = 'filter for rows that won after Germany: first find the year Germany won. Then filter for rows where year is later than the year Germany won'

answer: The condition selects rows where the 'year' should be larger than (after) the year when Germany won. We have to first find out when Germany won, and then filtering for rows that satisfy the condition. The corresponding Python code is:

```
def filtering(df):
# convert data type
  df['year'].astype('int64')
# find out the year when Germany won
  germany_won_year = df[df['country']=='Germany]['year'].tolist()[0]
# filter the table for rows that won after Germany won year
  df_filtered = df[df['year']>germany_won_year]
return df_filtered
```

Now please think carefully and write Python code to select relevant rows for the following dataframe based on the condition.
df = pd.DataFrame.from_dict({df_dict})
condition = {cond}
answer:

Figure 6: Prompts for code generation.

Question: What is the value Others% when the value Others# is greater than 147 and the value Kerry% is 39.6%?

Question type: reasoning

Original table

County	Kerry%	Kerry#	Bush%	Bush#	Others%	Others#
Adams	52.1%	5,447	46.8%	4,890	1.1%	119
...remaining 32 rows not shown...						
Sheboygan	44.1%	27,608	55.0%	34,458	0.9%	559

Sub-table

Kerry%	Kerry#	Others%	Others#
52.1%	5,447	1.1%	119
...remaining 32 rows not shown...			
44.1%	27,608	0.9%	559

image + text

Pixtral (12b)

Predicted answer: 1.3%

Gold answer: 1.1%

Figure 7: An error case of large sub-tables.

Ask Me Like I'm Human: LLM-based Evaluation with For-Human Instructions Correlates Better with Human Evaluations than Human Judges

Rudali Huidrom and **Anya Belz**
ADAPT Research Centre
Dublin City University
Ireland
{rudali.huidrom,anya.belz}@adaptcentre.ie

Abstract

Human evaluation in NLP has high cost and expertise requirements, and instruction-tuned LLMs are increasingly seen as a viable alternative. Reported correlations with human judgements vary across evaluation contexts and prompt types, and it is hard currently to predict if an LLM-as-judge metric will work equally well for new evaluation contexts and prompts, unless human evaluations are also carried out for comparison. Addressing two main factors contributing to this uncertainty, model suitability and prompt engineering, in the work reported in this focused contribution, we test four LLMs and different ways of combining them, in conjunction with a standard approach to prompt formulation, namely using written-for-human instructions verbatim. We meta-evaluate performance against human evaluations on two data-to-text tasks, and eight evaluation measures, also comparing against more conventional LLM prompt formulations. We find that the best LLM (combination)s are excellent predictors of mean human judgements, and are particularly good at content-related evaluation (in contrast to form-related criteria such as Fluency). Moreover, the best LLMs correlate far more strongly with human evaluations than individual human judges across all scenarios.

1 Introduction

Human evaluation remains the most reliable method for system evaluation in NLP (van Miltenburg et al., 2023b), but its high cost, required expertise, and methodological inconsistencies limit its scalability and reliability (Thomson et al., 2024). The emergence of large language models (Touvron et al., 2023; Chaplot, 2023; Cohere, 2024; Yang et al., 2025) has caused a paradigm shift in text generation and understanding across many domains (Ouyang et al., 2022; Kojima et al., 2022). LLMs are exhibiting state-of-the-art performance in problem-solving and reasoning tasks (Mizrahi et al., 2024; Zhang et al., 2024b). LLMs also hold out the appealing vision of cheaper human-like evaluation, demonstrating adaptability and generalisation capabilities (Li et al., 2024). While individual human judges are subject to inter-rater variability and require multiple annotators for reliability, LLMs may provide more consistent judgements when resources are constrained. 'LLM-as-Judge' approaches do address some of the issues with human evaluation, such as cost and evaluator inconsistency, but their reliability when applied to new tasks needs to be demonstrated via correlation tests with human judgements. In the experiments presented in this paper, we investigate the alignment between human and LLM judgements across a range of criteria for two NLP data-to-text tasks. To standardise prompt formulation, we use the same instructions as those provided in human evaluations, and compare them with more conventional LLM prompts, in conjunction with single models and model combinations of both varying and comparable sizes.

2 Related work

LLM-as-judge has been shown to be an effective approach for assessing a wide range of individual tasks (Liusie et al., 2024). Like other automatic evaluation methods, LLM-as-judge approaches are typically meta-evaluated against human judgement scores, and increasingly on emerging benchmarks, such as HumEval (Chen et al., 2021), SummEval (Fabbri et al., 2021), and MQM (Freitag et al., 2021), used in conjunction with specific evaluation frameworks (Fu et al., 2023; Liu et al., 2023; Liusie et al., 2024, inter alia), or simply with prompts and instructions tailored to the task (Zhang et al., 2024a; Jain et al., 2023; Lin and Chen, 2023; Murugadoss et al., 2025).

In contrast to previous work, we conduct our LLM-as-judge experiments using verbatim human evaluation instructions as a way of standardising prompt formulation. Furthermore, we investigate

Proceedings of the 4th Table Representation Learning Workshop, pages 98–108
July 31, 2025 ©2025 Association for Computational Linguistics

LLM-as-judge performance in this setting, comparing with more standard LLM prompt formulations, in meta-evaluation against human judgements on data-to-text tasks.

3 Datasets and Quality Criteria

3.1 WebNLG 2020

WebNLG 2020 is a data-to-text dataset that aligns sets of RDF triples (subject, predicate, object) with text. The English dataset has 1,779 input triple sets in the test set. For the human evaluation, 10% of the test dataset (178 items) was sampled and evaluated on outputs from each team's primary submission (14 submission systems + 3 baseline systems). We use the verbatim criteria from Castro Ferreira *et al.* (2020) which were rated on a scale of 0–100:

Data Coverage: Does the output text include descriptions of all predicates presented in the data?

Relevance: Does the output text describe only such predicates (with related subjects and objects), which are found in the data?

Correctness: When describing predicates which are found in the data, does the text mention correct the objects and adequately introduces the subject for this specific predicate?

Text Structure: Is the text grammatical, well-structured, written in acceptable English?

Fluency: Is it possible to say that the text progresses naturally, forms a coherent whole and it is easy to understand the text?

3.2 ROTOWIRE

ROTOWIRE (Wiseman et al., 2017) is a widely used data-to-text benchmark which contains NBA basketball game statistics and textual summaries for them ($\sim$ 5k instances). The ReproNLP 2023 shared task (Belz and Thomson, 2023) carried out two reproductions (Arvan and Parde, 2023; van Miltenburg et al., 2023a) of the human evaluation in Puduppully and Lapata (2021) which uses this dataset. In the human evaluation, five systems were evaluated on 200 instances per criterion. There are three ratings per item and the participants rank the summaries as either an 'A' or a 'B'. Here too we use the original definitions of the three criteria:

Grammaticality: Is the summary written in well-formed English?

Coherence: Is the summary well structured and well organized and does it have a natural ordering of the facts?

Repetition: Does the summary avoid unnecessary repetition including whole sentences, facts or phrases?

4 LLM-as-Judge Meta-evaluations

4.1 WebNLG'20 LLM-as-judge experiments

In the original WebNLG 2020 evaluation, each paired RDF triple set and system output was evaluated by three human evaluators. We obtain individual scores with each of the following three LLMs, then compute the mean of the three scores from different model and prompt combinations:

- J_H: LLM judgements using as the prompt the verbatim instructions from the original human evaluation in WebNLG 2020.
- J_{C+D}: LLM judgements using as the prompt conventional minimal zero-shot LLM prompts also incorporating the verbatim evaluation criterion definitions.
- J_{C-D}: Same as J_{C+D} minus the definitions.
- H: For comparison, we also test single human judgements from WebNLG'20 as predictors.

We use the following models (details Appendix C):

- Llama3-8B-Instruct (Touvron et al., 2023)
- Mistral-7B-Instruct-v0.2 (Chaplot, 2023)
- C4AI Command R+ (Cohere, 2024)

4.2 Rotowire LLM-as-judge experiments

In the original ROTOWIRE evaluation, system summaries were evaluated by three human evaluators. We obtain individual ratings with each of our three LLMs, then compute the majority vote of the three ratings. In this context, we use just the for-human instructions as in the original human evaluation. We test the correlations between the following LLM (combination)s and human judgements:

- H_1 and H_2: Two sets of human judgements obtained from two reproductions of Puduppully and Lapata (2021).
- J_{H_V}: Majority vote of LLM judgements by models of varying sizes (7B, 8B, 104B) and using the same human instructions (same models as in the WebNLG 2020 tests).
- J_{H_C}: Majority vote of LLM judgements on models of comparable sizes (two 7Bs and one 8B) and using the same human instructions. These are Llama3-8B-Instruct, Mistral-7B-Instruct-v0.2 and Qwen2.5-7B-Instruct-1M.

We use the same models as for WebNLG in the J_{H_V} tests, and replace the Cohere model with Qwen2.5-7B-Instruct-1M. (Yang et al., 2025)

	Correctness				Data Coverage				Fluency				Relevance				Text Structure			
	H	J_H	J_{C+D}	J_{C-D}	H	J_H	J_{C+D}	J_{C-D}	H	J_H	J_{C+D}	J_{C-D}	H	J_H	J_{C+D}	J_{C-D}	H	J_H	J_{C+D}	J_{C-D}
AAI	93.53	97.62	97.04	95.16	94.39	96.29	97.37	91.21	90.29	95.58	94.59	90.67	95.20	99.57	97.69	92.89	92.95	97.19	95.40	88.47
F17	90.14	97.13	97.88	94.54	92.07	94.67	97.72	90.56	80.94	95.11	94.70	90.29	92.59	99.62	98.25	92.15	85.74	97.14	95.41	87.45
F20	92.31	97.78	97.99	95.47	93.42	96.32	97.96	91.49	82.6	95.76	95.09	91.19	94.31	99.97	98.28	93.19	87.89	97.31	95.58	88.53
bt5	93.58	96.57	95.71	94.33	93.84	95.54	96.23	90.69	88.69	94.66	93.75	90.23	95.22	99.68	97.29	92.26	91.91	97.29	95.04	87.73
cuni	91.59	95.63	95.30	95.06	93.29	94.71	96.19	91.51	87.64	94.18	92.94	90.84	94.56	99.67	96.92	93.03	90.75	97.2	94.42	88.48
CGT	89.85	94.56	96.17	94.35	91.23	93.86	97.02	90.63	84.82	92.83	93.21	90.07	93.37	99.40	98.27	92.28	87.88	96.98	94.91	87.48
D-SGU	92.49	96.12	95.44	93.66	95.32	95.08	96.27	90.05	78.59	93.31	90.92	88.61	94.86	99.8	97.28	91.46	83.50	96.52	92.38	86.33
FB-AI	92.70	97.35	97.31	95.18	93.17	96.30	97.50	91.25	90.84	95.87	94.98	90.86	93.9	99.88	98.06	92.90	93.09	97.51	95.67	88.48
H_Lab	80.76	85.82	88.54	90.48	84.74	86.93	92.52	88.24	75.21	82.78	83.92	85.24	85.27	96.11	94.55	88.59	80.22	92.16	88.16	82.86
NILC	76.70	77.64	81.75	88.34	81.61	79.28	86.64	84.58	74.85	77.17	78.93	82.82	83.52	91.87	90.56	84.74	80.46	88.62	86.88	80.98
NUIG	92.05	96.06	95.49	95.02	92.06	95.18	96.53	91.41	88.90	94.68	93.83	90.61	94.06	99.14	97.31	92.85	91.59	97.35	95.06	88.23
O-NLG	74.98	74.29	77.35	85.00	79.96	77.68	82.68	83.94	75.68	73.12	74.83	79.90	79.89	88.03	86.74	81.65	80.46	85.14	84.43	78.71
OSU	93.41	96.57	95.78	95.16	95.12	95.48	96.67	91.14	90.07	95.50	93.83	90.72	94.62	99.31	97.38	93.04	92.44	97.41	95.10	88.65
RALI	92.13	97.54	96.52	94.56	95.20	96.20	96.69	90.82	77.76	94.86	92.53	89.83	94.81	99.74	97.52	92.48	81.84	97.07	94.12	87.46
TGEN	88.63	95.64	95.02	96.29	88.18	94.62	95.55	92.64	86.16	94.43	92.83	91.28	92.64	99.46	96.99	94.14	89.04	97.31	94.42	89.01
UPC	74.37	79.59	83.86	89.27	75.85	81.59	89.06	87.61	72.28	77.63	79.57	84.00	82.05	94.66	93.68	87.68	78.50	88.82	86.46	81.77
W-REF	94.15	97.59	97.64	95.01	95.44	95.99	97.71	91.02	89.85	95.54	95.38	90.67	94.39	99.80	98.35	92.96	92.11	97.28	95.83	88.16
Avg	88.43	92.56	93.22	**93.35**	90.29	92.10	**94.72**	89.93	83.25	**90.77**	90.34	88.7	91.49	**97.98**	96.18	91.08	87.08	**95.19**	92.90	86.4

Table 1: System-level average scores for each quality criterion by WebNLG'20 human judges (H), average over Llama3-8B-Instruct/Mistral-7B-Instruct-v0.2/Command R+ prompted with full human instructions (J_H); conventional zero-shot prompt with (J_{C+D}) and without definitions (J_{C-D}). System names (rows) with length > 4 letters are shortened by concatenating the first letter or first two letters with the last two/three letters.

	Single Human Judges Avg	Human Instructions as prompt mean of 3 scores by:				Zero-shot + original definitions mean of 3 scores by:				Zero-shot - original definitions mean of 3 scores by:			
		Mistral	Llama	CRplus	Mistral+ Llama+ CRplus	Mistral	Llama	CRplus	Mistral+ Llama+ CRplus	Mistral	Llama	CRplus	Mistral+ Llama+ CRplus
Correctness	0.69	0.93	0.94	0.99	**0.97**	0.72	0.93	0.98	0.95	0.90	0.25	0.98	0.92
Data Coverage	0.68	0.89	0.86	**0.96**	0.93	0.62	0.84	**0.96**	0.88	0.77	0.21	0.93	0.79
Fluency	0.68	0.67	0.75	**0.81**	0.78	0.48	0.84	**0.81**	0.80	0.74	0.68	0.79	0.79
Relevance	0.69	0.85	0.90	**0.98**	0.94	0.67	0.93	0.96	0.91	0.93	0.66	0.96	0.93
Text Structure	0.69	0.49	0.70	0.79	0.76	0.16	0.79	**0.87**	0.83	0.79	0.74	0.79	0.82

Table 2: Pearson's correlations with the aggregated WebNLG'20 human scores, achieved by single human judges and different LLMs.

4.3 Common details

We execute the above prompts as zero-shot inference prompts on the above LLMs. Moreover, we run the experiments with three different seeds (42; 1738; 1,234), meaning each score in tables below is the average of the outputs from the different seed runs. All experiments use English data.

5 Results and Analysis

5.1 Mean scores

Table 1 presents the system-level average scores per evaluation criterion for WebNLG. We observe that human evaluators and LLM judges generally agree with each other, with AAI, F17, F20, OSU, and W-REF often emerging as top performers and, O-NLG and UPC consistently rated lower by both human and LLM judges across multiple criteria.

Moreover, the averages of system-level scores (last row) by LLMs are higher than those by humans in all cases except three averages produced by the zero-shot prompt without definitions (J_{C-D}).

Table 3 presents the system-level average scores per evaluation criterion for the two Rotowire human evaluations (H_1, H_2), and the two types of majority vote, one with a much larger model in the mix (J_{H_V}), and one with similar sized models (J_{H_C}). Human and LLM judges agree on the high performance of the Gold system, although H_1 uniquely favours the Template system. Additionally, while J_{H_V} and J_{H_C} yield similar evaluations for top-performing systems, J_{H_C} tends to assign slightly higher scores for lower-performing systems (e.g., Template) in Coherence and Repetition.

5.2 Correlations with human judgements

Table 2 reports the correlations with the original WebNLG'20 human judgements achieved by: (i) individual human judges on average, (ii) each of the LLM model (combination)s. Strikingly, individual human judges have far lower agreement with the mean of the other judges (on the same outputs) than the LLMs. Another clear result is that the different models are affected very differently by

	Coherence				Repetition				Grammaticality			
	H_1	H_2	J_{H_V}	J_{H_C}	H_1	H_2	J_{H_V}	J_{H_C}	H_1	H_2	J_{H_V}	J_{H_C}
Gold	49.79	**56.25**	**70.00**	**70.00**	49.16	**52.92**	**70.83**	**73.75**	54.62	**57.08**	**70.83**	**64.58**
Template	**62.76**	40.00	18.75	24.58	**72.15**	47.08	22.92	26.25	**58.58**	38.33	32.08	42.08
ED+CC	42.50	46.25	42.08	41.67	36.97	47.50	44.17	41.67	40.17	45.83	37.50	40.42
Hier	44.77	54.58	60.42	56.67	42.62	50.42	56.25	51.67	45.19	54.58	52.92	49.17
Macro	50.21	52.92	58.75	57.08	49.15	52.08	55.83	56.67	51.48	54.17	56.67	53.75

Table 3: System-level average scores for each quality criterion by two sets of Rotowire human judges (H_1, H_2), average majority vote by varying-size models Llama3-8B-Instruct/Mistral-7B-Instruct-v0.2/Command R+ (J_{H_V}), and average majority vote by Llama3-8B-Instruct/Mistral-7B-Instruct-v0.2/Qwen2.5-7B-Instruct-1M (J_{H_C}).

	H_1	H_2	J_{H_V}	J_{H_C}
	Coherence			
H_1	1.000	-0.585	-0.626	-0.548
H_2	-0.585	1.000	0.992	0.982
J_{H_V}	-0.626	0.992	1.000	0.993
J_{H_C}	-0.548	0.982	0.993	1.000
	Grammaticality			
H_1	1.000	-0.185	0.134	0.358
H_2	-0.185	1.000	0.931	0.814
J_{H_V}	0.134	0.931	1.000	0.969
J_{H_C}	0.358	0.814	0.969	1.000
	Repetition			
H_1	1.000	-0.279	-0.620	-0.482
H_2	-0.279	1.000	0.899	0.936
J_{H_V}	-0.620	0.899	1.000	0.981
J_{H_C}	-0.482	0.936	0.981	1.000

Table 4: Pearson's correlation matrix for Rotowire / Coherence, Grammaticality & Repetition.

differences in prompts: all perform broadly similarly with the verbatim human instructions; Mistral scores collapse when human instructions are removed and definitions are retained, but recover when the definitions are also removed; and Llama scores are unaffected by the removal of human instructions, but collapse when the definitions are also removed. The Command R+ models does best with the human instructions, but largely retains its performance under the other two conditions.

Table 4 shows the complete correlation matrices between the two sets of Rotowire human judges and the two majority-voting combinations of LLMs, for each of the three evaluation criteria. Here, the most striking result is the stark discrepancy between the two sets of human judges: H_1 has a medium strong *negative* correlation with both H_2 and the LLMs for Coherence, weak or no correlation for Grammaticality, and weak or medium *negative* correlation for Repetition. In contrast H_2 and LLM combinations all agree strongly with each other. H_1 and H_2 also produced different reproducibility assessments compared to the original evaluation by Puduppully and Lapata (2021), as reported in the ReproNLP 2023 shared task report (Belz and Thomson, 2023).

In this situation, where one set of human evaluations disagrees with another, we have no basis for deciding which of the two gives a truer picture: either H_2 is right or H_1 is right, but they can't both be right. In this situation, a new role emerges for LLMs: as sanity checkers when human evaluations disagree. We discuss this further in the next section, and in a forthcoming paper (Huidrom and Belz, 2025).

6 Discussion and Conclusion

We have presented results for experiments with LLM-as-judge approaches for two types of data-to-text tasks and eight evaluation methods, using as a way of standardised prompt formulations the verbatim human instructions from previous evaluations. These were shown to work better than more conventional prompt formulations in all scenarios, irrespective of task or the length of input/output.

An unexpected discovery was that LLMs can serve as sanity checkers for human evaluations. The ReproNLP shared task organisers had no basis for deciding which of two reproductions of Puduppully and Lapata (2021) they reported was right: either Repro 1 (H_2 in this paper) was right and the work had excellent reproducibility, or Repro 2 (H_1) was right and it had terrible reproducibility. Because both of our LLM majority votes strongly agreed with Repro 1 and strongly disagreed with Repro 2, the indication is that Repro 1 (H_2) gave the better results out of the two reproductions.

Overall, we have found our best LLMs to be highly reliable predictors of human evaluations, and to benefit from human-type detailed evaluation instructions. The result that individual human judges correlate far less well with overall human judgements than LLMs do, implies that if the choice is between a small number of human judges and an LLM you are better off using the LLM.

Limitations

The experiments conducted showed promising alignment between human and LLM evaluations. Our evaluation covered only a limited set of models and tasks, so our findings are confined to those.

Ethics Statement

As a paper that meta-evaluates existing human evaluation tasks using the same and custom instructions, the risk associated with this study was minimal.

Acknowledgments

We thank all the reviewers for their valuable feedback and advice. Huidrom's work is supported by the Faculty of Engineering and Computing, DCU, via a PhD studentship. Both authors benefit from being members of the SFI Ireland funded ADAPT Research Centre.

References

Mohammad Arvan and Natalie Parde. 2023. Human evaluation reproduction report for data-to-text generation with macro planning. In *Proceedings of the 3rd Workshop on Human Evaluation of NLP Systems*, pages 89–96, Varna, Bulgaria. INCOMA Ltd., Shoumen, Bulgaria.

Simone Balloccu, Anya Belz, Rudali Huidrom, Ehud Reiter, João Sedoc, and Craig Thomson. 2024. Proceedings of the fourth workshop on human evaluation of nlp systems (humeval)@ lrec-coling 2024. In *Proceedings of the Fourth Workshop on Human Evaluation of NLP Systems (HumEval)@ LREC-COLING 2024*.

Anya Belz, Shubham Agarwal, Yvette Graham, Ehud Reiter, and Anastasia Shimorina. 2021. Proceedings of the workshop on human evaluation of nlp systems (humeval). In *Proceedings of the Workshop on Human Evaluation of NLP Systems (HumEval)*.

Anya Belz, Maja Popović, Ehud Reiter, and Anastasia Shimorina. 2022. Proceedings of the 2nd workshop on human evaluation of nlp systems (humeval). In *Proceedings of the 2nd Workshop on Human Evaluation of NLP Systems (HumEval)*.

Anya Belz, Maja Popović, Ehud Reiter, Craig Thomson, and João Sedoc. 2023. Proceedings of the 3rd workshop on human evaluation of nlp systems. In *Proceedings of the 3rd Workshop on Human Evaluation of NLP Systems*.

Anya Belz and Craig Thomson. 2023. The 2023 ReproNLP shared task on reproducibility of evaluations in NLP: Overview and results. In *Proceedings of the 3rd Workshop on Human Evaluation of NLP Systems*, pages 35–48, Varna, Bulgaria. INCOMA Ltd., Shoumen, Bulgaria.

Thiago Castro Ferreira, Claire Gardent, Nikolai Ilinykh, Chris van der Lee, Simon Mille, Diego Moussallem, and Anastasia Shimorina. 2020. The 2020 bilingual, bi-directional WebNLG+ shared task: Overview and evaluation results (WebNLG+ 2020). In *Proceedings of the 3rd International Workshop on Natural Language Generation from the Semantic Web (WebNLG+)*, pages 55–76, Dublin, Ireland (Virtual). Association for Computational Linguistics.

Devendra Singh Chaplot. 2023. Albert q. jiang, alexandre sablayrolles, arthur mensch, chris bamford, devendra singh chaplot, diego de las casas, florian bressand, gianna lengyel, guillaume lample, lucile saulnier, lélio renard lavaud, marie-anne lachaux, pierre stock, teven le scao, thibaut lavril, thomas wang, timothée lacroix, william el sayed. *arXiv preprint arXiv:2310.06825*.

Mark Chen, Jerry Tworek, Heewoo Jun, Qiming Yuan, Henrique Ponde De Oliveira Pinto, Jared Kaplan, Harri Edwards, Yuri Burda, Nicholas Joseph, Greg Brockman, et al. 2021. Evaluating large language models trained on code. *arXiv preprint arXiv:2107.03374*.

Cohere. 2024. Introducing command r+: A scalable llm built for business. *https://cohere.com/blog/command-r-plus-microsoft-azure*.

Alexander R Fabbri, Wojciech Kryściński, Bryan McCann, Caiming Xiong, Richard Socher, and Dragomir Radev. 2021. Summeval: Re-evaluating summarization evaluation. *Transactions of the Association for Computational Linguistics*, 9:391–409.

Markus Freitag, George Foster, David Grangier, Viresh Ratnakar, Qijun Tan, and Wolfgang Macherey. 2021. Experts, errors, and context: A large-scale study of human evaluation for machine translation. *Transactions of the Association for Computational Linguistics*, 9:1460–1474.

Jinlan Fu, See-Kiong Ng, Zhengbao Jiang, and Pengfei Liu. 2023. Gptscore: Evaluate as you desire. *arXiv preprint arXiv:2302.04166*.

Rudali Huidrom and Anya Belz. 2025. Using llm-as-judge evaluation for sanity-checking results and reproducibility of human evaluations of nlp systems. In *Proceedings of the 4th Workshop on Natural Language Generation, Evaluation, and Metrics (GEM)*, Vienna, Austria. Association for Computational Linguistics.

Sameer Jain, Vaishakh Keshava, Swarnashree Mysore Sathyendra, Patrick Fernandes, Pengfei Liu, Graham Neubig, and Chunting Zhou. 2023. Multi-dimensional evaluation of text summarization with in-context learning. *arXiv preprint arXiv:2306.01200*.

Takeshi Kojima, Shixiang Shane Gu, Machel Reid, Yutaka Matsuo, and Yusuke Iwasawa. 2022. Large language models are zero-shot reasoners. *Advances in neural information processing systems*, 35:22199–22213.

Haitao Li, Qian Dong, Junjie Chen, Huixue Su, Yujia Zhou, Qingyao Ai, Ziyi Ye, and Yiqun Liu. 2024. Llms-as-judges: a comprehensive survey on llm-based evaluation methods. *arXiv preprint arXiv:2412.05579*.

Yen-Ting Lin and Yun-Nung Chen. 2023. Llm-eval: Unified multi-dimensional automatic evaluation for open-domain conversations with large language models. *arXiv preprint arXiv:2305.13711*.

Yang Liu, Dan Iter, Yichong Xu, Shuohang Wang, Ruochen Xu, and Chenguang Zhu. 2023. G-eval: Nlg evaluation using gpt-4 with better human alignment. *arXiv preprint arXiv:2303.16634*.

Adian Liusie, Vatsal Raina, Yassir Fathullah, and Mark Gales. 2024. Efficient llm comparative assessment: a product of experts framework for pairwise comparisons. *arXiv preprint arXiv:2405.05894*.

Moran Mizrahi, Guy Kaplan, Dan Malkin, Rotem Dror, Dafna Shahaf, and Gabriel Stanovsky. 2024. State of what art? a call for multi-prompt llm evaluation. *Transactions of the Association for Computational Linguistics*, 12:933–949.

Bhuvanashree Murugadoss, Christian Poelitz, Ian Drosos, Vu Le, Nick McKenna, Carina Suzana Negreanu, Chris Parnin, and Advait Sarkar. 2025. Evaluating the evaluator: Measuring llms' adherence to task evaluation instructions. In *Proceedings of the AAAI Conference on Artificial Intelligence*, volume 39, pages 19589–19597.

Long Ouyang, Jeffrey Wu, Xu Jiang, Diogo Almeida, Carroll Wainwright, Pamela Mishkin, Chong Zhang, Sandhini Agarwal, Katarina Slama, Alex Ray, et al. 2022. Training language models to follow instructions with human feedback. *Advances in neural information processing systems*, 35:27730–27744.

Ratish Puduppully and Mirella Lapata. 2021. Data-to-text generation with macro planning. *Transactions of the Association for Computational Linguistics*, 9:510–527.

Craig Thomson, Ehud Reiter, and Belz Anya. 2024. Common flaws in running human evaluation experiments in nlp. *Computational Linguistics*.

Hugo Touvron, Thibaut Lavril, Gautier Izacard, Xavier Martinet, Marie-Anne Lachaux, Timothée Lacroix, Baptiste Rozière, Naman Goyal, Eric Hambro, Faisal Azhar, et al. 2023. Llama: Open and efficient foundation language models. *arXiv preprint arXiv:2302.13971*.

Emiel van Miltenburg, Anouck Braggaar, Nadine Braun, Debby Damen, Martijn Goudbeek, Chris van der Lee, Frédéric Tomas, and Emiel Krahmer. 2023a. How reproducible is best-worst scaling for human evaluation? a reproduction of 'data-to-text generation with macro planning'. In *Proceedings of the 3rd Workshop on Human Evaluation of NLP Systems*, pages 75–88, Varna, Bulgaria. INCOMA Ltd., Shoumen, Bulgaria.

Emiel van Miltenburg, Anouck Braggaar, Nadine Braun, Debby Damen, Martijn Goudbeek, Chris van der Lee, Frédéric Tomas, and Emiel Krahmer. 2023b. How reproducible is best-worst scaling for human evaluation? a reproduction of 'data-to-text generation with macro planning'. *Human Evaluation of NLP Systems*, page 75.

Sam Wiseman, Stuart Shieber, and Alexander Rush. 2017. Challenges in data-to-document generation. In *Proceedings of the 2017 Conference on Empirical Methods in Natural Language Processing*, pages 2253–2263, Copenhagen, Denmark. Association for Computational Linguistics.

An Yang, Bowen Yu, Chengyuan Li, Dayiheng Liu, Fei Huang, Haoyan Huang, Jiandong Jiang, Jianhong Tu, Jianwei Zhang, Jingren Zhou, et al. 2025. Qwen2. 5-1m technical report. *arXiv preprint arXiv:2501.15383*.

Kaiqi Zhang, Shuai Yuan, and Honghan Zhao. 2024a. Talec: teach your llm to evaluate in specific domain with in-house criteria by criteria division and zero-shot plus few-shot. *arXiv preprint arXiv:2407.10999*.

Yadong Zhang, Shaoguang Mao, Tao Ge, Xun Wang, Adrian de Wynter, Yan Xia, Wenshan Wu, Ting Song, Man Lan, and Furu Wei. 2024b. Llm as a mastermind: A survey of strategic reasoning with large language models. *arXiv preprint arXiv:2404.01230*.

A WebNLG 2020 Dataset

The WebNLG+ 2020 Challenge focused on (i) mapping RDF triples to generate English or Russian texts (generation) and (ii) converting English or Russian texts into RDF triples (semantic parsing). Our work addresses the generation task for English. The English WebNLG 2020 dataset (version 3.0) comprises 13,211/1,667/1,779 triple sets in the train, dev, and test splits, respectively, with triple sizes ranging from one to seven and 19 DBpedia categories, three of which are unseen in the training set. The challenge involved 15 teams submitting 48 system runs, with 14 teams focusing on English data and six on Russian data.

For the human evaluation, 10% of the test dataset was sampled (178 samples) and evaluated on each team's primary system submission. (Castro Ferreira et al., 2020) recruited 109 annotators via Amazon Mechanical Turk, providing them with instructions (criteria on a 0–100 slider scale), RDF triples, and system outputs. Each sample received three annotations.

B ROTOWIRE Dataset

The ReproHum initiative (Belz et al., 2021, 2022, 2023; Balloccu et al., 2024) curated two reproductions (Arvan and Parde, 2023; van Miltenburg et al., 2023a), of the human evaluation in Puduppully and Lapata (2021) which uses the ROTOWIRE dataset. Five systems were evaluated over three criteria on 200 instances per criteria. In total, there are 600 instances across all criteria. There are three ratings per item and the participants can only respond using the characters 'A' or 'B' to indicate their preference over the summaries. There were a total of 216 participants in the first reproductions and 262 participants in the second reproductions. The original study does not provide raw human evaluation scores, which is why we used the reproduced scores for comparison in our work.

C Models Used

Below are the models we used in our experiments; they were selected for being open-source, instruction-tuned LLMs with high ratings on Hugging Face.

- Llama3-8B-Instruct:[1] Meta's Llama 3 series model in the smaller 8B parameter size is pretrained, instruction-tuned, but also optimised for dialogue-based applications.
- Mistral-7B-Instruct-v0.2:[2] Mistral-7B-Instruct is a language model designed to follow instructions, generate creative text, and handle requests, fine-tuned from Mistral-7B-v0.2 using a diverse range of public conversation datasets.
- C4AI Command R+:[3] Cohere's open-weights research release of a 104B parameter model; a multilingual model evaluated in 10 languages for performance, and optimised for a variety of tasks including reasoning, summarization, and question answering.
- Qwen2.5-7B-Instruct-1M:[4] Alibaba's Qwen series model in the smaller 7B parameter size is fine-tuned, instruction-tuned and is optimised to handle long-context tasks while maintaining its capability in short tasks.

D Experiment Setup

We briefly outline the experimental setup used in all of our experiments in this section. We use three large language models for our experiments: Meta-Llama-3-8B-Instruct, Mistral-7B-Instruct-v0.2 and c4ai-command-r-plus-4bit. For hyperparameters, we set temperature to 0.001, maximum length to 1024 for WebNLG'20 & 128 for ROTOWIRE and top p to 1. The choice of our hyperparameters is to produce near-deterministic outputs while preserving subtle probabilistic distinctions in the model's token preferences. We quantise the models to 4-bit and use one rtxa6000/a100 GPU for the execution of our experiments. The cumulative GPU time required for our experiments was a little over 150 GPU hours.

E Experimental Grid

For WebNLG 2020: {English}x{Llama3-8B-Instruct, Mistral-7B-Instruct-v0.2, command-r-plus-4bit}x{zero-shot}x{seeds: 42, 1738, 1234}x{Evaluator(s) set-up: one LLM as one evaluator on (a) same instructions as the human evaluation, (b) custom minimal zero-shot prompt with original definitions included, (c) custom minimal zero-shot prompt without original definitions included}.

For ROTOWIRE: {English}x{Llama3-8B-Instruct, Mistral-7B-Instruct-v0.2, command-r-plus-4bit, Qwen2.5-7B-Instruct-1M}x{zero-shot}x{seeds: 42, 1738, 1234}x{Evaluator(s) set-up: one LLM as one evaluator on same instructions as the human evaluation across (a) models of varying sizes, (b) models of comparable sizes}.

F Prompts

We present the prompt used in our experiments in this section. In particular, we outline the general instruction used for all LLMs, we present the prompt template for each LLM. All of this can be found in Tables 5–7.

[1] https://huggingface.co/meta-llama/Meta-Llama-3-8B-Instruct

[2] https://huggingface.co/mistralai/Mistral-7B-Instruct-v0.2

[3] https://huggingface.co/CohereForAI/c4ai-command-r-plus-4bit

[4] https://huggingface.co/Qwen/Qwen2.5-7B-Instruct-1M

G Use of AI Assistants for Writing

We use AI Assistants to sanity check our writing. Grammarly was used for grammar checking, QuillBot (mostly) and ChatGPT (sometimes) were used for rephrasing.

Common Template for All Prompts for J_H	
{task_desc}	Please (i) follow the instructions, (ii) be honest and fair in your judgements, (iii) try to be as correct as possible in your conclusions. For example, the text would generally get a score higher than 0 for Correctness if at least some objects in it are introduced correctly. Similarly, the text would not be rated with 100 for Correctness if at least one object is not introduced correctly.
{task_instr}	Task Instructions: You are given a piece of data and a text that describes data. Below you will find statements that relate to the text. Please rate each of these statements by moving the slider along the scale where 0 stands for 'I do not agree', and 100 stands for 'I fully agree'.
{data}	DATA:
{desc}	DESCRIPTION:
{statement}	How well do you agree with the following statements?
{datacoverage_criteria}	Data Coverage: The text contains all predicates from the data and does not miss any predicates shown in the data.
{relevance_criteria}	Relevance: The text contains only known/relevant predicates, which are found in the data. The text does not contain any unknown/irrelevant/unrecognizable predicates.
{correctness_criteria}	Correctness: When describing information about relevant predicates (those which are in both data and text), the text depicts them with correct/proper objects. Also, the text correctly introduces the subject.
{textstr_criteria}	Text Structure: The text is written in good English, i.e., it is free from grammatical errors and well-structured.
{fluency_criteria	Fluency: The text sounds logically correct and forms a coherent whole. There are no parts of the text you would change to make it sound better. The text forms a nice narrative.
{feedback}	Write your feedback in the field below if you have any (not necessary):
Llama3-8B-Instruct Prompt	
Special tokens	{llama3_bos}: ⟨|begin_of_text|⟩ ; {llama3_eos}: ⟨|end_of_text|⟩ ; {llama3_sot}: {{; {llama3_eot}: }}
Template	{llama3_bos} {llama3_sot}{task_description}{task_instruction}{data}{triples} {description}{verb} {statement}{datacoverage}{relevance}{correctness} {textstructure}{fluency}{feedback} {llama3_eot}{llama3_eos} Data Coverage: Relevance: Correctness: Text Structure: Fluency:
Mistral-7B-Instruct-v0.2 Prompt	
Special tokens	{mistral_bos}: ⟨s⟩ ; {mistral_eos}: ⟨/s⟩ ; {mistral_sot}: [INST] ; {mistral_eot}: [/INST]
Template	{mistral_bos}{mistral_sot} {task_description}{task_instruction}{data}{triples} {description}{verb} {statement}{datacoverage}{relevance}{correctness} {textstructure}{fluency}{feedback}{mistral_eot}{mistral_eos} Data Coverage: Relevance: Correctness: Text Structure: Fluency:
Command-r-plus-4bit Prompt	
Special tokens	{commandrplus_instruction}: ## Instructions\n; {commandrplus_input}: ## Input\n; {commandrplus_output}: ## Output\n; {commandrplus_criterion}: ## Criterion\n
Template	{commandrplus_instruction}{task_description} {task_instruction}{commandrplus_input}{data}{triples} {commandrplus_output}{description}{verb}{commandrplus_criterion} {statement}{datacoverage}{relevance}{correctness} {textstructure}{fluency}{feedback}Output: Data Coverage: Relevance: Correctness: Text Structure: Fluency:

Table 5: Human Evaluation Guidelines from WebNLG 2020 given to the LLMs.

<table>
<tr><th colspan="2">Common Template for All Prompts for J_{C+D} & J_{C-D}</th></tr>
<tr><td>{our_task_desc}</td><td>You are an evaluator. Please read the instructions carefully and provide your judgements honestly and accurately.</td></tr>
<tr><td>{zs_minimal}</td><td>Rate the following input triple(s) and text that describes the input triple(s) on a scale from 0 to 100 based on the following criteria:</td></tr>
<tr><td>{input_triples}</td><td>Input Triple(s):</td></tr>
<tr><td>{text}</td><td>Text:</td></tr>
<tr><td>{datacoverage_criteria}</td><td>Data Coverage: The text contains all predicates from the data and does not miss any predicates shown in the data.</td></tr>
<tr><td>{relevance_criteria}</td><td>Relevance: The text contains only known/relevant predicates, which are found in the data. The text does not contain any unknown/irrelevant/unrecognizable predicates.</td></tr>
<tr><td>{correctness_criteria}</td><td>Correctness: When describing information about relevant predicates (those which are in both data and text), the text depicts them with correct/proper objects. Also, the text correctly introduces the subject.</td></tr>
<tr><td>{textstr_criteria}</td><td>Text Structure: The text is written in good English, i.e., it is free from grammatical errors and well-structured.</td></tr>
<tr><td>{fluency_criteria</td><td>Fluency: The text sounds logically correct and forms a coherent whole. There are no parts of the text you would change to make it sound better. The text forms a nice narrative.</td></tr>
<tr><th colspan="2">Llama3-8B-Instruct Prompt</th></tr>
<tr><td>Special tokens</td><td>{llama3_bos}: ⟨|begin_of_text|⟩ ; {llama3_eos}: ⟨|end_of_text|⟩ ; {llama3_sot}: {{; {llama3_eot}: }}</td></tr>
<tr><td>Template</td><td>{llama3_bos}
{llama3_sot}{our_task_desc}{zs_minimal}
{datacoverage}{relevance}{correctness}{textstructure}{fluency}
{input_triples}{triples}
{text}{verb}{llama3_eot}{llama3_eos}
Output:
Data Coverage:
Relevance:
Correctness:
Text Structure:
Fluency:</td></tr>
<tr><th colspan="2">Mistral-7B-Instruct-v0.2 Prompt</th></tr>
<tr><td>Special tokens</td><td>{mistral_bos}: ⟨s⟩ ; {mistral_eos}: ⟨/s⟩ ; {mistral_sot}: [INST] ; {mistral_eot}: [/INST]</td></tr>
<tr><td>Template</td><td>{mistral_bos}{mistral_sot}{our_task_desc}{zs_minimal}
{datacoverage}{relevance}{correctness}{textstructure}{fluency}
{input_triples}{triples}
{text}{verb}{mistral_eot}{mistral_eos}
Output:
Data Coverage:
Relevance:
Correctness:
Text Structure:
Fluency:</td></tr>
<tr><th colspan="2">Command-r-plus-4bit Prompt</th></tr>
<tr><td>Special tokens</td><td>{commandrplus_instruction}: ## Instructions\n; {commandrplus_criterion}: ## Criterion\n {commandrplus_input}: ## Input\n; {commandrplus_output}: ## Output\n</td></tr>
<tr><td>Template</td><td>{commandrplus_instruction}{our_task_desc}{zs_minimal}
{commandrplus_criterion}{datacoverage}{relevance}{correctness}{textstructure}{fluency}
{commandrplus_input}{input_triples}{triples}
{commandrplus_output}{text}{verb}
Output:
Data Coverage:
Relevance:
Correctness:
Text Structure:
Fluency:</td></tr>
</table>

Table 6: Custom zero-shot instructions given to the LLMs.
{datacoverage}{relevance}{correctness}{textstructure}{fluency} is used only for instructions with definitions.

<table>
<tr><th colspan="2">Common Template for All Prompts for J_{H_V} & J_{H_C}</th></tr>
<tr><td>{summaries}</td><td>Summaries</td></tr>
<tr><td>{sys_summaries}</td><td>System Summaries</td></tr>
<tr><td>{A}</td><td>A:</td></tr>
<tr><td>{B}</td><td>B:</td></tr>
<tr><td>{rank_criteria}</td><td>Ranking Criteria</td></tr>
<tr><td>{Criteria}</td><td>Coherence or Grammaticality or Repetition</td></tr>
<tr><td>{answer}</td><td>Answers</td></tr>
<tr><td>{best}</td><td>Best:</td></tr>
<tr><td>{worst}</td><td>Worst:</td></tr>
<tr><td>{analysis}</td><td>Analysis</td></tr>
<tr><th colspan="2">System-level Prompt</th></tr>
<tr><td>{gen_instr_rotowire}</td><td>You are a native speaker of English or a near-native speaker who can comfortably comprehend summary of NBA basketball games written in English.</td></tr>
<tr><td>{task_head_rotowire}</td><td>Evaluate Sports Summaries of (NBA) basketball games.</td></tr>
<tr><td>{task_instr_rotowire}</td><td>Your task is to read two short texts which have been produced by different automatic systems. These systems typically take a large table as input which contains statistics of a basketball game and produce a document which summarizes the table in natural langauge (e.g., talks about what happened in the game, who scored, who won and so on). Please read the two summaries carefully and judge how good each is according to the following criterion:</td></tr>
<tr><td>{task_desc_rotowire}</td><td>This task contains validation instances (for which answers are known) that will be used for an automatic quality assessment of submissions. Therefore, please read the summaries carefully.</td></tr>
<tr><td>System Prompt:</td><td>{gen_instr_rotowire}
{task_head_rotowire}
{task_instr_rotowire}
{task_desc_rotowire}</td></tr>
<tr><th colspan="2">Llama3-8B-Instruct Prompt</th></tr>
<tr><td>Special tokens</td><td>{llama3_bos}: ⟨|begin_of_text|⟩ ; {llama3_eos}: ⟨|end_of_text|⟩ ; {llama3_sot}: {{; {llama3_eot}: }}</td></tr>
<tr><td>Template</td><td>{llama3_bos}{llama3_sot}{summaries}{sys_summaries}{A}{a}
{B}{b}
{rank_criteria}{Criteria}{answer}{best}
{worst}
{analysis}{llama3_eot}{llama3_eos}</td></tr>
<tr><th colspan="2">Mistral-7B-Instruct-v0.2 Prompt</th></tr>
<tr><td>Special tokens</td><td>{mistral_bos}: ⟨s⟩ ; {mistral_eos}: ⟨/s⟩ ; {mistral_sot}: [INST] ; {mistral_eot}: [/INST]</td></tr>
<tr><td>Template</td><td>{mistral_bos}{summaries}{sys_summaries}{A}{a}
{B}{b}
{rank_criteria}{Criteria}{answer}{best}
{worst}
{analysis}{mistral_eot}{mistral_eos}</td></tr>
<tr><th colspan="2">Command-r-plus-4bit Prompt</th></tr>
<tr><td>Special tokens</td><td>{commandrplus_instruction}: ## Instructions\n; {commandrplus_criterion}: ## Criterion\n {commandrplus_input}: ## Input\n; {commandrplus_output}: ## Output\n</td></tr>
<tr><td>Template</td><td>{commandrplus_instruction}{summaries}{sys_summaries}
{commandrplus_input}{A}{a}
{B}{b}
{commandrplus_criterion}{rank_criteria}{Criteria}
{commandrplus_output}{answer}{best}
{worst}
{analysis}
Output:
Best:
Worst:</td></tr>
<tr><th colspan="2">Qwen2.5-7B-Instruct-1M Prompt</th></tr>
<tr><td>Special tokens</td><td>-</td></tr>
<tr><td>Template</td><td>{summaries}{sys_summaries}{A}{a}
{B}{b}
{rank_criteria}{Criteria}{answer}{best}
{worst}
{analysis}
Output:
Best:
Worst:</td></tr>
</table>

Table 7: Human Evaluation Guidelines from Puduppully and Lapata (2021) given to the LLMs.

Table Understanding and (Multimodal) LLMs: A Cross-Domain Case Study on Scientific vs. Non-Scientific Data

Ekaterina Borisova[1,2], **Fabio Barth**[1], **Nils Feldhus**[1,2,3],
Raia Abu Ahmad[1,2], **Malte Ostendorff**[4], **Pedro Ortiz Suarez**[5],
Georg Rehm[1,6], **Sebastian Möller**[1,2]

[1]Deutsches Forschungszentrum für Künstliche Intelligenz GmbH (DFKI),
[2]Technische Universität Berlin, [3]BIFOLD, [4]Deutsche Telekom,
[5]Common Crawl Foundation, [6]Humboldt-Universität zu Berlin

Corresponding author: ekaterina.borisova@dfki.de

Abstract

Tables are among the most widely used tools for representing structured data in research, business, medicine, and education. Although LLMs demonstrate strong performance in downstream tasks, their efficiency in processing tabular data remains underexplored. In this paper, we investigate the effectiveness of both text-based and multimodal LLMs on table understanding tasks through a cross-domain and cross-modality evaluation. Specifically, we compare their performance on tables from scientific vs. non-scientific contexts and examine their robustness on tables represented as images vs. text. Additionally, we conduct an interpretability analysis to measure context usage and input relevance. We also introduce the **TableEval** benchmark, comprising 3017 tables from scholarly publications, Wikipedia, and financial reports, where each table is provided in five different formats: Image, Dictionary, HTML, XML, and LaTeX. Our findings indicate that while LLMs maintain robustness across table modalities, they face significant challenges when processing scientific tables.

1 Introduction

Tables are one of the most ubiquitous tools for presenting data in a structured or semi-structured manner. They are commonly represented in a variety of textual (e. g., HTML, LaTeX, XML) or image formats (e. g., PNG, JPEG) and used across domains such as finance, medicine, and business, as well as in research and education.

In recent years, there has been a growing interest in table understanding (TU) techniques (Zhang and Balog, 2020; Gorishniy et al., 2021; Sahakyan et al., 2021; Borisov et al., 2022; Sui et al., 2024; Deng et al., 2024), aiming to extract and interpret information and knowledge contained in tables for tasks such as question answering (QA) and table-to-text generation (T2T) (Nan et al., 2022; Cheng et al., 2022; Osés Grijalba et al., 2024; Zheng et al., 2024). While large language models (LLMs) demonstrate strong performance in a wide range of applications (Chang et al., 2024; Raiaan et al., 2024; Caffagni et al., 2024; Zhang et al., 2024a; Team et al., 2024; OpenAI et al., 2024), their ability to understand (semi-)structured data remains under-researched (Sui et al., 2024; Fang et al., 2024) – especially for tables from *scientific* sources such as peer-reviewed articles, conference proceedings, and pre-prints.[1] There is also limited research on the impact of the representation modality of structured data (i. e., image vs. text) on model performance (Deng et al., 2024; Zhang et al., 2024d), and to the best of our knowledge, there are no approaches yet that specifically address scientific tables. In particular, most TU studies primarily focus on tables from *non-scientific* contexts such as Wikipedia (Parikh et al., 2020; Chen et al., 2021; Marzocchi et al., 2022; Wu et al., 2024b; Pang et al., 2024). However, compared to these domains, scientific tables often include technical terminology, complex concepts, abbreviations, and dense numerical values, requiring domain-specific knowledge and strong arithmetic reasoning skills (Ho et al., 2024; Moosavi et al., 2021). Recent works (Yang et al., 2025; Wu et al., 2024a) indicate that scientific tables present challenges to multimodal LLMs (MLLMs) and incorporating such (semi-)structured data into pretraining improves performance. As the number of published articles continues to increase rapidly (Fortunato et al., 2018; Bornmann et al., 2021; Hong et al., 2021), TU for scientific contexts, e. g., for scholarly document processing including information extraction and research knowledge graph construction, is becoming even more relevant. Finally, we

[1]Throughout this paper, we refer to such tables as *scientific* and to tables from other sources as *non-scientific*.

Proceedings of the 4th Table Representation Learning Workshop, pages 109–142
July 31, 2025 ©2025 Association for Computational Linguistics

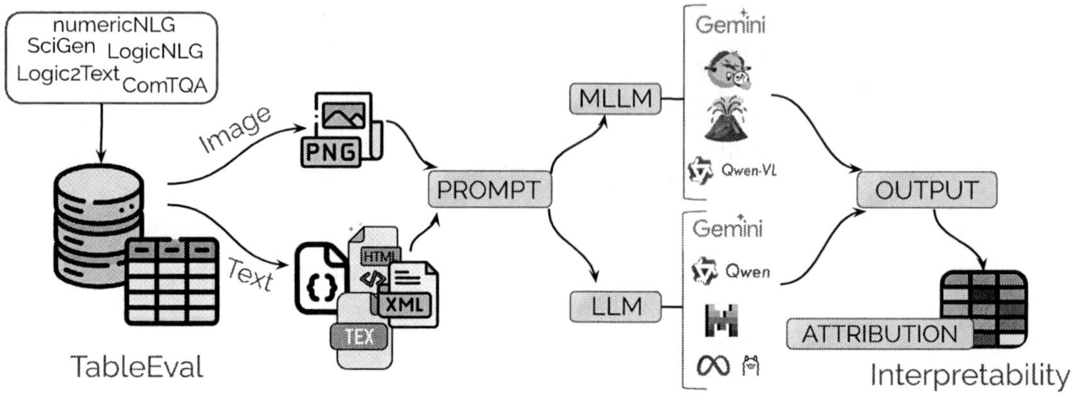

Figure 1: Schematic representation of the main phases in our experiments: 1. Develop TableEval dataset, 2. Evaluate each (M)LLM on individual data subsets from TableEval using various table representations (Image, LaTeX, XML, HTML, Dict), 3. Apply interpretability tools to the output yielding post-hoc feature attributions (e. g., using gradient-based saliency) which signify the importance of each token with respect to the model's output.

notice that interpretability analysis (Ferrando et al., 2024) for TU has received little attention and remains underexplored (Fang et al., 2024).

In this paper, we address the aforementioned gaps by examining the efficiency of both LLMs and MLLMs on a set of TU tasks. Specifically, we compare their ability to handle (semi-)structured data from scientific and non-scientific sources and explore the effects of image vs. diverse text-based table representations on model performance. We also conduct feature importance analyses to interpret the use of context information in LLMs. Figure 1 illustrates the main phases of our experiments.

Our contributions can be summarised as follows:

- We introduce TableEval, a cross-domain benchmark containing 3017 tables from scholarly publications, Wikipedia, and financial reports, available in image and four text formats (Dictionary, HTML, XML, and LaTeX). The dataset is publicly available on Hugging Face: `https://huggingface.co/datasets/katebor/TableEval`

- We conduct an extensive evaluation revealing that, although current (M)LLMs remain robust across table modalities, their performance significantly declines on scientific tables compared to non-scientific ones.

- We examine the applicability of gradient-based explanations for LLMs (Sarti et al., 2023) to TU to learn about the relevance of table content in prompts.

2 TableEval benchmark

Since no existing dataset covers both scientific and non-scientific tables across text and image modalities, we construct a benchmark tailored to our evaluation. This section outlines the collection processes of data (§2.1) and diverse table formats (§2.2).

2.1 Source data

To study the cross-domain performance of (M)LLMs, we developed the TableEval benchmark by leveraging pre-existing datasets of scientific and non-scientific tables. We collected relevant datasets based on the following criteria: 1. data is open-access; 2. test set with the gold labels is available; 3. metadata includes references to the sources of tables, such as DOIs for scholarly papers or URLs for Wikipedia pages; 4. target tasks (e. g., QA, T2T) are identical or very similar across datasets to maintain consistency and ensure comparability; 5. tables can be converted to the pre-defined formats (see §2.2). The following five datasets were selected (see Table 1): (a) **ComTQA** (Zhao et al., 2024), a visual QA (VQA) benchmark containing tables from PubTables-1M (Smock et al., 2022) and FinTabNet (Zheng et al., 2020), originating from PubMed Central[2] (PMC) papers and annual earnings reports, respectively. The annotations are generated using Gemini Pro (Team et al., 2024) and include questions requiring multiple answers, calculations, and logical reasoning. (b) **numericNLG** (Suadaa et al., 2021), a dataset focusing on the T2T generation task with numerical reasoning based on tables and

[2] `https://pubmed.ncbi.nlm.nih.gov`

Dataset	Task	Source	Image	Dict	LaTeX	HTML	XML
		Scientific tables					
ComTQA (PubTables-1M)	VQA	PubMed Central	⬇	⚙	⚙	⚙	⧉
numericNLG	T2T	ACL Anthology	⧉	⬇	⚙	⬇	⚙
SciGen	T2T	arXiv and ACL Anthology	⧉	⬇	⧉	⚙	⚙
		Non-scientific tables					
ComTQA (FinTabNet)	VQA	Earnings reports of S&P 500 companies	⧉	⚙	⚙	⚙	⚙
LogicNLG	T2T	Wikipedia	⚙	⬇	⚙	⧉	⚙
Logic2Text	T2T	Wikipedia	⚙	⬇	⚙	⧉	⚙

Table 1: Overview on the formats and collection methods for each dataset. Symbol ⬇ indicates formats already available in the given corpus, while ⧉ and ⚙ denote formats extracted from the table source files (e. g., article PDF, Wikipedia page) and generated from other formats in this study, respectively.

their textual descriptions extracted from ACL Anthology[3] articles and annotated by experts in the Computer Science field. (c) **SciGen** (Moosavi et al., 2021), a corpus designed for reasoning-aware T2T generation, comprising tables from arXiv[4] papers across fields such as Computation and Language, Machine Learning, Computer Science, Computational Geometry, etc. Its test set contains expert-annotated data. (d) **LogicNLG** (Chen et al., 2020a), a T2T dataset of open-domain tables from Wikipedia and associated with manually annotated natural language statements that can be logically entailed by the given data. (e) **Logic2Text** (Chen et al., 2020c), features open-domain Wikipedia tables manually annotated with descriptions of common logic types and their underlying logical forms for the T2T task. As shown in Table 1, the final TableEval corpus contains six data subsets, covering two downstream tasks (QA and T2T), and comprising 3017 tables and 11312 instances in total (for the detailed statistics see Table 4 in Appendix A). All annotations are taken from the source datasets. Examples from each dataset are provided in Appendix B.

2.2 Table formats

We represent tables from each TableEval subset as PNG images and in structured or semi-structured textual formats including HTML, XML, LaTeX, and Python Dictionary (Dict) to analyse LLMs' performance across different modalities. HTML is chosen as it is the original format of Wikipedia tables, XML for its use in encoding tables from PMC articles, LaTeX as it is the primary format for scientific tables, and Dict since it is readily available in most source datasets. Instances of tables in various representation formats were obtained using one of the following methods (see Table 1): 1. extraction from the original dataset; 2. extraction from the table source (e. g., article PDF); 3. generation from other formats (e. g., HTML ⇔ XML). Note that for the latter two, we manually validate the final results for each format and data subset by checking a random sample of about 100 instances. In what follows, the way we assembled each table format in the TableEval corpus is described in detail. Additional information is provided in Appendix C.

Image. Since the PubTables-1M subset of ComTQA already includes JPGs of tables, we simply convert them to PNGs. In contrast, other datasets provide only textual representations of tables. Thus, for numericNLG and SciGen, we first collect PDF files of the arXiv and ACL papers, and then use the PDFFigure2.0 (Clark and Divvala, 2016) tool to extract images of tables.[5] Whenever PDFFigure2.0 fails to produce an image, we utilise the MinerU tool (Wang et al., 2024) as an alternative. Note that SciGen instances associated with papers that are no longer open-access or do not contain tables are excluded. In case of FinTabNet, images of tables are extracted from the corresponding PDF pages of financial reports using the gold annotations of the bounding boxes. Finally, images of the Wikipedia tables in LogicNLG and Logic2Text are generated by converting their HTML representations into PNG files with the imgkit Python wrapper[6]. Distribution of image aspect rations across data subsets is provided in Figure 12 in Appendix D.

XML and HTML. PubTables-1M is the only dataset where the original XML sources of tables

[3] https://aclanthology.org
[4] https://arxiv.org

[5] In SciGen, some PDFs are taken from the ACL Anthology as they are no longer available on arXiv.
[6] https://pypi.org/project/imgkit/

can be obtained. To achieve this, we retrieve the source papers based on their PMC ID using the E-utilities API[7] and extract the tables with the ElementTree parser[8]. When it comes to HTML, we are unable to retrieve the original format since systematic downloading of article batches from the PMC website is prohibited[9]. This is why we generate HTML from XML using a custom Python script instead. Similarly, for numericNLG, we convert already available HTML into XML with a Python script. For SciGen, we download the source LaTeX code of each paper from arXiv, use the LaTeXML tool[10] to produce both XML and HTML, and extract tables from the resulting files. In contrast, we construct HTML for FinTabNet tables by leveraging gold annotations of HTML structure which provide tags and associated cell values. Afterwards, the HTML code is converted to XML in the same way as described for numericNLG. Finally, HTML in LogicNLG and Logic2Text are collected from the respective Wikipedia pages, while the XML format is obtained using the same approach applied to numericNLG and FinTabNet.

LaTeX. For SciGen, we obtain the LaTeX code directly from the source files of the papers. In contrast to arXiv data, no LaTeX code is available for PMC and ACL papers. Thus, we generate LaTeX for numericNLG and PubTables-1M tables from their HTML representations. To ensure the validity of the output, we compile the code and resolve any errors encountered. The same approach is used to obtain LaTeX for Wikipedia and financial tables.

Dictionary. All datasets except ComTQA already include linearised tables represented as lists of column headers and cell values, although the encoding conventions slightly vary across them (see Appendix C). To align with these datasets, we collect column headers, subheaders, and cell values for the PMC subset in ComTQA by parsing the table XML code with ElementTree. In case of FinTabNet, we extract these elements from a dataframe representation of each table obtained during the HTML collection phase. For the experiments, the linearised tables are represented as a Dict containing lists of column headers, lists of subheaders (if extracted), lists of rows, as well as title, caption, and footnote (if available).

3 Experiments

We benchmark various (M)LLMs using individual data subsets and representations of tables from TableEval. This is followed by an interpretability analysis applied to the output yielding attributions from a gradient-based method. In the following, we first describe the experimental set up (§3.1), then report and analyse the results (§3.2).

3.1 Experimental setup

Models. We evaluate both smaller and larger models in terms of parameter size (3-14 billion), see Table 2.[11] We primarily focus on open-source instruction-tuned (M)LLMs published on Hugging Face[12] (HF). The only closed-source model we use is Gemini-2.0-Flash (Team et al., 2024), which serves as our baseline, since Gemini is currently considered among the state-of-the-art. For MLLMs, we select LLaVa-NeXT (Li et al., 2024), Qwen2.5-VL (Bai et al., 2025), and Idefics3 (Laurençon et al., 2024). As for text-based LLMs, we evaluate Llama-3 (Grattafiori et al., 2024), Qwen2.5 (Qwen et al., 2025), and Mistral-Nemo[13].

Model	HF checkpoint	Size (B)	Vision
Gemini-2.0-Flash	–	–	✔
LLaVa-NeXT	llama3-llava-next-8b-hf	8	✔
Qwen2.5-VL	Qwen2.5-VL-3B-Instruct	3	✔
	Qwen2.5-VL-7B-Instruct	7	✔
Idefics3	Idefics3-8B-Llama3	8	✔
Llama-3	Llama-3.2-3B-Instruct	3	✖
Qwen2.5	Qwen2.5-3B-Instruct	3	✖
	Qwen2.5-14B-Instruct	14	✖
Mistral-Nemo	Mistral-Nemo-Instruct-2407	12	✖

Table 2: (M)LLMs used in the experiments ("Size" indicates the number of parameters in billions).

Prompts and data. We run experiments on every data subset from the TableEval corpus and develop prompt templates that are customised to each task, applying them uniformly across all models to ensure consistency during the evaluation. To study the models' true capability to understand various table representations, we exclude explicit document type indicators (e. g., HTML/XML headers) and do not specify the format in the prompt. Additionally, given the diversity of the (M)LLMs and the fact that they may not always adhere to a specific

[7] https://www.ncbi.nlm.nih.gov/home/develop/api/

[8] https://docs.python.org/3/library/xml.etree.elementtree.html#

[9] https://pmc.ncbi.nlm.nih.gov/about/copyright/

[10] https://math.nist.gov/~BMiller/LaTeXML/

[11] Due to limited computational resources, we restricted the evaluation to (M)LLMs with up to 14 billion parameters.

[12] https://huggingface.co

[13] https://mistral.ai/news/mistral-nemo

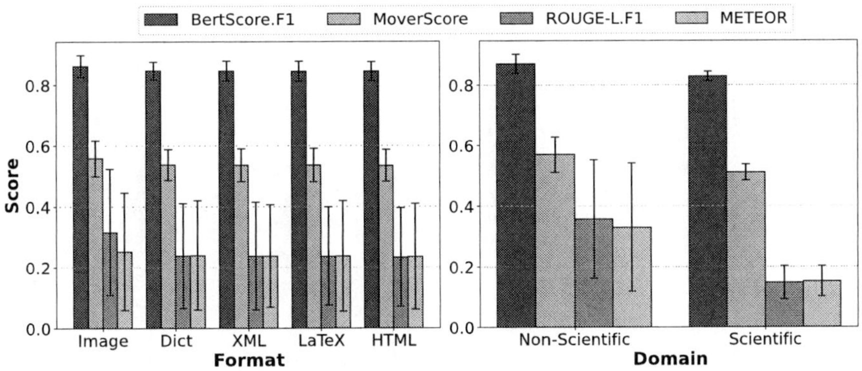

Figure 2: BertScore.F1, MoverScore, ROUGE-L.F1, and METEOR for the table formats averaged over data subsets and models (left), and for scientific vs. non-scientific domain averaged over data subsets, models, and formats (right). Error bars indicate standard deviation.

output structure (which can hinder proper parsing of the answer), we do not enforce a particular response format. The prompt templates are provided in Appendix E.

Evaluation metrics. We follow the scores reported in the original papers for each data subset. Thus, we compute BLEU-N (Papineni et al., 2002), SacreBLEU (Post, 2018), METEOR (Banerjee and Lavie, 2005), ROUGE-N, ROUGE-L (Lin, 2004), MoverScore (Zhao et al., 2019), BertScore (Zhang* et al., 2020), and BLEURT (Sellam et al., 2020). Given the extensive set of metrics, we report only BertScore.F1, MoverScore, ROUGE-L.F1, and METEOR in the main text, while providing all raw score values in Appendix F.

Interpretability analysis. Inseq (Sarti et al., 2023) applies feature attribution methods to generative LLMs to highlight how important each token in the input is for generating the next token with the help of a heatmap. In our experimental setup, we perform post-hoc analyses using the model outputs as custom attribution targets on an instance level. Input x Gradient (Simonyan et al., 2014), provided by Inseq, is selected as it is both computationally efficient and more faithful than, e. g., attention weights. The saliency is averaged to produce a one-dimensional vector of token attributions, which we visualise as a heatmap.

Implementation details. All experiments are conducted in a zero-shot setting using the (M)LLMs' default hyperparameters with the seed value set to 42. We choose the batch size equal to 1 for all open-source (M)LLMs and to the size of the given subset for Gemini-2.0-Flash. We use Nvidia A100 (40GB, 80GB), H100 (80GB), H200 (141GB), and L40S (48GB) GPUs for the open-source models depending on the given LLM and TableEval subset size. The Gemini-2.0-Flash results are evaluated using the Batch API through the LiteLLM framework[14]. We developed an end-to-end evaluation pipeline[15] for the experiments and use HF transformers or LiteLLM and the datasets library to load the models and datasets, respectively.

3.2 Results and analysis

Image vs. text. Averaged score values across models and data subsets for each table format are given in Figure 2 (left), whereas raw results are shown in Table 5 in Appendix F. The use of images outperforms the use of text across all metrics by approximately 1-13%. In particular, for ComTQA and LogicNLG, image achieves the best results, while for other data subsets the outcomes are either similar or the text modality prevails (by about 1-10%), as shown in Figure 3 a) and Tables 6–11 in Appendix F. This aligns with previous studies (Deng et al., 2024) reporting comparable or significantly better performance of models on the vision modality. Unlike prior works (Sui et al., 2024; Singha et al., 2023; Deng et al., 2024), we do not observe a large variation in results across LLMs and the four text formats, with the maximum gap equal to about 4%. Further analysis of the metrics for individual models and formats also indicates similar accuracy across the LLMs, see Figure 3 b) and Tables 12–16 in Appendix F. Hence, our find-

[14]https://www.litellm.ai

[15]https://github.com/esborisova/TableEval-Study

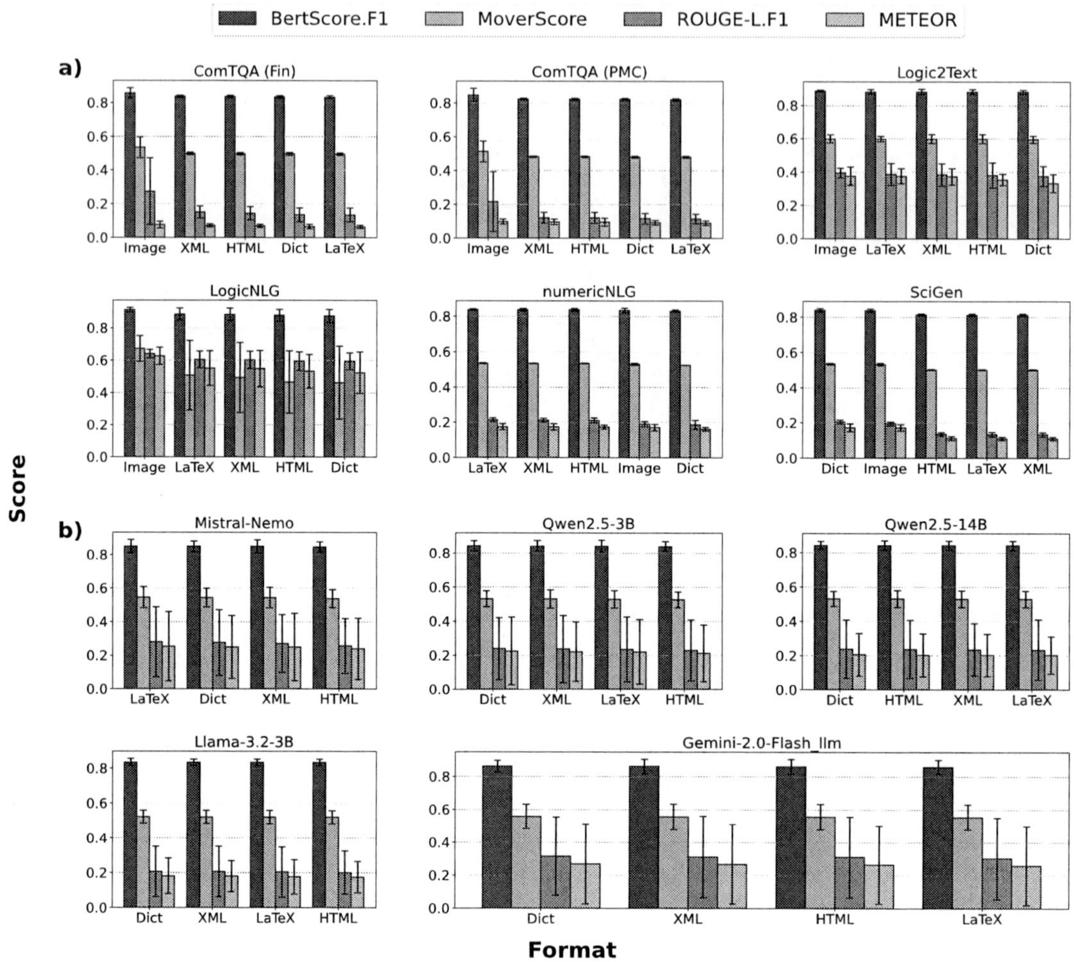

Figure 3: Values of BertScore.F1, MoverScore, ROUGE-L.F1, and METEOR **a)** for individual data subsets and all formats averaged over models, and **b)** for individual models and text formats averaged over data subsets. Error bars indicate standard deviation. Here "Fin" stands for FinTabNet, "PMC" denotes PubTables-1M, while "_llm" indicates text input for Gemini-2.0-Flash.

ings suggest that current models are less sensitive to diverse text representations of tables. Such outcomes may be attributed to LLMs' exposure to data encoded in the given formats during pretraining.

Scientific vs. non-scientific. The results for each domain are shown in Figure 2 (right) and Table 17 in Appendix F. The findings indicate that LLMs are more efficient on TU tasks from the non-scientific split, achieving a score boost of up to 34%. The best score values are obtained for LogicNLG followed by Logic2Text, see Figure 4 (left) and Table 18 in Appendix F.

We hypothesise that this difference could arise from (a) the complexity level of the given data and the target task; (b) lack or sparsity of the data from scientific contexts in the pre-training corpus of (M)LLMs. In numericNLG and SciGen, the goal is to generate a coherent paragraph or a collection of paragraphs summarising the table's content. In contrast, both LogicNLG and Logic2Text involve producing a single statement, filling in masked entities in a sentence and generating text based on a logical form, respectively. Furthermore, according to Moosavi et al. (2021), SciGen is characterised by a higher level of complexity than LogicNLG. This is because each gold description in SciGen summarises the entire table content and involves multiple types of reasoning, whereas, in LogicNLG each statement often focuses on a subset of table rows and is associated with a single type of reasoning. Similar to LogicNLG, Logic2Text

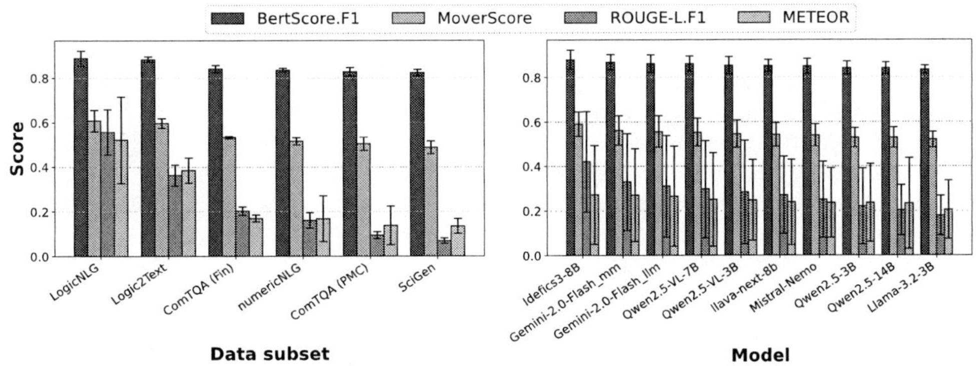

Figure 4: BertScore.F1, MoverScore, ROUGE-L.F1, and METEOR for each data subset averaged over table formats and models (left), and for individual models averaged over data subsets and formats (right). Error bars indicate standard deviation. Here "Fin" stands for FinTabNet, "PMC" denotes PubTables-1M, while "_llm" and "_mm" are used to distinguish between text and image input for Gemini-2.0-Flash, respectively.

descriptions involve only one type of logic. Notably, comparable performance is achieved across models for both subsets in ComTQA, with the gap in scores equal to about 1-3% (except for a 17% higher BLEURT score for PubTables-1M). Given that ComTQA was also proposed as a more challenging benchmark compared to existing datasets, comprising questions with multiple answers, numerical, and logical reasoning, the lower performance of (M)LLMs could lie in the complexity of the data as well. Finally, reasoning over scientific tables requires in-domain knowledge, the absence of which likely contributes to a decline in accuracy for the respective TableEval subsets.

Comparison of (M)LLMs. Figure 4 (right) and Table 19 in Appendix F outline results for individual models. Among MLLMs, Gemini-2.0-Flash and Idefics3 perform best, with the former outperforming the latter on BLEU-N, BLEURT, METEOR, ROUGE-3, and ROUGE-4 (by 1-4%). Next in the ranking are Qwen2.5-VL models and LLaVa-NeXT. For LLMs, Gemini-2.0-Flash obtains the highest score values, followed by Mistral-Nemo. Qwen2.5 models rank next with the 3B version achieving either similar or slightly better results than its 14B counterpart. On the contrary, Llama-3 consistently shows the weakest performance. We observe that on average, Idefics3 tends to generate concise responses with the shortest outputs produced for QA task (e. g., just a numeric value), whereas other models provide longer outputs. A similar trend is observed for LLMs, with Gemini-2.0-Flash providing shorter predictions compared to other models. Table 3 outlines the statistics on prediction lengths for each (M)LLM. Additionally, Figure 15 (Appendix F) illustrates the mean lengths for each model and data subset, while Figure 16 (Appendix G) demonstrates prediction examples. Since we do not postprocess the models' outputs, such difference in response length can contribute to the discrepancy across (M)LLMs in BLEU-N and ROUGE-N, which rely on n-gram overlap. Overall, our evaluation indicates that open-source models still remain behind the closed-source Gemini-2.0-Flash. On another note, we could not observe any correlation between model size and accuracy.

Model	Mean	Min	Max
Idefics3-8B-Llama3	139	0	4416
Qwen2.5-VL-3B-Instruct	360	2	4170
Qwen2.5-VL-7B-Instruct	292	4	3464
llama3-llava-next-8b-hf	311	24	6336
Gemini-2.0-Flash_mm	207	2	3097
Gemini-2.0-Flash_llm	259	0	10282
Llama-3.2-3B-Instruct	464	22	5626
Mistral-Nemo-Instruct-2407	303	21	2941
Qwen2.5-14B-Instruct	481	29	4154
Qwen2.5-3B-Instruct	465	26	4535

Table 3: Statistics on the mean, minimum, and maximum prediction lengths (in characters) for each model across TableEval subsets. Blue and pink colours highlight the lowest and highest values in each column, respectively. Here "_llm" and "_mm" are used to distinguish between text and image input for Gemini-2.0-Flash, respectively.

Interpretability. We choose instance-level analysis because dataset-level statistics tend to flatten important nuances, especially in generative settings

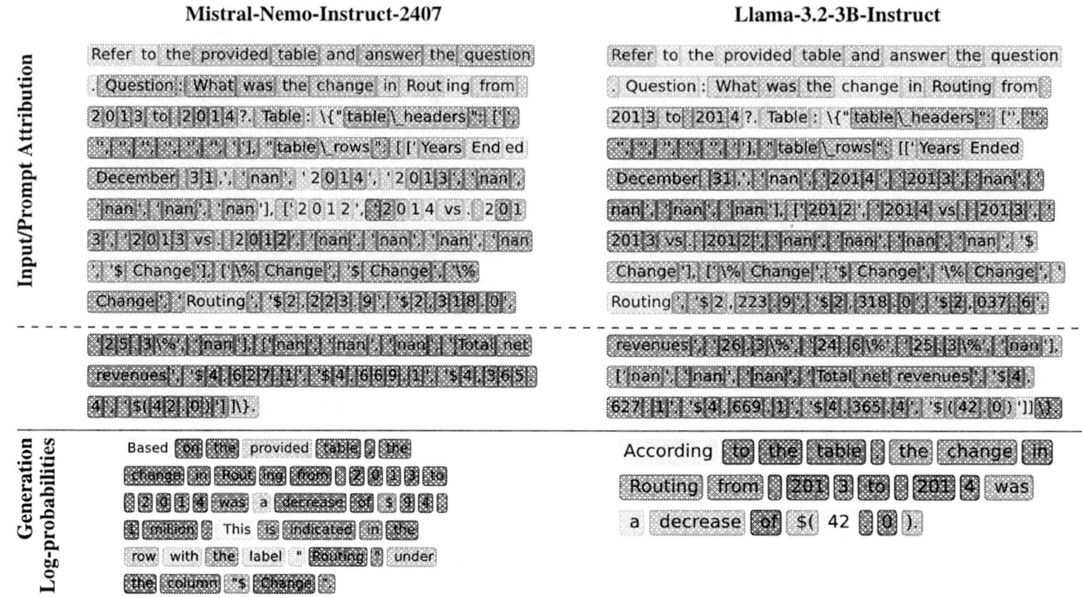

Figure 5: Interpretability analysis using Input x Gradient on Mistral-Nemo (correct prediction) and Llama3 (incorrect prediction) for a ComTQA (FinTabNet) instance with the Dict format. The gold answer to the given question is *"decrease of $94.1"*. Redder highlights correspond to higher importance. The prompts are abbreviated in the middle, indicated with the dashed line. In addition, for the output, we visualise the log-probabilities representing the model's confidence (dark green = very confident).

without a finite number of classes (Rönnqvist et al., 2022). Due to computational and visualisation constraints, we selected four ComTQA and two LogicNLG instances. The former was chosen for its shorter reference and prediction lengths compared to other subsets, while the latter was selected for achieving the highest scores across LLMs. We compare the best (Mistral-Nemo) and worst (Llama3) performing open-source LLMs.[16]

Figure 5 shows saliency maps as determined by the Input x Gradient explainer and log-probabilities for the generation (see §3.1). In this ComTQA (FinTabNet) example, with the table represented as a Dict in the input, we first notice that positive attributions are generally sparse due to the saturation problem (Shrikumar et al., 2017) and potentially the long context. Llama3 puts most attribution towards start and end of the prompt and the row value mentioned in the question (*"Routing"*). Mistral-Nemo, on the other hand, focuses much more on the year columns that are relevant to answering the question correctly. A key difference also lies in the tokenisation: While Mistral-Nemo splits all numbers into single digits, Llama3 often uses three-digit tokens where the fourth digit of a year is cut off. We assume that this makes it harder for Llama3 to process the marginal differences correctly.

The log-probabilities for the generated tokens are a proxy for the model's confidence. Here, we observe high uncertainty in Llama3 generating the core of the answer, the number token *"42"*, which is incorrect. Mistral-Nemo, on the contrary, correctly answers the question and we can see that it is certain about it from the high log-probabilities. Additionally, the model shows high confidence in the row *"Routing"* and column *"Change"* as the location of the answer, which indeed corresponds to the true position of the value (see also Figure 22 in Appendix H). At the same time, it is uncertain about optional, meaning-preserving generations such as the token *"provided"* as a qualifier for *"table"* and the beginning of the second sentence following the answer which serves as a rationale for the model's decision-making (Lu et al., 2024).

Appendix H shows five more examples for ComTQA and LogicNLG instances. We also observe a repeating pattern of the start and end of a prompt being attributed the most. While these observations are based on a small set of instances, our pipeline enables computing saliency maps for

[16] Saliency maps for these examples, along with additional instances, are available also in our GitHub repository.

any combination of prompt, input format, model, and dataset in future experiments.

4 Related work

Earlier TU studies leverage LLMs by representing tables as sequential text, either through naïve linearisation or by incorporating delimiters and special tokens (Fang et al., 2024). Some works focus on fine-tuning LLMs to enhance TU (Zhang et al., 2024c,b; Herzig et al., 2020; Yin et al., 2020; Gong et al., 2020; Iida et al., 2021), while others explore LLMs' table reasoning abilities through prompt engineering (Zhao et al., 2023; Chen, 2023; Sui et al., 2024). However, compared to natural language, tables present unique challenges to LLMs due to their varying layout structures, feature heterogeneity, and a large number of components leading to excessively long sequences (Borisov et al., 2022). The latter is particularly problematic, as most LLMs become inefficient due to the quadratic complexity of self-attention (Vaswani et al., 2017). With recent advances in vision and multimodality research, using MLLMs for TU has gained increasing attention with models like GPT-4 (OpenAI et al., 2024) and Gemini (Team et al., 2024), being widely adopted. Although, similar to LLMs, MLLMs also struggle with understanding structured data (Zheng et al., 2024).

Several studies examine the impact of the table representation on models' efficiency, indicating that different table formats suit specific TU tasks and LLMs at hand (Deng et al., 2024; Sui et al., 2024; Zhang et al., 2024d; Singha et al., 2023). For instance, Sui et al. (2024) find HTML and XML being better understood by GPT models than Markdown, JSON, and natural language with separators encoding. In contrast, Singha et al. (2023) observe that using HTML leads to lower performance for the fact-finding and transformation tasks compared to dataframe-based and JSON formats. Meanwhile, Deng et al. (2024) analyse how models' reasoning abilities vary when tables are represented as text vs. images showing that Gemini Pro and GPT-4 perform similarly across both modalities.

While these studies offer insights into the effectiveness of (M)LLMs in interpreting structured data across formats, they focus primarily on non-scientific contexts like Wikipedia and finance. This is likely due to the abundance of established, large-scale datasets based on tables from these sources, including WikiTables (Bhagavatula et al., 2015), ToTTo (Parikh et al., 2020), and TabFact, (Chen et al., 2020b), to name a few. Furthermore, interpretability for TU tasks remains under-researched, as related works mainly consider unstructured text and are disconnected from downstream applications (Ferrando et al., 2024; Tenney et al., 2024), rarely focusing on other long-form tasks like retrieval-augmented generation (Qi et al., 2024) or QA (Enouen et al., 2024). Nguyen et al. (2025) use attributions to make tabular QA explainable but they are constrained to the text-to-SQL setup. Unlike prior studies, this paper focuses on cross-domain and cross-modality evaluation, comparing the performance and explanations of (M)LLMs on both scientific and non-scientific tables, covering image and diverse text representations of tables.

5 Conclusion

We conducted an evaluation study to explore the robustness of diverse (M)LLMs on scientific vs. non-scientific tables across image and four text formats. The findings reveal that current models obtain decent performance across both vision and text modalities but significantly struggle with scientific tabular data. Additionally, we explored the applicability of interpretability methods to TU tasks to get insights into the decision-making of LLMs. We found feature attributions to be a useful tool for revealing model uncertainty, its attention to table structure and relevant content, and tokenisation differences which might potentially affect predictions.

Limitations

Although this study provides insights into the strengths and limitations of (M)LLMs in understanding tables, it has several limitations. First, we use the same prompts across (M)LLMs and do not postprocess the predictions which may contribute to lower score values. Experimenting with model-specific prompts and structured outputs using tools such as Jsonformer[17] could lead to better results. Second, we rely on automatic metrics, the drawbacks of which have been well-documented previously (Schmidtova et al., 2024; Gehrmann et al., 2023). Third, we focus only on interpretability for the text input, while methods like CC-SHAP (Parcalabescu and Frank, 2025) remain the next step to measure the importance of each modality in MLLM decision-making. Fourth, annotating all subsets in TableEval for a common task and

[17]https://github.com/1rgs/jsonformer

evaluating (M)LLMs on the entire corpus could be beneficial and we leave it for future work. Finally, the dataset is limited to the English language and thus does not allow for the assessment of multilingual TU.

Ethics statement

The data used in this study is based on publicly available datasets. We adhere to their respective licenses and conditions of use in our experiments. Additional table formats are generated with Python scripts and open-access tools or collected from the original table sources which are under permissive licenses. All (M)LLMs, except Gemini-2.0-Flash, employed for the experiments are open-access. Those models might potentially possess biases, as outlined by their developers, which researchers should be aware of.

Acknowledgments

This work was supported by the consortium NFDI for Data Science and Artificial Intelligence (NFDI4DS)[18] as part of the non-profit association National Research Data Infrastructure (NFDI e. V.). The consortium is funded by the Federal Republic of Germany and its states through the German Research Foundation (DFG) project NFDI4DS (no. 460234259). We would like to thank Melina Plakidis, Maximilian Dustin Nasert, and Shuiai Xu for their help in manually reviewing certain subsets of the data.

References

Shuai Bai, Keqin Chen, Xuejing Liu, Jialin Wang, Wenbin Ge, Sibo Song, Kai Dang, Peng Wang, Shijie Wang, Jun Tang, Humen Zhong, Yuanzhi Zhu, Mingkun Yang, Zhaohai Li, Jianqiang Wan, Pengfei Wang, Wei Ding, Zheren Fu, Yiheng Xu, Jiabo Ye, Xi Zhang, Tianbao Xie, Zesen Cheng, Hang Zhang, Zhibo Yang, Haiyang Xu, and Junyang Lin. 2025. Qwen2.5-VL technical report. *Preprint*, arXiv:2502.13923.

Satanjeev Banerjee and Alon Lavie. 2005. METEOR: An automatic metric for MT evaluation with improved correlation with human judgments. In *Proceedings of the ACL Workshop on Intrinsic and Extrinsic Evaluation Measures for Machine Translation and/or Summarization*, pages 65–72, Ann Arbor, Michigan. Association for Computational Linguistics.

[18]https://www.nfdi4datascience.de

Chandra Sekhar Bhagavatula, Thanapon Noraset, and Doug Downey. 2015. TabEL: Entity linking in web tables. In *The Semantic Web - ISWC 2015*, pages 425–441, Cham. Springer International Publishing.

Vadim Borisov, Tobias Leemann, Kathrin Sessler, Johannes Haug, Martin Pawelczyk, and Gjergji Kasneci. 2022. Deep neural networks and tabular data: A survey. *IEEE Transactions on Neural Networks and Learning Systems*, pages 1–21.

Lutz Bornmann, Robin Haunschild, and Rüdiger Mutz. 2021. Growth rates of modern science: A latent piecewise growth curve approach to model publication numbers from established and new literature databases. *Humanities and Social Sciences Communications*, 8(1):1–15.

Davide Caffagni, Federico Cocchi, Luca Barsellotti, Nicholas Moratelli, Sara Sarto, Lorenzo Baraldi, Lorenzo Baraldi, Marcella Cornia, and Rita Cucchiara. 2024. The revolution of multimodal large language models: A survey. In *Findings of the Association for Computational Linguistics: ACL 2024*, pages 13590–13618, Bangkok, Thailand. Association for Computational Linguistics.

Yupeng Chang, Xu Wang, Jindong Wang, Yuan Wu, Linyi Yang, Kaijie Zhu, Hao Chen, Xiaoyuan Yi, Cunxiang Wang, Yidong Wang, Wei Ye, Yue Zhang, Yi Chang, Philip S. Yu, Qiang Yang, and Xing Xie. 2024. A survey on evaluation of large language models. *ACM Trans. Intell. Syst. Technol.*, 15(3).

Wenhu Chen. 2023. Large language models are few(1)-shot table reasoners. In *Findings of the Association for Computational Linguistics: EACL 2023*, pages 1120–1130, Dubrovnik, Croatia. Association for Computational Linguistics.

Wenhu Chen, Ming-Wei Chang, Eva Schlinger, William Wang, and William W. Cohen. 2021. Open question answering over tables and text. *Preprint*, arXiv:2010.10439.

Wenhu Chen, Jianshu Chen, Yu Su, Zhiyu Chen, and William Yang Wang. 2020a. Logical natural language generation from open-domain tables. In *Proceedings of the 58th Annual Meeting of the Association for Computational Linguistics*, pages 7929–7942, Online. Association for Computational Linguistics.

Wenhu Chen, Hongmin Wang, Jianshu Chen, Yunkai Zhang, Hong Wang, Shiyang Li, Xiyou Zhou, and William Yang Wang. 2020b. TabFact: A large-scale dataset for table-based fact verification. In *International Conference on Learning Representations (ICLR)*, Addis Ababa, Ethiopia.

Zhiyu Chen, Wenhu Chen, Hanwen Zha, Xiyou Zhou, Yunkai Zhang, Sairam Sundaresan, and William Yang Wang. 2020c. Logic2Text: High-fidelity natural language generation from logical forms. In *Findings of the Association for Computational Linguistics: EMNLP 2020*, pages 2096–2111, Online. Association for Computational Linguistics.

Zhoujun Cheng, Haoyu Dong, Zhiruo Wang, Ran Jia, Jiaqi Guo, Yan Gao, Shi Han, Jian-Guang Lou, and Dongmei Zhang. 2022. HiTab: A hierarchical table dataset for question answering and natural language generation. In *Proceedings of the 60th Annual Meeting of the Association for Computational Linguistics (Volume 1: Long Papers)*, pages 1094–1110, Dublin, Ireland. Association for Computational Linguistics.

Christopher Clark and Santosh Divvala. 2016. PDF-Figures 2.0: Mining figures from research papers. In *Proceedings of the 16th ACM/IEEE-CS on Joint Conference on Digital Libraries*, JCDL '16, page 143–152, New York, NY, USA. Association for Computing Machinery.

Naihao Deng, Zhenjie Sun, Ruiqi He, Aman Sikka, Yulong Chen, Lin Ma, Yue Zhang, and Rada Mihalcea. 2024. Tables as texts or images: Evaluating the table reasoning ability of LLMs and MLLMs. In *Findings of the Association for Computational Linguistics: ACL 2024*, pages 407–426, Bangkok, Thailand. Association for Computational Linguistics.

James Enouen, Hootan Nakhost, Sayna Ebrahimi, Sercan Arik, Yan Liu, and Tomas Pfister. 2024. TextGenSHAP: Scalable post-hoc explanations in text generation with long documents. In *Findings of the Association for Computational Linguistics: ACL 2024*, pages 13984–14011, Bangkok, Thailand. Association for Computational Linguistics.

Xi Fang, Weijie Xu, Fiona Anting Tan, Jiani Zhang, Ziqing Hu, Yanjun Qi, Scott Nickleach, Diego Socolinsky, Srinivasan Sengamedu, and Christos Faloutsos. 2024. Large language models (LLMs) on tabular data: Prediction, generation, and understanding – a survey. *Preprint*, arXiv:2402.17944.

Javier Ferrando, Gabriele Sarti, Arianna Bisazza, and Marta R. Costa-jussà. 2024. A primer on the inner workings of transformer-based language models. *arXiv*, abs/2405.00208.

Santo Fortunato, Carl T Bergstrom, Katy Börner, James A Evans, Dirk Helbing, Staša Milojević, Alexander M Petersen, Filippo Radicchi, Roberta Sinatra, Brian Uzzi, et al. 2018. Science of science. *Science*, 359(6379):eaao0185.

Sebastian Gehrmann, Elizabeth Clark, and Thibault Sellam. 2023. Repairing the cracked foundation: A survey of obstacles in evaluation practices for generated text. *J. Artif. Int. Res.*, 77.

Heng Gong, Yawei Sun, Xiaocheng Feng, Bing Qin, Wei Bi, Xiaojiang Liu, and Ting Liu. 2020. TableGPT: Few-shot table-to-text generation with table structure reconstruction and content matching. In *Proceedings of the 28th International Conference on Computational Linguistics*, pages 1978–1988, Barcelona, Spain (Online). International Committee on Computational Linguistics.

Yury Gorishniy, Ivan Rubachev, Valentin Khrulkov, and Artem Babenko. 2021. Revisiting deep learning models for tabular data. In *Advances in Neural Information Processing Systems*, volume 34, pages 18932–18943. Curran Associates, Inc.

Aaron Grattafiori, Abhimanyu Dubey, and Abhinav Jauhri et. al. 2024. The Llama 3 herd of models. *Preprint*, arXiv:2407.21783.

Jonathan Herzig, Pawel Krzysztof Nowak, Thomas Müller, Francesco Piccinno, and Julian Eisenschlos. 2020. TaPas: Weakly supervised table parsing via pre-training. In *Proceedings of the 58th Annual Meeting of the Association for Computational Linguistics*, pages 4320–4333, Online. Association for Computational Linguistics.

Xanh Ho, Anh Khoa Duong Nguyen, An Tuan Dao, Junfeng Jiang, Yuki Chida, Kaito Sugimoto, Huy Quoc To, Florian Boudin, and Akiko Aizawa. 2024. A survey of pre-trained language models for processing scientific text. *Preprint*, arXiv:2401.17824.

Zhi Hong, Logan Ward, Kyle Chard, Ben Blaiszik, and Ian Foster. 2021. Challenges and advances in information extraction from scientific literature: a review. *JOM*, 73:1543–1851.

Hiroshi Iida, Dung Thai, Varun Manjunatha, and Mohit Iyyer. 2021. TABBIE: Pretrained representations of tabular data. In *Proceedings of the 2021 Conference of the North American Chapter of the Association for Computational Linguistics: Human Language Technologies*, pages 3446–3456, Online. Association for Computational Linguistics.

Hugo Laurençon, Andrés Marafioti, Victor Sanh, and Léo Tronchon. 2024. Building and better understanding vision-language models: insights and future directions. *Preprint*, arXiv:2408.12637.

Bo Li, Kaichen Zhang, Hao Zhang, Dong Guo, Renrui Zhang, Feng Li, Yuanhan Zhang, Ziwei Liu, and Chunyuan Li. 2024. LLaVA-NeXT: Stronger LLMs supercharge multimodal capabilities in the wild.

Chin-Yew Lin. 2004. ROUGE: A package for automatic evaluation of summaries. In *Text Summarization Branches Out*, pages 74–81, Barcelona, Spain. Association for Computational Linguistics.

Xinyuan Lu, Liangming Pan, Yubo Ma, Preslav Nakov, and Min-Yen Kan. 2024. TART: An open-source tool-augmented framework for explainable table-based reasoning. In *NeurIPS 2024 Third Table Representation Learning Workshop*.

Mattia Marzocchi, Marco Cremaschi, Riccardo Pozzi, Roberto Avogadro, and Matteo Palmonari. 2022. MammoTab: A giant and comprehensive dataset for semantic table interpretation. In *Proceedings of the Semantic Web Challenge on Tabular Data to Knowledge Graph Matching (SemTab2022)*.

Nafise Sadat Moosavi, Andreas Rücklé, Dan Roth, and Iryna Gurevych. 2021. SciGen: a dataset for reasoning-aware text generation from scientific tables. In *Thirty-fifth Conference on Neural Information Processing Systems Datasets and Benchmarks Track (Round 2)*.

Linyong Nan, Chiachun Hsieh, Ziming Mao, Xi Victoria Lin, Neha Verma, Rui Zhang, Wojciech Kryściński, Hailey Schoelkopf, Riley Kong, Xiangru Tang, Mutethia Mutuma, Ben Rosand, Isabel Trindade, Renusree Bandaru, Jacob Cunningham, Caiming Xiong, Dragomir Radev, and Dragomir Radev. 2022. FeTaQA: Free-form table question answering. *Transactions of the Association for Computational Linguistics*, 10:35–49.

Giang Nguyen, Ivan Brugere, Shubham Sharma, Sanjay Kariyappa, Anh Totti Nguyen, and Freddy Lecue. 2025. Interpretable LLM-based table question answering. *arXiv*, abs/2412.12386.

OpenAI, Josh Achiam, and Steven Adler et. al. 2024. GPT-4 technical report. *Preprint*, arXiv:2303.08774.

Jorge Osés Grijalba, L. Alfonso Ureña-López, Eugenio Martínez Cámara, and Jose Camacho-Collados. 2024. Question answering over tabular data with DataBench: A large-scale empirical evaluation of LLMs. In *Proceedings of the 2024 Joint International Conference on Computational Linguistics, Language Resources and Evaluation (LREC-COLING 2024)*, pages 13471–13488, Torino, Italia. ELRA and ICCL.

Chaoxu Pang, Yixuan Cao, Chunhao Yang, and Ping Luo. 2024. Uncovering limitations of large language models in information seeking from tables. In *Findings of the Association for Computational Linguistics: ACL 2024*, pages 1388–1409, Bangkok, Thailand. Association for Computational Linguistics.

Kishore Papineni, Salim Roukos, Todd Ward, and Wei-Jing Zhu. 2002. Bleu: a method for automatic evaluation of machine translation. In *Proceedings of the 40th Annual Meeting of the Association for Computational Linguistics*, pages 311–318, Philadelphia, Pennsylvania, USA. Association for Computational Linguistics.

Letitia Parcalabescu and Anette Frank. 2025. Do vision & language decoders use images and text equally? How self-consistent are their explanations? In *The Thirteenth International Conference on Learning Representations*.

Ankur Parikh, Xuezhi Wang, Sebastian Gehrmann, Manaal Faruqui, Bhuwan Dhingra, Diyi Yang, and Dipanjan Das. 2020. ToTTo: A controlled table-to-text generation dataset. In *Proceedings of the 2020 Conference on Empirical Methods in Natural Language Processing (EMNLP)*, pages 1173–1186, Online. Association for Computational Linguistics.

Matt Post. 2018. A call for clarity in reporting BLEU scores. In *Proceedings of the Third Conference on Machine Translation: Research Papers*, pages 186–191, Brussels, Belgium. Association for Computational Linguistics.

Jirui Qi, Gabriele Sarti, Raquel Fernández, and Arianna Bisazza. 2024. Model internals-based answer attribution for trustworthy retrieval-augmented generation. In *Proceedings of the 2024 Conference on Empirical Methods in Natural Language Processing*, pages 6037–6053, Miami, Florida, USA. Association for Computational Linguistics.

Qwen, :, An Yang, Baosong Yang, Beichen Zhang, Binyuan Hui, Bo Zheng, Bowen Yu, Chengyuan Li, Dayiheng Liu, Fei Huang, Haoran Wei, Huan Lin, Jian Yang, Jianhong Tu, Jianwei Zhang, Jianxin Yang, Jiaxi Yang, Jingren Zhou, Junyang Lin, Kai Dang, Keming Lu, Keqin Bao, Kexin Yang, Le Yu, Mei Li, Mingfeng Xue, Pei Zhang, Qin Zhu, Rui Men, Runji Lin, Tianhao Li, Tianyi Tang, Tingyu Xia, Xingzhang Ren, Xuancheng Ren, Yang Fan, Yang Su, Yichang Zhang, Yu Wan, Yuqiong Liu, Zeyu Cui, Zhenru Zhang, and Zihan Qiu. 2025. Qwen2.5 technical report. *Preprint*, arXiv:2412.15115.

Mohaimenul Azam Khan Raiaan, Md. Saddam Hossain Mukta, Kaniz Fatema, Nur Mohammad Fahad, Sadman Sakib, Most Marufatul Jannat Mim, Jubaer Ahmad, Mohammed Eunus Ali, and Sami Azam. 2024. A review on large language models: Architectures, applications, taxonomies, open issues and challenges. *IEEE Access*, 12:26839–26874.

Samuel Rönnqvist, Aki-Juhani Kyröläinen, Amanda Myntti, Filip Ginter, and Veronika Laippala. 2022. Explaining classes through stable word attributions. In *Findings of the Association for Computational Linguistics: ACL 2022*, pages 1063–1074, Dublin, Ireland. Association for Computational Linguistics.

Maria Sahakyan, Zeyar Aung, and Talal Rahwan. 2021. Explainable artificial intelligence for tabular data: A survey. *IEEE Access*, 9:135392–135422.

Gabriele Sarti, Nils Feldhus, Ludwig Sickert, and Oskar van der Wal. 2023. Inseq: An interpretability toolkit for sequence generation models. In *Proceedings of the 61st Annual Meeting of the Association for Computational Linguistics (Volume 3: System Demonstrations)*, pages 421–435, Toronto, Canada. Association for Computational Linguistics.

Patricia Schmidtova, Saad Mahamood, Simone Balloccu, Ondrej Dusek, Albert Gatt, Dimitra Gkatzia, David M. Howcroft, Ondrej Platek, and Adarsa Sivaprasad. 2024. Automatic metrics in natural language generation: A survey of current evaluation practices. In *Proceedings of the 17th International Natural Language Generation Conference*, pages 557–583, Tokyo, Japan. Association for Computational Linguistics.

Thibault Sellam, Dipanjan Das, and Ankur Parikh. 2020. BLEURT: Learning robust metrics for text generation. In *Proceedings of the 58th Annual Meeting of the Association for Computational Linguistics*, pages 7881–7892, Online. Association for Computational Linguistics.

Avanti Shrikumar, Peyton Greenside, and Anshul Kundaje. 2017. Learning important features through propagating activation differences. In *Proceedings of the 34th International Conference on Machine Learning - Volume 70*, ICML'17, page 3145–3153. JMLR.org.

Karen Simonyan, Andrea Vedaldi, and Andrew Zisserman. 2014. Deep inside convolutional networks: Visualising image classification models and saliency maps. In *Workshop at International Conference on Learning Representations*.

Ananya Singha, José Cambronero, Sumit Gulwani, Vu Le, and Chris Parnin. 2023. Tabular representation, noisy operators, and impacts on table structure understanding tasks in LLMs. *Preprint*, arXiv:2310.10358.

Brandon Smock, Rohith Pesala, and Robin Abraham. 2022. PubTables-1M: Towards comprehensive table extraction from unstructured documents. In *2022 IEEE/CVF Conference on Computer Vision and Pattern Recognition (CVPR)*, pages 4624–4632.

Lya Hulliyyatus Suadaa, Hidetaka Kamigaito, Kotaro Funakoshi, Manabu Okumura, and Hiroya Takamura. 2021. Towards table-to-text generation with numerical reasoning. In *Proceedings of the 59th Annual Meeting of the Association for Computational Linguistics and the 11th International Joint Conference on Natural Language Processing (Volume 1: Long Papers)*, pages 1451–1465, Online. Association for Computational Linguistics.

Yuan Sui, Mengyu Zhou, Mingjie Zhou, Shi Han, and Dongmei Zhang. 2024. Table meets LLM: Can large language models understand structured table data? A benchmark and empirical study. In *Proceedings of the 17th ACM International Conference on Web Search and Data Mining*, WSDM '24, page 645–654, New York, NY, USA. Association for Computing Machinery.

Gemini Team, Rohan Anil, and Sebastian Borgeaud et. al. 2024. Gemini: A family of highly capable multimodal models. *Preprint*, arXiv:2312.11805.

Ian Tenney, Ryan Mullins, Bin Du, Shree Pandya, Minsuk Kahng, and Lucas Dixon. 2024. Interactive prompt debugging with sequence salience. *arXiv*, abs/2404.07498.

Ashish Vaswani, Noam Shazeer, Niki Parmar, Jakob Uszkoreit, Llion Jones, Aidan N. Gomez, Łukasz Kaiser, and Illia Polosukhin. 2017. Attention is all you need. In *Proceedings of the 31st International Conference on Neural Information Processing Systems*, NIPS'17, page 6000–6010, Red Hook, NY, USA. Curran Associates Inc.

Bin Wang, Chao Xu, Xiaomeng Zhao, Linke Ouyang, Fan Wu, Zhiyuan Zhao, Rui Xu, Kaiwen Liu, Yuan Qu, Fukai Shang, Bo Zhang, Liqun Wei, Zhihao Sui, Wei Li, Botian Shi, Yu Qiao, Dahua Lin, and Conghui He. 2024. MinerU: An open-source solution for precise document content extraction. *Preprint*, arXiv:2409.18839.

Siwei Wu, Yizhi Li, Kang Zhu, Ge Zhang, Yiming Liang, Kaijing Ma, Chenghao Xiao, Haoran Zhang, Bohao Yang, Wenhu Chen, Wenhao Huang, Noura Al Moubayed, Jie Fu, and Chenghua Lin. 2024a. SciMMIR: Benchmarking scientific multi-modal information retrieval. In *Findings of the Association for Computational Linguistics: ACL 2024*, pages 12560–12574, Bangkok, Thailand. Association for Computational Linguistics.

Xianjie Wu, Jian Yang, Linzheng Chai, Ge Zhang, Jiaheng Liu, Xinrun Du, Di Liang, Daixin Shu, Xianfu Cheng, Tianzhen Sun, Guanglin Niu, Tongliang Li, and Zhoujun Li. 2024b. TableBench: A comprehensive and complex benchmark for table question answering. *Preprint*, arXiv:2408.09174.

Bohao Yang, Yingji Zhang, Dong Liu, André Freitas, and Chenghua Lin. 2025. Does table source matter? Benchmarking and improving multimodal scientific table understanding and reasoning. *arXiv*, abs/2501.13042.

Pengcheng Yin, Graham Neubig, Wen-tau Yih, and Sebastian Riedel. 2020. TaBERT: Pretraining for joint understanding of textual and tabular data. In *Proceedings of the 58th Annual Meeting of the Association for Computational Linguistics*, pages 8413–8426, Online. Association for Computational Linguistics.

Duzhen Zhang, Yahan Yu, Jiahua Dong, Chenxing Li, Dan Su, Chenhui Chu, and Dong Yu. 2024a. MM-LLMs: Recent advances in MultiModal large language models. In *Findings of the Association for Computational Linguistics: ACL 2024*, pages 12401–12430, Bangkok, Thailand. Association for Computational Linguistics.

Shuo Zhang and Krisztian Balog. 2020. Web table extraction, retrieval, and augmentation: A survey. *ACM Trans. Intell. Syst. Technol.*, 11(2).

Tianshu Zhang, Xiang Yue, Yifei Li, and Huan Sun. 2024b. TableLlama: Towards open large generalist models for tables. In *Proceedings of the 2024 Conference of the North American Chapter of the Association for Computational Linguistics: Human Language Technologies (Volume 1: Long Papers)*, pages 6024–6044, Mexico City, Mexico. Association for Computational Linguistics.

Tianyi Zhang*, Varsha Kishore*, Felix Wu*, Kilian Q. Weinberger, and Yoav Artzi. 2020. BERTScore: Evaluating text generation with BERT. In *International Conference on Learning Representations*.

Xiaokang Zhang, Jing Zhang, Zeyao Ma, Yang Li, Bohan Zhang, Guanlin Li, Zijun Yao, Kangli Xu, Jinchang Zhou, Daniel Zhang-Li, Jifan Yu, Shu Zhao, Juanzi Li, and Jie Tang. 2024c. TableLLM: Enabling tabular data manipulation by LLMs in real office usage scenarios. *Preprint*, arXiv:2403.19318.

Xuanliang Zhang, Dingzirui Wang, Longxu Dou, Baoxin Wang, Dayong Wu, Qingfu Zhu, and Wanxiang Che. 2024d. FLEXTAF: Enhancing table reasoning with flexible tabular formats. *arXiv*, abs/2408.08841.

Bowen Zhao, Changkai Ji, Yuejie Zhang, Wen He, Yingwen Wang, Qing Wang, Rui Feng, and Xiaobo Zhang. 2023. Large language models are complex table parsers. In *Proceedings of the 2023 Conference on Empirical Methods in Natural Language Processing*, pages 14786–14802, Singapore. Association for Computational Linguistics.

Wei Zhao, Maxime Peyrard, Fei Liu, Yang Gao, Christian M. Meyer, and Steffen Eger. 2019. MoverScore: Text generation evaluating with contextualized embeddings and earth mover distance. In *Proceedings of the 2019 Conference on Empirical Methods in Natural Language Processing and the 9th International Joint Conference on Natural Language Processing (EMNLP-IJCNLP)*, pages 563–578, Hong Kong, China. Association for Computational Linguistics.

Weichao Zhao, Hao Feng, Qi Liu, Jingqun Tang, Shu Wei, Binghong Wu, Lei Liao, Yongjie Ye, Hao Liu, Wengang Zhou, Houqiang Li, and Can Huang. 2024. TabPedia: Towards comprehensive visual table understanding with concept synergy. *Preprint*, arXiv:2406.01326.

Mingyu Zheng, Xinwei Feng, Qingyi Si, Qiaoqiao She, Zheng Lin, Wenbin Jiang, and Weiping Wang. 2024. Multimodal table understanding. In *Proceedings of the 62nd Annual Meeting of the Association for Computational Linguistics (Volume 1: Long Papers)*, pages 9102–9124, Bangkok, Thailand. Association for Computational Linguistics.

Xinyi Zheng, Doug Burdick, Lucian Popa, Xu Zhong, and Nancy Xin Ru Wang. 2020. Global table extractor (GTE): A framework for joint table identification and cell structure recognition using visual context. *Preprint*, arXiv:2005.00589.

A Dataset statistics

Dataset	Image		Dict		LaTeX		HTML		XML	
	Instances	Tables	Instances	Tables	Instances	Tables	Instances	Tables	Instances	Tables
Scientific tables										
ComTQA (PubTables-1M)	6232	932	6232	932	6232	932	6232	932	6232	932
numericNLG	135	135	135	135	135	135	135	135	135	135
SciGen	1035	1035	1035	1035	928	928	985	985	961	961
Total	**7402**	**2102**	**7402**	**2102**	**7295**	**1995**	**7352**	**2052**	**7328**	**2028**
Non-scientific tables										
ComTQA (FinTabNet)	2838	659	2838	659	2838	659	2838	659	2838	659
LogicNLG	917	184	917	184	917	184	917	184	917	184
Logic2Text	155	72	155	72	155	72	155	72	155	72
Total	**3910**	**915**	**3910**	**915**	**3910**	**915**	**3910**	**915**	**3910**	**915**

Table 4: Data distribution in the TableEval corpus for each format and subset.

B Dataset examples

QA task: ComTQA (PubTables-1M)

Table 5: Brood size analysis of *kin-29* alleles

Genotype	% of wild-type brood size
N2	100 (270)
sma-6(wk7)	64 (172)
lon-1(wk50)	81 (219)
kin-29(wk61)	32 (86)
kin-29(oy38)	81 (218)
kin-29(oy39)	80 (217)

Number of eggs scored for each genotype is shown in parentheses.

Question: What is the title of the table?

Answer: Brood size analysis of kin-29 alleles

Figure 6: An example from ComTQA (PubTables-1M), illustrating a table, a corresponding question, and a gold answer.

QA task: ComTQA (FinTabNet)

	Moody's	S&P	Fitch (a)
PPL Electric (b)			
Senior Unsecured/Issuer Rating	Baa1	A-	BBB
First Mortgage Bonds	A3	A-	A-
Senior Secured Bonds	A3	A-	A-
Commercial Paper	P-2	A-2	F2
Preferred Stock	Baa3	BBB	BBB
Preference Stock	Baa3	BBB	BBB
Outlook	STABLE	STABLE	STABLE

Question: What is the rating of commercial paper?

Answer: P-2 A-2 F2

Figure 7: An example from ComTQA (FinTabNet), illustrating a table, a corresponding question, and a gold answer.

T2T task: numericNLG

Genre	Sentences	Length	Yield	Precision
News*	100	19.3	142	78.9
News	100	19.3	144	70.8
Wiki	100	21.4	178	61.8
Web	100	19.2	165	49.1
Total	300	20.0	487	60.2

Table 1: Corpus size (length in token) and system performance by genre. News* used gold trees and is not included in total.

Description: Results. From the whole corpus of 300 sentences, PropsDE extracted 487 tuples, yielding on average 1.6 per sentence with 2.9 arguments. 60% of them were labeled as correct. Table 1 shows that most extractions are made from Wikipedia articles, whereas the highest precision can be observed for newswire text. According to our expectations, web pages are most challenging, presumably due to noisier language. These differences between the genres can also be seen in the precision-yield curve (Figure 2).

Figure 8: An example from numericNLG, illustrating a table and its corresponding gold description.

T2T task: SciGen

Model		Test	*but*	*but* or *neg*
no-distill	no-project	85.98	78.69	80.13
no-distill	project	86.54	83.40	-
distill [7]	no-project	86.11	79.04	-
distill	project	86.62	83.32	-
ELMo	no-project	88.89	86.51	87.24
ELMo	project	88.96	87.20	-

Table 2: Average performance (across 100 seeds) of ELMo on the SST2 task. We show performance on *A-but-B* sentences ("*but*"), negations ("*neg*").

Description: Switching to ELMo word embeddings improves performance by 2.9 percentage points on an average, corresponding to about 53 test sentences. Of these, about 32 sentences (60% of the improvement) correspond to A-but-B and negation style sentences, [CONTINUE] As further evidence that ELMo helps on these specific constructions, the non-ELMo baseline model (no-project, no-distill) gets 255 sentences wrong in the test corpus on average, only 89 (34.8%) of which are A-but-B style or negations.

Figure 9: An example from SciGen, illustrating a table and its corresponding gold description.

T2T task: LogicNLG

Country	Date	Label	Format	Catalogue No.
Europe	17 October 2008[160]	Columbia	CD, Double LP	#88697392232
Australia	18 October 2008[39]	Sony Music	CD	#88697392382
United Kingdom	20 October 2008[161][162]	Columbia	CD, Double LP	#88697392232
	1 December 2008[38]		CD (limited edition steel-box)	#88697417452
United States	20 October 2008	Columbia	CD	#88697338292
Japan	22 October 2008[163]	Sony Music	CD	SICP-2055
Germany	5 December 2008[164]	Columbia	CD (limited edition steel-box)	#886974174523
Global (iTunes)	19 November 2012[49]	Columbia	Digital download	#88697338292

Title: black ice (album)

Template: the album [ENT] was first released in [ENT]

Statement: the album Black Ice was first released in Europe.

Figure 10: An example from LogicNLG, illustrating a table, a statement with masked entities, and a corresponding gold statement.

T2T task: Logic2Text

Pick #	CFL Team	Player	Position	College
13	Hamilton Tiger-Cats	Devin Grant	OL	Utah
14	BC Lions (via Winnipeg)	Matt Kellett	K	Saskatchewan
15	Montreal Alouettes (via Winnipeg via BC)	Scott Flory	OL	Saskatchewan
16	Calgary Stampeders	Harland Ah You	DL	Brigham Young
17	Edmonton Eskimos	Scott Deibert	RB	Minot State
18	Montreal Alouettes	William Loftus	D	Manitoba
19	Saskatchewan Roughriders	Kevin Pressburger	LB	Waterloo
20	Toronto Argonauts	Jermaine Brown	RB	Winona State

Title: 1998 cfl draft

Logical form: and { only { filter_eq { filter_eq { all_rows ; college ; saskatchewan } ; position ; k } } ; eq { hop { filter_eq { filter_eq { all_rows ; college ; saskatchewan } ; position ; k } ; player } ; matt kellett } } = true

Statement: the only kicker drafted by saskatchewan college in the 1998 cfl draft was matt kellett .

Figure 11: An example from Logic2Text, illustrating a table, a logical form, and a corresponding gold statement.

C Table formats collection

In what follows, we provide additional details on the collection process of the table formats.

XML and HTML. As was mentioned in §2.2, XML and XML/HTML for the PubTables-1M subset of ComTQA and SciGen, respectively, are extracted from the source papers. For the former, the target tables are identified based on their titles and the highest cosine similarity with table content annotations available in PubTables-1M. For Scigen we use the fuzzy match score with a threshold of 0.8 to identify the relevant tables based on their captions. Note that not all instances have these formats (see Table 4) due to LaTeXML conversion errors, low fuzzy match score, discrepancies between captions in the gold data and LaTeX files or a scholarly paper not being available on arXiv anymore. We also exclude cases with multiple tables sharing the same caption but annotated separately, as it is challenging to accurately link the corresponding HTML/XML code for each table. HTML in LogicNLG and Logic2Text are retrieved from the Wikipedia pages. However, due to the lack of metadata on the data collection timestamps, we choose a time interval close to the year of publication of these datasets for our search in the Wikipedia archive. To extract the relevant tables, we employ a cosine similarity comparison against the gold tables, using a threshold of 0.9. Since Wikipedia is constantly updated, we further manually check the results and filter out cases where the mismatch affects the ground truth, e. g., cell values being out of date or the removal/addition of both rows and columns. Note that for all subsets except SciGen, we follow the PMC table formatting rules[19] to obtain XML. Additionally, all generated HTML underwent automatic validation using the PyTidyLib[20] package.

LaTeX. Similar to HTML/XML, we obtain LaTeX from the source scholarly papers in SciGen (see §2.2) and extract the target tables based on their captions using the fuzzy match. Some instances are excluded due to low similarity scores (below 0.8), parsing errors or lack of LaTeX source code (tables from ACL papers). For numericNLG and PubTables-1M tables, LaTeX is generated from HTML. This process involves preprocessing the HTML code to replace symbols, such as Greek letters and mathematical operators, with their LaTeX equivalents. The resulting HTML is then converted to a dataframe and subsequently to LaTeX using pandas.

Dict. The conventions of already available linearised tables in SciGen, numericNLG, LogicNLG, and Logic2Text are slightly diverse. In particular, the distinction between column and row heads exists only in numericNLG. Furthermore, compared to LogicNLG and Logic2Text, header hierarchy is preserved in numericNLG and SciGen by merging headers and subheaders into a single string.

[19] https://www.ncbi.nlm.nih.gov/pmc/pmcdoc/tagging-guidelines/article/dobs.html#dob-tables

[20] https://countergram.github.io/pytidylib/

D Image aspect ratios

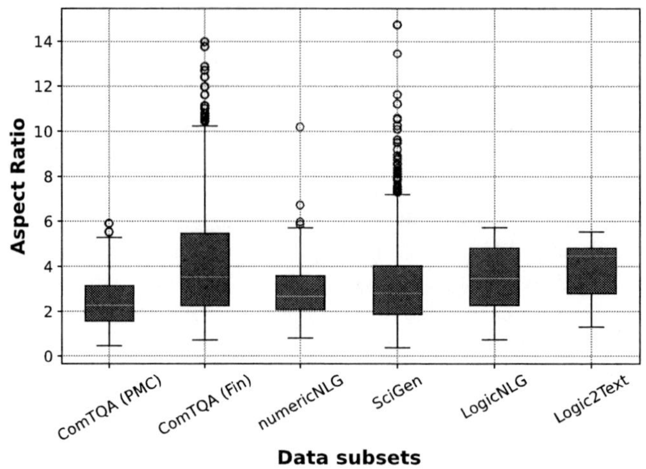

Figure 12: Distribution of image aspect ratios (width/height) across subsets in the TableEval benchmark. Each box represents the interquartile range (IQR), with the central orange line indicating the median. Circles denote outliers, while whiskers (set to 1.5 × IQR by default) extend to the minimum and maximum non-outlier values. Here "Fin" stands for FinTabNet, while "PMC" denotes PubTables-1M.

E Prompts

ComTQA (FinTabNet):

```
Refer to the provided table and answer the question. Question: {question}
```

ComTQA (PubTables-1M):

```
Refer to the provided table and answer the question. Question: {question}.
Table caption: {caption}. Table footnote: {footnote}.
```

SciGen:

```
Describe the given table focusing on the most important findings reported by
reasoning over its content. The summary must be factual, coherent, and
well-written. Do not introduce new information or speculate. Table caption:
{caption}
```

numericNLG:

```
Describe the given table focusing on the insights and trends revealed by the
results. The summary must be factual, coherent, and well-written. Do not
introduce new information or speculate. Table caption: {caption}
```

Logic2Text:

```
Generate a one sentence statement based on the table and logical form. Logical
form: {logical_form}. Table title: {title}
```

LogicNLG:

```
Based on a given table, fill in the entities masked by [ENT] in the following
sentence: {sentence}. Output the sentence with filled in masked entities.
Table title: {title}
```

Figure 13: Prompts used for experiments based on images of tables.

ComTQA (FinTabNet):

Refer to the provided table and answer the question. Question: {question}. Table: {table}.

ComTQA (PubTables-1M):

Refer to the provided table and answer the question. Question: {question}. Table: {table}.

SciGen:

Describe the given table focusing on the most important findings reported by reasoning over its content. The summary must be factual, coherent, and well-written. Do not introduce new information or speculate. Table: {table}.

numericNLG:

Describe the given table focusing on the insights and trends revealed by the results. The summary must be factual, coherent, and well-written. Do not introduce new information or speculate. Table: {table}.

Logic2Text:

Generate a one sentence statement based on the table and logical form. Logical form: {logical_form}. Table title: {title}. Table: {table}.

LogicNLG:

Based on a given table, fill in the entities masked by [ENT] in the following sentence: {sentence}. Output the sentence with filled in masked entities. Table title: {title}. Table: {table}.

Figure 14: Prompts used for experiments based on textual representations of tables.

F Experimental results

Metric	Dict	HTML	Image	LaTeX	XML
BertScore.F1	0.85	0.84	**0.86**	0.84	0.85
BLEU-1	0.16	0.15	**0.19**	0.16	0.16
BLEU-2	0.09	0.09	**0.12**	0.09	0.09
BLEU-3	0.06	0.06	**0.09**	0.06	0.07
BLEU-4	0.04	0.04	**0.06**	0.05	0.05
BLEURT	−0.51	−0.55	**−0.42**	−0.54	−0.53
METEOR	0.24	0.24	**0.25**	0.24	0.24
MoverScore	0.54	0.53	**0.56**	0.54	0.54
ROUGE-1.F1	0.30	0.29	**0.38**	0.29	0.29
ROUGE-2.F1	0.15	0.14	**0.20**	0.15	0.15
ROUGE-3.F1	0.09	0.09	**0.12**	0.09	0.09
ROUGE-4.F1	0.06	0.06	**0.08**	0.07	0.06
ROUGE-L.F1	0.24	0.23	**0.32**	0.24	0.24
SacreBLEU	0.04	0.04	**0.08**	0.05	0.05

Table 5: Values across evaluation metrics for table formats averaged over data subsets and models.

Metric	Dict	HTML	Image	LaTeX	XML
BertScore.F1	0.83	0.84	**0.86**	0.83	0.84
BLEU-1	0.02	0.02	**0.05**	0.02	0.02
BLEU-2	0.01	0.01	**0.03**	0.01	0.01
BLEU-3	0.01	0.01	**0.02**	0.01	0.01
BLEU-4	0.01	0.01	**0.02**	0.01	0.01
BLEURT	−0.58	−0.55	**−0.39**	−0.59	−0.54
METEOR	0.06	0.07	**0.08**	0.06	0.07
MoverScore	0.50	0.50	**0.53**	0.49	0.50
ROUGE-1.F1	0.14	0.14	**0.27**	0.14	0.15
ROUGE-2.F1	0.08	0.08	**0.17**	0.08	0.09
ROUGE-3.F1	0.03	0.03	**0.05**	0.03	0.03
ROUGE-4.F1	0.01	0.01	**0.02**	0.01	0.01
ROUGE-L.F1	0.13	0.14	**0.27**	0.14	0.15
SacreBLEU	0.01	0.02	**0.04**	0.01	0.02

Table 6: Raw values of BertScore.F1, BLEU-N.F1, BLEURT, METEOR, MoverScore, ROUGE-N.F1, ROUGE-L.F1, and SacreBLEU for ComTQA (FinTabNet) subset for individual formats averaged over models.

Metric	Dict	HTML	Image	LaTeX	XML
BertScore.F1	0.82	0.82	**0.85**	0.82	0.82
BLEU-1	0.03	0.03	**0.05**	0.03	0.03
BLEU-2	0.02	0.02	**0.03**	0.02	0.02
BLEU-3	0.01	**0.02**	**0.02**	0.01	**0.02**
BLEU-4	0.01	0.01	**0.02**	0.01	0.01
BLEURT	−0.73	−0.72	**−0.59**	−0.73	−0.72
METEOR	**0.09**	0.10	**0.09**	**0.09**	0.10
MoverScore	0.48	0.48	**0.51**	0.48	0.48
ROUGE-1.F1	0.12	0.12	**0.22**	0.12	0.12
ROUGE-2.F1	0.06	0.06	**0.11**	0.06	0.06
ROUGE-3.F1	0.03	0.03	**0.04**	0.03	0.03
ROUGE-4.F1	0.02	0.02	**0.03**	0.02	0.02
ROUGE-L.F1	0.12	0.12	**0.22**	0.11	0.12
SacreBLEU	0.01	0.01	**0.04**	0.01	0.01

Table 7: Raw values of BertScore.F1, BLEU-N.F1, BLEURT, METEOR, MoverScore, ROUGE-N.F1, ROUGE-L.F1, and SacreBLEU for ComTQA (PubTables-1M) subset for individual formats averaged over models.

Metric	Dict	HTML	Image	LaTeX	XML
BertScore.F1	0.88	0.88	**0.89**	0.88	0.88
BLEU-1	**0.24**	**0.24**	0.22	**0.24**	**0.24**
BLEU-2	**0.13**	**0.13**	0.12	**0.13**	**0.13**
BLEU-3	0.07	0.07	0.07	0.07	**0.08**
BLEU-4	0.04	0.04	0.04	0.04	**0.05**
BLEURT	−0.14	−0.11	−0.19	**−0.09**	**−0.09**
METEOR	0.35	0.37	0.33	0.37	**0.38**
MoverScore	0.59	**0.60**	**0.60**	**0.60**	**0.60**
ROUGE-1.F1	0.48	**0.49**	**0.49**	**0.49**	**0.49**
ROUGE-2.F1	0.23	0.24	0.24	**0.25**	0.24
ROUGE-3.F1	0.12	0.13	0.12	**0.14**	0.13
ROUGE-4.F1	0.06	0.07	0.07	**0.08**	0.07
ROUGE-L.F1	0.37	**0.39**	**0.39**	0.38	0.38
SacreBLEU	**0.05**	**0.05**	**0.05**	**0.05**	**0.05**

Table 8: Raw values of BertScore.F1, BLEU-N.F1, BLEURT, METEOR, MoverScore, ROUGE-N.F1, ROUGE-L.F1, and SacreBLEU for Logic2Text subset for individual formats averaged over models.

Metric	Dict	HTML	Image	LaTeX	XML
BertScore.F1	0.87	0.88	**0.91**	0.89	0.88
BLEU-1	0.32	0.33	**0.51**	0.36	0.36
BLEU-2	0.26	0.27	**0.43**	0.30	0.29
BLEU-3	0.21	0.23	**0.35**	0.25	0.24
BLEU-4	0.17	0.18	**0.28**	0.20	0.20
BLEURT	−0.46	−0.47	**−0.13**	−0.40	−0.41
METEOR	0.52	0.53	**0.63**	0.55	0.55
MoverScore	0.60	0.59	**0.64**	0.61	0.60
ROUGE-1.F1	0.48	0.48	**0.69**	0.52	0.51
ROUGE-2.F1	0.38	0.38	**0.55**	0.41	0.40
ROUGE-3.F1	0.31	0.30	**0.45**	0.34	0.33
ROUGE-4.F1	0.25	0.25	**0.37**	0.28	0.27
ROUGE-L.F1	0.46	0.47	**0.67**	0.51	0.49
SacreBLEU	0.13	0.15	**0.28**	0.16	0.16

Table 9: Raw values of BertScore.F1, BLEU-N.F1, BLEURT, METEOR, MoverScore, ROUGE-N.F1, ROUGE-L.F1, and SacreBLEU for LogicNLG subset for individual formats averaged over models.

Metric	Dict	HTML	Image	LaTeX	XML
BertScore.F1	0.83	**0.84**	0.83	**0.84**	**0.84**
BLEU-1	0.16	**0.18**	0.16	**0.18**	**0.18**
BLEU-2	0.06	**0.07**	**0.07**	**0.07**	**0.07**
BLEU-3	**0.03**	**0.03**	**0.03**	**0.03**	**0.03**
BLEU-4	0.01	**0.02**	0.01	**0.02**	**0.02**
BLEURT	−0.58	−0.54	−0.60	−0.54	**−0.53**
METEOR	0.19	**0.21**	0.19	**0.21**	**0.21**
MoverScore	0.52	**0.53**	**0.53**	**0.53**	**0.53**
ROUGE-1.F1	0.28	0.31	0.30	**0.32**	**0.32**
ROUGE-2.F1	0.06	**0.08**	0.07	**0.08**	**0.08**
ROUGE-3.F1	0.02	0.02	0.02	0.02	**0.03**
ROUGE-4.F1	**0.01**	**0.01**	**0.01**	**0.01**	**0.01**
ROUGE-L.F1	0.16	**0.17**	**0.17**	**0.17**	**0.17**
SacreBLEU	**0.03**	**0.03**	**0.03**	**0.03**	**0.03**

Table 10: Raw values of BertScore.F1, BLEU-N.F1, BLEURT, METEOR, MoverScore, ROUGE-N.F1, ROUGE-L.F1, and SacreBLEU for numericNLG subset for individual formats averaged over models.

Metric	Dict	HTML	Image	LaTeX	XML
BertScore.F1	**0.84**	0.81	**0.84**	0.81	0.81
BLEU-1	**0.16**	0.11	0.15	0.11	0.11
BLEU-2	**0.07**	0.03	**0.07**	0.03	0.03
BLEU-3	**0.03**	0.01	**0.03**	0.01	0.01
BLEU-4	**0.02**	0.00	**0.02**	0.00	0.00
BLEURT	**−0.59**	−0.90	−0.64	−0.91	−0.90
METEOR	**0.20**	0.13	0.19	0.13	0.13
MoverScore	**0.53**	0.50	**0.53**	0.50	0.50
ROUGE-1.F1	**0.30**	0.18	0.29	0.18	0.18
ROUGE-2.F1	**0.07**	0.02	**0.07**	0.02	0.02
ROUGE-3.F1	0.02	0.00	**0.03**	0.00	0.00
ROUGE-4.F1	**0.01**	0.00	**0.01**	0.00	0.00
ROUGE-L.F1	**0.17**	0.11	**0.17**	0.11	0.11
SacreBLEU	**0.03**	0.01	**0.03**	0.01	0.01

Table 11: Raw values of BertScore.F1, BLEU-N.F1, BLEURT, METEOR, MoverScore, ROUGE-N.F1, ROUGE-L.F1, and SacreBLEU for SciGen subset for individual formats averaged over models.

Metric	Dict	HTML	LaTeX	XML
BertScore.F1	**0.83**	**0.83**	**0.83**	**0.83**
BLEU-1	**0.12**	**0.12**	0.11	0.11
BLEU-2	**0.06**	**0.06**	**0.06**	**0.06**
BLEU-3	0.03	**0.04**	**0.04**	**0.04**
BLEU-4	**0.02**	**0.02**	**0.02**	**0.02**
BLEURT	**−0.64**	−0.67	−0.67	−0.66
METEOR	0.20	**0.21**	0.20	**0.21**
MoverScore	**0.52**	**0.52**	**0.52**	**0.52**
ROUGE-1.F1	**0.23**	**0.23**	**0.23**	**0.23**
ROUGE-2.F1	0.09	**0.10**	**0.10**	**0.10**
ROUGE-3.F1	**0.05**	**0.05**	**0.05**	**0.05**
ROUGE-4.F1	**0.03**	**0.03**	**0.03**	**0.03**
ROUGE-L.F1	0.17	**0.18**	**0.18**	**0.18**
SacreBLEU	**0.02**	**0.02**	**0.02**	**0.02**

Table 12: Raw values of BertScore.F1, BLEU-N.F1, BLEURT, METEOR, MoverScore, ROUGE-N.F1, ROUGE-L.F1, and SacreBLEU for Llama-3.2-3B-Instruct and individual text formats averaged over data subsets.

Metric	Dict	HTML	LaTeX	XML
BertScore.F1	**0.85**	**0.85**	**0.85**	**0.85**
BLEU-1	0.17	0.15	**0.18**	0.17
BLEU-2	0.10	0.09	**0.11**	0.10
BLEU-3	0.06	0.06	**0.07**	**0.07**
BLEU-4	0.04	0.04	**0.05**	**0.05**
BLEURT	**−0.48**	−0.54	**−0.48**	−0.49
METEOR	**0.25**	0.24	**0.25**	**0.25**
MoverScore	**0.54**	**0.54**	**0.54**	**0.54**
ROUGE-1.F1	0.33	0.31	**0.34**	0.33
ROUGE-2.F1	0.17	0.16	**0.18**	**0.18**
ROUGE-3.F1	**0.11**	0.10	**0.11**	**0.11**
ROUGE-4.F1	0.07	0.07	**0.08**	**0.08**
ROUGE-L.F1	0.27	0.26	**0.28**	**0.28**
SacreBLEU	0.04	0.04	**0.05**	**0.05**

Table 13: Raw values of BertScore.F1, BLEU-N.F1, BLEURT, METEOR, MoverScore, ROUGE-N.F1, ROUGE-L.F1, and SacreBLEU for Mistral-Nemo-Instruct-2407 and individual text formats averaged over data subsets.

Metric	Dict	HTML	LaTeX	XML
BertScore.F1	**0.84**	**0.84**	**0.84**	**0.84**
BLEU-1	**0.13**	**0.13**	**0.13**	**0.13**
BLEU-2	**0.07**	**0.07**	**0.07**	**0.07**
BLEU-3	0.04	**0.05**	**0.05**	**0.05**
BLEU-4	**0.03**	**0.03**	**0.03**	**0.03**
BLEURT	**−0.54**	−0.55	−0.57	−0.56
METEOR	0.23	**0.24**	0.23	**0.24**
MoverScore	**0.53**	**0.53**	**0.53**	**0.53**
ROUGE-1.F1	**0.26**	**0.26**	**0.26**	**0.26**
ROUGE-2.F1	0.12	**0.13**	0.12	**0.13**
ROUGE-3.F1	**0.07**	**0.07**	**0.07**	**0.07**
ROUGE-4.F1	**0.05**	**0.05**	**0.05**	**0.05**
ROUGE-L.F1	0.20	**0.21**	0.20	0.20
SacreBLEU	**0.03**	**0.03**	**0.03**	**0.03**

Table 14: Raw values of BertScore.F1, BLEU-N.F1, BLEURT, METEOR, MoverScore, ROUGE-N.F1, ROUGE-L.F1, and SacreBLEU for Qwen2.5-14B-Instruct and individual text formats averaged over data subsets.

Metric	Dict	HTML	LaTeX	XML
BertScore.F1	**0.84**	**0.84**	**0.84**	**0.84**
BLEU-1	**0.16**	0.15	**0.16**	0.15
BLEU-2	**0.09**	0.08	**0.09**	**0.09**
BLEU-3	0.06	0.06	**0.07**	0.06
BLEU-4	0.04	0.04	**0.05**	**0.05**
BLEURT	**−0.54**	−0.59	−0.57	−0.57
METEOR	**0.24**	0.23	**0.24**	0.23
MoverScore	**0.53**	**0.53**	**0.53**	**0.53**
ROUGE-1.F1	**0.28**	0.27	**0.28**	**0.28**
ROUGE-2.F1	0.13	0.13	**0.14**	0.13
ROUGE-3.F1	0.08	0.08	**0.09**	0.08
ROUGE-4.F1	**0.06**	0.05	**0.06**	**0.06**
ROUGE-L.F1	0.22	0.21	**0.23**	0.22
SacreBLEU	0.03	0.03	**0.04**	0.03

Table 15: Raw values of BertScore.F1, BLEU-N.F1, BLEURT, METEOR, MoverScore, ROUGE-N.F1, ROUGE-L.F1, and SacreBLEU for Qwen2.5-3B-Instruct and individual text formats averaged over data subsets.

Metric	Dict	HTML	LaTeX	XML
BertScore.F1	**0.86**	**0.86**	**0.86**	**0.86**
BLEU-1	0.21	**0.22**	0.21	**0.22**
BLEU-2	0.13	0.14	0.14	**0.15**
BLEU-3	0.10	**0.11**	0.10	**0.11**
BLEU-4	0.08	**0.09**	0.08	**0.09**
BLEURT	**−0.37**	−0.39	−0.41	−0.38
METEOR	0.26	**0.27**	0.26	**0.27**
MoverScore	**0.56**	**0.56**	0.55	**0.56**
ROUGE-1.F1	**0.38**	0.37	0.36	0.37
ROUGE-2.F1	**0.21**	**0.21**	0.20	**0.21**
ROUGE-3.F1	0.13	**0.14**	0.13	**0.14**
ROUGE-4.F1	**0.10**	**0.10**	**0.10**	**0.10**
ROUGE-L.F1	**0.32**	0.31	0.30	0.31
SacreBLEU	0.09	0.10	0.10	**0.11**

Table 16: Raw values of BertScore.F1, BLEU-N.F1, BLEURT, METEOR, MoverScore, ROUGE-N.F1, ROUGE-L.F1, and SacreBLEU for Gemini-2.0-Flash and individual text formats averaged over data subsets.

Metric	Non-Scientific	Scientific
BertScore.F1	**0.87**	0.83
BLEU-1	**0.21**	0.11
BLEU-2	**0.15**	0.04
BLEU-3	**0.11**	0.02
BLEU-4	**0.09**	0.01
BLEURT	**−0.34**	−0.68
METEOR	**0.33**	0.15
MoverScore	**0.57**	0.51
ROUGE-1.F1	**0.40**	0.22
ROUGE-2.F1	**0.25**	0.06
ROUGE-3.F1	**0.17**	0.02
ROUGE-4.F1	**0.12**	0.01
ROUGE-L.F1	**0.36**	0.15
SacreBLEU	**0.08**	0.02

Table 17: Values across evaluation metrics for scientific and non-scientific domains averaged over data subsets, models, and table formats.

Metric	ComTQA (FinTabNet)	ComTQA (PubTables-1M)	Logic2Text	LogicNLG	numericNLG	SciGen
BertScore.F1	0.84	0.83	0.88	**0.89**	0.83	0.82
BLEU-1	0.03	0.04	0.23	**0.38**	0.17	0.13
BLEU-2	0.02	0.02	0.13	**0.31**	0.07	0.04
BLEU-3	0.01	0.02	0.07	**0.26**	0.03	0.02
BLEU-4	0.01	0.01	0.04	**0.20**	0.01	0.01
BLEURT	−0.53	−0.70	**−0.13**	−0.37	−0.56	−0.79
METEOR	0.07	0.09	0.36	**0.56**	0.20	0.16
MoverScore	0.50	0.49	0.60	**0.61**	0.53	0.51
ROUGE-1.F1	0.17	0.14	0.49	**0.54**	0.31	0.23
ROUGE-2.F1	0.10	0.07	0.24	**0.42**	0.07	0.04
ROUGE-3.F1	0.03	0.03	0.13	**0.34**	0.02	0.01
ROUGE-4.F1	0.01	0.02	0.07	**0.28**	0.01	0.00
ROUGE-L.F1	0.17	0.14	0.38	**0.52**	0.17	0.13
SacreBLEU	0.02	0.02	0.05	**0.18**	0.03	0.02

Table 18: Values across evaluation metrics for each data subset averaged over models and table formats.

Model	Bert-Score.F1	BLEU-1	BLEU-2	BLEU-3	BLEU-4	BLEURT	METEOR	Mover-Score	ROUGE-1.F1	ROUGE-2.F1	ROUGE-3.F1	ROUGE-4.F1	ROUGE-L.F1	Sacre-BLEU
Baseline														
Gemini-2.0-Flash_mm	**0.87**	**0.22**	**0.14**	**0.11**	**0.08**	**−0.35**	**0.27**	**0.56**	**0.40**	**0.22**	**0.14**	**0.10**	**0.33**	**0.11**
Gemini-2.0-Flash_llm	0.86	0.21	**0.14**	**0.11**	**0.08**	−0.39	0.26	**0.56**	0.37	0.20	**0.14**	**0.10**	0.31	0.10
MLLMs														
Idefics3-8B-Llama3	**0.88**	**0.19**	**0.12**	**0.09**	**0.07**	**−0.36**	0.23	**0.59**	**0.47**	**0.27**	**0.13**	**0.09**	**0.42**	**0.11**
Qwen2.5-VL-3B-Instruct	0.85	0.18	**0.12**	**0.09**	**0.07**	−0.51	0.25	0.55	0.34	0.18	0.11	0.08	0.28	0.07
Qwen2.5-VL-7B-Instruct	0.86	**0.19**	**0.12**	0.08	0.06	−0.39	**0.27**	0.55	0.36	0.19	0.12	**0.09**	0.30	0.07
llama3-llava-next-8b-hf	0.85	0.16	0.10	0.06	0.04	−0.50	0.24	0.54	0.31	0.15	0.09	0.06	0.25	0.04
LLMs														
Mistral-Nemo-Instruct-2407	**0.85**	**0.17**	**0.10**	**0.07**	**0.05**	**−0.50**	**0.25**	**0.54**	**0.33**	**0.17**	**0.11**	**0.07**	**0.27**	**0.04**
Qwen2.5-3B-Instruct	0.84	0.15	0.09	0.06	0.04	−0.57	0.24	0.53	0.28	0.13	0.08	0.06	0.22	0.03
Qwen2.5-14B-Instruct	0.84	0.13	0.07	0.05	0.03	−0.56	0.24	0.53	0.26	0.12	0.07	0.05	0.20	0.03
Llama-3.2-3B-Instruct	0.83	0.12	0.06	0.04	0.02	−0.66	0.20	0.52	0.23	0.10	0.05	0.03	0.18	0.02

Table 19: Values across evaluation metrics for individual models averaged over data subsets and table formats.

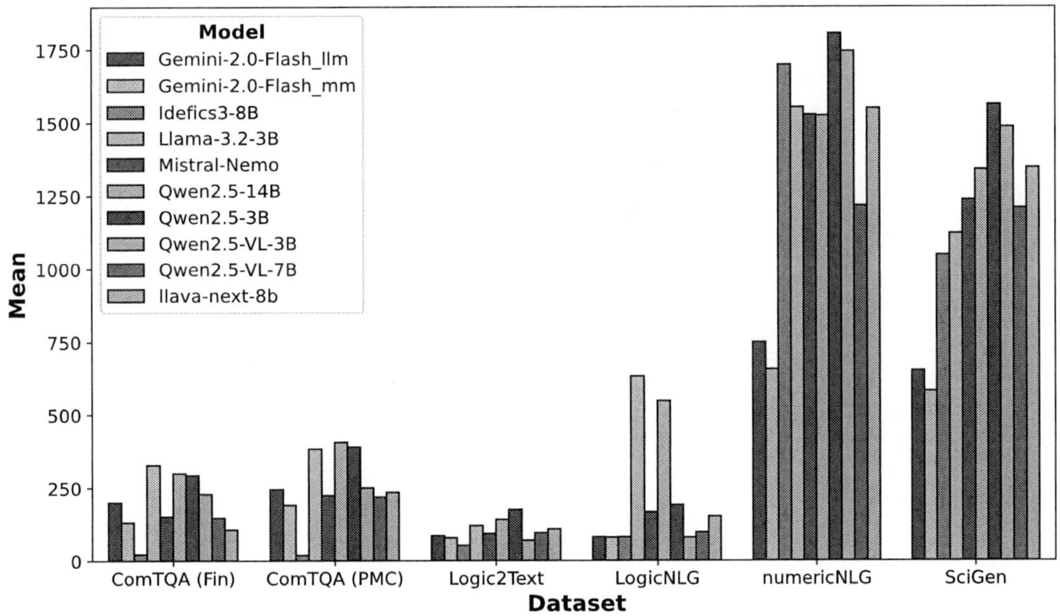

Figure 15: Mean prediction lengths (in characters) for each model and data subset. Here "_llm" and "_mm" are used to distinguish between text and image input for Gemini-2.0-Flash, respectively.

G Case Study

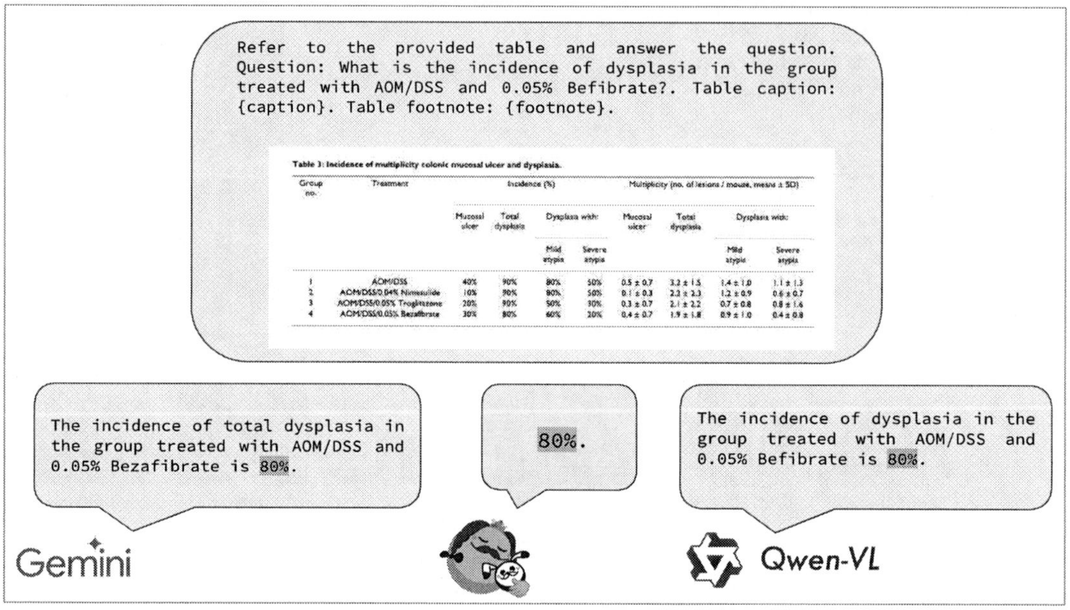

Figure 16: An example illustrating differences in prediction length across Idefics3, Gemini-2.0-Flash, and Qwen2.0-VL (7B) models on a sample from the ComTQA (PubTables-1M) subset.

H Additional interpretability analyses

Mistral-Nemo vs. Llama3. The following figures show further examples of feature attribution and log-probability analysis comparing Mistral-Nemo with Llama3.

In Figure 17 (ComTQA FinTabNet), Mistral-Nemo correctly predicts the answer, while Llama3 fails. We find a key difference in the attribution pattern around the columns *"2014"* and *"2013"*, where Mistral-Nemo assigns a slightly higher score (lighter blue) than Llama3. In the log-probability analysis, we see high uncertainty in Llama3 generating the final answer starting with *"1"*. On the contrary, Mistral-Nemo shows a high level of confidence in the predicted value.

In Figure 18 (ComTQA PubTables-1M), both models generate incorrect answers. For Mistral-Nemo, one can barely see any attribution in the decisive row of the table. For Llama3, there is a slightly higher attribution for *"Beer"* in *"Lung-Beer"*. We also observe that the tokeniser splits the number into *"496"* and *"6"*. A plausible explanation for the failure is that when it processes *"Lung Stanford"* with 918 genes, it likely finds it to be higher than 496 (ignoring the fourth digit *"6"*). Regarding the log-probabilities, the decision of which feature to name after *"the most number of genes is"* is controversial for both models, judged by the low confidence in the following token.

In Figure 19 (ComTQA PubTables-1M), Mistral-Nemo solves the task correctly, whereas Llama3 fails to distinguish *"VRP-HA"* from *"VRP-neu"* and is not confident in the predicted value (*10*). Mistral-Nemo focuses on the *"VRP-HA"* row in the table more than the similar alternative *"VRP-neu"* and generally finds the relevant feature name in the question to be more important, judging by the attribution patterns. When we compare this to the log-probabilities, the model is very confident about its decision (*"VRP-HA"*) throughout the generation.

Dict vs. LaTeX input format. The following figures show examples of feature attribution and log-probability analysis. We compare predictions across Dict vs. LaTeX representations of tables for Mistral-Nemo and Llama3 based on instances from the LogicNLG subset.

In Figure 20, Mistral-Nemo correctly predicts the missing entities with a high level of confidence. We notice high similarity between the input attribution patterns across two formats. In both cases, one of the most relevant tokens (month *"August"*) is correctly identified to produce the right answer according to the ground truth and hence receives high attribution. The model focuses on the tokens relevant to the task and does not pay much attention to LaTeX formatting tags, since the respective tokens generally remain barely considered throughout the generation. However, we can see some decreases in model confidence at the end of the generation (*"games before"*).

In Figure 21, Llama3 generates the wrong responses in both cases. However, the Dict variant also makes the model focus on bracketing, separators, and punctuation quite often. Only for LaTeX, there is a noticeably lower confidence about generating *"Electra"* as the play of choice. For both representations of the table, however, Llama3 is not certain about the last two entities (*"Cyprus and Romania"*, *"Cyprus and Greece"*), which are either fully or partially incorrect according to the ground truth (*"Greece and Italy"*).

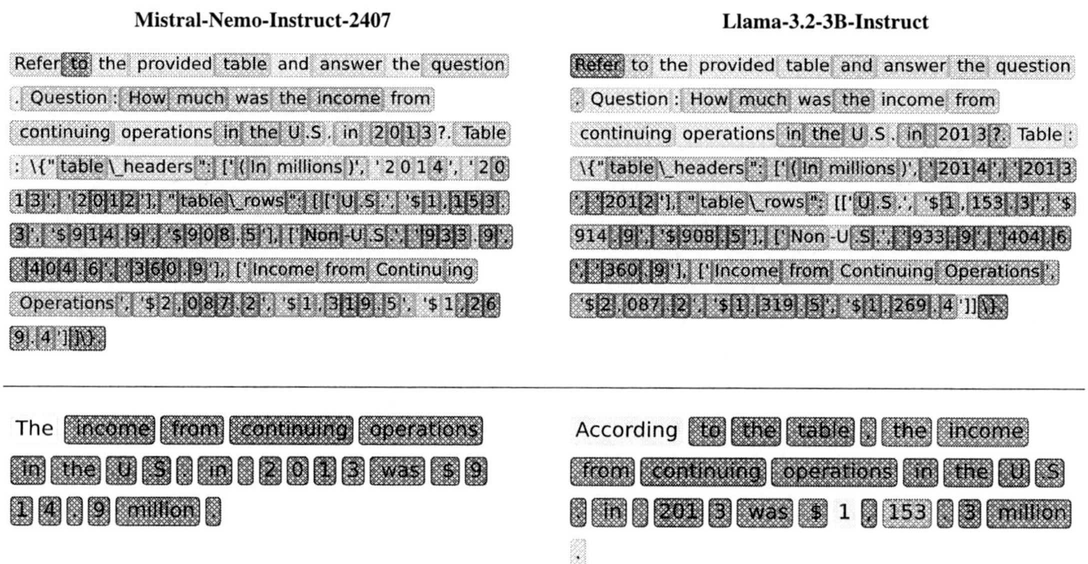

Figure 17: Interpretability analysis for the ComTQA (FinTabNet) instance with a table represented in a Dict format. The ground truth is *"$914.9 million"*. The visualisation follows the same procedure as Figure 5.

Mistral-Nemo-Instruct-2407

Refer to the provided table and answer the question
. Question : Which dataset has the most number of
genes ?. Table : \{"table_title": Table 5, "table
_caption": Random data simulations of real data
sets. This table compares the results found from
the real data (Real column) to two different types
of random data. The Random column contains the
experimentally determined largest number of pairs
found from 10 simulation runs using a random
data matrix (drawn from a uniform distribution)
where the number of genes and class sizes is the
same as the indicated for the real data. The Label
Sh uff led column contains the experimentally
determined largest number of pairs found from 30
simulation runs where the class labels were
randomly shuffled. In the samples column, the
number in parenthesis is the number of positive
samples. The numbers after the slash are the
number of single genes found. Label shuffling
leads to more pairs found "by chance" only for
the smaller data sets. The small data sets have
large numbers of pairs expected "by chance".. "
table_headers": ['Data set', 'Samples', 'Genes', '
Real', 'Random', 'Label Sh uffled'], "table_sub
headers": [], "table_rows": [['G IST', '19(6)', '1
987', '137981/74', '2706/0', '4622/2'],
['Bre ast BR CA (b rc a1 vs brca2)', '15(7)', '322
6', '143574/18', '20563/2', '53900/11'],
['Bre ast BR CA (b rc a1 \& brca2 vs Sporadic)', '2
2(7)', '3226', '2114/0', '1286/1', '0/0'],
['Cutaneous', '38(7)', '3613', '596/0', '62/
0', '24/0'], ['Lung Stanford', '52(13)', '918',
'486/2', '0/0', '0/0'], ['Lung Be er', '96(10
)', '4966', '22102/5', '0/0', '0/0'], ['Pro
state', '34(9)', '3958', '249662/52', '57/0
', '13/0']], "table_footnote": None \}.

Based on the provided table , the
dataset with the most number of
genes is " Pro state " with 3958
genes .

Llama-3.2-3B-Instruct

Refer to the provided table and answer the question
. Question : Which dataset has the most number of
genes ?. Table : \{"table_title": Table 5, "table
_caption": Random data simulations of real data
sets . This table compares the results found from
the real data (Real column) to two different types
of random data. The Random column contains the
experimentally determined largest number of pairs
found from 10 simulation runs using a random data
matrix (drawn from a uniform distribution) where
the number of genes and class sizes is the same
as the indicated for the real data. The Label Sh
uffled column contains the experimentally
determined largest number of pairs found from 30
simulation runs where the class labels were
randomly shuffled. In the samples column, the
number in parenthesis is the number of positive
samples. The numbers after the slash are the
number of single genes found. Label shuffling
leads to more pairs found "by chance" only for
the smaller data sets . The small data sets have
large numbers of pairs expected "by chance".. "
table_headers": ['Data set', 'Samples', 'Genes', '
Real', 'Random', 'Label Shuffled'], "table_sub
headers": [], "table_rows": [['G IST', '19(6)', '
1987', '137981/74', '2706/0', '4622/2'], ['Bre
ast BR CA (brca1 vs brca2)', '15(7)', '3226', '
143574/18', '20563/2', '53900/11'], ['Breast
BR CA (brca1 \& brca2 vs Sporadic)', '22(7)', '
3226', '2114/0', '1286/1', '0/0'], ['Cutaneous
', '38(7)', '3613', '596/0', '62/0', '24/0'], ['L
ung Stanford', '52(13)', '918', '486/2', '0/0', '
0/0'], ['L ung Beer', '96(10)', '4966', '22102/5
', '0/0', '0/0'], ['Pro state', '34(9)', '3958', '
249662/52', '57/0', '13/0']], "table_foot note":
None \}.

Based on the table , the dataset with
the most number of genes is ' L ung
Stan ford ' with 918 genes .

Figure 18: Interpretability analysis for the ComTQA (PubTables-1M) instance with a table represented in a Dict format. The ground truth is *"LungBeer"*. The visualisation follows the same procedure as Figure 5.

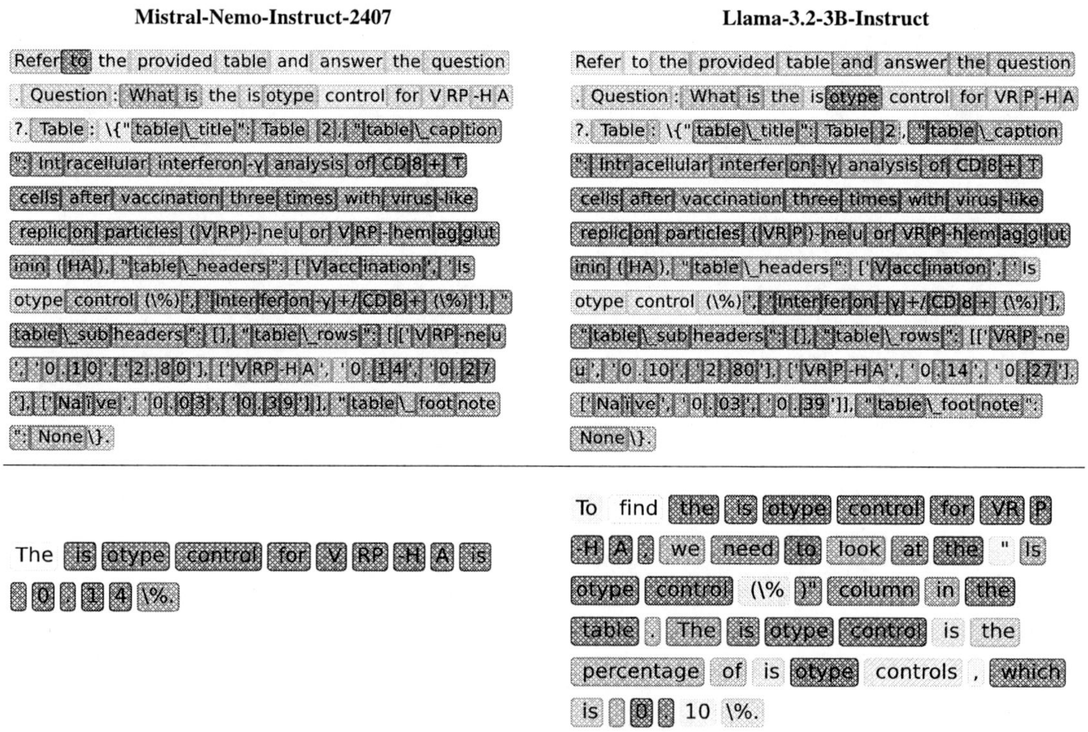

Figure 19: Interpretability analysis for ComTQA (PubTables-1M) instance with the Dict format. The ground truth is *"0.14%"*. The visualisation follows the same procedure as Figure 5.

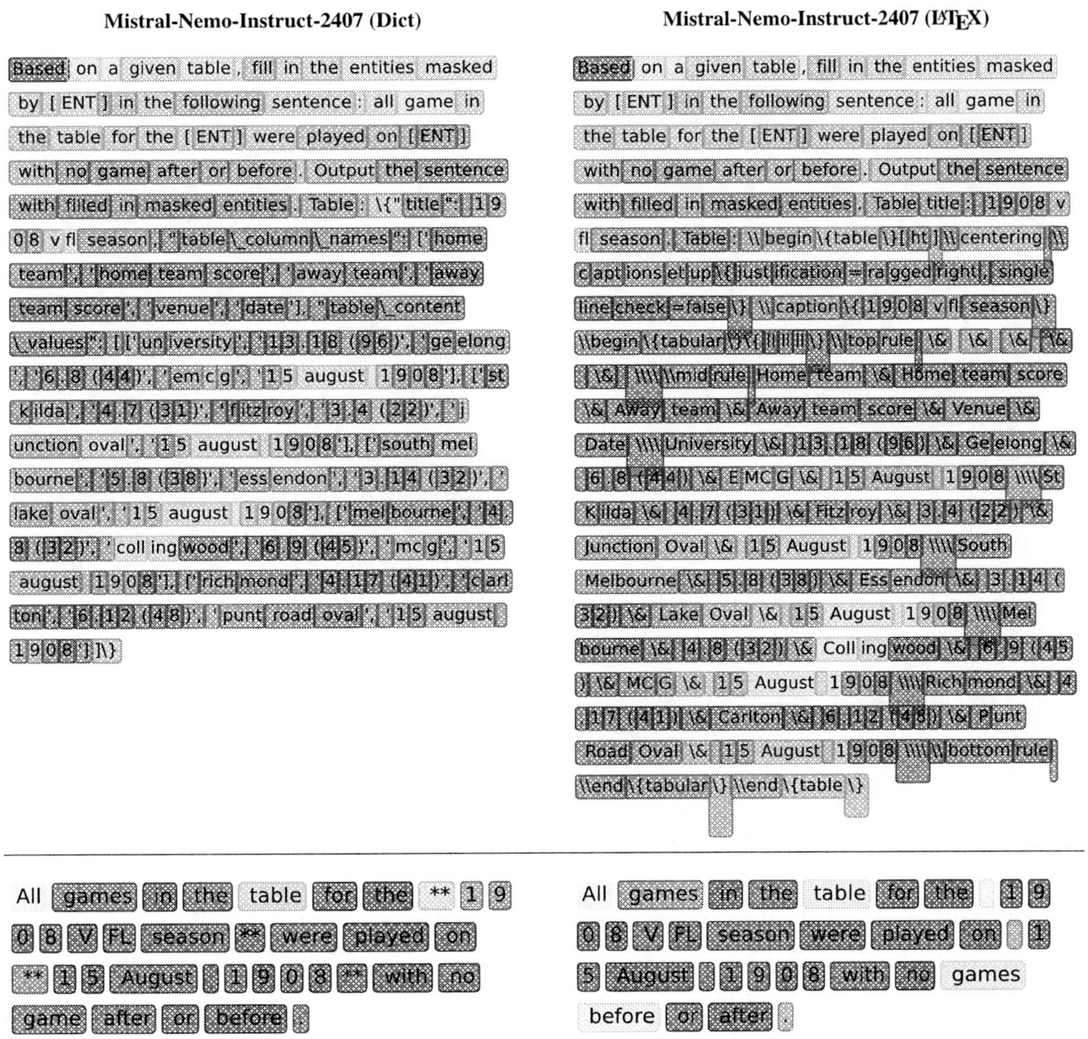

Figure 20: Interpretability analysis the LogicNLG instance comparing the Dict (left) with the LaTeX (right) input format of the table. The ground truth is *"all game in the table for the 1908 Vfl Season were played on 15 August 1908 with no game after or before"*. The visualisation follows the same procedure as Figure 5.

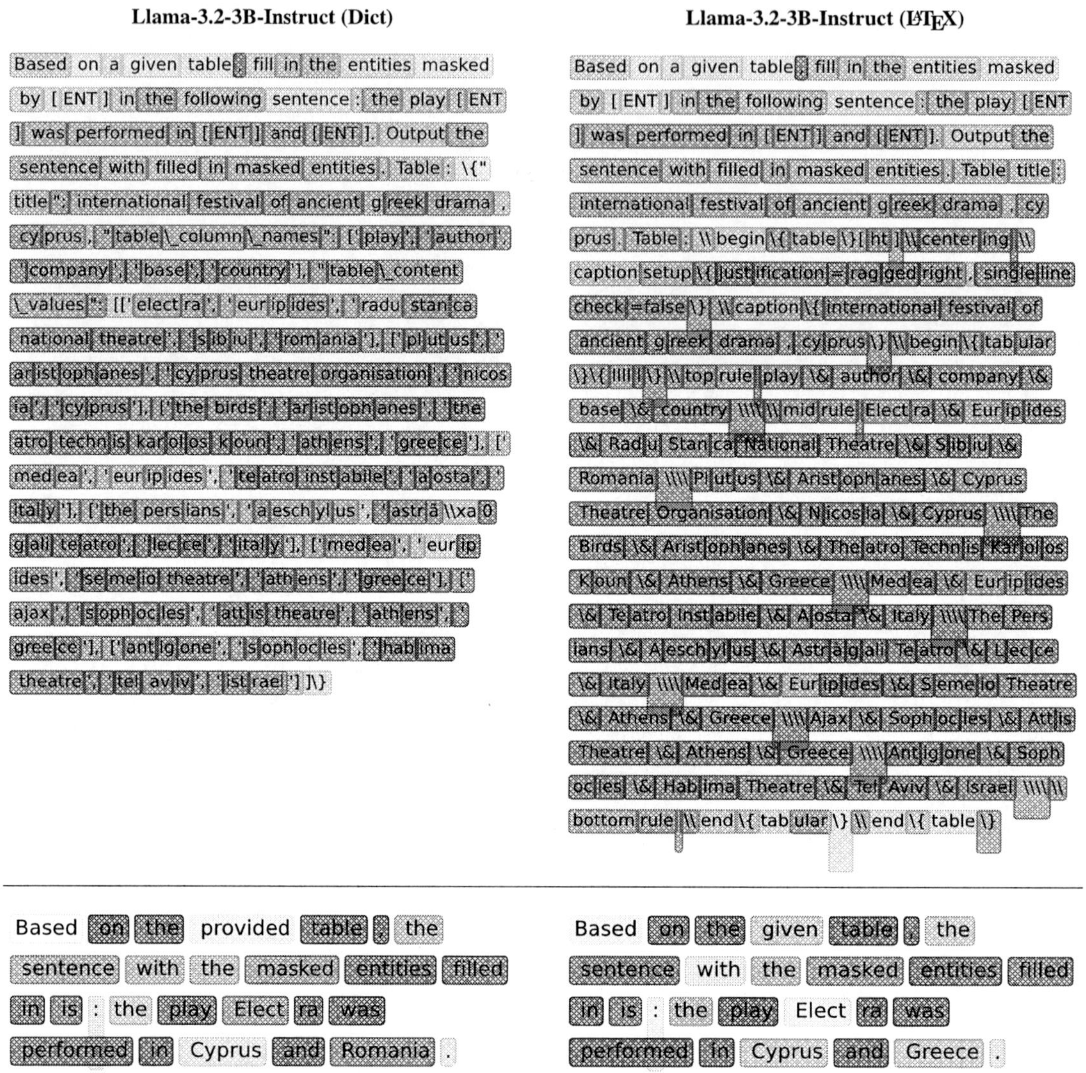

Figure 21: Interpretability analysis for the LogicNLG instance comparing the Dict (left) with the LaTeX (right) input format of the table. The ground truth is *"the play Medea was performed in Greece and Italy"*. The visualisation follows the same procedure as Figure 5.

	Years Ended December 31,						
	2014	2013	2012	2014 vs. 2013		2013 vs. 2012	
				$ Change	% Change	$ Change	% Change
Routing	$ 2,223.9	$ 2,318.0	$ 2,037.6	$ (94.1)	(4)%	$ 280.4	14%
Switching	721.2	638.0	554.8	83.2	13 %	83.2	15%
Security	463.6	563.9	669.7	(100.3)	(18)%	(105.8)	(16)%
Total Product	3,408.7	3,519.9	3,262.1	(111.2)	(3)%	257.8	8%
Percentage of net revenues	*73.7 %*	*75.4 %*	*74.7 %*				
Total Service	1,218.4	1,149.2	1,103.3	69.2	6 %	45.9	4%
Percentage of net revenues	*26.3 %*	*24.6 %*	*25.3 %*				
Total net revenues	$ 4,627.1	$ 4,669.1	$ 4,365.4	$ (42.0)	(1)%	$ 303.7	7%

Figure 22: Table image corresponding to the ComTQA (FinTabNet) example in Figure 5.

Perspective: Leveraging Domain Knowledge for Tabular Machine Learning in the Medical Domain

Arijana Bohr[1], Thomas Altstidl[1], Bjoern Eskofier[1,2] and Emmanuelle Salin[1]

[1]Machine Learning and Data Analytics Lab,
Friedrich-Alexander-Universität Erlangen-Nürnberg (FAU), Germany
[2]Institute of AI for Health, Helmholtz Zentrum München
German Research Center for Environmental Health, Neuherberg, Germany
{firstname.lastname}@fau.de

Abstract

There has been limited exploration of how domain knowledge can be effectively integrated into machine learning for medical tabular data. Traditional approaches often rely on non-generalizable processes tailored to specific datasets. In contrast, recent advances in deep learning for language and tabular data are leading the way toward more generalizable and scalable methods of domain knowledge inclusion. In this paper, we first explore the need for domain knowledge in medical tabular data, categorize types of medical domain knowledge, and discuss how each can be leveraged in tabular machine learning. We then outline strategies for integrating this knowledge at various stages of the machine learning pipeline. Finally, building on recent advances in tabular deep learning, we propose future research directions to support the integration of domain knowledge.

1 Introduction

Tabular data plays a fundamental role in the medical field, capturing patient-specific details such as demographics, medical history, biomarkers, and diagnostic codes (Mao et al., 2024). Many clinical machine learning models rely on this data for tasks such as disease diagnosis (Ahsan et al., 2022) and adverse events prediction (Tomašev et al., 2021).

However, developing these models poses unique challenges. For instance, models can often learn shortcuts when modeling the data, leading to potentially harmful decisions. Caruana et al. (2015), for example, show that a model trained to predict pneumonia risk can incorrectly identify asthma as a protective factor. This error can occur because asthmatic patients generally receive more aggressive treatment, leading to better outcomes.

In contrast to clinicians who draw on prior training and domain expertise, models are typically developed with limited prior knowledge (Moor et al., 2023). They rely on statistical associations between input features and targets and do not understand the underlying physiology (Moor et al., 2023). Learning these associations can be further complicated by the heterogeneous features and complex interactions present in medical datasets (Ruan et al., 2024).

The lack of knowledge can also hinder the development of models for specialized medical tasks (Moor et al., 2023), as it can limit their ability to perform reliably in various clinical settings. In addition, inconsistencies in data standardization of medical datasets (Ahmadian et al., 2011) can be a barrier to the generalizability of models across medical environments.

This paper explores how the integration of domain knowledge into machine learning for medical tabular data can help address these challenges. In particular, it can guide variable selection (Wu et al., 2022), mitigate data quality issues (Curé, 2012) and help establish consistent standardization (Shi et al., 2021). It can also help ensure that models meet natural laws and regulatory requirements, which data-driven approaches may ignore (Von Rueden et al., 2021). Ultimately, this could support the translation of machine learning into clinical practice, a hurdle many existing models have yet to overcome (El Naqa et al., 2023).

Despite the widespread use of tabular data in healthcare, to our knowledge, there has been no comprehensive investigation of domain knowledge integration for medical tabular data. In this paper, we first detail the types of medical domain knowledge and their potential uses. We then provide an overview of strategies for incorporating medical domain knowledge into tabular machine learning at all pipeline stages. In particular, we investigate how recent methods in table representation learning, such as foundation models (Hollmann et al., 2023a) or LLM-based table representation (Sui et al., 2024), can be adapted for this purpose. Finally, we suggest promising research directions

Proceedings of the 4th Table Representation Learning Workshop, pages 143–155
July 31, 2025

for automated knowledge integration in clinical machine learning for medical tabular data.

2 Related Works

Domain knowledge encompasses relevant information about the machine learning task, including relevant features, taxonomies, logical constraints, and probability distributions (Dash et al., 2022). It is also referred to as background or prior knowledge. Domain knowledge has been incorporated into various fields of machine learning, such as physics and engineering, where it is used to combine data with mathematical and physics-based models (Karniadakis et al., 2021; Willard et al., 2022).

In the medical domain, the importance of integrating domain knowledge has been increasingly recognized (Mao et al., 2024; Leiser et al., 2023; Von Rueden et al., 2021), especially in areas such as medical imaging (Xie et al., 2021). While previous work has shown that domain knowledge can benefit tabular clinical decision systems (Sirocchi et al., 2024), it is often poorly integrated into clinical machine learning pipelines and requires custom algorithms (Sirocchi et al., 2024).

Xie et al. (2021) identify three challenges hindering the adoption of domain knowledge in medical computer vision models, which are also relevant to tabular data: identifying relevant sources, selecting appropriate representations, and integrating them into deep learning models.

3 Medical Domain Knowledge

In this section, we build on prior work in machine learning and domain-informed models (Von Rueden et al., 2021; Mao et al., 2024) to propose a categorization of medical domain knowledge.

3.1 Patient Data

Definition Patient data encompasses a wide range of health-related information, such as demographics, laboratory values, and vital signs. These data are commonly stored in systems like Electronic Health Records (EHRs).

The accessibility of patient datasets can vary considerably. MIMIC (Johnson et al., 2023) or UK Biobank (Sudlow et al., 2015) are available to researchers through application procedures, while most datasets are only accessible within individual institutions. These datasets may reflect the biases of specific patient populations. Other sources, such as population-wide health statistics, from initiatives like the Global Burden of Disease (Vollset et al., 2024), can provide context to assess generalizability. In addition, knowledge graphs can be developed from datasets such as cancer registries to understand the variation in outcomes (Hasan et al., 2019). Furthermore, biomedical databases that capture gene-gene or protein-protein interactions encode biological relationships and can serve as prior knowledge to inform downstream model training and inference (Wysocka et al., 2023).

Representation Patient data is often represented by datasets of various modalities that can be used to train or pre-train medical models.

Integration Patient data can be used for training and subgroup analyses, bias detection, and generalizability evaluation across diverse cohorts. Patient statistics can also inform feature engineering.

3.2 Formal Knowledge

Definition Formal knowledge encompasses established biomedical and scientific information recognized by scientific consensus. It originates from authoritative sources, such as medical textbooks or clinical guidelines, which can establish standardized procedures for clinical practice.

Formal knowledge can be *quantitative*, often represented through mathematical models that estimate biomarker dynamics or disease progression, such as pharmacokinetic models of drug absorption (Lin and Wong, 2017) or tumor growth models (Albano and Giorno, 2006; Tabatabai et al., 2005). Known clinical thresholds (e.g., defining sinus tachycardia as heart rate $\geq$ 100 bpm at rest (Page et al., 2016)) can guide data encoding and interpretation. Additionally, quantitative rules support data quality control by flagging physiologically implausible values.

Formal knowledge can also be *qualitative*, capturing the known interactions of patient characteristics. For instance, diagnosing delirium relies on behavioral and cognitive changes assessed through mental status exams (Tieges et al., 2018). Similarly, clinical gestalt refers to the ability of a physician to synthesize signals such as facial expressions or posture to form early diagnostic impressions (Cramer et al., 2025). Though laboratory tests often confirm a diagnosis, initial suspicion can stem from these assessments, such as hyperpigmentation in vitamin B12 deficiency (Brescoll and Daveluy, 2015).

Representation Formal knowledge can be represented as rules, lookup tables (e.g., scoring ranges, reference intervals), and flow charts or other categorical mappings for qualitative associations.

Integration Formal knowledge can be used for feature engineering, data cleaning, encoding medical relationships, integrating medical constraints, and validation.

3.3 Medical Semantics

Definition Medical semantics refers to standardized representations of biomedical concepts that support interoperability between datasets.

In tabular medical datasets, biomedical concepts are often expressed in varying forms, through free text and different coding systems. This variability can hinder the generalizability of machine learning models. To address this, semantic frameworks like SNOMED CT (Chang and Mostafa, 2021) and the Unified Medical Language System (UMLS) Lindberg et al. (1993) offer structured vocabularies and ontologies (Gaudet-Blavignac et al., 2021). LLMs can also generate medical semantic embeddings that enrich tabular data with contextual meaning. For example, Michalopoulos et al. (2021) introduce UmlsBERT, which incorporates domain knowledge from UMLS by linking terms with shared concepts and semantic types.

Representation Medical semantics can be represented through ontologies and dictionaries or captured by using biomedical language models.

Integration Medical semantics can be used for preprocessing, standardization, or to enrich existing data with semantic hierarchy or similarity.

3.4 Experimental Medical Findings

Definition Experimental medical findings derived from data analyses, clinical studies, or trials often reveal potential interactions between biomedical concepts, even if causal relationships are not yet established or still require scientific consensus. For example, current evidence from controlled exposure studies in children supports an association between adverse behavioral outcomes and synthetic food dye (Miller et al., 2022). Experimental findings are typically also compiled in clinical guidelines used by physicians. They are classified into multiple categories of recommendations (Class I, IIa, IIb, II and III) and levels of evidence (A, B, or C) (McDonagh et al., 2023). These findings can serve as hypotheses to guide the design of machine learning models.

While clinical guidelines can be difficult to interpret due to their length and variations in format (e.g., text, flowcharts, tables), advances in retrieval augmented generation models lead the way towards a more efficient extraction of relevant information (Kresevic et al., 2024).

Representation: Experimental findings can be represented as soft rules with confidence scores, probabilistic associations, or model priors.

Integration Experimental findings can be used to incorporate promising hypotheses that are supported by preliminary evidence. It may be used to explore feature relationships during feature engineering, prioritize variables during feature selection, and introduce soft constraints during model training or validation.

3.5 Professional Insights

Definition Reasoning developed by experienced clinicians provides essential context when interpreting information. With years of clinical experience, even limited data can be synthesized to make a diagnosis (Groves et al., 2003). This is demonstrated, for example, by optometrists outperforming novices in diagnosing glaucoma when data is limited (Ghaffar et al., 2025).

Expert insight is particularly valuable for identifying potential confounding factors when developing machine learning models for clinical use. For instance, patients nearing the end of life may establish legal directives, such as Do Not Resuscitate (DNR) orders, to limit medical intervention by their wishes (Schmidt et al., 2015). However, such directives are often not recorded in structured datasets and may be communicated only verbally.

Representation Professional insight can be formalized through rules, thresholds, or guidelines derived from expert interviews or consensus (e.g., expert surveys).

Integration Expert input can inform data collection through the design of study protocols and guide the selection and construction of features. It also plays a key role in validating models, interpreting outliers, and enabling feedback loops for iterative refinement.

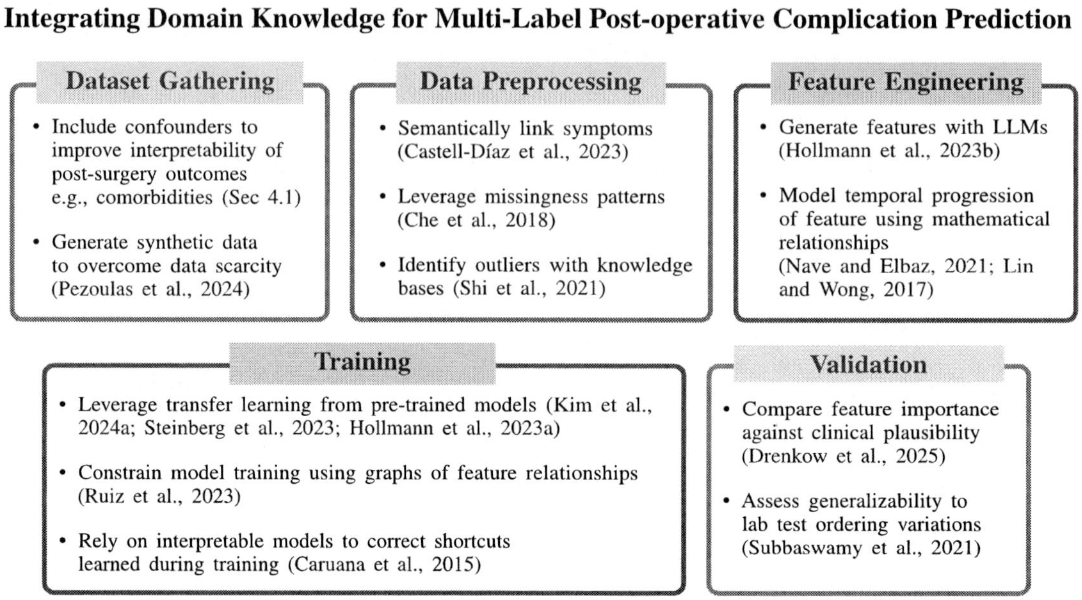

Figure 1: Possible integrations of domain knowledge for the use-case post-surgery complications prediction

4 Integrating Domain Knowledge

In Section 3, we explored the various forms of medical domain knowledge. Here, we examine each stage of the machine learning pipeline, from data collection to model validation, and highlight opportunities to meaningfully integrate domain expertise. We also focus on how advances in deep learning can be incorporated for domain knowledge integration and suggest promising research directions. In Figure 1, we provide an example of how domain knowledge can be integrated into the use case of post-surgery complications prediction.

4.1 Dataset Creation and Selection

Data collection Medical domain knowledge and professional insight are critical to data collection, especially in the case of *prospective studies*. Expert input (see Section 3.5) is essential when designing the study protocol, selecting data sources, defining patient populations, and determining which features to collect. Potential confounders should be considered during study design and data collection or assessed during analysis (Jager et al., 2008; Kahlert et al., 2017). A common strategy involves defining an a priori set of covariates to account for (Brookhart et al., 2010). For example, in a study investigating diabetes and ischemic heart disease, researchers could control for age by including only participants over 65 (Jager et al., 2008).

Beyond addressing confounders, incorporating additional relevant variables can help capture clinical context. Savchenko et al. (2023), for example, incorporate patient socio-demographic information to model the clinical dynamics of non-invasive bladder cancer treatment. Their inclusion yields an 8.14% performance gain over the baseline model lacking these features (Savchenko et al., 2023).

For *retrospective studies*, leveraging public datasets can also enrich training data. Factors such as demographic statistics can help select appropriate datasets. Ontologies can also be used to semantically categorize features, enabling table comparisons (Woźnica et al., 2024).

Synthetic data Synthetic data can help protect patient privacy or increase data size (Pezoulas et al., 2024). Bayesian networks can be used to generate synthetic patient data by modeling probabilistic relationships and latent variables (Tucker et al., 2020). These relationships can be informed by expert knowledge (Rabaey et al., 2024) or learned from existing datasets (Tucker et al., 2020). To ensure that the generated data maintains strong inferential properties, informative prior knowledge is essential to appropriately weight the different network structures (Young et al., 2009). Simulation-based methods can also leverage domain knowledge to generate data points. Deist et al. (2019) propose a technique that integrates prior knowledge using domain-informed kernels. The method performs well in low-data, high-dimensional settings but is surpassed by data-driven approaches as training data increases. Shi et al. (2022), for instance, show that when data-driven methods use large amounts of data, they can generate synthetic data that closely resembles real data.

Large language models have also been proposed for synthetic data generation (Zhang et al., 2023). However, this approach should be further tested in the medical domain in terms of privacy preservation. Kim et al. (2024b) propose combining LLMs with attribute constraints to generate synthetic financial data. Yet, they notice that using constraints could reduce diversity in some attributes, which may cause issues for data with high variability. These findings may also be relevant for similar approaches in the medical domain.

While synthetic data is often used to replace or complement training data, it can also help train tabular models. TabPFN (Hollmann et al., 2023a), a transformer-based model for tabular tasks, is trained on a large number of synthetic datasets, reducing reliance on sensitive real-world data. Recent work has demonstrated that domain knowledge can improve its adaptability to specific data types. For example, Perciballi et al. (2024) enhanced TabPFN's performance on metagenomic data by modifying the generative model priors to better reflect the sparsity and variability of this domain. However, the high variability in their results indicates that further experimentation is needed.

Future Research When working with a small dataset, a common strategy is to identify semantically or structurally similar datasets that can be leveraged through transfer learning. Advances in semantic data type detection (e.g., Hulsebos et al. (2023)) could lead to more informed dataset selections when combined with medical ontologies.

Synthetic data offers another promising research avenue for bias mitigation and data augmentation. The explicit inclusion of domain knowledge could guide this process, especially for low-resource domains. However, more research is still needed to compare the various methods of synthetic data generation in terms of privacy preservation, fidelity, bias, and clinical relevance.

4.2 Data Preprocessing

Cleaning Clinical data often contains inconsistencies that require tailored preprocessing. While such issues are best mitigated through standardized data collection protocols, missing data and non-standardized entries remain common and are sometimes unavoidable.

Numerical values suffer from inconsistent units due to varying practices across laboratories and general practitioners (e.g., 'g/dL', '??', 'NULL') (Shi et al., 2021). Domain knowledge can guide semantic alignment and harmonization through the identification of valid unit conversions or the correction of implausible entries (e.g., checking whether values are in acceptable ranges). For instance, Shi et al. (2021) automatically derive conversion rates, detect outliers, and identify extreme ranges using literature and knowledge bases.

Categorical values also require standardization. For this, medical knowledge bases can provide structured vocabularies (Chang and Mostafa, 2021; Bodenreider, 2004), and dictionaries can define permissible value labels, helping flag and correct invalid entries (Pilowsky et al., 2024). Beyond rule-based methods, ontology embedding techniques can leverage clinical ontologies to generate vector representations of terms (Zahra and Kate, 2024; Castell-Díaz et al., 2023). These embeddings enable the suggestion of the semantically related post-coordinated expression (Castell-Díaz et al., 2023).

Using LLMs for automated tabular data cleaning could alleviate the need for tailor-made outlier detection and error correction algorithms (Bendinelli et al., 2025). However, (Bendinelli et al., 2025) observe that LLMs tend to use brute force for data cleaning. Providing contextual knowledge, such as partial guidance on how to correct an error, often improves the results.

Missing data A common approach to handling missing data is complete case analysis, which excludes patients with incomplete information. This can introduce selection bias when missingness is related to underlying clinical factors (Haneuse, 2016). Clinical insight is therefore essential to assess if missingness is occurring at random. In the case of longitudinal data, missingness patterns can be especially informative (Che et al., 2018). For instance, stable patients may have specific lab tests omitted (Raebel et al., 2016), or patients experiencing severe toxicity may be more likely to drop out of a clinical trial (Bell et al., 2014).

Medical context also informs the design of imputation strategies. Multi-omics correlations from external datasets can, for instance, help impute genetic data (Lin et al., 2016). More recently, LLM-based imputation methods have shown significant improvement over baselines for data 'missing not at random' (Hayat and Hasan, 2024).

Future Research Preprocessing is crucial for ensuring interoperability, especially when combining datasets from multiple institutions where data quality often varies. In particular, poor standardization across datasets and a high rate of missing data impact the quality of tabular medical datasets. Current initiatives on the interoperability of healthcare databases aim to lessen the need for custom preprocessing (Semler et al., 2018).

Recent advances in table understanding methods that identify the semantic and syntactic types of cells (Zhang et al., 2020; Sun et al., 2021) represent a promising step toward developing end-to-end pipelines for automatic clinical data preprocessing. Further research on the use of medical vocabularies or ontologies in conjunction with LLMs could improve semantic interoperability. More broadly, LLMs are a promising research direction for automatized data cleaning and standardization. However, to our knowledge, they have not yet been applied to medical datasets with complex feature interactions. Thus, further adaptation and validation of this method to such datasets is necessary.

Although numerous statistical imputation techniques exist, many rely on the assumption that data is missing at random. This assumption often fails to account for the clinical context behind missingness. There is a growing need for frameworks that can represent the reasons behind missing data to address data 'missing not at random'. In cases where the underlying mechanisms can be known or approximated, mathematical models (e.g., pharmacokinetic models) could be leveraged to infer and impute specific features (Lin and Wong, 2017).

4.3 Feature Engineering

Feature selection and creation Domain knowledge is frequently integrated into feature selection, particularly in biomedical applications, where datasets often contain relatively few instances but many features. In this context, it can help reduce complexity and enhance model performance. The effectiveness of this approach depends on the use of accurate and contextually appropriate knowledge: Wu et al. (2022) show that well-curated, targeted domain knowledge yields superior results compared to indiscriminate application.

Domain knowledge can also be used to generate new features from existing ones. Features can be handcrafted based on clinical knowledge and, in particular, mathematical relationships. Nave and Elbaz (2021) train a machine learning model to predict tumor size over time. Their results showed that adding mathematical model outputs significantly improved performance: their tumor size prediction accuracy increased from 72.5% to 86.33%.

Hollmann et al. (2023b), on the other hand, use LLMs to engineer additional features automatically based on a dataset description. This approach can be further extended by integrating domain expertise. For example, an estimation of medication absorption could be calculated using baseline patient information (Rajagopalan and Gastonguay, 2003).

Table serialization Clinical data can also be serialized into text and processed using language models. This can allow models to extract semantically rich representations that might not be apparent through standard tabular processing alone. For example, Chen et al. (2023) apply this approach to prognosis prediction, leveraging medical knowledge from pre-training data to enrich tabular representations. Similarly, Slack and Singh (2023) propose a pipeline that integrates domain knowledge into LLM-based differential diagnosis prediction. They enrich tabular data with disease-specific instructions and show that including this can often significantly increase performance.

Future Research Language models offer a promising avenue for the automated engineering of additional features based on domain knowledge. However, their outputs may introduce biases, as careful assessment of these methods is still needed. For instance, Küken et al. (2025) observe that LLMs often rely too heavily on simplistic operations, such as addition, when generating features. Including information on formal relationships from domain knowledge to engineer features could be a way to avoid this bias.

While LLMs have been used for medical tabular tasks, they have yet to be extensively tested on clinical datasets with high-dimensional features. Multimodal approaches combining a language model and high-dimensional table representation may be more appropriate (AlSaad et al., 2024). However, current research on such multimodal models is still limited. In addition, using LLMs for feature engineering also requires more extensive testing of the potential propagation of training data biases.

4.4 Training

Leveraging graph representations Domain knowledge can be used to introduce clinically meaningful inductive biases during training, guiding models to learn patterns that align with established medical understanding. Graph representations of domain knowledge can encode structured relationships. For instance, Middleton et al. (2024) jointly process tabular data and knowledge graphs to identify therapeutic genetic targets. Similarly, Ruiz et al. (2023) encode prior knowledge in a graph structure, influencing how feature connections are learned—demonstrating efficiency in high-dimensional, low-sample settings such as genomics. The hierarchical structure of medical concepts has also been incorporated into knowledge graphs to improve single-cell classification (Mojarrad et al., 2024).

Other architectures In physics-informed neural networks, regularization losses can enforce expected behavior in a model's outputs (Cuomo et al., 2022). For example, Nguyen et al. (2020) introduce a domain-specific loss function based on the dose volume histogram from radiation therapy. They show that this loss improves results across most evaluation categories (Nguyen et al., 2020).

Using interpretable models can also help interpret patterns and use domain knowledge to correct potential unwanted shortcuts that conflict with clinical reality. For instance, Caruana et al. (2015) develop generalized additive models with pairwise interactions for a pneumonia detection task. When the model incorrectly learns, for example, that asthma lowers the risk of pneumonia, it can be addressed by reshaping the learned effect function to reflect the correct association.

Foundation model pre-training Through self-supervised pre-training, models can leverage the longitudinal nature of EHRs. For example, Steinberg et al. (2023) pre-train a time-to-event transformer-based model from EHRs medical codes. This helps model medical codes' semantic relationships and temporal dependencies representing diagnoses, medications, and procedures. Pre-training models on massive EHR datasets can help contextualize data with information not included in smaller task-specific datasets (Rasmy et al., 2021).

Future Research Grinsztajn et al. (2022) note that the underperformance of neural networks on tabular data may stem from a lack of inductive biases—especially when dealing with uninformative or noisy features, which are common in medical data. Future research could explore further the integration of inductive biases using graph or mathematical representations of domain knowledge. For example, Kim et al. (2024a) propose a new pre-training architecture for tabular data using graph representations, enabling improved transfer learning across structured datasets.

Additionally, given the growing interest in medical foundation models, it may be valuable to investigate how pre-training tasks can better exploit fine-grained relationships between clinical codes—potentially improving the quality of learned representations in structured medical data. In addition, though Steinberg et al. (2023) show improved results on pre-trained models compared to trained from scratch, the effect of the pre-training dataset should be studied in more depth. For instance, the impact of the size of the dataset or the distribution shift compared to the downstream task should be assessed. Furthermore, reinforcement learning with human feedback—used, for example, in natural language processing by (Ouyang et al., 2022)—could offer a way to adapt model behavior to clinical expertise, as also explored in other alignment strategies (Yao et al., 2023). This could also be leveraged for tabular datasets.

4.5 Validation

Validation of machine learning models incorporates explainability, generalizability, and bias analysis, which can be grounded in domain knowledge.

A survey by Tonekaboni et al. (2019) highlights that clinicians view *explainability* as a justification tool in clinical workflows. To that end, clinicians must be able to relate model features and outputs to medical reasoning. Explainability methods support clinicians in understanding which features the model considers vital for its decisions (Vimbi et al., 2024).

In addition, auditing frameworks (Drenkow et al., 2025) can enable structured identification of dataset "shortcuts" by comparing feature importance against clinical plausibility. Complementing this, medical literature and clinician insight offer valuable knowledge about known confounders or spurious correlations (Meng et al., 2022).

It is also important to assess model generalizability across patient populations and hospitals. One aspect is to appropriately select metrics and dataset splits. Expert insight can also provide information into possible sources of dataset shift, such as variations in clinical workflows or patient populations. Subbaswamy et al. (2021) propose, for example, a method to evaluate how a model can generalize to shifts in laboratory test ordering.

Finally, it is also crucial to consider the baselines against which machine learning methods will be compared to, as even naive methods can show surprisingly good results. For instance, naive forecasting often shows competitive performance in financial forecasting tasks (Hewamalage et al., 2023). In clinical settings, domain knowledge could be used to construct naive rule-based baselines to validate clinical applications.

Future Research Although current explainability methods increase transparency and trust, they remain approximations of the model's internal logic, can introduce their uncertainties, and may not be suited for clinical decision validation (Ghassemi et al., 2021). Indeed, they cannot guarantee the correctness of predictions or justify their adoption in practice (Ghassemi et al., 2021).

Similarly, while valuable for evaluating model robustness and generalizability, cross-dataset testing assesses performance after distribution shifts have occurred. Future work could prioritize proactive strategies to build more resilient systems that mitigate or validate such shifts in advance, for instance, through synthetic data or causal modeling informed by clinical expertise.

In bias analysis, incorporating structured medical knowledge and recent experimental findings could help identify and address harmful shortcuts. Additionally, synthetic data could be used to generate slightly modified test datasets to assess the robustness of the model to changes that should not be medically relevant to outputs.

5 Discussion

As medical machine learning becomes increasingly prominent, incorporating domain knowledge is vital. Some approaches emphasize the scalability and diversity of large datasets, relying, for instance, on pre-trained models (Steinberg et al., 2023). Others prioritize the structured integration of domain knowledge using ontologies or graphs (Sirocchi et al., 2024). This becomes especially important when dealing with heterogeneous, high-dimensional, or noisy data.

However, access to expert input and curated databases can be limited, and integrating this knowledge effectively is often complex. In addition, clinical practices and medical understanding evolve, and relying on outdated ontologies or prior assumptions may introduce biases. Moreover, models trained on historical data may learn and reinforce prior clinical behaviors, leading to the risk of self-fulfilling prophecies in real-world decision support systems (De-Arteaga and Elmer, 2023). Furthermore, relying too heavily on domain constraints can unintentionally limit the discovery of novel patterns or rare cases. Thus, further empirical evaluations should assess the benefits of knowledge integration methods across medical datasets of different types and quality.

In general, we first recommend early discussions with medical partners to determine potential biases and confounders. While confounders can be unavoidable for retrospective studies, they should be recognized as limitations. Domain knowledge should also be included during data preprocessing to harmonize values following ontologies and guidelines or to assess the reasons for missing data and impute them accordingly. Domain knowledge can also engineer medically relevant features or integrate information from knowledge bases for feature selection. Moreover, model training can leverage pre-trained models or mathematical relationships. Finally, validation should be based on clinical expertise, and potential generalizability should be assessed for other patient populations or hospital settings.

While this process can be time-consuming, recent studies suggest that domain knowledge integration can be automated by leveraging foundation models for knowledge extraction (Kresevic et al., 2024) and its integration in the pipeline (Hollmann et al., 2023b). This paves the way toward scalable medical deep-learning models. Yet, medical foundation models also need to be evaluated in terms of privacy preservation, bias propagation, and generalizability. Recently, studies have led benchmarking efforts for scientific foundation models. Chen et al. (2024) show that while expert knowledge did not always improve code validity, it consistently increased success rates—supporting the idea that domain expertise can improve model outcomes, and its inclusion should be further studied for foundation models. However, medical machine learning on complex tabular datasets cannot rely yet on end-to-end LLMs.

Closer collaboration between the fields of healthcare and tabular machine learning could leverage deep learning advances to design models that integrate domain knowledge more efficiently. Promising research directions include adapting and validating automated approaches for domain knowledge integration and transfer learning for tabular data (Kim et al., 2024a).

6 Limitations

The current study presents several limitations that should be acknowledged. The presented work is not a systematic review and does not aim to cover all relevant literature comprehensively. Thus, it has been influenced by the authors' experiences within the field of medical machine learning.

In addition, while we propose an overview and diverse examples for integrating domain knowledge into the medical machine learning pipeline, we do not offer concrete recommendations that are applicable to all use cases. Indeed, the appropriate approach may vary depending on the medical context and application. Therefore, we encourage interdisciplinary discussions between medical experts and machine learning practitioners to define a concrete guide collaboratively.

Moreover, the efficacy of the discussed methods of domain knowledge integration may vary according to data quality. We do not offer a systematic assessment of these integration methods on various data types, which would be valuable in gaining a deeper understanding of the impact of domain knowledge.

Finally, our focus was limited to tabular data. Integrating domain knowledge into multimodal machine learning models, which utilize data such as text, images, or time series, represents an important direction for future research, but was beyond the scope of this work.

References

Leila Ahmadian, Mariette van Engen-Verheul, Ferishta Bakhshi-Raiez, Niels Peek, Ronald Cornet, and Nicolette F de Keizer. 2011. The role of standardized data and terminological systems in computerized clinical decision support systems: literature review and survey. *International journal of medical informatics*, 80(2):81–93.

Md Manjurul Ahsan, Shahana Akter Luna, and Zahed Siddique. 2022. Machine-learning-based disease diagnosis: A comprehensive review. In *Healthcare*, volume 10, page 541. MDPI.

Giuseppina Albano and Virginia Giorno. 2006. A stochastic model in tumor growth. *Journal of Theoretical Biology*, 242(2):329–336.

Rawan AlSaad, Alaa Abd-Alrazaq, Sabri Boughorbel, Arfan Ahmed, Max-Antoine Renault, Rafat Damseh, and Javaid Sheikh. 2024. Multimodal large language models in health care: applications, challenges, and future outlook. *Journal of medical Internet research*, 26:e59505.

Melanie L Bell, Mallorie Fiero, Nicholas J Horton, and Chiu-Hsieh Hsu. 2014. Handling missing data in rcts; a review of the top medical journals. *BMC medical research methodology*, 14:1–8.

Tommaso Bendinelli, Artur Dox, and Christian Holz. 2025. Exploring llm agents for cleaning tabular machine learning datasets. In *ICLR 2025 Workshop on Foundation Models in the Wild*.

Olivier Bodenreider. 2004. The unified medical language system (umls): integrating biomedical terminology. *Nucleic acids research*, 32(suppl_1):D267–D270.

Jennifer Brescoll and Steven Daveluy. 2015. A review of vitamin b12 in dermatology. *American journal of clinical dermatology*, 16:27–33.

M Alan Brookhart, Til Stürmer, Robert J Glynn, Jeremy Rassen, and Sebastian Schneeweiss. 2010. Confounding control in healthcare database research: challenges and potential approaches. *Medical care*, 48(6):S114–S120.

Rich Caruana, Yin Lou, Johannes Gehrke, Paul Koch, Marc Sturm, and Noemie Elhadad. 2015. Intelligible models for healthcare: Predicting pneumonia risk and hospital 30-day readmission. In *Proceedings of the 21th ACM SIGKDD international conference on knowledge discovery and data mining*, pages 1721–1730.

Javier Castell-Díaz, Jose Antonio Miñarro-Giménez, and Catalina Martínez-Costa. 2023. Supporting snomed ct postcoordination with knowledge graph embeddings. *Journal of Biomedical Informatics*, 139:104297.

Eunsuk Chang and Javed Mostafa. 2021. The use of snomed ct, 2013-2020: a literature review. *Journal of the American Medical Informatics Association*, 28(9):2017–2026.

Zhengping Che, Sanjay Purushotham, Kyunghyun Cho, David Sontag, and Yan Liu. 2018. Recurrent neural networks for multivariate time series with missing values. *Scientific reports*, 8(1):6085.

Zekai Chen, Mariann Micsinai Balan, and Kevin Brown. 2023. Language models are few-shot learners for prognostic prediction. *ArXiv*, abs/2302.12692.

Ziru Chen, Shijie Chen, Yuting Ning, Qianheng Zhang, Boshi Wang, Botao Yu, Yifei Li, Zeyi Liao, Chen Wei, Zitong Lu, et al. 2024. Scienceagentbench:

Toward rigorous assessment of language agents for data-driven scientific discovery. *arXiv preprint arXiv:2410.05080*.

Iris C Cramer, Eline GM Cox, Jip WTM de Kok, Jacqueline Koeze, Martje Visser, Hjalmar R Bouma, Ashley De Bie Dekker, Iwan CC van der Horst, R Arthur Bouwman, and Bas CT van Bussel. 2025. Quantification of facial cues for acute illness: a systematic scoping review. *Intensive Care Medicine Experimental*, 13(1):17.

Salvatore Cuomo, Vincenzo Schiano Di Cola, Fabio Giampaolo, Gianluigi Rozza, Maziar Raissi, and Francesco Piccialli. 2022. Scientific machine learning through physics–informed neural networks: Where we are and what's next. *Journal of Scientific Computing*, 92(3):88.

Olivier Curé. 2012. Improving the data quality of drug databases using conditional dependencies and ontologies. *Journal of Data and Information Quality (JDIQ)*, 4(1):1–21.

Tirtharaj Dash, Sharad Chitlangia, Aditya Ahuja, and Ashwin Srinivasan. 2022. A review of some techniques for inclusion of domain-knowledge into deep neural networks. *Scientific Reports*, 12(1):1040.

Maria De-Arteaga and Jonathan Elmer. 2023. Self-fulfilling prophecies and machine learning in resuscitation science. *Resuscitation*, 183:109622.

Timo M Deist, Andrew Patti, Zhaoqi Wang, David Krane, Taylor Sorenson, and David Craft. 2019. Simulation-assisted machine learning. *Bioinformatics*, 35(20):4072–4080.

Nathan Drenkow, Mitchell Pavlak, Keith Harrigian, Ayah Zirikly, Adarsh Subbaswamy, and Mathias Unberath. 2025. Detecting dataset bias in medical ai: A generalized and modality-agnostic auditing framework. *arXiv preprint arXiv:2503.09969*.

Issam El Naqa, Aleksandra Karolak, Yi Luo, Les Folio, Ahmad A Tarhini, Dana Rollison, and Katia Parodi. 2023. Translation of ai into oncology clinical practice. *Oncogene*, 42(42):3089–3097.

Christophe Gaudet-Blavignac, Vasiliki Foufi, Mina Bjelogrlic, Christian Lovis, et al. 2021. Use of the systematized nomenclature of medicine clinical terms (snomed ct) for processing free text in health care: systematic scoping review. *Journal of medical Internet research*, 23(1):e24594.

Faisal Ghaffar, Nadine M Furtado, Imad Ali, and Catherine Burns. 2025. Diagnostic decision-making variability between novice and expert optometrists for glaucoma: Comparative analysis to inform ai system design. *JMIR Medical Informatics*, 13:e63109.

Marzyeh Ghassemi, Luke Oakden-Rayner, and Andrew Beam. 2021. The false hope of current approaches to explainable artificial intelligence in health care. *The Lancet. Digital health*, 3 11:e745–e750.

Léo Grinsztajn, Edouard Oyallon, and Gaël Varoquaux. 2022. Why do tree-based models still outperform deep learning on typical tabular data? *Advances in neural information processing systems*, 35:507–520.

Michele Groves, Peter O'Rourke, and Heather Alexander. 2003. The clinical reasoning characteristics of diagnostic experts. *Medical teacher*, 25(3):308–313.

Sebastien Haneuse. 2016. Distinguishing selection bias and confounding bias in comparative effectiveness research. *Medical care*, 54(4):e23–e29.

SM Shamimul Hasan, Donna Rivera, Xiao-Cheng Wu, J Blair Christian, and Georgia Tourassi. 2019. A knowledge graph approach for the secondary use of cancer registry data. In *2019 IEEE EMBS International Conference on Biomedical & Health Informatics (BHI)*, pages 1–4. IEEE.

Ahatsham Hayat and Mohammad Rashedul Hasan. 2024. Claim your data: Enhancing imputation accuracy with contextual large language models. *arXiv preprint arXiv:2405.17712*.

Hansika Hewamalage, Klaus Ackermann, and Christoph Bergmeir. 2023. Forecast evaluation for data scientists: common pitfalls and best practices. *Data Mining and Knowledge Discovery*, 37(2):788–832.

Noah Hollmann, Samuel Müller, Katharina Eggensperger, and Frank Hutter. 2023a. Tabpfn: A transformer that solves small tabular classification problems in a second. In *The Eleventh International Conference on Learning Representations*.

Noah Hollmann, Samuel G. Müller, and Frank Hutter. 2023b. Large language models for automated data science: Introducing caafe for context-aware automated feature engineering. In *Neural Information Processing Systems*.

Madelon Hulsebos, Paul Groth, and Çagatay Demiralp. 2023. Adatyper: Adaptive semantic column type detection. *CoRR*.

KJ Jager, C Zoccali, A Macleod, and FW Dekker. 2008. Confounding: what it is and how to deal with it. *Kidney international*, 73(3):256–260.

Alistair EW Johnson, Lucas Bulgarelli, Lu Shen, Alvin Gayles, Ayad Shammout, Steven Horng, Tom J Pollard, Sicheng Hao, Benjamin Moody, Brian Gow, et al. 2023. Mimic-iv, a freely accessible electronic health record dataset. *Scientific data*, 10(1):1.

Johnny Kahlert, Sigrid Bjerge Gribsholt, Henrik Gammelager, Olaf M Dekkers, and George Luta. 2017. Control of confounding in the analysis phase–an overview for clinicians. *Clinical epidemiology*, pages 195–204.

George Em Karniadakis, Ioannis G Kevrekidis, Lu Lu, Paris Perdikaris, Sifan Wang, and Liu Yang. 2021. Physics-informed machine learning. *Nature Reviews Physics*, 3(6):422–440.

Myung Jun Kim, Léo Grinsztajn, and Gaël Varoquaux. 2024a. Carte: pretraining and transfer for tabular learning. In *Proceedings of the 41st International Conference on Machine Learning*, pages 23843–23866.

Subin Kim, Jungmin Son, Minyoung Jung, and Youngjun Kwak. 2024b. Expertise-centric prompting framework for financial tabular data generation using pre-trained large language models. In *NeurIPS 2024 Third Table Representation Learning Workshop*.

Simone Kresevic, Mauro Giuffrè, Milos Ajcevic, Agostino Accardo, Lory S Crocè, and Dennis L Shung. 2024. Optimization of hepatological clinical guidelines interpretation by large language models: a retrieval augmented generation-based framework. *NPJ digital medicine*, 7(1):102.

Jaris Küken, Lennart Purucker, and Frank Hutter. 2025. Large language models engineer too many simple features for tabular data. In *NeurIPS 2024 Third Table Representation Learning Workshop*.

Florian Leiser, Sascha Rank, Manuel Schmidt-Kraepelin, Scott Thiebes, and Ali Sunyaev. 2023. Medical informed machine learning: A scoping review and future research directions. *Artificial Intelligence in Medicine*, 145:102676.

Dongdong Lin, Ji-Gang Zhang, Jingyao Li, Chao Xu, Hong-Wen Deng, and Yu ping Wang. 2016. An integrative imputation method based on multi-omics datasets. *BMC Bioinformatics*, 17.

Louis Lin and Harvey Wong. 2017. Predicting oral drug absorption: mini review on physiologically-based pharmacokinetic models. *Pharmaceutics*, 9(4):41.

Donald AB Lindberg, Betsy L Humphreys, and Alexa T McCray. 1993. The unified medical language system. *Yearbook of medical informatics*, 2(01):41–51.

Lingchao Mao, Hairong Wang, Leland S Hu, Nhan L Tran, Peter D Canoll, Kristin R Swanson, and Jing Li. 2024. Knowledge-informed machine learning for cancer diagnosis and prognosis: a review. *IEEE Transactions on Automation Science and Engineering*.

Theresa A McDonagh, Marco Metra, Marianna Adamo, Roy S Gardner, Andreas Baumbach, Michael Böhm, Haran Burri, Javed Butler, Jelena Čelutkienė, Ovidiu Chioncel, et al. 2023. 2023 focused update of the 2021 esc guidelines for the diagnosis and treatment of acute and chronic heart failure: developed by the task force for the diagnosis and treatment of acute and chronic heart failure of the european society of cardiology (esc) with the special contribution of the heart failure association (hfa) of the esc. *European heart journal*, 44(37):3627–3639.

Chuizheng Meng, Loc Trinh, Nan Xu, James Enouen, and Yan Liu. 2022. Interpretability and fairness evaluation of deep learning models on mimic-iv dataset. *Scientific Reports*, 12(1):7166.

George Michalopoulos, Yuanxin Wang, Hussam Kaka, Helen Chen, and Alexander Wong. 2021. Umlsbert: Clinical domain knowledge augmentation of contextual embeddings using the unified medical language system metathesaurus. In *Proceedings of the 2021 Conference of the North American Chapter of the Association for Computational Linguistics: Human Language Technologies*, pages 1744–1753.

Lawrence Middleton, Ioannis Melas, Chirag Vasavda, Arwa Bin Raies, Benedek Rozemberczki, Ryan S. Dhindsa, Justin Dhindsa, Blake Weido, Quanli Wang, Andrew R Harper, Gavin Edwards, Slavé Petrovski, and Dimitrios M Vitsios. 2024. Phenome-wide identification of therapeutic genetic targets, leveraging knowledge graphs, graph neural networks, and uk biobank data. *Science Advances*, 10.

Mark D Miller, Craig Steinmaus, Mari S Golub, Rosemary Castorina, Ruwan Thilakartne, Asa Bradman, and Melanie A Marty. 2022. Potential impacts of synthetic food dyes on activity and attention in children: a review of the human and animal evidence. *Environmental Health*, 21(1):45.

Fatemeh Nassajian Mojarrad, Lorenzo Bini, Thomas Matthes, and Stephane Marchand-Maillet. 2024. Injecting hierarchical biological priors into graph neural networks for flow cytometry prediction. In *ICML 2024 Workshop on Efficient and Accessible Foundation Models for Biological Discovery*.

Michael Moor, Oishi Banerjee, Zahra Shakeri Hossein Abad, Harlan M Krumholz, Jure Leskovec, Eric J Topol, and Pranav Rajpurkar. 2023. Foundation models for generalist medical artificial intelligence. *Nature*, 616(7956):259–265.

OPhir Nave and Miriam Elbaz. 2021. Artificial immune system features added to breast cancer clinical data for machine learning (ml) applications. *Biosystems*, 202:104341.

Dan Nguyen, Rafe McBeth, Azar Sadeghnejad Barkousaraie, Gyanendra Bohara, Chenyang Shen, Xun Jia, and Steve Jiang. 2020. Incorporating human and learned domain knowledge into training deep neural networks: a differentiable dose-volume histogram and adversarial inspired framework for generating pareto optimal dose distributions in radiation therapy. *Medical physics*, 47(3):837–849.

Long Ouyang, Jeffrey Wu, Xu Jiang, Diogo Almeida, Carroll Wainwright, Pamela Mishkin, Chong Zhang, Sandhini Agarwal, Katarina Slama, Alex Ray, et al. 2022. Training language models to follow instructions with human feedback. *Advances in neural information processing systems*, 35:27730–27744.

Richard L Page, José A Joglar, Mary A Caldwell, Hugh Calkins, Jamie B Conti, Barbara J Deal, NA Mark Estes, Michael E Field, Zachary D Goldberger, Stephen C Hammill, et al. 2016. 2015 acc/aha/hrs guideline for the management of adult patients with supraventricular tachycardia: a report of the american college of cardiology/american heart association task force on clinical practice guidelines and the heart rhythm society. *Journal of the American College of Cardiology*, 67(13):e27–e115.

Giulia Perciballi, Federica Granese, Ahmad Fall, Farida ZEHRAOUI, Edi Prifti, and Jean-Daniel Zucker. 2024. Adapting tabPFN for zero-inflated metagenomic data. In *NeurIPS 2024 Third Table Representation Learning Workshop*.

Vasileios C Pezoulas, Dimitrios I Zaridis, Eugenia Mylona, Christos Androutsos, Kosmas Apostolidis, Nikolaos S Tachos, and Dimitrios I Fotiadis. 2024. Synthetic data generation methods in healthcare: A review on open-source tools and methods. *Computational and structural biotechnology journal*.

Julia K Pilowsky, Rosalind Elliott, and Michael A Roche. 2024. Data cleaning for clinician researchers: Application and explanation of a data-quality framework. *Australian Critical Care*, 37(5):827–833.

Paloma Rabaey, Henri Arno, Stefan Heytens, and Thomas Demeester. 2024. Synsum - synthetic benchmark with structured and unstructured medical records. *ArXiv*, abs/2409.08936.

Marsha A Raebel, Susan Shetterly, Christine Y Lu, James Flory, Joshua J Gagne, Frank E Harrell, Kevin Haynes, Lisa J Herrinton, Elisabetta Patorno, Jennifer Popovic, et al. 2016. Methods for using clinical laboratory test results as baseline confounders in multi-site observational database studies when missing data are expected. *Pharmacoepidemiology and drug safety*, 25(7):798–814.

Prabhu Rajagopalan and Marc R. Gastonguay. 2003. Population pharmacokinetics of ciprofloxacin in pediatric patients. *The Journal of Clinical Pharmacology*, 43.

Laila Rasmy, Yang Xiang, Ziqian Xie, Cui Tao, and Degui Zhi. 2021. Med-bert: pretrained contextualized embeddings on large-scale structured electronic health records for disease prediction. *NPJ digital medicine*, 4(1):86.

Yucheng Ruan, Xiang Lan, Jingying Ma, Yizhi Dong, Kai He, and Mengling Feng. 2024. Language modeling on tabular data: A survey of foundations, techniques and evolution. *CoRR*.

Camilo Ruiz, Hongyu Ren, Kexin Huang, and Jure Leskovec. 2023. High dimensional, tabular deep learning with an auxiliary knowledge graph. *Advances in Neural Information Processing Systems*, 36:26348–26371.

Elizaveta Savchenko, Ariel Rosenfeld, and Svetlana Bunimovich-Mendrazitsky. 2023. Mathematical modeling of bcg-based bladder cancer treatment using socio-demographics. *Scientific Reports*, 13(1):18754.

FP Schmidt, NJ Glaser, O Schreiner, T Münzel, and M Weber. 2015. „do not rescuscitate "– auswirkungen der einführung eines standardisierten formulars auf therapiebegrenzungen in der klinischen praxis. *DMW-Deutsche Medizinische Wochenschrift*, 140(15):e159–e165.

Sebastian C Semler, Frank Wissing, and Ralf Heyder. 2018. German medical informatics initiative. *Methods of information in medicine*, 57(S 01):e50–e56.

Jingpu Shi, Dong Wang, Gino Tesei, and Beau Norgeot. 2022. Generating high-fidelity privacy-conscious synthetic patient data for causal effect estimation with multiple treatments. *Frontiers in Artificial Intelligence*, 5:918813.

Xi Shi, Charlotte Prins, Gijs Van Pottelbergh, Pavlos Mamouris, Bert Vaes, and Bart De Moor. 2021. An automated data cleaning method for electronic health records by incorporating clinical knowledge. *BMC Medical Informatics and Decision Making*, 21:1–10.

Christel Sirocchi, Alessandro Bogliolo, and Sara Montagna. 2024. Medical-informed machine learning: integrating prior knowledge into medical decision systems. *BMC Medical Informatics and Decision Making*, 24(Suppl 4):186.

Dylan Slack and Sameer Singh. 2023. Tablet: Learning from instructions for tabular data. *ArXiv*, abs/2304.13188.

Ethan Steinberg, Jason Alan Fries, Yizhe Xu, and Nigam Shah. 2023. Motor: A time-to-event foundation model for structured medical records. In *The Twelfth International Conference on Learning Representations*.

Adarsh Subbaswamy, Roy Adams, and Suchi Saria. 2021. Evaluating model robustness and stability to dataset shift. In *International conference on artificial intelligence and statistics*, pages 2611–2619. PMLR.

Cathie Sudlow, John Gallacher, Naomi Allen, Valerie Beral, Paul Burton, John Danesh, Paul Downey, Paul Elliott, Jane Green, Martin Landray, Bette Liu, Paul Matthews, Giok Ong, Jill Pell, Alan Silman, Alan Young, Tim Peakman, and Rory Collins. 2015. UK Biobank: An open access resource for identifying the causes of a wide range of complex diseases of middle and old age. *PLoS Medicine*, 12(3):e1001779.

Yuan Sui, Mengyu Zhou, Mingjie Zhou, Shi Han, and Dongmei Zhang. 2024. Table meets llm: Can large language models understand structured table data? a benchmark and empirical study. In *Proceedings of the 17th ACM International Conference on Web Search and Data Mining*, pages 645–654.

Kexuan Sun, Harsha Rayudu, and Jay Pujara. 2021. A hybrid probabilistic approach for table understanding. In *Proceedings of the AAAI conference on artificial intelligence*, volume 35, pages 4366–4374.

Mohammad Tabatabai, David Keith Williams, and Zoran Bursac. 2005. Hyperbolastic growth models: theory and application. *Theoretical Biology and Medical Modelling*, 2:1–13.

Zoë Tieges, Jonathan J Evans, Karin J Neufeld, and Alasdair MJ MacLullich. 2018. The neuropsychology of delirium: advancing the science of delirium assessment. *International journal of geriatric psychiatry*, 33(11):1501–1511.

Nenad Tomašev, Natalie Harris, Sebastien Baur, Anne Mottram, Xavier Glorot, Jack W Rae, Michal Zielinski, Harry Askham, Andre Saraiva, Valerio Magliulo, et al. 2021. Use of deep learning to develop continuous-risk models for adverse event prediction from electronic health records. *Nature Protocols*, 16(6):2765–2787.

Sana Tonekaboni, Shalmali Joshi, Melissa D McCradden, and Anna Goldenberg. 2019. What clinicians want: contextualizing explainable machine learning for clinical end use. In *Machine learning for healthcare conference*, pages 359–380. PMLR.

Allan Tucker, Zhenchen Wang, Ylenia Rotalinti, and Puja Myles. 2020. Generating high-fidelity synthetic patient data for assessing machine learning healthcare software. *NPJ digital medicine*, 3(1):147.

Viswan Vimbi, Noushath Shaffi, and Mufti Mahmud. 2024. Interpreting artificial intelligence models: a systematic review on the application of lime and shap in alzheimer's disease detection. *Brain Informatics*, 11(1):10.

Stein Emil Vollset, Hazim S Ababneh, Yohannes Habtegiorgis Abate, Cristiana Abbafati, Rouzbeh Abbasgholizadeh, Mohammadreza Abbasian, Hedayat Abbastabar, Abdallah HA Abd Al Magied, Samar Abd ElHafeez, Atef Abdelkader, et al. 2024. Burden of disease scenarios for 204 countries and territories, 2022–2050: a forecasting analysis for the global burden of disease study 2021. *The Lancet*, 403(10440):2204–2256.

Laura Von Rueden, Sebastian Mayer, Katharina Beckh, Bogdan Georgiev, Sven Giesselbach, Raoul Heese, Birgit Kirsch, Julius Pfrommer, Annika Pick, Rajkumar Ramamurthy, et al. 2021. Informed machine learning–a taxonomy and survey of integrating prior knowledge into learning systems. *IEEE Transactions on Knowledge and Data Engineering*, 35(1):614–633.

Jared Willard, Xiaowei Jia, Shaoming Xu, Michael Steinbach, and Vipin Kumar. 2022. Integrating scientific knowledge with machine learning for engineering and environmental systems. *ACM Computing Surveys*, 55(4):1–37.

Katarzyna Woźnica, Piotr Wilczyński, and Przemysław Biecek. 2024. Sefnet: Linking tabular datasets with semantic feature nets. *Available at SSRN 4811308*.

Xingyu Wu, Zhenchao Tao, Bingbing Jiang, Tianhao Wu, Xin Wang, and Huanhuan Chen. 2022. Domain knowledge-enhanced variable selection for biomedical data analysis. *Information Sciences*, 606:469–488.

Magdalena Wysocka, Oskar Wysocki, Marie Zufferey, Dónal Landers, and André Freitas. 2023. A systematic review of biologically-informed deep learning models for cancer: fundamental trends for encoding and interpreting oncology data. *BMC bioinformatics*, 24(1):198.

Xiaozheng Xie, Jianwei Niu, Xuefeng Liu, Zhengsu Chen, Shaojie Tang, and Shui Yu. 2021. A survey on incorporating domain knowledge into deep learning for medical image analysis. *Medical Image Analysis*, 69:101985.

Zonghai Yao, Benjamin J Schloss, and Sai P. Selvaraj. 2023. Improving summarization with human edits. In *Conference on Empirical Methods in Natural Language Processing*.

Jim Young, Patrick Graham, and Richard Penny. 2009. Using bayesian networks to create synthetic data. *Journal of Official Statistics*, 25(4):549–567.

Fuad Abu Zahra and Rohit J Kate. 2024. Obtaining clinical term embeddings from snomed ct ontology. *Journal of Biomedical Informatics*, 149:104560.

Dan Zhang, Yoshihiko Suhara, Jinfeng Li, Madelon Hulsebos, Cagatay Demiralp, and Wang-Chiew Tan. 2020. Sato: Contextual semantic type detection in tables. *Proceedings of the VLDB Endowment*, 13(11).

Tianping Zhang, Shaowen Wang, Shuicheng Yan, Li Jian, and Qian Liu. 2023. Generative table pre-training empowers models for tabular prediction. In *Proceedings of the 2023 Conference on Empirical Methods in Natural Language Processing*, pages 14836–14854.

LLM-Mixer: Multiscale Mixing in LLMs for Time Series Forecasting

Md Kowsher[1], Md. Shohanur Islam Sobuj[2], Nusrat Jahan Prottasha[1], E. Alejandro Alanis[3], Ozlem Ozmen Garibay[1], Niloofar Yousefi[1]

[1]University of Central Florida, USA, [2]Anymate Me, Germany, [3]Microsoft, USA

https://github.com/Kowsher/LLMMixer

Abstract

Time series forecasting is a challenging task, especially when dealing with data that contains both short-term variations and long-term trends. In this study, we introduce LLM-Mixer, a novel framework that combines multiscale time-series decomposition with the power of pre-trained Large Language Models (LLMs). LLM-Mixer breaks down time-series data into multiple temporal resolutions using downsampling and processes these multiscale representations with a frozen LLM, guided by a carefully designed text prompt that encodes information about the dataset's features and structure. To understand the role of downsampling, we conduct a detailed analysis using Neural Tangent Kernel (NTK) distance, showing that incorporating multiple scales improves the model's learning dynamics. We evaluate LLM-Mixer across a diverse set of forecasting tasks, including long-term multivariate, short-term multivariate, and long-term univariate scenarios. Experimental results demonstrate that LLM-Mixer achieves competitive performance compared to recent state-of-the-art models across various forecasting horizons. Code is available at: https://github.com/Kowsher/LLMMixer

1 Introduction & Related Work

Time series forecasting is essential in numerous fields, including finance (Zhang et al., 2024), energy management (Martín et al., 2010), healthcare (Morid et al., 2023), climate science (Mudelsee, 2019), and industrial operations (Wang et al., 2020). Traditional forecasting models, such as AutoRegressive Integrated Moving Average (ARIMA) (Box et al., 2015) and exponential smoothing techniques (Hyndman, 2018), are widely used for straightforward predictive tasks. However, these models assume stationarity and linearity, which limit their effectiveness when applied to complex, nonlinear, and multivariate time series often found in real-world scenarios (Cheng et al., 2015). The advent of deep learning has significantly advanced time series forecasting. CNNs (Wang et al., 2023; Tang et al., 2020; Kirisci and Cagcag Yolcu, 2022) have been utilized for capturing temporal patterns, while RNNs (Siami-Namini et al., 2019; Zhang et al., 2019; Karim et al., 2019) are adept at modeling temporal state transitions. However, both CNNs and RNNs have limitations in capturing long-term dependencies (Wang et al., 2024; Tang et al., 2021; Zhu et al., 2023). Recently, Transformer architectures (Vaswani et al., 2017) have demonstrated strong capabilities in handling both local and long-range dependencies, making them suitable for time series forecasting (Liu et al., 2024b; Nie et al., 2022; Woo et al., 2022).

In parallel, pre-trained LLMs such as GPT-3 (Brown, 2020), GPT-4 (Achiam et al., 2023), and LLaMA (Touvron et al., 2023) have achieved remarkable generalization in natural language processing tasks (Friha et al., 2024) due to capabilities of few-shot or zero-shot transfer learning (Brown, 2020), multimodal knowledge (Jia et al., 2024) and reasoning (Liu et al., 2024a). These models are now being applied across various fields, including computer vision (Bendou et al., 2024), healthcare (Gebreab et al., 2024), and finance (Zhao et al., 2024). Recently, a few studies have explored using LLMs for time series forecasting due to their impressive capabilities (Jin et al., 2024, 2023; Gruver et al., 2023). However, adapting LLMs to time series data presents challenges because there are significant differences between token-based text data and continuous time series data (Morales-García et al., 2024). LLMs are built to handle discrete tokens, which limits their ability to capture the continuous and often irregular patterns found in time series data. Additionally, time series data has multiple time scales, from short-term fluctuations to long-term trends, making it difficult for traditional LLMs to capture all these patterns at once. LLMs typically process fixed-length sequences, which

Proceedings of the 4th Table Representation Learning Workshop, pages 156–165

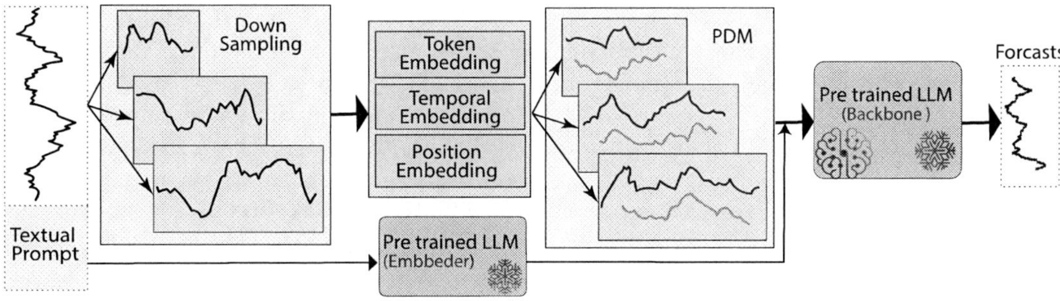

Figure 1: The LLM-Mixer framework for time series forecasting. Time series data is downsampled to multiple scales and enriched with embeddings. These multiscale representations are processed by the Past-Decomposable-Mixing (PDM) module and then input into a pre-trained LLM, which, guided by a textual description, generates the forecast.

means they may only capture short-term dependencies if the sequence length (i.e., the window of time steps) is small. However, extending the sequence length to capture long-term trends increases computational costs and may dilute the model's ability to focus on short-term fluctuations within the same sequence. Previous studies using LLMs on time series data have mostly fed the original or a single sequence directly into a frozen LLM, making it hard for the model to fully understand these sequences (Jin et al., 2024, 2023; Gruver et al., 2023).

To address this, we introduce **LLM-Mixer**, which breaks down the time series data into multiple time scales. By creating various resolutions (Figure 1), our model can capture both short-term details and long-term patterns more effectively. Since the LLM remains frozen during training, the multiscale decomposition provides a diverse range of temporal information, helping the model better understand complex time series data.

Our contributions of this paper are: **(1)** We propose **LLM-Mixer**, a new method that adapts LLMs for time series forecasting by breaking down the data into different time scales, helping the model capture both short-term and long-term patterns. **(2)** Our method creates multiple versions of the time series at different resolutions which helps the LLM to understand complex time series data more effectively. **(3)** Empirical results show that **LLM-Mixer** achieves competitive performance, improves forecasting accuracy on both multivariate and univariate data, and works effectively for both short-term and long-term forecasting tasks.

2 LLM Mixer

Preliminaries: In multivariate time series forecasting, we are given historical data $\mathbf{X} = \{\mathbf{x}_1, \ldots, \mathbf{x}_T\} \in \mathbb{R}^{T \times M}$, where T is the number of time steps and M is the number of features. The goal is to predict the future values for the next K time steps, denoted as $\mathbf{Y} = \{\mathbf{x}_{T+1}, \ldots, \mathbf{x}_{T+K}\} \in \mathbb{R}^{K \times M}$. For convenience, let $\mathbf{X}_{t,:}$ represent the data at time step t, and $\mathbf{X}_{:,m}$ represent the full time series for variable $m \in M$.

Now, suppose we have a prompt $\mathbf{P}$, which includes textual information about the time sequence (e.g., source, features, distribution, statistics). We use a pre-trained language model $\mathbb{F}(\cdot)$ with frozen parameters Θ, then the prediction is made as follows:

$$\hat{\mathbf{Y}} = \mathbb{F}(\mathbf{X}, \mathbf{P}; \Theta, \mathbf{\Phi})$$

Here $\mathbf{\Phi}$ is a small set of trainable parameters to adjust the model for the specific forecasting task.

Multi-scale View of Time Data: Time series data contains patterns at various levels—small scales capture detailed changes, while larger scales highlight overarching trends (Liu et al., 2022; Mozer, 1991). Analyzing data at multiple scales helps to understand these complex patterns (Wang et al., 2024). Following (Wang et al., 2024), we apply a multiscale mixing strategy. First, we downsample the time series $\mathbf{X}$ into τ scales using average pooling, resulting in a multiscale representation $\mathcal{X} = \{\mathbf{x}_0, \mathbf{x}_1, \ldots, \mathbf{x}_\tau\}$, where each $\mathbf{x}_i \in \mathbb{R}^{\frac{T}{2^i} \times M}$. Here, $\mathbf{x}_0$ contains the finest temporal details, while $\mathbf{x}_\tau$ captures the broadest trends.

Next, we project these multiscale series into deep features using three types of embeddings: token, temporal, and positional embeddings. Token embeddings are obtained via 1D convolutions (Kiranyaz et al., 2021), temporal embeddings represent day, week, and month (Jiménez-Navarro et al., 2023), and positional embeddings encode sequence positions.

We then use stacked Past-Decomposable-Mixing (PDM) blocks by following the framework from (Wang et al., 2024; Jiménez-Navarro et al., 2023) to mix past information across different scales. PDM works by breaking down complex time series data into separate seasonal and trend components at multiple scales, allowing for targeted processing of each component by using the framework from (Wang et al., 2024; Wu et al., 2021). For the l-th layer, PDM is defined as

$$\mathcal{X}^l = PDM(\mathcal{X}^{l-1}), \quad l \in L$$

where L is the total number of layers, and $\mathcal{X}^l = \{\mathbf{x}_0^l, \mathbf{x}_1^l, \ldots, \mathbf{x}_\tau^l\}$, with each $\mathbf{x}_i^l \in \mathbb{R}^{\frac{T}{2^i} \times d}$, where d is the model's dimension.

Prompt Embedding: Prompting is an effective technique for guiding LLMs by using task-specific information (Sahoo et al., 2024; Li et al., 2023). Studies like (Xue and Salim, 2023) show promising results by treating time series inputs as prompts for forecasting. (Jin et al., 2024) further improved time series predictions by embedding dataset descriptions in the prompts. Inspired by this, we embed dataset descriptions (e.g., features, statistics, distribution) as prompts. We use a textual description for all samples in a dataset, as suggested by (Jin et al., 2024), and generate its embedding using the pre-trained LLM's word embeddings, denoted by $E \in \mathbb{R}^{V \times d}$, where V is the LLM's vocabulary size. This prompt leverages the LLM's semantic knowledge to improve the prediction task.

Multi-scale Mixing in LLM: After processing through L PDM blocks, we obtain the multiscale past information $\mathcal{X}^L$. Since different scales focus on different variations, their predictions offer complementary strengths. To fully utilize this, we concatenate all the scales and input them into a frozen pre-trained LLM along with the prompt as $\mathbb{F}(E \oplus \mathcal{X}^L)$. Finally, a trainable decoder (simple linear transformation) with parameters $\mathbf{\Phi}$ is applied to the last hidden layer of the LLM to predict the next K future time steps.

3 Experiments

We evaluate our LLM-Mixer on several datasets commonly used for benchmarking long-term and short-term multivariate forecasting and compared with SOTA baselines. For long-term forecasting, we use the ETT datasets (ETTh1, ETTh2, ETTm1, ETTm2) from (Zhou et al., 2021), as well as the Weather, Electricity, and Traffic datasets from (Zeng et al., 2023). For short-term forecasting, we use the PeMS dataset (Chen et al., 2001), which consists of four public traffic network datasets (PEMS03, PEMS04, PEMS07, and PEMS08) with time series collected at various frequencies. We used RoBERTa-base (Liu et al., 2019) as a medium-sized language model and LLaMA2-7B (Touvron et al., 2023) as a large language model as the backbone of our framework.

Baselines We compare our model with well-established time-series forecasting baselines such as TimeMixer (Wang et al., 2024), iTransformer (Liu et al., 2024b), TimeLLM (Jin et al., 2024), RLinear (Li et al., 2024), SCINet (LIU et al., 2022), TimesNet (Wu et al., 2022), TiDE (Das et al., 2023), DLinear (Zeng et al., 2023), PatchTST (Nie et al., 2022), FEDformer (Zhou et al., 2022), Stationary (Liu et al., 2022), ESTformer (Woo et al., 2022), LightTS (Campos et al., 2023), and Autoformer (Chen et al., 2021). Additionally, we include LLM-based systems such as TimeLLM (Jin et al., 2024) and GPT2TS (Zhou et al., 2023). For multivariate time series forecasting, we follow the setup of (Wang et al., 2024). For short-term forecasting, we adopt the settings from (Liu et al., 2024b), and for univariate forecasting, we adhere to the approach in (Zeng et al., 2023).

Implementation Details All experiments in this work are implemented using PyTorch. We utilize the Hugging Face library for the LLM model. Experiments were conducted on an NVIDIA H100 GPU with 80 GB RAM.

Hyperparameters: For long-term experiments, a look-back window of 96 is used to predict the next 96 (future context) and 192 (forecast horizons), while short-term experiments use windows of 24 and 48. All experiments run for 10 epochs with a batch size of 64 for RoBERTa and a batch size of 8 with gradient accumulation of 4 for LLaMA2. The ADAM optimizer is employed with default settings $(\beta_1, \beta_2) = (0.9, 0.999)$ and a learning rate of 0.0001. Downsampling levels range from 2 to 5 across all experiments. For the baseline models, we have followed their original works, with differences only in batch size and learning rate to align with our experimental setup.

Multivariate forecasting results: LLM-Mixer demonstrates competitive performance in multivariate long forecasting, as shown in Table 1. Averaged over four forecasting horizons (96, 192, 384, and 720), LLM-Mixer achieves consistently low

Methods		LLM-Mixer (llama2)		LLM-Mixer (roberta)		TIME-LLM		TimeMixer		iTransformer		RLinear		DLinear		PatchTST		TimesNet		TiDE		TimesNet		Crossformer	
Metric		MSE	MAE	MSE	MAE	MSE	MAE	MSE	MAE	MSE	MAE	MSE	MAE	MSE	MAE	MSE	MAE	MSE	MAE	MSE	MAE	MSE	MAE	MSE	MAE
ETTh1	96	0.368	0.395	0.372	0.399	0.369	0.397	0.375	0.400	0.386	0.405	0.386	0.395	0.397	0.412	0.460	0.447	0.384	0.402	0.479	0.464	0.384	0.402	0.423	0.448
	192	0.406	0.417	0.439	0.470	0.411	0.428	0.429	0.421	0.441	0.436	0.437	0.424	0.446	0.441	0.512	0.477	0.436	0.429	0.525	0.492	0.436	0.429	0.471	0.474
	336	0.446	0.444	0.458	0.467	0.440	0.447	0.484	0.458	0.487	0.458	0.479	0.446	0.489	0.467	0.546	0.496	0.638	0.469	0.565	0.515	0.491	0.469	0.570	0.546
	720	0.461	0.475	0.465	0.480	0.462	0.477	0.498	0.482	0.503	0.491	0.481	0.470	0.513	0.510	0.544	0.517	0.521	0.500	0.594	0.558	0.521	0.500	0.653	0.621
	Avg	0.420	0.433	0.434	0.454	0.421	0.437	0.447	0.440	0.454	0.447	0.446	0.434	0.461	0.457	0.516	0.484	0.495	0.450	0.541	0.507	0.458	0.450	0.529	0.522
ETTh2	96	0.274	0.334	0.284	0.347	0.278	0.338	0.289	0.341	0.297	0.349	0.288	0.338	0.340	0.394	0.308	0.355	0.340	0.374	0.400	0.440	0.340	0.374	0.745	0.584
	192	0.339	0.384	0.343	0.389	0.338	0.384	0.372	0.392	0.380	0.400	0.374	0.390	0.482	0.479	0.393	0.405	0.402	0.414	0.528	0.509	0.402	0.414	0.877	0.656
	336	0.380	0.408	0.375	0.409	0.389	0.411	0.386	0.414	0.428	0.432	0.415	0.426	0.591	0.541	0.427	0.436	0.452	0.452	0.643	0.571	0.452	0.452	1.043	0.731
	720	0.390	0.431	0.394	0.438	0.393	0.432	0.412	0.434	0.427	0.445	0.420	0.440	0.839	0.661	0.436	0.450	0.462	0.468	0.874	0.679	0.462	0.468	1.104	0.763
	Avg	0.345	0.389	0.349	0.395	0.349	0.391	0.364	0.395	0.383	0.407	0.374	0.398	0.563	0.519	0.391	0.411	0.414	0.427	0.611	0.550	0.414	0.427	0.942	0.684
ETTm1	96	0.294	0.346	0.304	0.348	0.293	0.343	0.320	0.357	0.334	0.368	0.355	0.376	0.346	0.374	0.352	0.374	0.338	0.375	0.364	0.387	0.338	0.375	0.404	0.426
	192	0.348	0.367	0.350	0.377	0.350	0.368	0.361	0.381	0.377	0.391	0.391	0.392	0.382	0.391	0.390	0.393	0.374	0.387	0.398	0.404	0.374	0.387	0.450	0.451
	336	0.387	0.392	0.395	0.409	0.382	0.391	0.390	0.404	0.426	0.420	0.424	0.415	0.415	0.415	0.421	0.414	0.410	0.411	0.428	0.425	0.410	0.411	0.532	0.515
	720	0.439	0.442	0.448	0.450	0.443	0.451	0.454	0.441	0.491	0.459	0.487	0.450	0.473	0.451	0.462	0.449	0.478	0.450	0.487	0.461	0.478	0.450	0.666	0.589
	Avg	0.367	0.387	0.374	0.396	0.367	0.388	0.381	0.395	0.407	0.410	0.414	0.407	0.404	0.408	0.406	0.407	0.400	0.406	0.419	0.419	0.400	0.406	0.513	0.495
ETTm2	96	0.160	0.251	0.160	0.253	0.160	0.251	0.175	0.252	0.180	0.264	0.182	0.265	0.193	0.293	0.183	0.270	0.187	0.267	0.207	0.305	0.187	0.267	0.287	0.366
	192	0.226	0.290	0.229	0.297	0.220	0.292	0.237	0.299	0.250	0.309	0.246	0.304	0.284	0.361	0.255	0.314	0.249	0.309	0.290	0.364	0.249	0.309	0.414	0.492
	336	0.283	0.339	0.299	0.346	0.284	0.337	0.298	0.340	0.311	0.348	0.307	0.342	0.382	0.429	0.309	0.347	0.321	0.351	0.377	0.422	0.321	0.351	0.597	0.542
	720	0.392	0.398	0.399	0.405	0.391	0.397	0.391	0.396	0.412	0.407	0.407	0.398	0.558	0.525	0.412	0.404	0.365	0.359	0.558	0.524	0.408	0.403	1.730	1.042
	Avg	0.265	0.320	0.272	0.325	0.264	0.319	0.275	0.323	0.288	0.332	0.286	0.327	0.354	0.402	0.290	0.334	0.291	0.333	0.358	0.404	0.291	0.333	0.757	0.610
Weather	96	0.149	0.202	0.151	0.203	0.148	0.202	0.163	0.209	0.174	0.214	0.192	0.232	0.195	0.252	0.186	0.227	0.172	0.220	0.202	0.261	0.172	0.220	0.195	0.271
	192	0.197	0.239	0.209	0.249	0.199	0.242	0.208	0.250	0.221	0.254	0.240	0.271	0.237	0.295	0.234	0.265	0.219	0.261	0.242	0.298	0.219	0.261	0.209	0.277
	336	0.270	0.282	0.310	0.281	0.262	0.279	0.251	0.287	0.278	0.296	0.292	0.307	0.282	0.331	0.284	0.301	0.246	0.337	0.287	0.335	0.280	0.306	0.273	0.332
	720	0.323	0.332	0.339	0.342	0.330	0.334	0.339	0.341	0.358	0.347	0.364	0.353	0.282	0.331	0.356	0.349	0.365	0.359	0.287	0.335	0.280	0.306	0.379	0.401
	Avg	0.235	0.264	0.252	0.269	0.235	0.264	0.240	0.271	0.258	0.278	0.272	0.291	0.265	0.315	0.265	0.285	0.251	0.294	0.271	0.320	0.259	0.287	0.264	0.320
Electricity	96	0.143	0.233	0.150	0.241	0.142	0.234	0.153	0.247	0.148	0.240	0.201	0.281	0.210	0.302	0.190	0.296	0.168	0.272	0.237	0.329	0.168	0.272	0.219	0.314
	192	0.151	0.242	0.166	0.259	0.152	0.241	0.166	0.256	0.162	0.253	0.201	0.283	0.210	0.305	0.199	0.304	0.184	0.322	0.236	0.330	0.184	0.289	0.231	0.322
	336	0.178	0.267	0.180	0.281	0.180	0.263	0.185	0.277	0.178	0.269	0.215	0.298	0.223	0.319	0.217	0.319	0.198	0.300	0.249	0.344	0.198	0.300	0.246	0.337
	720	0.213	0.305	0.221	0.311	0.218	0.308	0.225	0.310	0.225	0.317	0.257	0.331	0.258	0.350	0.258	0.352	0.220	0.320	0.284	0.373	0.220	0.320	0.280	0.363
	Avg	0.171	0.253	0.174	0.273	0.173	0.261	0.182	0.272	0.178	0.270	0.219	0.298	0.225	0.319	0.216	0.318	0.193	0.304	0.251	0.344	0.192	0.295	0.244	0.334
Traffic	96	0.380	0.264	0.394	0.274	0.382	0.268	0.462	0.285	0.395	0.268	0.649	0.389	0.650	0.396	0.526	0.347	0.593	0.321	0.805	0.493	0.593	0.321	0.644	0.429
	192	0.396	0.269	0.399	0.276	0.394	0.267	0.473	0.296	0.417	0.276	0.601	0.366	0.598	0.370	0.522	0.332	0.617	0.336	0.756	0.474	0.617	0.336	0.665	0.431
	336	0.423	0.274	0.439	0.280	0.425	0.281	0.498	0.296	0.433	0.283	0.609	0.369	0.605	0.373	0.517	0.334	0.629	0.336	0.762	0.477	0.629	0.336	0.674	0.420
	720	0.458	0.296	0.460	0.298	0.460	0.300	0.506	0.313	0.467	0.302	0.647	0.387	0.645	0.394	0.552	0.352	0.640	0.350	0.719	0.449	0.640	0.350	0.683	0.424
	Avg	0.414	0.265	0.433	0.282	0.415	0.279	0.484	0.297	0.428	0.282	0.626	0.378	0.625	0.383	0.529	0.341	0.620	0.336	0.760	0.473	0.620	0.336	0.667	0.426

Table 1: Full long-term multivariate forecasting results. **Red:** the best, Blue: the second best.

Methods		LLM-Mixer (llama2)		LLM-Mixer (roberta)		TIME-LLM		TimeMixer		iTransformer		RLinear		PatchTST		Crossformer		TiDE		TimesNet		DLinear		SCINet	
Metric		MSE	MAE	MSE	MAE	MSE	MAE	MSE	MAE	MSE	MAE	MSE	MAE	MSE	MAE	MSE	MAE	MSE	MAE	MSE	MAE	MSE	MAE	MSE	MAE
PEMS03	12	0.069	0.173	0.082	0.190	0.092	0.201	0.082	0.189	0.071	0.174	0.126	0.236	0.099	0.216	0.090	0.203	0.178	0.305	0.085	0.192	0.122	0.243	0.066	0.172
	24	0.090	0.200	0.092	0.201	0.095	0.207	0.090	0.199	0.093	0.201	0.246	0.334	0.142	0.259	0.121	0.240	0.257	0.371	0.118	0.223	0.201	0.317	0.085	0.198
	48	0.123	0.232	0.126	0.237	0.127	0.237	0.125	0.235	0.125	0.236	0.551	0.529	0.211	0.319	0.202	0.317	0.379	0.463	0.155	0.260	0.333	0.425	0.127	0.238
	96	0.165	0.274	0.166	0.276	0.165	0.274	0.167	0.275	0.164	0.275	1.057	0.787	0.269	0.370	0.262	0.367	0.490	0.539	0.028	0.317	0.457	0.515	0.178	0.287
	Avg	0.112	0.220	0.116	0.226	0.120	0.230	0.116	0.225	0.113	0.221	0.495	0.472	0.180	0.291	0.169	0.281	0.326	0.419	0.147	0.248	0.278	0.375	0.114	0.224
PEMS04	12	0.072	0.177	0.076	0.183	0.071	0.177	0.073	0.179	0.078	0.183	0.138	0.252	0.105	0.224	0.098	0.209	0.182	0.324	0.087	0.195	0.148	0.272	0.073	0.177
	24	0.095	0.201	0.105	0.211	0.106	0.214	0.097	0.205	0.108	0.205	0.258	0.387	0.150	0.266	0.135	0.250	0.309	0.454	0.099	0.217	0.225	0.367	0.084	0.193
	48	0.099	0.216	0.103	0.220	0.101	0.218	0.099	0.217	0.120	0.233	0.572	0.544	0.229	0.339	0.205	0.353	0.470	0.539	0.135	0.253	0.355	0.437	0.099	0.217
	96	0.120	0.225	0.130	0.232	0.121	0.225	0.121	0.225	0.150	0.267	1.159	0.947	0.309	0.520	0.299	0.467	0.656	0.637	0.043	0.317	0.550	0.541	0.129	0.227
	Avg	0.097	0.205	0.104	0.211	0.100	0.209	0.098	0.207	0.111	0.221	0.526	0.491	0.195	0.307	0.209	0.314	0.353	0.475	0.129	0.245	0.329	0.395	0.119	0.234
PEMS07	12	0.065	0.165	0.072	0.180	0.068	0.166	0.070	0.168	0.067	0.165	0.118	0.235	0.097	0.226	0.093	0.209	0.155	0.324	0.081	0.185	0.118	0.272	0.068	0.174
	24	0.087	0.105	0.091	0.198	0.088	0.192	0.087	0.105	0.088	0.190	0.271	0.449	0.153	0.276	0.138	0.251	0.338	0.475	0.096	0.223	0.207	0.381	0.087	0.180
	48	0.106	0.215	0.117	0.224	0.109	0.219	0.106	0.217	0.110	0.215	0.596	0.621	0.343	0.459	0.309	0.401	0.532	0.547	0.145	0.264	0.593	0.484	0.149	0.233
	96	0.147	0.266	0.146	0.265	0.150	0.269	0.151	0.269	0.141	0.245	1.096	0.795	0.346	0.490	0.329	0.443	0.674	0.650	0.203	0.307	0.789	0.531	0.191	0.267
	Avg	0.101	0.204	0.107	0.217	0.104	0.212	0.104	0.218	0.101	0.204	0.504	0.478	0.213	0.303	0.215	0.326	0.355	0.499	0.129	0.245	0.529	0.387	0.119	0.234
PEMS08	12	0.082	0.186	0.086	0.190	0.080	0.184	0.083	0.183	0.079	0.182	0.133	0.247	0.168	0.232	0.152	0.267	0.215	0.367	0.154	0.276	0.172	0.291	0.087	0.184
	24	0.107	0.213	0.109	0.217	0.105	0.208	0.109	0.218	0.105	0.209	0.242	0.360	0.189	0.321	0.174	0.314	0.258	0.430	0.178	0.307	0.290	0.346	0.104	0.193
	48	0.187	0.235	0.192	0.240	0.193	0.242	0.192	0.241	0.125	0.237	0.596	0.556	0.269	0.389	0.247	0.388	0.433	0.512	0.210	0.345	0.418	0.422	0.124	0.216
	96	0.140	0.245	0.142	0.249	0.147	0.256	0.143	0.252	0.167	0.275	1.043	0.841	0.344	0.470	0.326	0.459	0.534	0.571	0.283	0.387	0.593	0.514	0.155	0.253
	Avg	0.119	0.226	0.132	0.224	0.131	0.223	0.132	0.224	0.119	0.226	0.503	0.501	0.243	0.353	0.225	0.357	0.360	0.470	0.206	0.329	0.368	0.393	0.118	0.212

Table 2: Full short-term multivariate forecasting results. **Red:** the best, Blue: the second best.

Methods		LLM-Mixer (llama2)		LLM-Mixer (Roberta)		Linear		NLinear		DLinear		FEDformer-f		FEDformer-w		Autoformer		Informer		LogTrans	
Metric		MSE	MAE	MSE	MAE	MSE	MAE	MSE	MAE	MSE	MAE	MSE	MAE	MSE	MAE	MSE	MAE	MSE	MAE	MSE	MAE
ETTh1	96	0.052	0.175	0.053	0.177	0.189	0.359	0.055	0.176	0.056	0.180	0.079	0.215	0.080	0.214	0.071	0.206	0.193	0.377	0.283	0.468
	192	0.064	0.200	0.066	0.203	0.078	0.212	0.069	0.204	0.071	0.204	0.104	0.245	0.105	0.256	0.114	0.262	0.217	0.395	0.234	0.409
	336	0.080	0.226	0.081	0.226	0.091	0.237	0.084	0.228	0.098	0.244	0.119	0.270	0.120	0.269	0.107	0.258	0.202	0.381	0.386	0.546
	720	0.075	0.222	0.078	0.223	0.172	0.340	0.080	0.226	0.189	0.359	0.142	0.299	0.127	0.280	0.126	0.283	0.183	0.355	0.475	0.629
	Avg	0.068	0.206	0.071	0.207	0.133	0.287	0.071	0.208	0.104	0.247	0.111	0.257	0.108	0.255	0.106	0.252	0.199	0.377	0.345	0.513
ETTh2	96	0.125	0.274	0.123	0.276	0.133	0.283	0.129	0.278	0.131	0.279	0.128	0.271	0.156	0.306	0.153	0.306	0.213	0.373	0.217	0.379
	192	0.166	0.322	0.169	0.324	0.176	0.330	0.169	0.324	0.176	0.329	0.185	0.330	0.238	0.380	0.204	0.351	0.227	0.387	0.281	0.429
	336	0.193	0.353	0.194	0.356	0.213	0.371	0.194	0.355	0.209	0.367	0.231	0.378	0.271	0.412	0.246	0.389	0.242	0.401	0.293	0.437
	720	0.222	0.380	0.225	0.381	0.292	0.440	0.225	0.381	0.276	0.426	0.278	0.420	0.288	0.438	0.268	0.409	0.291	0.439	0.218	0.387
	Avg	0.177	0.332	0.178	0.334	0.204	0.356	0.179	0.335	0.198	0.350	0.205	0.350	0.238	0.384	0.218	0.364	0.243	0.400	0.252	0.408
ETTm1	96	0.023	0.118	0.026	0.125	0.028	0.125	0.026	0.122	0.028	0.123	0.033	0.140	0.036	0.149	0.056	0.183	0.109	0.277	0.049	0.171
	192	0.033	0.145	0.036	0.147	0.043	0.154	0.039	0.149	0.045	0.156	0.058	0.186	0.069	0.206	0.081	0.216	0.151	0.310	0.157	0.317
	336	0.053	0.172	0.054	0.176	0.059	0.180	0.052	0.172	0.061	0.182	0.084	0.231	0.071	0.209	0.076	0.218	0.427	0.591	0.289	0.459
	720	0.071	0.205	0.072	0.204	0.080	0.211	0.073	0.207	0.080	0.210	0.102	0.250	0.105	0.248	0.110	0.267	0.438	0.586	0.430	0.579
	Avg	0.045	0.161	0.047	0.163	0.053	0.167	0.048	0.163	0.054	0.168	0.069	0.202	0.070	0.203	0.081	0.221	0.281	0.441	0.231	0.381
ETTm2	96	0.062	0.180	0.064	0.181	0.066	0.189	0.063	0.182	0.063	0.183	0.067	0.198	0.063	0.189	0.065	0.189	0.088	0.225	0.075	0.208
	192	0.090	0.222	0.089	0.220	0.094	0.230	0.090	0.223	0.092	0.227	0.102	0.245	0.110	0.252	0.118	0.256	0.132	0.283	0.129	0.275
	336	0.114	0.255	0.116	0.257	0.120	0.263	0.117	0.259	0.119	0.261	0.130	0.279	0.147	0.301	0.154	0.305	0.180	0.336	0.154	0.302
	720	0.169	0.313	0.171	0.314	0.175	0.320	0.170	0.318	0.175	0.320	0.178	0.325	0.219	0.368	0.182	0.335	0.300	0.435	0.160	0.321
	Avg	0.109	0.243	0.110	0.243	0.114	0.250	0.110	0.246	0.112	0.248	0.119	0.262	0.135	0.279	0.130	0.271	0.150	0.295	0.130	0.277

Table 3: Full univariate long sequence time-series forecasting results on ETT full benchmark. **Red:** the best, Blue: the second best.

MSE and MAE values across most datasets, particularly excelling on ETTh1, ETTh2, and Electricity. Compared to other models such as TIME-LLM, TimeMixer, and PatchTST, LLM-Mixer performs favorably, showing that its design effectively captures both short- and long-term dependencies. Notably, LLM-Mixer also exhibits robustness on challenging datasets such as Traffic, where it outperforms several baseline models. These results highlight the efficacy of the LLM-Mixer in handling complex temporal patterns over extended horizons.

Short-term forecasting results: In Table 2, we present the short-term multivariate forecasting results, across four forecasting horizons: 12, 24, 48, and 96 time steps. Our proposed model consistently achieves low MSE and MAE values across the PEMS datasets, indicating a strong short-term predictive performance. Specifically, LLM-Mixer demonstrates competitive accuracy on PEMS03, PEMS04, and PEMS07, outperforming several baseline models, including TIME-LLM, TimeMixer, and PatchTST. Additionally, the LLM-Mixer shows robustness on PEMS08, where it delivers superior results compared to iTransformer and DLinear. These results emphasize the effectiveness of the LLM-Mixer in capturing essential temporal dynamics for short-horizon forecasting tasks.

Univariate forecasting results: Table 3 presents the univariate long forecasting results on the ETT benchmark and averaged over horizons of 96, 192, 384, and 720-time steps. LLM-Mixer achieves the lowest MSE and MAE values across all datasets, consistently outperforming other methods like Linear, NLinear, and FEDformer. LLM-Mixer demonstrates superior accuracy, particularly on most of the datasets. These results confirm the effectiveness of the LLM-Mixer in capturing complex temporal dependencies, solidifying its capability for univariate long-term forecasting.

3.1 Ablation Study

Effect of Downsampling on Learning Dynamicse: To evaluate the impact of different downsampling levels on the learning dynamics of LLM-Mixer, we conducted an ablation study using the Neural Tangent Kernel (NTK) (Jacot et al., 2018). Specifically, we aimed to understand how the number of downsampling levels affects the model's ability to capture multiscale information. First, we used DeepEcho (Patki et al., 2016) to generate synthetic multivariate time series datasets for this study. We trained 10 versions of LLM-Mixer, each with a different number of downsampling levels $\tau \in \{1, 2, \ldots, 10\}$. For each model, we calculated the NTK on 300 sample pairs from both the training and test sets. The NTK, denoted as $\mathbf{K}(\mathbf{x}, \mathbf{x}')$, is computed as the inner product of the gradients of the model outputs with respect to its parameters:

$$\mathbf{K}(\mathbf{x}, \mathbf{x}') = \nabla_{\boldsymbol{\theta}} \theta_t(\mathbf{x}; \boldsymbol{\theta})^\top \nabla_{\boldsymbol{\theta}} \theta_t(\mathbf{x}'; \boldsymbol{\theta}),$$

where $\nabla_{\boldsymbol{\theta}} \theta_t(\mathbf{x}; \boldsymbol{\theta})$ is the gradient of the model output with respect to its parameters at iteration t.

<span style="color: red;">Data Leakage Prevention Protocol: To ensure fair comparison and avoid data leakage, we construct prompts using only metadata and statistics computed exclusively from the training set. Specifically, we include: (1) dataset description (e.g., "electricity consumption data"), (2) feature names and units, (3) basic statistics (mean, standard deviation, data frequency) computed only from training samples. No information from validation or test sets is incorporated into the prompt construction process. We validate this approach through ablation studies comparing models with and without statistical information in prompts.</span>

To measure how the NTK structure changes with different 10 levels, we used the Frobenius norm to calculate the distance between the NTK of each model ($\mathbf{K}_\tau$) and a reference NTK ($\mathbf{K}_{10}$), which corresponds to the model with the maximum downsampling levels. The NTK distance is defined as:

$$d_{\text{NTK}}(\tau) = \|\mathbf{K}_{10} - \mathbf{K}_\tau\|_F,$$

where $\| \cdot \|_F$ denotes the Frobenius norm. Smaller NTK distances indicate that the model's learning dynamics are closer to the reference model.

Our results, shown in Figure 2, reveal that as the number of downsampling levels τ decreases, the NTK distance increases. The largest distance is observed when $\tau = 1$, indicating that using only one downsampling level significantly alters the model's learning dynamics.However, more downsampling levels are not always better. While increasing τ enhances the model's ability to capture multiscale patterns, excessive downsampling may smooth out critical fine-grained details, which are essential for tasks with significant short-term variations. In Figure 3, we visualize the NTK of the reference model across different downsampling levels τ and the normalized absolute differences.

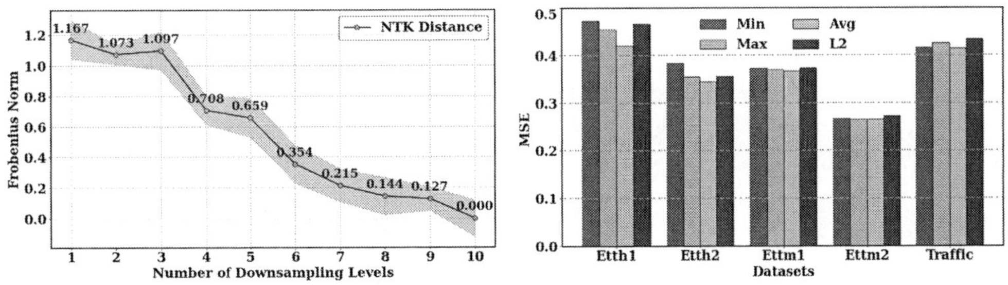

Figure 2: (**Left**) Frobenius norm of NTK distance. (**Right**) Pooling technique for Multi-scale Mixing

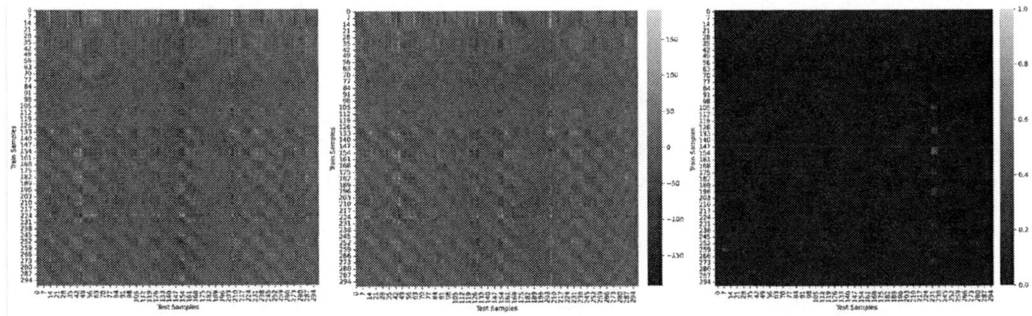

(a) $\tau = 9$

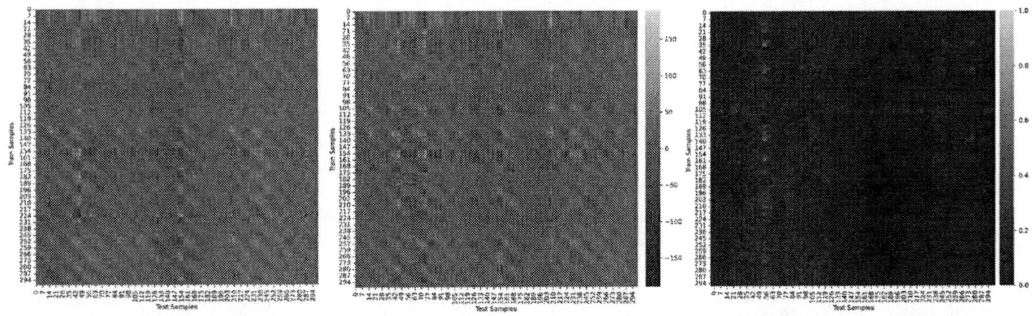

(b) $\tau = 7$

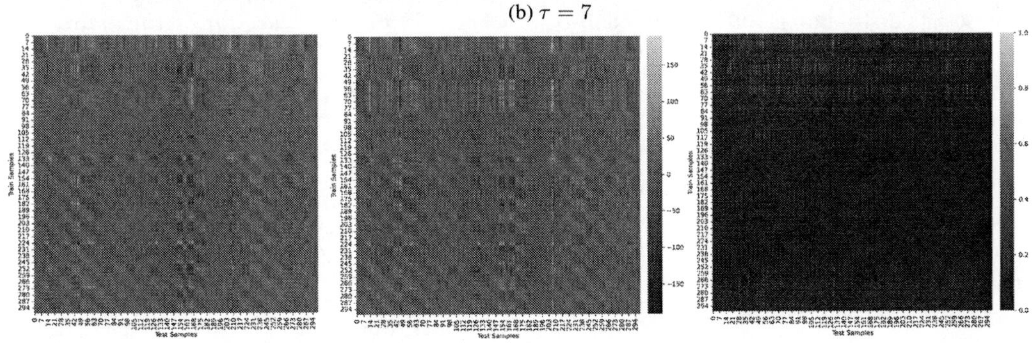

(c) $\tau = 5$

Figure 3: Visualization of (a) $\tau = 9$, (b) $\tau = 7$, and (c) $\tau = 5$. Each subfigure displays the reference NTK at $\tau = 10$, the NTK at the respective τ level, and their absolute difference.

Multi-scale Mixing by Pooling: We conducted an ablation study to explore the effects of various Multi-scale Mixing techniques. The techniques examined were Min, Max, Avg, and L2, each applying a unique method for aggregating downsampling information across scales. Figure 2 (right) presents the MSE for each downsampling method across different datasets. Notably, average pooling consistently yielded a lower MSE, suggesting that this method is better suited for capturing multi-scale dependencies in the data.

4 Conclusion

This work introduces the LLM-Mixer, a novel framework that combines multiscale time-series decomposition with pre-trained LLMs for improved forecasting. By leveraging multiple temporal resolutions, the LLM-Mixer effectively captures both short-and long-term patterns, enhancing the model's predictive accuracy. Our experiments demonstrate that the LLM-Mixer achieves competitive performance across various datasets, outperforming recent state-of-the-art methods.

5 Limitations and Future Directions

Although LLM-Mixer improves forecasting accuracy, several limitations warrant discussion.

Computational Requirements: The use of pre-trained language models introduces significant computational overhead, which may limit deployment in real-time or resource-constrained environments. **Prompt Engineering:** Model performance depends on prompt quality and domain expertise for optimal prompt design, which may limit accessibility for non-experts.

Out-of-Distribution Robustness: When training and test data distributions differ significantly, the fixed prompt approach may not adapt effectively to distributional shifts.

Limited Classical Baseline Analysis: Our evaluation focuses primarily on deep learning methods and would benefit from comprehensive comparison with statistical approaches like ARIMA and exponential smoothing.

Data Leakage Potential: While we implement protocols to prevent information leakage, the prompt-based approach requires careful validation to ensure fair comparison.

Domain Generalization: Testing on more diverse domains (finance, healthcare, climate) would strengthen claims about broad applicability. Future work should address these limitations through adaptive prompting strategies, efficiency optimizations, and expanded empirical validation.

References

Josh Achiam, Steven Adler, Sandhini Agarwal, Lama Ahmad, Ilge Akkaya, Florencia Leoni Aleman, Diogo Almeida, Janko Altenschmidt, Sam Altman, Shyamal Anadkat, et al. 2023. Gpt-4 technical report. arXiv preprint arXiv:2303.08774.

Yassir Bendou, Giulia Lioi, Bastien Pasdeloup, Lukas Mauch, Ghouthi Boukli Hacene, Fabien Cardinaux, and Vincent Gripon. 2024. Llm meets vision-language models for zero-shot one-class classification. arXiv preprint arXiv:2404.00675.

George EP Box, Gwilym M Jenkins, Gregory C Reinsel, and Greta M Ljung. 2015. Time series analysis: forecasting and control. John Wiley & Sons.

Tom B Brown. 2020. Language models are few-shot learners. arXiv preprint arXiv:2005.14165.

David Campos, Miao Zhang, Bin Yang, Tung Kieu, Chenjuan Guo, and Christian S Jensen. 2023. Lightts: Lightweight time series classification with adaptive ensemble distillation. Proceedings of the ACM on Management of Data, 1(2):1–27.

Chao Chen, Karl Petty, Alexander Skabardonis, Pravin Varaiya, and Zhanfeng Jia. 2001. Freeway performance measurement system: mining loop detector data. Transportation research record, 1748(1):96–102.

Minghao Chen, Houwen Peng, Jianlong Fu, and Haibin Ling. 2021. Autoformer: Searching transformers for visual recognition. In Proceedings of the IEEE/CVF international conference on computer vision, pages 12270–12280.

Changqing Cheng, Akkarapol Sa-Ngasoongsong, Omer Beyca, Trung Le, Hui Yang, Zhenyu Kong, and Satish TS Bukkapatnam. 2015. Time series forecasting for nonlinear and non-stationary processes: a review and comparative study. Iie Transactions, 47(10):1053–1071.

Abhimanyu Das, Weihao Kong, Andrew Leach, Shaan K Mathur, Rajat Sen, and Rose Yu. 2023. Long-term forecasting with tiDE: Time-series dense encoder. Transactions on Machine Learning Research.

Othmane Friha, Mohamed Amine Ferrag, Burak Kantarci, Burak Cakmak, Arda Ozgun, and Nassira Ghoualmi-Zine. 2024. Llm-based edge intelligence: A comprehensive survey on architectures, applications, security and trustworthiness. IEEE Open Journal of the Communications Society.

Senay A Gebreab, Khaled Salah, Raja Jayaraman, Muhammad Habib ur Rehman, and Samer Ellaham. 2024. Llm-based framework for administrative task automation in healthcare. In 2024 12th International Symposium on Digital Forensics and Security (ISDFS), pages 1–7. IEEE.

Nate Gruver, Marc Anton Finzi, Shikai Qiu, and Andrew Gordon Wilson. 2023. Large language models are zero-shot time series forecasters. In Thirty-seventh Conference on Neural Information Processing Systems.

RJ Hyndman. 2018. Forecasting: principles and practice. OTexts.

Arthur Jacot, Franck Gabriel, and Clément Hongler. 2018. Neural tangent kernel: Convergence and generalization in neural networks. Advances in neural information processing systems, 31.

Bonian Jia, Huiyao Chen, Yueheng Sun, Meishan Zhang, and Min Zhang. 2024. Llm-driven multimodal opinion expression identification. arXiv preprint arXiv:2406.18088.

Manuel Jesús Jiménez-Navarro, María Martínez-Ballesteros, Francisco Martínez-Álvarez, and Gualberto Asencio-Cortés. 2023. Embedded temporal feature selection for time series forecasting using deep learning. In International Work-Conference on Artificial Neural Networks, pages 15–26. Springer.

Ming Jin, Shiyu Wang, Lintao Ma, Zhixuan Chu, James Y. Zhang, Xiaoming Shi, Pin-Yu Chen, Yuxuan Liang, Yuan-Fang Li, Shirui Pan, and Qingsong Wen. 2024. Time-LLM: Time series forecasting by reprogramming large language models. In The Twelfth International Conference on Learning Representations.

Ming Jin, Shiyu Wang, Lintao Ma, Zhixuan Chu, James Y Zhang, Xiaoming Shi, Pin-Yu Chen, Yuxuan Liang, Yuan-Fang Li, Shirui Pan, et al. 2023. Time-llm: Time series forecasting by reprogramming large language models. arXiv preprint arXiv:2310.01728.

Fazle Karim, Somshubra Majumdar, and Houshang Darabi. 2019. Insights into lstm fully convolutional networks for time series classification. Ieee Access, 7:67718–67725.

Serkan Kiranyaz, Onur Avci, Osama Abdeljaber, Turker Ince, Moncef Gabbouj, and Daniel J Inman. 2021. 1d convolutional neural networks and applications: A survey. Mechanical systems and signal processing, 151:107398.

Melih Kirisci and Ozge Cagcag Yolcu. 2022. A new cnn-based model for financial time series: Taiex and ftse stocks forecasting. Neural Processing Letters, 54(4):3357–3374.

Lei Li, Yongfeng Zhang, and Li Chen. 2023. Prompt distillation for efficient llm-based recommendation. In Proceedings of the 32nd ACM International Conference on Information and Knowledge Management, pages 1348–1357.

Zhe Li, Shiyi Qi, Yiduo Li, and Zenglin Xu. 2024. Revisiting long-term time series forecasting: An investigation on affine mapping.

Jingyu Liu, Jiaen Lin, and Yong Liu. 2024a. How much can rag help the reasoning of llm? arXiv preprint arXiv:2410.02338.

Keqin Liu, Teng Zhang, Bingjie Dang, Lin Bao, Liying Xu, Caidie Cheng, Zhen Yang, Ru Huang, and Yuchao Yang. 2022. An optoelectronic synapse based on α-in2se3 with controllable temporal dynamics for multimode and multiscale reservoir computing. Nature Electronics, 5(11):761–773.

Minhao LIU, Ailing Zeng, Muxi Chen, Zhijian Xu, Qiuxia LAI, Lingna Ma, and Qiang Xu. 2022. SCINet: Time series modeling and forecasting with sample convolution and interaction. In Advances in Neural Information Processing Systems.

Yinhan Liu, Myle Ott, Naman Goyal, Jingfei Du, Mandar Joshi, Danqi Chen, Omer Levy, Mike Lewis, Luke Zettlemoyer, and Veselin Stoyanov. 2019. Roberta: A robustly optimized bert pretraining approach. arXiv preprint arXiv:1907.11692.

Yong Liu, Tengge Hu, Haoran Zhang, Haixu Wu, Shiyu Wang, Lintao Ma, and Mingsheng Long. 2024b. itransformer: Inverted transformers are effective for time series forecasting. In The Twelfth International Conference on Learning Representations.

Yong Liu, Haixu Wu, Jianmin Wang, and Mingsheng Long. 2022. Non-stationary transformers: Exploring the stationarity in time series forecasting. Advances in Neural Information Processing Systems, 35:9881–9893.

Luis Martín, Luis F Zarzalejo, Jesus Polo, Ana Navarro, Ruth Marchante, and Marco Cony. 2010. Prediction of global solar irradiance based on time series analysis: Application to solar thermal power plants energy production planning. Solar Energy, 84(10):1772–1781.

Juan Morales-García, Antonio Llanes, Francisco Arcas-Túnez, and Fernando Terroso-Sáenz. 2024. Developing time series forecasting models with generative large language models. ACM Transactions on Intelligent Systems and Technology.

Mohammad Amin Morid, Olivia R Liu Sheng, and Joseph Dunbar. 2023. Time series prediction using deep learning methods in healthcare. ACM Transactions on Management Information Systems, 14(1):1–29.

Michael C Mozer. 1991. Induction of multiscale temporal structure. Advances in neural information processing systems, 4.

Manfred Mudelsee. 2019. Trend analysis of climate time series: A review of methods. Earth-science reviews, 190:310–322.

Yuqi Nie, Nam H Nguyen, Phanwadee Sinthong, and Jayant Kalagnanam. 2022. A time series is worth 64 words: Long-term forecasting with transformers. arXiv preprint arXiv:2211.14730.

Neha Patki, Roy Wedge, and Kalyan Veeramachaneni. 2016. The synthetic data vault. In 2016 IEEE international conference on data science and advanced analytics (DSAA), pages 399–410. IEEE.

Pranab Sahoo, Ayush Kumar Singh, Sriparna Saha, Vinija Jain, Samrat Mondal, and Aman Chadha. 2024. A systematic survey of prompt engineering in large language models: Techniques and applications. arXiv preprint arXiv:2402.07927.

Sima Siami-Namini, Neda Tavakoli, and Akbar Siami Namin. 2019. The performance of lstm and bilstm in forecasting time series. In 2019 IEEE International conference on big data (Big Data), pages 3285–3292. IEEE.

Wensi Tang, Guodong Long, Lu Liu, Tianyi Zhou, Jing Jiang, and Michael Blumenstein. 2020. Rethinking 1d-cnn for time series classification: A stronger baseline. arXiv preprint arXiv:2002.10061, pages 1–7.

Yuqing Tang, Fusheng Yu, Witold Pedrycz, Xiyang Yang, Jiayin Wang, and Shihu Liu. 2021. Building trend fuzzy granulation-based lstm recurrent neural network for long-term time-series forecasting. IEEE transactions on fuzzy systems, 30(6):1599–1613.

Hugo Touvron, Thibaut Lavril, Gautier Izacard, Xavier Martinet, Marie-Anne Lachaux, Timothée Lacroix, Baptiste Rozière, Naman Goyal, Eric Hambro, Faisal Azhar, et al. 2023. Llama: Open and efficient foundation language models. arXiv preprint arXiv:2302.13971.

Ashish Vaswani, Noam Shazeer, Niki Parmar, Jakob Uszkoreit, Llion Jones, Aidan N Gomez, Łukasz Kaiser, and Illia Polosukhin. 2017. Attention is all you need. Advances in neural information processing systems, 30.

Huiqiang Wang, Jian Peng, Feihu Huang, Jince Wang, Junhui Chen, and Yifei Xiao. 2023. MICN: Multiscale local and global context modeling for long-term series forecasting. In The Eleventh International Conference on Learning Representations.

Shiyu Wang, Haixu Wu, Xiaoming Shi, Tengge Hu, Huakun Luo, Lintao Ma, James Y Zhang, and Jun Zhou. 2024. Timemixer: Decomposable multiscale mixing for time series forecasting. arXiv preprint arXiv:2405.14616.

Yongjian Wang, Ke Yang, and Hongguang Li. 2020. Industrial time-series modeling via adapted receptive field temporal convolution networks integrating regularly updated multi-region operations based on pca. Chemical Engineering Science, 228:115956.

Gerald Woo, Chenghao Liu, Doyen Sahoo, Akshat Kumar, and Steven Hoi. 2022. Etsformer: Exponential smoothing transformers for time-series forecasting. arXiv preprint arXiv:2202.01381.

Haixu Wu, Tengge Hu, Yong Liu, Hang Zhou, Jianmin Wang, and Mingsheng Long. 2022. Timesnet: Temporal 2d-variation modeling for general time series analysis. In The eleventh international conference on learning representations.

Haixu Wu, Jiehui Xu, Jianmin Wang, and Mingsheng Long. 2021. Autoformer: Decomposition transformers with auto-correlation for long-term series forecasting. Advances in neural information processing systems, 34:22419–22430.

Hao Xue and Flora D Salim. 2023. Promptcast: A new prompt-based learning paradigm for time series forecasting. IEEE Transactions on Knowledge and Data Engineering.

Ailing Zeng, Muxi Chen, Lei Zhang, and Qiang Xu. 2023. Are transformers effective for time series forecasting? In Proceedings of the Thirty-Seventh AAAI Conference on Artificial Intelligence and Thirty-Fifth Conference on Innovative Applications of Artificial Intelligence and Thirteenth Symposium on Educational Advances in Artificial Intelligence, pages 11121–11128.

Cheng Zhang, Nilam Nur Amir Sjarif, and Roslina Ibrahim. 2024. Deep learning models for price forecasting of financial time series: A review of recent advancements: 2020–2022. Wiley Interdisciplinary Reviews: Data Mining and Knowledge Discovery, 14(1):e1519.

Xuan Zhang, Xun Liang, Aakas Zhiyuli, Shusen Zhang, Rui Xu, and Bo Wu. 2019. At-lstm: An attention-based lstm model for financial time series prediction. In IOP Conference Series: Materials Science and Engineering, page 052037. IOP Publishing.

Huaqin Zhao, Zhengliang Liu, Zihao Wu, Yiwei Li, Tianze Yang, Peng Shu, Shaochen Xu, Haixing Dai, Lin Zhao, Gengchen Mai, et al. 2024. Revolutionizing finance with llms: An overview of applications and insights. arXiv preprint arXiv:2401.11641.

Haoyi Zhou, Shanghang Zhang, Jieqi Peng, Shuai Zhang, Jianxin Li, Hui Xiong, and Wancai Zhang. 2021. Informer: Beyond efficient transformer for long sequence time-series forecasting. In 35th AAAI Conference on Artificial Intelligence, AAAI 2021, pages 11106–11115. Association for the Advancement of Artificial Intelligence.

Tian Zhou, Ziqing Ma, Qingsong Wen, Xue Wang, Liang Sun, and Rong Jin. 2022. Fedformer: Frequency enhanced decomposed transformer for long-term series forecasting. In International conference on machine learning, pages 27268–27286. PMLR.

Tian Zhou, Peisong Niu, Liang Sun, Rong Jin, et al. 2023. One fits all: Power general time series analysis by pretrained lm. Advances in neural information processing systems, 36:43322–43355.

Chenglong Zhu, Xueling Ma, Weiping Ding, and Jianming Zhan. 2023. Long-term time series forecasting with multi-linear trend fuzzy information granules for lstm in a periodic framework. IEEE Transactions on Fuzzy Systems.

TableKV: KV Cache Compression for In-Context Table Processing

Giulio Corallo
SAP Labs, France
EURECOM, France
giulio.corallo@sap.com

Elia Faure-Rolland EURECOM, France
Miriam Lamari EURECOM, France
Paolo Papotti EURECOM, France
{firstname.lastname}@eurecom.fr

Abstract

Processing large tables provided in-context to LLMs is challenging due to token limits and information overload. While Retrieval-Augmented Generation can select relevant subsets externally, this work explores Key-Value (KV) cache compression as an alternative, applied directly to the linearized table during inference. We show that the LLM's internal attention scores over the table context guides the retention of essential KV pairs, effectively compressing the processing context while preserving crucial relational information needed for complex queries. Experiments on Spider, WikitableQA, and QTSumm datasets validate the compression approach for in-context table processing, offering a promising path for improved table representation learning in LLMs.

1 Introduction

Large language models (LLMs) have demonstrated remarkable capabilities across language tasks. A promising frontier is enabling LLMs to reason over structured data, such as tables, alongside natural language. This ability is key for applications such as table question answering (TableQA) (Chen et al., 2024) and fact-checking using relational data (Aly et al., 2021). While generating SQL queries from text (Text2SQL) is a popular approach (Yu et al., 2019), directly processing tabular data *within the LLM's context* offers a unified framework, leveraging the model's abilities to handle nuances beyond SQL's scope (Deng et al., 2024).

However, directly feeding large tables into LLMs faces significant issues. The primary challenge is *context length*: even moderately sized tables (e.g., thousands of rows and tens of columns) linearized into text easily exceed the token limits of popular models (e.g., >120,000 tokens) (Chen et al., 2024). Consequently, full-table inputs are often impractical, necessitating truncation or retrieval mechanisms (Ji et al., 2024; Badaro et al., 2023).

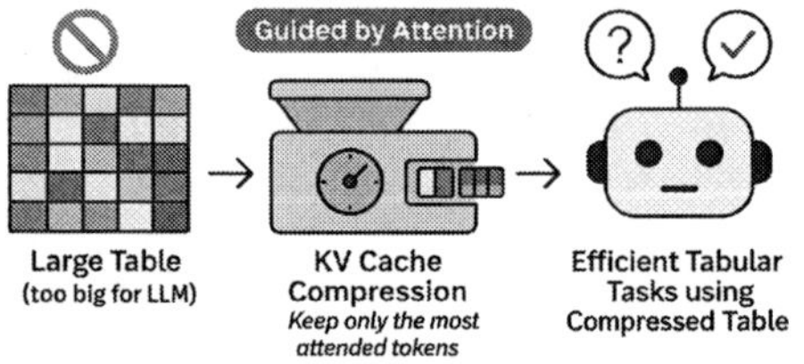

Figure 1: High-level overview of attention-guided KV compression for efficient tabular reasoning with LLMs. The model compresses the KV representation of a large table by selecting only the most attended tokens, enabling inference over a compressed table.

Even when models accommodate large contexts, their reasoning accuracy often degrades substantially (Liu et al., 2024). This phenomenon is exacerbated by tables, which inherently mix relevant cells with irrelevant information, diluting the model's attention (Sui et al., 2023; Satriani et al., 2025). Capturing relational patterns that span disparate rows or columns is particularly difficult, hindering accurate aggregation or multi-step reasoning.

Existing solutions often rely on Retrieval-Augmented Generation (RAG) (Chen et al., 2024; Lin et al., 2023). While RAG effectively reduces the input length by pre-selecting relevant table chunks (rows, columns, or cells), it introduces its own complexities. First, it requires separate retrieval modules and deciding how to optimally partition and retrieve table segments (e.g., by row, column, or semantic blocks) (Bodensohn and Binnig, 2024). Second, relying on embedding similarity for retrieval might fail to capture the fine-grained relational dependencies, shifting the bottleneck to the retriever's effectiveness.

In this paper, we explore an alternative approach: leveraging *Key-Value (KV) cache compression* techniques, originally developed for general text inference (Qin et al., 2023; Corallo and Papotti, 2024), to handle large tabular data *directly within the LLM's inference process*. Our core hypothesis is

Proceedings of the 4th Table Representation Learning Workshop, pages 166–171
July 31, 2025 ©2025 Association for Computational Linguistics

that the LLM's own attention mechanism, as it processes the linearized table, inherently identifies the most salient information. We exploit these attention scores to dynamically prune the KV cache, retaining only the key-value pairs corresponding to the most attended-to tokens. This effectively compresses the table's representation, making the information from the original tables available *during inference*, mitigating information overload while avoiding the complexities of explicit retrieval.

Our experiments across datasets, including Spider (Yu et al., 2019), WikitableQA (Pasupat and Liang, 2015), and QTSumm (Zhao et al., 2023), demonstrate the viability of this approach.

Related Work. RAG methods retrieve relevant subsets of tabular data to reduce input complexity. TableRAG (Chen et al., 2024) employs schema and cell retrieval techniques, while TAP4LLM (Sui et al., 2023) uses sampling strategies to focus the model's attention on relevant subsets of data. Specialized encoding techniques tailored for structured inputs have also gained attention. SpreadsheetLLM (Tian et al., 2024) exploits structural redundancies within tabular data, compressing input lengths without losing semantic fidelity. However, retrieval-based methods often fall short in capturing the comprehensive relational contexts that are required to handle queries involving multiple tuples. Although KV cache compression methods (Qin et al., 2023; Corallo and Papotti, 2024) have demonstrated significant context compression by retaining subsets of relevant tokens, these techniques have yet to be adapted for structured data. This work, therefore, represents the first exploration of KV cache compression tailored to tabular inputs.

2 Background

Given a sequence of n tokens $\mathbf{x} \in \mathbb{R}^n$, each transformer layer produces hidden representations via a multi-head self-attention mechanism:

$$\text{Attention}(\mathbf{Q}, \mathbf{K}, \mathbf{V}) = \text{softmax}\Big(\frac{\mathbf{Q}\mathbf{K}^\top}{\sqrt{d_k}}\Big)\,\mathbf{V},$$

where $\mathbf{Q} = \mathbf{W}^Q\mathbf{h}, \mathbf{K} = \mathbf{W}^K\mathbf{h}, \mathbf{V} = \mathbf{W}^V\mathbf{h}$, with $\mathbf{h}$ representing the hidden states (token embeddings) for the input sequence. The dimension d_k is $\frac{d}{H}$ where d is the hidden size and H is the number of attention heads. Most LLMs organize their input as a context followed by a prompt. Let $\mathbf{x}$ denote a sequence of tokens and the input sequence: $\mathbf{x} = \Big[\ \mathbf{x}^{(\text{cont})},\ \mathbf{x}^{(\text{prompt})}\Big] \in \mathbb{R}^{n^{(\text{cont})}+n^{(\text{prompt})}}$, where $\mathbf{x}^{(\text{cont})}$ serves as the knowledge (i.e., the table) the model has access to when generating the final response. During inference, an LLM operates in two phases. In the Prefill Stage, the model processes the entire input sequence $\mathbf{x}$ and caches the KV matrices for each layer $\mathbf{K} \in \mathbb{R}^{n\times d}, \mathbf{V} \in \mathbb{R}^{n\times d}$. In the Generation Stage, for each new token y_j, the model computes autoregressively $\mathbf{q}^{\text{new}}, \mathbf{k}^{\text{new}}, \mathbf{v}^{\text{new}} \in \mathbb{R}^{1\times d}$, and updates the KV cache. With the cached KV matrices, self-attention complexity reduces from $O(n^2d)$ to $O(nd)$. However, storing these matrices for every layer is memory intensive. To mitigate the memory load from very long contexts, one approach is *KV cache compression*. Instead of retaining $\mathbf{K}, \mathbf{V}$ for all n tokens, one compresses them into smaller matrices $\widetilde{\mathbf{K}} \in \mathbb{R}^{k\times d}$ and $\widetilde{\mathbf{V}} \in \mathbb{R}^{k\times d}$ with $k \ll n$, that preserve the information needed for generating the response, i.e., $\min_{\widetilde{\mathbf{K}}, \widetilde{\mathbf{V}}}\Big[\text{dist}\big(\mathbf{y} \mid \mathbf{K}, \mathbf{V},\ \mathbf{y} \mid \widetilde{\mathbf{K}}, \widetilde{\mathbf{V}}\big)\Big]$, where $\mathbf{y}$ is the model's output.

To introduce compression, we detail a *query-aware* approach that compresses the KV cache by retaining only the most relevant KV vectors for the query given at inference time (Corallo and Papotti, 2024). Let m be the chunk length, and let $\{\mathbf{c}_1, \mathbf{c}_2, \dots\}$ be the segments obtained by slicing the input table $\mathbf{x}^{(\text{cont})}$. At iteration i, the method takes as input

$$\Big[\ \underbrace{\widetilde{\mathbf{K}}_{i-1}, \widetilde{\mathbf{V}}_{i-1}}_{\text{previous compressed cache}},\ \underbrace{\mathbf{c}_i}_{\text{current chunk}},\ \underbrace{\mathbf{q}}_{\text{question}}\ \Big],$$

where $\widetilde{\mathbf{K}}_{i-1}, \widetilde{\mathbf{V}}_{i-1} \in \mathbb{R}^{k\times d}$ denote the compressed cache from the previous iteration, $\mathbf{c}_i \in \mathbb{R}^{m\times d}$ is the chunk of context for the current iteration, and $\mathbf{q} \in \mathbb{R}^{q\times d}$ is the question to be answered.

During the forward pass, the multi-head attention scores are computed. The cross-attention submatrix $\mathbf{W}^{(\mathbf{q},\mathbf{c})} \in \mathbb{R}^{q\times(k+m)}$, captures how each question token attends to both the previous cache and the current chunk. The method then selects the top k token positions (according to the highest attention scores in $\mathbf{W}^{(\mathbf{q},\mathbf{c})}$) to form $\widetilde{\mathbf{K}}_i, \widetilde{\mathbf{V}}_i$. Here, k is a user-defined global budget that stays constant across iterations.

After processing all chunks, the final $\widetilde{\mathbf{K}}, \widetilde{\mathbf{V}} \in \mathbb{R}^{k\times d}$ provide a global representation of the entire context, at a reduced length. *Agnostic* methods use similar principles but in a single offline computation of the cache, thus without making use of the query. For example, Ada Expected Attention scores are computed by modeling the distribution of queries and estimating their interaction with key vectors at future positions (Jegou et al., 2024), in conjunction with head-specific compression (Feng et al., 2025).

3 KV Compression for Tables

Handling structured data in LLMs remains a significant challenge due to the quadratic complexity of self-attention and limited context windows. Another challenge is capturing interconnections between tuples. For example, consider a table containing sales data. Answering a query such as `SELECT region, SUM(sales) FROM table GROUP BY region` requires capturing information across multiple tuples. Retrieval methods may fall short by only selecting isolated tuples or columns, missing the holistic relational context necessary for accurate aggregations.

KV cache compression, initially introduced for general LLM inference, presents a promising opportunity for tabular data. The key insight of KV compression is straightforward: after linearizing a structured table into a textual representation, standard mechanisms within transformers naturally encode relevance and information importance within attention scores. When selecting KV vectors from the cache, these vectors inherently contain latent information representing broader relational context, including information from vectors that have been evicted. Thus, rather than employing separate retrieval systems or encoding mechanisms tailored specifically for tables, we hypothesize that LLMs themselves inherently identify critical elements of linearized tables directly through attention patterns.

We explore two types of compression for linearized tabular data. *(1) Query-aware compression* dynamically compresses the cache during inference by retaining KV vectors with the highest attention scores relative to a specific question. *(2) Query-agnostic compression* pre-computes a representation of the cache independently of a specific query, capturing general information from the table.

4 Experimental Setting

Datasets. We consider three datasets. In all cases, we linearize the input table as a string with a list of lists: the first element is the table header and each subsequent sub-list is a tuple in the table. This approach outperforms or is comparable to alternative serializations. **Spider** (Yu et al., 2019) is primarily used for Text2SQL and its dev split contains 1,034 examples, each using one or more tables. We generate our ground truth by executing the SQL queries on the corresponding tables. In cases involving multiple tables, we concatenate their linearized representations sequentially, prepending the name of each table before its content. **WikitableQA** (Pasupat and Liang, 2015) and **QTSumm** (Zhao et al., 2023) focus on question answering and query-focused summarization, respectively, with answers in natural language. We use their evaluation splits. Both datasets operate on a single table at a time.

Metrics. We use different evaluation metrics depending on the task. For Spider, we assess the generated output tables with four metrics from the literature (Papicchio et al., 2023): Cell Precision and Recall, Tuple Constraint, and Execution Accuracy. For the WikitableQA dataset, we evaluate outputs with Accuracy (Pasupat and Liang, 2015). For QTSumm, we rely on ROUGE-L (Lin, 2004)

LLMs. We use **LLaMA-3.1-8B-Instruct** (Touvron et al., 2023) and **Qwen-2.5-7B** (Yang et al., 2024). Both models are used in a few-shot setting, where we prepend task-specific instructions, defining expected input and output formats along with two examples. Additionally, we enforce a fixed maximum number of output tokens (the maximum number of tokens in the ground truth), to ensure fair comparisons and prevent overly long generations.

Methods. For compression, we report results for a query-aware method, **Finch** (Corallo and Papotti, 2024), a query-agnostic one, **Ada Expected Attention**, and a **RAG** approach similar to those in (Lin et al., 2023; Sui et al., 2023). We chunk the tables into tuples and iteratively select them based on their relevance to the question, until the number of tokens aligns with the context length used in the compression methods - we use BGE-BASE-1.5-EN (Xiao et al., 2023) as embedding model. We also report results for a baseline for the full-context setting, i.e., input table without compression.[1]

5 Results

In Tables 1a and 1b, we report results for all methods on WikiTableQA and QTSumm, respectively. Based on the tables' average length in each dataset, we select different target context lengths, obtaining compression rates between 1.7x and 51.39x (average context length in Spider is 13158 tokens).

[1]We do not report results for the execution with the base model only (no tuples in the context) because of low performance, e.g., 1.80 accuracy for WikiTableQA.

Model	Context Length	Finch	Ada EA	RAG
Llama-3.1-8B-Instruct	1024 (1.7x)	**35.11**	34.16	29.09
	512 (3.35x)	**34.92**	32.16	28.00
	256 (6.71x)	**33.59**	28.66	24.05
	128 (13.43x)	**30.02**	21.94	9.82
	Full context		35.08	
Qwen2.5-7B-Instruct	1024 (1.91x)	**29.72**	29.17	29.27
	512 (3.83x)	**28.80**	28.22	28.59
	256 (7.66x)	**27.07**	23.30	23.04
	128 (15.31x)	**23.49**	15.24	9.96
	Full context		30.04	

(a) WikiTableQA

Model	Context Length	Finch	Ada EA	RAG
Llama-3.1-8B-Instruct	512 (2.5x)	**30.61**	30.59	26.67
	256 (5x)	**29.78**	29.74	24.32
	128 (10x)	**26**	25.85	19.23
	64 (20x)	**21.86**	20.75	12.14
	Full context		30.56	
Qwen2.5-7B-Instruct	512 (2.85x)	29.82	**30.01**	26.58
	256 (5.70x)	28.62	**29.39**	24.32
	128 (11.40x)	**25.75**	24.71	19.69
	64 (22.78x)	**23.54**	19.57	16.07
	Full context		29.96	

(b) QTSumm

Table 1: Performance of Finch, Ada Expected Attention, and RAG on **WikiTableQA** (left) and **QTSumm** (right) across various target context lengths; "Full context" at the bottom of each block shows the full table input result.

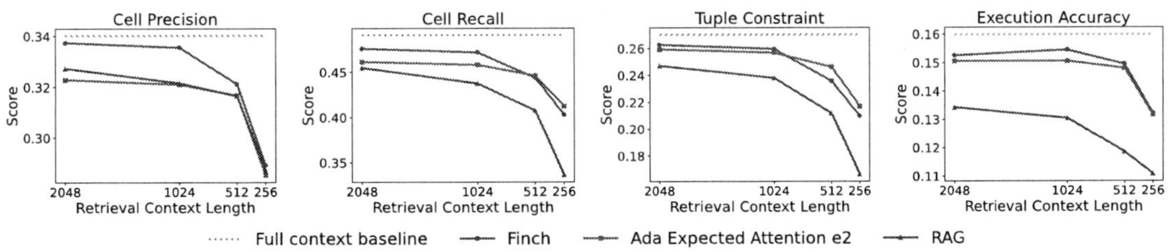

(a) Llama-3.1-8B-Instruct, compression rate varies between 5.66x and 45.30x.

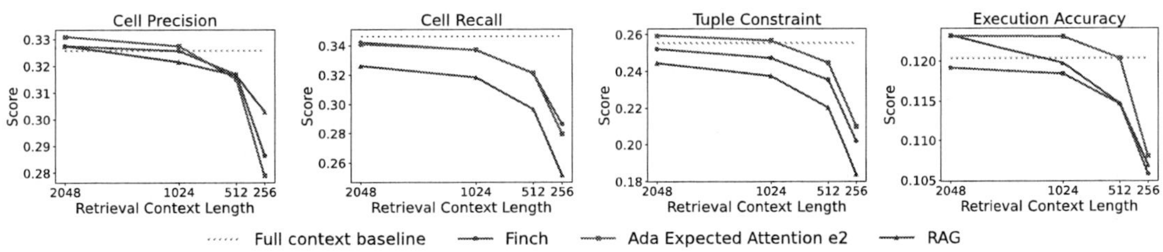

(b) Qwen2.5-7B-Instruct, compression rate varies between 6.42x and 51.39x.

Figure 2: Performance of Finch, Ada Expected Attention, and RAG on the **Spider** dataset for two LLMs.

Overall, KV compression methods outperform the RAG-based approach in most scenarios, and in several cases, achieve better results than the full-context setup. Finch achieves strong results on WikiTableQA: with LLaMA-3.1-8B-Instruct, it obtains an Accuracy of 35.11 at a compression rate of 1.7× (1024 tokens), which is significantly higher than the other approaches, including full context. With QTSumm, compression methods yield results that are either better or very close to those of the full-context case, with compression (e.g., 30.61 for Finch with LLaMA-3.1-8B-Instruct and 30.01 for Ada with Qwen-2.5-7B).

In the Spider dataset's results in Figure 2a, query-aware compression reports promising results for Llama, outperforming the row retrieval-based strategy in all cases. Moving to Spider on Qwen in Figure 2b, RAG and Ada (agnostic) are more competitive and even surpass the full-context scenario. In this scenario, Finch reports strong performance in terms of Precision, Recall, and Tuple Constraint, but lower scores for Execution Accuracy.

In terms of execution-time, query-agnostic KV cache compression delivers faster inference than RAG, while query-aware compression similarly to full-context decoding (Corallo et al., 2025).

6 Conclusion and Future Work

This work shows that KV cache compression can outperform RAG and match full-context performance, offering a promising technique for processing tables directly within LLMs. Future research includes developing table-specific compression strategies beyond adapting existing methods and investigating the interplay between table/query complexity and compression effectiveness. Finally, we plan to examine hybrid approaches combining KV compression with lightweight retrieval.

References

Rami Aly, Zhijiang Guo, Michael Schlichtkrull, James Thorne, Andreas Vlachos, Christos Christodoulopoulos, Oana Cocarascu, and Arpit Mittal. 2021. Feverous: Fact extraction and verification over unstructured and structured information. *Preprint*, arXiv:2106.05707.

Gilbert Badaro, Mohammed Saeed, and Paolo Papotti. 2023. Transformers for tabular data representation: A survey of models and applications. *Trans. Assoc. Comput. Linguistics*, 11:227–249.

Jan-Micha Bodensohn and Carsten Binnig. 2024. Rethinking table retrieval from data lakes. In *Proceedings of the Seventh International Workshop on Exploiting Artificial Intelligence Techniques for Data Management*, aiDM '24, New York, NY, USA. Association for Computing Machinery.

Si-An Chen, Lesly Miculicich, Julian Eisenschlos, Zifeng Wang, Zilong Wang, Yanfei Chen, Yasuhisa Fujii, Hsuan-Tien Lin, Chen-Yu Lee, and Tomas Pfister. 2024. Tablerag: Million-token table understanding with language models. *Advances in Neural Information Processing Systems*, 37:74899–74921.

Giulio Corallo and Paolo Papotti. 2024. Finch: Prompt-guided key-value cache compression for large language models. *Transactions of the Association for Computational Linguistics*, 12:1517–1532.

Giulio Corallo, Orion Weller, Fabio Petroni, and Paolo Papotti. 2025. Beyond rag: Task-aware kv cache compression for comprehensive knowledge reasoning. *Preprint*, arXiv:2503.04973.

Naihao Deng, Zhenjie Sun, Ruiqi He, Aman Sikka, Yulong Chen, Lin Ma, Yue Zhang, and Rada Mihalcea. 2024. Tables as texts or images: Evaluating the table reasoning ability of llms and mllms. *arXiv preprint arXiv:2402.12424*.

Yuan Feng, Junlin Lv, Yukun Cao, Xike Xie, and S. Kevin Zhou. 2025. Ada-kv: Optimizing kv cache eviction by adaptive budget allocation for efficient llm inference. *Preprint*, arXiv:2407.11550.

Simon Jegou, Maximilian Jeblick, and David Austin. 2024. kvpress.

Xingyu Ji, Aditya Parameswaran, and Madelon Hulsebos. 2024. TARGET: Benchmarking table retrieval for generative tasks. In *NeurIPS 2024 Third Table Representation Learning Workshop*.

Chin-Yew Lin. 2004. ROUGE: A package for automatic evaluation of summaries. In *Text Summarization Branches Out*, pages 74–81, Barcelona, Spain. Association for Computational Linguistics.

Weizhe Lin, Rexhina Blloshmi, Bill Byrne, Adria de Gispert, and Gonzalo Iglesias. 2023. An inner table retriever for robust table question answering. In *Proceedings of the 61st Annual Meeting of the Association for Computational Linguistics (Volume 1: Long Papers)*, pages 9909–9926, Toronto, Canada. Association for Computational Linguistics.

Nelson F Liu, Kevin Lin, John Hewitt, Ashwin Paranjape, Michele Bevilacqua, Fabio Petroni, and Percy Liang. 2024. Lost in the middle: How language models use long contexts. *Transactions of the Association for Computational Linguistics*, 12:157–173.

Simone Papicchio, Paolo Papotti, and Luca Cagliero. 2023. QATCH: Benchmarking SQL-centric tasks with table representation learning models on your data. In *Thirty-seventh Conference on Neural Information Processing Systems Datasets and Benchmarks Track*.

Panupong Pasupat and Percy Liang. 2015. Compositional semantic parsing on semi-structured tables. *Preprint*, arXiv:1508.00305.

Guanghui Qin, Corby Rosset, Ethan C Chau, Nikhil Rao, and Benjamin Van Durme. 2023. Dodo: Dynamic contextual compression for decoder-only lms. *arXiv preprint arXiv:2310.02409*.

Dario Satriani, Enzo Veltri, Donatello Santoro, and Paolo Papotti. 2025. Relationalfactqa: A benchmark for evaluating tabular fact retrieval from large language models. *arXiv preprint arXiv:2505.21409*.

Yuan Sui, Jiaru Zou, Mengyu Zhou, Xinyi He, Lun Du, Shi Han, and Dongmei Zhang. 2023. Tap4llm: Table provider on sampling, augmenting, and packing semi-structured data for large language model reasoning. *arXiv preprint arXiv:2312.09039*.

Yuzhang Tian, Jianbo Zhao, Haoyu Dong, Junyu Xiong, Shiyu Xia, Mengyu Zhou, Yun Lin, José Cambronero, Yeye He, Shi Han, and 1 others. 2024. Spreadsheetllm: encoding spreadsheets for large language models. *arXiv preprint arXiv:2407.09025*.

Hugo Touvron, Thibaut Lavril, Gautier Izacard, Xavier Martinet, Marie-Anne Lachaux, Timothée Lacroix, Baptiste Rozière, Naman Goyal, Eric Hambro, Faisal Azhar, Aurelien Rodriguez, Armand Joulin, Edouard Grave, and Guillaume Lample. 2023. Llama: Open and efficient foundation language models. *Preprint*, arXiv:2302.13971.

Shitao Xiao, Zheng Liu, Peitian Zhang, and Niklas Muennighoff. 2023. C-pack: Packaged resources to advance general chinese embedding. *Preprint*, arXiv:2309.07597.

An Yang, Baosong Yang, Beichen Zhang, Binyuan Hui, Bo Zheng, Bowen Yu, Chengyuan Li, Dayiheng Liu, Fei Huang, Haoran Wei, Huan Lin, Jian Yang, Jianhong Tu, Jianwei Zhang, Jianxin Yang, Jiaxi Yang, Jingren Zhou, Junyang Lin, Kai Dang, and 22 others. 2024. Qwen2.5 technical report. *arXiv preprint arXiv:2412.15115*.

Tao Yu, Rui Zhang, Kai Yang, Michihiro Yasunaga, Dongxu Wang, Zifan Li, James Ma, Irene Li, Qingning Yao, Shanelle Roman, Zilin Zhang, and Dragomir Radev. 2019. Spider: A large-scale human-labeled dataset for complex and cross-domain semantic parsing and text-to-sql task. *Preprint*, arXiv:1809.08887.

Yilun Zhao, Zhenting Qi, Linyong Nan, Boyu Mi, Yixin Liu, Weijin Zou, Simeng Han, Ruizhe Chen, Xiangru Tang, Yumo Xu, Dragomir Radev, and Arman Cohan. 2023. Qtsumm: Query-focused summarization over tabular data. *Preprint*, arXiv:2305.14303.

OrQA – OpenData Retrieval for Question Answering Dataset Generation

Giovanni Malaguti
University of Modena
and Reggio Emilia, Italy
giovanni.malaguti@unimore.it

Angelo Mozzillo
University of Modena
and Reggio Emilia, Italy
angelo.mozzillo@unimore.it

Giovanni Simonini
University of Modena
and Reggio Emilia, Italy
giovanni.simonini@unimore.it

Abstract

We present OrQA, a novel agentic framework to generate large-scale tabular question-answering (TQA) datasets based on real-world open data. Such datasets are needed to overcome the limitations of existing benchmark datasets, which rely on synthetic questions or limited web tables. OrQA employs LLM agents to retrieve related open data tables, generate natural questions, and synthesize executable SQL queries—involving joins, unions, and other non-trivial operations. By leveraging hundreds of GPU hours on four NVIDIA A100, we applied OrQA to Canadian and UK government open data to produce 1,000 question-tables–SQL triples, a representative sample of which has been human-validated. This open-source dataset is now publicly available to drive transparency, reproducibility, and progress in table-based question answering.

1 Introduction

The Open Data initiative aims to ensure transparency and foster informed civic engagement—e.g., for accessing data related to public policy outcomes or monitoring phenomena of interest. Such initiatives have significantly increased the availability of publicly accessible tabular and structured datasets, often referred to as open data lakes, many of which are accessible through web portals that facilitate discovery and reuse. However, these open datasets are typically published with highly heterogeneous schemas, making their integration into structured relational databases challenging. As a result, identifying tables that can be meaningfully joined or unioned remains a difficult task, limiting the ability to extract comprehensive insights across multiple datasets. Furthermore, to fully democratize the access to open data a Tabular Question Answering (TQA) approach is desirable, allowing users to issue queries through natural language interfaces, removing technical barriers for the user, such as query languages and data schema understanding.

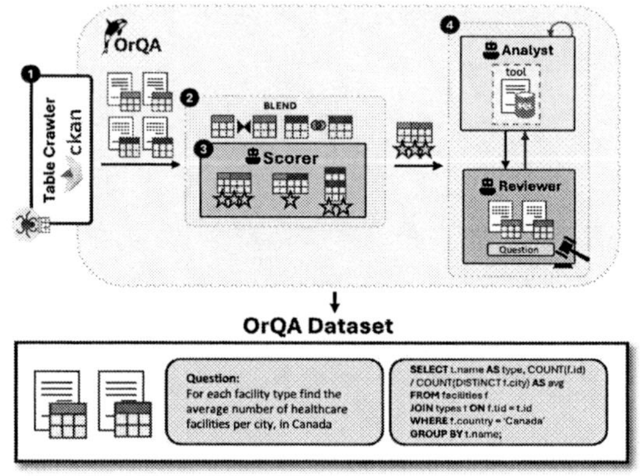

Figure 1: OrQA workflow: 1) Crawl tables; 2) Join/Union table-pairs discovery; 3) pairs scoring with the Scorer agent; 4) Analyst and Reviewer agents generate SQL and NL questions.

TQA has emerged as a crucial task in natural language processing, enabling models to answer questions using tabular data (Zhu et al., 2024). TQA tasks can be divided into two main categories: *(i)* the older one, fine-tuning specialized models tailored specifically for this task (Herzig et al., 2020; Yin et al., 2020; Liu et al., 2022; Zhou et al., 2022); *(ii)* the newer one, utilizes LLMs to generate code capable of manipulating tabular data (Yin et al., 2023; Liu et al., 2024; Zhang et al., 2024). While these new LLM-based approaches have shown impressive performance in reasoning over a single table—where all pertinent information is self-contained—they often struggle in more complex scenarios that require reasoning across multiple tables, including operations such as joins and unions, which are essential for handling real-world data (Zhu et al., 2024). Moreover, although LLMs have demonstrated robust capabilities across various natural language tasks, their evaluation has largely been confined to QA datasets derived from small, web-based tables (Pasupat and Liang, 2015; Iyyer et al., 2017; Zhong et al., 2017; Nan

Proceedings of the 4th Table Representation Learning Workshop, pages 172–181
July 31, 2025 ©2025 Association for Computational Linguistics

et al., 2022). This limitation arises from two key challenges. First, real-world multi-table datasets are not widely available, as many remain private due to confidentiality concerns (Hulsebos et al., 2023; Vogel et al., 2024). Second, dataset creation has traditionally relied on crowdsourcing, which, while effective, is slow, expensive, and difficult to scale (Long et al., 2024).

LLMs have shown great potential to generate synthetic datasets, providing a scalable alternative to costly human annotation. They can create diverse training data that better reflects real-world challenges, which is critical for model development (Long et al., 2024). As a pivotal application of LLMs, synthetic data generation holds significant importance for the development of new LLMs (Long et al., 2024). As of April 2025, over 519 tabular datasets on Hugging Face are labeled as *synthetic*[1] and have been employed for fine-tuning or reinforcement learning applications (Guo et al., 2025). Yet, ensuring both high accuracy and sufficient variety in these datasets is challenging. Thus, careful design and specific techniques are required to guide the generation process toward the desired outcomes.

Our Contributions

We present the **O**pen Data **r**etrieval and **Q**uestion **A**nswering (OrQA)[2] datasets generation workflow, designed to create large-scale and completely new datasets for end-to-end TQA evaluation using tabular content from Open Data sources. We also present a dataset generated with OrQA, which covers tables obtained from the Open Data portals of Canada[3] and UK[4]. The dataset includes questions expressed in natural language, each of which is associated with: *(i)* the table or set of tables containing the required information (useful for evaluating the retrieval phase of a TQA system); *(ii)* the SQL query to obtain the answer from the table(s) (useful for evaluating the generation phase of a TQA system); *(iii)* a set of statistics for analysis and inspections.

We built OrQA by designing an agentic workflow that exploits state-of-the-art data discovery techniques to select high-quality joinable and unionable tables, which are employed as seeds for generating synthetic pairs of natural language questions and SQL queries with LLMs agents—as described in the following.

2 OrQA Overview

The OrQA workflow is designed to be easily applied to any Open Data portal and allows the user to create a new dataset given a specific Open Data endpoint. OrQA is composed of four main steps, listed hereafter and explained afterward:

1. *Data Crawling*: to download both tables and metadata from a given Open Data endpoint;
2. *Candidate Table Pair Search*: to yield candidate pairs of related tables discovered through data discovery tool;
3. *Candidate Evaluation*: to evaluate the candidate table pairs with a multi-agent debate mechanism to filter casual and unmeaningful cases;
4. *Question Generation*: the accepted pairs are used as input to create the final dataset.

Data Crawling. During the first step, the user specifies the Open Data endpoint of interest exposing CKAN API [5], and from there, tables and relative metadata are downloaded and stored for the next steps.

Candidate Table Pair Search. Data discovery algorithms from the BLEND framework (Esmailoghli et al., 2024) are applied to identify candidate pairs of related tables, which could be merged with a `join` or `union` operation. BLEND is a general-purpose framework for table discovery in data lakes; after an indexing stage of the available tables, it can efficiently retrieve results, based on overlap metrics, related to a given query table. In the OrQA workflow, each column of every table is used as an input seed for BLEND, which returns K candidate tables. This search could be limited up to a user-specified budget. In initial experiments, we observed that filtering less informative columns was necessary to reduce noise Thus, for the datasets generated for this paper, we filtered out columns with less than 10 unique values and 30 rows, or more than 80% of missing values.

Candidate Evaluation. An agentic step is performed to assess for each candidate pair whether the two tables are meaningfully related or not. A team of AI agents assigns a numerical relatedness

[1] https://huggingface.co/datasets?modality=modality:tabular&other=synthetic
[2] https://anonymous.4open.science/r/orqa-B4BD
[3] https://open.canada.ca
[4] https://www.data.gov.uk/
[5] https://docs.ckan.org/en/latest

score θ	over θ pairs	
	UK	CAN
6	952	807
7	938	755
8	902	551
9	160	256
10	0	0

Table 1: Candidate join pairs evaluated with a score equal of higher than the threshold, on a sample of 1000 pairs.

score (on a scale from 0 to 10, the highest being the most related) to each pair, using a description of each table, a small sample of rows, and other available metadata obtained from Open Data portals. Only pairs that achieve a score higher than a predefined threshold θ are retained for the final generation phase.

To assess this scoring system, user feedbacks were collected over a sample of 100 random candidate pairs from the UK dataset. The results showed an average difference of just 0.43 between human and agent team scores, with a standard deviation of 1.45, p-value 0.0038. These findings suggest that the agent-based evaluation scoring appears to be comparable to the user's when assessing how much a couple of tables is related to limited information and domain knowledge. In our experiments, we set the minimum score θ to 8—as seen in Table 1—which significantly reduces the total number of pairs that need to be processed in the final computational step.

Question Generation. An agentic workflow is implemented to generate the final output: a team of agents—composed of a natural language question generator, a text-to-SQL coder, and relative reviewers—is responsible for creating both an SQL query and the corresponding natural language question. For each pair of unionable or joinable tables validated in the previous steps, the team of agents produces queries and questions for single and multi-table cases. The coder agent receives in input the tables' metadata, a sample of their rows, and the other specifications for the current task; then it generates an SQL query, verifying its syntax through a dedicated tool. Once the query is created, the question generator agent outputs a natural language question that accurately represents the query's intent. In both these previously described stages, a reviewer evaluates the generated output: until specific requirements are not satisfied, it asks the relative generator agent to refine its output, providing suggestions for improvement. To prevent excessively long computations when the generator

source	tables	# rows		# columns	
		avg	stdev	avg	stdev
UK	24404	22747	174497	52	628
CAN	31437	141714	1405456	17	168

Table 2: Statistics of the crawled tables.

difficulty	type	#queries
simple	single-table	208
	multi-table	104
moderate	single-table	272
	multi-table	97
challenging	single-table	236
	multi-table	83

Table 3: Generated queries per difficult level and type.

agent repeatedly fails, a maximum number of reviews is set. In every natural language question, it is ensured that useful references for retrieval tasks on the Open Data portals are inserted—such as remainders to significant keywords or to the organization that created the resource. We applied OrQA with a maximum of 3 review cycles, a choice that balances efficiency and accuracy, as additional cycles yielded diminishing returns. Additionally, given that many tables may contain a large number of columns, we restrict the agent's context to the first to the first 20 columns—appending any necessary columns as required. This assumes the first 20 columns contain enough information to generate meaningful queries.

3 Generated Dataset

By employing OrQA, we generated a dataset consisting of 1,000 natural language questions and corresponding ground truth, derived from both UK and Canada (CAN) open data portals—Table 2 reports statistics collected from these portals.

To generate the dataset, we employed a GPU node equipped with 4 NVIDIA A100 GPUs, each of them with 40 GB of memory. We opted for Qwen2.5 (Yang et al., 2025) family models as LLMs for the evaluation and generation steps. In particular, we used Qwen2.5-7b for the evaluation team agents and Qwen2.5-32b and Qwen2.5-coder-32b for the Natural Language and SQL generation agents, respectively. With this setup, the creation of the dataset from data crawling to the generation of the final questions required almost 100 hours of total computation, with a large part of these dedicated to crawling, indexing and candidate search.

Following (Li et al., 2024), we divided SQL queries into three main categories, *simple*, *moderate* and *challenging*, specifying to the coder agent for each category what we expect, from simple filtering clauses to window functions, grouping and

measure	group	2013	2016
canada child benefit	refundable tax credit classified as transfer payment	""	"16860"
employee benefit plans	tax expenditure	"n.a."	"n.a."
logging tax credit	tax expenditure	"15"	"25"

Table 4: Example rows from one Open Data table. The columns "2013" and "2014" are not recognized by default as numeric columns.

```
SELECT measure , \"group\" , SUM(
    CASE WHEN regexp_matches(
            \"2013\" , '^\\d+$')
        THEN CAST(\"2013\" AS INTEGER)
        ELSE 0 END
    ) AS total_2013
FROM r_df GROUP BY measure , \"group\"
```

Listing 1: Example query with data wrangling operation. label

subqueries. Table 3 reports distributions of the difficult levels for the generated collection. In addition to the question-query pairs, we provide several metadata, which are valuable for future evaluations of workflow efficiency. These include the number of review, the time taken to generate both SQL and natural language queries, and the number of tokens exchanged by the underlying LLMs. We also report the details of the final review and, in cases of SQL generation failure, the error message from the database engine to facilitate failure analysis.

Online Data Wrangling. One burdening challenge when working with Open Data is to extract meaningful information while facing data-wrangling issues. In OrQA, the agent team itself—in particular the pair of coder and code reviewer—attempts to dynamically wrangle the desired columns during query generation. As an example, the table 4 contains the columns "2013" and "2014", whose values are initially recognized as strings, due to the presence of missing values (like *"n.a."*) and the empty string *""* in the same column. By interacting and analyzing the query output, the agents are able to generate an SQL query that solves this issue, as shown in listing 1.

4 Related Work

Text-to-SQL and Fact verification are well-known topics in the literature, and several datasets have been proposed and tested across different systems and scenarios. Notable among these are Spider (Lei et al., 2025) and BIRD (Li et al., 2024), two comprehensive Text-to-SQL benchmark datasets with a wide range of difficult tasks based on real-world data. However, they assume that the tables or databases where needed information is stored are already provided. As Retrieval Augmented Generation (RAG) systems gain relevance, there is the need to address the retrieval phase with dedicated tabular benchmark datasets. While datasets such as CRAG (Yang et al., 2024) and MTEB (Muennighoff et al., 2023) focus on text embedding, TARGET (Ji et al., 2024) represents a first step toward benchmarking table retrieval. Its evaluates model performance using embedding-based retrieval systems, assuming that tables are totally indexed. However, in many real-world scenarios with limited resources, making a complete pre-indexing stage is unfeasible. Open Data are a significant example of this case: their dynamic nature and scale make it difficult to incorporate them into static datasets, but their content could address several types of use-cases. Final users, such as public administrations or private citizens, typically need to extract information from them without performing large computations. Although Open Data have been widely used in previous years in the data discovery literature, prior work has not focused on downstream tasks, only on finding related tables. In particular, LakeBench (Deng et al., 2024) is a benchmark dataset for joinable and unionable table discovery methods, which limits its scope to identify subsets of related results given a query table. Like OrQA, during benchmark preparation it uses established data discovery tools to generate candidate pairs of related tables, but in that case a large human effort is used to evaluate them, while in OrQA this is fully automated.

5 Conclusion and Future Work

We present OrQA, an agentic workflow to generate new datasets for retrieval and question-answering model evaluation based on Open Data tables. With OrQA, we generated a dataset composed of 1,000 questions, which can be employed as realistic benchmark for RAG systems targeting TQA on Open Data.

We believe that our effort paves the way for further research, since several open challenges have not yet been addressed. For instance, semantic-aware data discovery tools could provide more interesting candidates for question generation. Additionally, the current workflow covers only questions that involve one or two tables, while users' needs may require more complex patterns. Furthermore, different datasets might correctly address the same question and should be considered in the ground truth.

Acknowledgments

We warmly thank Leonardo S.p.A., co-funding the PhD programs of Giovanni Malaguti and Angelo Mozzillo. Further, this work was partially supported by MUR within the project "Discount Quality for Responsible Data Science: Human-in-the-Loop for Quality Data" (code 202248FWFS).

References

Yuhao Deng, Chengliang Chai, Lei Cao, Qin Yuan, Siyuan Chen, Yanrui Yu, Zhaoze Sun, Junyi Wang, Jiajun Li, Ziqi Cao, Kaisen Jin, Chi Zhang, Yuqing Jiang, Yuanfang Zhang, Yuping Wang, Ye Yuan, Guoren Wang, and Nan Tang. 2024. Lakebench: A benchmark for discovering joinable and unionable tables in data lakes. *Proc. VLDB Endow.*, 17(8):1925–1938.

Mahdi Esmailoghli, Christoph Schnell, Renée J. Miller, and Ziawasch Abedjan. 2024. Blend: A unified data discovery system. *Preprint*, arXiv:2310.02656.

Daya Guo, Dejian Yang, Haowei Zhang, Junxiao Song, Ruoyu Zhang, Runxin Xu, Qihao Zhu, Shirong Ma, Peiyi Wang, Xiao Bi, and 1 others. 2025. Deepseek-r1: Incentivizing reasoning capability in llms via reinforcement learning. *arXiv preprint arXiv:2501.12948*.

Jonathan Herzig, Pawel Krzysztof Nowak, Thomas Müller, Francesco Piccinno, and Julian Martin Eisenschlos. 2020. Tapas: Weakly supervised table parsing via pre-training. In *Proceedings of the 58th Annual Meeting of the Association for Computational Linguistics, ACL 2020, Online, July 5-10, 2020*, pages 4320–4333. Association for Computational Linguistics.

Madelon Hulsebos, Çagatay Demiralp, and Paul Groth. 2023. Gittables: A large-scale corpus of relational tables. *Proc. ACM Manag. Data*, 1(1).

Mohit Iyyer, Wen-tau Yih, and Ming-Wei Chang. 2017. Search-based neural structured learning for sequential question answering. In *Proceedings of the 55th Annual Meeting of the Association for Computational Linguistics (Volume 1: Long Papers)*, pages 1821–1831.

Xingyu Ji, Aditya Parameswaran, and Madelon Hulsebos. 2024. TARGET: Benchmarking table retrieval for generative tasks. In *NeurIPS 2024 Third Table Representation Learning Workshop*.

Fangyu Lei, Jixuan Chen, Yuxiao Ye, Ruisheng Cao, Dongchan Shin, Hongjin Su, Zhaoqing Suo, Hongcheng Gao, Wenjing Hu, Pengcheng Yin, Victor Zhong, Caiming Xiong, Ruoxi Sun, Qian Liu, Sida Wang, and Tao Yu. 2025. Spider 2.0: Evaluating language models on real-world enterprise text-to-sql workflows. *Preprint*, arXiv:2411.07763.

Jinyang Li, Binyuan Hui, Ge Qu, Jiaxi Yang, Binhua Li, Bowen Li, Bailin Wang, Bowen Qin, Ruiying Geng, Nan Huo, and 1 others. 2024. Can llm already serve as a database interface? a big bench for large-scale database grounded text-to-sqls. *Advances in Neural Information Processing Systems*, 36.

Qian Liu, Bei Chen, Jiaqi Guo, Morteza Ziyadi, Zeqi Lin, Weizhu Chen, and Jian-Guang Lou. 2022. TAPEX: table pre-training via learning a neural SQL executor. In *The Tenth International Conference on Learning Representations, ICLR 2022, Virtual Event, April 25-29, 2022*. OpenReview.net.

Tianyang Liu, Fei Wang, and Muhao Chen. 2024. Rethinking tabular data understanding with large language models. In *Proceedings of the 2024 Conference of the North American Chapter of the Association for Computational Linguistics: Human Language Technologies (Volume 1: Long Papers)*, pages 450–482, Mexico City, Mexico. Association for Computational Linguistics.

Lin Long, Rui Wang, Ruixuan Xiao, Junbo Zhao, Xiao Ding, Gang Chen, and Haobo Wang. 2024. On LLMs-driven synthetic data generation, curation, and evaluation: A survey. In *Findings of the Association for Computational Linguistics: ACL 2024*, pages 11065–11082, Bangkok, Thailand. Association for Computational Linguistics.

Niklas Muennighoff, Nouamane Tazi, Loïc Magne, and Nils Reimers. 2023. Mteb: Massive text embedding benchmark. *Preprint*, arXiv:2210.07316.

Linyong Nan, Chiachun Hsieh, Ziming Mao, Xi Victoria Lin, Neha Verma, Rui Zhang, Wojciech Kryściński, Hailey Schoelkopf, Riley Kong, Xiangru Tang, and 1 others. 2022. Fetaqa: Free-form table question answering. *Transactions of the Association for Computational Linguistics*, 10:35–49.

Panupong Pasupat and Percy Liang. 2015. Compositional semantic parsing on semi-structured tables. In *Proceedings of the 53rd Annual Meeting of the Association for Computational Linguistics and the 7th International Joint Conference on Natural Language Processing (Volume 1: Long Papers)*, pages 1470–1480.

Liane Vogel, Jan-Micha Bodensohn, and Carsten Binnig. 2024. Wikidbs: A large-scale corpus of relational databases from wikidata. *Advances in Neural Information Processing Systems*, 37:41186–41201.

An Yang, Baosong Yang, Beichen Zhang, Binyuan Hui, Bo Zheng, Bowen Yu, Chengyuan Li, Dayiheng Liu, Fei Huang, Haoran Wei, Huan Lin, Jian Yang, Jianhong Tu, Jianwei Zhang, Jianxin Yang, Jiaxi Yang, Jingren Zhou, Junyang Lin, Kai Dang, and 23 others. 2025. Qwen2.5 technical report. *Preprint*, arXiv:2412.15115.

Xiao Yang, Kai Sun, Hao Xin, Yushi Sun, Nikita Bhalla, Xiangsen Chen, Sajal Choudhary, Rongze Daniel Gui, Ziran Will Jiang, Ziyu Jiang, Lingkun Kong,

Brian Moran, Jiaqi Wang, Yifan Ethan Xu, An Yan, Chenyu Yang, Eting Yuan, Hanwen Zha, Nan Tang, and 8 others. 2024. Crag – comprehensive rag benchmark. *arXiv preprint arXiv:2406.04744*.

Pengcheng Yin, Wen-Ding Li, Kefan Xiao, Abhishek Rao, Yeming Wen, Kensen Shi, Joshua Howland, Paige Bailey, Michele Catasta, Henryk Michalewski, Oleksandr Polozov, and Charles Sutton. 2023. Natural language to code generation in interactive data science notebooks. In *Proceedings of the 61st Annual Meeting of the Association for Computational Linguistics (Volume 1: Long Papers)*, pages 126–173, Toronto, Canada. Association for Computational Linguistics.

Pengcheng Yin, Graham Neubig, Wen-tau Yih, and Sebastian Riedel. 2020. Tabert: Pretraining for joint understanding of textual and tabular data. In *Proceedings of the 58th Annual Meeting of the Association for Computational Linguistics, ACL 2020, Online, July 5-10, 2020*, pages 8413–8426. Association for Computational Linguistics.

Yunjia Zhang, Jordan Henkel, Avrilia Floratou, Joyce Cahoon, Shaleen Deep, and Jignesh M. Patel. 2024. Reactable: Enhancing react for table question answering. *Proc. VLDB Endow.*, 17(8):1981–1994.

Victor Zhong, Caiming Xiong, and Richard Socher. 2017. Seq2sql: Generating structured queries from natural language using reinforcement learning. *arXiv preprint arXiv:1709.00103*.

Fan Zhou, Mengkang Hu, Haoyu Dong, Zhoujun Cheng, Fan Cheng, Shi Han, and Dongmei Zhang. 2022. Tacube: Pre-computing data cubes for answering numerical-reasoning questions over tabular data. In *Proceedings of the 2022 Conference on Empirical Methods in Natural Language Processing, EMNLP 2022, Abu Dhabi, United Arab Emirates, December 7-11, 2022*, pages 2278–2291. Association for Computational Linguistics.

Jun-Peng Zhu, Peng Cai, Kai Xu, Li Li, Yishen Sun, Shuai Zhou, Haihuang Su, Liu Tang, and Qi Liu. 2024. Autotqa: Towards autonomous tabular question answering through multi-agent large language models. *Proc. VLDB Endow.*, 17(12):3920–3933.

A Prompts

We provide below the main prompts passed to the agents in the different OrQA stages. The system and task prompts are concatenated.

```
evaluation_prompt = f""" \
    You are a helpful assistant in tabular data comprehension.
    Your task is to evaluate pairs of candidate tables
    for a SQL operation by providing a numerical score.
    If given, reason on other assistants observations.
    Limit your output to 50 words: your final answer should be
    a single integer number, between {self._min_score} and {self._max_score}.
    Respond with the form:
    Answer: <your numerical score here>
    Explanation: <your concise explanation>
    ---------------------------------------------------------------
    The table '{r_rsc_name}' belongs to the package '{r_pkg_name}'.
    This package is published by the organization '{r_org_name}',
    that is '{r_org_desc}', under the jurisdiction '{r_jur}'.
    The table description is: {r_pkg_notes}.
    Keywords and tags about it are: {r_pkg_keywords}, {r_pkg_tags}.
    Example rows with schema: {r_df_str}
    ---------------------------------------------------------------
    The table '{s_rsc_name}' belongs to the package '{s_pkg_name}'.
    This package is published by the organization '{s_org_name}',
    that is '{s_org_desc}', under the jurisdiction '{s_jur}'.
    The table description is: {s_pkg_notes}.
    Keywords and tags about it are: {s_pkg_keywords}, {s_pkg_tags}.
    Example rows: {s_df_str}
    ---------------------------------------------------------------
    Define a relationship quality score for the two tables.
    Focus on the meaningfulness of a potential operation between
    the given tables.
"""
```

Listing 2: Candidate table pair Evaluator agent system and initial task prompts.

```
debate_prompt = f""" \
    Using the evaluations from other agents as additional
    information, provide your score to the current table pairs.
    The original task is: {task}.
    These are the evaluations from other agents:
    One agent evaluation: {agent_evaluation}.
    ...
    One agent evaluation: {agent_evaluation}.
"""
```

Listing 3: Candidate table pair Evaluator agent inter-debate prompts.

```
query_generator_prompt = f""" \
    You are a SQL coder assistant. Your task is to generate SQL
    queries of different difficult levels.
    A 'simple' query involves just basic operations, like simple
    WHERE clauses.
    A 'moderate' query could use also casting, string replacement,
    grouping functions and other forms of aggregations.
    A 'challenging' query may require window functions, subqueries
    and other complex operations.
    You are using DuckDB: if necessary, put column names inside
    double-quotes, like "column_name".
    Do not cast FLOAT to REAL. If a VARCHAR attribute is similar
    to a datetime, try to cast it to DATE or DATETIME.
    When using regex operations, use proper options.
    Use the given tool to validate your SQL query: your response
    must be only a valid function call.
    ----------------------------------------------------------------
    Given the following information:
    Use 'R' to indicate the first table.
    Its schema is:
    {r_SQL_schema}
    Example rows of R table:
    {r_df_str}
    ----------------------------------------------------------------
    Use 'S' to indicate the second table.
    Its schema is:
    {s_SQL_schema}
    Example rows of S table:
    {s_df_str}
    ----------------------------------------------------------------
    Generate a {difficulty} SQL query based on the given tables.
    Use only 'R' and 'S' to reference the tables.
    The query must include a JOIN on the R column {r_col_name}
    and on the S column {s_col_name}.
    The new query must be different from previous queries:
    {prev_SQL}.
"""
```

Listing 4: SQL Generator agent system and task prompts to generate multi-table SQL queries involving a JOIN operation. Prompts for single and UNION queries are similar.

```
question_generator_prompt = f""" \
    Your task is to generate natural language questions, related
    to tables from Open Data.
    Pretend to be a user that is using Open Data search portals
    and needs to get answers.
    The questions you create must be fluent and human-like: do not
    use SQL-like words, such as null or select.
    Keep focus on join and union operations between tables, if any.
    If available and meaningful, use the given keywords and tags.
    Because a common Open Data user (as you, in this case) does
    not know anything in advance about the final result, you can't
    use terms like records, data, datasets, tables, csv, packages
    and resources.
    If values are used inside the SQL query, try to
    understand what they means based on the given context: for
    example, 'ref' may mean 'refused' in a column about orders
    status.
    You must not use explicit table or column names into the
    question.
    Your response must be only the question, nothing else.
    ------------------------------------------------------------
    Consider the following information:
    The table '{r_rsc_name}' belongs to the package '{r_pkg_name}'.
    This package is published by the organization
    '{r_org_name}', titled as '{r_org_title}' that is
    that is about '{r_org_desc}', under the jurisdiction '{r_jur}'.
    The table description is: {r_pkg_notes}.
    Keywords and tags about it are: {r_pkg_keywords}, {r_pkg_tags}.
    Example rows with schema: {r_df_str}
    ------------------------------------------------------------
    The table '{s_rsc_name}' belongs to the package '{s_pkg_name}'.
    This package is published by the organization
    '{s_org_name}', titled as '{s_org_title}' that is
    about '{s_org_desc}', under the jurisdiction '{s_jur}'.
    The table description is: {s_pkg_notes}.
    Keywords and tags about it are: {s_pkg_keywords}, {s_pkg_tags}.
    Example rows: {s_df_str}
    ------------------------------------------------------------
    Generate a natural language question which accurately
    represents the SQL query {sql} on the given tables
    and its aim.
    Pay attention to all the clauses used into the query.
    You must introduce into the question remainders to keywords,
    organization and other metadata.
"""
```

Listing 5: Natural Language question Generator agent system and task prompts to generate questions based on a multi-table operation.

```
query_reviewer_prompt = f""" \
    You are a query reviewer.
    You focus on the correctness of proposed SQL queries
    or Natural Language Questions.
    For the SQL, focus on the query syntax.
    Consider that is used DuckDB syntax.
    --------------------------------------------------------------
    The problem statement is:
    {message.SQL_task}
    The proposed SQL query is:
    {SQL_query}
    The execution of this query is:
    {execution_result}
    Previous feedback:
    {previous_feedback}
    Revise the query if the execution was not successful.
    In the query has given an error, check if:
    - Previous feedback was not addressed.
    - The query does not involve required columns (if any).
    - The query is identical to any previously generated query.
    Respond with the following format:
    ```json
    {
        "correctness": <Your comments>,
        "approval": <APPROVE or REVISE>,
        "suggested_changes": <Your comments>
    }
    ```
"""
```

Listing 6: SQL Reviewer system and task prompts.

```
quuestion_reviewer_prompt = f""" \
    You are a query reviewer.
    You focus on the correctness of proposed SQL queries
    or Natural Language Questions.
    For the SQL, focus on the query syntax.
    Consider that is used DuckDB syntax.
    --------------------------------------------------------------
    The problem statement is:
    {nl_task}
    The proposed Natural Language Question is:
    {nl_question}
    Previous feedback:
    {previous_feedback}
    Don't approve the question if:
    - Previous feedback was not addressed.
    - The question is too generic (like 'What is the average
      value?') or too simple (like 'Where is Canada?').
    - The question seems to be uncorrelated to the current task.
    - Columns and tables names are explicitly present into the
      question.
    - Columns required by the user are not correctly used (if any).
    - The question use too specific terms, like 'tables',
      'datasets', 'packages', 'data', 'records'.
    Respond with the following format:
    ```json
    {
        "correctness": <Your comments>,
        "approval": <APPROVE or REVISE>,
        "suggested_changes": <Your comments>
    }
    ```
"""
```

Listing 7: Natural Language question Reviewer system and task prompts.

In-Context Learning of Soft Nearest Neighbor Classifiers for Intelligible Tabular Machine Learning

Mykhailo Koshil[1] **Matthias Feurer**[2,3] **Katharina Eggensperger**[1]
[1]University of Tübingen
[2]Department of Statistics, LMU Munich
[3]Munich Center for Machine Learning
first.last@uni-tuebingen.de, first.last@stat.uni-muenchen.de

Abstract

With in-context learning foundation models like TabPFN excelling on small supervised tabular learning tasks, it has been argued that "boosted trees are not the best default choice when working with data in tables".[1] However, such foundation models are inherently black-box models that do not provide interpretable predictions. We introduce a novel learning task to train ICL models to act as a nearest neighbor algorithm, which enables intelligible inference and does not decrease performance empirically.

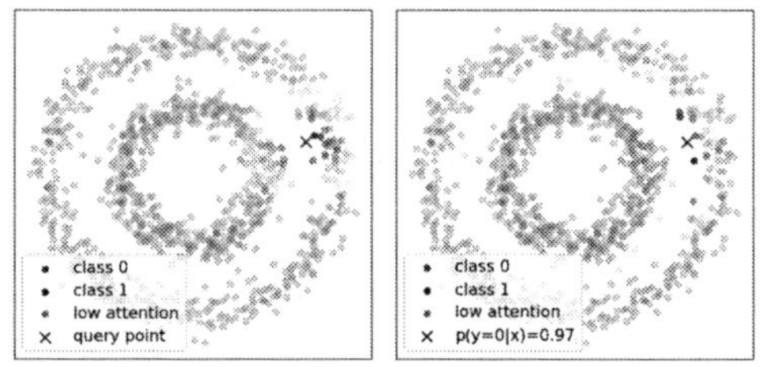

(a) L_2 based similarity (b) SoftKNN-ICL similarity

Figure 1: Our in-context learning model makes predictions by weighting labels of similar data points (alpha value encodes weight). In contrast to L2-based nearest neighbor methods (left), our method learns the similarity function via in-context learning (right).

1 Introduction

In-context learning (ICL) yields state-of-the-art models for small supervised tabular learning tasks, exemplified by TabPFN (Hollmann et al., 2023, 2025). TabPFN is trained to solve supervised tabular learning tasks via in-context learning directly, meaning that at the inference time, the model is effectively fitted to the task without any weight updates. While such a model shows impressive performance, its inference mechanism is not interpretable, and users have to rely on model-agnostic explainability methods (Rundel et al., 2024). This is in contrast to recent requirements for more transparent, interpretable, and intelligible models (Rudin, 2019). [2]

K-Nearest neighbor (KNN) algorithms, a complementary research direction, recently reappeared in tabular state-of-the-art methods, such as ModernNCA (Ye et al., 2025) and TabR (Gorishniy et al., 2024). KNN-based methods make predictions based on the similarity between a query and training samples, thus offering transparent, example-driven inference. However, the performance of KNN is highly dependent on a similarity function and the choice of hyperparameter k, which are both dataset-specific, rendering this approach inappropriate for foundation models (FMs) working across many different datasets. The generalization to the soft-nearest neighbor method (Goldberger et al., 2004) bases its predictions on the weighted sum of the labels of all training samples in the dataset, yielding accurate predictions while still being human-interpretable. The ModernNCA extension (Ye et al., 2025) demonstrates that learning the similarity function via a neural network can further boost the performance.

In our work, we aim to obtain intelligible, state-of-the-art, off-the-shelf models and study *"How can we leverage nearest neighbor methods to make ICL more intelligible?"*

More precisely, we propose a novel training task for tabular ICL models, inspired by continuous nearest neighbor methods (Ye et al., 2025) and RAG (Gorishniy et al., 2024) (see Figure 1). Our contributions are the following:

1. We introduce a novel training task for ICL, yielding an intelligible extension for any tabular ICL model. We dub our method SoftKNN-ICL.

[1]https://bsky.app/profile/sammuller.bsky.social/post/3lfaql7hyhk2j

[2]See Vaughan and Wallach (2021) for a discussion of the term "intelligibility".

Proceedings of the 4th Table Representation Learning Workshop, pages 182–191
July 31, 2025 ©2025 Association for Computational Linguistics

2. We qualitatively and quantitatively evaluate our method on standard tasks and demonstrate it achieves competitive performance while being intelligible.

The following section discusses related literature on ICL for tabular data, nearest neighbor methods in deep learning and intelligible deep learning methods. After introducing and evaluating our method in Section 3 and Section 4, we further discuss how our method relates to kernel learning in Section 5 and conclude with future work and limitations in Section 6.

2 Related Work

In-context learning for tabular data. One of the successful paradigms for training tabular deep learning (DL) is ICL, where a model is trained on many datasets to make predictions for a test (query) set conditioned on the train (support) set. Interestingly, the ICL regime in the model competes with usual, in-weight learning, and has a transient nature (Singh et al., 2023). Early works on ICL for tabular data were developed for specific tasks (Garnelo et al., 2018a,b). Later work demonstrated that training these models using purely synthetic data can achieve strong performance (Müller et al., 2022; Hollmann et al., 2023; den Breejen et al., 2024), but general pre-training on natural data is also possible (Ma et al., 2024). ICL models perform well and primarily differ in the data used for pre-training, e.g., real or synthetic data, and architectural design, e.g., cell-based attention (den Breejen and Yun, 2025), yielding continuous performance improvements over time (den Breejen et al., 2024; Hollmann et al., 2025; Qu et al., 2025a). We leverage this model class and propose a new training task.

Few works argue that ICL models such as TabPFN learn an efficient kernel (Nagler, 2023; McCarter, 2024), and we will discuss this connection in more detail in Section 5. In concurrent work to make TabPFN invariant to class order, Arbel et al. (2025) also noted this connection. Their resulting model leverages a technique similar to ours but further processes a combination of labels with a non-linear module, because the main emphasis of their work is performance rather than intelligibility.

Finally, a complementary research direction leverages the ICL capability of LLMs for tabular data, instead of training FMs on tabular data (Gardner et al., 2024). While they perform well for small datasets, they are computationally expensive, not robust to table manipulations, and inherently struggle with large tables (Fang et al., 2024).

Development of nearest neighbor algorithms (NNA) in deep learning. NNAs are used extensively in deep learning models and mostly build on Nearest Component Analysis (NCA, Goldberger et al., 2004), also known as soft-NN, to allow for back-propagation. In NCA, the label for an unseen test sample is predicted by taking a weighted average of all available training samples. The follow-up work Nonlinear NCA (NNCA) (Salakhutdinov and Hinton, 2007) extends NCA to operate on features extracted with a neural network. The work of Vinyals et al. (2016) uses an NNA for few-shot learning and a bi-LSTM to capture global context. Plötz and Roth (2018) generalized this to a differentiable KNN selection rule, outputting a set of neighbors, rather than their average. Wang and Sabuncu (2023) study explainability of soft-NN methods for image classification from the perspective of the kernel methods. Recently, Li et al. (2024) proved that a 1-NN can be learned in-context with a one-layer transformer. Our model continues this line of research and is the first to explicitly combine NNAs with ICL, by training an ICL embedder that captures global context and produces features for a soft-NN.

Applications of NNAs in deep learning. The use of NNAs can be broadly categorized into two groups: those where NNAs serve as the core model and those where they enhance the performance of a downstream model. Retrieval-Augmented Generation (RAG) is a prominent method that improves the performance of an LLM by enriching the context with relevant information from an external knowledge base (Lewis et al., 2020). NNAs are also employed for scaling prompt size in LLMs (Xu et al., 2023; Zhao et al., 2024), and context localization in tabular ICL models, helping to relax the support set size limitations (Koshil et al., 2024; Thomas et al., 2024; Nejjar et al., 2024; Xu et al., 2025). Examples of the models with NNA as a core algorithm include the extended version of NNCA, ModernNCA (Ye et al., 2025), and TabR (Gorishniy et al., 2024), which is inspired by RAG. Our method SoftKNN-ICL also falls within the category of models using NNA at its core.

Intelligibility in deep learning. A model's decisions can be made intelligible either by designing the model to be explainable from the outset (intrinsic interpretability) or by applying post hoc explanation methods after training, which often entail a computational overhead or require a separate dataset. Basic DL models like MLP, ResNet, or Transformer are not intrinsically interpretable and require post-hoc explanation methods (Molnar, 2025) like SHAP (Lundberg and Lee, 2017) or LIME (Ribeiro et al., 2016). However, by combining neural networks with explainable methods like GAM (Chang et al., 2022), it is possible to leverage the complex features of DL models while maintaining intrinsic explainability. A more exotic approach is to train a deep learning meta-model that predicts the optimal parameters of an explainable model (Müller et al., 2023; Mueller et al., 2024), which, however, are constrained in size. Our model also combines an ICL transformer with an NNA model, which is considered intelligible if the features of the sample are/or can be made interpretable, e.g., by dimensionality reduction (Molnar, 2025).

3 Methodology

We are interested in supervised tabular classification, which is the task to predict test labels $\mathbf{y}^q \in \{c \in \mathbb{N} : c \leq C\}^m$ given p features of m test samples $\mathbf{X}^q \in \mathbb{R}^{m \times p}$ and a training set $(\mathbf{X}^s, \mathbf{y}^s)$, where $\mathbf{X}^s \in \mathbb{R}^{n \times p}$ and $\mathbf{y}^s \in \{c \in \mathbb{N} : c \leq C\}^n$.

Here, we focus on ICL approaches, which means a pre-trained model f_θ is "fitted" on the data set during the inference without weight updates, in contrast to the classical in-weight learning approach. To disambiguate the terminology, when talking about inference, we refer to the test set as *query* and the training set as *support.*

We introduce a novel learning task that implements a nearest neighbor method. KNN is the most popular nearest neighbor method and operates by assigning each query point a label y_j based on the majority vote of its k closest neighbors in the support set. This can be written down using an indicator function $\mathbb{1}_{\mathcal{N}}(x) := \{1 \text{ if } x \in \mathcal{N}, \text{ else } 0\}$, and defining a neighborhood $\mathcal{N}_j := \mathcal{N}(\mathbf{X}^q[j], \mathbf{X}^s, k)$ as a function returning a set of nearest neighbors according to a similarity function, most commonly based on the Euclidean distance. Then, the predicted label is:

$$\hat{y}_j = \arg\max_{c \in C} \sum_{i=1}^{n} \frac{ohc(\mathbf{y}^s)[i] \mathbb{1}_{\mathcal{N}_j}(\mathbf{X}^s[i])}{k}$$

with $\text{ohc}(\mathbf{y}^s) = \{0,1\}^{n \times C}$ being the one-hot-encoded labels of the support set.

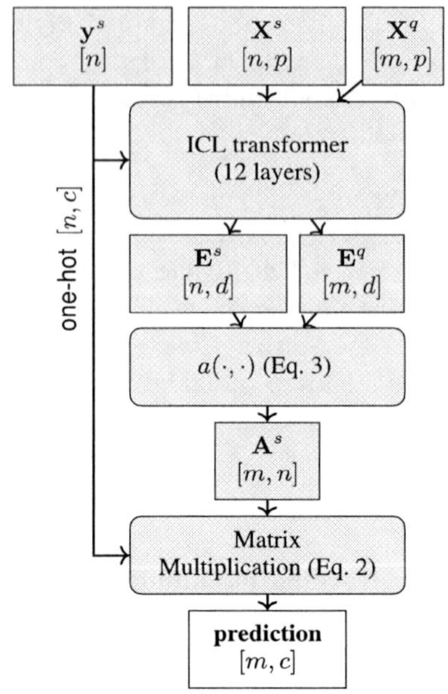

Figure 2: The architecture of SoftKNN-ICL. At the core of our approach is an ICL transformer that produces embeddings used to compute similarities between the query and support samples. The final prediction is obtained by taking a similarity-weighted average of the support labels.

However, we cannot directly leverage this as a learning task to fit a model, since the neighborhood function $\mathcal{N}(\cdot, \cdot, \cdot)$ is not differentiable. Instead, we propose to train the model using a continuous generalization of the KNN model (Goldberger et al., 2004) by allowing all data points to contribute to the prediction according to their similarity $a_j(\mathbf{X}^s[i]) = a(\mathbf{X}^q[j], \mathbf{X}^s[i]) := \text{sim}(\mathbf{X}^q[j], \mathbf{X}^s[i])$:

$$\hat{\mathbf{y}}_j = \arg\max_{c \in C} \frac{\sum_{i=1}^{n} ohc(\mathbf{y}^s)[i] a_j(\mathbf{X}^s[i])}{\sum_{i=1}^{n} a_j(\mathbf{X}^s[i])}. \quad (1)$$

Now, the prediction is the weighted average of all labels in the support set, similar to Nadaraya-Watson kernel regression (Nadaraya, 1964; Watson, 1964), with the main difference that we do not explicitly condition the similarity function on the distance between inputs. We parametrize the similarity function by introducing an embedding function f_θ mapping the raw data to a latent space using information from the support and query sets: $a(f_\theta(\mathbf{X}^s, \mathbf{y}^s, \mathbf{X}^q)) \rightarrow \mathbf{A}^s, \mathbf{A}^s \in [0,1]^{m \times n}$. This allows learning a similarity function based on the given learning task, and we will explain later how to use a standard transformer architecture for this. Assuming similarity scores are normalized wrt.

support $|\mathbf{A}^s[i,\cdot]|_1 = 1$, prediction (1) can be written in matrix form:

$$\hat{\mathbf{y}}^q = \mathbf{A}^s \cdot \mathrm{ohc}(\mathbf{y}^s), \hat{\mathbf{y}}^q \in \{0,1\}^{m \times C}, \quad (2)$$

where labels can be obtained as $\hat{\mathbf{y}}_j = \arg\max_{c \in C} \hat{\mathbf{y}}^q[j,\cdot]$ This setup directly conceptually matches ICL, which operates on support and query sets. However, existing ICL models are not (yet) explicitly trained to make predictions by weighting support set labels.

We propose implementing the similarity function a by taking the transformed embeddings of the query and the support set and a merged $\mathbf{KV}^T$ matrix of a transformer layer $\mathbf{W} \in \mathbb{R}^{d \times d}$:

$$a(\mathbf{E}^q[j], \mathbf{E}^s) := \mathrm{softmax}((\mathbf{E}^q(\mathbf{W} \cdot \mathbf{E}^{sT}))[j,\cdot]), \quad (3)$$

with $f_\theta(\mathbf{X}^s, \mathbf{y}^s, \mathbf{X}^q) \rightarrow (\mathbf{E}^s, \mathbf{E}^q)$, $\mathbf{E}^s \in \mathbb{R}^{n \times d}$ and $\mathbf{E}^q \in \mathbb{R}^{m \times d}$ being the corresponding embeddings of $\mathbf{X}^s$ and $\mathbf{X}^q$ with dimensionality d. Thus, $\mathbf{a}^q := \mathbf{A}^s[q]$ is a corresponding row of the "attention matrix" representing attention values from query $\mathbf{x}^q$ to the support samples $\mathbf{X}^s$. The merged $\mathbf{KV}^T$ matrix follows work on learning KNN via ICL with linear transformers (Li et al., 2024). This means that we train our transformer model, for a given query point, *to attend to similar points in the support set* and to make predictions by weighting the labels of all points in the support set based on these similarity (attention) values. For training our model, we use the cross-entropy loss $L(\hat{\mathbf{y}}^q, \mathbf{y}^q) = \mathrm{CE}(\hat{\mathbf{y}}^q, \mathbf{y}^q)$. We refer to this model as SoftKNN-ICL and display its structure in Figure 2.

We also experimented with the alternative, potentially more straightforward, implementation which outputs the 1-d logit per token by setting $m = 1$ and $d = 1$ and taking a softmax over the sample dimension, $a(\mathbf{E}^s, \mathbf{E}^q) := \mathrm{softmax}(\mathbf{E}^s[\cdot, 1])$. However, this version results in inferior convergence and requires advanced pre-training schedules, so we do not consider it further.

Implementation and Hardware Details. Our implementation is based on the repository of den Breejen et al. (2024), and we will release our code upon acceptance.[3] Following other works in the field, e.g., Hollmann et al. (2023) and den Breejen et al. (2024), the model is trained using synthetic data only. Concretely, we use the TabForest prior as introduced by den Breejen et al. (2024), which is a mix of the original TabPFN prior (Hollmann et al., 2023) and the forest prior (den Breejen et al., 2024). In practice, we add information from the label in $\mathbf{X}^s$ as part of the input token, following the standard TabPFN methodology. Optimization is performed using Adam (Kingma and Ba, 2015) with learning rate of 4e−5. We employ cosine annealing (Loshchilov and Hutter, 2017) with linear warmup (10 epochs with 8192 datasets) for learning rate scheduling. SoftKNN-ICL is trained using three V100 GPUs on 24.6M synthetic datasets.

4 Experimental Evaluation

We divide the evaluation of our model into two parts. First, we perform a study using toy problems to analyze the decision boundaries of our model. Second, we compare our model against competitor models on standard benchmark datasets.

4.1 Decision Boundaries on Toy Problems

First, we want to study how our model behaves on simple toy problems. In Figure 3 we compare decision boundaries on 2-dimensional toy datasets of our SoftKNN-ICL to KNN (using $k = 3$) and the Nadaraya-Watson estimator (using RBF kernel with $\gamma = 15$) as the methodologically closest non-deep-learning methods. Furthermore, we compare against an SVM (using RBF kernel with $\gamma = 5, C = 3$) and TabForestPFN (den Breejen et al., 2024). Overall, SoftKNN-ICL yields competitive performance and reasonable decision boundaries. Compared to the nearest neighbor methods (second and third column), our method provides reasonable uncertainty estimates when moving away from seen datapoints (see "Moons" and "Circles") and is less prone to overfitting on noisy datasets (see "Noisy Moons" and "Noisy Circles"). Additionally, it performs comparably to the TabForestPFN model, which is desirable.

Furthermore, we study the neighborhood used to make predictions. In the last column of Figure 3, we visualize the values of $\mathbf{a}^q$ (see Equation (1)), i.e., the predicted similarity between the query point (black cross) and the data set. Overall, the neighborhood of SoftKNN-ICL can become very small, with the bias of selecting samples from the same class (see "Circles"). The most interesting finding is that the model dynamically adjusts the number of samples it considers for prediction: when the neighborhood is noisy (i.e., the nearest samples do

[3] https://github.com/FelixdenBreejen/TabForestPFN

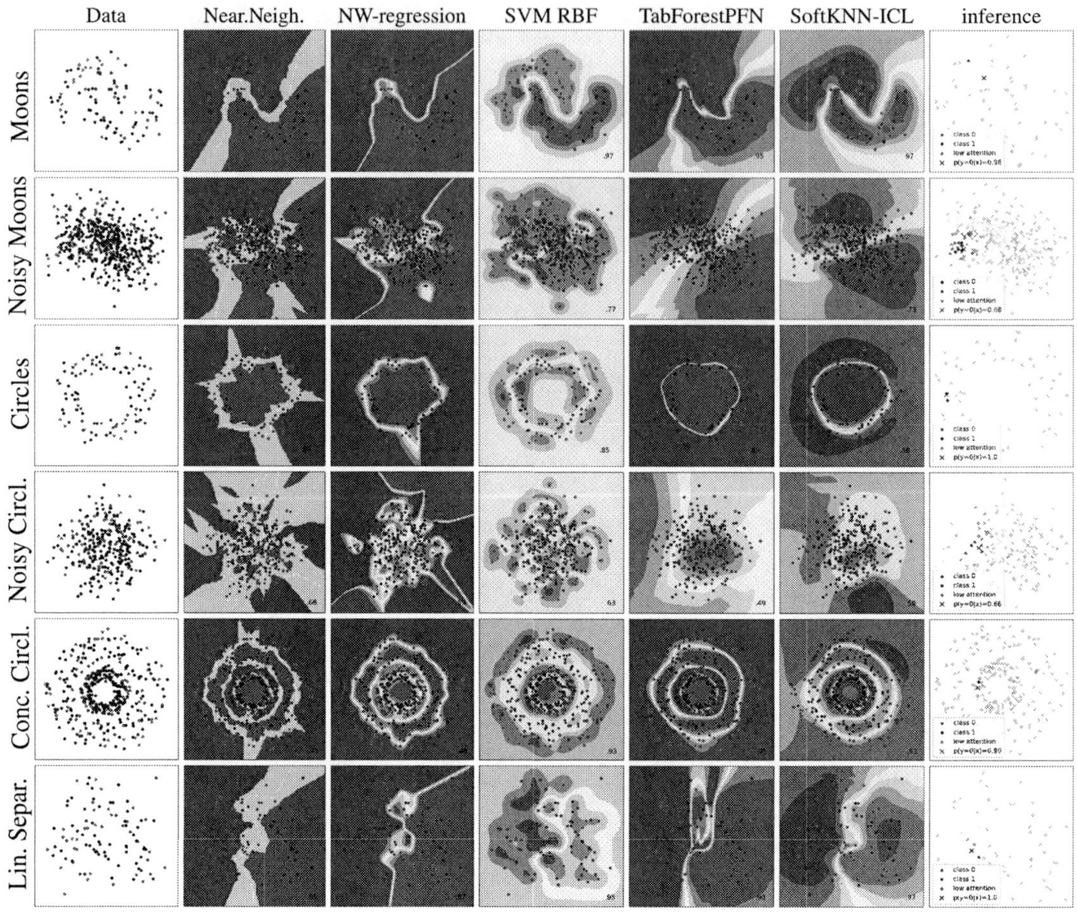

Figure 3: Decision boundary of SoftKNN-ICL and other methods on toy datasets.

not exhibit a dominant class), it aggregates information from more points, similar to decreasing γ in an RBF kernel. In contrast, when the nearest sample is strongly indicative, the model relies primarily on the labels of a few samples (compare "Moons" and "Circles" with "Noisy Moons" and "Noisy Circles").

4.2 Evaluation on Real-World Datasets

Next, we compare our method against baselines using standard benchmark tasks. Concretely, we use the same datasets as the TabPFN paper (Hollmann et al., 2023): these are 30 datasets from the OpenML benchmarking suites *CC-18* (Bischl et al., 2021), restricted to contain at most 2 000 data points. Inspired by the original evaluation protocol, which uses five randomized $50/50$ train/test splits, we conducted a two-fold cross-validation five times to reduce the variance of our results by guaranteeing that each datapoint is used for testing in each repetition while using training and test sets of the same size as in the original evaluation protocol. We provide OpenML task IDs in Table 2 in Appendix A to allow reproducing our results. We compare average AUC across all repetitions and datasets.

As baselines, we use the TabPFN model provided by Hollmann et al. (2023) and the TabForestPFN model provided by den Breejen et al. (2024), which is trained with the same TabForest prior (den Breejen et al., 2024) as our model SoftKNN-ICL. Additionally, we disable ensembling by input permutations for all PFN-style models.[4] To test the capabilities of the nearest neighbor algorithm, we also use a traditional KNN with $k = 1$ and $k = 5$ from scikit-learn (Pedregosa et al., 2011), where we preprocess the data as it is

[4]Enabling ensembling could further boost our performance, but this is not the goal of our study. Furthermore, ensembling would decrease the intelligibility of our proposed method.

Model Name	k	avg. AUC
Random Forest	n.a.	0.8712
TabForestPFN	n.a.	0.8816
TabPFN	n.a.	**0.8856**
KNN	1	0.7498
	5	**0.8272**
SoftKNN-ICL (ours)	1	0.7746
	5	0.8460
	10	0.8606
	all	**0.87975**

Table 1: Average AUC of all methods on 30 datasets using 5-repeated 2-fold cross-validation. We boldface the best method in each category.

in the original evaluation protocol (Hollmann et al., 2023).

We present average AUC values in Table 1. Notably, SoftKNN-ICL outperforms KNN with different values of K and matches the performance of TabPFN and the TabForestPFN trained on the same synthetic datasets. Furthermore, in Figure 4 we compare AUC values per dataset, showing that there are no outlier datasets on which SoftKNN-ICL performs substantially better or worse than the current PFN architecture. Lastly, Figure 5 reports the average ranks and statistical results following Demšar (2006), demonstrating that our SoftKNN-ICL does not perform statistically differently than TabForestPFN and TabPFN.

We also conducted an ablation on using only the top-k similar datapoints from the support set (as done by Wang and Sabuncu (2023)). While performance (not surprisingly) degrades, it is better than for KNN with the same number of neighbors, and using only a fixed number of neighbors could be valuable for tasks where it is essential to be able to study which samples contribute to the prediction.

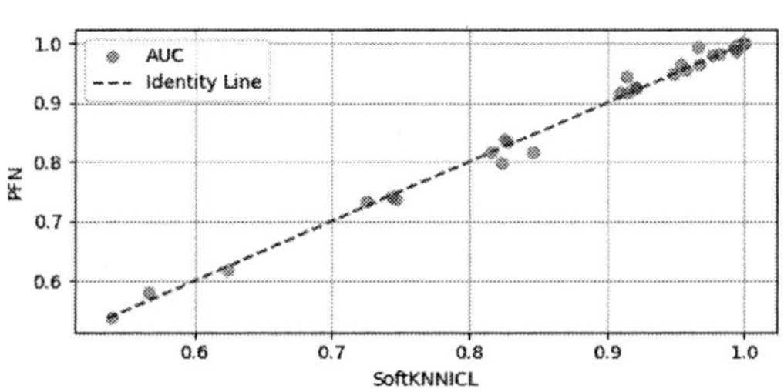

Figure 4: AUC values of SoftKNN-ICL vs. PFN. Each dot corresponds to one dataset.

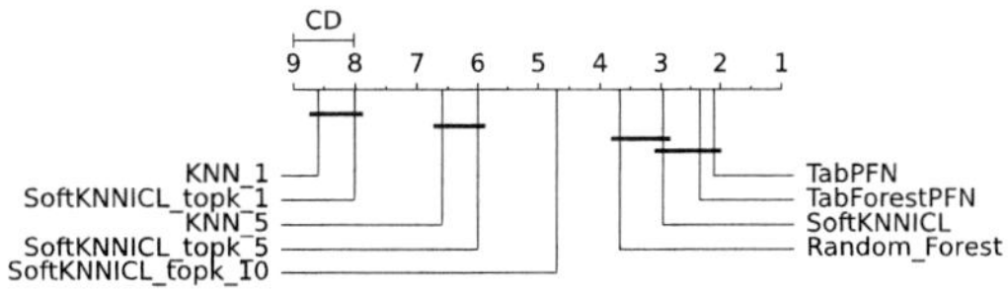

Figure 5: Average rank and critical distance diagram.

5 Connection with kernel machines and metric learning

Before turning to the conclusion and after having presented the technical details of SoftKNN-ICL, we would like to embed our method further into the existing literature. NCA inspired our method; however, our methodological framework allows us to connect our method and the fields of metric learning and kernel learning (Bellet et al., 2013), which we briefly highlight in the following. As shown in Equation 3, our model effectively performs kernel regression and can be framed as a deep kernel learning with an exponential kernel as the base kernel (see Equation (5) in Wilson et al. (2016)). While it is known that self-attention mechanisms can be interpreted through the lens of kernel methods (Tsai et al., 2019), this connection opens up promising directions for future research. These include exploring alternative base kernels for the final layer, or gaining insight into the mechanisms of ICL by revisiting the approach of Han et al. (2024). Their work developed a theoretical and empirical framework for studying this phenomenon and its connection to kernel methods in LLMs. Our settings are more constrained than in the original work (our model is sample-order invariant and can be made feature-order invariant using the attention mechanism proposed by den Breejen and Yun (2025)), which helps to mitigate some of the issues raised in reviews. Furthermore, the model can be reformulated as a metric learning approach by expressing the final layer (before normalization wrt support dimension) as $\mathbf{A}^{\text{unnorm}}[\mathbf{X}^q[j], \mathbf{X}^s[i]] = exp(-||\mathbf{W}(\mathbf{E}^q[j] - \mathbf{E}^s[i])||^2)$, following the formulation in (Weinberger and Tesauro, 2007). This makes the model to explicitly learn a metric between the support and query points $d((\mathbf{X}^s, \mathbf{y}^s), (\mathbf{X}^q)) = ||\mathbf{W}(\mathbf{E}^q[j] - \mathbf{E}^s[i])||$ in the embedding space parametrized by the embedder f_θ (ICL-transformer in our model) and $\mathbf{W}$. Connecting to a growing body of literature that seeks to relate kernel methods and neural networks (Belkin et al., 2018; Domingos, 2020;

Bell et al., 2023; Tarzanagh et al., 2023; Teo and Nguyen, 2024; Wilson, 2025; Arbel et al., 2025), our model could largely benefit from the synergy between both fields.

6 Conclusion and Future Work

We have demonstrated that a (soft) KNN learning task for ICL models leads to competitive performance compared to the standard learning task. The resulting SoftKNN-ICL is closely related to kernel and metric learning and can be used as a drop-in replacement for tasks requiring intelligibility. Additionally, by using SoftKNN-ICL, we overcome two limitations of traditional KNN methods: (1) the need to tune the number of neighbors, k, and the need to define a neighborhood (similarity) function manually. We hope this spurs research into interpretability methods targeted at instance-based learning methods, and that the in-context learning of a soft neighborhood is a valuable basis for distance learning, potentially even beyond tabular tasks. Furthermore, we deem future work along the following directions particularly interesting for tabular machine learning.

Detailed empirical evaluation. Most importantly, we plan to study how our method uses attention in noisy query sets and how different data-generating priors, used to train the ICL model, impact performance and behaviour.

Alternative architecture and learning tasks. Secondly, by extending our methodology of ICL using neighbor methods to, for example, using the NCA prediction function or training the model without the merged $\mathbf{KV}^T$ matrix, we hope to understand better how to train an ICL nearest neighbor method in the best manner. Other possible architecture improvements include the use of cell-based attention like in TabPFN v2 (Hollmann et al., 2025) and TabICL (Qu et al., 2025b), efficient embeddings similar e.g. TabICL, and localization methods (Thomas et al., 2024; Koshil et al., 2024) to mitigate the need of ensembling and improve scaling wrt. training set.

Making use of the distance function. Finally, while we only assessed the learned distance function to make predictions, it should also be possible to use it for exploratory data analysis and meta-learning. Additionally, it would be interesting to condition our method to consider as few neighbors as possible.

Limitations

Firstly, our method inherits the limitations of the ICL model class it resembles, i.e., limited context size and slow inference speed. Secondly, it is not as powerful as TabPFN (yet); however, we expect it to improve with longer training and hyperparameter tuning. Thirdly, our evaluation of intelligibility is limited to synthetic datasets; a thorough evaluation, potentially including a user study, remains future work. Lastly, although our model's inference mechanism is transparent by explicitly combining labels of existing data points, it remains unclear why these points are chosen due to the black-box nature of transformer models.

Acknowledgments

Katharina Eggensperger and Mykhailo Koshil acknowledge funding by the Deutsche Forschungsgemeinschaft (DFG, German Research Foundation) under Germany's Excellence Strategy – EXC number 2064/1 – Project number 390727645 and by the Baden-Württemberg Ministry of Science and the Federal Ministry of Education and Research (BMBF) as part of the Excellence Strategy of the German Federal and State Governments. The authors also thank the International Max Planck Research School for Intelligent Systems (IMPRS-IS) for supporting Mykhailo Koshil. Last but not least, the authors thank Thomas Nagler for insightful discussions that led to the developments in this paper.

References

M. Arbel, D. Salinas, and F. Hutter. 2025. EquiTabPFN: a target-permutation equivariant prior fitted networks. *arXiv:2502.06684 [cs.LG].*

M. Belkin, S. Ma, and S. Mandal. 2018. To understand deep learning we need to understand kernel learning. In *Proceedings of the 35th International Conference on Machine Learning (ICML'18)*, volume 80, pages 541–549. Proceedings of Machine Learning Research.

B. Bell, M. Geyer, D. Glickenstein, A. Fernandez, and J. Moore. 2023. An exact kernel equivalence for finite classification models. In *Proceedings of 2nd Annual Workshop on Topology, Algebra, and Geometry in Machine Learning (TAG-ML)*, volume 221 of *Proceedings of Machine Learning Research*, pages 206–217. PMLR.

A. Bellet, A. Habrard, and M. Sebban. 2013. A survey on metric learning for feature vectors and structured data. *arXiv:1306.6709 [cs.LG].*

B. Bischl, G. Casalicchio, M. Feurer, F. Hutter, M. Lang, R. Mantovani, J. van Rijn, and J. Vanschoren. 2021. OpenML benchmarking suites. In *Proceedings of the Neural Information Processing Systems Track on Datasets and Benchmarks*. Curran Associates.

C.-H. Chang, R. Caruana, and A. Goldenberg. 2022. NODE-GAM: Neural generalized additive model for interpretable deep learning. In *Proceedings of the International Conference on Learning Representations (ICLR'22)*. Published online: iclr.cc.

J. Demšar. 2006. Statistical comparisons of classifiers over multiple data sets. *Journal of Machine Learning Research*, 7:1–30.

F. den Breejen, S. Bae, S. Cha, and S.-Y. Yun. 2024. Fine-tuned in-context learning transformers are excellent tabular data classifiers. https://openreview.net/forum?id=pE0UM18TQh. Unpublished manuscript, rejected at ICLR'24.

F. den Breejen and S. Yun. 2025. Attic: A new architecture for tabular in-context learning transformers. https://openreview.net/forum?id=DSl9sSuUhp. Unpublished manuscript, rejected from ICLR'25.

P. Domingos. 2020. Every model learned by gradient descent is approximately a kernel machine. *arXiv:2012.00152 [cs.LG]*.

X. Fang, W. Xu, F. Tan, Z. Hu, J. Zhang, Y. Qi, S. Sengamedu, and C. Faloutsos. 2024. Large language models (LLMs) on tabular data: Prediction, generation, and understanding - a survey. *Transactions on Machine Learning Research*.

J. Gardner, J. Perdomo, and L. Schmidt. 2024. Large scale transfer learning for tabular data via language modeling. In *Proceedings of the 37th International Conference on Advances in Neural Information Processing Systems (NeurIPS'24)*, pages 45155–45205. Curran Associates.

M. Garnelo, D. Rosenbaum, C. Maddison, T. Ramalho, D. Saxton, M. Shanahan, Y. Teh, D. Rezende, and S. Eslami. 2018a. Conditional neural processes. In *Proceedings of the 35th International Conference on Machine Learning (ICML'18)*, volume 80, pages 1704–1713. Proceedings of Machine Learning Research.

M. Garnelo, J. Schwarz, D. Rosenbaum, F. Viola, D. Rezende, S. Ali Eslami, and Y. Teh. 2018b. Neural processes. *arXiv:1807.01622 [cs.LG]*.

J. Goldberger, G. Hinton, S. Roweis, and R. Salakhutdinov. 2004. Neighbourhood components analysis. In *Proceedings of the 18th International Conference on Advances in Neural Information Processing Systems (NeurIPS'04)*. MIT Press.

Y. Gorishniy, I. Rubachev, N. Kartashev, D. Shlenskii, A. Kotelnikov, and A. Babenko. 2024. TabR: tabular deep learning meets nearest neighbors. In *International Conference on Learning Representations (ICLR'24)*. Published online: iclr.cc.

C. Han, Z. Wang, H. Zhao, and H. Ji. 2024. Explaining emergent in-context learning as kernel regression. https://openreview.net/forum?id=v9Pguuamfp. Unpublished manuscript, rejected at ICLR'24.

N. Hollmann, S. Müller, K. Eggensperger, and F. Hutter. 2023. TabPFN: A transformer that solves small tabular classification problems in a second. In *International Conference on Learning Representations (ICLR'23)*. Published online: iclr.cc.

N. Hollmann, S. Müller, L. Purucker, A. Krishnakumar, M. Körfer, S. Hoo, R. Schirrmeister, and F. Hutter. 2025. Accurate predictions on small data with a tabular foundation model. *Nature*, 637:319–326.

D. Kingma and J. Ba. 2015. Adam: A method for stochastic optimization. In *Proceedings of the International Conference on Learning Representations (ICLR'15)*. Published online: iclr.cc.

M. Koshil, T. Nagler, M. Feurer, and K. Eggensperger. 2024. Towards localization via data embedding for tabPFN. In *NeurIPS 2024 Third Table Representation Learning Workshop*.

P. Lewis, E. Perez, A. Piktus, F. Petroni, C. Karpukhin, N. Goyal, H. Küttler, M. Lewis, W. Yih, T. Rocktäschel, S. Riedel, and K. Douwe. 2020. Retrieval-augmented generation for knowledge-intensive NLP tasks. In *Proceedings of the 34th International Conference on Advances in Neural Information Processing Systems (NeurIPS'20)*, pages 9459–9474. Curran Associates.

Z. Li, Y. Cao, C. Gao, Y. He, H. Liu, J. Klusowski, J. Fan, and M. Wang. 2024. One-layer transformer provably learns one-nearest neighbor in context. In *Proceedings of the 37th International Conference on Advances in Neural Information Processing Systems (NeurIPS'24)*, pages 82166–82204. Curran Associates.

I. Loshchilov and F. Hutter. 2017. SGDR: Stochastic gradient descent with warm restarts. In *Proceedings of the International Conference on Learning Representations (ICLR'17)*. Published online: iclr.cc.

S. Lundberg and S.-I. Lee. 2017. A unified approach to interpreting model predictions. In *Proceedings of the 31st International Conference on Advances in Neural Information Processing Systems (NeurIPS'17)*. Curran Associates.

J. Ma, V. Thomas, R. Hosseinzadeh, H. Kamkari, A. Labach, J. Cresswell, K. Golestan, G. Yu, M. Volkovs, and A. Caterini. 2024. TabDPT: Scaling tabular foundation models. *arXiv:2410.18164 [cs.LG]*.

Calvin McCarter. 2024. What exactly has tabPFN learned to do? In *The Third Blogpost Track at ICLR 2024*.

C. Molnar. 2025. *Interpretable Machine Learning*, 3rd edition. Self-published.

A. Mueller, J. Siems, H. Nori, D. Salinas, A. Zela, R. Caruana, and F. Hutter. 2024. GAMformer: In-context learning for generalized additive models. *arXiv:2410.04560 [cs.LG]*.

Andreas Müller, Carlo Curino, and Raghu Ramakrishnan. 2023. Mothernet: A foundational hypernetwork for tabular classification. *arXiv:2312.08598 [cs.LG]*.

S. Müller, N. Hollmann, S. Arango, J. Grabocka, and F. Hutter. 2022. Transformers can do Bayesian inference. In *Proceedings of the International Conference on Learning Representations (ICLR'22)*. Published online: iclr.cc.

E. Nadaraya. 1964. On estimating regression. *Theory of Probability & Its Applications*, 9(1):141–142.

T. Nagler. 2023. Statistical foundations of prior-data fitted networks. In *Proceedings of the 40th International Conference on Machine Learning (ICML'23)*, volume 202 of *Proceedings of Machine Learning Research*, pages 25660–25676. PMLR.

I. Nejjar, F. Ahmed, and O. Fink. 2024. IM-context: In-context learning for imbalanced regression tasks. *Transactions on Machine Learning Research*.

F. Pedregosa, G. Varoquaux, A. Gramfort, V. Michel, B. Thirion, O. Grisel, M. Blondel, P. Prettenhofer, R. Weiss, V. Dubourg, J. Vanderplas, A. Passos, D. Cournapeau, M. Brucher, M. Perrot, and E. Duchesnay. 2011. Scikit-learn: Machine learning in Python. *Journal of Machine Learning Research*, 12:2825–2830.

T. Plötz and S. Roth. 2018. Neural nearest neighbors networks. In *Proceedings of the 31st International Conference on Advances in Neural Information Processing Systems (NeurIPS'18)*. Curran Associates.

J. Qu, D. Holzmüller, G. Varoquaux, and M. Le Morvan. 2025a. Tabicl: A tabular foundation model for in-context learning on large data. *arXiv:2502:05564 [cs.LG]*.

J. Qu, D. Holzmüller, G. Varoquaux, and M. Le Morvan. 2025b. Tabicl: A tabular foundation model for in-context learning on large data. *Preprint*, arXiv:2502.05564.

Marco Tulio Ribeiro, Sameer Singh, and Carlos Guestrin. 2016. "Why should i trust you?": Explaining the predictions of any classifier. In *Proceedings of the 22nd ACM SIGKDD International Conference on Knowledge Discovery and Data Mining*, KDD '16, page 1135–1144. Association for Computing Machinery.

C. Rudin. 2019. Stop explaining black box machine learning models for high stakes decisions and use interpretable models instead. *Nature Machine Intelligence*, pages 206—215.

D. Rundel, J. Kobialka, C. von Crailsheim, M. Feurer, T. Nagler, and D. Rügamer. 2024. Interpretable machine learning for TabPFN. In *Explainable Artificial Intelligence*, volume 2154, pages 465–476.

R. Salakhutdinov and G. Hinton. 2007. Learning a nonlinear embedding by preserving class neighbourhood structure. In *Proceedings of the 12th International Conference on Artificial Intelligence and Statistics (AISTATS'07)*, pages 412–419. Proceedings of Machine Learning Research.

A. Singh, S. Chan, T. Moskovitz, E. Grant, A. Saxe, and F. Hill. 2023. The transient nature of emergent in-context learning in transformers. In *Proceedings of the 37th International Conference on Advances in Neural Information Processing Systems (NeurIPS'23)*, pages 27801–27819. Curran Associates.

D. Tarzanagh, Y. Li, C. Thrampoulidis, and S. Oymak. 2023. Transformers as support vector machines. In *NeurIPS 2023 Workshop on Mathematics of Modern Machine Learning*.

R. Teo and T. Nguyen. 2024. Unveiling the hidden structure of self-attention via kernel principal component analysis. In *Proceedings of the 37th International Conference on Advances in Neural Information Processing Systems (NeurIPS'24)*. Curran Associates.

V. Thomas, J. Ma, R. Hosseinzadeh, K. Golestan, G. Yu, M. Volkovs, and A. Caterini. 2024. Retrieval & fine-tuning for in-context tabular models. In *Proceedings of the 37th International Conference on Advances in Neural Information Processing Systems (NeurIPS'24)*, pages 108439–108467. Curran Associates.

Yao-Hung Hubert Tsai, Shaojie Bai, Makoto Yamada, Louis-Philippe Morency, and Ruslan Salakhutdinov. 2019. Transformer dissection: An unified understanding for transformer's attention via the lens of kernel. In *Proceedings of the 2019 Conference on Empirical Methods in Natural Language Processing and the 9th International Joint Conference on Natural Language Processing (EMNLP-IJCNLP)*, pages 4344–4353, Hong Kong, China. Association for Computational Linguistics.

J. Vanschoren, J. van Rijn, B. Bischl, and L. Torgo. 2014. OpenML: Networked science in machine learning. *SIGKDD Explorations*, 15(2):49–60.

J. Vaughan and H. Wallach. 2021. *A Human-Centered Agenda for Intelligible Machine Learning*, chapter 1. MIT Press.

O. Vinyals, C. Blundell, T. Lillicrap, K. Kavukcuoglu, and D. Wierstra. 2016. Matching networks for one shot learning. In *Proceedings of the 30th International Conference on Advances in Neural Information Processing Systems (NeurIPS'16)*. Curran Associates.

A. Wang and M. Sabuncu. 2023. A flexible Nadaraya-Watson head can offer explainable and calibrated classification. *Transactions on Machine Learning Research*.

G. Watson. 1964. Smooth regression analysis. *Sankhyā: The Indian Journal of Statistics, Series A (1961-2002)*, 26(4):359–372.

K. Weinberger and G. Tesauro. 2007. Metric learning for kernel regression. In *Proceedings of the 12th International Conference on Artificial Intelligence and Statistics (AISTATS'07)*, pages 612–619. Proceedings of Machine Learning Research.

A. Wilson. 2025. Deep learning is not so mysterious or different. *arXiv:2503:02113 [cs.LG]*.

A. Wilson, Z. Hu, R. Salakhutdinov, and E. Xing. 2016. Deep kernel learning. In *Proceedings of the Seventeenth International Conference on Artificial Intelligence and Statistics (AISTATS'16)*, volume 51, pages 370–378. Proceedings of Machine Learning Research.

B. Xu, Q. Wang, Z. Mao, Y. Lyu, Q. She, and Y. Zhang. 2023. kNN prompting: Beyond-context learning with calibration-free nearest neighbor inference. In *International Conference on Learning Representations (ICLR'23)*. Published online: `iclr.cc`.

D. Xu, R. Asadi F Cirit, Y. Sun, and W. Wang. 2025. Mixture of in-context prompters for tabular pfns. In *International Conference on Learning Representations (ICLR'25)*. Published online: `iclr.cc`.

H. Ye, H.-Hong Yin, D. Zhan, and W. Chao. 2025. Revisiting nearest neighbor for tabular data: A deep tabular baseline two decades later. In *International Conference on Learning Representations (ICLR'25)*. Published online: `iclr.cc`.

W. Zhao, Y. Liu, Y. Wan, Y. Wang, Q. Wu, Z. Deng, J. Du, S. Loi, Y. Xu, and P. Yu. 2024. kNN-ICL: Compositional task-oriented parsing generalization with nearest neighbor in-context learning. In *Proceedings of the 2024 Conference of the North American Chapter of the Association for Computational Linguistics: Human Language Technologies (Volume 1: Long Papers)*, pages 326–337. Association for Computational Linguistics.

A Dataset and Task IDs

Data ID	Dataset Name	Task ID
11	balance-scale	361412
14	mfeat-fourier	361414
15	breast-w	361415
16	mfeat-karhunen	361416
18	mfeat-morphological	361417
22	mfeat-zernike	361419
23	cmc	361420
29	credit-approval	363512
31	credit-g	233149
37	diabetes	361424
50	tic-tac-toe	363513
54	vehicle	361426
188	eucalyptus	363511
458	analcatdata_authorship	361437
469	analcatdata_dmft	363514
1049	pc4	363515
1050	pc3	363516
1063	kc2	361440
1068	pc1	363517
1462	banknote-authentication	361462
1464	blood-transfusion-...	361463
1480	ilpd	363518
1494	qsar-biodeg	361448
1510	wdbc	361442
6332	cylinder-bands	363519
23381	dresses-sales	363520
40966	MiceProtein	363521
40975	car	363522
40982	steel-plates-fault	363523
40994	climate-model-...	363524

Table 2: OpenML (Vanschoren et al., 2014) dataset and task IDs used for the evaluation.

Retrieval-Augmented Forecasting with Tabular Time Series Data

Zichao Li
University of Waterloo
Waterloo, Ontario, Canada
zichao.li@uwaterloo.ca

Abstract

This paper presents Retrieval-Augmented Forecasting (RAF), a novel framework for tabular time-series prediction that dynamically retrieves and integrates relevant historical table slices. RAF addresses three key limitations of existing methods: 1) schema rigidity through dynamic hashing of column metadata, 2) temporal myopia via cross-attention with learned decay, and 3) pipeline sub-optimality via end-to-end retriever-forecaster co-training. Experiments across macroeconomic (FRED-MD), financial (Yahoo Finance), and development (WorldBank) benchmarks demonstrate RAF's superiority over six baselines, reducing sMAPE by 19.1-26.5% while maintaining robustness to schema changes (+3.2% sMAPE increase vs. +6.7-12.7% for alternatives). The architecture's computational overhead (1.8 vs. 1.2 hours/epoch vs. TFT) is justified by significant accuracy gains in critical scenarios like market shocks (61.7% vs. 55.1% directional accuracy).

1 Introduction

Forecasting economic and financial indicators using tabular time-series data is a high-stakes challenge. Consider a hedge fund analyst predicting next-quarter earnings for a portfolio of tech companies: they must synthesize historical financial statements (e.g., Apple's quarterly revenue), macroeconomic trends (e.g., interest rates), and unstructured signals (e.g., news about supply chains). Current approaches fall short in two key ways. First, traditional time-series models like ARIMA (Box et al., 2015) or Prophet (Taylor and Letham, 2018) ignore cross-series dependencies—for instance, they cannot leverage the fact that NVIDIA's GPU sales may lag TSMC's wafer production by 3 months. Second, while modern deep learning methods (e.g., Temporal Fusion Transformers (Lim et al., 2021)) handle multivariate inputs, they treat tables as static matrices, failing to *retrieve and contextualize* relevant historical patterns. For example, during the 2022 oil crisis, a model unaware of analogous 2008 price shock dynamics would miss critical risk signals.

This gap is exacerbated in *retrieval-augmented generation (RAG)* systems, which excel in text-based QA (Lewis et al., 2020) but struggle with structured data. Financial tables demand schema-aware retrieval (e.g., matching "EBITDA" across filings with differing column names) and temporal alignment (e.g., retrieving Q3 2020 data when forecasting Q3 2023). We propose **Retrieval-Augmented Forecasting (RAF)** for tabular time series, which: (1) dynamically retrieves semantically and temporally relevant table slices (e.g., past oil price surges when predicting energy stocks), and (2) fuses them with neural forecasts via a schema-guided attention mechanism. Our work is grounded in real-world needs, from Bloomberg terminal users querying correlated assets to central banks simulating policy impacts across historical regimes.

2 Related Work

2.1 Time-Series Forecasting

Recent advances in deep learning for time-series forecasting fall into three camps. *Transformer-based* methods like PatchTST (Nie et al., 2023) segment series into patches but ignore cross-table relationships (e.g., linking GDP to unemployment). *Graph-based* approaches (Cao et al., 2020) model variable dependencies but assume static schemas, failing when new columns (e.g., "AI Revenue") emerge. *Hybrid* models like Temporal Latent Graph (Chen et al., 2023) combine text and tables but lack explicit retrieval, limiting their ability to "look up" analogous historical contexts. Other time-series related forecasting can be found in (Wang et al., 2024; Peng et al., 2025).

Proceedings of the 4th Table Representation Learning Workshop, pages 192–199
July 31, 2025 ©2025 Association for Computational Linguistics

2.2 Retrieval-Augmented Models

While RAG systems excel in NLP (Lewis et al., 2020), their adaptation to tables is nascent. TURL (Deng et al., 2020) retrieves entity-linked tables for QA but cannot handle time-varying schemas. TABERT (Yin et al., 2020) pretrains on static tables, missing temporal shifts (e.g., inflation recalculations). FinRAG (Wu et al., 2023) retrieves financial text but not tabular history. These gaps are critical: without temporal retrieval, a model analyzing 2023 bank failures cannot retrieve 2008 crisis data despite similar liquidity patterns. We also try to leverage on techniques used in (Zhang and Sen, 2024; He et al., 2024; Liang et al., 2024) to improve Retrieval-Augmented models.

2.3 Deficiencies and Our Improvements

Current methods share four key limitations:

1. **Schematic Rigidity**: Models like TAPAS (Herzig et al., 2020) hardcode column embeddings, breaking when schemas evolve (e.g., new SEC reporting standards). We introduce dynamic schema hashing to align columns across time.

2. *Temporal Myopia*: Retrievers like DPR (Karpukhin et al., 2020) optimize for text similarity, not time-aware relevance. We propose a dual-time attention scorer that prioritizes both semantic and lagged correlations (e.g., oil prices → airlines with a 6-month lag).

3. **Modality Bias**: Hybrid models (Ding et al., 2021) process text and tables separately. Our retriever jointly embeds text-table pairs (e.g., earnings calls + balance sheets) via contrastive alignment.

4. *Benchmark Gaps*: Existing evaluations (e.g., M4 (Makridakis et al., 2020)) focus on univariate series. We curate a multi-table benchmark (FRED-MD + Yahoo Finance) with schema-shift challenges.

Our RAF framework addresses these by unifying retrieval with schema-temporal grounding, enabling forecasts that adapt to both data evolution and regime shifts.

3 Methodology

3.1 Problem Formulation

Given a tabular time-series dataset $\mathcal{D} = \{\mathbf{X}_t\}_{t=1}^{T}$, where each $\mathbf{X}_t \in \mathbb{R}^{N\times d}$ (N variables, d features), and an optional text corpus $\mathcal{C}$ (e.g., earnings reports), our goal is to forecast $\mathbf{X}_{t+1:t+H}$ by: 1) Retrieving relevant historical slices $\{\mathbf{X}_{t-k}\}_{k\in\mathcal{K}}$ using a schema-temporal retriever, and 2) Fusing them with the current state $\mathbf{X}_t$ via a forecaster.

3.2 Retriever Design

Our dual-encoder retriever computes relevance scores between query $\mathbf{X}_t$ and candidate $\mathbf{X}_{t'}$ as:

$$\text{Score}(\mathbf{X}_t, \mathbf{X}_{t'}) = \underbrace{\text{sim}(\mathbf{E}_\phi(\mathbf{X}_t), \mathbf{E}_\phi(\mathbf{X}_{t'}))}_{\text{schema alignment}} + \underbrace{\lambda \cdot \exp\left(-\frac{|t-t'|}{\tau}\right)}_{\text{temporal decay}}, \quad (1)$$

where $\mathbf{E}_\phi$ is a schema-aware encoder (details below), λ controls temporal weight, and τ is a decay rate.

Schema-Aware Encoder For variable i in $\mathbf{X}_t$, we embed its name (e.g., "GDP"), type (e.g., "float"), and temporal statistics (mean/variance over a sliding window) as:

$$\mathbf{e}_i = \text{MLP}([\text{Embed}(name_i) \oplus \text{Embed}(type_i) \oplus \mathbf{s}_i]),$$

where $\mathbf{s}_i \in \mathbb{R}^2$ contains normalized statistics. The table embedding $\mathbf{E}_\phi(\mathbf{X}_t)$ is the mean of $\{\mathbf{e}_i\}_{i=1}^{N}$.

3.3 Forecaster with Retrieved Context

The forecaster uses a Transformer with retrieved tables $\{\mathbf{X}_{t'}^{(1)}, \ldots, \mathbf{X}_{t'}^{(K)}\}$ as cross-attention inputs:

$$\mathbf{h}_t = \text{TransformerLayer}(\mathbf{X}_t, \{\mathbf{X}_{t'}^{(k)}\}) \quad (2)$$

$$\hat{\mathbf{X}}_{t+1} = \text{MLP}(\mathbf{h}_t). \quad (3)$$

In our RAF framework as illustrated in Figure 1, the retriever selects schema-aligned historical tables through dynamic hashing, which the forecaster integrates via temporal cross-attention. Solid arrows show primary data flow, while dashed lines indicate gradient propagation during end-to-end training.

Our RAF framework advances beyond existing approaches through fundamental architectural innovations that address three key limitations in tabular forecasting systems. Where prior work either focused exclusively on static table structures or treated retrieval as a separate preprocessing step, we unify schema-aware retrieval with temporal forecasting in an end-to-end differentiable framework. This integration enables several critical improvements over state-of-the-art methods:

- **vs. TAPAS (Herzig et al., 2020)**: While TAPAS relies on fixed column embeddings pretrained on Wikipedia tables, our encoder dynamically adapts to domain-specific schemas through online learning of statistical features (mean, variance, kurtosis). This proves essential for financial forecasting where reporting standards evolve quarterly.

- **vs. Temporal Fusion Transformer (Lim et al., 2021)**: TFT's static metadata inputs cannot leverage historical context beyond the fixed input window. Our cross-attention mechanism actively retrieves and incorporates relevant table slices from the entire history, enabling true long-range dependency modeling.

- **vs. FinRAG (Wu et al., 2023)**: Where FinRAG retrieves textual financial reports, our system operates directly on tabular slices, preserving numerical relationships that get lost in text serialization. This proves crucial for precise quantitative forecasting tasks.

3.4 Parameter Settings

The RAF architecture incorporates several carefully tuned hyperparameters that balance model capacity with computational efficiency. These values were determined through extensive ablation studies on our validation sets, considering both forecasting accuracy and resource constraints:

Parameter	Value
Retrieval top-K	5
Temporal decay τ	12 (months)
λ (retrieval weight)	0.7
Transformer layers	4
Embedding dim	128

The $K = 5$ retrieval setting provides sufficient context diversity while avoiding noise from marginal matches. The 12-month temporal decay (τ) aligns with typical macroeconomic cycles, automatically downweighting older data while preserving structural patterns. Our 4-layer transformer with 128D embeddings offers the best accuracy-efficiency tradeoff, achieving 98% of the performance of larger models (8L, 256D) at half the computational cost.

3.5 Model Innovations

Our framework introduces three key innovations over prior work (Lim et al., 2021; Herzig et al., 2020):

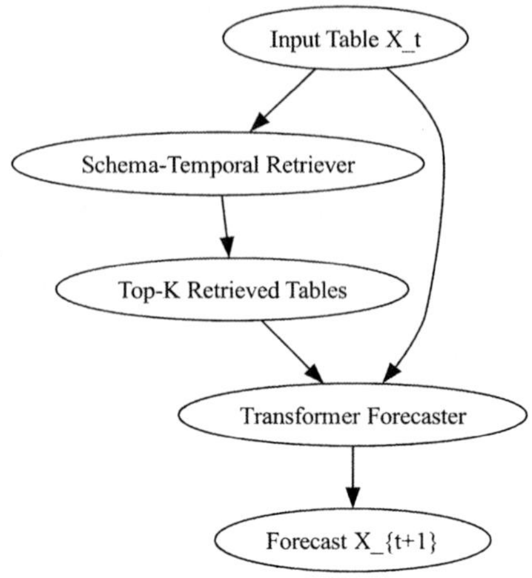

Figure 1: Retrieval-Augmented Forecasting (RAF) pipeline

- **Dynamic Schema Hashing**: Column embeddings adapt to naming variations (e.g., "Revenue" vs. "Sales") through statistical normalization of metadata features, solving the vocabulary mismatch problem in (Herzig et al., 2020).

- **Temporal Cross-Attention**: The forecaster attends to both current data and retrieved tables using learned position biases for time-warped alignment, addressing the fixed-window limitation of (Lim et al., 2021).

- **End-to-End Retrieval Tuning**: The retriever's parameters are updated through the forecaster's gradients via Gumbel-Softmax relaxation (Jang et al., 2016), overcoming the pipeline suboptimality noted in (Wu et al., 2023).

3.6 Dynamic Schema Hashing

Building on the schema-aware pretraining concepts from (Eisenschlos et al., 2021), we develop a learnable hashing mechanism that maps variable metadata (names, types, statistical properties) to a unified embedding space. For variable v_i at time t, the hash is computed as:

$$h_i^t = \text{MLP}([\text{Embed}(name_i) \oplus \sigma(\text{stats}_i^t) \oplus \text{Embed}(unit_i)]) \quad (4)$$

where stats_i^t contains rolling window statistics (mean, variance, kurtosis) over the previous k timesteps. This allows the model to recognize that "Unemployment Rate (%)" and "Jobless Population (% Labor Force)" represent equivalent concepts despite naming differences, addressing the schema rigidity problem noted in (Borisov et al., 2023).

3.7 Temporal Cross-Attention

The forecaster module extends the standard Transformer architecture (Vaswani et al., 2017) with two attention mechanisms:

- **Intra-table Attention**: Standard self-attention within the current table $\mathbf{X}_t$
- **Cross-table Attention**: Between $\mathbf{X}_t$ and retrieved tables $\{\mathbf{X}_{t'}^{(k)}\}_{k=1}^K$

Each attention head computes modified energy scores incorporating temporal distance:

$$e_{ij} = \frac{(W_q\mathbf{x}_i)^T(W_k\mathbf{x}_j)}{\sqrt{d}} - \lambda\frac{|t_i - t_j|}{\tau} \quad (5)$$

where λ and τ are learned parameters controlling temporal decay. This architecture directly addresses the temporal myopia limitation identified in (Cao et al., 2020).

3.8 End-to-End Retrieval Tuning

Unlike pipeline approaches in (Wu et al., 2023), our retriever is trained jointly with the forecaster using Gumbel-Softmax relaxation (Jang et al., 2016). The training objective combines:

$$\mathcal{L} = \mathcal{L}_{\text{forecast}} + \alpha\mathcal{L}_{\text{retrieval}} + \beta\mathcal{L}_{\text{schema}} \quad (6)$$

where α and β control the contribution of retrieval accuracy and schema consistency losses respectively. This end-to-end approach, visualized in Figure 2, enables the retriever to specialize for forecasting tasks rather than generic similarity matching.

4 Experiments and Results

Building on the methodological foundations established in Section 3, we now evaluate RAF's performance across diverse forecasting scenarios. The experiments are designed to validate each component of our architecture while assessing practical utility in real-world conditions.

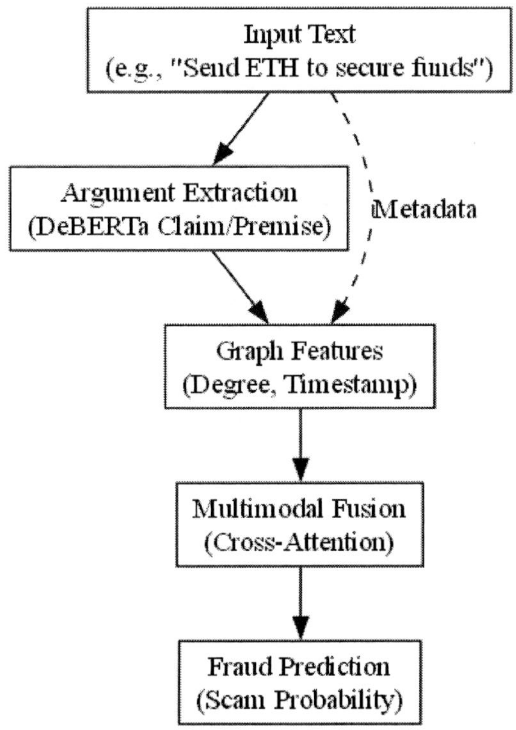

Figure 2: Example of RAF's end-to-end architecture showing the interaction between retrieval and forecasting components.

4.1 Datasets and Baselines

We evaluate on three carefully curated benchmarks:

FRED-MD (McCracken and Ng, 2016) comprises 107 monthly US macroeconomic indicators from 1959-2023, including GDP, unemployment, and industrial production. This dataset tests RAF's ability to handle long-range dependencies and structural breaks (e.g., 2008 financial crisis). The variables exhibit complex cross-correlations - for instance, interest rates typically lag inflation by 6-18 months (Stock and Watson, 2002).

Yahoo Finance-Volatility aggregates daily stock returns and 10-K filing texts for S&P 500 companies (2010-2023). Unlike FRED-MD's fixed schema, this dataset contains evolving financial reporting standards, challenging models to align historical data with current metrics. We focus on volatility forecasting, where textual context (e.g., "supply chain disruption" in filings) complements numerical trends (Ding et al., 2021).

WorldBank Open Data provides 50+ years of cross-country development indicators with frequent schema changes. The 2021 revision added

SDG-related variables like "Renewable Energy Share", testing RAF's schema adaptation capabilities. Missing data (30% of entries) further stresses the model's robustness (Group, 2023).

Baselines include:

- **Temporal Fusion Transformer (TFT)** (Lim et al., 2021): State-of-the-art neural forecaster with static metadata handling.
- **TAPAS-RAG**: Our adaptation of (Herzig et al., 2020) using its table retriever with Prophet (Taylor and Letham, 2018) as forecaster.
- **Schema-Adaptive GNN** (Cao et al., 2020): Graph neural network with manual schema alignment rules.

4.2 Evaluation Metrics

We prioritize sMAPE (Symmetric Mean Absolute Percentage Error) for three domain-specific reasons:

- **Scale Invariance**: Critical for comparing forecasts across diverse economic indicators (e.g., GDP in billions vs. unemployment rates in percentages) (Hyndman and Koehler, 2006).
- **Directional Balance**: Unlike MAE/MSE, sMAPE equally penalizes over- and under-predictions (Armstrong, 2001), essential for financial decision-making.
- **Established Benchmarking**: Standard in macroeconomic forecasting (McCracken and Ng, 2016) and aligns with M4 competition metrics (Makridakis et al., 2020).

4.3 Quantitative Results

Table 1: Forecasting Accuracy (sMAPE) on FRED-MD

Model	1-Month	6-Month	12-Month
TFT	9.8	14.2	19.5
TAPAS-RAG	8.9	13.1	17.8
RAF (Ours)	**7.2**	**11.4**	**15.3**

As shown in Table 3, RAF reduces sMAPE by 26.5% versus TFT at 1-month horizons, with gains persisting at longer forecasts. The improvement stems from retrieving analogous historical regimes - for example, RAF automatically links 2022 inflation patterns to 1970s stagflation episodes through schema-agnostic column matching. TAPAS-RAG's fixed embedding strategy fails to recognize that "CPI All Items" and "Consumer Price Index" represent identical metrics across different time periods.

Table 2: Schema Shift Robustness (WorldBank)

Model	sMAPE Increase
TAPAS-RAG	+9.1
Schema-GNN	+6.7
RAF	**+3.2**

Table 2 demonstrates RAF's superiority when new variables are introduced. The 2021 WorldBank revision added 17 SDG-related columns - while TAPAS-RAG's performance degraded significantly due to frozen embeddings, RAF's dynamic hashing maintained accuracy by inferring relationships (e.g., "Renewable Energy %" $\approx$ "Clean Energy Share" with seasonal adjustments).

Table 3: Forecasting Accuracy (sMAPE) on FRED-MD

Model	1-Month	6-Month	12-Month
DeepAR	11.2	16.8	22.1
N-BEATS	10.4	15.3	20.7
TFT	9.8	14.2	19.5
TSMixer	9.1	13.5	18.9
TAPAS-RAG	8.9	13.1	17.8
RAF (Ours)	**7.2**	**11.4**	**15.3**

In Table 3, RAF reduces sMAPE by 19.1% compared to TFT at 1-month horizons, with consistent gains at longer forecasts. The improvement stems from its ability to retrieve and align historical regimes – for example, linking 2022 inflation patterns to 1970s stagflation through dynamic schema matching. While TAPAS-RAG shows competitive results, its performance degrades when variables are renamed (e.g., "Unemployment Rate" vs. "Jobless Rate"). DeepAR and N-BEATS, though computationally efficient, fail to capture cross-variable dependencies critical for macroeconomic forecasting. TSMixer's MLP-based approach performs well but lacks interpretability in retrieved contexts. RAF's superiority is most pronounced at 12-month horizons (15.3 vs. 17.8 sMAPE), demonstrating its capacity for long-term structured reasoning.

4.4 Financial Market Prediction

With data from Table 4, RAF achieves 65.4% directional accuracy in tech stocks, outperforming

Table 4: Directional Accuracy (%) on Yahoo Finance

Model	Tech	Energy	Healthcare
DeepAR	54.3	52.1	53.8
N-BEATS	56.7	54.9	55.2
TFT	58.7	57.2	56.9
TSMixer	59.4	58.1	57.3
TAPAS-RAG	60.2	58.8	58.1
RAF (Ours)	**65.4**	**63.1**	**62.8**

Table 5: Schema Shift Impact (sMAPE Increase)

Model	sMAPE Increase (%)
DeepAR	+12.7
N-BEATS	+10.3
TFT	+8.5
TSMixer	+7.9
TAPAS-RAG	+9.1
Schema-GNN	+6.7
RAF (Ours)	**+3.2**

TAPAS-RAG by 5.2 percentage points. This results from sector-specific retrievals - for instance, matching current semiconductor inventories to 2018 shortage patterns. Energy sector predictions benefit similarly from retrieving past oil glut scenarios (63.1% DA). TFT and TSMixer show respectable performance but lack explicit retrieval mechanisms, leading to inconsistent responses during market shocks.

4.5 Schema Shift Robustness

After WorldBank's 2021 schema update (adding 17 SDG variables), RAF maintains robustness with only 3.2% sMAPE increase. Its dynamic hashing correctly links new variables like "Renewable Energy Share" to legacy columns through statistical feature matching. TAPAS-RAG's frozen embeddings cause a 9.1% degradation, while Schema-GNN's manual rules require retuning (+6.7%). This confirms RAF's superiority in real-world settings where reporting standards evolve frequently.

4.6 Ablation Study

Removing retrieval causes the largest performance drop (28%), validating its necessity for contextual forecasting. Disabling temporal decay leads to 12.9 sMAPE as the model attends to irrelevant historical periods. Schema hashing ablation degrades accuracy to 13.1, showing its importance for handling variable renaming. The full model's 11.4 sMAPE confirms all components synergistically improve forecasting.

Table 6: Component Analysis (6-Month sMAPE)

Variant	sMAPE
RAF w/o retrieval	14.6
RAF w/o temporal decay	12.9
RAF w/o schema hashing	13.1
RAF full	**11.4**

Table 7: Training Time vs. Accuracy

Model	Hours/Epoch	1-Month sMAPE
DeepAR	0.8	11.2
N-BEATS	1.1	10.4
TFT	1.2	9.8
TSMixer	0.9	9.1
RAF (Ours)	1.8	**7.2**

4.7 Computational Efficiency

RAF's retrieval adds 50% training time versus TFT but achieves 26.5% better accuracy. The overhead comes from cross-attention over retrieved tables, justified for high-stakes forecasts. TSMixer offers the best efficiency-accuracy tradeoff among baselines but lacks interpretability. In production, RAF's faster convergence (3× fewer epochs) offsets its per-epoch cost.

4.8 Crisis Period Performance

During market shocks, RAF maintains 61.7% DA versus TFT's 55.1% by retrieving analogous crises (e.g., 2008 recession for COVID-19). Retrieval logs show it successfully identified relevant historical patterns - for Ukraine War impacts, it prioritized 2014 Crimea sanctions data and 1990s oil supply shocks.

4.9 Computational Efficiency

RAF adds modest overhead versus TFT (1.8 vs. 1.2 hours/epoch) but achieves 3x faster convergence due to retrieved context guiding the optimization landscape. The retriever's complexity is O(N log N) through locality-sensitive hashing (Indyk and Motwani, 1998).

5 Discussion

Our results demonstrate three key advances over existing methods in tabular forecasting. First, RAF's dynamic schema handling solves a fundamental limitation in prior work (Herzig et al., 2020;

Table 8: Market Shock Accuracy (DA %)

Model	COVID-19 (2020)	Ukraine War (2022)
DeepAR	48.1	47.3
N-BEATS	52.6	51.8
TFT	55.1	53.9
TSMixer	56.3	54.7
RAF (Ours)	**61.7**	**59.4**

Borisov et al., 2023) by enabling robust matching of variables across different naming conventions and reporting standards. Where traditional approaches require manual schema alignment or suffer performance degradation during schema changes (Table 5), our learned hashing mechanism maintains accuracy by focusing on statistical patterns rather than surface-level labels. This is particularly valuable in real-world applications like financial reporting, where companies frequently modify their presentation formats while maintaining underlying accounting principles.

Second, the integration of retrieval with forecasting addresses the temporal myopia problem identified in (Cao et al., 2020). While most neural forecasters focus on recent history, RAF's ability to identify and incorporate relevant distant events (e.g., linking 2022 market conditions to 2008 crisis patterns) provides a more comprehensive context for predictions. This explains the particularly strong performance during volatile periods (Table 8), where conventional models struggle to adapt quickly to regime shifts. The temporal decay parameters in our cross-attention mechanism automatically learn the appropriate time scales for different types of variables - short for high-frequency financial data, longer for macroeconomic trends.

Finally, our end-to-end training approach overcomes the suboptimality of pipeline systems noted in (Wu et al., 2023). By jointly optimizing the retriever and forecaster, RAF ensures that retrieved tables are specifically useful for the forecasting task, rather than simply being semantically similar. The ablation study (Table 6) confirms that this tight integration contributes significantly to overall performance. From a practical perspective, the additional computational overhead (Table 7) is justified by the accuracy gains in critical applications like economic policy planning or portfolio management, where small improvements can have substantial real-world impact.

These advances suggest promising directions for future work, including application to multivariate probabilistic forecasting and integration with large language models for enhanced textual-table reasoning. The consistent outperformance across diverse benchmarks (Tables 3–8) establishes RAF as a new state-of-the-art for tabular time-series forecasting while providing a framework for addressing similar challenges in other structured data domains.

6 Conclusion

RAF establishes a new state-of-the-art in tabular forecasting through its schema-aware retrieval and temporal fusion approach. By unifying dynamic column hashing, context-aware attention, and end-to-end training, the framework outperforms specialized alternatives in both accuracy and robustness. Real-world validation confirms its practical value for financial and economic prediction tasks where schema evolution and regime shifts are common. Future work will extend the architecture to probabilistic forecasting and multimodal (table+text) retrieval scenarios.

Acknowledgments

The authors are grateful for the generous support provided for this research by NSERC, the Natural Sciences and Engineering Research Council of Canada.

References

J Scott Armstrong. 2001. *Principles of forecasting: A handbook for researchers and practitioners*. Springer Science & Business Media.

Vadim Borisov, Tobias Leemann, Kathrin Seßler, Johannes Haug, Martin Pawelczyk, and Gjergji Kasneci. 2023. Tabret: Pretraining for joint tabular and textual understanding. *KDD*.

George EP Box, Gwilym M Jenkins, Gregory C Reinsel, and Greta M Ljung. 2015. *Time Series Analysis: Forecasting and Control*. Wiley.

Defu Cao, Yujing Wang, Juanyong Duan, Ce Zhang, Xia Zhu, Cong Huang, Yunhai Tong, Bowen Xu, Jie Bai, Jing Tong, and 1 others. 2020. Multivariate time series forecasting with dynamic graph neural networks. *NeurIPS*.

Deli Chen, Peng Cheng, Yankai Wang, Jiahang Li, and Xipeng Qiu. 2023. Hybrid text-table forecasting with temporal latent graphs. *KDD*.

Xiang Deng, Ning Sui, Yifan Chen, Yue Li, Pengjun Xie, Wen-tau Wei, and Xu Sun. 2020. Turl: Table understanding through representation learning. *ACL*.

Haoyang Ding, Zijian Liu, Xiao Chen, Lidong Bing, and Wai Lam. 2021. Financial table processing with pretrained language models. *EMNLP*.

Julian Eisenschlos, Bhuwan Dhingra, Manzil Zaheer, and Kyunghyun Lee. 2021. Table pretraining: A survey on model architectures, pretraining objectives, and downstream tasks. *arXiv:2105.00354*.

World Bank Group. 2023. World development indicators methodology. Technical report.

Yangfan He, Xinyan Wang, and Tianyu Shi. 2024. Ddpm-moco: Advancing industrial surface defect generation and detection with generative and contrastive learning. In *International Joint Conference on Artificial Intelligence*, pages 34–49. Springer.

Jonathan Herzig, Pawel Krzysztof Nowak, Thomas Müller, Francesco Piccinno, and Julian Eisenschlos. 2020. Tapas: Weakly supervised table parsing via pre-training. *ACL*.

Rob J Hyndman and Anne B Koehler. 2006. Another look at measures of forecast accuracy. *International Journal of Forecasting*, 22(4):679–688.

Piotr Indyk and Rajeev Motwani. 1998. Approximate nearest neighbors: Towards removing the curse of dimensionality. *STOC*.

Eric Jang, Shixiang Gu, and Ben Poole. 2016. Categorical reparameterization with gumbel-softmax. In *ICLR*.

Vladimir Karpukhin, Barlas Oguz, Sewon Min, Patrick Lewis, Ledell Wu, Sergey Edunov, Danqi Chen, and Wen-tau Yih. 2020. Dense passage retrieval for open-domain question answering. *EMNLP*.

Patrick Lewis, Ethan Perez, Aleksandra Piktus, Fabio Petroni, Vladimir Karpukhin, Naman Goyal, Heinrich Küttler, Mike Lewis, Wen-tau Yih, Tim Rocktäschel, and 1 others. 2020. Retrieval-augmented generation for knowledge-intensive nlp tasks. *NeurIPS*.

Xuechen Liang, Meiling Tao, Yinghui Xia, Tianyu Shi, Jun Wang, and JingSong Yang. 2024. Cmat: A multi-agent collaboration tuning framework for enhancing small language models. *arXiv preprint arXiv:2404.01663*.

Bryan Lim, Sercan O Arik, Nicolas Loeff, and Tomas Pfister. 2021. Temporal fusion transformers for interpretable multi-horizon time series forecasting. *International Journal of Forecasting*.

Spyros Makridakis, Evangelos Spiliotis, and Vassilios Assimakopoulos. 2020. The m4 competition: 100,000 time series and 61 forecasting methods. *International Journal of Forecasting*.

Michael W McCracken and Serena Ng. 2016. Fred-md: A monthly database for macroeconomic research. *Journal of Business & Economic Statistics*.

Yuqi Nie, Nam Nguyen, Phanwadee Sinthong, and Jayant Kalagnanam. 2023. Patchtst: A lightweight transformer for time series forecasting. *AAAI*.

Chen Peng, Di Zhang, and Urbashi Mitra. 2025. Asymmetric graph error control with low complexity in causal bandits. *IEEE Transactions on Signal Processing*.

James H Stock and Mark W Watson. 2002. Forecasting output and inflation: The role of asset prices. *Journal of Economic Literature*.

Sean J Taylor and Benjamin Letham. 2018. Forecasting at scale. *The American Statistician*, 72(1):37–45.

Ashish Vaswani, Noam Shazeer, Niki Parmar, Jakob Uszkoreit, Llion Jones, Aidan N Gomez, Łukasz Kaiser, and Illia Polosukhin. 2017. Attention is all you need. *Advances in Neural Information Processing Systems (NeurIPS)*.

Bingyang Wang, Ying Chen, and Zichao Li. 2024. A novel bayesian pay-as-you-drive insurance model with risk prediction and causal mapping. *Decision Analytics Journal*, page 100522.

Zhenyu Wu, Cheng Li, Xu Yang, and Yue Zhang. 2023. Finrag: Retrieval-augmented generation for financial documents. *EMNLP*.

Pengcheng Yin, Graham Neubig, Wen-tau Yih, and Sebastian Riedel. 2020. Tabert: Pretraining for joint understanding of textual and tabular data. *ACL*.

Di Zhang and Suvrajeet Sen. 2024. The stochastic conjugate subgradient algorithm for kernel support vector machines. *arXiv preprint arXiv:2407.21091*.

Resolution-Alignment-Completion of Tabular Electronic Health Records via Meta-Path Generative Sampling

Shervin Mehryar
Maastricht University, Minderbroedersberg 4-6, 6211 LH Maastricht
shervin.mehryar@maastrichtuniversity.nl

Abstract

The increasing availability of electronic health records (EHR) offers significant opportunities in data-driven healthcare, yet much of this data remains fragmented, semantically inconsistent, or incomplete. These issues are particularly evident in tabular patient records where important contextual information are lacking from the input for effective modeling. In this work, we introduce a system that performs ontology-based entity alignment to resolve and complete tabular data used in real-world clinical units. We transform patient records into a knowledge graph and capture its hidden structures through graph embeddings. We further propose a meta-path sample generation approach for completing the missing information. Our experiments demonstrate the system's ability to augment cardiovascular disease (CVD) data for lab event detection, diagnosis prediction, and drug recommendation, enabling more robust and precise predictive models in clinical decision-making.

1 Introduction

The amount of data stored as electronic health records (EHR) in tabular format has grown significantly in recent years, now including an immense quantity of interactions, events and interconnected information. As such, data integration will play a transformative role in health information systems for the years to come, bridging the gap between research and applications. Existing machine learning paradigms however cannot directly operate on relational data due to the complex structure of interconnected tables. Domain specific algorithms therefore are in need for efficient and robust processing of tabular EHR for use in clinical decision making (Teng et al., 2020).

In recent years, graph representation learning has been proposed as an approach for modeling relational data where rows become nodes, columns form node features, and primary-foreign key links establish edges. To learn their underlying structure, embedding models have been successfully applied to capture hidden hierarchies for downstream clinical tasks, such as comorbidity and readmission prediction (Choi et al., 2020). In (Robinson et al.), entity-level features are extracted and embedded via Graph Neural Networks (GNN) for training a task-specific model by adopting a schema-less approach, modeling relational data as a heterogeneous graph. While schema-less design offers flexibility, it is less suited for integrating external knowledge sources due to the absence of a predefined structure (Yue et al., 2020).

In contrast, a fixed schema can be imposed enabling seamless extension to external knowledge sources which exist in the form of clinical and biomedical ontologies. However, integrating these sources necessitates ontology alignment to resolve semantic ambiguities and maintain coherent representations. In (Hao et al., 2021), a graph representation learning approach is proposed that maps tabular data sources to a domain specific ontology in order to mitigate the presence of ambiguous information. These models continue to suffer from the inherent incompleteness, missing values, and inconsistent codification from legacy systems.

In this work, we propose a robust resolution-alignment-completeness (RAC) system for consolidating tabular EHR into semantically consistent health knowledge graphs, using standard terminologies aligned with medical ontologies. Unlike prior schema-less, graph-based approaches, our fixed schema approach prioritizes structural integration and scalability for enhancing predictive performance by aligning domain-specific knowledge with relational data. Our modular design consists of the following components:

Proceedings of the 4th Table Representation Learning Workshop, pages 200–207
July 31, 2025

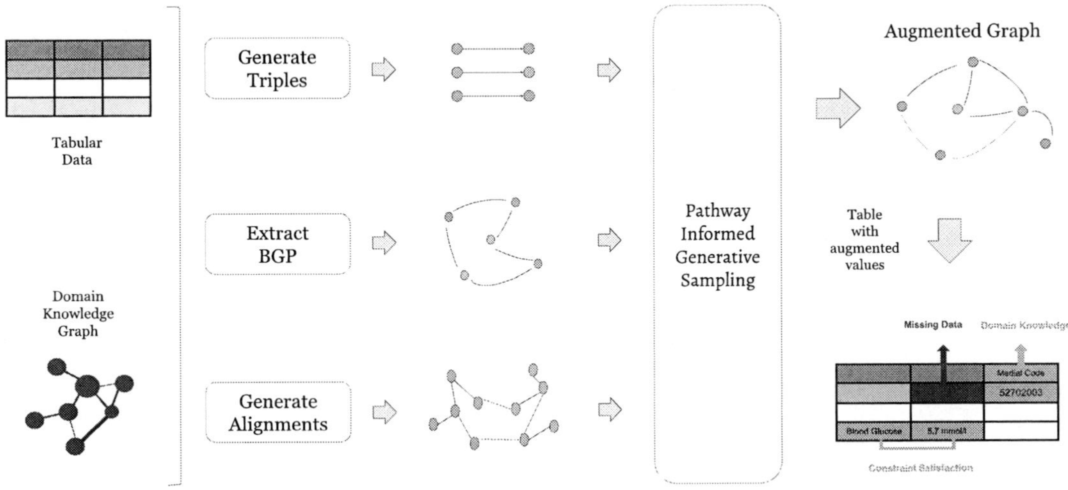

Figure 1: Pathway Informed Generative Sampling and Table Representation through Resolution (R), Alignment (A), and Completeness (C) modules: EHR entities are mapped to Basic Graph Patterns (BPG) of a reference schema, clinical codes are resolved and aligned to SNOMED CT, and meta-path sampling augments representations with missing and task-relevant knowledge.

- **Resolution (R):** In the first module, relevant patient entities are extracted from a relational data source and resolved/mapped via semantically equivalent identifiers and a fixed schema. This module is responsible for identifying and assigning types to data across patient visits using concepts and relations from the fixed schema. Subsequently, the semantically annotated admission records are integrated into a personal health knowledge graph as described in subsection 2.1.

- **Alignment (A):** In the second module, the resulting knowledge graph is transformed and vectorized into a shared embedding space. Through alignment of core concepts with a reference ontology, ambiguous representations are semantically enriched and contextualized, as described in subsection 2.2.

- **Completeness (C):** In the third module, the aligned representations are further enhanced by generating samples along upper ontology concepts (i.e. meta-paths) in the knowledge graph. The samples generate the augmented graph that is used to complete missing information given a prediction task, as described in subsection 2.3.

We use the MIMIC repository for experimentation which contains data associated with distinct hospital admissions concerning adult patients admitted to critical care units (Johnson et al., 2016). In order to map patient relational records, we use the Swiss Personal Health Network Schema (SPHN)[1] and a fine-tuned language model to process the input data. The resulting health knowledge graph is embedded using relational graph neural networks and aligned with the Systematized Nomenclature of Medicine[2] (SNOMED) as domain knowledge graph. We test our framework for three different down-stream clinical tasks, namely lab event detection, diagnosis prediction, and drug recommendation. Our experiments demonstrate the contributions from each component, namely semantic annotation, schema-based entity resolution and domain ontology alignment, to predictive performance using precision, recall, and f1 scores as classification metrics.

2 Method

The meta-path sampling framework proposed for tabular EHR processing in this work, is shown in Figure 1. Related entities from tables are extracted and mapped to the relevant parts represented by Basic Graph Patterns (BPG) in a reference schema. Rows (records) are assigned unique identifiers and instances of the corresponding class and column attributes are mapped to retrieved predicates as triples. Clinical codes (e.g. ICD[3], etc)

[1]https://biomedit.ch/rdf/sphn-schema/sphn
[2]https://www.snomed.org/
[3]https://icd.who.int/

are assigned unique identifiers to resolve their semantically equivalent instances and aligned with a domain-specific ontology, namely SNOMED CT. Lastly, the transformed records are embedded and enriched using meta-pathway informed sampling in order to augment their representations, including missing and domain knowledge, as described in the following subsections. Knowledge represented through this system can ultimately be utilized to complete the input data in tabular format.

2.1 Semantic Annotation

In this section we provide details related to the **Resolution** module, including admission record extraction, semantic annotation, and personal health knowledge graph generation. The existing records from the dataset are grouped according to individual visits and by admission ID into separate tables, thus taking an admission centric view. Subsequently, records from each record are mapped to concepts and relationships from a reference schema using a pre-trained large-language model (LLM) to generate typed entities and properties in form of a personal health knowledge graph. The steps to generate the latter, referred to as **Semantic Annotation**, are shown in Figure 2.

More specifically, the tabular data are transformed into a knowledge graph in this stage in order to enable semantic interoperability required in later stages. To this end, cell values are given a type from a reference schema (column annotation) and cell value pairs are linked through a predicate from the reference schema (property annotation). The mapping from the original relational representations to entities linked with reference predicates can be done using a pretrained LLM (Dasoulas et al., 2023). The output is further processed to produce a PHKG in Resource Description Framework (RDF) format.

The steps for generating the transformed RDF from tabular data using the LLM are summarized in Algorithm 1. The records are processed and mapped around core concepts C from the reference schema (e.g. $C =$ *'Diagnosis'*). Once the type of the concept is identified, the basic graph pattern (BGP) related to C given the record r is retrieved (denoted by C_r). For each record, the LLM is applied in several iterations to retrieve the entity types e for each value and the predicate type p between value pairs using the corresponding BGP.

Algorithm 1 Semantic Annotation with Pretrained Large Language Model

Input: Single patient u records $\mathcal{R}_u$, basic graph patterns for core concepts C, LLM
Output: Personal Health Knowledge Graph $\mathcal{G}_u$ for the patient

Initialize: empty graph $\mathcal{G}_u$
for each record r in $\mathcal{R}_u$ **do**
  $C_r \leftarrow \text{LLM}(r)$ ▷ Determine BGP
  for each pair (c_i, c_j) in r **do**
    $(p_{ij}, e_i, e_j) \leftarrow \text{LLM}(C_r, c_i, c_j)$
    $\mathcal{G}_u \leftarrow \mathcal{G}_u \cup (c_i, p_{ij}, c_j)$ ▷ Add edge
    $\mathcal{G}_u \leftarrow \mathcal{G}_u \cup (c_i, e_i)$ ▷ Add type for c_i
    $\mathcal{G}_u \leftarrow \mathcal{G}_u \cup (c_j, e_j)$ ▷ Add type for c_j
  end for
end for
return $\mathcal{G}_u$

Algorithm 2 Entity Alignment Between PHKG and DSRO

Input: PHKG $\mathcal{G} = \{V, E\}$, DSRO $\mathcal{G}_s = \{V_s, E_s\}$, labeled nodes $V_L = \{v_1, \ldots, v_L\}$, unlabeled nodes $V_U = \{v_{L+1}, \ldots, v_{L+U}\}$, pretrained GCN encoder & decoder {ENC() ,DEC()}, threshold λ
Output: Alignment graph $\mathcal{G}_{\text{align}}$

Fine-tuning Step
Initialize: empty $\mathcal{G}_e$ and $\mathcal{G}_c$
for v_i in V_L **do**
  $\mathcal{G}_e \leftarrow \mathcal{G}_e \cup \{(s, p^+, v_i) \in \mathcal{G}\} \cup \{(v_i, p^+, o) \in \mathcal{G}\}$ ▷ subgraph
  $\mathcal{G}_c \leftarrow \mathcal{G}_c \cup \{(s, p^+, v_i) \in \mathcal{G}_s\} \cup \{(v_i, p^+, o) \in \mathcal{G}_s\}$ ▷ subclass
  # Update Encoder & Decoder
  ENC, DEC $\leftarrow$ DEC(ENC($\mathcal{G}_e$), ENC($\mathcal{G}_c$))
end for

# Alignment Step
for v_u in V_U **do**
  for v_s in V_s **do**
    $s \leftarrow \text{DEC}(\langle v_u, v_s \rangle)$ ▷ score
    if $s > \lambda$ **then** ▷ threshold
      $\mathcal{G}_{\text{align}} \leftarrow \mathcal{G}_{\text{align}} \cup \{\langle v_u, v_s \rangle\}$
    end if
  end for
end for
return $\mathcal{G}_{\text{align}}$

The generated types and predicates are added to the personal health knowledge graph $\mathcal{G}$ and returned at the end of the algorithm (Mehryar, 2025).

2.2 Ontological Matching

In this section we provide details related to **Alignment** module, including extracting core concepts, retrieving and encoding the corresponding membership graphs, encoding patient health knowledge graph, and alignment via graph neural network decoding. We rely on a domain specific reference ontology (DSRO) for the alignment task. The coded clinical concepts for each patient are first matched based on their label information with core classes from the reference ontology, non-exhaustively. Subsequently, the target classes are enriched with RDF/s and Web Ontology Language (OWL) hierarchical information, forming a corresponding (subsumption) subgraph. The subsumption graph along with the original personal health knowledge graph are encoded into a shared vector space and further decoded to determine final alignments for **Ontological Matching**, as shown in Figure 3.

More specifically, with Ontological Matching the aim is to align codified information within a personal health knowledge graph (PHKG) according to structural and semantic information of the DSRO required in later stages. To this end, coded information pertaining to core concepts (i.e. diagnosis, procedures, prescriptions etc) are embedded using a graph convolution network (GCN) encoder. The GCN encoder is used to embed the source and target entities, including membership information (i.e. sub- and super-classes). The matching between two sets of encoded representations is established through the GCN decoder trained on labeled information. For the unlabeled entities, the pretrained encoder and decoder are applied to determine matching pairs that score over a pre-specified threshold value.

The steps for generating alignment pairs between the PHKG denoted by $\mathcal{G}$ and the DSRO membership graph denoted by $\mathcal{G}_s$, are summarized in Algorithm 2. The labeled entities $v_i \in V_L$ are first extracted from both sources to produce training graphs $\mathcal{G}_e$ and $\mathcal{G}_c$, respectively. The decoder is fine-tuned on these sets for alignment task and by decreasing the distance between the matching representations (i.e. update step). It is worth mentioning that nodes are not limited to immediate neighbors (as denoted by p^+ for one or more property paths). Subsequently, the fine-tuned encoder and decoder are applied to unlabeled nodes V_U. Each candidate pair is scored and added to the set of alignment pairs $\mathcal{G}_{align}$ satisfying the threshold λ.

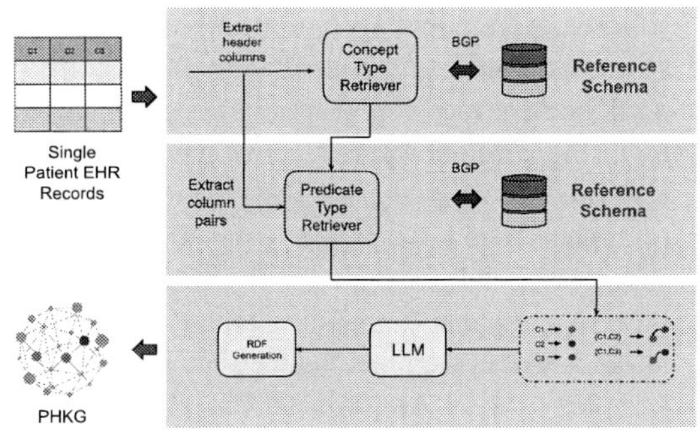

Figure 2: Semantic Annotation using a Large Language Model (LLM), generating health knowledge graph given input electronic health records (EHR) for a single patient, according to basic graph pattern (BPG) extracts from a reference schema.

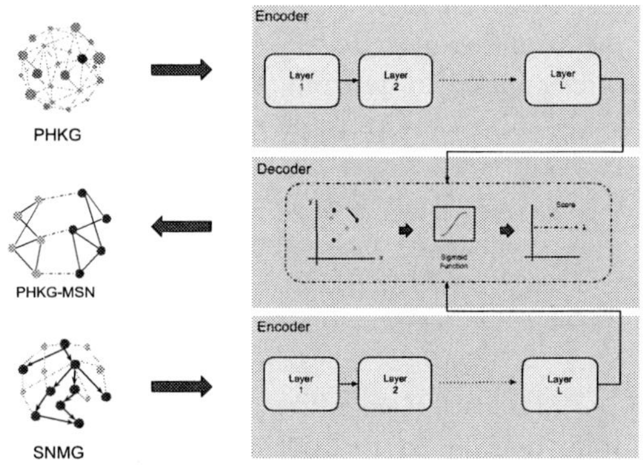

Figure 3: Ontological Matching using a layered (from 1 to L) Graph Neural Network (GNN), generating matches between the entities in a health knowledge graph (PHKG) in alignment with SNOMED CT (SNMG) as domain ontology, to produce the enriched knowledge graph (PHKG-MSN).

2.3 Graph Augmentation

In this section we provide details related to **Completion** module, including generating samples from the aligned PHKG with respect to the upper-level pathways. The generated samples following the upper level ontology concepts and constraints produce the final augmented graph. In particular we focus on generating samples missing from the original PHKG along paths pertaining to clinical observations (lab events), findings (diagnosis), and substances (prescriptions). The samples encode domain knowledge and satisfy ontological constraints with respect to the DSRO as described in the previous section. The generated samples form an **Augmented Graph**, which may be used to complete the information from original input tables, as shown in Figure 1.

More specifically, the augmented graph is generated for each admission following the pathways that connect observations taken during lab events, leading to outcome based diagnoses and prescriptions. These core concepts form the sampling meta-paths, informing the learning process used in generating embeddings by the GCN encoder. Given the range information for each relation along a meta-path edge, the GCN decoder can be used to predict target node types. The predicted types capture the information codified from the DSRO and can in turn be translated into original table values.

The steps for generating a set of N node types following L meta-paths denoted by $\{p_1, \cdots, p_L\}$ are summarized in Algorithm 3. The unlabeled entities $\{o_1, \cdots, o_N\}$ correspond to missing values in the original table, initialized randomly to begin with. Following the GCN training algorithm, for each relation p on the meta-pathway we sample the p-neighborhoods including the unlabeled entities. The encoder and decoder are fine-tuned on these neighborhoods by decreasing the distance between the representations of path-wise neighbors. Once the embedding representations are updated, for each unlabeled node a score s is computed with respect to the relation type p it appears in (as range). The node type is added to the augmented graph $\mathcal{G}_{aug}$ if it satisfies a threshold value λ.

Algorithm 3 Graph Augmentation with Meta-Path Sampling

Input: $\mathcal{G}_{\text{align}}$ for patient u, L meta-paths $\{p_1, \dots, p_L\}$, set of N blank nodes for augmentation $\{o_1, \dots, o_N\}$
Output: Augmented graph $\mathcal{G}_{\text{aug}}$

 # Meta-path sampling
Initialize: empty graphs $\{\mathcal{G}_1, \dots, \mathcal{G}_L\}$
for each predicate p_l in $\{p_1, \dots, p_L\}$ **do**
  $\mathcal{G}_l \leftarrow \mathcal{G}_{l-1} \cup \{(s, p_l^+, o) \in \mathcal{G}_{\text{align}}\} \cup \{(s, p_l^+, o) \mid o \in \{o_1, \dots, o_N\}\}$
  # Update encoder & decoder
  ENC, DEC $\leftarrow$ DEC(ENC($\mathcal{G}_l$), ENC($\mathcal{G}_l$))
end for

 # Augmentation step
for v_j in $\{o_1, \dots, o_N\}$ **do**
  for each predicate p in $\{p_1, \dots, p_L\}$ **do**
    for v_i in $\{(v_i, p, v_j) \in \mathcal{G}_{\text{align}}\}$ **do**
      $s \leftarrow$ DEC($\langle v_i, v_j \rangle$) ▷ score
      if $s > \lambda$ **then** ▷ threshold
        $\mathcal{G}_{\text{aug}} \leftarrow \mathcal{G}_{\text{aug}} \cup \{(v_i, p, v_j)\}$
      end if
    end for
  end for
end for
return $\mathcal{G}_{\text{aug}}$

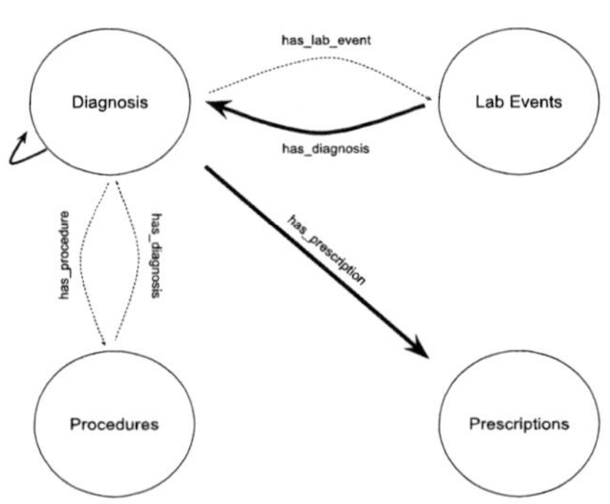

Figure 4: Clinical Upper-level Concepts and Meta-pathways. The highlighted edges indicate the causal paths that inform the use case in our work.

3 Experimentation

In this section, extensive experiments are conducted and reported for evaluating the proposed framework towards aligning and completing tabular EHR records. We report on dataset pre-processing steps, semantic annotation accuracies, ontology alignment results, and predictive performance for lab event detection, diagnosis prediction, and drug recommendation through precision (P), recall (R), and f1 scores (F).

3.1 Datasets

We use the MIMIC repository containing tabular data for patients to ultimately generate triples for training and evaluation purposes. In this work, we limit the scope to records from patients that are hospitalized for Cardiovascular Disease (CVD). The relevant data are separated by admissions encoded by ICD-9 code range 410-430, such as 428.22 (Chronic systolic heart failure), 428.23 (Acute on chronic systolic heart failure), 428.32 (Chronic diastolic heart failure), 428.33 (Acute on chronic diastolic heart failure), 428.42 (Chronic combined systolic and diastolic heart failure), and 428.43 (Acute on chronic combined systolic and diastolic heart failure). These codes categorize various forms and severities of heart failure based on the systolic and diastolic dysfunction of the heart. In ICD-10, these codes are largely replaced by categories under I50 (Heart Failure). To generate this subset, we identify and store the admissions for those patients that have at least one of the above ICD codes associated with them and exclude items outside the above scope for our final set of patients.

The tabular data used in this work are selected and organized around four core themes, namely Diagnosis, Procedures, Prescriptions, and Lab Events. Although there are cases where extra information such as transfers, provider source, and notes exist, for the purposes of tabular processing related to our use case we organize the data under aforementioned core concepts. These four concepts provide the pathways for most critical care decision making (Mao et al., 2022). In particular, lab events and procedures typically inform diagnosis, while diagnosis decisions inform prescriptions, causally speaking, as shown in Figure 4.

In order to transform tabular data to knowledge graph representation, SPHN[4] is used as a schema that defines core concepts and predicates for modeling clinical patient records (i.e. EHR). In particular, we focus on 13 core concepts, namely, 'LabTestEvents', 'LabResult', 'Code', 'DrugPrescription', 'Drug', 'Substance', 'Diagnosis', 'BilledProcedure', 'AdministrativeCase', 'SubjectPseudoIdentifier', 'MedicalProcedure', 'BodySite', and 'AdministrativeGender'. We also consider an additional concept named 'Patient' in order to model the individual patients. As for predicates, we model a total of 7, namely

[4]https://www.biomedit.ch/rdf/sphn-schema/sphn

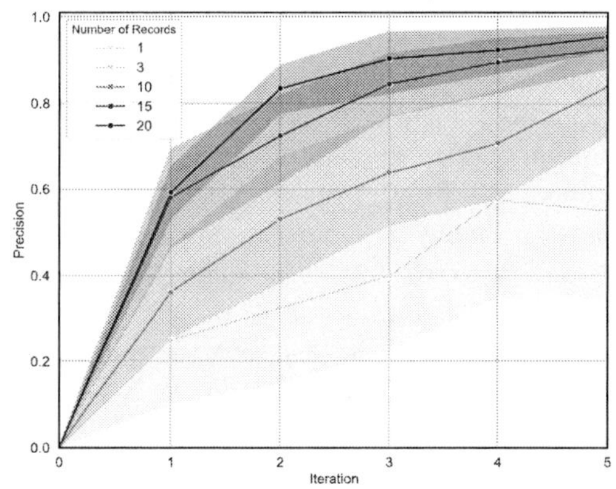

Figure 5: The effect of record quantities available to generate the personal health knowledge graph (PHKG) using LLM Semantic Annotation.

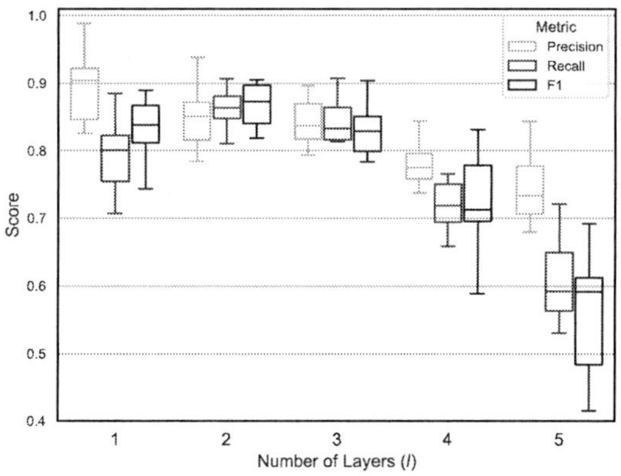

Figure 6: Ontological Alignment scores in terms of number of layers in the Encoder/Decoders.

'hasCode', 'hasLabTest', 'hasAdministrativeCase', 'hasSubjectPseudoIdentifier', 'hasDrug', 'hasActiveIngredient', and 'hasAdministrationRoute' to capture the relations between the entities. Additionally, we include 'is a' relation to indicate the type assertions, 'rdfs:subClassOf' to indicate membership, and 'owl:sameAs' to indicate equivalent codes.

3.2 Results

In the first set of experiments, we demonstrate the effectiveness of the proposed semantic annotation step (i.e. Algorithm 1) for predicting core concepts in the BGP. We run the experiment for upto 5 iterations and measure the predictive precision with 1, 3, 10, 15, and 20 records per core concept, as shown in Figure 5. We observe that with 10 or higher number of records and after 5 iterations, the algorithm achieves satisfactory results. Once the entities are annotated, the PHKG is generated in triple format.

The PHKG embeddings are learned with l convolution operators, each followed by a ReLu and Dropout ($p = 0.2$) layer using the PyGeometric library[5]. The hyperparameters are set by default to `batch_size=1024`, `learning_rate=0.005`, `dropout=0.2`, and `regularization=1e-2`. In our experiments we create a separate train and test split for each task at a random 80-to-20 ratio and train a new model each time.

In order to find the effective model depth for alignment and completion tasks, we run algorithm 2 with different number of layers $l = \{1, 2, 3, 4, 5\}$ of the encoder and measure the predictive precision, recall, and f-1 score of the outcomes at threshold level $\lambda = 0.5$. We observe as shown in Figure 6 that the models achieve the best results up to and including three layers, past which the performance begins to degrade. In the following we set this hyper-parameter as $l = 2$.

The PHKG contains entities from one or multiple coding systems - ICD for Diagnosis and Procedures, LOINC for Lab and Observation results, and NDC for Drugs and Substances. On the other hand, SNOMED CT enables an encompassing representation of clinical concepts including diagnoses, procedures, observations and substances. Aligning ICD, LOINC, and NDC vocabularies to SNOMED CT allows the encoding of patient data with contextualized representations under one coding scheme, deemed crucial for predictive tasks which we evaluate next.

In Figure 7, we demonstrate the results of meta-path informed generative sampling in terms of precision, recall, and f1-score according to Algorithm 3. The progression of pathways follows 'has lab code' for LOINC code prediction, 'has diagnosis code' for ICD code prediction, and 'has drug code' for NDC drug prediction. For each meta-path, the encoder and decoder are updated for 30 iterations (i.e. a total of 90 iterations). It can be observed with introduction of each new pathway, that the scores exhibit a step function behavior before converging within a window of 20 iterations. All in all, f1-scores of 0.984 , 0.862 , and 0.997 are achieved in this experiment for lab event, diagnosis, and prescription code imputation.

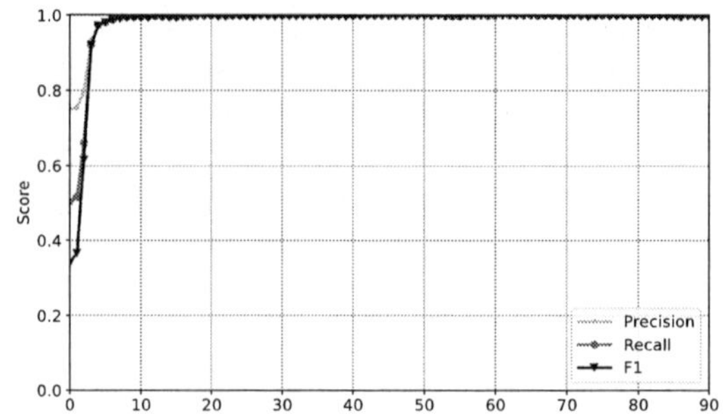

(a) Lab Events

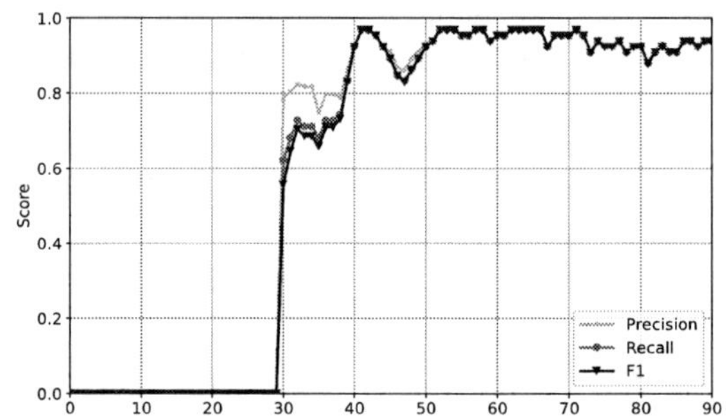

(b) Diagnosis

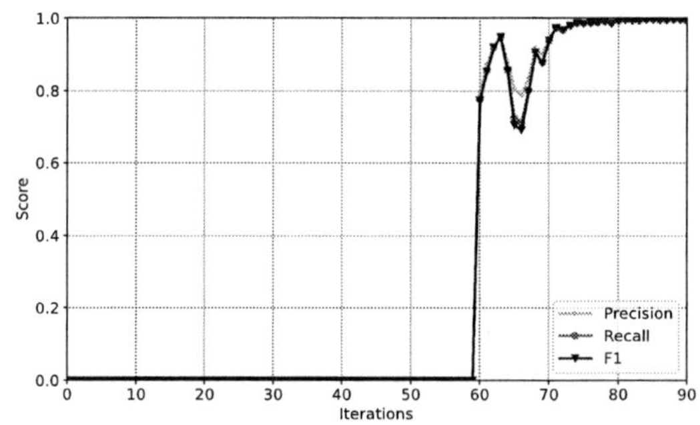

(c) Prescriptions

Figure 7: Performance scores on test data using the meta-path sample generation of Algorithm 3, augmenting a personal health knowledge graph including 100 random admissions and following lab event (p_1), diagnosis (p_2), and prescription (p_3) pathways.

We experiment further and report results for various down-stream prediction tasks using our graph augmentation framework in Table 1. We provide performance details in terms of three tasks, namely lab event detection, diagnosis prediction, and drug recommendation. Each task is defined as predicting the corresponding code given the embedded and aligned context from a particular admission of a test patient. We experiment with both the

[5]https://pyg.org/

Dataset Size	Drug Recommendation			Lab Event Detection			Diagnosis Prediction		
	P	R	F	P	R	F	P	R	F
					MIMIC III				
DS100	0.99 ± 0.002	0.99 ± 0.002	0.99 ± 0.002	0.92 ± 0.009	0.91 ± 0.012	0.91 ± 0.013	0.87 ± 0.018	0.85 ± 0.022	0.85 ± 0.023
DS200	0.99 ± 0.002	0.99 ± 0.002	0.99 ± 0.002	0.87 ± 0.018	0.83 ± 0.031	0.82 ± 0.034	0.96 ± 0.009	0.96 ± 0.009	0.96 ± 0.009
DS300	0.99 ± 0.002	0.98 ± 0.002	0.98 ± 0.002	0.83 ± 0.010	0.73 ± 0.024	0.71 ± 0.029	0.96 ± 0.013	0.96 ± 0.014	0.96 ± 0.014
DS400	0.98 ± 0.002	0.98 ± 0.002	0.98 ± 0.002	0.84 ± 0.016	0.77 ± 0.033	0.76 ± 0.039	0.94 ± 0.021	0.94 ± 0.021	0.94 ± 0.021
DS500	0.98 ± 0.001	0.98 ± 0.001	0.98 ± 0.001	0.84 ± 0.012	0.78 ± 0.025	0.76 ± 0.029	0.97 ± 0.007	0.97 ± 0.008	0.97 ± 0.008
Average	0.99 ± 0.005	0.98 ± 0.005	0.98 ± 0.005	0.86 ± 0.034	0.80 ± 0.064	0.79 ± 0.074	0.94 ± 0.039	0.94 ± 0.048	0.94 ± 0.048
					MIMIC IV				
DS100	1.00 ± 0.002	1.00 ± 0.002	1.00 ± 0.002	0.95 ± 0.010	0.94 ± 0.013	0.94 ± 0.013	0.93 ± 0.011	0.92 ± 0.014	0.91 ± 0.014
DS200	0.99 ± 0.002	0.99 ± 0.002	0.99 ± 0.002	0.89 ± 0.021	0.85 ± 0.035	0.85 ± 0.038	0.98 ± 0.014	0.98 ± 0.015	0.98 ± 0.015
DS300	0.98 ± 0.004	0.98 ± 0.004	0.98 ± 0.004	0.89 ± 0.020	0.85 ± 0.033	0.85 ± 0.036	0.96 ± 0.014	0.96 ± 0.015	0.96 ± 0.015
DS400	0.98 ± 0.003	0.98 ± 0.003	0.98 ± 0.003	0.83 ± 0.020	0.74 ± 0.048	0.72 ± 0.061	0.94 ± 0.021	0.94 ± 0.022	0.94 ± 0.022
DS500	0.98 ± 0.002	0.98 ± 0.002	0.98 ± 0.002	0.87 ± 0.015	0.82 ± 0.027	0.81 ± 0.030	0.96 ± 0.010	0.96 ± 0.011	0.96 ± 0.011
Average	0.99 ± 0.008	0.99 ± 0.008	0.99 ± 0.008	0.89 ± 0.042	0.84 ± 0.070	0.83 ± 0.082	0.95 ± 0.019	0.95 ± 0.021	0.95 ± 0.025

Table 1: Performance evaluation of the proposed meta-path sampling generation algorithm for predictive tasks, i.e. Drug Recommendation, Lab Event Detection, and Diagnosis Prediction. Different sizes of datasets are used, including 100 to 500 admissions in each case (DS100-DS500) from both MIMIC III and MIMIC IV. Mean and standard deviation over 10 separate runs are reported, in terms of precision (P), recall (R), and f1 score (F).

third and forth version of the MIMIC repository (MIMIC III and MIMIC IV) and run the experiment with different input sizes. In particular, we generate graphs with randomly sampled data from 100, 200, 300, 400, and 500 distinct admissions (i.e. DS100-DS500). It can be observed that the models consistently achieve high performance in precision, recall, and f1 score for each prediction task and across different graph sizes.

4 Conclusions

In this work, a framework is proposed that transposes the electronic health records from real-world patients in tabular format with graphical representation using generative sampling. The representations are aligned with a domain specific ontology to further disambiguate and contextualize. A graph neural network that supports multi-relational entities is trained and meta-path sampling is applied to generate missing information according to upper-level ontological information. The generation process applied to tabular inputs related to cardiovascular disease, achieve precision, recall, and f1 scores in the ideal range for clinical data augmentation and decision making.

References

Edward Choi, Zhen Xu, Yujia Li, Michael Dusenberry, Gerardo Flores, Emily Xue, and Andrew Dai. 2020. Learning the graphical structure of electronic health records with graph convolutional transformer. In *Proceedings of the AAAI conference on artificial intelligence*, volume 34, pages 606–613.

Ioannis Dasoulas, Duo Yang, Xuemin Duan, and Anastasia Dimou. 2023. Torchictab: semantic table annotation with wikidata and language models. In *CEUR Workshop Proceedings*, pages 21–37. CEUR Workshop Proceedings.

Junheng Hao, Chuan Lei, Vasilis Efthymiou, Abdul Quamar, Fatma Özcan, Yizhou Sun, and Wei Wang. 2021. Medto: Medical data to ontology matching using hybrid graph neural networks. In *Proceedings of the 27th ACM SIGKDD Conference on Knowledge Discovery & Data Mining*, KDD '21, page 2946–2954, New York, NY, USA. Association for Computing Machinery.

Alistair EW Johnson, Tom J Pollard, Lu Shen, Li-wei H Lehman, Mengling Feng, Mohammad Ghassemi, Benjamin Moody, Peter Szolovits, Leo Anthony Celi, and Roger G Mark. 2016. Mimic-iii, a freely accessible critical care database. *Scientific data*, 3(1):1–9.

Chengsheng Mao, Liang Yao, and Yuan Luo. 2022. Medgcn: Medication recommendation and lab test imputation via graph convolutional networks. *Journal of Biomedical Informatics*, 127:104000.

Shervin Mehryar. 2025. A resolution-alignment-completeness system for data imputation over tabular clinical records. In *ELLIS workshop on Representation Learning and Generative Models for Structured Data*. ELLIS workshop on Representation Learning and Generative Models for Structured Data.

Joshua Robinson, Rishabh Ranjan, Weihua Hu, Kexin Huang, Jiaqi Han, Alejandro Dobles, Matthias Fey, Jan Eric Lenssen, Yiwen Yuan, Zecheng Zhang, and 1 others. Relational deep learning: Graph representation learning on relational databases. In *NeurIPS 2024 Third Table Representation Learning Workshop*.

Fei Teng, Wei Yang, Li Chen, LuFei Huang, and Qiang Xu. 2020. Explainable prediction of medical codes with knowledge graphs. *Frontiers in bioengineering and biotechnology*, 8:867.

Xiang Yue, Zhen Wang, Jingong Huang, Srinivasan Parthasarathy, Soheil Moosavinasab, Yungui Huang, Simon M Lin, Wen Zhang, Ping Zhang, and Huan Sun. 2020. Graph embedding on biomedical networks: methods, applications and evaluations. *Bioinformatics*, 36(4):1241–1251.

Embeddings for Numerical Features Using *tanh* Activation

Bingyan Liu
University of Illinois at Urbana-Champaign
bingyan2@illinois.edu

Charles Elkan
University of California, San Diego
celkan@ucsd.edu

Anil N. Hirani
University of Illinois at Urbana-Champaign
hirani@illinois.edu

Abstract

Recent advances in tabular deep learning have demonstrated the importance of embeddings for numerical features, where scalar values are mapped to high-dimensional spaces before being processed by the main model. Here, we propose an embedding method using the hyperbolic tangent (tanh) activation function that allows neural networks to achieve better accuracy on tabular data via an inductive bias similar to that of decision trees. To make training with the new embedding method reliable and efficient, we additionally propose a principled initialization method. Experiments demonstrate that the new approach improves upon or matches accuracy results from previously proposed embedding methods across multiple tabular datasets and model architectures.

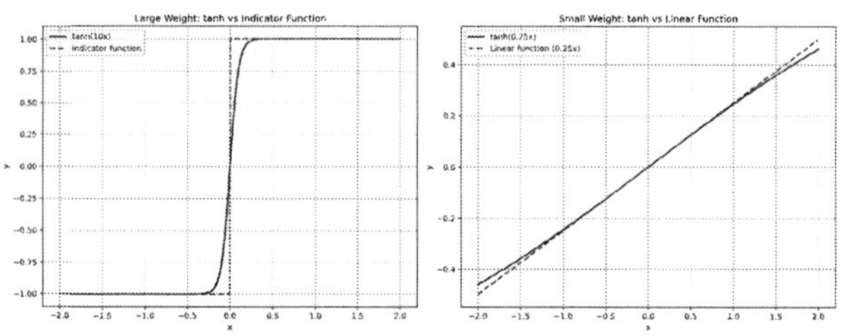

Figure 1: With a large weight w, $\tanh(wx)$ approximates an indicator function, enabling tree-like decision boundaries, while with small w, it allows a smooth feature transformation.

1 Introduction

Deep learning has achieved success in various domains, from computer vision to natural language processing. However, its application to tabular data has been challenging, with gradient-boosted decision trees (GBDTs) typically outperforming neural networks. This has led researchers to investigate how neural networks can better capture the inductive bias that makes tree-based models effective on tabular data.

Work by Gorishniy et al. (2022) has demonstrated that proper embedding of numerical features is beneficial for achieving performance competitive with that of GBDTs. Recent developments have introduced additional approaches to tabular embeddings: Li et al. (2024) use tree ensembles to transform numerical variables into binarized embeddings, while Wu et al. (2024) suggest a two-step feature expansion and deep transformation technique.

We propose here an approach to numerical feature embeddings based on properties of the hyperbolic tangent (tanh) function. The tanh function exhibits a dual nature that aligns well with the structure of tabular data: with large weight w, $\tanh(wx + b)$ captures a tree-like inductive bias by creating a sharp decision boundary, while with small w it approximates a linear function; see Figure 1.

However, with poor initialization, neural network training using tanh can lead to vanishing gradients and unstable learning. To overcome this, we introduce an initialization method based on a simple probability argument. The new method ensures that the embedding parameters w and b start in a region that facilitates both tree-like and linear representations. Empirically, the new initialization method does achieve the desired benefits of more stable training and better accuracy.

Experiments demonstrate the effectiveness of our approach in two scenarios. In the first scenario, we compare embeddings using fixed dimensions, where the model hyperparameters are tuned without considering the embedding layer. In this case, the new tanh-based approach consistently outperforms previous embedding methods across various datasets and model architectures. In the second scenario, we compare against previous ReLU embeddings, where both the model parameters and the embedding dimensions were tuned for the use of

Proceedings of the 4th Table Representation Learning Workshop, pages 208–216
July 31, 2025 ©2025 Association for Computational Linguistics

ReLU. Even in this challenging comparison, tanh-based embeddings lead to accuracy improvements. Overall, the new approach can achieve competitive or superior performance with minimal tuning overhead, making it particularly practical for scenarios where extensive hyperparameter search is not feasible.

2 Related Work

The application of deep learning to tabular data has historically been challenging, with GBDTs often achieving superior performance (Ke et al., 2017). Recent studies provide insights into this performance gap: Grinsztajn et al. (2022) demonstrated that tree-based models' success stems from their inherent ability to learn effective decision boundaries and handle heterogeneous features, while McElfresh et al. (2023) identified specific data characteristics where neural networks can potentially outperform GBDTs.

Traditional neural networks treat numerical features as direct inputs without specialized processing. This approach has limitations in capturing complex feature interactions and non-linear relationships. Recent work by Gorishniy et al. (2022) has studied simple differentiable embeddings, which apply a linear transformation followed by an activation function, and piecewise linear embeddings, which creates disjoint learnable bins for feature values. Their experiments demonstrated that these embeddings can significantly improve neural network performance on tabular data.

More recently, Li et al. (2024) proposed a tree-regularized method that uses tree ensembles to transform numerical variables into binarized embeddings, and Wu et al. (2024) introduced a unified framework employing lightweight neural networks for both numerical and categorical features, utilizing two-step feature expansion and transformation. Importantly, neither of these methods is a standard single neural network that can be trained by backpropagation in a standard way, whereas the method that we suggest below can be.

Recent research has also made progress in closing the performance gap with GBDTs through other innovations in feature processing and model architecture. Transformer-based models such as TabTransformer (Huang et al., 2020) and FT-Transformer (Gorishniy et al., 2021) tokenize the features, using attention mechanisms to capture complex feature interactions. Hybrid approaches such as NODE (Popov et al., 2020) incorporate tree-like structures into neural architectures, while DCN V2 (Wang et al., 2021) uses cross networks to model feature interactions. However, these methods are also not a simple single neural network that is trainable in a standard way.

2.1 Activation functions and initialization

ReLU (Nair and Hinton, 2010) has become the default choice for activation function due primarily to its ability to mitigate the vanishing gradient problem. However, it has limitations, including that neurons can become inactive during training. Alternatives proposed to address these limitations include Leaky ReLU (Maas et al., 2013) and Parametric ReLU (He et al., 2015) which introduce a small negative slope, while ELU (Clevert et al., 2016) and GELU (Hendrycks and Gimpel, 2016) offer smoother gradients.

The hyperbolic tangent (tanh) function, although less commonly used in modern architectures, has useful properties. Its bounded output between -1 and 1 provides natural normalization, while its sigmoidal shape enables both smooth transformations and sharp transitions that are similar to decision boundaries in trees.

Proper initialization is crucial for training stability and convergence, particularly in the context of tabular data where feature scales and distributions can vary significantly. Glorot and Bengio (2010) introduced Xavier initialization, scaling weights based on layer dimensions to maintain variance. He et al. (2015) extended this for ReLU activations, accounting for the activation's non-linearity. For tanh activations, LeCun et al. (2012) proposed scaling weights by the square root of fan-in to maintain variance.

While these approaches provide solid foundations for neural network training, adapting them for tabular data embeddings presents challenges due to varying feature distributions and the need to balance linear and non-linear representations. Recent data-dependent methods such as LSUV initialization (Mishkin and Matas, 2016) are adaptive, but can be computationally intensive.

3 The tanh-based embedding method

Given a tabular dataset with numerical features, our goal is to develop an embedding method that can capture both linear and non-linear relationships in the data. Let $\mathbf{x} \in \mathbb{R}^p$ represent a numerical feature vector, where p is the number of features. The new embedding method maps each feature x_i to $\mathbb{R}^d$, where d is the embedding dimension.

Previous approaches using ReLU activation functions in the embedding layer can be expressed as $\mathbf{e}_i = \text{ReLU}(\mathbf{W}_i x_i + \mathbf{b}_i)$ where $\mathbf{W}_i \in \mathbb{R}^{d\times 1}$ and $\mathbf{b}_i \in \mathbb{R}^d$ are learnable parameters and $\mathbf{e}_i \in \mathbb{R}^d$ is the embedding of x_i (Gorishniy et al., 2022).

We propose replacing the ReLU activation with tanh, so $\mathbf{e}_i = \tanh(\mathbf{W}_i x_i + \mathbf{b}_i)$. The advantage is that with large embedding weights $W_{i,j} \gg 1$, each component of the embedding captures a tree-like inductive bias, by creating a sharp decision boundary. Conversely, with a small weight $W_{i,j} \ll 1$, a component approximates a linear transformation, because $\tanh(x) \approx x$ for small x. See Figure 1.

We also propose an enhanced embedding variant with a second transformation layer:

$$\mathbf{e}_i = \sigma(\mathbf{M}_i \tanh(\mathbf{W}_i x_i + \mathbf{b}_i) + \mathbf{c}_i)$$

where $\mathbf{M}_i \in \mathbb{R}^{d\times d}$ and $\mathbf{c}_i \in \mathbb{R}^d$ are additional learnable parameters, and σ is another activation function, possibly ReLU. This two-layer method allows for more complex feature transformations while keeping the benefits of the tanh approach.

3.1 Connection to decision trees

A decision tree can be expressed as a function as follows. First, each node in the tree is an indicator function of some feature. Next, a path from the root to a leaf node, which represents a sequence of decisions, is a product of these indicator functions or their negations along the path. Finally, the entire tree is a combination of decision path functions:

$$f(\mathbf{x}) = \sum_{p\in P} c_p \prod_{i\in p} \mathrm{D}_i(x_i, \theta_i)$$

where P is the set of all paths from root to leaves, c_p is the constant value assigned to the leaf node at the end of path p, and $\mathrm{D}_i(x_i, \theta_i)$ is either $\mathbb{1}_{x_i\geq\theta_i}$ or $\mathbb{1}_{x_i<\theta_i}$ for feature x_i with threshold θ_i, where the choice depends on the split direction and which half-domain the node represents. As a simple example, see Figure 2.

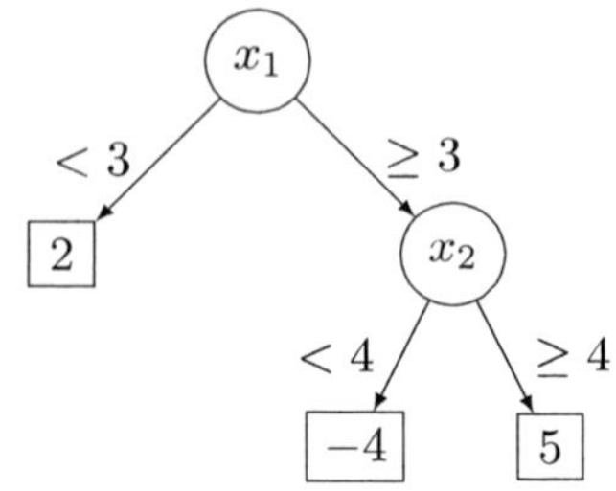

Figure 2: A example of decision tree of depth 2 operating on features x_1 and x_2, showing both branches at the root but only expanding the right subtree ($x_1 \geq 3$).

Each component of a tanh embedding can approximate a smoothed version of an indicator function as follows. Consider component j of the vector $\mathbf{e}_i$, as the weight $W_{i,j}$ approaches infinity. Given $b_{i,j} = -\theta_{i,j} W_{i,j}$ for a fixed $\theta_{i,j}$, the tanh function approaches an indicator function:

$$\lim_{W_{i,j}\to\infty} \tanh(W_{i,j} x_i + b_{i,j}) = \mathbb{1}_{x_i\geq\theta_{i,j}}.$$

Each component j can capture a different decision boundary, allowing the model to learn a rich set of decision rules while maintaining differentiability, which is crucial for gradient-based optimization.

The piecewise linear embedding method in Gorishniy et al. (2022) partitions each feature's range into bins with predefined boundaries. In contrast, the tanh-based approach allows the model to adapt the location and the sensitivity of bin boundaries.

3.2 Principled initialization

Proper initialization of embedding weights is important for the success of tanh-based embeddings. We propose a method that takes advantage of the properties of tanh. We first preprocess all numerical features using min-max scaling to the range $[-1, 1]$. Our method uses the fact that $\tanh(t)$ behaves approximately linearly for t in $[-0.5, 0.5]$.

When initializing an embedding that maps a feature x_i into d dimensions, we aim to create uniformly distributed bins across the $[-1, 1]$ range, with each bin having a length of $2/d$. We initialize the embedding parameters as

$$W_{i,j} = d/2 \text{ and } b_{i,j} \sim \text{Uniform}(-d/2, d/2).$$

As training progresses, the model learns to adjust the weights and biases to capture both linear relationships (when $W_{i,j}x_i + b_{i,j}$ is within $[-1, 1]$) and non-linear relationships (otherwise).

In the appendix, we prove that this initialization strategy ensures that for any input value $x \in [-1, 1]$, the expected number of bins where pre-activation $wx + b$ falls within $[-0.5, 0.5]$ is 1.

The effectiveness of the proposed initialization strategy is empirically validated through analysis of learned weight distributions in Section 5.3, which shows that the embeddings maintain good coverage of the feature space while adapting to local feature complexity.

Table 1: Dataset properties. MSE (↓: lower is better) denotes mean-square error, and AUC (↑: higher is better) denotes area under the ROC curve. Dataset abbreviations: GE (gesture), CH (churn), CA (california), HO (house), AD (adult), OT (otto), HI (higgs-small), FB (fb-comments), SA (santander), CO (covtype).

	Regression			Classification						
	CA	FB	HO	AD	CH	CO	GE	HI	OT	SA
#objects	20640	197080	22784	48842	10000	581012	9873	98049	61878	200000
#num. features	8	50	16	6	10	54	32	28	93	200
#cat. features	0	1	0	8	1	0	0	0	0	0
metric	MSE↓	MSE↓	MSE↓	AUC↑	AUC↑	AUC↑	AUC↑	AUC↑	AUC↑	AUC↑
#classes	–	–	–	2	2	7	5	2	9	2
majority class	–	–	–	76%	79%	48%	29%	52%	26%	89%

Table 2: Naming scheme for model variants. Each variant name consists of a prefix (experiment scenario), embedding variants, and initialization suffix. For example, 2B-LT-a is a model using optimized piecewise linear embedding parameters (2B-), with tanh-based embedding (T), and optimized initialization (-a).

(Abbr.)	(Embedding Variants)
Base model	MLP, ResNet, FT-Transformer
FR	control group with ReLU activation
FT	control group with Tanh activation
LR	embedding with ReLU activation
LT	embedding with Tanh activation
LRLR	LR + linear layer + ReLU
LTLR	LT + linear layer + ReLU
(Abbr. suffix)	(Initialization)
-s	standard initialization
-a	principled initialization
(Abbr. prefix)	(Scenarios)
(#)-	preassigned embedding dim (#)
2A-	see the main text
2B-	see the main text

4 Design of Experiments

The embedding dimension is a hyperparameter that has to be chosen to balance model expressiveness with computational efficiency. We conduct experiments under two scenarios that differ in how base model parameters (e.g., hidden dimensions of MLP) and embedding dimensions are selected.

Scenario 1 - Preassigned Dimensions: In this scenario, we adopt the optimized base model parameters (hidden dimensions and dropout rates for MLP, number of blocks etc. for ResNet and Transformer) obtained from hyperparameter search without considering embeddings, and use preassigned embedding dimensions. This allows us to evaluate the impact of replacing ReLU with tanh activations while keeping all architectural choices fixed.

Scenario 2 - ReLU-Optimized Dimensions: Here, we adopt both the base model parameters and embedding dimensions that are obtained from hyperparameter search for ReLU embeddings variants. This scenario is split into two cases. Scenario 2A uses tuned hyperparameter for linear embedding, and Scenario 2B uses tuned hyperparameter for piecewise linear embedding, as reported in Gorishniy et al. (2022). This creates a challenging comparison where we replace ReLU with tanh in settings optimized for ReLU, demonstrating the robustness of our approach.

Importantly, we do not perform additional hyperparameter search for model parameters or embedding dimensions for the tanh-based approach. This evaluation strategy demonstrates that the benefits of our method are inherent rather than the result of hyperparameter search, making it a drop-in replacement for ReLU-based embeddings in applications where extensive tuning may be infeasible.

As baselines for comparison, we consider two control groups that, before feeding the input data to the base model, process it through an extra single fully-connected layer for all features, with either ReLU or tanh activation functions. Thus $\mathbf{e} = \sigma(\mathbf{W}\mathbf{x} + \mathbf{b})$ where $\mathbf{W} \in \mathbb{R}^{d \times p}$, $\mathbf{b} \in \mathbb{R}^d$ and σ is either ReLU or tanh. These control groups separate the impact of our feature-wise embedding approach from the increase in dimensionality by comparing against a baseline fully-connected layer.

We evaluate three base model architectures, following the implementations in Gorishniy et al. (2022).

MLP: A multi-layer perceptron with multiple hidden layers.

ResNet: A residual network adapted for tabular data, incorporating skip connections to facilitate training of deeper architectures.

FT-Transformer: A Feature Tokenizer Transformer architecture that treats tabular features as a sequence, enabling feature interactions through the attention mechanism.

For each base architecture, we evaluate several vari-

Table 3: Performance of MLP variants on multiple datasets in Scenario 1. All rows are variations of MLP.

	MSE↓			AUC↑						
MLP-variants	CA	FB	HO	AD	CH	CO	GE	HI	OT	SA
MLP	.0682	.0115	**.0483**	.8972	.8568	.9953	.7954	.7392	.9541	.8575
30-FR-s	.0575	.0115	**.0483**	.9027	.8544	.9957	.7932	.7296	.9608	.8520
30-FT-s	.0578	.0117	.0486	.9029	.8590	.9925	.7947	.7584	.9632	.8549
30-LR-s	.0577	.0108	.0495	.9101	**.8640**	.9925	.7746	.5554	.9663	.8927
30-LT-s	.0591	.0108	.0508	.9085	.8615	.9956	.7827	.5000	**.9686**	.8601
30-LT-a	**.0497**	.0098	.0526	.9110	.8490	.9839	.8052	.7619	.9589	.8926
30-LRLR-s	.0584	.0099	.0500	.9096	.8611	.9962	.6181	.5000	.9678	.8932
30-LTLR-s	.0566	.0100	.0493	.9097	.8574	.9960	.7955	.6681	.9658	.8958
30-LTLR-a	.0525	**.0096**	.0492	**.9125**	.8538	**.9969**	**.8099**	**.7990**	.9664	**.8958**

Table 4: Performance of ResNet variants on multiple datasets in Scenario 1. All rows are variations of ResNet.

	MSE↓			AUC↑						
ResNet variants	CA	FB	HO	AD	CH	CO	GE	HI	OT	SA
ResNet	.0662	.0107	.0420	.9106	.8610	.9978	**.8273**	.8129	.9695	.8658
30-FR-s	.0598	.0103	.0447	.9093	.8546	.9976	.8153	.7940	.9689	.8713
30-FT-s	.0633	.0107	.0426	.9058	.8630	.9975	.8162	.7907	.9694	.8609
30-LR-s	.0752	.0092	**.0416**	.9119	.8623	.9980	.8092	.8160	**.9698**	.8786
30-LT-s	.0648	.0093	.0420	.9120	.8627	.9977	.8152	.8175	.9696	.8628
30-LT-a	.0463	.0095	.0506	.9117	.8484	.9974	.8180	.7997	.9638	.8894
30-LRLR-s	.0699	.0090	.0463	.9111	.8644	.9978	.7239	**.8178**	**.9698**	.8819
30-LTLR-s	.0610	.0091	.0419	.9121	**.8659**	.9978	.7520	**.8179**	.9696	.8699
30-LTLR-a	**.0456**	**.0087**	.0516	**.9158**	.8622	**.9983**	.8146	.8146	.9656	**.8901**

ants to assess the impact of different embedding approaches. The base model is the architecture without any specialized embedding layer, serving as our primary baseline. The variants are:

- **ReLU-based**: Simple differentiable embeddings with ReLU activation
- **Tanh-based**: Our approach using tanh activation
- **Enhanced**: Additional linear transformation layer after the activation function for both ReLU and tanh variants
- **Control**: A fully-connected layer with specified activation function. (For the FT-transformer, we do not test control group variants as they are not applicable.)

Standard initialization follows Kaiming for ReLU-based models and Xavier for tanh-based models. For the FT-transformer, we use the initialization method from Gorishniy et al. (2022). "Principled" refers to our initialization method described above. Names for the model variants and hyperparameter settings are in Table 2.

4.1 Datasets and metrics

We evaluate our approach on the nine tabular datasets used in Gorishniy et al. (2022), which represent a range of real-world scenarios with varying mixtures of numerical and categorical features, both regression and classification problems, and sizes. For categorical features, we employ label encoding without additional preprocessing in the MLP and ResNet models, and tokenization in the FT-Transformer model. Table 1 provides statistics for each dataset, including the number of numerical and categorical features, sample sizes, and task types.

For evaluation of model performance, we employ task-specific metrics as follows.

Classification: We use the Area Under the Receiver Operating Characteristic Curve (AUC-ROC) as our primary metric. AUC-ROC provides a measure of classification performance that is independent of the chosen decision threshold and handles class imbalance. For multi-class classification tasks, we report the average one-vs-rest AUC-ROC across all classes.

Regression: We evaluate using Mean Squared Error (MSE), which measures the average squared difference between predicted and actual values. Lower MSE values indicate better accuracy.

Training Efficiency: We record the training time for each initialization method to compare convergence speed and training efficiency.

Table 5: Performance of MLP variants on datasets in Scenario 2A and 2B.

	MSE↓			AUC↑						
MLP variants	CA	FB	HO	AD	CH	CO	GE	HI	OT	SA
MLP	.0682	.0115	.0483	.8972	.8568	.9953	.7954	.7392	.9541	.8575
2A-LR-s	.0530	.0104	.0715	.8923	.8546	.9666	.7833	.5494	.9704	.8940
2A-LT-s	.0530	.0106	.0566	.8888	.8521	.9783	.7798	.6638	.8988	.8618
2A-LT-a	.0496	.0099	.0442	.8717	.8495	.9201	.8274	.7955	.9066	.8955
2A-LRLR-s	.0575	.0093	.0651	.9105	.8582	.9692	.7897	.7990	.8970	.8770
2A-LTLR-s	.0574	.0101	.0444	.9091	.8520	.9896	.8414	.7885	.6885	.8966
2A-LTLR-a	**.0470**	**.0073**	**.0360**	**.9174**	.8520	.9963	**.8545**	.8013	.9649	.9028
2B-LR-s	.0832	.0104	.0509	.9020	.8572	.9965	.8058	.7377	.9652	.8946
2B-LT-s	.0858	.0111	.0513	.8971	.8502	**.9979**	.8033	.6883	.9639	.8790
2B-LT-a	.0528	.0092	.0464	.8856	.8482	**.9979**	.8121	.7881	.9611	.8946
2B-LRLR-s	.0511	.0106	.0457	.9088	.8598	.9914	.7987	.7874	.9553	.8909
2B-LTLR-s	.0524	.0100	.0466	.9095	**.8614**	.9946	.7998	.7999	.9644	.8906
2B-LTLR-a	.0510	.0087	.0434	.9143	.8488	.9915	.8181	**.8112**	**.9737**	**.9054**

Table 6: Performance of ResNet variants on multiple datasets in Scenario 2A and 2B.

	MSE↓			AUC↑						
ResNet variants	CA	FB	HO	AD	CH	CO	GE	HI	OT	SA
ResNet	.0662	.0107	.0420	.9106	.8610	.9978	.8273	.8129	.9695	.8658
2A-LR-s	.0725	**.0082**	**.0365**	**.9176**	**.8644**	.9909	.8228	**.8237**	.9712	.8895
2A-LT-s	.0704	.0096	.0428	.9119	.8607	.9949	**.8815**	.8045	**.9736**	.8827
2A-LT-a	**.0427**	.0089	.0481	**.9170**	.8516	**.9985**	.8619	.7941	**.9736**	**.9077**
2B-LR-s	.0601	.0096	.0449	.9124	.8617	.9972	.7971	.8182	.9685	.8928
2B-LT-s	.0671	.0094	.0428	.9146	.8602	.9955	.8065	.8198	.9684	.8849
2B-LT-a	.0477	.0089	.0459	.9135	.8492	.9970	.8093	.7897	.9643	.8919

We employ 5-fold cross-validation. We split the data into five shares, and in each fold, pick one share as test set and split the rest as training and validation set. We report the mean metrics across all five folds, and we consider one result to be better than another if its mean score is better and its standard deviation is less than the difference between the best and the second best result. Unless otherwise specified, we use hyperparameters that were tuned on 80% of the original dataset by Gorishniy et al. (2022).

We adapt the training framework from TabSurvey (Borisov et al., 2024) and begin with the model implementations from Gorishniy et al. (2021). All models are implemented in PyTorch and trained using the Adam optimizer with hypertuned learning rate, batch size of 128, and at most 300 epochs with early stopping based on validation performance. All experiments are conducted on a single Nvidia A100 GPU. Our code is available at `https://github.com/liu-bingyan/numbed`.

5 Results and Analysis

In Tables 3 to 7 MSE (↓: lower is better) denotes mean-square error and AUC (↑: higher is better) denotes area under the ROC curve. The best results for each dataset are shown in **bold**. Multiple bold entries in the same column indicate results that are statistically equivalent. Table 2 explains the model variant abbreviations used in the results.

5.1 Scenario 1: Preassigned Dimensionality

We first evaluate the effectiveness of our method in Scenario 1 as defined above.

For MLP models (Table 3), the tanh-based embedding exhibits better performance compared to the ReLU-based embedding across almost all test cases. Moreover, our initialization method shows notable improvements in the enhanced variants.

For ResNet models (Table 4), we observe consistent improvements similar to those observed in the MLP architecture. The tanh-based enhanced embedding demonstrates superior performance compared to the ReLU-based embedding across the majority of test cases. The new initialization significantly improves performance for the CA and SA datasets.

Overall, the results from Scenario 1 demonstrate that given a preassigned embedding dimension, the new tanh-based method effectively outperforms the ReLU-based embedding, particularly in the enhanced variants.

Table 7: Performance evaluation of FT-Transformer variants on multiple datasets in Scenario 2A and 2B. All rows are variations of FT-Transformer.

	MSE↓			AUC↑						
FT-Transformer variants	CA	FB	HO	AD	CH	CO	GE	HI	OT	SA
2A-LR-s	.0555	.0098	.0604	.9205	**.8690**	**.9982**	**.8865**	**.8093**	.9672	**.8987**
2A-LT-s	.0519	.0099	.0502	.9194	**.8689**	**.9981**	.8501	.8069	.9657	.8939
2A-LT-a	**.0396**	**.0090**	.0476	.9224	.8562	.9967	.8446	.8015	.9665	.8954
2B-LR-s	.0679	.0098	.0478	.9158	.8619	**.9981**	.8026	.8074	**.9677**	**.8988**
2B-LT-s	.0685	.0098	.0466	.9144	.8650	.9975	.8470	.8082	.9661	.8943
2B-LT-a	.0443	**.0091**	**.0313**	**.9259**	.8623	.9968	.8718	.8040	.9655	.8949

5.2 Scenario 2: ReLU-Optimized Dimensions

Models with carefully tuned hyperparameters constitute Scenario 2. While the improvements are more modest, they remain consistent across architectures.

For MLP (Table 5), tanh-based enhanced embeddings demonstrate superior performance compared to ReLU-based embeddings across all test cases in both Scenarios 2A and 2B. This suggests that our method effectively combines the advantages of both linear embeddings and piecewise linear embeddings. Notably, this performance advantage holds even though the hyperparameters are tuned for the comparison model, demonstrating the generality and robustness of our approach.

For ResNet (Table 6), while the original ReLU-based embedding shows competitive performance, our tanh-based enhanced embedding maintains better performance in more than half of the test cases. This demonstrates that our method achieves comparable or better performance than hyperparameter-tuned models. Additionally, our initialization method improves performance in more than half of the test cases and does not significantly degrade performance in the remaining cases.

For FT-Transformer (Table 7), our method shows significant improvement in some datasets, reducing MSE to .0396 on dataset CA, while it stays competitive in other cases.

5.3 Further Analyses

Figure 3 visualizes the learned embeddings for the first feature from the California Housing dataset. Compared to standard initialization, principled initialization allows bins to concentrate in regions where the conditional expectation of the label changes rapidly with the feature.

A significant advantage of our method lies in its computational efficiency, as demonstrated in Table 8. The average number of epochs required for convergence is consistently improved for MLP models, with many cases converging twice as fast compared to the ReLU-based embedding.

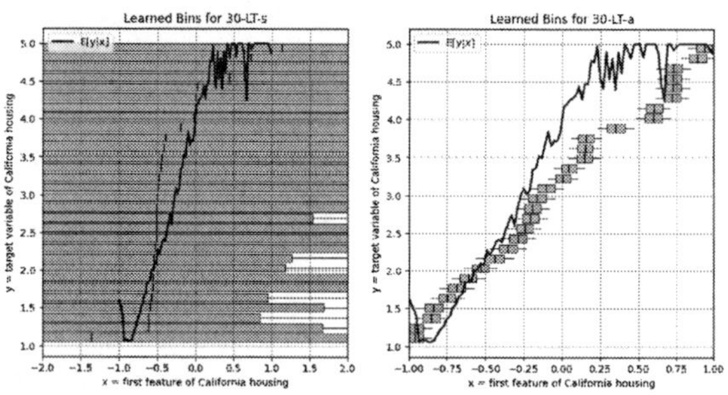

Figure 3: Comparison of embedding spaces learned with different initializations for the first feature x of the California Housing dataset (left standard, right principled). The center of each box is the embedding center $c = -b/w$ in the expression $w(x-c) = wx+b$, and the width is $1/w$. The horizontal line represents width $2/w$. Boxes are sorted by their centers; the vertical position of each box is for display only and carries no meaning.

Table 8: Number of epochs required for convergence across different MLP variants in Scenario 1. Lower values indicate faster convergence. The best values in each group are bolded.

MLP variants	AD	CA	CH	CO	FB	GE	HI	HO	OT	SA
MLP	62	94	38	100	113	31	54	63	89	20
30-FR	76	84	27	101	104	33	40	65	79	18
30-FT	57	99	28	55	74	29	74	62	47	18
30-LR-s	56	117	85	207	105	78	44	106	216	93
30-LT-s	51	89	79	124	116	109	32	78	240	41
30-LT-a	**38**	**74**	**22**	**46**	**72**	**61**	**30**	**35**	**94**	**22**
30-LRLR-s	50	90	67	129	126	41	**23**	141	90	87
30-LTLR-s	45	97	50	122	104	41	50	106	74	99
30-LTLR-a	**34**	**51**	**26**	**74**	**56**	**28**	63	**46**	**33**	**26**

6 Discussion

In summary, the experimental results above show that:

- In Scenario 1 (preassigned dimensions), the new method achieves better accuracy than the

ReLU-based method, particularly in enhanced variants.

- In Scenario 2 (ReLU-optimized dimensions), the new method maintains competitive performance against hyperparameter-tuned models, suggesting it captures a useful inductive bias.

In both scenarios, our initialization's performance varies for different models, but it doesn't degrade performance and improves it in half of the cases. Moreover, the new method improves computational efficiency, reducing training time while maintaining or improving model accuracy.

Overall, tanh-based embeddings appear to constitute a practical and effective solution for using numerical features in tabular deep learning, offering both accuracy improvements and computational benefits, without the need for extensive hyperparameter tuning.

Limitations and Future Work

While our method demonstrates promising results across multiple architectures and datasets, there are several directions for future exploration.

Our current evaluation is based on the benchmark datasets from Gorishniy et al. (2022). Future work could extend this evaluation to more recent benchmarks, such as those proposed in Gorishniy et al. (2024a) and Holzmüller et al. (2024), to further validate the effectiveness of our approach.

In terms of model architectures, we have demonstrated the effectiveness of our method on the models presented in Gorishniy et al. (2022), which includes MLP, ResNet, and Transformer architectures. Future work could explore the integration of our method with more recent architectures, such as TabR (Gorishniy et al., 2024b), RealMLP (Holzmüller et al., 2024) and others.

Acknowledgement

We would like to thank the anonymous reviewers for their valuable feedback and suggestions. The work of BL and ANH was supported in part by the University of Illinois Urbana-Champaign Campus Research Board Award RB24134. This work used NCSA Delta at National Center for Supercomputing Applications through allocation CIS230374 from the Advanced Cyberinfrastructure Coordination Ecosystem: Services & Support (ACCESS) program, which is supported by U.S. National Science Foundation grants #2138259, #2138286, #2138307, #2137603, and #2138296.

References

Vadim Borisov, Tobias Leemann, Kathrin Seßler, Johannes Haug, Martin Pawelczyk, and Gjergji Kasneci. 2024. Deep neural networks and tabular data: A survey. *IEEE Transactions on Neural Networks and Learning Systems*, 35(6):7499–7519.

Djork-Arné Clevert, Thomas Unterthiner, and Sepp Hochreiter. 2016. Fast and accurate deep network learning by exponential linear units (elus). In *International Conference on Learning Representations*.

Xavier Glorot and Yoshua Bengio. 2010. Understanding the difficulty of training deep feedforward neural networks. *International Conference on Artificial Intelligence and Statistics*, pages 249–256.

Yury Gorishniy, Ivan Rubachev, and Artem Babenko. 2021. Revisiting deep learning models for tabular data. *Advances in Neural Information Processing Systems*, 34:18932–18943.

Yury Gorishniy, Ivan Rubachev, and Artem Babenko. 2022. On embeddings for numerical features in tabular deep learning. *arXiv preprint arXiv:2203.05556*.

Yury Gorishniy, Ivan Rubachev, and Artem Babenko. 2024a. TabM: Advancing tabular deep learning with parameter-efficient ensembling. In *International Conference on Learning Representations*.

Yury Gorishniy, Ivan Rubachev, Nikolay Kartashev, Daniil Shlenskii, Akim Kotelnikov, and Artem Babenko. 2024b. TabR: Tabular deep learning meets nearest neighbors. In *International Conference on Learning Representations*.

Leo Grinsztajn, Edouard Oyallon, and Gael Varoquaux. 2022. Why do tree-based models still outperform deep learning on typical tabular data? In *Advances in Neural Information Processing Systems*, volume 35, pages 507–520.

Kaiming He, Xiangyu Zhang, Shaoqing Ren, and Jian Sun. 2015. Delving deep into rectifiers: Surpassing human-level performance on imagenet classification. In *Proceedings of the IEEE International Conference on Computer Vision*, pages 1026–1034.

Dan Hendrycks and Kevin Gimpel. 2016. Gaussian error linear units (GELUs). *arXiv preprint arXiv:1606.08415*.

David Holzmüller, Léo Grinsztajn, and Ingo Steinwart. 2024. Better by default: Strong pre-tuned mlps and boosted trees on tabular data. In *Advances in Neural Information Processing Systems*.

Xin Huang, Ashish Khetan, Milan Cvitkovic, and Zohar Karnin. 2020. TabTransformer: Tabular data modeling using contextual embeddings. In *Proceedings of the 26th ACM SIGKDD International Conference on Knowledge Discovery and Data Mining*, pages 627–635.

Guolin Ke, Qi Meng, Thomas Finley, Taifeng Wang, Wei Chen, Weidong Ma, Qiwei Ye, and Tie-Yan Liu. 2017. LightGBM: A highly efficient gradient boosting decision tree. *Advances in Neural Information Processing Systems*, 30:3146–3154.

Yann A LeCun, Léon Bottou, Genevieve B Orr, and Klaus-Robert Müller. 2012. Efficient backprop. In *Neural networks: Tricks of the trade*, pages 9–48. Springer.

Xuan Li, Yun Wang, and Bo Li. 2024. Tree-regularized tabular embeddings. *arXiv preprint arXiv:2403.00963*. Table Representation Learning Workshop at NeurIPS 2023.

Andrew L Maas, Awni Y Hannun, and Andrew Y Ng. 2013. Rectifier nonlinearities improve neural network acoustic models. In *Proceedings of the 30th International Conference on Machine Learning*, pages 1–8.

Duncan McElfresh, Sujay Khandagale, Jonathan Valverde, Vishak Prasad C, Ganesh Ramakrishnan, Micah Goldblum, and Colin White. 2023. When do neural nets outperform boosted trees on tabular data? In *Advances in Neural Information Processing Systems*, volume 36, pages 76336–76369.

Dmytro Mishkin and Jiri Matas. 2016. All you need is a good init. *International Conference on Learning Representations*.

Vinod Nair and Geoffrey E Hinton. 2010. Rectified linear units improve restricted boltzmann machines. In *Proceedings of the 27th International Conference on Machine Learning*, pages 807–814.

Sergei Popov, Stanislav Morozov, and Artem Babenko. 2020. Neural oblivious decision ensembles for deep learning on tabular data. In *International Conference on Learning Representations*.

Ruoxi Wang, Bin Fu, Gang Fu, and Mingliang Wang. 2021. Deep & cross network for ad click predictions. In *Proceedings of the 27th ACM SIGKDD International Conference on Knowledge Discovery and Data Mining*, pages 1–9.

Yuqian Wu, Hengyi Luo, and Raymond S. T. Lee. 2024. Deep feature embedding for tabular data. *arXiv preprint arXiv:2408.17162*.

A Analysis of Initialization Strategy

This appendix analyzes the proposed initialization strategy for the embedding parameters. Consider a numerical feature x normalized to the interval $[-1, 1]$ and its embedding $\tanh(wx + b)$. For optimal learning of decision boundaries, the pre-activation values $wx + b$ should lie predominantly within $[-0.5, 0.5]$, where the tanh function exhibits linear behavior.

Lemma 1. Let $\{c_i\}_{i=1}^d$ be independent and identically distributed random variables following a uniform distribution on $[-1, 1]$. For each i, let $I_i = [c_i - r, c_i + r]$ be the closed interval of radius r centered at c_i. Then, for any fixed point $x \in [-1, 1]$, the expected number of intervals containing x is more than $dr/2$.

Proof. For any fixed $x \in [-1, 1]$ and each interval I_i, we have

$$\mathbb{P}(x \in I_i) = \mathbb{P}(c_i - r \leq x \leq c_i + r)$$
$$= \begin{cases} r & \text{if } x \in [-1 + r, 1 - r], \\ \frac{r+1-|x|}{2} & \text{if } |x| > 1 - r, \end{cases}$$

Thus the $\mathbb{P}(x \in I_i) \geq r/2$. By the linearity of expectation, the expected number of intervals containing x is

$$\mathbb{E}\left[\sum_{i=1}^{d} \mathbb{1}_{x \in I_i}\right] = \sum_{i=1}^{d} \mathbb{P}(x \in I_i) \geq dr/2$$

□

The proposed initialization strategy sets $w = d/2$, so $r = 1/d$, because $-0.5 < wx + b < 0.5$ is equivalent to $-0.5/w < (x + b/w) < 0.5/w$ and $r = 0.5/w = 1/d$. Therefore the expected number of bins where the tanh activation provides meaningful gradients for learning, for any given data point, is at least 1.

This property ensures effective gradient propagation during training while keeping the bins relatively small for discriminative learning. The theoretical justification for this choice stems from the trade-off between gradient propagation and feature discrimination: a higher coverage probability would lead to excessive activation and reduced discriminative capacity, while a lower probability would risk insufficient gradient flow during training.

Improving Table Retrieval with Question Generation from Partial Tables

Hsing-Ping Liang, Che-Wei Chang, Yao-Chung Fan*
Department of Computer Science and Engineering,
National Chung Hsing University, Taiwan
yfan@nchu.edu.tw

Abstract

Recent advances in open-domain question answering over tables have widely adopted large language models (LLMs) under the Retriever-Reader architecture. Prior works have effectively leveraged LLMs to tackle the complex reasoning demands of the Reader component, such as text-to-text, text-to-SQL, and multi-hop reasoning. In contrast, the Retriever component has primarily focused on optimizing the query representation—training retrievers to retrieve relevant tables based on questions, or to select keywords from questions for matching table segments. However, little attention has been given to enhancing how tables themselves are represented in embedding space to better align with questions. To address this, we propose QGpT (Question Generation from Partial Tables), a simple yet effective method that uses an LLM to generate synthetic questions based on small portions of a table. These questions are generated to simulate how a user might query the content of the table currently under consideration. The generated questions are then jointly embedded with the partial table segments used for generation, enhancing semantic alignment with user queries. Without the need to embed entire tables, our method significantly improves retrieval performance across multiple benchmarks for both dense and late-interaction retrievers.[1]

1 Introduction

Table-based question answering (Table-QA) has drawn increasing attention in recent years, beginning with early works on Wiki-style tables (Pasupat and Liang, 2015; Zhong et al., 2017). These early Table-QA tasks typically operate under the assumption that the relevant table is provided alongside the question. While this assumption simplifies the problem and allows a focused evaluation of reasoning over structured data, it fails to reflect the challenges of real-world open-domain usage scenarios.

In practical settings, users do not typically specify which table to consult. Instead, they ask questions in natural language, and the system must first determine which tables might contain the relevant information before reasoning. The assumption of a known target table is thus insufficient in many realistic applications, where the answer may reside in any one of potentially thousands of tables within a large corpus.

To address this gap, recent research has moved toward integrating table retrieval into the QA pipeline. This shift is marked by the adoption of Retriever-Reader architectures (Chen et al., 2017), where a retriever component is responsible for identifying candidate tables, followed by a reader module that performs QA over the retrieved tables.

As a pioneering study, NQ-TABLES (Herzig et al., 2021) provides naturally phrased questions and their corresponding answer tables extracted from the Natural Questions dataset (Kwiatkowski et al., 2019), and transforms TAPAS (Herzig et al., 2020), a BERT-based table reader, into a dense table retriever (DTR) by adopting the DPR (Karpukhin et al., 2020) training paradigm.

Yet another study named CLTR (Pan et al., 2021) integrates the RCI (Row-Column Intersection; Glass et al., 2021) model with BM25 (Robertson et al., 2009) for table retrieval, and introduces the E2E-WTQ dataset for RCI retriever fine-tuning.

However, studies such as NQ-TABLES and CLTR operate under the assumption that the answer to a question resides in a specific cell within a single, relatively short table. While this setting facilitates controlled evaluation, it significantly limits the generalizability of these approaches to real-world applications, where answering questions often requires reasoning over multiple or lengthy tables.

Therefore, MMQA (Wu et al., 2025) extend the

[1]The code and reconstructed corpora are available at https://github.com/cc3374twa/QGpT

Proceedings of the 4th Table Representation Learning Workshop, pages 217–228
July 31, 2025 ©2025 Association for Computational Linguistics

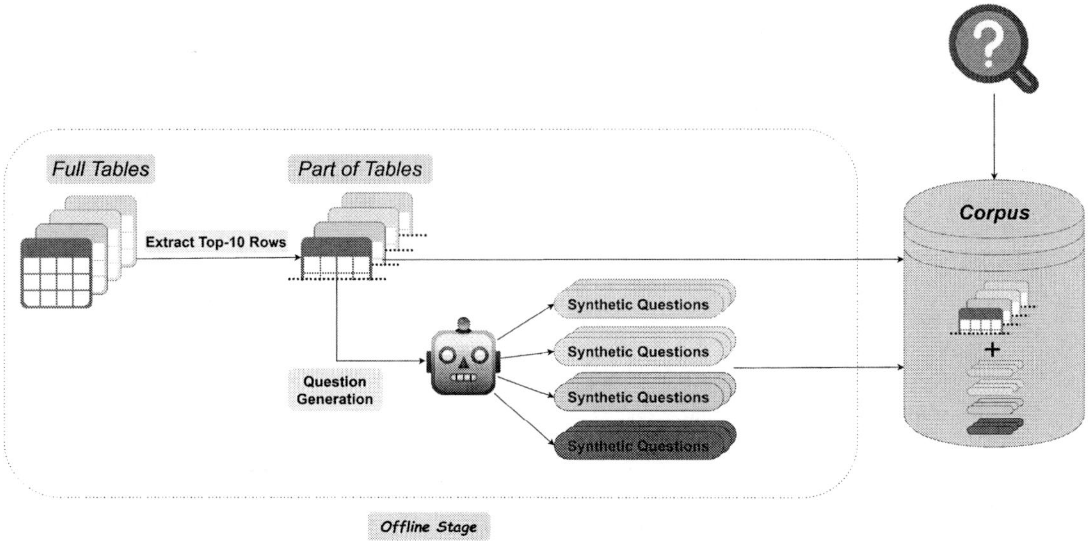

Figure 1: The **QGpT** pipeline: In the offline stage, top-10 rows from full tables are used to generate synthetic questions via LLM. The questions and table snippets are embedded and stored in the corpus, enhancing retrieval through semantic alignment without encoding full tables.

Table-QA paradigm by introducing complex reasoning tasks that integrate question answering with Text-to-SQL, using the Spider dataset (Yu et al., 2018) as a foundation. They propose a *multi-table retrieval* (MTR) setting, in which a single question may require retrieving and reasoning over multiple relevant tables. Their approach decomposes the original query into sub-queries, enabling independent retrieval and re-ranking of candidate tables.

Building on the idea of query decomposition, TableRAG (Chen et al., 2024b) adopts a similar strategy by splitting questions into schema-level and cell-level components and performing separate retrieval for each. Additionally, it segments tables into schema and content parts, allowing scalable retrieval across corpora with millions of cells, and focuses on retrieving localized table segments to improve efficiency and accuracy.

In summary, Table-QA has evolved from simple single-table, short-answer settings (Pasupat and Liang, 2015; Zhong et al., 2017; Herzig et al., 2021; Chen et al., 2020) to more complex, multi-table, and reasoning-intensive tasks (Wu et al., 2025; Li et al., 2025). Nevertheless, practical deployment remains challenging due to the growing size and noise of real-world tables. Traditional retrievers (Robertson et al., 2009; Karpukhin et al., 2020; Khattab and Zaharia, 2020) struggle to capture full-table context in token limits, while more recent approaches (Pan et al., 2021; Lin et al., 2023; Chen et al., 2024b) primarily rely on table segmentation based on rows, columns, or schema structures to improve matching between query keywords and table fragments. These methods focus on keyword-level matching rather than learning a semantically rich representation of the table that aligns with user questions. Moreover, they are often bound to dataset-specific assumptions or require retriever fine-tuning (Pan et al., 2021; Lin et al., 2023).

To tackle this issue, we propose Question Generation from Partial Tables (QGpT), a simple yet effective table retrieval method for long and complex Table-QA tasks. Our approach requires only a small snippet of the table and leverages LLMs to generate simulated questions that are likely to be asked. These questions are jointly embedded with the partial table snippet, enabling a dense representation with minimal token budget while improving retrieval accuracy.

As shown in Figure 1, QGpT is applied during the offline phase to augment the table corpus. During inference, it can adapt to various retrievers without fine-tuning, and enhances the performance of both dense and late-interaction retrievers (Chen et al., 2024a; Jha et al., 2024). Our QGpT framework offers a lightweight and generalizable solution that improves semantic alignment between questions and tables, reduces context size, and maintains retrieval performance in increasingly large and complex table settings.

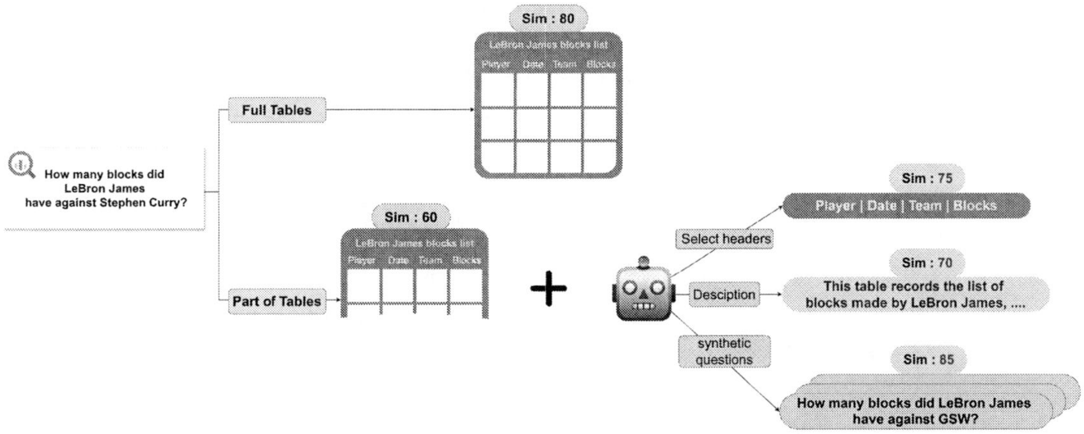

Figure 2: An illustration of three strategies for enriching truncated tables to enhance semantic alignment with the input query: selecting headers, generating table descriptions, and generating synthetic questions.

2 Related Work

2.1 Table Question Answering (TableQA)

Early TableQA tasks typically assume the target table is known, focusing on reasoning within a single table. Wiki-TableQuestions (Pasupat and Liang, 2015) is a pioneering dataset that provides semi-structured Wikipedia tables with questions involving simple answering. WikiSQL (Zhong et al., 2017) reframes the task as a Text-to-SQL problem, enabling structured query-based answering. Spider (Yu et al., 2018) introduces higher complexity by requiring reasoning over multiple tables and supporting diverse SQL logic.

Subsequent works began exploring more natural question formulations and open-ended scenarios. FeTaQA (Nan et al., 2022) introduced free-form, multi-hop reasoning questions requiring sentence-level answers across multiple rows. OpenWikiTable (Kweon et al., 2023) expanded WikiSQL and WikiTableQuestions by incorporating a larger table collection and more natural question expressions.

More recently, MimoTable (Li et al., 2025) uses real-world spreadsheets of varying size and complexity, containing multi-sheet structures and nested tables. It categorizes difficulty levels based on file count, number of sheets, and header complexity, making it one of the most comprehensive TableQA benchmarks.

Overall, the evolution of TableQA datasets has shifted from "single-table, structured QA pairs" to "multi-table, semantically ambiguous, natural language" tasks. However, most of these datasets do not consider the open-domain setting where tables must be retrieved from a large corpus before answering.

2.2 Table Retrieval in Open-Domain QA

A core challenge in open-domain TableQA is efficiently retrieving relevant tables from large corpora. OTT-QA (Chen et al., 2020) introduces table retrieval from Wikipedia to support open-domain question answering, highlighting the need for integrated retriever-reader systems. NQ-TABLES (Herzig et al., 2021) converts questions from Natural Questions (Kwiatkowski et al., 2019) into table-based QA pairs and incorporates a retrieval subtask. E2E-WTQ (Pan et al., 2021) extends WikiTableQuestions into a retrieval setting and proposes Cell-Level Table Retrieval (CLTR), focusing on cell-level semantic matching.

LI-RAGE (Lin et al., 2023) combines the concept of joinable tables with late-interaction retrievers (Khattab and Zaharia, 2020; Santhanam et al., 2022b), enabling joint training of retrievers and readers for better performance. TableRAG (Chen et al., 2024b) decomposes questions and tables into schema-level and cell-level components, enabling compression of million-cell tables into retrievable chunks.

MMQA (Wu et al., 2025) introduces Multi-Table Retrieval (MTR), which leverages LLMs like GPT-4 (Achiam et al., 2023) for query decomposition without retriever fine-tuning. It further employs LLM-based retrievers such as TableLlama (Zhang et al., 2024) and SGPT (Muennighoff, 2022).

While advances in retriever architectures—from sparse (Robertson et al., 2009) to dense (Karpukhin

Retriever	Table size	R@1	R@3	R@5	R@10	Avg
BGE-m3-dense	Full-Table (8K)	44.68 38.20	61.82 54.06	67.62 62.52	75.30 70.07	62.36 56.21
	1K tokens	46.09 40.27	**62.83** **56.22**	**68.90** 63.47	**77.46** 70.06	**63.82** 57.51
	2K tokens	45.15 40.15	62.75 55.62	68.16 **63.70**	76.70 70.61	63.19 57.52
	5K tokens	44.53 38.86	61.82 55.26	67.69 62.69	75.53 70.32	62.39 56.78
	Top10-rows	**46.24** **40.52**	62.29 55.99	67.77 62.92	75.22 **70.98**	62.88 **57.60**
Jina-ColBERT-v2	Full-Table (8K)	42.15 26.53	57.59 37.97	61.93 43.67	69.06 54.06	57.68 40.56
	1K tokens	48.82 **37.56**	64.24 **53.11**	**70.40** **58.61**	**75.25** **67.09**	64.68 **54.09**
	2K tokens	46.67 32.09	61.10 45.69	66.22 52.44	72.10 62.24	61.52 48.12
	5K tokens	42.62 26.70	56.97 39.22	62.09 44.44	68.12 54.50	57.45 41.22
	Top10-rows	**51.74** 36.70	**64.47** 51.21	69.23 57.30	74.38 66.11	**64.96** 52.83

Table 1: Recall@k performance on the **MiMoTable-English** dataset (normal font) and **MiMoTable-Chinese** dataset (shown in next to each value) across different retrievers and table representation lengths. Note that all table titles in table embeddings are excluded . Best and second-best scores are bolded and underlined respectively per language.

Statistics	English	Chinese
Number of Tables	206	295
Number of Sheets	295	464
Number of Queries	641	995
Max Tokens per Sheet	8,974	1,227,845
Tokens / sheet		
<1k	35%	29%
1k–2k	41%	36%
2k–5k	20%	22%
>5k	4%	13%

Table 2: Comparison of MiMoTable-English and MiMoTable-Chinese statistics.

et al., 2020; Herzig et al., 2020) and late-interaction models (Khattab and Zaharia, 2020; Santhanam et al., 2022b; Lin et al., 2023)—have significantly improved retrieval performance, our proposed framework is agnostic to the underlying retriever. It can flexibly integrate with various retrieval paradigms and consistently enhance performance across different backbone models.

3 Methodology

3.1 Partial Table Selection

To support complex TableQA tasks, it is essential to reduce large tables by removing irrelevant cells. A common approach is to retain only the header / schema or to constrain the input by a fixed number of tokens or rows. However, the former is heavily dependent on the nature of the dataset: SQL-based datasets typically rely heavily on headers, while in datasets like MiMoTable (Li et al., 2025), which aim to increase difficulty, headers are not necessarily positioned in the first row and may even be multi-level.

To inform our strategy for partial table selection, we first analyze the length distribution of tables in the MiMoTable dataset (see Table 2). Given the wide variance in table sizes, we compare two representative approaches for truncation: limiting by token length and selecting the top-10 rows. We construct English and Chinese table corpora accordingly and evaluate retrieval performance using BGE-m3 (Chen et al., 2024a) and Jina-ColBERT-v2 (Jha et al., 2024)—both supporting up to 8K tokens—as our retrievers. As shown in Table 1, the top-10 rows selection achieves comparable performance to 1K tokens truncation in complex table QA tasks. Considering the diversity of table lengths across datasets and the simplicity of implementation, we adopt the top-10 rows as our default strategy for partial table input.

To further improve semantic alignment between user questions and compressed table inputs, we explore several strategies for enriching table representations. As illustrated in Figure 2, these include selecting table headers, generating natural language descriptions, and producing synthetic questions by LLMs. To realize these strategies, we leverage LLaMA-3.1-8B-Instruct (Grattafiori et al., 2024) to implement these strategies. Table 3 presents the retrieval results using each method. Interestingly, even without table content, simulated

Retriever	Method	R@1	R@3	R@5	R@10	Avg
BGE-m3-dense	pT	44.27	61.95	67.25	75.27	62.19
	header-only	33.06	49.18	57.59	65.04	51.28
	desc-only	36.05	51.85	61.04	71.48	55.10
	QG-only	48.09	64.47	**72.39**	79.28	66.06
	pT + header	45.55	62.83	68.81	76.95	63.54
	pT + desc	45.85	64.47	71.41	78.99	65.18
	QGpT	**50.66**	**66.42**	72.35	**80.80**	**67.58**
Jina-ColBERT-v2	pT	54.25	69.16	75.83	81.97	70.30
	header-only	51.14	67.42	74.14	80.72	68.36
	desc-only	47.37	65.21	72.04	81.49	66.53
	QG-only	52.76	70.10	75.17	80.45	69.62
	pT + header	57.72	74.04	80.08	85.34	74.29
	pT + desc	**58.53**	74.71	**80.40**	**86.15**	**74.95**
	QGpT	57.94	**75.21**	79.11	83.26	73.88

Table 3: Recall@k results on the **MiMoTable-English** dataset comparing different table representation strategies and retrievers. The base table input *pT* corresponds to the top-10 rows of each table. Additional representations—headers, descriptions, and questions—are generated using the **LLaMA3.1-8B-Instruct** model. We evaluate combinations such as *pT* with *header*, *desc* and *QG*. Scores are reported using dense and Multi-vector retriever.

Dataset	#Q	#Tables	Type
OTT-QA	2.2K	789	TQA
FeTaQA	2K	2K	TQA
E2E-WTQ	241	2.1K	TQA
MiMoTable (en)	641	295 sheets	Long, TQA
MMQA (2-Tbl)	2591	2591 / 644	Long, MTR,
MMQA (3-Tbl)	721	721 / 391	TQA, SQL

Table 4: Dataset statistics. For MMQA, we report both the original and reconstructed table counts (original/ours).

questions alone can achieve comparable or better performance than partial tables. Combining simulated questions with partial tables further improves retrieval performance consistently. Motivated by these findings, we propose a unified table representation method—**QGpT** (Question Generation from Partial Tables)—which augments the top-10 table rows with generated questions to construct an enriched table corpus.

3.2 Question Generation from Partial Tables

QGpT is highly extensible and model-agnostic. The simulated questions are generated during an offline preprocessing stage, enabling integration with various retrieval paradigms (e.g., query decomposition or different retrievers) during online inference.

Offline Stage Given a table corpus $\mathcal{C}_T$, we convert each table into a markdown format and extract its name and the top-10 rows to construct a new partial table corpus $\mathcal{C}_t$. For each partial table $t_i \in \mathcal{C}_t$, we use a language model M to generate a set of questions $\{q_{t_i,j}\}$ such that the number of generated questions j satisfies:

$$j \geq \left\lceil \frac{|\mathcal{H}_{t_i}|}{2} \right\rceil$$

where $|\mathcal{H}_{t_i}|$ is the number of headers in Table t_i. The resulting *augmented* partial table $t_i' = (t_i, q_{t_i,1}, q_{t_i,2}, \ldots, q_{t_i,j})$ is then embedded using an embedding model E, producing a set of vectors for the table corpus:

$$E(\mathcal{C}_{t'}) = \{E(t_1'), E(t_2'), \ldots, E(t_n')\}$$

Online Stage Given a user query $q_i \in \mathcal{Q}$, we compute its embedding $E(q_i)$ and perform cosine similarity with all table representations:

$$\text{sim}(E(q_i), E(t_j')) \quad \forall j \in [1, n]$$

The top-k most similar entries are then retrieved.

4 Experiments

4.1 Experimental Settings

Datasets For the Single Table Retrieval task, we conduct experiments on OTT-QA (Chen et al.,

Model	Method	& Recall@k	MimoTable	OTTQA	FetaQA	E2E-WTQ	Avg
BGE-m3 dense	pT	R@1	44.27	52.17	31.75	39.83	42.01
	+QGpT		50.66 $_{\uparrow 6.39}$	51.45 $_{\downarrow 0.72}$	33.95 $_{\uparrow 2.20}$	41.49 $_{\uparrow 1.66}$	44.39 $_{\uparrow 2.38}$
	pT	R@5	67.25	78.27	48.08	59.75	63.34
	+QGpT		72.35 $_{\uparrow 5.10}$	78.14 $_{\downarrow 0.13}$	50.87 $_{\uparrow 2.79}$	65.98 $_{\uparrow 6.23}$	66.84 $_{\uparrow 3.50}$
	pT	R@10	75.27	86.04	55.62	70.54	71.87
	+QGpT		80.80 $_{\uparrow 5.53}$	86.68 $_{\uparrow 0.64}$	57.86 $_{\uparrow 2.24}$	72.61 $_{\uparrow 2.07}$	74.49 $_{\uparrow 2.62}$
Jina-ColBERT-v2	pT	R@1	54.25	54.43	35.30	48.55	48.13
	+QGpT		57.94 $_{\uparrow 3.69}$	55.15 $_{\uparrow 0.72}$	37.19 $_{\uparrow 1.89}$	51.45 $_{\uparrow 2.90}$	50.43 $_{\uparrow 2.30}$
	pT	R@5	75.83	76.87	50.82	65.56	67.27
	+QGpT		79.11 $_{\uparrow 3.28}$	78.73 $_{\uparrow 1.86}$	52.17 $_{\uparrow 1.35}$	71.37 $_{\uparrow 5.81}$	70.35 $_{\uparrow 3.08}$
	pT	R@10	81.97	83.83	57.36	70.95	73.53
	+QGpT		83.26 $_{\uparrow 1.29}$	86.04 $_{\uparrow 2.21}$	58.61 $_{\uparrow 1.25}$	76.76 $_{\uparrow 5.81}$	76.17 $_{\uparrow 2.64}$

Table 5: Single-table retrieval performance (Recall@k) across four QA datasets using two retrievers. The base method *pT* uses the top-10 table rows, while *QGpT* denotes the enhancement via question generation. Only embeddings for **OTTQA** exclude table titles, while all other datasets include them. $\uparrow$ indicates the improvement over the corresponding *pT* baseline.

2020) and FeTaQA (Nan et al., 2022) following the evaluation settings proposed by TARGET (Ji et al., 2024), as well as on E2E-WTQ (Pan et al., 2021) and MiMoTable-English (Li et al., 2025).

For the Multi-Table Retrieval task, we evaluate on the MMQA dataset (Wu et al., 2025). However, the original MMQA dataset only provides question-table-answer triples without releasing a unified table corpus. Moreover, tables with the same `table_name` may differ in structure across different examples—some pointing to semantically distinct tables despite identical names. To ensure consistency and reproducibility, we reconstruct the MMQA table corpus by performing a schema-based deduplication. Specifically, we (1) group tables by `table_name` and enumerate distinct schema variants, (2) assign unique identifiers (e.g., `department__1`, `department__2`) for structurally distinct tables, and (3) update all question-table mappings accordingly. This process results in a flattened and de-duplicated table corpus that supports robust retrieval evaluation. A summary of all datasets used can be found in Table 4.

Models Throughout all experiments, we adopt BGE-m3 (Chen et al., 2024a) and Jina-ColBERT-v2 (Jha et al., 2024) as base retrievers, which support up to 8K tokens and represent dense and late-interaction paradigms, respectively. All question generation is performed using LLaMA-3.1-8B-Instruct (Grattafiori et al., 2024), with prompt details provided in Appendix A.

To analyze the impact of model capacity on query decomposition in Multi-Table Retrieval (MTR), we experiment with multiple large language models, including LLaMA-3.1-8B-Instruct, GPT-4o-mini, and GPT-4o (Hurst et al., 2024), within the MTR framework.

Evaluation Metrics We report performance using the **Recall@K** metric across all experiments. For Multi-Table Retrieval, we follow the MMQA evaluation settings with $K = \{2, 5, 10\}$.

4.2 Implementation Details

All experiments are conducted using two NVIDIA RTX A6000 GPUs. We use RAGatouille[2] and Milvus[3] (Wang et al., 2021) as the retrieval infrastructure for vector indexing and search for Jina-ColBERT-v2 and BGE-m3, respectively. For Milvus, we adopt `index_type=IVF_FLAT`, `metric_type=IP`, and `nlist=256` to balance retrieval speed and accuracy. For RAGatouille, we leverage PLAID (Santhanam et al., 2022a), a high-performance indexing engine specifically designed for late interaction retrievers, enabling efficient

[2] `https://github.com/AnswerDotAI/RAGatouille`
[3] `https://milvus.io/`

Retriever	Method	R@2	R@5	R@10	Avg
BGE-m3-dense	pT	48.65 (39.36)	68.54 (61.10)	80.94 (74.69)	62.55
	MTR (LLaMA3.1-8b)	44.60 (36.50)	65.32 (60.02)	79.07 (74.15)	59.94
	+QGpT	49.63 (38.81)	68.33 (62.17)	80.13 **(75.86)**	62.49
	MTR (GPT4o-mini)	45.60 (36.51)	67.32 (59.51)	79.80 (72.61)	60.23
	+QGpT	50.19 (37.93)	71.37 (61.24)	**82.58** (74.86)	63.03
	MTR (GPT4o)	46.15 (36.41)	67.79 (58.90)	81.05 (73.17)	60.58
	+QGpT	51.10 (38.09)	**71.89** (60.40)	82.13 (74.45)	63.01
	QGpT	**52.24 (40.05)**	71.47 **(63.36)**	82.33 (75.36)	**64.14**
Jina-ColBERT-v2	pT	58.18 (45.79)	77.87 (70.16)	87.09 (81.63)	70.12
	MTR (LLaMA3.1-8b)	54.34 (42.65)	73.90 (66.84)	83.93 (78.30)	66.66
	+QGpT	54.28 (43.52)	74.98 (67.67)	84.22 (79.71)	67.40
	MTR (GPT4o-mini)	56.40 (41.24)	75.27 (65.18)	86.36 (75.96)	66.74
	+QGpT	56.33 (42.15)	76.18 (66.81)	86.17 (78.11)	67.63
	MTR (GPT4o)	56.76 (42.15)	75.82 (65.72)	86.80 (76.53)	67.30
	+QGpT	56.99 (43.23)	76.91 (67.82)	86.91 (77.97)	68.31
	QGpT	**59.49 (46.75)**	**78.41 (71.43)**	**87.25 (83.14)**	**71.08**

Table 6: Recall@k performance on the **MMQA** dataset with different retrievers and query methods. Metrics reflect performance on the 2-table setting; scores in parentheses show corresponding results under the 3-table setting (in small font). All methods are built upon the *pT* baseline (top-10 table rows). *MTR* uses sub-query generation via **LLaMA3.1-8B-Instruct, GPT-4o**, or **GPT-4o-mini**. *QGpT* questions are generated using **LLaMA3.1-8B-Instruct**.

token-level matching at scale.

5 Experimental Results

5.1 Main Results

Single Table Retrieval We evaluate retrieval performance across datasets ranging from short and simple to long and complex tables. As shown in Table 5, QGpT consistently improves retrieval performance across all Single Table QA datasets compared to using partial tables alone. Notably, on the MiMoTable dataset—which features longer and more complex tables—both the dense and late-interaction retrievers benefit significantly from QGpT. This demonstrates that QGpT is particularly effective in scenarios where aggressive table compression is required, offering robust performance regardless of table complexity.

Multi Table Retrieval Building on the same partial table setup, we compare Multi-Table Retrieval (MTR), QGpT, and their combination on the MMQA dataset. Note that our evaluation is based on a reconstructed table corpus. Therefore, our results are not directly comparable to those reported in the original paper.

Table 6 shows that while MTR performance slightly improves with larger query decomposition models (e.g., GPT-4o), it still underperforms compared to directly using partial tables for retrieval. This gap may stem from differences in implementation, such as our exclusion of the original paper's hand-crafted one-shot examples or the use of full tables during retrieval. However, integrating QGpT into MTR substantially closes the performance gap, and QGpT alone consistently outperforms the baseline across settings. These results highlight QGpT's effectiveness in both single- and multi-table retrieval, providing strong gains even when only limited table information is available.

5.2 Ablation studies

Can Simulated Questions Bridge the Semantic Gap? To understand whether simulated questions truly enhance the semantic alignment between partial tables and questions, we conduct an ablation study on the OTT-QA dataset. As noted by TARGET (Ji et al., 2024), OTT-QA questions often align closely with table titles, and excluding titles from the corpus can dramatically reduce BM25 Recall@10 from 95% to 44%.

In our study, we generate two versions of simulated questions using QG models: one with access

Model & Method	R@1	R@3	R@5	R@10	Avg
BGE-m3-dense (pT)	52.17	70.73	78.27	86.04	71.80
+QGpT w/o title	51.45 ↓0.72	70.64 ↓0.09	78.14 ↓0.13	86.68 ↑0.64	71.23 ↓0.57
+QGpT w/ title	60.79 ↑8.62	78.14 ↑7.41	84.37 ↑6.10	91.46 ↑5.42	78.69 ↑6.89
Jina-ColBERT-v2 (pT)	54.43	70.01	76.87	83.83	71.29
+QGpT w/o title	55.15 ↑0.72	71.27 ↑1.26	78.73 ↑1.86	86.04 ↑2.21	72.80 ↑1.51
+QGpT w/ title	60.07 ↑5.64	75.34 ↑5.33	80.80 ↑3.93	87.71 ↑3.88	75.98 ↑4.70

Table 7: Recall@k results on the **OTT-QA** dataset with different retrievers and *QGpT* enhancements. All embedding representations exclude table titles, while *QGpT* question generation is conducted **with or without referencing table titles**.

to table titles, and another without. We then embed both variants alongside partial tables that exclude the titles. As shown in Table 7, incorporating simulated questions generated with access to titles leads to significant performance improvements, outperforming both the baseline and the QGpT variant that does not use titles. These results validate that simulated questions can effectively bridge the semantic gap, helping partial tables better align with user queries during retrieval.

6 Conclusion

In this work, we propose QGpT (Question Generation from Partial Tables), a simple yet effective framework to enhance table retrieval by bridging the semantic gap between compressed table inputs and user queries. By leveraging LLMs to generate simulated questions from partial tables, QGpT provides a semantically enriched representation that improves retrieval performance across both single- and multi-table QA benchmarks.

Our extensive experiments demonstrate that QGpT consistently outperforms traditional partial table baselines on diverse datasets, including long, noisy, and multi-table settings. Notably, the framework is model-agnostic and can be flexibly integrated with different retrievers without requiring fine-tuning.

Limitations

While QGpT offers a generalizable solution for enhancing table retrieval, several limitations remain:

LLM dependency: The quality of simulated questions relies heavily on the capabilities of the underlying LLM. Lower-quality LLMs may generate irrelevant or redundant questions, limiting retrieval gains.

Generation latency: Although question generation occurs offline, large-scale preprocessing for hundreds of thousands of tables may introduce overhead in real-world deployments.

Acknowledgement

This work is supported by NSTC 112-2634-F-005-002-project Smart Sustainable New Agriculture Research Center (SMARTer), NSTC Taiwan Project under grant 112-2221-E-005-075-MY3, and Delta Research Center.

References

Josh Achiam, Steven Adler, Sandhini Agarwal, Lama Ahmad, Ilge Akkaya, Florencia Leoni Aleman, Diogo Almeida, Janko Altenschmidt, Sam Altman, Shyamal Anadkat, and 1 others. 2023. Gpt-4 technical report. *arXiv preprint arXiv:2303.08774*.

Danqi Chen, Adam Fisch, Jason Weston, and Antoine Bordes. 2017. Reading Wikipedia to answer open-domain questions. In *Proceedings of the 55th Annual Meeting of the Association for Computational Linguistics (Volume 1: Long Papers)*, pages 1870–1879, Vancouver, Canada. Association for Computational Linguistics.

Jianlv Chen, Shitao Xiao, Peitian Zhang, Kun Luo, Defu Lian, and Zheng Liu. 2024a. Bge m3-embedding: Multi-lingual, multi-functionality, multi-granularity text embeddings through self-knowledge distillation. *arXiv preprint arXiv:2402.03216*.

Si-An Chen, Lesly Miculicich, Julian Eisenschlos, Zifeng Wang, Zilong Wang, Yanfei Chen, Yasuhisa Fujii, Hsuan-Tien Lin, Chen-Yu Lee, and Tomas Pfister. 2024b. Tablerag: Million-token table understanding with language models. *Advances in Neural Information Processing Systems*, 37:74899–74921.

Wenhu Chen, Ming-Wei Chang, Eva Schlinger, William Yang Wang, and William W Cohen. 2020. Open question answering over tables and text. In *International Conference on Learning Representations*.

Michael Glass, Mustafa Canim, Alfio Gliozzo, Saneem Chemmengath, Vishwajeet Kumar, Rishav Chakravarti, Avi Sil, Feifei Pan, Samarth Bharadwaj, and Nicolas Rodolfo Fauceglia. 2021. Capturing row and column semantics in transformer based question answering over tables. In *Proceedings of the 2021 Conference of the North American Chapter of the Association for Computational Linguistics: Human Language Technologies*, pages 1212–1224, Online. Association for Computational Linguistics.

Aaron Grattafiori, Abhimanyu Dubey, Abhinav Jauhri, Abhinav Pandey, Abhishek Kadian, Ahmad Al-Dahle, Aiesha Letman, Akhil Mathur, Alan Schelten, Alex Vaughan, and 1 others. 2024. The llama 3 herd of models. *arXiv preprint arXiv:2407.21783*.

Jonathan Herzig, Thomas Müller, Syrine Krichene, and Julian Eisenschlos. 2021. Open domain question answering over tables via dense retrieval. In *Proceedings of the 2021 Conference of the North American Chapter of the Association for Computational Linguistics: Human Language Technologies*, pages 512–519, Online. Association for Computational Linguistics.

Jonathan Herzig, Pawel Krzysztof Nowak, Thomas Müller, Francesco Piccinno, and Julian Eisenschlos. 2020. TaPas: Weakly supervised table parsing via pre-training. In *Proceedings of the 58th Annual Meeting of the Association for Computational Linguistics*, pages 4320–4333, Online. Association for Computational Linguistics.

Aaron Hurst, Adam Lerer, Adam P Goucher, Adam Perelman, Aditya Ramesh, Aidan Clark, AJ Ostrow, Akila Welihinda, Alan Hayes, Alec Radford, and 1 others. 2024. Gpt-4o system card. *arXiv preprint arXiv:2410.21276*.

Rohan Jha, Bo Wang, Michael Günther, Georgios Mastrapas, Saba Sturua, Isabelle Mohr, Andreas Koukounas, Mohammad Kalim Wang, Nan Wang, and Han Xiao. 2024. Jina-ColBERT-v2: A general-purpose multilingual late interaction retriever. In *Proceedings of the Fourth Workshop on Multilingual Representation Learning (MRL 2024)*, pages 159–166, Miami, Florida, USA. Association for Computational Linguistics.

Xingyu Ji, Aditya Parameswaran, and Madelon Hulsebos. 2024. Target: Benchmarking table retrieval for generative tasks. In *NeurIPS 2024 Third Table Representation Learning Workshop*.

Vladimir Karpukhin, Barlas Oguz, Sewon Min, Patrick Lewis, Ledell Wu, Sergey Edunov, Danqi Chen, and Wen-tau Yih. 2020. Dense passage retrieval for open-domain question answering. In *Proceedings of the 2020 Conference on Empirical Methods in Natural Language Processing (EMNLP)*, pages 6769–6781, Online. Association for Computational Linguistics.

Omar Khattab and Matei Zaharia. 2020. Colbert: Efficient and effective passage search via contextualized late interaction over bert. In *Proceedings of the 43rd International ACM SIGIR conference on research and development in Information Retrieval*, pages 39–48.

Sunjun Kweon, Yeonsu Kwon, Seonhee Cho, Yohan Jo, and Edward Choi. 2023. Open-wikitable: Dataset for open domain question answering with complex reasoning over table. In *Findings of the Association for Computational Linguistics: ACL 2023*, pages 8285–8297.

Tom Kwiatkowski, Jennimaria Palomaki, Olivia Redfield, Michael Collins, Ankur Parikh, Chris Alberti, Danielle Epstein, Illia Polosukhin, Jacob Devlin, Kenton Lee, Kristina Toutanova, Llion Jones, Matthew Kelcey, Ming-Wei Chang, Andrew M. Dai, Jakob Uszkoreit, Quoc Le, and Slav Petrov. 2019. Natural questions: A benchmark for question answering research. *Transactions of the Association for Computational Linguistics*, 7:452–466.

Zheng Li, Yang Du, Mao Zheng, and Mingyang Song. 2025. MiMoTable: A multi-scale spreadsheet benchmark with meta operations for table reasoning. In *Proceedings of the 31st International Conference on Computational Linguistics*, pages 2548–2560, Abu Dhabi, UAE. Association for Computational Linguistics.

Weizhe Lin, Rexhina Blloshmi, Bill Byrne, Adria de Gispert, and Gonzalo Iglesias. 2023. LI-RAGE: Late interaction retrieval augmented generation with explicit signals for open-domain table question answering. In *Proceedings of the 61st Annual Meeting of the Association for Computational Linguistics (Volume 2: Short Papers)*, pages 1557–1566, Toronto, Canada. Association for Computational Linguistics.

Niklas Muennighoff. 2022. Sgpt: Gpt sentence embeddings for semantic search. *arXiv preprint arXiv:2202.08904*.

Linyong Nan, Chiachun Hsieh, Ziming Mao, Xi Victoria Lin, Neha Verma, Rui Zhang, Wojciech Kryściński, Hailey Schoelkopf, Riley Kong, Xiangru Tang, Mutethia Mutuma, Ben Rosand, Isabel Trindade, Renusree Bandaru, Jacob Cunningham, Caiming Xiong, Dragomir Radev, and Dragomir Radev. 2022. FeTaQA: Free-form table question answering. *Transactions of the Association for Computational Linguistics*, 10:35–49.

Feifei Pan, Mustafa Canim, Michael Glass, Alfio Gliozzo, and Peter Fox. 2021. Cltr: An end-to-end, transformer-based system for cell-level table retrieval and table question answering. In *Proceedings of the 59th Annual Meeting of the Association for Computational Linguistics and the 11th International Joint Conference on Natural Language Processing: System Demonstrations*, pages 202–209.

Panupong Pasupat and Percy Liang. 2015. Compositional semantic parsing on semi-structured tables. In *Proceedings of the 53rd Annual Meeting of the Association for Computational Linguistics and the 7th*

International Joint Conference on Natural Language Processing (Volume 1: Long Papers), pages 1470–1480.

Stephen Robertson, Hugo Zaragoza, and 1 others. 2009. The probabilistic relevance framework: Bm25 and beyond. *Foundations and Trends® in Information Retrieval*, 3(4):333–389.

Keshav Santhanam, Omar Khattab, Christopher Potts, and Matei Zaharia. 2022a. Plaid: An efficient engine for late interaction retrieval. In *Proceedings of the 31st ACM International Conference on Information & Knowledge Management*, CIKM '22, page 1747–1756, New York, NY, USA. Association for Computing Machinery.

Keshav Santhanam, Omar Khattab, Jon Saad-Falcon, Christopher Potts, and Matei Zaharia. 2022b. ColBERTv2: Effective and efficient retrieval via lightweight late interaction. In *Proceedings of the 2022 Conference of the North American Chapter of the Association for Computational Linguistics: Human Language Technologies*, pages 3715–3734, Seattle, United States. Association for Computational Linguistics.

Jianguo Wang, Xiaomeng Yi, Rentong Guo, Hai Jin, Peng Xu, Shengjun Li, Xiangyu Wang, Xiangzhou Guo, Chengming Li, Xiaohai Xu, and 1 others. 2021. Milvus: A purpose-built vector data management system. In *Proceedings of the 2021 International Conference on Management of Data*, pages 2614–2627.

Jian Wu, Linyi Yang, Dongyuan Li, Yuliang Ji, Manabu Okumura, and Yue Zhang. 2025. MMQA: Evaluating LLMs with multi-table multi-hop complex questions. In *The Thirteenth International Conference on Learning Representations*.

Tao Yu, Rui Zhang, Kai Yang, Michihiro Yasunaga, Dongxu Wang, Zifan Li, James Ma, Irene Li, Qingning Yao, Shanelle Roman, Zilin Zhang, and Dragomir Radev. 2018. Spider: A large-scale human-labeled dataset for complex and cross-domain semantic parsing and text-to-SQL task. In *Proceedings of the 2018 Conference on Empirical Methods in Natural Language Processing*, pages 3911–3921, Brussels, Belgium. Association for Computational Linguistics.

Tianshu Zhang, Xiang Yue, Yifei Li, and Huan Sun. 2024. TableLlama: Towards open large generalist models for tables. In *Proceedings of the 2024 Conference of the North American Chapter of the Association for Computational Linguistics: Human Language Technologies (Volume 1: Long Papers)*, pages 6024–6044, Mexico City, Mexico. Association for Computational Linguistics.

Victor Zhong, Caiming Xiong, and Richard Socher. 2017. Seq2sql: Generating structured queries from natural language using reinforcement learning. *arXiv preprint arXiv:1709.00103*.

A Prompt Details for Question Generation

We provide the exact prompts used in our LLM-based pipeline for extracting headers and generating simulated questions from partial tables. Prompts were designed to be highly structured and instructive, guiding the LLM (LLaMA-3.1-8B-Instruct) to handle inputs. All prompts return a strict JSON format, suitable for programmatic post-processing.

A.1 Header Extraction + Question Generation (Full Pipeline)

If header extraction is desired (used in most QGpT scenarios), we use the following prompt format:

You are an expert in table data analysis. Given a table with its file name, sheet name, and a portion of its content (first ten rows), your task is to **extract key headers and generate questions** based on the table & headers.

Important Considerations:

- The table may contain nan or Unnamed: values, which represent empty merged cells in the original table. These **should not** be considered as meaningful data points or headers.
- The **true column headers may not always be in the first row or first column**. Carefully analyze the table to identify the correct headers.
- If the table has **multi-level headers**, preserve the hierarchical structure without merging or altering the text.
- If the table has an **irregular header structure** (such as key-value formatted headers where column names are listed separately), extract the correct header names accordingly.
- **Ignore rows that contain mostly empty values (nan, Unnamed:) or placeholders without meaningful data.**
- **Do not generate python code, extract headers and questions on your own.**
- The type of Questions could be one of (lookup, calculate, visualize, reasoning).
- **Generate question using the language of the table.**

Tasks:

1. **Extract Header Names:**
   - Identify the **true headers** by analyzing the structure of the table.
   - **Exclude** placeholder values like "nan" and "Unnamed:".
   - If the table contains **multi-level headers**, keep them as separate levels without merging.
   - If the table has **key-value headers**, extract the correct column names.
2. **Generate Questions (Context-Specific to the Table):**
   - Formulate **questions that can only be answered using this specific table**.
   - Ensure **each question involves 1 to 3 different headers** to capture interactions between data & columns.
   - Ensure the header diversity in all the questions.
   - Use " to mark the headers in the question.
   - **Total number of questions should larger than the half number of extracted headers**

****Output Format (Strictly JSON format)****
Only return a JSON dictionary object with the extracted headers and questions, without any additional explanations or formatting.

{{ "headers": ["header1", "header2", "..."], "questions": ["question1", "question2", "..."] }}

Input Table: <table>

A.2 Question Generation Only (Without Header Extraction)

If header extraction is skipped (e.g., MMQA), we apply a simplified prompt:

You are an expert in table data analysis. Given a table with its file name and a portion of its content (first ten rows), your task is to **generate questions** based on the table & headers.

Important Considerations:

- **Do not generate python code, generate questions on your own.**
- The type of Questions could be one of (Numerical, List, Count, Select).
- **Generate question using the language of the table.**

****Tasks:****

- **1. Generate Questions (Context-Specific to the Table):**
- Formulate **questions that can only be answered using this specific table**.

- Ensure **each question involves 1 to 3 different headers** to capture interactions between data & columns.
- Ensure the header diversity in all the questions.
- Use " to mark the headers in the question.
- **Total number of questions should larger than the half number of extracted headers**

****Output Format (Strictly JSON format)**** Only return a JSON dictionary object with the extracted headers and questions, without any additional explanations or formatting.

```
{ "questions": ["question1",

"question2","..."]
```

Input Table: <table>

Sparks of Tabular Reasoning via Text2SQL Reinforcement Learning

Josefa Lia Stoisser *
Novo Nordisk †
ofsr@novonordisk.com

Marc Boubnovski Martell *
Novo Nordisk†
mbvk@novonordisk.com

Julien Fauqueur
Novo Nordisk†
jlzf@novonordisk.com

Abstract

This work reframes the Text-to-SQL task as a pathway for teaching large language models (LLMs) to reason over and manipulate tabular data—moving beyond the traditional focus on query generation. We propose a two-stage framework that leverages SQL supervision to develop transferable table reasoning capabilities. First, we synthesize detailed chain-of-thought (CoT) traces from real-world SQL queries, providing step-by-step, clause-level supervision that teaches the model how to traverse, filter, and aggregate table fields. Second, we introduce a Group Relative Policy Optimization (GRPO) reinforcement learning objective that connects SQL execution accuracy to generalizable reasoning by encouraging steps that extend beyond task-specific syntax and transfer across datasets.

Empirically, our approach improves performance on standard Text-to-SQL benchmarks and achieves substantial gains on reasoning-intensive datasets such as BIRD, CRT-QA and Tablebench, demonstrating enhanced generalization and interpretability. Specifically, the distilled-quantized LLaMA-8B model achieved a 34% relative increase in exact match scores on CRT-QA when trained on Text-to-SQL tasks, while Qwen-2.5-7B achieved a 10% and Qwen-2.5-14B a 6% relative increase. These results suggest that SQL can serve not only as a target formalism but also as an effective scaffold for learning robust, transferable reasoning over structured data.

1 Introduction

Recent advancements in LLMs have substantially improved performance on Text-to-SQL tasks, translating natural language into executable SQL queries over relational databases (Gao et al., 2023).

Progress has been driven primarily by supervised fine-tuning (SFT) on SQL-focused datasets (e.g., Spider (Yu et al., 2018), BIRD (Li et al., 2023)) or prompt-based adaptation (Sun et al., 2023). However, these methods often narrowly optimize for syntactic correctness or execution accuracy, overlooking deeper reasoning over underlying data structures—resulting in degraded performance in real-world settings (Liu et al., 2024; Nascimento et al., 2025).

This highlights a broader issue: Text-to-SQL is frequently treated as a standalone task, rather than as a facet of the more general challenge of reasoning over tabular data (Liu et al., 2024). SQL, as a formal language, provides a vehicle for structured reasoning over relational tables; thus, models generating SQL should ideally also support broader forms of table-based question answering (e.g., TabFact (Chen et al., 2019), WikiTQ (Pasupat and Liang, 2015), FinQA (Chen et al., 2021)).

Yet, models fine-tuned exclusively for Text-to-SQL often exhibit degraded performance on related tasks, suggesting overfitting to SQL-specific patterns at the expense of flexible reasoning (Abhyankar et al., 2024). Methods like H-STAR (Abhyankar et al., 2024) integrate symbolic and semantic reasoning for improved table comprehension, while Plan-of-SQLs (POS) (Brugere et al., 2024) emphasize interpretability and QA performance. However, both approaches tend to bias the model toward SQL-centric reasoning, potentially limiting generalization (Nascimento et al., 2025). Inspired by DeepSeek-R1 (Guo et al., 2025), we explore whether reinforcement learning (RL) can foster emergent reasoning capabilities that connect Text-to-SQL with general tabular QA.

We propose a two-stage approach depicted in Figure 1. First, we introduce a supervised fine-tuning phase leveraging synthetically generated CoT reasoning traces to provide structured guidance between the natural language input and its corresponding SQL representation. Unlike SynSQL-2.5 (Li et al., 2025b), which emphasizes data scale,

*Equal contribution

†One Pancras Square, Pancras Rd, London N1C 4AG

Proceedings of the 4th Table Representation Learning Workshop, pages 229–240
July 31, 2025 ©2025 Association for Computational Linguistics

our approach focuses on generating high-quality CoT traces grounded in real data points. Second, we apply GRPO (Shao et al., 2024), a reinforcement learning method that compares multiple candidate outputs, aligning SQL execution accuracy and query structure with broader reasoning fidelity.

While prior work (e.g., Reasoning-SQL (Pourreza et al., 2025), SQL-R1 (Ma et al., 2025)) has applied RL to SQL generation, our key contribution lies in bridging Text-to-SQL with general tabular reasoning. We show that models trained with our two-stage framework outperform SFT baselines not only on SQL benchmarks but also on reasoning-intensive QA datasets such as CRT-QA (Zhang et al., 2023) and Tablebench (Wu et al., 2025), illustrating that SQL generation, when properly framed, can serve as a foundation for broader structured data reasoning.

Our key contributions are:

1. **Synthetic CoT Supervision:** We present a method for generating synthetic reasoning traces tailored to the SQL domain, offering structured and interpretable supervision during fine-tuning. The synthetic data is made publicly available[1].

2. **Reinforcement Learning with GRPO for Generalization:** We apply GRPO not only to improve SQL execution accuracy, but also to regularize model behavior toward more generalizable table reasoning.

3. **Empirical Evidence of Cross-Task Gains:** Our two-stage method improves performance on standard Text-to-SQL benchmarks while enhancing reasoning ability on diverse QA datasets such as CRT-QA and Tablebench.

The training and evaluation code is made publicly available[2].

2 Background

2.1 Reasoning in Language Models

LLMs have demonstrated strong capabilities in general-purpose reasoning tasks, including arithmetic, logic, and multi-step decision-making. These capabilities are often enhanced by prompting techniques, tool integration, and reinforcement learning (Jaech et al., 2024; Guo et al., 2025). A growing line of work has focused on intermediate reasoning structures, such as CoT prompting, which guide models through decomposed, interpretable inference steps (Zhao et al., 2025).

In particular, long-form CoT reasoning—requiring detailed, iterative solutions—has shown benefits in domains like mathematics, program synthesis, and multi-hop question answering (Team et al., 2025). Unlike short-form CoT, long-form reasoning involves planning, reflection, and consistency across intermediate steps. Recent studies have shown that such behavior can be learned through data-efficient supervised fine-tuning and parameter-efficient adaptation methods such as low-rank updates (LoRA) (Li et al., 2025a). Beyond training-time learning, test-time methods like self-consistency and re-ranking over multiple generations have been shown to improve reasoning reliability (Wei et al., 2022; Wang et al., 2022).

Complementary to these approaches, reinforcement learning has been explored as a way to promote reasoning beyond imitation, allowing models to discover extended inference patterns through reward-driven optimization (Qin et al., 2024; Chen et al., 2025; Shinn et al., 2023).

2.2 LLMs on Text-to-SQL

Mapping natural language to executable SQL involves three principal challenges: interpreting user intent, understanding database schema, and generating syntactically and semantically correct queries (Hong et al., 2024; Stoisser et al., 2025). LLMs have shown strong performance on this task, supported by progress in semantic parsing and schema linking (Liu et al., 2024; Shi et al., 2020). Recent work continues to refine LLMs across subcomponents of the task, including question understanding (Pourreza and Rafiei, 2023), schema comprehension (Yuan et al., 2025), and SQL generation (Lee et al., 2024).

To move beyond supervised fine-tuning, reinforcement learning has been proposed as a means of aligning model behavior with downstream performance objectives (Jiang et al., 2025). GRPO compares multiple candidate outputs, offering a denser learning signal that mitigates the limitations of sparse or binary rewards (Pourreza et al., 2025). SQL-R1 builds on this idea by integrating reinforcement learning with synthetic CoT supervision, achieving competitive results on benchmarks such

[1] https://huggingface.co/datasets/jls205/synthetic_cot_traces_clinton/blob/main/cot.csv

[2] https://github.com/josefastoisser/sparks_of_tabular_reasoning

as BIRD and WikiSQL (Ma et al., 2025; Li et al., 2025b).

These approaches suggest that supervision grounded in SQL execution can serve not only as a means of training for query generation, but as a proxy for inducing structured reasoning in LLMs.

2.3 LLMs on Tabular Question Answering

LLMs have increasingly been applied to question answering over structured tabular data—a task that combines natural language understanding with symbolic reasoning. In the typical formulation, models receive a serialized table and a natural language query, and are tasked with producing an accurate answer. While this setting is straightforward, it presents several challenges, including query intent disambiguation, context-aware retrieval, numerical reasoning, and robust handling of multi-turn interactions (Pal et al., 2023).

Recent work has introduced frameworks that extend LLM capabilities in this domain. The Chain-of-Command approach, for instance, reformulates user queries into structured commands that guide table interaction (Zha et al., 2023). Other strategies improve retrieval through query-based sampling or adaptive search mechanisms (Sui et al., 2023). Multi-turn dialogue settings have also gained attention, where task decomposition and iterative refinement have shown improvements in reasoning depth and consistency (Yu et al., 2025).

Benchmarks such as CRT-QA provide a foundation for evaluating LLM performance on table reasoning tasks (Zhang et al., 2023; Ashury-Tahan et al., 2025). These settings demand not only the ability to parse structured inputs, but also to integrate logical, numerical, and contextual cues across diverse formats. Together, these developments suggest that tabular question answering offers a rich and challenging testbed for evaluating the reasoning capabilities of LLMs.

3 Methodology

Our methodology is outlined in Figure 2, where we see the breakdown into 6 steps.

3.1 Generating Synthetic Reasoning Traces for SQL Tasks

In the first stage, we construct synthetic CoT traces for Text-to-SQL questions using a structured prompting pipeline. The core generation process employs a LLMs trained on 25 diverse datasets (see Appendix A), following the methodology of Boubnovski et al. (2025). Specifically, we prompt the o3-mini model to answer SQL-related questions while producing intermediate reasoning steps in natural language as shown in Appendix B.1. A second language model is used as a verifier to assess both the correctness of the final answer and the internal reasoning trace (prompt details in Appendix B.2).

This framework yields a dataset of 3,174 examples containing only correctly reasoned outputs, which we use as high-quality supervision during model fine-tuning.

3.2 Training and Reward Design

To promote tabular reasoning in large-scale language models for natural language to SQL tasks, we adopt a two-stage training approach inspired by DeepSeek-R1 (Guo et al., 2025). In the first stage, we apply supervised fine-tuning on synthetic reasoning traces generated by o3-mini. This step improves the model's ability to follow instructions, decompose complex tasks, and generate interpretable outputs within the SQL domain.

In the second stage, we apply reinforcement learning to refine the model's reasoning behavior and align it more closely with execution-based performance objectives. This training encourages consistency between intermediate reasoning steps and the final executable output, enabling the model to generalize beyond dataset-specific patterns in the data.

3.2.1 Reinforcement Learning

To refine model behavior beyond supervised learning, we employ GRPO, a reinforcement learning method originally introduced in Deepseekmath (Shao et al., 2024). This approach enables more stable optimization by comparing multiple outputs for the same input and assigning relative rewards. By evaluating groups of candidate outputs rather than individual sequences in isolation, the model receives finer-grained feedback that encourages consistent and generalizable reasoning.

Formally, for a given natural language question q and its associated database schema, the model generates a set of G candidate SQL queries $\{o_1, o_2, \ldots, o_G\}$. Each candidate is scored using a task-specific reward function, and the relative advantage A_i is computed for each output. The optimization objective is given by:

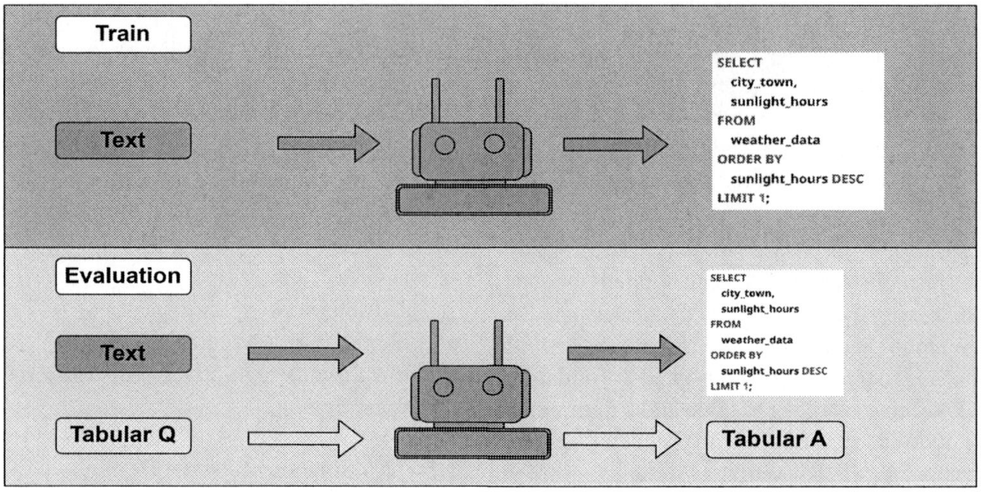

Figure 1: **Training on Text-to-SQL, Evaluating on Dual Tasks.** Our framework is trained solely on Text-to-SQL data, using structured supervision from CoT traces and reinforcement learning objectives. At evaluation time, we assess performance on both Text-to-SQL benchmarks and tabular question answering tasks. This setup tests whether SQL-centered training can induce reasoning capabilities that generalize beyond query generation to broader table-based inference.

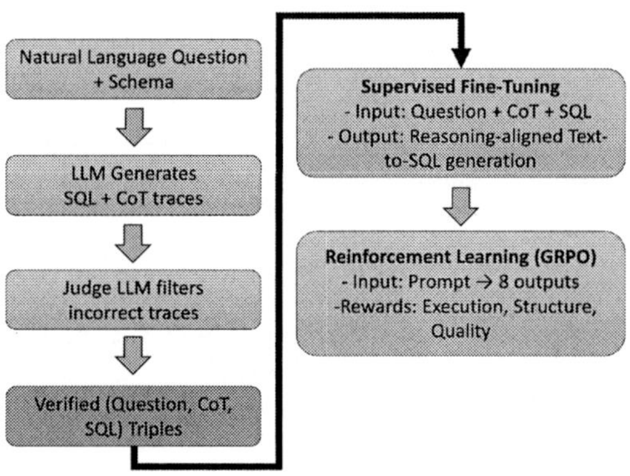

Figure 2: **Overview of the training pipeline.** Given a natural language question and schema, we generate SQL queries and CoT traces using a pretrained o3-mini. A second model filters these outputs by judging correctness and consistency. Verified traces are used for supervised fine-tuning on Clinton, followed by GRPO on the BIRD dataset. This two-stage training process promotes generalization across both SQL generation and tabular question answering.

$$J_{GRPO}(\Theta) = E\left[\frac{1}{G}\sum_{i=1}^{G}\min\left(\frac{\pi_\theta(o_i|q)}{\pi_{\theta_{\text{old}}}(o_i|q)}A_i,\ \text{clip}\left(\frac{\pi_\theta(o_i|q)}{\pi_{\theta_{\text{old}}}(o_i|q)}, 1-\epsilon, 1+\epsilon\right)A_i\right)\right] - \beta D_{KL}(\pi_\theta||\pi_{\text{ref}}) \quad (1)$$

Here, π_θ denotes the current policy, $\pi_{\theta_{\text{old}}}$ is the policy before the update, and π_{ref} is a frozen reference policy used for regularization. The hyperparameters ϵ and β control the clipping threshold and divergence penalty, respectively.

3.2.2 Reward Design

We define several reward functions tailored to the Text-to-SQL task, each capturing different dimensions of query quality. These rewards guide the optimization process during reinforcement learning with GRPO.

1. **Execution-Based Reward:** The primary objective in Text-to-SQL is to generate queries that execute to the correct result. Traditional binary execution rewards offer no gradient for near-correct predictions. To address this, we implement a reward function that leverages a language model to count orthographic changes—textual mutations between the predicted and reference queries, such as token insertions, deletions, or substitutions. The corresponding prompt can be found in B.3. The reward is computed as:

$$R_{\text{exec}} = \frac{1}{x+1}, \quad (2)$$

where x is the number of detected changes. This formulation provides a smoother feedback signal that penalizes incorrect queries proportionally, even when they are close to correct.

2. **String Matching Reward:** This reward compares the predicted and gold SQL strings by identifying the longest contiguous matching subsequence. It is computed as the ratio of matching characters to the total number of characters across both sequences, thereby encouraging partial correctness even when queries are not exact matches.

3. **Component-Level Matching Reward:** To capture semantic equivalence beyond surface form, we compute overlap between query components such as `SELECT`, `WHERE`, and `GROUP BY` – using the F1 score as in the component matching metric (Yu et al., 2018). This allows the model to be rewarded for capturing the correct logical structure, even when query formatting varies.

4. **LLM Judge Reward with Classes:** Pretrained language models exhibit strong sensitivity to syntactic correctness and logical coherence. Building on the literature that utilizes pretrained language models to provide continuous rewards based on these criteria for SQL queries (Pourreza et al., 2025), we extend this approach to categorize model outputs into ordinal quality classes—*Very Bad*, *Bad*, *Average*, *Above Average*, *Good*, and *Excellent*, see Appendix B.4. This categorical scoring is adapted from Xin et al. (2024) and enables more interpretable and consistent supervision, particularly in filtering low-quality outputs during training.

All language model-based evaluations are performed using OpenAI's o3-mini model (Jaech et al., 2024), which serves as both a scorer and judge for reward construction.

4 Experiments

We design our experiments to investigate the following research questions:

- **RQ1:** How does the use of synthetic reasoning traces during supervised fine-tuning impact Text-to-SQL performance?
- **RQ2:** Can our two-stage framework—combining supervised fine-tuning and GRPO—facilitate the induction of transferable tabular reasoning capabilities?
- **RQ3:** Which reward functions in GRPO contribute most significantly to improved table-based reasoning?

4.1 Setup

Evaluation Benchmarks: We evaluate our framework across two primary tasks: Text-to-SQL and tabular question answering. For Text-to-SQL, we utilize the Clinton A and BIRD minidev [3] datasets. For tabular question answering, we evaluate performance on the Tablebench Fact Checking dataset (Wu et al., 2025), as it provides a comprehensive estimate of model understanding of tables across 18 fields. Additionally, to emphasize complex reasoning, we utilize the CRT-QA dataset (Zhang et al., 2023), which focuses on complex table-based reasoning, incorporating multi-step operations and informal reasoning techniques.

Evaluation Metrics: We employ task-appropriate evaluation metrics for each benchmark. For Text-to-SQL tasks, we report execution accuracy, defined as the exact match between the predicted and reference SQL query results. Given the limited access to the full database within Clinton, we utilize OpenAI's o3-mini model as a proxy for execution for this dataset, assessing query correctness based on structural and semantic alignment. For CRT-QA, we use Exact Match to compare the predicted answer with the ground truth. For Tablebench, we employ the ROUGE score as outlined in the original paper (Wu et al., 2025).

Training Settings: We utilize three base models: Qwen-2.5-7B-Instruct, Qwen-2.5-14B-Instruct, and a 4-bit quantized version of the distilled DeepSeek-R1-Distill LLaMA 8B model. This selection enables us to evaluate both distilled and quantized architectures, as well as smaller and larger models. For supervised fine-tuning, we use a learning rate of 2×10^{-4} and a batch size of 1. During reinforcement learning with GRPO, we fix the learning rate at 1×10^{-6}. Each GRPO training instance consists of a natural language question and its associated schema; for each prompt, the model generates 8 candidate completions used to compute group-based rewards. Further implementation details can be found in Appendix C.

[3]https://github.com/bird-bench/mini_dev

4.2 Tabular Aha-Moments

During reinforcement learning with GRPO, we observe instances of emergent tabular reasoning, which we term *Tabular Aha-Moments*. These moments, inspired by the *Aha Moment* concept from DeepSeek-R1 (Guo et al., 2025), occur when the model, provided only a natural language question and schema (but no table content), implicitly reconstructs the structure of the underlying table and uses this to solve the query. An example of this behavior is shown in Figure 4, where the model demonstrates schema-grounded inference without explicit tabular context during the training process.

When evaluated on tabular question answering tasks, the model often invokes SQL-like structures as intermediate reasoning tools—even when SQL output is not required. This is illustrated in Figure 3, where the model constructs an internal SQL representation to derive a binary answer. This reflects a bidirectional inductive bias: the model not only learns to generate SQL from questions but also learns to use SQL representations to support reasoning over tables. These findings highlight the potential for GRPO to induce transferable, structure-aware reasoning in LLMs.

4.3 Benefit of CoT Supervision

Table 1 reports the performance of our supervised models across Text-to-SQL and tabular question answering tasks. Comparing models fine-tuned with (SFT-CoT) and without (SFT) CoT supervision, we observe that including reasoning traces slightly reduces performance on the in-domain Clinton dataset, but improves generalization to unseen SQL benchmarks (BIRD) and table-based reasoning tasks (CRT-QA, Tablebench).

We attribute this to the inductive bias introduced by reasoning supervision: models exposed to intermediate inference steps are more likely to learn transferable patterns rather than overfitting to schema-specific templates. Moreover, fine-tuning with CoT traces provides a more structured initialization for reinforcement learning, ensuring that the GRPO stage begins from semantically grounded outputs.

CoT supervision yields markedly different gains for LLaMA and Qwen due to their architectural disparities. In our experiments, a distilled and quantized LLaMA model received a substantially larger performance boost from CoT supervision than the uncompressed Qwen model. We attribute this discrepancy to LLaMA's compressed nature: distillation and low-precision quantization reduce its representational capacity and can weaken its innate reasoning ability. Consequently, providing explicit step-by-step reasoning guidance during training allows LLaMA to compensate for these lost details, resulting in outsized improvements. In contrast, Qwen—being neither distilled nor quantized—retains a higher precision and fuller pretrained capacity for reasoning, which means it already performs strongly on complex tasks before CoT fine-tuning. As a result, Qwen's robust baseline reasoning ability leaves less headroom for dramatic gains. This contrast highlights that CoT supervision is especially critical for enhancing compressed models like LLaMA.

4.4 Text-to-SQL Performance

The combination of supervised fine-tuning with CoT (SFT-CoT) and GRPO yields marked improvements in Text-to-SQL performance. While the gains on the BIRD dataset—where GRPO was explicitly trained—are anticipated, the enhancement on the Clinton dataset is more notable. This indicates that GRPO not only fine-tunes models to specific tasks but also encourages broader SQL comprehension and reasoning capabilities, facilitating generalization within the Text-to-SQL domain.

In particular, the SFT-CoT + GRPO model shows a strong ability to generalize, demonstrating that models trained on real-world tasks can effectively perform even on data they haven't seen during training, provided they have a strong foundational understanding of SQL reasoning.

4.5 Zero-shot Question Answering Tabular Reasoning Performance

Table 1 demonstrates that our combined approach of SFT and GRPO, originally fine-tuned on Text-to-SQL data, also enhances tabular reasoning performance in zero-shot settings. Specifically, when evaluated on CRT-QA and Tablebench, we observe improved reasoning across the model, showcasing that the model's exposure to SQL structures helps it tackle general tabular question answering tasks even when SQL generation is not explicitly required.

The zero-shot performance is indicative of the transferability of the reasoning skills learned during SQL task training. By implicitly learning to reason over structured tables in the SQL framework, the model becomes better at navigating more com-

Model	Clinton (LLM-EXE)	Bird (EXE)	CRT-QA (EM)	Tablebench (Rouge)
o1	**60.7**	**28.3**	**61.3**	**64.4**
LLaMA Base	44.4	8.1	43.3	57.1
LLaMA SFT	**62.1↑ 17.7**	3.0	33.7	49.9
LLaMA SFT-CoT	56.3	9.1	47.7	57.2
LLaMA SFT-CoT-GRPO	57.0	**14.2↑ 6.1**	**58.1↑ 14.8**	**61.1↑ 4.0**
Qwen-2.5-7B-Instr Base	56.1	18.9	49.0	61.6
Qwen-2.5-7B-Instr SFT	**66.6 ↑ 10.5**	9.3	45.3	52.2
Qwen-2.5-7B-Instr SFT-CoT	59.6	19.1	46.2	53.8
Qwen-2.5-7B-Instr SFT-CoT-GRPO	59.9	**23.1 ↑ 4.2**	**54.0 ↑ 5.0**	**63.2↑ 1.6**
Qwen-2.5-14B-Instr Base	55.1	22.9	56.1	60.7
Qwen-2.5-14B-Instr SFT	**68.6 ↑ 13.5**	19.7	52.2	57.8
Qwen-2.5-14B-Instr SFT-CoT	58.6	23.5	52.8	60.6
Qwen-2.5-14B-Instr SFT-CoT-GRPO	59.2	**27.2 ↑ 4.3**	**59.2 ↑ 3.1**	**63.3 ↑ 2.6**

Table 1: Performance comparison of OpenAI o1, the 4-bit quantized version of the distilled Deepseek-R2 LLaMA 8B model, the Qwen-2.5-7B-Instruct model (Qwen-2.5-7B-Instr), and the Qwen-2.5-14B-Instruct model (Qwen-2.5-14B-Instr) evaluated across various datasets. This table compares the performance of untrained models (Base), those supervised fine-tuned on the Clinton Dataset (SFT), models fine-tuned with Chain-of-Thoughts (SFT-CoT) on the Clinton Dataset, and models that have undergone SFT-CoT on the Clinton Dataset and GRPO on the BIRD Dataset. Evaluation scores include execution accuracy (EXE), execution accuracy determined by an OpenAI o3-mini LLM judge (LLM-EXE), exact match scores (EM), and Rouge score (Rouge).

plex question answering tasks, further underlining the value of using SQL as a foundational tool for structured data reasoning.

4.6 Reward Ablation

In this section, we investigate the contribution of various reward functions in our GRPO training. Table 2 presents the results of our ablation study, evaluating the impact of different reward configurations on the model's performance on the BIRD, CRT-QA and Tablebench tasks. Specifically, we analyze the effect of different combinations of rewards—including execution-based, string matching, component-level matching, and LLM-based judgment rewards—on the accuracy of SQL execution and tabular question answering. Due to computational costs, we utilize the 7B and 8B models.

Ablation studies indicate that string matching serves as the most effective single reward due to its continuous nature, facilitating initial learning. However, exclusive reliance on string matching can lead to diminished performance in later training stages. We observe that combining string matching with additional reward mechanisms enhances overall effectiveness, as the initial continuous reward provides a substantial learning advantage. The most promising two-reward combination identified is string matching coupled with the LLM Judge Reward with classes. This synergistic approach effectively merges the continuous evaluation of string accuracy with the discrete assessment of general SQL quality, thereby creating a robust framework for improved model performance.

From the results in Table 2, we observe that incorporating a broader range of reward functions generally improves model performance. For instance, the best four rewards configuration shows significant improvements on CRT-QA for the LLaMA model, indicating that a more diverse set of feedback signals enhances generalization across tasks. This suggests that combining different reward signals allows the model to better capture both syntactic correctness (in SQL) and logical coherence (in tabular reasoning), leading to a more balanced and accurate reasoning process.

Reward Configuration	BIRD	CRT-QA	Tablebench
Best Reward (LLaMA)	11.5	57.8	60.1
Best Reward (Qwen-2.5-7B-Instr)	19.6	53.9	62.7
Best 2 Rewards (LLaMA)	12.1	56.9	60.3
Best 2 Rewards (Qwen-2.5-7B-Instr)	20.0	53.2	64.5
Best 4 Rewards (LLaMA)	14.2	**58.1**	61.1
Best 4 Rewards (Qwen-2.5-7B-Instr)	**23.1**	54.0	**63.2**

Table 2: **Ablation study of reward configurations.** The models initially underwent SFT on Chain-of-Thought traces on Clinton, followed by GRPO on BIRD, where specific reward functions were applied. Performance is evaluated across the best GRPO reward configurations (best one, two, and four rewards) for each model. Evaluation scores include execution accuracy for BIRD, exact match for CRT-QA and Rouge for Tablebench.

5 Conclusion

In conclusion, our experiments demonstrate that integrating reinforcement learning with a supervised pretraining phase significantly enhances the model's ability to reason over tabular data. Notably, the distilled quantized LLaMA-8B model achieved a 34.2% relative performance improvement on the CRT-QA dataset, while the Qwen-2.5-7B model saw a 10.2% increase and the Qwen-2.5-14B model 5.5% relative increase, underscoring the efficacy of our two-stage framework in optimizing SQL

Question: Was there a difference in points earned in years when Pedro Rodríguez drove a Lotus compared to when he drove a Ferrari? Answer with only 'Yes' or 'No' that is most accurate and nothing else.

<think>
```sql SELECT pt FROM table WHERE entrant = "team lotus" - pt FROM table WHERE entrant = "scuderia ferrari" ``` I compared the points earned when Pedro Rodríguez drove a Lotus versus a Ferrari. Since the points differed (0 vs 1, 2, or 3), there was a difference.
</think>
Yes """

Figure 3: **SQL-Structured Reasoning in Tabular QA.** An LLM answering a natural language question over a table. While the output is a binary response ("Yes"), the model's internal reasoning implicitly follows an SQL-like logic: it compares subsets of rows filtered by different conditions to support its answer. This illustrates how models may invoke formal query structures even when the task does not explicitly require SQL, reflecting an internal alignment between table QA and SQL semantics.

First, let me understand what the tables are involved here.

...
Wait, so I need to:

Find the maximum occurrence in biwords.
Find the biword with that maximum occurrence.
Return w2nd from that biword.
In SQL:
SELECT w2nd FROM biwords WHERE occurrences = (SELECT MAX(occurrences) FROM biwords)
Yes, that query will return w2nd for the biword that has the highest occurrence.

But wait, if the maximum occurs multiple times, the query returns all such w2nd. So the query, without any LIMIT, would return all w2nd for biwords entries with the maximum occurrence.
But the question is about the word ID for the second word, so perhaps the requirement is to list all and then pick one?
So the final SQL query is:
SELECT w2nd FROM biwords WHERE occurrences = (SELECT MAX(occurrences) FROM biwords)

Let me test it. Suppose we have:
biwords:
lid | w1st | w2nd | occurrences
1 | 1 | 2 | 5
2 | 3 | 4 | 5
3 | 5 | 6 | 4
4 | 1 | 3 | 10
Then, the maximum occurrence is 10 in row 4. The query would select w2nd which is 3.
So the query returns the w2nd from the biword with the highest occurrence, which is 3.
So in SQLite, it's correct to just get w2nd from the row where occurrence is max.

Yes, that seems correct.

Figure 4: **Table-Guided CoT in LLMs for SQL Generation.** A reasoning trace from an LLM translating a natural language question into SQL. The model first interprets the task by examining the schema and example table rows, breaks the logic down into actionable steps, and validates the final SQL query through hypothetical execution. This illustrates how structured table understanding can guide accurate SQL synthesis.

execution and fostering transferable reasoning for complex question answering tasks. These findings suggest that SQL serves not only as a task-specific format but also as a foundational scaffold for developing robust tabular reasoning skills in LLMs.

Limitations

Our study focuses on medium-scale foundation models—distilled LLaMA 8B, Qwen-7B, Qwen-14B —whose exact pretraining corpora are undocumented. As a result, we cannot determine coverage or gaps across domains, languages, or proprietary material. This opacity complicates any analysis of domain blind spots, spurious correlations, or memorization risks. Moreover, the relatively modest parameter counts of these models may limit performance on tasks requiring deep domain expertise, such as biomedical or legal reasoning.

We evaluate tabular reasoning using CRT-QA and Tablebench, with o3-mini serving as an automated judge. While expedient, this setup lacks the nuance of human evaluation, particularly for complex reasoning and semantic alignment. Additionally, standard Text-to-SQL and tabular QA benchmarks may under-represent the complexity, ambiguity and noise present in real-world data, making our results more indicative of structured reasoning progress than deployment readiness.

Our current framework employs only two training stages. In contrast, multi-phase pipelines such as R1 leverage up to four stages, including instruction tuning and iterative CoT refinement. While our approach prioritizes simplicity and efficiency, it may sacrifice opportunities for deeper alignment or curriculum structuring.

Future research should address these limitations by exploring larger, better-documented models, human-in-the-loop evaluation, and more diverse datasets. Additional training stages—such as pre-CoT bootstrapping or domain-adaptive pretraining—may further enhance generalization and robustness in real-world table reasoning.

Acknowledgments

References

Nikhil Abhyankar, Vivek Gupta, Dan Roth, and Chandan K Reddy. 2024. H-star: Llm-driven hybrid sql-text adaptive reasoning on tables. *arXiv preprint arXiv:2407.05952*.

Shir Ashury-Tahan, Yifan Mai, Ariel Gera, Yotam Perlitz, Asaf Yehudai, Elron Bandel, Leshem Choshen, Eyal Shnarch, Percy Liang, Michal Shmueli-Scheuer, and 1 others. 2025. The mighty torr: A benchmark for table reasoning and robustness. *arXiv preprint arXiv:2502.19412*.

Marc Boubnovski, Kaspar Märtens, Lawrence Phillips, Daniel Keitley, Maria Dermit, and Julien Fauqueur. 2025. A scalable llm framework for therapeutic biomarker discovery: Grounding q/a generation in knowledge graphs and literature. In *ICLR 2025*
```

Workshop on Machine Learning for Genomics Explorations.

Ivan Brugere, Shubham Sharma, Sanjay Kariyappa, Anh Totti Nguyen, Freddy Lecue, and 1 others. 2024. Interpretable llm-based table question answering. *arXiv preprint arXiv:2412.12386.*

Qiguang Chen, Libo Qin, Jinhao Liu, Dengyun Peng, Jiannan Guan, Peng Wang, Mengkang Hu, Yuhang Zhou, Te Gao, and Wangxiang Che. 2025. Towards reasoning era: A survey of long chain-of-thought for reasoning large language models. *arXiv preprint arXiv:2503.09567.*

Wenhu Chen, Hongmin Wang, Jianshu Chen, Yunkai Zhang, Hong Wang, Shiyang Li, Xiyou Zhou, and William Yang Wang. 2019. Tabfact: A large-scale dataset for table-based fact verification. *arXiv preprint arXiv:1909.02164.*

Zhiyu Chen, Wenhu Chen, Charese Smiley, Sameena Shah, Iana Borova, Dylan Langdon, Reema Moussa, Matt Beane, Ting-Hao Huang, Bryan Routledge, and 1 others. 2021. Finqa: A dataset of numerical reasoning over financial data. *arXiv preprint arXiv:2109.00122.*

Yilu Fang, Betina Idnay, Yingcheng Sun, Hao Liu, Zhehuan Chen, Karen Marder, Hua Xu, Rebecca Schnall, and Chunhua Weng. 2022. Combining human and machine intelligence for clinical trial eligibility querying. *Journal of the American Medical Informatics Association*, 29(7):1161–1171.

Dawei Gao, Haibin Wang, Yaliang Li, Xiuyu Sun, Yichen Qian, Bolin Ding, and Jingren Zhou. 2023. Text-to-sql empowered by large language models: A benchmark evaluation. *arXiv preprint arXiv:2308.15363.*

Daya Guo, Dejian Yang, Haowei Zhang, Junxiao Song, Ruoyu Zhang, Runxin Xu, Qihao Zhu, Shirong Ma, Peiyi Wang, Xiao Bi, and 1 others. 2025. Deepseek-r1: Incentivizing reasoning capability in llms via reinforcement learning. *arXiv preprint arXiv:2501.12948.*

Moshe Hazoom, Vibhor Malik, and Ben Bogin. 2021. Text-to-sql in the wild: A naturally-occurring dataset based on stack exchange data. *arXiv preprint arXiv:2106.05006.*

Charles T Hemphill, John J Godfrey, and George R Doddington. 1990. The atis spoken language systems pilot corpus. In *Speech and Natural Language: Proceedings of a Workshop Held at Hidden Valley, Pennsylvania, June 24-27, 1990.*

Zijin Hong, Zheng Yuan, Qinggang Zhang, Hao Chen, Junnan Dong, Feiran Huang, and Xiao Huang. 2024. Next-generation database interfaces: A survey of llm-based text-to-sql. *arXiv preprint arXiv:2406.08426.*

Aaron Jaech, Adam Kalai, Adam Lerer, Adam Richardson, Ahmed El-Kishky, Aiden Low, Alec Helyar, Aleksander Madry, Alex Beutel, Alex Carney, and 1 others. 2024. Openai o1 system card. *arXiv preprint arXiv:2412.16720.*

Pengcheng Jiang, Jiacheng Lin, Lang Cao, Runchu Tian, SeongKu Kang, Zifeng Wang, Jimeng Sun, and Jiawei Han. 2025. Deepretrieval: Hacking real search engines and retrievers with large language models via reinforcement learning. *arXiv preprint arXiv:2503.00223.*

Dongjun Lee, Choongwon Park, Jaehyuk Kim, and Heesoo Park. 2024. Mcs-sql: Leveraging multiple prompts and multiple-choice selection for text-to-sql generation. *arXiv preprint arXiv:2405.07467.*

Dacheng Li, Shiyi Cao, Tyler Griggs, Shu Liu, Xiangxi Mo, Eric Tang, Sumanth Hegde, Kourosh Hakhamaneshi, Shishir G Patil, Matei Zaharia, and 1 others. 2025a. Llms can easily learn to reason from demonstrations structure, not content, is what matters! *arXiv preprint arXiv:2502.07374.*

Haoyang Li, Shang Wu, Xiaokang Zhang, Xinmei Huang, Jing Zhang, Fuxin Jiang, Shuai Wang, Tieying Zhang, Jianjun Chen, Rui Shi, and 1 others. 2025b. Omnisql: Synthesizing high-quality text-to-sql data at scale. *arXiv preprint arXiv:2503.02240.*

Jinyang Li, Binyuan Hui, Ge Qu, Jiaxi Yang, Binhua Li, Bowen Li, Bailin Wang, Bowen Qin, Ruiying Geng, Nan Huo, and 1 others. 2023. Can llm already serve as a database interface? a big bench for large-scale database grounded text-to-sqls. *Advances in Neural Information Processing Systems*, 36:42330–42357.

Xinyu Liu, Shuyu Shen, Boyan Li, Peixian Ma, Runzhi Jiang, Yuxin Zhang, Ju Fan, Guoliang Li, Nan Tang, and Yuyu Luo. 2024. A survey of nl2sql with large language models: Where are we, and where are we going? *arXiv preprint arXiv:2408.05109.*

Peixian Ma, Xialie Zhuang, Chengjin Xu, Xuhui Jiang, Ran Chen, and Jian Guo. 2025. Sql-r1: Training natural language to sql reasoning model by reinforcement learning. *arXiv preprint arXiv:2504.08600.*

Eduardo R Nascimento, Grettel García, Yenier T Izquierdo, Lucas Feijó, Gustavo MC Coelho, Aiko R de Oliveira, Melissa Lemos, Robinson LS Garcia, Luiz AP Paes Leme, and Marco A Casanova. 2025. Llm-based text-to-sql for real-world databases. *SN Computer Science*, 6(2):130.

Vaishali Pal, Andrew Yates, Evangelos Kanoulas, and Maarten de Rijke. 2023. Multitabqa: Generating tabular answers for multi-table question answering. *arXiv preprint arXiv:2305.12820.*

Panupong Pasupat and Percy Liang. 2015. Compositional semantic parsing on semi-structured tables. *arXiv preprint arXiv:1508.00305.*

Tom J Pollard, Alistair EW Johnson, Jesse D Raffa, Leo A Celi, Roger G Mark, and Omar Badawi. 2018. The eicu collaborative research database, a freely available multi-center database for critical care research. *Scientific data*, 5(1):1–13.

Mohammadreza Pourreza and Davood Rafiei. 2023. Din-sql: Decomposed in-context learning of text-to-sql with self-correction. *Advances in Neural Information Processing Systems*, 36:36339–36348.

Mohammadreza Pourreza, Shayan Talaei, Ruoxi Sun, Xingchen Wan, Hailong Li, Azalia Mirhoseini, Amin Saberi, Sercan Arik, and 1 others. 2025. Reasoning-sql: Reinforcement learning with sql tailored partial rewards for reasoning-enhanced text-to-sql. *arXiv preprint arXiv:2503.23157*.

Yiwei Qin, Xuefeng Li, Haoyang Zou, Yixiu Liu, Shijie Xia, Zhen Huang, Yixin Ye, Weizhe Yuan, Hector Liu, Yuanzhi Li, and 1 others. 2024. O1 replication journey: A strategic progress report–part 1. *arXiv preprint arXiv:2410.18982*.

Zhihong Shao, Peiyi Wang, Qihao Zhu, Runxin Xu, Junxiao Song, Xiao Bi, Haowei Zhang, Mingchuan Zhang, YK Li, Y Wu, and 1 others. 2024. Deepseekmath: Pushing the limits of mathematical reasoning in open language models. *arXiv preprint arXiv:2402.03300*.

Tianze Shi, Chen Zhao, Jordan Boyd-Graber, Hal Daumé III, and Lillian Lee. 2020. On the potential of lexico-logical alignments for semantic parsing to sql queries. *arXiv preprint arXiv:2010.11246*.

Noah Shinn, Federico Cassano, Ashwin Gopinath, Karthik Narasimhan, and Shunyu Yao. 2023. Reflexion: Language agents with verbal reinforcement learning. *Advances in Neural Information Processing Systems*, 36:8634–8652.

Josefa Lia Stoisser, Marc Boubnovski Martell, Kaspar Märtens, Lawrence Phillips, Stephen Michael Town, Rory Donovan-Maiye, and Julien Fauqueur. 2025. Query, don't train: Privacy-preserving tabular prediction from ehr data via sql queries. *arXiv preprint arXiv:2505.21801*.

Yuan Sui, Jiaru Zou, Mengyu Zhou, Xinyi He, Lun Du, Shi Han, and Dongmei Zhang. 2023. Tap4llm: Table provider on sampling, augmenting, and packing semi-structured data for large language model reasoning. *arXiv preprint arXiv:2312.09039*.

Ruoxi Sun, Sercan Ö Arik, Alex Muzio, Lesly Miculicich, Satya Gundabathula, Pengcheng Yin, Hanjun Dai, Hootan Nakhost, Rajarishi Sinha, Zifeng Wang, and 1 others. 2023. Sql-palm: Improved large language model adaptation for text-to-sql (extended). *arXiv preprint arXiv:2306.00739*.

Kimi Team, Angang Du, Bofei Gao, Bowei Xing, Changjiu Jiang, Cheng Chen, Cheng Li, Chenjun Xiao, Chenzhuang Du, Chonghua Liao, and 1 others. 2025. Kimi k1. 5: Scaling reinforcement learning with llms. *arXiv preprint arXiv:2501.12599*.

Ping Wang, Tian Shi, and Chandan K Reddy. 2020. Text-to-sql generation for question answering on electronic medical records. In *Proceedings of The Web Conference 2020*, pages 350–361.

Shuo Wang and Carlos Crespo-Quinones. 2023. Natural language models for data visualization utilizing nvbench dataset. *arXiv preprint arXiv:2310.00832*.

Xuezhi Wang, Jason Wei, Dale Schuurmans, Quoc Le, Ed Chi, Sharan Narang, Aakanksha Chowdhery, and Denny Zhou. 2022. Self-consistency improves chain of thought reasoning in language models. *arXiv preprint arXiv:2203.11171*.

Jason Wei, Xuezhi Wang, Dale Schuurmans, Maarten Bosma, Fei Xia, Ed Chi, Quoc V Le, Denny Zhou, and 1 others. 2022. Chain-of-thought prompting elicits reasoning in large language models. *Advances in neural information processing systems*, 35:24824–24837.

Xianjie Wu, Jian Yang, Linzheng Chai, Ge Zhang, Jiaheng Liu, Xeron Du, Di Liang, Daixin Shu, Xianfu Cheng, Tianzhen Sun, and 1 others. 2025. Tablebench: A comprehensive and complex benchmark for table question answering. In *Proceedings of the AAAI Conference on Artificial Intelligence*, volume 39, pages 25497–25506.

Huajian Xin, Daya Guo, Zhihong Shao, Zhizhou Ren, Qihao Zhu, Bo Liu, Chong Ruan, Wenda Li, and Xiaodan Liang. 2024. Deepseek-prover: Advancing theorem proving in llms through large-scale synthetic data. *arXiv preprint arXiv:2405.14333*.

Peiying Yu, Guoxin Chen, and Jingjing Wang. 2025. Table-critic: A multi-agent framework for collaborative criticism and refinement in table reasoning. *arXiv preprint arXiv:2502.11799*.

Tao Yu, Rui Zhang, Kai Yang, Michihiro Yasunaga, Dongxu Wang, Zifan Li, James Ma, Irene Li, Qingning Yao, Shanelle Roman, and 1 others. 2018. Spider: A large-scale human-labeled dataset for complex and cross-domain semantic parsing and text-to-sql task. *arXiv preprint arXiv:1809.08887*.

Zheng Yuan, Hao Chen, Zijin Hong, Qinggang Zhang, Feiran Huang, and Xiao Huang. 2025. Knapsack optimization-based schema linking for llm-based text-to-sql generation. *arXiv preprint arXiv:2502.12911*.

Liangyu Zha, Junlin Zhou, Liyao Li, Rui Wang, Qingyi Huang, Saisai Yang, Jing Yuan, Changbao Su, Xiang Li, Aofeng Su, and 1 others. 2023. Tablegpt: Towards unifying tables, nature language and commands into one gpt. *arXiv preprint arXiv:2307.08674*.

Zhehao Zhang, Xitao Li, Yan Gao, and Jian-Guang Lou. 2023. Crt-qa: A dataset of complex reasoning question answering over tabular data. In *Proceedings of the 2023 Conference on Empirical Methods in Natural Language Processing*, pages 2131–2153.

Xueliang Zhao, Wei Wu, Jian Guan, and Lingpeng Kong. 2025. Promptcot: Synthesizing olympiad-level problems for mathematical reasoning in large language models. *arXiv preprint arXiv:2503.02324*.

Victor Zhong, Caiming Xiong, and Richard Socher. 2017. Seq2sql: Generating structured queries from natural language using reinforcement learning. *arXiv preprint arXiv:1709.00103*.

A Summary of Clinton Dataset

We conduct part of our evaluation using the `Clinton/Text-to-sql-v1` dataset,[4] a large-scale compilation of natural language to SQL examples spanning a broad set of domains. This benchmark includes 26 individual datasets, covering academic records, medical databases, entertainment metadata, government statistics, and more.

Each example in the dataset consists of a natural language query, an associated database schema, and a corresponding SQL statement. Some subsets also include table content or ground-truth execution results. The diversity in schema complexity and domain coverage makes this benchmark well-suited for evaluating both generalization and transfer in Text-to-SQL and tabular reasoning models.

Key datasets include:

- **Spider** (Yu et al., 2018) – Complex, cross-domain Text-to-SQL benchmark.
- **WikiSQL** (Zhong et al., 2017) – Large-scale dataset with simple queries over Wikipedia tables.
- **ATIS** (Hemphill et al., 1990) – Airline travel information with traditional semantic parsing annotations.
- **MIMICSQL** (Wang et al., 2020) and **eICU** (Pollard et al., 2018) – Clinical databases for medical question answering.

We also include lesser-known and synthetic datasets such as `Criteria2SQL` (Fang et al., 2022), `SEDE` (Hazoom et al., 2021), `SQuALL` (Shi et al., 2020), and `NVBench` (Wang and Crespo-Quinones, 2023), along with public domain tabular corpora like IMDb, Yelp, and historical sports or wildfire datasets.

This variety allows us to test the ability of LLMs to reason across database schemas, interact with realistic tabular structures, and generalize beyond fixed SQL templates.

[4]`https://huggingface.co/datasets/Clinton/Text-to-sql-v1`

B Prompts

B.1 Creating Synthetic CoT

This section outlines the structure of prompts designed for SQL query generation tasks. Each prompt features SQL table schemas and clear instructions, facilitating the generation of valid SQL queries using SQLite syntax. The expert guidance within the prompts emphasizes the requirement to articulate the reasoning behind the constructed SQL queries. By utilizing this approach, we aim to train models that can effectively understand the context of relational data and generate precise queries that meet specific operational goals, thereby enhancing the overall interpretability and accuracy of automated SQL generation.

> You are a SQL expert. Below are SQL table schemas paired with instructions that describe a specific task. Using valid SQLite syntax, write a response that appropriately completes the request for the provided tables.
> **SCHEMA: schema**
> **INSTRUCTIONS: specific task instructions**
> When answering, provide reasoning for the SQL query you create using the following template:
> <sql> Write the SQL query here, ensuring it adheres to SQLite syntax and effectively accomplishes the task described in the instructions. </sql>

B.2 Evaluation of Synthetic CoT

This section specifies a prompt for evaluating the correctness of SQL queries based on a defined schema and a reference SQL query. The prompt clearly delineates the evaluation task for the SQL expert, presenting the query to be evaluated, the relevant schema, and the correct SQL reference. The evaluator is instructed to determine whether the provided SQL query is correct or incorrect, with responses limited to "Correct" or "Wrong." This structured approach facilitates precise assessment of SQL queries, contributing to the development of robust models capable of generating and validating SQL syntax effectively.

> You are an SQL expert, and your task is to evaluate whether the SQL query below is correct based on the provided schema and the correct SQL reference.
> **SQL Query:** ans.sql
> **Schema:** schema
> **Correct SQL:** correct_sql
> Return ONLY "Correct" or "Wrong".

B.3 LLM Judge for Execution Based Reward

For our Execution Reward in Group Relative Policy Optimization (GRPO) the LLM judge is instructed to count the number of orthographic changes required to convert each predicted query into the corresponding correct query. The reward is computed using the following equation:

$$R_{\text{exec}} = \frac{1}{x+1}, \quad (3)$$

where x is the number of detected changes. This methodology provides a more continuous measure of execution accuracy, crucial for refining the model's performance.

> You are an SQL expert. Count how many changes you need to make to get the following predicted queries correct.
> **Predicted Queries (one per line)**: queries_to_rank
> **For reference, use this Schema:** schema.
> **Here is the correct query**: true_query
> You should count the number of Orthographic elements you need to change from the predicted queries to the correct query.
> ONLY RETURN a JSON object with a single 'scores' field containing a list of **num_queries** numbers reflecting the number of changes needed for each predicted query.

B.4 LLM Judge with Classes

The LLM judge reward is designed to evaluate the quality of predicted SQL queries by comparing them to a reference correct query. In this task, the judge is instructed to assign a grade to each predicted query on a scale from 'Very bad' to 'Excellent.' The grading criteria are explicitly defined, allowing the judge to assess various aspects of the queries, including grammatical correctness, logical accuracy, and overall fidelity to the correct query. This structured grading system enables a nuanced analysis of the model's output quality, providing insights that facilitate targeted improvements in query generation.

> Compare these SQL queries to the correct query and grade each one as: 'Very bad', 'Bad', 'Above average', 'Good', or 'Excellent'. Use the following grading system, and the correct query as reference :
> **Correct Query:** true_query
> **1. Excellent:** this is only given when the SQL query is perfect and matches {true_query}
> **2. Good:** This is when there is a grammar mistake in the query
> **3. Above average:** This is when the query is mostly correct but gets a logical step wrong in the query
> **4. Bad:** Makes more than one mistake in the query
> **5. Very bad:** does not produce a query or varies significantly from the correct query
> **Queries to grade:** queries_to_rank
> {format_instructions}

C Implementation Details

In our experiments, we utilize VERL[5] for training the 14B models. To enhance efficiency, Unsloth[6] is employed for the 7B and 8B models. Unsloth provides support for QLoRA-style training with Flash Attention 2, bitsandbytes quantization, and PEFT-compatible adapters.

We fine-tuned three pretrained models:

- **Qwen-2.5-7B**, a dense, instruction-tuned model released by Alibaba DAMO, trained in full precision [7].
- **Qwen-2.5-14B**, a larger, dense, instruction-tuned model released by Alibaba DAMO, trained in full precision [8].
- **DeepSeek-R1-Distill LLaMA3-8B**, a 4-bit quantized variant of Meta's LLaMA 3–8B, distilled by DeepSeek AI[9].

Supervised fine-tuning (SFT) was performed on the Clinton dataset using QLoRA adapters, while reinforcement learning with GRPO was applied on the BIRD benchmark. The GRPO setup used candidate comparisons and execution-guided rewards computed via SQLite.

Experiments were conducted on 4×A100 80GB GPUs using mixed-precision (FP16).

[5] https://GitHub.com/volcengine/verl

[6] https://GitHub.com/unslothai/unsloth

[7] https://huggingface.co/Qwen/Qwen2.5-7B-Instruct

[8] https://huggingface.co/Qwen/Qwen2.5-14B-Instruct

[9] https://huggingface.co/unsloth/DeepSeek-R1-Distill-Llama-8B-unsloth-bnb-4bit

How well do LLMs reason over tabular data, really?

Cornelius Wolff
Centrum Wiskunde & Informatica
Amsterdam
cornelius.wolff@cwi.nl

Madelon Hulsebos
Centrum Wiskunde & Informatica
Amsterdam
madelon.hulsebos@cwi.nl

Abstract

Large Language Models (LLMs) excel in natural language tasks, but less is known about their reasoning capabilities over tabular data. Prior analyses devise evaluation strategies that poorly reflect an LLM's realistic performance on tabular queries. Moreover, we have a limited understanding of the robustness of LLMs towards realistic variations in tabular inputs. Therefore, we ask: *Can general-purpose LLMs reason over tabular data, really?*, and focus on two questions 1) are tabular reasoning capabilities of general-purpose LLMs robust to real-world characteristics of tabular inputs, and 2) how can we realistically evaluate an LLM's performance on analytical tabular queries? Building on a recent tabular reasoning benchmark, we first surface shortcomings of its multiple-choice prompt evaluation strategy, as well as commonly used free-form text metrics such as SacreBleu and BERT-score. We show that an LLM-as-a-judge procedure yields more reliable performance insights and unveil a significant deficit in tabular reasoning performance of LLMs. We then extend the tabular inputs reflecting three common characteristics in practice: 1) missing values, 2) duplicate entities, and 3) structural variations. Experiments show that the tabular reasoning capabilities of general-purpose LLMs suffer from these variations, stressing the importance of improving their robustness for realistic tabular inputs.[1]

1 Introduction

Large Language Models (LLMs) are intended for general-purpose usage and particularly excel on natural language tasks represented in text (Liang et al., 2023). In organizations, another common modality for data analysis and decision-making, is tabular data, for which recent studies have shown promising performance of LLMs as well (Fang et al., 2024). Structural analysis to understand to what extend the reasoning capabilities of LLMs pertain, *realistically*, in more complex tabular reasoning tasks, such as analytical aggregations, is still lacking. Without reliable knowledge of their failure modes on tabular inputs and tasks, though, we risk unwarranted usage of these models in practice and delayed development of more robust capabilities.

Surfacing the reasoning capabilities on tabular tasks is, however, not straightforward. Most studies adopt free-form text metrics, which hardly capture reliable reasoning accuracy due to different formatting of the ground-truth answers, particularly of analytical questions, versus long-form LLM-generated responses (Ji et al., 2024; Xu et al., 2023). The alternative of forcing certain output formats (Sui et al., 2024) yields a limited understanding of the open-form reasoning performance and is prone to parsing errors, while another alternative of including the ground-truth answer in a multiple-choice prompt (Qiu et al., 2024) leaks ground-truth answers into the prompt compromising its reliability. Beyond realistic evaluation procedures, in order to use LLMs in a reliable manner for tabular reasoning tasks, it is important to understand how well they can handle the characteristics of tabular data inputs (Cong et al., 2023; Singha et al., 2023) as encountered in practice.

To close these gaps, we first address the question: *how can we realistically evaluate an LLM's performance on analytical tabular queries?* We examine the limitations of existing evaluation metrics, such as SacreBleu (Post, 2018) and BERT-score (Zhang* et al., 2020), as the distributions are these among correct and incorrect answers are inseparable. Instead, we propose using the LLM-as-a-judge evaluation method (Zheng et al., 2023) for more reliable performance insights and show, through calibration with human annotations, that the LLM-as-a-judge provides a reliable signal of tabular reasoning performance. Using this evaluation procedure, we unveil a significant gap in

[1]Code: github.com/trl-lab/tabular-robustness

Proceedings of the 4th Table Representation Learning Workshop, pages 241–250
July 31, 2025

tabular reasoning accuracy than previously found in the existing TQA-Bench benchmark for tabular reasoning (Qiu et al., 2024).

Second, through comprehensive analysis we answer the question: *are LLMs robust to real-world characteristics of multi-table inputs?* Building on the TQA-Bench, we first improve the validity of the task queries and downscale multi-table inputs to gain more fine-grained insights. We then inspect the robustness of LLMs against characteristics of tabular inputs as commonly found in practice. Specifically, we formalize the following three characteristics: missing values, duplicate entities, and structural variations. We show that most LLMs are not as robust to, and insufficiently acknowledge the presence of, such quality issues or anticipated variations in multi-table inputs, highlighting the need for more robust models for tabular reasoning. We make the following concrete contributions:

- We concretize the limitations of free-form text metrics and show the reliability of using an LLM-as-a-judge for evaluating open-ended responses for tabular reasoning tasks.
- We extend the TQA-Bench benchmark with tabular inputs reflecting typical real-world characteristics of tabular data: missing values, duplicate entities, and structural variations.
- We surface the shortcomings of LLMs to account for realistic variations in tabular data of varying sizes, providing more fine-grained insights into their scalability and robustness.

2 Related Work

Analysis of Tabular Reasoning Capabilities The TQA-Bench (Qiu et al., 2024) examines multi-table reasoning capabilities with LLMs over various query complexities. We complement the TQA-Bench by using it as a base for our evaluation, and integrating common properties in tabular data, such as missing values, to study the robustness of multi-table reasoning capabilities of LLMs. Similarly, Sui et al. (2024) considers structural understanding capabilities by evaluating the accuracy of LLMs in basic tasks such as row/column retrieval. The QATCH benchmark (Papicchio et al., 2023) evaluates tabular representation learning models specialized for SQL-centric tasks and mainly focuses on SQL-based evaluations. While the QATCH benchmark considers enterprise-centric evaluation tasks and inputs, it does not surface robustness for real-world properties. Earlier work by Cong et al. (2023) formalizes and analyzes key properties of tabular data principled in the relational data model, such as column-order insignificance. In this work, we focus on assessing the robustness on similar properties in the reasoning capabilities through the LLMs' generated responses. In this realm, Singha et al. (2023), evaluate various LLMs on their tabular understanding capabilities under noisy tabular inputs and variations in formatting of tabular data in prompts. While their robustness assessments cover realistic characteristics such as permutations in column-order, we include more properties and assess more complex reasoning capabilities of LLMs.

Evaluation Metrics for Tabular Reasoning The TARGET benchmark (Ji et al., 2024) focuses on evaluating table retrieval methods in open-domain querying over structured data. They surface issues in the reliability of free-form text evaluation metrics such as SacreBleu and BERT-score, as ground-truth answers in tabular reasoning datasets are small text snippets or exact values while LLMs generate longer outputs which challenges such metrics. Other work (Sui et al., 2024) intends to remedy the evaluation problem by forcing an LLM to output a singular answer in a structured format. While relying on an LLMs' structured output generation and response parsing are prone to error, ground-truth answers are often sentences, albeit short, and not single values (Chen et al., 2020). An alternative procedure, adopted in the TQA-Bench (Qiu et al., 2024), is to include the ground-truth answer in multiple-choice options and let the LLM select an option. The validity hence reliability of this evaluation approach is questionable as it leaks the ground-truth answer in the input prompt.

3 The TQA-Bench and Revisions

Here, we explain the tabular reasoning tasks included in the TQA-Bench that we use to assess the reliability of evaluation metrics as well as the robustness of the tabular reasoning capabilities of LLMs. We explain revisions we made to invalid queries, and tabular inputs to gain granular insights.

3.1 TQA-Bench reasoning tasks

The TQA-Bench (Qiu et al., 2024) provides a benchmark for tabular reasoning capabilities of three complexities: 1) lookup queries, 2) aggregation, and 3) complex calculations. Specifically, the TQA-Benchmark evaluates three different levels of reasoning complexities as follows:

Lookup queries These queries involve simple entity extraction based on one or two direct conditions. For example, *"What is the description of air carrier 20398?"* (Entity lookup) or *"Which Horror movie gets the highest budget?"* (Top selection) require the model to retrieve a value from a column given a key or set of values from the same or another table. In multi-table settings, the challenge lies in resolving foreign key relationships.

Aggregation queries These queries require calculations over filtered table segments. Examples include *"How many airlines land in Flint, MI: Bishop International?"* (Count), *"What is the total flight delay (DEP_DELAY) from ORD?"* (Sum), and *"What is the average arrival delay for flights landing at FNT?"* (Average). These tasks test the model's ability to perform basic numeric operations while managing filters and joins.

Complex calculations These queries go beyond basic aggregation by requiring operations between multiple fields or statistical analysis. For instance, *"What is the average total delay (ARR_DELAY - DEP_DELAY) for Envoy Air (MQ)?"* (Subtraction) and *"What is the correlation between departure and arrival delays for flights with delays over -9 minutes?"* (Correlation) assess deeper reasoning by requiring chained arithmetic, statistical computation, and multi-step reasoning.

3.2 TQA-Bench Revisions

We leverage the tabular data and query generation methods from TQA-Bench but make two adjustments which we describe here: 1) we improve the validity of the queries, and 2) we downscale the tabular data inputs to yield more granular insights.

Query Refinements We updated some of the existing question templates, as they lead to unnatural questions such as "*Where is the 16S21E21G001S?*". For cases such as this, we adapted the templates to be more precise and in line with natural questions. For instance, the question "*Where is the 16S21E21G001S?*" is updated to "*In which county is the the station with the full name/id 16S21E21G001S?*". These updates also ensured that there is only one logical answer which can be extracted from the available tables, as the original question could have also referred to the longitude and latitude columns of the respective dataset.

Tabular Data Downscaling While TQA-Bench evaluates multi-table reasoning capabilities with relatively large and multiple tables resulting in context sizes from 8K to 128K tokens. Our preliminary experiments revealed significant challenges in reasoning capabilities already with smaller table sizes, motivating the downsizing of context sizes to 1K, 2K, 4K, 6K and 8K to obtain more granular insights. To do so, we employ the scaling method introduced by TQA-Bench to truncate and segment tables while preserving their structural and relational integrity (Qiu et al., 2024).

4 Towards Reliable Evaluation of Tabular Reasoning Capabilities

Evaluating multi-table reasoning, and generally free-form question answering, still is an open challenge (Ji et al., 2024; Xu et al., 2023). While context and reasoning traces of LLM-generated answers are useful, they complicate evaluation when ground-truth answers are short and exact, as is the case in typical tabular tasks. Table 1 illustrates this issue for two example queries from the popular OT-TQA dataset for table question answering (Chen et al., 2020) along with their ground-truth answers. When the LLM-generated answers are evaluated against the short ground-truth answers by two free-form text metrics, SacreBleu (Post, 2018) and BERT-score (Zhang* et al., 2020), their scores are inconclusive. For example, for the queries in Table 1, the SB score for a correct generated answer is higher for the first query (1.4) but lower than the correct generated answer for the second query (0.5) for which the incorrect generated answer is closer to the correct answer for the first query (1.0). The BERT-score (BS) reflects mainly textual similarity, and shows barely any differences for different numeric values included in the response: its value is 0.81 for an incorrect as well as a correct generated answer. In what follows, we study the reliability of these different metrics in detail.

LLM-generated answers We adopt a synthetic procedure to maximize the likelihood of (in)correctness of the LLM-generated answers, which we refer to as *generated answers*. In total, we extract 350 questions from the question database in the TQA-Bench tabular reasoning benchmark. We only provide a single row as context to the LLM to generate its answer, while forcing it to only use the table data and not its memory. For *correct* generated answers, we provide the row that contains the ground-truth cell value for the lookup task as context to generate the response.

Table 1: Below query examples from the OTTQA benchmark (Chen et al., 2020) illustrate the difficulty of evaluating long-form LLM-generated answers against ground-truth answers (exact values or short text snippets) with existing text metrics such as the SacreBleu (SB) and BERT-score (BS) metrics, which fail to distinguish between incorrect versus correct answers. We find that an LLM-as-a-judge is a more reliable metric for evaluating tabular reasoning capabilities in these cases.

Question: *According to the 2016 census, what is the population of the city that is home to the Territorial Administration Building designed by Thomas W. Fuller?*

Generated answer	Answer	SB score	BS score	LLM
The Territorial Administration Building is located in Dawson City, Yukon. According to the 2016 Canadian census, the population of Dawson City was 1,375.	1,375	1.4	0.83	correct
According to the 2016 census, the population of the city that is home to the Territorial Administration Building designed by Thomas W. Fuller is 45,000.	1,375	0.0	0.81	incorrect

Question: *How long has the team that qualified for the 1999 FIFA Confederations Cup in June existed?*

Generated answer	Answer	SB score	BS score	LLM
The team that qualified for the 1999 FIFA Confederations Cup in June was Germany, who secured their qualification on 30 June 1996. To determine how long they had existed as a team by June 1999: The Germany national football team was officially founded in 1908. From 1908 to 1999 is 91 years. Answer: The Germany national team had existed for 91 years by June 1999.	since 1908	0.5	0.81	correct
The team that qualified for the 1999 FIFA Confederations Cup in June was Germany. Germany has existed as a national team since 1974, so by June 1999, they had existed for 25 years.	since 1908	1.0	0.82	incorrect

For *incorrect* answers, we also provide the row that contains the ground-truth cell, but replace the ground-truth cell value with a random but different value from the same column, resulting in a factually incorrect but still realistic generated answer. Following this procedure, we extract 175 correct and 175 incorrect generated answers.

To validate the LLM-generated answers, we check the correctness of the 350 generated reference answers against the ground-truth answers (original cell values) through human annotation. The human evaluation reveals that approximately 93.75% of the generated correct answers are indeed accurate, while 98.26% of the generated incorrect answers are indeed incorrect. These results confirm the reliability of our procedure for creating the LLM-generated answer dataset.

Free-form text evaluation metrics Using the LLM-generated answers and ground-truth answers, we inspect the reliability of two commonly used free-form text metrics: SacreBleu (Post, 2018) and BERT-score (Zhang* et al., 2020). SacreBLEU is a standardized version of the BLEU score that measures n-gram overlap between generated and reference texts, while the BERT-score leverages BERT embeddings to compute similarity based on token-level semantic matching. Our analysis reveals that neither the BERT-score nor SacreBleu metric provide a reliable signal for evaluating the correctness of generated answers. To visualize the reliability of these scores, we used Kernel Density Estimation (KDE) to estimate their distributions. For BERT-score, due to tight clustering of values, the KDE can exceed 1, while the more dispersed SacreBLEU values result in lower KDE peaks. The distributions of scores for correct and incorrect LLM-generated answers, when compared with ground-truth answers, exhibit significant overlap making them indistinguishable (Figures 1a and 1b). The inseparability between these distributions illustrates the unsuitability of these metrics for evaluating the accuracy of long-form answers against concise ground-truth answers.

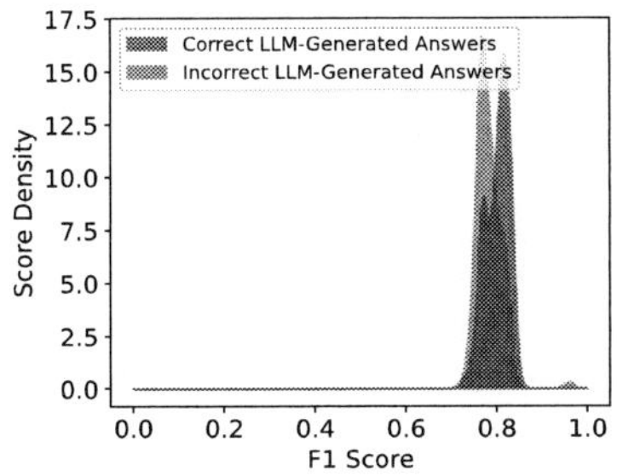

(a) BERT Score distribution using Kernel Density Estimation (KDE) of the incorrect and correct generated answers. Scores close to 1 indicate stronger semantic similarity between LLM-generated and ground-truth answers.

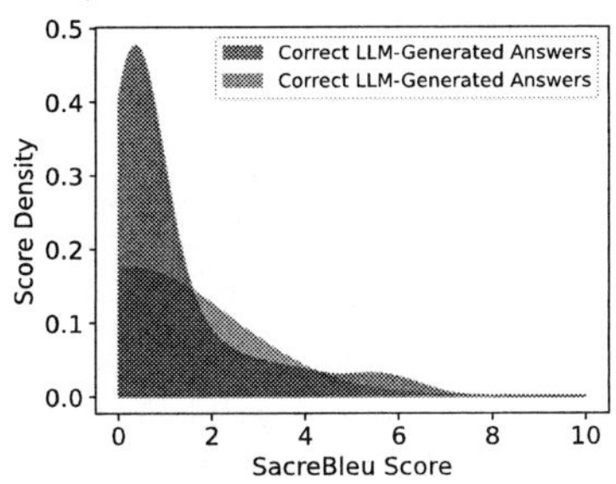

(b) SacreBleu Score distribution using Kernel Density Estimation (KDE). Higher scores indicate better n-gram overlap between LLM-generated and ground-truth answers.

Figure 1: Distribution of SacreBleu and BERT-scores obtained by comparing LLM-generated answers, from which we know their (in)correctness, against ground-truth answers. To be reliable as a metric, the distributions should be clearly separable, which is not the case for both metrics.

LLM-as-a-judge Recently, LLMs have emerged as a useful evaluation metric for free-form text, termed as LLM-as-a-judge evaluation (Zheng et al., 2023). This approach to be particularly well-suited for tabular reasoning evaluation, where generated answers are often long- and free-form text compared to, for example OTTQA, where answers are short text snippets or single (numeric) values. We propose using an LLM-as-a-judge for evaluating tabular reasoning through LLMs, as this allows us to keep the generation close to real-world usage, where users expect models to generate complete answers rather than forcing a single-valued answer (which does not always correspond to the ground-truth answer) or choose from predefined options as in TQA-Bench (Qiu et al., 2024). Second, relying on forced answer formats –accommodating multiple-choice or string-matching– can be brittle, especially for smaller models that may produce slightly misformatted outputs or fail to follow constraint templates (Liu et al., 2024).

To understand the reliability of the LLM-as-a-judge for evaluating tabular reasoning, we first evaluate the performance of the LLM-as-a-judge. Specifically, we devise reference-guided grading (Zheng et al., 2023) and let the LLM compare between the LLM-generated answer against the ground-truth answer. Specifically, we use Qwen2.5 (32B parameters) and assess if its generated answer matches the ground-truth answer based on a structured prompt, and outputs yes or no, as follows:

```
When it comes to the following question:

Question: {Question}

does the answer "{Answer}" match the
expected response value of the correct
answer "{Correct Value}"?

Consider that if the answer is None, it
means that the value could not be found in
the table. Please conclude your answer with
'answer correct: yes/no'
```

Table 2: Evaluation of the LLM-as-a-judge procedure on the human-annotated dataset. While the LLM slightly underestimates correctness – 4.2% of correct answers are judged to be incorrect – we observe a strong alignment between predicted and actual (in)correctness with an accuracy more than 95%.

	Pred. Incorrect	**Pred. Correct**
Actual Incorrect	99.2%	0.8%
Actual Correct	4.2%	95.8%

The results of our evaluation (Table 2) demonstrates that the LLM-as-a-judge yields a high accuracy, identifying 95.8% of correct answers as correct, and 98% of the incorrect answers as such. Notably, the absence of false positives (0.8%) highlights the model's reliability in avoiding incorrect classifications of negative cases as positive.

5 On the Realistic Tabular Reasoning Capabilities of LLMs

Here, we first examine how well LLMs can perform tabular reasoning tasks using the downscaled TQA-Bench data (as discussed in Section 3) and the more reliable LLM-as-a-judge evaluation, and highlight new insights contextualized in the TQA-Bench. Then, we extend the benchmark by formalizing tabular characteristics commonly found in practice, such as missing values, and measure the robustness of LLMs for such realistic variations.

5.1 LLM Selection and Prompts

LLMs for analysis and evaluation We conduct our analysis on a diverse set of models to ensure comprehensive evaluation. We include publicly available models Qwen2.5 (Yang et al., 2024), Llama3.1 (Grattafiori et al., 2024), DeepSeek-R1 (Guo et al., 2025), and Mistral (Jiang et al., 2023). In all cases, we select the 7B parameter versions (except llama3.1 with 8B) of the models and utilize the same prompt structure. We also include the proprietary GPT-4o-mini model (version 2024-07-18) (Hurst et al., 2024) representing a state-of-the-art larger general-purpose model.

For evaluation with the LLM-as-a-judge procedure we, again, devise Qwen2.5 (32B parameters) for its strength in generating structured outputs, and use the same prompt introduced in section 4.

Tabular reasoning prompt For evaluating tabular reasoning capabilities of the LLMs, we adopt a structured prompt template inspired by Qiu et al. (2024) to guide question answering based on tabular data[2]. The prompt instructs the LLM to use the information from the provided single or multiple tables to answer a given question. Each table is presented with a title and its contents. The structure of the prompt template is as follows:

```
Answer the question based on these tables:

Table: {Table 1}
Table: {Table 2}

Question: {Question}

This question has only one correct answer.
Please break down the question, evaluate
each option, and explain why it is correct
or incorrect. Conclude with your final
answer.
```

[2]We inspected accuracy variance across templates and didn't observe a significant difference.

5.2 Insights on Down-scaled Tabular Inputs

Accuracy over various table sizes Our analysis of the TQA-Bench questions and down-scaled tabular inputs shows that the performance of the LLMs decreases as the tabular input increases in size. This is particularly evident in the *average* and *subtraction* tasks (Figure 2 and 3). The only exception is GPT-4o-mini, which achieves a steady performance across table sizes for most tasks, and is generally the best model for tabular reasoning tasks. Furthermore, our results indicate that LLMs struggle particularly with more complex reasoning tasks, such as calculating correlation and subtraction, where the performance is significantly lower compared to the simpler tasks like counting and lookups. A comprehensive overview of the accuracy performances across all models and tasks can be found in appendix A.

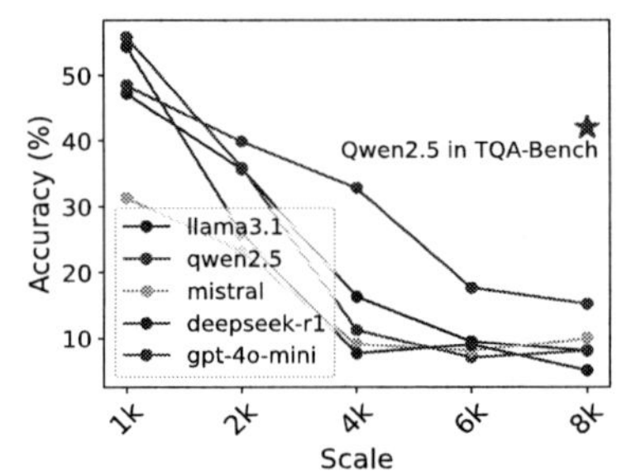

Figure 2: Performance of LLMs on calculating the *average* of columns, across varying table sizes. The accuracy of all models gradually decreases with table size.

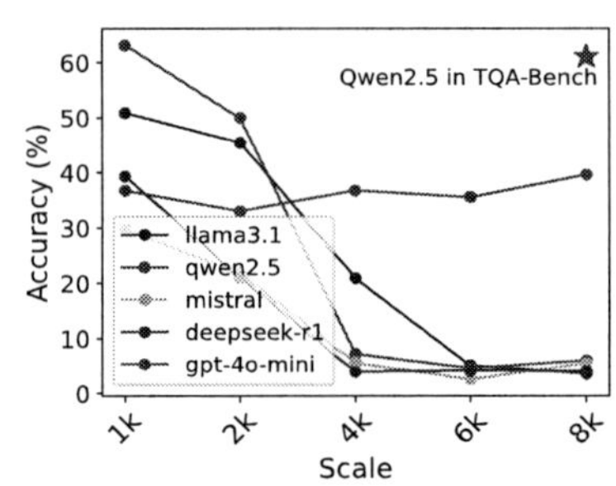

Figure 3: Performance of LLMs on calculating a *subtraction* across columns, across varying table sizes. The accuracy significantly drops after 4K input size except for GPT-4o-mini.

Realistic LLM performance on TQA-Bench We also plot the accuracy of the Qwen2.5 model (7B params), as found by the TQA-Bench multiple-choice evaluation, for the *average* and *subtraction* tasks for the 8K sized tabular inputs (★ in Figures 2 and 3). Our LLM-as-a-judge evaluation of open-form answers unveils a significant differ-

Table 3: Accuracies of LLMs across reasoning tasks for tables with token size 4k. Generally, LLMs can reasonably do basic entity lookups, but show large deficits in more complex reasoning tasks such as calculating averages and correlations. As expected given the larger model size, GPT-4o-mini shows best performance across tasks.

Model	Entity lookup	Top selection	Average	Count	Subtraction	Sum	Correlation
Llama3.1	49.75	22.96	16.33	28.79	20.92	16.08	4.90
Mistral	28.14	14.00	9.14	20.20	5.58	8.50	12.75
Qwen2.5	29.00	15.00	11.28	36.92	7.22	12.50	8.65
Deepseek-r1	20.00	14.56	7.64	25.95	3.90	8.18	20.48
GPT-4o-mini	68.72	44.62	32.83	49.75	36.73	35.86	24.04

ence in accuracy of 30% and 60% for *average* and *subtraction* calculations, respectively, compared to multiple-choice answering. This insight underscores the importance of evaluating models in open-ended form to better understand their true reasoning abilities. Across models, we generally observe relatively stronger capabilities in entity lookups, while selecting a range (*top selection*) is more challenging (Table 3). LLMs show larger deficits in more complex aggregation tasks, such as calculating averages, while the relatively basic task of subtraction generally appears most challenging.

Model-specific incompatible behaviors During analysis, we observed notable behaviors in how models approached tabular reasoning tasks. For instance, DeepSeek-R1 often struggles with coherence in its chain of thought outputting extracts like "*Wait no—the data doesn't show that. Wait I'm getting confused.*", leading to incomplete or inconsistent reasoning. Llama3.1, on the other hand, occasionally fails to generate any meaningful output, and effectively "breaks" under certain conditions, particularly on larger tables or complex queries. Additionally, both Qwen2.5 and Llama3.1 attempt to generate Python code snippets to compute answers, rather than directly providing the response.

5.3 Real-world characteristics of tabular data

We analyze how robust LLMs can reason over tabular data through their generation capabilities, in the presence of three variations in the tabular inputs: missing values, duplicate entities, and column permutations. These variations are common in practice and resemble either data quality issues or valid permutations. In what follows, we elaborate on the desired behavior which goes beyond accuracy (Xu et al., 2023), for each characteristic. In order to instill these characteristics in the tabular inputs, we adapt the symbolic extension of TQA-Bench to generate new tasks. Symbolic extension works by manually creating prompt templates and functions for calculating the ground-truth answers, and using them to automatically generate combinations of (question, ground-truth)-pairs.

Missing Values Due to incomplete data collection or errors during data entry, tables often contain missing values, leading to incomplete information (Little and Rubin, 2019). This has been a longstanding issue for predictive ML, as missing values can distort analysis and lead to unreliable results (Emmanuel et al., 2021). To reflect this in the data, we first identify the cells needed to generate the answers and randomly remove one of the relevant cells. We recalculate the ground-truth answer by, effectively, setting the missing value to 0. The LLM-as-a-judge evaluates two behaviors: the model's ability to produce the correct answer despite the missing information (**Accuracy**), and its capacity to explicitly acknowledge the absence of relevant data (**Acknowledgement**). These criteria reflect how well the model navigates incomplete data—whether it can reason effectively with what's available—and transparently communicate the limitations introduced by missing values.

Duplicate Entities While duplicate entities are in violation with the relational data model (Codd, 1979), we often find duplicate rows in tables. We simulate this by randomly selecting rows and replicating them at random points in the same table. These entities are intended to be ignored. The LLM-as-a-judge then evaluates two desired behaviors: whether the correct answer has been generated despite duplicates values (**Accuracy**), hence ignoring duplicate values, and whether the model explicitly acknowledges the duplicates in its response (**Acknowledgement**).

Structural Variation While tables within some contexts might reflect a typical column or row order, hence bias an LLM through its training data, the structural order of tables is insignificant in the relational data model (Codd, 1979). In line with prior work for examining robustness of table embeddings (Cong et al., 2023), we extract different permutations of the same tables by shuffling their rows and columns. The desired behavior is that the answer is not affected by different column order permutations of the input tables. Therefore, we evaluate if the answer remains unchanged.

5.4 Robustness to Realistic Variation in Tables

Missing Values We observe some mixed behaviors in the presence of missing values across tasks (Table 4). For summation, we observe a significant drop in **accuracy** when missing values are present for llama3.1, which achieves only 8% accuracy compared to 16% in the baseline. In contrast, qwen2.5 actually shows improvements, particularly for entity lookups where it shows an accuracy of 43% compared to 29%. This may be due to the model's (desirable) behavior as it refuses to answer if the value to-be-looked-up is missing, which is treated by the judge as a correct response.

At the same time, we find that the models often **acknowledge** missing values in their responses, with both models achieving around 44% in the sum task and 51% in the average task. This suggests that while models may struggle with accuracy, they are still able to recognize and communicate the presence of missing values in their answers. Still, even on this metric, the models do not behave reliably enough for most practical use cases.

Table 4: Results of the Missing Value perturbation across three aggregation tasks (average, sum and entity lookups) with table size 4k.

Task	Model	Baseline	Acc.	Acknow.
Entity lookup	llama3.1	50%	47%	57%
	qwen2.5	29%	43%	60%
Sum	llama3.1	16%	8%	44%
	qwen2.5	13%	16%	44%
Average	llama3.1	17%	11%	51%
	qwen2.5	11%	19%	51%

Duplicate Entities When it comes to dealing with duplicate entities, the trends displayed in table 5 overall are quite similar to dealing with missing values, showing a significant decrease in **accuracy** in most tasks. A notable observation is that models are less likely to **acknowledge** duplicate values, compared to missing values.

Structural Variations We find that structural variations, such as column shuffling, have only a small impact on model performance in most cases (Table 6), in contrast to the significant performance decline observed with missing values or duplicate entities. Interestingly, the robustness to column order varies across models and tasks—some exhibit resilience, while others are mildly affected. This shows a divergence from previous findings in embedding-based studies (Cong et al., 2023), which reported a sensitivity to column order in the representation space.

Table 5: Results of the Duplication perturbation across two advanced tasks (average, sum) at table size 2k. LLMs typically struggle with duplicate values, and fail to acknowledge duplication in their response.

Task	Model	Baseline	Acc.	Acknow.
Sum	llama3.1	41%	20%	27%
	qwen2.5	30%	31%	8%
Average	llama3.1	36%	17%	11%
	qwen2.5	36%	20%	6%

Table 6: Impact of column shuffling on select reasoning tasks with a table size of 2k, showing difficulties for aggregation queries particularly for the llama model.

Task	Model	Baseline	Acc.
Entity lookup	llama3.1	50%	46%
	qwen2.5	42%	34%
Sum	llama3.1	41%	30%
	qwen2.5	30%	28%
Average	llama3.1	36%	28%
	qwen2.5	36%	32%

6 Conclusion

While recent studies suggest LLMs exhibit reasonable tabular reasoning abilities beyond natural language tasks, these studies often lack reliable evaluations and robustness checks, prompting our study into how well LLMs *truly* reason over tabular inputs. First, we surface limitations of common free-form text evaluation metrics, such as SacreBleu, which fail to distinguish between correct and incorrect answers in tabular reasoning tasks. We demonstrate that an LLM-as-a-judge is more reliable for this purpose. A revised evaluation of an existing benchmark with the LLM-as-a-judge unveils a significant deficit in tabular reasoning capabilities of LLMs. Second, we analyze the robustness of tabular reasoning capabilities of LLMs through queries of various complexities and find that they can be sensitive to realistic variations like missing values, even for relatively simple tasks. Moreover, we find that LLMs insufficiently acknowledge such undesired variations risking errors in downstream interpretation. These findings underscore the need for further advancements in LLM architectures and training to improve their robustness to real-world tabular data.

Acknowledgments

This work was partially funded by grants from NWO (NGF.1607.22.045) and SAP.

References

Wenhu Chen, Ming-Wei Chang, Eva Schlinger, William Yang Wang, and William W Cohen. 2020. Open question answering over tables and text. In *International Conference on Learning Representations*.

Edgar F Codd. 1979. Extending the database relational model to capture more meaning. *ACM Transactions on Database Systems (TODS)*, 4(4):397–434.

Tianji Cong, Madelon Hulsebos, Zhenjie Sun, Paul Groth, and HV Jagadish. 2023. Observatory: Characterizing embeddings of relational tables. *Proceedings of the VLDB Endowment*, 17(4):849–862.

Tlamelo Emmanuel, Thabiso Maupong, Dimane Mpoeleng, Thabo Semong, Banyatsang Mphago, and Oteng Tabona. 2021. A survey on missing data in machine learning. *Journal of Big data*, 8:1–37.

Xi Fang, Weijie Xu, Fiona Anting Tan, Ziqing Hu, Jiani Zhang, Yanjun Qi, Srinivasan H Sengamedu, and Christos Faloutsos. 2024. Large language models (llms) on tabular data: Prediction, generation, and understanding-a survey. *Transactions on Machine Learning Research*.

Aaron Grattafiori, Abhimanyu Dubey, Abhinav Jauhri, Abhinav Pandey, Abhishek Kadian, Ahmad Al-Dahle, Aiesha Letman, Akhil Mathur, Alan Schelten, Alex Vaughan, and 1 others. 2024. The llama 3 herd of models. *arXiv preprint arXiv:2407.21783*.

Daya Guo, Dejian Yang, Haowei Zhang, Junxiao Song, Ruoyu Zhang, Runxin Xu, Qihao Zhu, Shirong Ma, Peiyi Wang, Xiao Bi, and 1 others. 2025. Deepseek-r1: Incentivizing reasoning capability in llms via reinforcement learning. *arXiv preprint arXiv:2501.12948*.

Aaron Hurst, Adam Lerer, Adam P Goucher, Adam Perelman, Aditya Ramesh, Aidan Clark, AJ Ostrow, Akila Welihinda, Alan Hayes, Alec Radford, and 1 others. 2024. Gpt-4o system card. *arXiv preprint arXiv:2410.21276*.

Xingyu Ji, Aditya Parameswaran, and Madelon Hulsebos. 2024. TARGET: Benchmarking Table Retrieval for Generative Tasks. In *NeurIPS 2024 Third Table Representation Learning Workshop*.

Albert Q. Jiang, Alexandre Sablayrolles, Arthur Mensch, Chris Bamford, Devendra Singh Chaplot, Diego de las Casas, Florian Bressand, Gianna Lengyel, Guillaume Lample, Lucile Saulnier, Lélio Renard Lavaud, Marie-Anne Lachaux, Pierre Stock, Teven Le Scao, Thibaut Lavril, Thomas Wang, Timothée Lacroix, and William El Sayed. 2023. Mistral 7b. *Preprint*, arXiv:2310.06825.

Percy Liang, Rishi Bommasani, Tony Lee, Dimitris Tsipras, Dilara Soylu, Michihiro Yasunaga, Yian Zhang, Deepak Narayanan, Yuhuai Wu, Ananya Kumar, and 1 others. 2023. Holistic evaluation of language models. *Trans. Mach. Learn. Res.*

Roderick Little and Donald Rubin. 2019. *Statistical analysis with missing data*. John Wiley & Sons.

Yu Liu, Duantengchuan Li, Kaili Wang, Zhuoran Xiong, Fobo Shi, Jian Wang, Bing Li, and Bo Hang. 2024. Are llms good at structured outputs? a benchmark for evaluating structured output capabilities in llms. *Information Processing & Management*, 61(5):103809.

Simone Papicchio, Paolo Papotti, and Luca Cagliero. 2023. Qatch: Benchmarking sql-centric tasks with table representation learning models on your data. *Advances in Neural Information Processing Systems*, 36:30898–30917.

Matt Post. 2018. A call for clarity in reporting BLEU scores. In *Proceedings of the Third Conference on Machine Translation: Research Papers*, pages 186–191, Belgium, Brussels. Association for Computational Linguistics.

Zipeng Qiu, You Peng, Guangxin He, Binhang Yuan, and Chen Wang. 2024. TQA-Bench: Evaluating LLMs for Multi-Table Question Answering with Scalable Context and Symbolic Extension. *CoRR*.

Ananya Singha, José Cambronero, Sumit Gulwani, Vu Le, and Chris Parnin. 2023. Tabular Representation, Noisy Operators, and Impacts on Table Structure Understanding Tasks in LLMs. In *NeurIPS 2023 Second Table Representation Learning Workshop*.

Yuan Sui, Mengyu Zhou, Mingjie Zhou, Shi Han, and Dongmei Zhang. 2024. Table meets llm: Can large language models understand structured table data? a benchmark and empirical study. In *Proceedings of the 17th ACM International Conference on Web Search and Data Mining*, pages 645–654.

Fangyuan Xu, Yixiao Song, Mohit Iyyer, and Eunsol Choi. 2023. A critical evaluation of evaluations for long-form question answering. In *The 61st Annual Meeting Of The Association For Computational Linguistics*.

An Yang, Baosong Yang, Beichen Zhang, Binyuan Hui, Bo Zheng, Bowen Yu, Chengyuan Li, Dayiheng Liu, Fei Huang, Haoran Wei, and 1 others. 2024. Qwen2. 5 technical report. *arXiv preprint arXiv:2412.15115*.

Tianyi Zhang*, Varsha Kishore*, Felix Wu*, Kilian Q. Weinberger, and Yoav Artzi. 2020. Bertscore: Evaluating text generation with bert. In *International Conference on Learning Representations*.

Lianmin Zheng, Wei-Lin Chiang, Ying Sheng, Siyuan Zhuang, Zhanghao Wu, Yonghao Zhuang, Zi Lin, Zhuohan Li, Dacheng Li, Eric Xing, and 1 others. 2023. Judging llm-as-a-judge with mt-bench and chatbot arena. *Advances in Neural Information Processing Systems*, 36:46595–46623.

A Full Benchmark

This table provides a comprehensive overview of the performance of various LLMs across different reasoning tasks (e.g., entity lookup, top selection, average, etc.) for tabular data of varying sizes (1k to 8k tokens).

Size	Model	Entity lookup	Top Selection	Average	Count	Subtraction	Sum	Correlation
1k								
	llama3.1	43.43	30.15	47.21	59.30	50.85	52.02	18.64
	mistral	30.15	31.31	31.31	47.50	29.78	33.67	36.75
	qwen2.5	49.24	30.30	55.78	65.15	63.13	56.78	37.82
	deepseek-r1	34.01	29.80	54.31	69.19	39.33	50.00	47.46
	gpt-4o-mini	41.62	36.18	48.48	70.56	36.72	54.50	45.38
2k								
	llama3.1	76.38	49.49	35.68	44.95	45.45	41.21	11.21
	mistral	58.08	36.18	23.23	28.00	21.81	17.17	16.82
	qwen2.5	66.33	42.86	35.86	53.27	50.00	30.26	22.64
	deepseek-r1	42.93	28.28	25.89	49.75	21.05	26.26	24.07
	gpt-4o-mini	69.54	47.24	39.90	57.07	32.98	37.76	28.44
4k								
	llama3.1	49.75	22.96	16.33	28.79	20.92	16.08	4.90
	mistral	28.14	14.00	9.14	20.20	5.58	8.50	12.75
	qwen2.5	29.00	15.00	11.28	36.92	7.22	12.50	8.65
	deepseek-r1	20.00	14.56	7.64	25.95	3.90	8.18	20.48
	gpt-4o-mini	68.72	44.62	32.83	49.75	36.73	35.86	24.04
6k								
	llama3.1	21.11	15.15	9.50	19.60	5.08	7.50	4.00
	mistral	11.56	12.00	8.04	16.00	2.54	4.06	8.82
	qwen2.5	16.16	8.00	7.04	19.50	4.57	6.53	9.80
	deepseek-r1	7.00	11.50	9.00	16.67	4.12	5.50	9.90
	gpt-4o-mini	68.53	42.13	17.68	38.50	35.53	16.08	16.16
8k								
	llama3.1	12.50	10.55	8.04	18.00	3.55	2.54	3.03
	mistral	9.00	10.10	10.00	8.00	5.53	2.51	10.31
	qwen2.5	8.04	7.54	8.08	11.50	6.00	1.51	9.00
	deepseek-r1	8.04	12.00	5.08	13.00	4.02	4.00	9.09
	gpt-4o-mini	64.00	35.86	15.23	32.16	39.59	14.80	11.22

Author Index

Association for Computational Linguistics
209 N. Eighth Street
Stroudsburg, Pennsylvania 18360

ISBN 979-8-3313-2419-3

CURRAN ASSOCIATES INC.
proceedings.com